...onal

Voluntary Work

VICTORIA PYBUS

Distributed in the USA by
The Globe Pequot Press, Guilford, Connecticut

VACATION WORK
PUBLICATIONS

Publi .... treet, Oxford
www

THE INTERNATIONAL DIRECTORY OF VOLUNTARY WORK
By Victoria Pybus

First published 1979
Second Edition 1982
Third Edition 1985
Fourth Edition 1989
Fifth Edition 1993
Sixth Edition 1997
Seventh Edition 2000
Eighth Edition 2003
Ninth Edition 2005

ISBN 1-85458-313-1
ISSN 0143-3474

Cover design by mccdesign

Typeset by Brendan Cole

Illustrations by John Taylor

Publicity by Charles Cutting

Printed and bound in Italy by Legoprint SpA, Trento

Contents

PART 1 – RESIDENTIAL WORK

PART TWO – NON-RESIDENTIAL WORK

Preface

In recent years it has been said that volunteering has come increasingly under pressure from the relentless advance of globalisation. In the industrialised countries national volunteering is in decline as societies become more detached from religion, and consumerism has taken over from religion as the guiding force. The rise of individualism and the loss of traditional communities have also contributed to the decline in volunteering. There is much in today's press about the lack of civic involvement of young people and there are constantly new government initiatives to promote volunteering in the community by making it 'cool' and appealing to the idealism of young people, and by pointing out that those who help others are also helping themselves by acquiring skills and credibility that will give them the edge over the competition when applying to future employers.

So much for volunteering on the home front, but what about international volunteering? This has turned out to be something of a cash cow for organisations and the projects they support. Many are now in the business of organising this popular rite of passage for young people, who can afford to finance a period of volunteering fitted into an adventure involving world travel, sporting activities and some paid work on their gap year. In the USA such schemes are advertised to students as internships or study tours, and allow them to gain university credits in the process. But this is the tip of the international volunteering iceberg. There are thousands of selfless international volunteers working long-term or on short projects, with skills and qualifications or with none. Prospective volunteers with smaller financial resources and less than impressive CVs should not be disheartened, there are plenty of alternatives that can be done on a budget provided that you can scrape together the airfares and have access to some funds for emergencies. Volunteering on farms, retreats, archaeological digs and working with the disabled are some of the possibilities where board and lodging are given free or at minimal cost.

Some types of volunteering may be in retreat but others are becoming growing trends. In many industrialised countries people are retiring earlier, are wealthier, and active much longer than their forbears. In recognition of this, volunteer agencies are beginning to admit older volunteers that they would not previously have considered. For voluntary service abroad, good health is nearly always vital as medical facilities may be distant from the work site, or below the standard of the home country, but otherwise there is nothing to stop older people from offering their services to volunteer agencies and their skills and experience can still be put to good use. The other area of growth in volunteering is online volunteering (sometimes called virtual or cyber volunteering) where volunteers carry out work online, from translating to setting up a website for farmers in a particular region. In this way, volunteers can help people in developing countries without ever leaving their own home area. It also opens up exciting opportunities for disabled volunteers.

This book is divided into two main sections: residential and non-residential work. The former is sub-divided into categories of voluntary work open to all volunteers with a range of diverse skills and attributes, and includes a section for voluntary organisations, which specifically recruit professionals and longer-term volunteers. However, these definitions are not rigid, for example, a Romanian orphanage may need people with experience in child care, fully-qualified medical personnel, experienced decorators and plumbers, and a pair of willing hands to help in all areas of running the orphanage. Whether you are trained in a particular discipline or not, the overriding characteristic essential to all volunteers is a desire and enthusiasm to help. The organisations featured in the first half of this book mostly provide free, or at cost, board and lodging to volunteers and some offer a stipend to cover out-of-pocket expenses. For those with long-term contracts a salary equivalent to the local rates is usually paid.

No person is an island. Our world comprises interdependent and co-dependent entities. In such an environment the importance of voluntary services cannot be overstated. Giving up any amount of time to help others in some way from assisting an elderly person with their shopping or just acting as a companion for them, to more high profile work in social, medical or international relief fields, can have a 'pebble-dropped-in-water' effect which promotes a national and international awareness and respect for others and the global society in which we live.

Victoria Pybus
Oxford, October 2004

PART ONE

RESIDENTIAL WORK

WORLDWIDE

UNITED KINGDOM

EUROPE

UNITED STATES OF AMERICA

CANADA

MEXICO, CENTRAL & SOUTH AMERICA

ISRAEL,PALESTINIAN-RULED TERRITORIES & EGYPT

AFRICA

ASIA

AUSTRALIA & NEW ZEALAND

Residential Work

This section of the Directory examines the different types of voluntary work for which the volunteer is required to live and work away from home. This usually means a full-time commitment, which can be from as little as a weekend to several years.

For the purposes of classification, organisations requiring resident volunteers have been divided. International Volunteering is sub-divided beginning with a Worldwide section followed by the United Kingdom (own section), and Europe (subdivided into countries), The USA and Canada each have their own section, followed by the rest of the Americas and then the Israel-Egypt region, Africa, Asia and Australia and New Zealand). A new category *Professional and Longer-term Volunteering* has been created for those projects requiring people with specific qualifications ranging from medicine to construction, and from IT to financial services, among others, or those that require volunteers prepared to commit for one or more years. Note that most longer-term positions tend to need skilled and qualified volunteers due to the need for skilled workers in ongoing development projects.

Any opportunities not classified under Professional and Longer-term are open to all people who can commit for, in most cases, a few weeks or a couple of months.

Some organisations recruit both skilled and unskilled workers. In these cases such organisations will be fully described under the category in which they are most active. If you like the sound of an organisation but are not sure if they take volunteers with general skills it may be worth checking their website or telephoning to see if support staff are required for general administration or basic care-giving tasks.

Applicants for voluntary work outside their own country are reminded that visas and work permits are sometimes necessary. The fact that the majority of voluntary work is unpaid often, but not always exempts them from these requirements. Regulations around the world change frequently, so volunteers going abroad are advised to check with the appropriate embassy before departure.

International Volunteering

For a volunteer with little or no skills or qualifications, but who has willing hands, dedication or just enthusiasm, the opportunities for voluntary work are endless. This chapter of the book covers both long-term (a year or more) and short-term placements for such volunteers.

Amongst the numerous short-term voluntary opportunities open to unskilled workers are various workcamps. A workcamp is a project that sets out to accomplish some specific goal over the course of one or more seasons with the help of groups of volunteers who arrive to help, usually for, one, two, three or more weeks. This project may involve conservation work, forestry, restoring an ancient monument, building a community amenity, or one of many other types of job that would not be done if volunteers were not prepared to undertake it. Workcamps take place all over east and west Europe, North America, North Africa, and sometimes further afield. While each camp will have some specific objective, such as clearing a derelict pond and the surrounding woodland and converting it into public parkland, or restoring an ancient building, they also achieve something by their very existence. Many organisations select the participants on a camp to represent as many nationalities as possible, in order to give those taking part the opportunity to meet and work alongside people from different cultures and backgrounds.

Many volunteers on short-term assignments – and this applies particularly to students on workcamps, archaeological digs and kibbutzim – see their involvement principally as a working holiday or a means of staying somewhere rather more cheaply than would otherwise be possible. Indeed in some countries with a very high cost of living such as those of Scandinavia, Switzerland workcamps may be the only affordable way to visit them for some young people. While in some former Soviet Union countries, short-term voluntary work may be the only way of getting more than a tourist's view of the way of life. Although English is the standard language in most international workcamps, the environment can provide invaluable practise for students of other languages. The hours of work expected of volunteers on a workcamp can be light, involving working in the mornings: at least part of the remainder of the time may be filled with organised 'educational' activities such as outings, lectures etc., intended to give participants a taste of the local culture.

It is not possible to generalise about the financial arrangements for non-professional voluntary work. In some cases pocket money is paid in addition to travel expenses and free accommodation. In other cases no money changes hands at all, or volunteers may find themselves making a contribution towards the cost of food and accommodation. Increasingly, it seems the burden of financing the actual project itself has been transferred to the volunteers. Many projects run in very poor countries such as Nepal and India expect the volunteer to 'fundraise' a hefty amount from £300 to £3000 and then work for free as well. The method of operation and cost or subsidisation of the volunteer all depends on the source and extent of available funds. Officially sponsored organisations, like Community Service Volunteers, usually have the funds to provide at least the bare necessities. As another example, kibbutzim, by their very nature, are expected to provide volunteers with free board and accommodation, but could not reasonably be expected to meet everyone's travel expenses, particularly when applicants literally come from all over the globe. Stays on kibbutzim therefore tend to be marketed as 'working holidays', as do many archaeological digs for the same reason – no funds are available to cover all costs. Indeed, participants in most archaeological digs have to pay for their own board and lodging and daily expenses in return for the privilege of working hard physically for six or more hours a day.

Because of the great number of organisations requiring volunteers with all kinds of skills and experience – great or small, or none at all, it has been necessary to subdivide them geographically. One or two organisations thus fall into more than one classification and will therefore be listed more than once. However, the organisations which are truly international in their recruitment policies and activities have been listed separately under the heading *Worldwide*.

As there is a preponderance of worldwide, British and European organisations, the sections on Worldwide Volunteering, the United Kingdom and Europe have been further sub-divided, Worldwide and the UK by types of work, and Europe by country. These divisions are far from clear-cut, especially in the Worldwide and UK chapters. Many of the entries under *Religious Projects,* for instance, cut across several of the other classifications: and there is a great deal of overlap between child care and work with the sick and disabled. The subheadings are therefore to be considered as a rough guide only. Entries are otherwise listed in simple alphabetical order within their respective sections or subdivisions.

Worldwide

Archaeology

Archaeology is the study of historic or prehistoric sites by excavation, (i.e. digging on sites where their remains are buried and then analysing them). Many a volunteer starts in their teens by attending a course at a local college, progressing to local or national digs and then spreading their wings to take part in digs abroad from Asia to Central America and from Malta to Israel. However, you don't have to have digging or archaeological qualifications and experience to take part in an excavation, as tuition, guidance and lectures are often given on site to volunteers. Note however that not all digs will take volunteers who have no previous archaeological experience or they will restrict them to certain beginners' weeks. Many local archaeological societies also have specially organised 'training digs' which are offered to newcomers. Once you have done some courses and have experience, you are likely to get more interesting jobs and so feel more involved in a particular project.

Publications. The magazine *Current Archaeology,* which deals with UK archaeology, and its new sister magazine *Current World Archaeology,* which deals with the international archaeological scene, can be obtained by subscription from the website www.archaeology.co.uk. This website also lists all main digs in the UK plus a detailed description of the background and progress of each, dig dates and contact details. Current Archaeology can also be contacted by post (Current Archaeology, 9 Nassington Road, London, NW3 2TX; 08456-447707; e-mail current@archaeology.co.uk). *Archaeo-Volunteers, the World Guide to Archaeological and Heritage Volunteering* is a book listing 200 organisations and opportunities they offer worldwide (£10.99 from www.vacationwork.co.uk; 01865-241978).

Websites. Archaeology Resources is a site mainly sourced from the UK but run from Canada (www.wordy.canadianwebs.com/page/arch.html) where you can find all matters relating to archaeology including dating methods, journals and publications, archaeology associations and archaeological sites and excavations and a database including the National Monument Record (Britain) and Sites and Monument Records (Britain). Also check out Archaeology Fieldwork and Field Schools at www.cyberpursuits.com/archaeo/fieldwrk.asp which has about 80 links to fieldwork opportunities and archaeology organisations worldwide.
      Other useful UK websites are:
www.cix.co.archaeology/begin/career/htm: lists UK amateur archaeological societies, which are very useful contacts for the beginner.
www.archaeolink.com/archaeology_volunteer_opportunit.htm: – lists international opportunities.

www.ukarchaeology.org.uk: lists UK opportunities and courses in archaeology.

The following contacts are useful in the USA:
www.archaeological.org: the website of the Archaeological Institute of America (AIA) is an excellent resource of amateur archaeological societies in the USA and also lists the requirements of over 200 archaeological excavations worldwide. A useful publication available from the AIA is the *Archaeological Fieldwork Opportunities Bulletin* (AFOB) (ISBN 1-931909-10-5), which costs $19.95 from David Brown Books in the USA and £14.95 from Oxbow Books in the UK.
www.simonides.org/users/bibliotheca/links/archaeological/groups.html: describes itself as an A-Z of Archaeological Societies in the USA and worldwide.

France is another country with a huge number of archaeological digs, which require about 5,000 'diggers' annually during the summer months. Every May a comprehensive list of archaeological excavations is published by the Ministry of Culture (Direction de l'Architecture et du Patrimoine, Sous-Direction de l'Archaeologie, 4 rue d'Aboukir, 75002 Paris, France; tel 01-40 15 77 81) on their website www.culture.fr/fouilles.
Anthony Blake worked during summer on a dig near Le Mans: *Archaeology is hard work. Applicants must be aware of what working from 8.30am-noon and 2-6pm in baking heat means! That said, I thoroughly enjoyed the working holiday: excellent company (75% French, so fine opportunity to practise French), weekends free after noon on Saturday, good lunches in SNCF canteen, evening meals quite haphazard as prepared by fellow diggers. Accommodation simple but adequate.*

ARCHAEOLOGY ABROAD
31-34 Gordon Square, London WC1H OPY; tel/fax 020-8537-0849; e-mail arch.abroad@ucl.ac.uk; www.britarch.ac.uk/archabroad
This organisation provides two information bulletins annually about forthcoming opportunities for archaeological fieldwork and excavations abroad. Publications are available by subscription. Subscribers are eligible to apply for Fieldwork Awards to help them with their expenses. Enquiries should be sent to the Honorary Secretary at the above address enclosing a stamped self-addressed envelope or via e-mail to the address above.

Children & Youth

For many people the idea of doing voluntary work with deprived and traumatised children, seems to be the most worthwhile of all, as effects can be instant on children's morale. Just shining the light of attention and interacting with them gives hope in otherwise bleak future prospects. Work can involve teaching, usually English or sports, in places where education and athletics, things which westerners take for granted, are in the developmental stage nationally, or otherwise impossible without outside help (for instance, in a refugee camp in a war-torn country). Learning English, becoming an athlete or sports hero is perceived in many poor communities as the golden passport to a better future. Many teachers have remarked that the children of poverty often have an eagerness to learn that almost overwhelms teachers used to the semi-attentive classrooms of their own consumerism-oriented countries.

Working with children traumatised by conflict, who have probably lost their homes and families and who have been habituated to violence in wars or in the home, can involve the introduction of processes to break the cycle of violence and to help such children learn to socialise and acquire learning skills that will enable them to be receptive to learning and education. There are also thousands of children who have been orphaned, or abandoned, and then institutionalised, where they languish almost forgotten in shamefully deprived conditions lacking not just in material things but also the external stimuli that each human being needs to develop and achieve their potential. Much of the desperately-needed remedial work is done by professionals working through the main global organisations such as UNICEF, Save the Children, etc who employ psychotherapists and other qualified personnel. However for the determined volunteer there are opportunities to be found by seeking out the smaller grass roots organisations whose focus is on children in local orphanages or schools. Loving care and attention, and access to western-style education is often the greatest need. You can start your search by looking on the internet for umbrella sites such as www.evolunteer.co.uk or where small organisations post their requirements for teachers in Nepal, and carers for orphanages in eastern Europe, Brazil etc. Bear in mind that this work can be very tough on the volunteer, and draining emotionally and physically, and it requires the support of a good team, which may not be forthcoming with some of the smaller organisations, whose main focus will be on the children they are trying to help.

> **Vicky Wright taught English to children in Nepal:**
> *As my time drew to a close, I began to reflect and summarise with the children on what we had covered in class, and the amount that their English had improved made me so proud I almost cried. Many of them who were too shy or insecure with their conversational skills when I arrived, were insisting on talking to me all the time and demonstrating their enthusiasm, occasionally even becoming a little hard to control!*

ACTION FOR CHILDREN IN CONFLICT (AfC)
2 Frilford Farms, Hinton road, Longworth, Oxon, OX13 5EA; tel 01865-821380; fax 01865-822150; e-mail info@actionchildren.org.

Action for Children in Conflict (AfC), works with child survivors of conflict in the UK and overseas, with an ultimate objective of helping to break the cycles of violence, hatred and despair by providing psychological, emotional and educational support. Conflicts are all too often about issues long since past. Unless intervention is applied, they pass on from generation to generation.

In Sierra Leone, AfC works with children and young people who have been affected by the recently ended ten-year civil war. Volunteers are needed to provide counselling, basic education, skills training, family tracing and social healing and re-integration through sport, drama and art.

In Kenya and Tanzania, volunteers work with orphans and street children. Overseas volunteers go for a minimum of 8 weeks.

In the UK, there is always a need for volunteers to develop and promote the charity and to work in the UK office for a minimum of four weeks. For UK volunteers, accommodation and pocket money can be provided. Overseas volunteers fundraise to cover their own costs before they travel. AfC will provide all the assistance it can in helping people to fundraise.

Further details on the website and an application form to download, or write or e-mail.

HOPE AND HOMES FOR CHILDREN
East Clyffe, Salisbury, Wiltshire SP3 4LZ; tel 01722 790111; fax 01733 790024; e-mail hhc@hopeand homes.org; www.hopeandhomes.org

Hope and Homes for Children is a charity that works with orphaned and abandoned children in fourteen countries in eastern Europe and in Africa. The type of work depends on the country and varies from closing orphanages in Romania by finding permanent families for the children, and supporting AIDS orphans in Africa.

Volunteers are currently needed to help some of the world's most desperate children in Romania, Albania and Bosnia and give them love, care and stimulation and helping to prepare them for reintegration back into the community. Volunteers with special needs qualifications and experience in physiotherapy, play, music, art and occupational therapy are required. Also volunteers to work with babies, stimulating them with educational activities and charting their development. Also volunteers to work with pre-school children helping them to coordinate play together and do simple pre-school activities.

Volunteers are provided with accommodation.

Applications to Julia Hall at the above address.

MONDO CHALLENGE
Galliford Building, Gayton Road, Milton Malsor, Northampton NN7 3AD; ☎01604-858225; fax 01605-859323; e-mail businesslink@compuserve.com; www.yangrima.org.

Mondo Challenge is a young and rapidly expanding non-profit organisation that sends volunteers on business development and teaching adventures all over the world. It is currently running over 40 projects spanning through India, Nepal, Sri Lanka, The Gambia, Senegal, Tanzania, Kenya and Chile with new projects sprouting in Bolivia and Ecuador. Current projects include raising AIDS/HIV awareness in Tanzania, teaching Buddhist monks IT in Sri Lanka and bee-keeping programmes in The Gambia. Mondo Challenge sends about 200 volunteers a year abroad and the average age is 30 years. Volunteers include gap students and mature volunteers of all types particularly those taking career breaks.

Volunteers need not be qualified teachers but in order to succeed must be able to adapt to new and exciting situations with open minds and enthusiasm. Business development volunteers need a minimum of three years' business experience before they are able to take up the Mondo Challenge. Volunteers also have to pay a fee of about £900 for the recommended three-month stay. Cost varies for other lengths of stay. Volunteers pay for their own travel and accommodation. The latter is provided at low cost (approximately £15 per week) by local families.

Volunteers are given pre-departure training and information packs and the back-up of the UK-based team and their project coordinators located in the country where they are working. An induction is provided on arrival by the in-country coordinator to help volunteers feel more at home in the community where they will be based.

With an increasing number of early retired volunteers applying to MondoChallenge over the past two years, it is worth noting that MondoChallenge has no problem accepting applications from those who have retired and are now looking for something worthwhile and reasonably challenging to do with their time.
em]Further information from the above address.

Christine Graves was an older MondoChallenge volunteer in India
Why should all the travelling and volunteering be left to the young. We have got the experience and plenty of youthful energy to be doing something worthwhile. I just loved teaching the children and living with local families. Conditions were simple but perfectly safe and I had the most wonderful time (twice).

Vicky Wright, 18 took a year out after A-levels before Cambridge University and taught English near Kalimpong in the foothills of the Himalayas.
To begin with I had doubts about how much of an impact my teaching would make and felt there would be little difference between a local teacher and myself. However, I soon came to realise that the styles were very different. Quite shockingly, the normal method of teaching is based around punishment (the cane), which makes the children frightened of getting things wrong. They are also taught by rote and learn words by spelling them first before saying them. Consequently they don't know how to break down the long words to pronounce the syllabic sounds separately.

These methods it seemed had been used for so long that it was how the teachers themselves had been taught and their teachers before them that I felt quite unsettled. I didn't know how to change what seemed to be an ingrained system, and I really didn't want to be the Westerner who was convinced she new best, effectively promoting colonialism through western methodology. So I came to the idea of a teacher training programme and contacted Mondo Challenge with my proposal. I thought that by showing the staff that there are other ways they wouldn't feel the need to cane the children so much. Rather than punishing them for being naughty, I would reward those who were good with sweets or by playing games. Natalie, (the other volunteer at the school) and I also gave some children detention a few times as punishment. However, this faded with time as they simply weren't naughty enough.

Understandably it is hard for the children to be taught in English, which is their second language after Nepali. However, in the long run it is advantageous as all the Indian schools at age 14/15 switch from being taught everything in Nepali to everything in English. Something which I found slightly bizarre is that they don't even learn English, but an 'Indian English' with altered pronunciation which has evolved over the years.

Outside the classroom I did feel a slight culture shock for about two weeks. Communication with the rest of the family was difficult and they spoke little English. Eating curry and rice for breakfast took some getting used to as did the squat toilet, the bamboo houses, the bucket of water 'shower', wearing flip-flops when it was raining and the 'super strong' Hit beer which as a local custom is forced upon you at every house you visit.

Over the entire three months of being in the village they did not celebrate one birthday, which suggests how little importance they attach to their own birthdays in this culture. Instead, their celebrations are focused on religion and marriage and quite luckily we had hit prime time as the majority are held between the cold season and the wet season (i.e. after February and before June). Weddings were a joyous occasion and being a foreign novelty we were invited to them all.

The last week, as did the three months, flew by and before I knew it I was sitting on a stage watching the children whilst being smothered in garlands. It was a really enjoyable last day and I was glad that the 'farewell' programme took a more informal style compared to others I had been to during my stay. My leaving the next morning was a tearful affair as I have made valuable and close relationships, especially with Natalie and the family. I hope to return in the not-too-distant future.

OUTREACH INTERNATIONAL
Bartletts Farm, Hayes Road, Compton Dundon, Somerset TA11 6PF; tel/fax 01458-274957; e-mail gap@outreachinternational.co.uk; www. outreachinternational.co.uk

A specialist placement organisation with carefully selected projects with enough variety to ensure that the interests and skills of individual volunteers can be put to good use.

Volunteers are needed to participate in local initiatives in Mexico, Ecuador and Cambodia allowing them to live in communities and work alongside local people. Cambodian placements include working with young landmine and polio victims and children who have become victims of human trafficking. Volunteers teach English, computer skills and art skills. Physiotherapists and volunteers with therapy skills would be appreciated in Cambodia. Other professional people with experience in computers, marketing, art and craft teaching would be particularly sought after to help local initiatives. Mexican projects are on the Pacific coast in traditional villages. The projects are with orphans, disabled children, teaching in local schools or working with giant sea turtles. In Ecuador, volunteers work in an orphanage and also carry out conservation work in the Amazon Rainforest.

Placements are for 3+ months. Applicants will be invited to interview within 3 weeks of applying. Cost of £3,100 for 3 months includes air tickets, full insurance, language course, in-country support, food, accommodation and all project costs. Additional months are approximately £400 per month. Applicants should be confident young people with a desire to offer their help to a damaged society. Commonsense is more important than formal qualifications. Some projects are more suitable for school leavers while others are more appropriate for people with some years or work experience.

PERSONAL OVERSEAS DEVELOPMENT
Gap Year Programmes and Career Breaks, Linden Cottage, The Burgage, Prestbury, Cheltenham, Gloucestershire; ☎01242-250901; e-mail info@thepodsite.co.uk; www.thepodsite.co.uk
Personal Overseas Development coordinates career breaks, time off and gap years for people wishing to volunteer their time and skills where it is needed. They arrange placements for people wanting to do something worthwhile in their year out, or a break from work. They provide opportunities for voluntary work and personal development with charities schools and other organisations in a developing world environment. This could be two weeks working in an orphanage as part of your travels, two months training to be a divemaster, or five months teaching English to children in a local school. Currently, programmes are organised in Tanzania Africa, Peru South America and Thailand SE Asia.

Gap Year Programmes last two to six months and Career Breaks from two weeks to a year. Programmes available include teaching English, orphanage work and diving. Career Breaks can be incorporated into travel plans so that you can choose how much is organised by PoD. You can apply your existing skills in a Third World environment or learn new ones. Friends and couples who want to work together can be accommodated on the same placement or different placements in the same location. Costs from about £350-£2,195 including training, being met on arrival and introduced to the area and placement, accommodation, ongoing support and insurance. Costs do not include flights, visas or food.

RIGHT TO PLAY
Thomson Building, Box 64, 65 Queen Street West, Suite 1900, Toronto, Ontario M5H 2MH; ☎+1 416-498 1922, ext. 224; fax +1 416-498 1942; e-mail pshea@righttoplay.com; www.righttoplay.com/opportunities.asp.
Right to Play's aim is to have a healthy impact on children and their communities with special focus on fostering healthy physical and psycho-social development of refugee children, children living in poverty, former child combatants and children orphaned by HIV/AIDS. Right to play recognises the need to promote the rights of women, girls and the disabled and to support their full participation in RTP's programmes. Complete information can be found on the website.

RTP recruits volunteers globally to staff their projects in about 22 countries. An honorarium of $8000 per annum plus accommodation, insurance etc. is provided.

Skills required for all projects: project management and implementation experience with overseas experience preferred; a high degree of professionalism; written and verbal communication skills, and comfort using these in a cross-cultural environment; training emphasis on training a low-literacy adult and youth population in non-traditional ways; comfort representing yourself and Right to Play to high level officials: UN agencies, directors, teachers and children and ease moving through different sections of the population in your host community; ability to be flexible and respond to project's needs; some locations require volunteers to live with minimal communications services and basic living arrangements.

Typically, volunteers should come from one of the following backgrounds: experience working with people with disabilities, experience working with children and developing children's activities; experience with HIV/AIDS awareness and health promotion, teacher trainers and coaches; communications backgrounds working with all forms of media; experience in community development and capacity building; experience in curriculum development; sport and physical activity background. Volunteers should have fluency in written and spoken English. Any of the following languages are an advantage: French, Portuguese, Russian, Spanish, Swahili, Amharic or Thai.

Applications: look on the website for general opportunities. Applications may be sent any time but there are two deadlines annually

---

Kat Powell describes a Right to Play community event day in Tanzania's refugee camps

I was a project coordinator, and today was a big day for many youth and young adults in the Lukole A & B UNHCR camps. We were near the end of the training of the new Right to Play community coaches, with this Track and Field event as the culmination. It was an amazing experience to see the excitement on the faces of the coaches, participants, and community spectators. There were activities for female and male youth, young adults and people with disabilities. It was the first time ever that people with disabilities had been invited to participate in a community event; something the coaches could be proud of. Throughout the day, the support and energy generated amongst the coaches, participants and spectators was contagious.

As the Track & Field event came to a close, the coaches received many thank-yous from their friends, family, and neighbours for this special day. The coaches said that even though it had been difficult to organise, they would gladly do it again, as they could see the power of sports to draw a community together and put smiles on faces. It is this crowd of smiles that my volunteer partner and I carried in our memories; that and proof of the importance of sport and play for the well-being of the community.

YOUTH CAREER COUNCIL (YCC)
Youth Avenue, Ishaque Shaheed Road, PO Box 108, Chakinal-48800, Pakistan; ☎ +92-573 51401; fax +92-573 21990; e-mail farakh –raja@hotmail.com
YCC is a branch of the Farakh Welfare Network, a multi-dimensional NGO cum voluntary movement operating in over 50 countries worldwide and devoted to serving the community through social welfare. YCC works mainly as an advisory service for young people encouraging further education, job placement, and career advancement. YCC also organises bilateral international youth exchange programmes such as 'International Youth Ambassadors', 'Global Cultural Friends' and 'Youth Volunteers for Peace'. The main objective of these programmes is character-building and to help young people become global-minded citizens.

The programmes which recruit over 700 volunteers annually, last from two weeks to two years. Volunteers participate in activities from casual labouring to office work in fields such as agriculture, health, economics, care, education, environment, media, vocational training, emergency relief, organisational strengthening, engineering, IT, marketing, business, industry, and community development. Minimum age 15. Applicants must be in good health. Partial expenses or pocket money are occasionally provided.

Applications with CV and photo to the above address.

Conservation, the Environment and Heritage

Volunteers are sought by a myriad of organisations to prop up the relics of our collective past, preserve the best parts of the environment from degradation and prevent the annihilation of more species from the planet. The tasks for volunteers are varied and far flung: assisting on study expeditions collecting data, helping to protect endangered species, planting trees, preserving old farming methods, and restoring ancient buildings for new usage, or to preserve them as museums, to name but a few. Whilst we cannot turn back the clock and reduce the impact of our ever encroaching species on the resources of this world, nor its urge to sweep away the old and build anew, we can keep trying to minimise the desecration of the natural world and shore up the remaining monuments of our historic heritages. Once gone, the world is poorer for their absence and clones and theme parks to recreate them are an admission of defeat.

There is something for volunteers of all interests and abilities, when it comes to volunteering in conservation/environment or heritage projects from the trained and skilled, to those wanting to learn ancient techniques, to those happy to do some donkey work in an inspirational setting. Some volunteers are more driven by a need to protect the ecology of the planet, while others mourn to see neglected historic buildings crumble and feel a stirring of their DIY instincts on a grand scale. The range of international projects is vast and everyone can do a bit, locally or internationally to resist the arrival of bland landscapes and a less astonishing natural world.

James Donnan took part in Kentwell's recreation of Tudor life:

The magic of Kentwell re-enactments is in bringing history to life in an engaging and entertaining way. This is not about being an anonymous player in a massive battle display, it is about presenting the reality of everyday Tudor life.

There are useful resources on the internet for conservation, environment and heritage work which you can browse by typing 'conservation abroad volunteering' etc into a search engine. Useful websites include:

Volunteering with Animals or in Conservation: www.chimps.nl/volunteer.htm: compiled by an experienced volunteer who searched the web when looking for a project to volunteer on and compiled a directory of many useful sites, which are now listed at this site for the benefit of all. The websites are listed under categories including General Volunteer Sites and Worldwide Green Volunteer Opportunities and also by country and continent. A great resource for those wanting to find a project.

Green Volunteers. www.greenvolunteers.org/network.html: site with hundreds of green projects around the world, but you have to buy the book *Green Volunteers* (ISBN 88-900167-9-5; £10.99) available from Vacation Work Publications (01865-241978; www.vacationwork.co.uk) first to get the contacts listed in the e-mail newsletter and to access the Green Volunteers Network. You are also promised free updates to the guide for many years to come.

Ecovolonteer: www.ecovolunteer.org: Ecovolunteer is a travel agent with a difference. They cooperate with local organisations around the world that are dedicated to the protection of nature and its inhabitants and help them find volunteers who want to do the same by organising trips for volunteers to places that are not accessible to tourists where it is possible to help with local conservation projects.

International Hands-on Workshops for Architectural and Site Conservation: www.heritageconservation.net/, is a non-profit organisation promoting the conservation of historic architecture and sites. The aim is to preserve architectural heritage around the globe. Hands-on workshops provide training in a variety of conservation techniques. Heritage network is in the process of developing a network of conservation specialists who are able to provide technical assistance when needed. These experts will work with interested laypersons worldwide to create an atmosphere of international cooperation. Volunteer participants can also work under the guidance of experts at conservation sites learning much-needed preservation skills. The emphasis is on vernacular structures and smaller monuments, which are often overlooked by big funding. A useful source of contacts.

Transitions Abroad: www.transitionsabroad.com, the website of the North American magazine has a section Responsible/Eco Travel Programs which includes a listing of conservation and environmental volunteer organisations.

BIOSPHERE EXPEDITIONS
Sprat's Water, nr. Carlton Colville, The Broads National Park, Suffolk NR33 8BP; ☎01502-583085; fax 01502-587414; e-mail info@biosphere-expeditions. org; www.biosphere-expeditions.org; Also has an office in Germany (e-mail deutschland@biosphere-expeditions.org)
Biosphere Expeditions is an award-winning, non-profit organisation offering hands-on wildlife conservation expeditions as an adventure with a purpose for everyone to all corners of the earth. The projects are not tours, photographic safaris or excursions but genuine wildlife expeditions placing those with no research experience alongside scientists who are at the forefront of conservation work. No special skills required and there are no age limits. Ages participating so far: youngest 16, oldest 83.

Projects run all year round and you can join from two weeks to two months with most joining for two to four weeks. Expedition contributions vary depending on the expedition. Biosphere always works with local people and at least two thirds of the volunteer's contribution goes towards the project directly. In 2004 these were wolf conservation (Poland), wolf and bird conservation (Ukraine), Amazon wildlife survey (Peru) and cheetah conservation (Namibia). Cost to volunteer is from about £1,000. Volunteers have to make their own travel arrangements to the in-country assembly point. Accommodation is provided.

For more information contact the above address.

BSES EXPEDITIONS
At The Royal Geographical Society, 1 Kensington Gore, London SW7 2AR; ☎020-7591 3141; fax 020-7591 3140; e-mail info@bses.org.uk; www.bses. org.uk
In 2005, BSES Expeditions are planning three 5/6 weeks summer expeditions to remote wilderness environments includingn the Andean White Mountains, Peru and Towards the North Pole (Svalbard) in the Arctic Circle. Approximately 200 fit, 'Young Explorers'

aged between sixteen and a half and twenty are needed to participate in scientific and conservation work, mountaineering and wilderness training. 'Young Explorers' aged 18 to 23 can volunteer for 3-month (April-June) gap year expedition for 2005 which is 'Wilderness, Wildlife and Zulu Warriors' getting to explore the Drakensburg Mountains, the Greater St. Lucia Wetlands and gain the first qualification towards becoming a Game Ranger or, January to March 2006, 'Journey to the End of the Earth' visiting Chile, Tierra del Fuego and exploring the awe-inspiring Cordillera Darwin mountain range. Those aged 21 and above with previous expedition experience can become leaders/ assistant leaders of the science projects and treks, assisting with logistics and base camp management. Qualified doctors are also needed for each expedition.

Participants for the 5/6 weeks summer expeditions will need to raise a contribution of approximately £3,000 each to cover travel, insurance and accommodation. Gap year participants will need to raise approximately £5,500 as their contribution for this expedition.

Applications should be received at the above address by mid-October of the year prior to explorer's departure.

BTCV
Conservation Centre, 163 Balby Road, Balby, Doncaster, DN4 ORH; ☎01302-572244; fax 01302-310167; e-mail information@btcv.org.uk; www.btcv.org. uk

BTCV is the UK's leading practical conservation charity for improving and protecting the environment. It aims to harness people's energies and talents to protect the environment by practical action. BTCV offers a programme of over 80 international working holidays each year lasting from one to six weeks throughout Europe, North America, Africa and Asia. These holidays offer people of all ages and all backgrounds the chance to work with and get to know local people in places off the beaten tourist track and to make a real difference to protecting the environment.

Holidays offer a variety of sometimes unusual assignments e.g. turtle monitoring in Thailand, radio tracking wolves in Slovakia and habitat management work in Tasmania. The working day is typically from 9am to 5.30pm and the evenings are free. Average costs are between £220 and £1,450 inclusive of accommodation, training and food. No experience necessary.

For a copy of the holidays brochure please e-mail or telephone.

CHELON – MARINE TURTLE CONSERVATION & RESEARCH PROGRAMME
Via le Val Padana, 134/B, 00141 Roma, Italy; tel/fax (research office) 0681 25301; chelon@tin.it

CHELON is among the main research bodies in Europe focusing on the biology and conservation of sea turtles. It works in conjunction with national and international organisations to develop awareness and understanding for marine turtles. Current and future projects take place primarily in the Italian peninsula, in the Mediterranean basin, Greece and Turkey, and in Thailand.

Several people every year actively contribute to the projects by participating in the 'research camps' held in the areas of special scientific value. A minimum commitment of two weeks is required from May to September for projects in the Mediterranean, and for projects in Thailand from December to April. Longer-term participants are also welcome. Volunteers help researchers gather data on nesting behaviour, and carry out observation, protection and tagging of turtles. Help is also needed with conservation awareness activities directed at local people and tourists. Lessons on marine turtle conservation and biology are scheduled too. In Turkey and Thailand training courses are available for Biological and Natural Science students.

Applicants should be at least 18 and able to speak English or Italian. Volunteers stay in their own tents in Greece and Turkey and in huts at the Golden Buddha Beach resort in Thailand. Projects cost US$600 for two weeks which covers food and accommodation. Travel expenses to/from research sites, personal expenses and insurance are not included.

For further information on specific projects contact CHELON at the above address.

CONCORDIA
Heversham House, 20/22 Boundary Road, Hove, East Sussex BN3 4ET; ☎01273-422218; fax 01273-421182; e-mail info@concordia-iye.org.uk; www.concordia-iye.org.uk

Concordia is a small charity committed to international youth exchange. Concordia International Volunteer Programme offers young people the opportunity to join an international team of volunteers working on community-based projects in over 40 countries including the UK. The projects differ enormously and include nature conservation, restoration, archaeology, construction, work with special needs adults and children, teaching/organising youth/children's holiday schemes. Projects generally last for 2-4 weeks with the main season from June to September with some spring and winter projects as well. Generally, the work does not require special skills or experience, though real motivation and commitment to the project are a must. Volunteers pay a subscription fee of £6-£10, a project fee of £85 (£60 for projects in the UK) for the standard programme in eastern/western Europe, North America, Korea and Japan, and £250 for projects in Latin America, Africa and South-east Asia. They also fund their own travel. Board and accommodation are free of charge.

CORAL CAY CONSERVATION LIMITED
The Tower, 13th Floor, 125, High Street, Colliers Wood, London SW19 2JG; ☎0870 750 0667; fax (0870) 750 0667; e-mail info@coralcay.org; www.coralcay.org

Coral Cay Conservation (CCC) is an international award-winning, non-profit organisation, which uses volunteers to assist with coral reef and tropical forest survey programmes and management initiatives. It is dedicated to providing resources to help sustain livelihoods and alleviate poverty through the protection, restoration, and management of coral reefs and tropical forests. Each year hundreds of international volunteers participate on CCC projects worldwide, working together as teams to assist local communities and counterpart agencies in gathering vital data.

CCC currently runs projects in the Philippines, Malaysia, Fiji and Honduras. In each of these locations, the pristine reefs and rainforests are under threat from development and rapidly growing tourism industries. Therefore there is an urgent need to complete the survey work, which will allow management plans for the sustainable use of the natural resources to be established.

No previous experience is required and full training (including SCUBA tuition, where necessary) is provided at each location. CCC projects run continuously throughout the year and volunteers (aged 16 years and over) may join projects for 2 weeks upwards. Costs start at £350 for forest expeditions and £700 for marine expeditions. A free information pack is available on request.

CCC also offers a range of voluntary non-salaried project staff positions, including: Project Scientist, Expedition Leader, Science Officer, Medical Officer, SCUBA Instructor and mountain leader. For further details about staff opportunities contact the Staff Recruitment Department at CCC.

> **Lucy Misch, 20, spent six weeks on the Fiji Coral Reef Conservation Project with Coral Cay**
>
> *People often ask me which was the best part of my gap year. I tell them that Fiji was the most intense and amazing experience I had because I learnt how to recognise and talk about a vast array of species in the Indo-Pacific. I saw things I had only ever seen on TV. I made friends that I will never lose contact with, and I also began to realise how I could live without my creature comforts. When I think back to the fun we had on the surveys there are too many moments to record. One time we were on our first deep survey dive of the day and were about half way down when a large sting-ray came swooping out of the blue. We just watched in awe as this massive creature moved majestically through the water. It circled us once and then disappeared. It was a stunning moment.*
>
> *This experience is something you will never repeat, and is an experience that you shouldn't miss out on. Diving for me has become a passion, and now as a fully-fledged instructor I teach throughout my university term. Every holiday I travel and teach diving, educating people about the coral reefs and helping other divers and snorkellers enjoy their holiday with fish identification.*

EARTHWATCH
267 Banbury Road, Oxford, OX2 7HT; ☎01865-318831; fax 01865-311388/38; e-mail projects@earthwatch.org.uk; www.uk.earthwatch.org/europe
Earthwatch is an international science and education charity, which supports over 140 scientific research projects in 50 countries, through individual membership, volunteers' financial contributions and corporate funding. To date, Earthwatch has enabled more than 65,000 volunteers to contribute over £35 million and 10 million hours to environmental and cultural field research in support of 2,800 field research projects in 118 countries' projects worldwide.

Earthwatch provides an opportunity for anyone to work directly in the field with scientists. Projects range from Hawksbill Sea Turtles of Barbados to Kenya's Black Rhino with prices ranging from £155 to £2,115 excluding flights, with teams lasting from three to eighteen days. Anyone over 16 years can volunteer, and no experience is required, as any training, where needed, is given on site.

Membership of Earthwatch is £30 per year, and members receive regular mailings on Earthwatch events, activities and volunteering opportunities, along with preferential rates on some projects.
US applicants should contact: Earthwatch, 3 Clocktower Place, Suite 100, P.O. Box 75, Maynard, MA 01754, USA; ☎800 776-0188 (freephone); fax 978-461-2332; www.earthwatch.org.

ECOVOLUNTEER PROGRAM
Meyersweg 29, 7553 AX Hengelo, Netherlands; ☎ +31-74 250 8250; fax +31-74 250 6572; e-mail info@ecovolunteer.org; www.ecovolunteer.org
The Ecovolunteer Program organises wildlife conservation projects and wildlife research projects operated by local conservation organisations worldwide. Work varies from practical fieldwork to production and support jobs in wildlife rescue centres, to visitor education, maintenance work, and household duties, dependent on each individual project.

500-600 volunteers were recruited in past years for projects lasting from 1-4 weeks. About 30 projects will be run in 2005. The minimum age of volunteers is 18; participants must be in good physical health. Accommodation is provided.

Applications should be made to the national Ecovolunteer agency of the country in which the applicant is resident (see list below). A list of the national agencies can also be found on the Ecovolunteer website or obtained from the above address.

Austria: Business & Ethnic Travel Center, Troststrasse 50/3/302, 1100 Vienna; ☎01-607 91 00 26; fax 01-607 91 03; e-mail info@betc.at

Belgium: Tierra Natuurreizen vzw, Heidebergstraat 309, 3010 Leuven; tel/fax 016 25.56.16; e-mail tierra@skynet.be Dutch language www.ecovolunteer.be; French language http://fr.ecovolunteer.be

Brasil: Mont Blanc Turismo, Rua Flavio Pinto Severo 430, Niteroi RJ; ☎021-2608 1477; http: br.ecovoluntarios.org/

Germany: One World Reisen mit Sinnen, Roseggerstrasse 59, 44137 Dortmund; ☎0231-164480; e-mail oneworld@reisenmitsinnen.de; covolunteer.de

Hungary: EcoVista Andrassy ut 1, 1061 Budapest; ☎01 429 9697; e-mail eco@vista.hu; www.vadonprogram.co.hu

Italy: Pithekos, Onlus, Via Savona 26, 20144 Milano, Italy; ☎39-(0)2 89405267; e-maill asspithekos@tiscalinet.it

Netherlands: JoHo, Stille Rijn 8, 2312 Leiden; ☎071-5131357; e-mail travel@joho.nl; www.joho.ecovolunteer.nl

Spain: Años Luz, Ronda de Sant Pere 26 Bajo, 08010 Barcelona; ☎093-310 1828; e-mail bcn@aluz.com; http://es.ecovoluntarios.org

Switzerland:= Arcatour SA, Bahnhofstrasse 28, 6301 Zug, Switzerland; ☎729 1420; 729 1421; e-mail arcatour@arcatour.ch

United Kingdom: WildWings, First Floor, 577/579 Fishponds Road, Fishponds, Bristol BS16 3AF; ☎0117-965 8333; e-mail wildinfo@wildwings.co.uk; www.ecovolunteer.org.uk

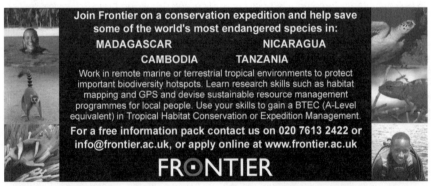

FRONTIER
50-52 Rivington Street, London, EC2A 3QP; ☎020-7631 2422; fax 020-7613 2992; e-mail info@frontier.ac.uk; www.frontier.ac.uk.
Frontier is an environmental organisation that recruits about 300 volunteers a year to participate in conservation expeditions in remote and unexplored areas of the world. The projects address high priority resource management and habitat conservation issues in Cambodia, Madagascar and Tanzania. Volunteers work on coral reefs, in rainforests and game reserves.

Volunteers can participate in long-term conservation projects for 4, 8, 10 or 20 weeks.

Projects focus on threatened tropical eco-systems (rainforest, savanna, coral reef and mangrove areas); the work includes biodiversity surveys, disturbance and resource-use assessments, socio-economic work and practical projects such as environmental education alongside local students and scientists. There are also 4-week expeditions organised to Madagascar.

Full training is given making all participants eligible to gain an internationally recognised BTEC qualification. No previous experience needed. Volunteers must be aged at least 17. Projects run year round. Volunteers must raise from £1,200 for 4 weeks, £1,700 for 8 weeks, £2,100 for 10 weeks and £3,200 for 20 weeks' expedition (excluding flight and visa costs). Help, advice and a briefing weekend are provided prior to departure. The contribution covers food and basic lodging, equipment, staff costs etc.

Prospective volunteers should contact Frontier for a free information pack or find out more through the Frontier website.

GLOBAL VISION INTERNATIONAL
Amwell Farmhouse, Nomansland, Wheathampstead, St. Albans, Herts. AL4 8EJ; ☎ 0870 608 8898; fax 01582-834002; e-mail info@gvi.co.uk; www.gvi. co.uk

GVI is a non-political, non-religious organisation which specialises in providing overseas expeditions. Through alliance with aid reliant environmental organisations throughout the world, GVI volunteers fulfil a critical role in the fields of environmental research, conservation, education and community development. Volunteers work in dramatic locations and receive excellent training.

GVI volunteers come from all walks of life and from all over the world. Ages from 18-80 are welcome. Projects include Coral Reef conservation in Mexico and the Seychelles and wildlife conservation research in the Amazon rainforest and South Africa. There are 30 projects to choose from worldwide including Street Children of Guatemala, turtle protection in Panama, work with the Diane Fossey Gorilla fund, community development in Nepal and river dolphin research in Brazil. Or you can work alongside ecologists and biological research specialists as an intern at National Parks and protected areas throughout South Africa, Mexico and Venezuela. Ask for an application pack from the above address.

Further opportunities run all over the world with departures throughout the year from 2 weeks to 2 years for everyone ages 18-65. No experience required as comprehensive training is provided. Costs start at £695 (for 4 weeks in South Africa). Further information and application at the website.

THE INSTITUTE FOR EARTH EDUCATION (IEE)
Cedar Cove, PO Box 115, Greenville, WV 24945, USA; ☎ +1 304 832-6404; fax +1 304 832-6077; e-mail IEE1@aol.com; www.eartheducation.org

Earth Education is the process of helping people to live more harmoniously and joyously with the natural world. Founded in 1974, the Institute for Earth Education (IEE) is an international, non-profit educational organisation made up of a volunteer network of individuals and member organisations committed to fostering earth education programmes throughout societies without relying upon government and corporate support. Currently there are branches underway in the United States, Australia, United Kingdom, Canada, Finland, France, Germany, Italy, Japan and the Netherlands. Internships are available for anyone wishing to discover the world's alternative to agency- and industry-sponsored environmental education at Cedar Cove, the home base of IEE, which serves the largest international group of educators in the environmental movement.

Internships in earth education, organic gardening and landcare are normally 2-12 months, all year round. Duties include earth education study, environmental living practicum; development/maintenance of the centre; assisting with operations of a non-profit organisation. Organic gardening interns are responsible for planting, sowing, harvesting, and preserving organic produce in the community garden. Landcare interns assist in the master planning, housing rehabilitation, trail design, establishing teepee and tree-house villages, developing wild cave tours, and some basic maintenance. Lodging, and an allowance for food are provided.

Those interested should apply to Internships at the above address.

MAST INTERNATIONAL
R395 VoTech Building, 1954 Buford Avenue, University of Minnesota, St Paul, MN 55108, USA; ☎800-346-6278 (in the USA or Canada); +1 612 624-3740 (elsewhere); fax +1 612 625 7031; e-mail mast@umn.edu; www.mast. coafes.umn.edu
The MAST International programme provides qualified individuals the opportunity to gain practical hands-on experience in agriculture, horticulture, agri-business, forestry or related areas. It involves a cross-cultural experience living and working in another culture and develops a global perspective and a broader understanding of the world. MAST operates in the following countries: Argentina, Australia, Denmark, Estonia, Finland, France, Germany, Hungary, the Netherlands, New Zealand, Morocco, South Africa, Spain, Sweden, Switzerland and elsewhere. Over 5,000 trainees from more thatn 65 countries have participated since the programme started in 1949.

Applicants must be between 18 and 30, in good health, have a minimum of six months practical or work experience in the field in which they are seeking additional training, and a knowledge of the host country's language is preferred (essential in France, Spain, Argentina and Morocco).

Volunteer trainees pay a MAST programme fee, a non-refundable application fee made payable to the University of Minnesota must be submitted with each application. Participants generally receive room and board and an allowance dependent on the country and type of placement. All international and domestic travel plus personal expenses are at the cost of the participant.

Applications should be received a minimum of three months prior to the preferred start date (four months for Germany and Denmark). An interview will be arranged once the application arrives in the MAST office. Pre-departure orientations are held throughout the year.

OCEANIC SOCIETY EXPEDITIONS
230-E Fort Mason, San Francisco, CA 94123, USA; ☎+1 415-441-1106; fax +1 415-474-3395; e-mail office@oceanicsociety.org; www.oceanic-society.org
OSE has researchers stationed all over the world and enables volunteer, paying participants to work on research programmes up close to marine wildlife and other aquatic species alongside biologists conducting on-going vital research in unique sites of biological significance. Service project members actively contribute to field projects by performing simple but labour intensive tasks. They receive hands-on experience in the sciences, and often become ambassadors for scientific research and conservation.

No previous experience is necessary as on-site training given. Activities range from data collection and analysis to taking photographic or collecting acoustic data from marine wildlife and ecology. Participants must be in good health and mobile enough to climb in and out of skiffs. They should be prepared for a variety of travel and climatic conditions. Normal period of recruitment is 1-3 weeks. Participants pay for their food, travel and lodging. Accommodation is provided within these costs.

OSE publishes *Whale Magazine* that is available to members. Membership costs $35 per annum. Participants receive a detailed information pack prior to joining in a research programme. Ocean Society is also an environmental, educational institution and information on current conservation issues and research can be accessed via their website.

Apply by contacting the office direct on 800 326 7491 or fill out an application form at the website or e-mail them.

TREKFORCE EXPEDITIONS
34 Buckingham Palace Road, London SW1W ORE; ☎020-7828 2275; e-mail info@trekforce.org.uk; www.trekforce.org.uk
Trekforce is a registered charity that offers a once-in-a-lifetime opportunity to play a part in international conservation. Eight-week, team-based expeditions run in Central and South America and South East Asia concentrating on endangered rainforests and working with the local communities. Also offered are four or five month programmes incorporating two months of project work, up to one month learning new languages and two months teaching in schools in rural communities.

Trekforce also offer extended programmes of three to five months incorporating a two-month project, up to one month learning a new language and two months teaching in a rural school.

Each volunteer has to raise their own Trekforce funds and help and advice are provided for this. Training includes a briefing day in the UK prior to departure and then full training in safety, first aid, outdoor skills, etc. once in the country.

Anyone aged 18-38 can apply. You can find out more by attending an informal introduction day. For information on recent projects, visit the website.

Ian Benton on why he chose Trekforce's Belize expedition in 2004
I chose Trekforce because I wanted to do more than just travel around the world. I wanted to immerse myself in a culture in a way that only living in a country can do. Trekforce offered to deliver all that in a professional and fun way. It was obvious that they are an organisation that could provide some real challenges, and give you the opportunity to do things that you have never done before.

UNIVERSITY RESEARCH EXPEDITIONS PROGRAM (UREP)
University of California, Davis, CA 95616, USA; ☎ + 1 530 752-8811; fax + 1 530 757-85967; e-mail urep@unexmail.ucdavis.edu; www/extension.ucdavis.edu/urep
UREP provides opportunities for people to participate in scientific discoveries by acting as field assistants on a University of California research expedition. Research topics offered in a large number of countries include animal studies, archaeology, arts and culture, earth sciences, ecology, and plant studies. Over 200 volunteers are needed each year for over 20 different projects. Most projects are offered from February to September and last around two weeks.

Volunteers must be in good health, at least 16 years old, have a desire to learn, enthusiasm and be willing to undertake team work. Specific skills or experiences are not essential but may be an advantage. Volunteers make a large contribution (typically $1,200-$1,800) to cover the project's costs. This contribution covers research equipment and supplies, preparatory materials, camping and field gear, ground transportation and meals and accommodation. Travel to the site is not included.

For more information contact UREP at the above address.

WWOOF (Worldwide Opportunities on Organic Farms)
WWOOF UK, P.O. Box 2675, Lewes, East Sussex, BN7 1RB; ☎01273-476286; e-mail hello@wwoof.org; www.wwoof.org.uk

WWOOF UK was started in 1971 and has since become a worldwide exchange network where bed, board and practical experience are given in return for help on organic farms. Stays of varied length are possible. WWOOF provides excellent opportunities for organic training, changing to a rural life, cultural exchange and being part of the organic movement.

For further details of WWOOF UK, WWOOF independents and other national WWOOF organisations, please send a stamped, addressed envelope to WWOOF UK at the above address.

Each of the groups listed below is an independent group with its own aims, system, fees and rules. They are all similar in that they offer volunteers the chance to learn in a practical way the growing methods of their host. The minimum age for Wwoofing in the UK is 16 and abroad it is 18 years. Volunteers must pay their own travel expenses but food and accommodation is provided. Each group will supply a worklist booklet to members from which volunteers can choose a farm; send International Reply Coupons when writing to an overseas group.

WWOOF schemes:

Australia: WWOOF (Aus), RSD, Buchan, Vic 3885; ☎+61-3 5155 0218; fax +61-3 5155-0342; e-mail wwoof@wwoof.com.au; www.woof.com.au. Fix-it yourself basis only. $50 (single), $60 for two people travelling together using one book (The Australian WWOOF book).

Austria: WWOOF (Austria), Hildegard Gottlieb, Einoedhofweg 48, 8042 Graz, Austria; tel/fax +43 (0)676-5051639; e-mail: wwoof.welcome@telering.at; web: www.wwoof.welcome.at.tf. Austrian farm list (about 140 farms) is US$25 or €20 plus two international reply coupons.

Canada: WWOOF (Canada), 4429 Carlson Road, Nelson, British Columbia Canada V1L 6X3; ☎+1 250-354 4417; e-mail wwoofcan@shaw.can; web: www.wwoof.ca.

Czech Republic: WWOOF Czech Republic, Jana Lojkova, Area Viva, Dubecno 50, 28902 Knezice, Czech Republic; tel +42 (0)776 22 60 14; e-mail areaviva@quickcz or areaviva@seznam.cz; web www.wwoof.ecn.cz. . For Czech farm list send $15, or GBP£10 or 15 euros.

Denmark: WWOOF Denmark, Bent & Inga Nielsen, Asenvej 35, 9881 Bindslev, Denmark; tel +45 9893 8607; e-mail info@wwoof.dk; web: www.wwoof.dk.

Finland: WWOOF (Finland) is currently without a representative. WWOOF independents will list WWOOF hosts in Finland for the time being.

Germany: WWOOF (Germany), Postfach 210 259, 01263 Dresden, Germany; e-mail info@wwoof.de; web: www.wwoof.de. Membership 18 euros (no other currency) plus two international reply coupons.

Ghana: WWOOF (Ghana), Ebenezer Nortey-Mensah, PO Box 154 TF, Fair Trade Centre, Accra, Ghana; tel/fax +233 21-761091. Send $25 plus three IRCs.

Hawaii: 50 hosts on four islands – see website www.wwoofhawaii.org. Some hosts are also listed in WWOOF Independents listings.

Italy: Bridget Matthews,109 via Casavecchia, 57022 Castegneto Carducci, LI, Italy; e-mail info@wwoof.it; web: www.wwoof.it. The list costs 25 euros (only currency) payable only in cash or by bank draft.

Japan: WWOOF Japan, Kita 16-jo, Higashi 16-chome, 3-22, Higashi-ku, Sapporo, 065-0016 Japan; e-mail info@wwoofjapan.com; web: wwoofjapan.com. The Japan list has about 50 hosts and expanding. It costs $50 Australian, $40 American or 4000 Japanese yen and is available as a PDF file downloadable document to WWOOFers..

Korea: 1008 Seoul B/D 45 Jongno-1Ga, Jongno-Gu; 110-121 South Korea; ☎+82 2 723 4458; fax +82 2 723 9996; e-mail wwoof@wwoofkorea.com; www.wwoofkorea. com. Not all on list are organic farms. Membership $50 inclusive of international postage.

Nepal: FD Regmi, GPO Box 9594, Kathmandu, Nepal; tel +9771-4363418; fax +9771-4479965; e-mail fdregmi@wlink.com.np. Membership $20 or for two people travelling together $30.

New Zealand: WWOOF (NZ), Jane & Andrew Strange, PO Box 1172, Nelson, NZ; tel/fax +64 3 5449890; e-mail support@wwoof.co.nz; web: www.wwoof.co.nz. write enclosing £16 cash for list (£20 for couple).

Wwoof Slovenia: Polona Gostan, Pajerjeva 10, 4208 Sencur, Slovenia; e-mail polona. gostan@s5.net; web: www.wwoofslovenia.cjb.net. Membership 10 euros.

Sweden: Andreas Hedren, Palstrop Hunna, 340 30 Vislanda, Sweden; ☎+470 75 43 75.

*Switzerland:*WWOOF,Postfach 59, CH-8124, Maur, Switzerland; e-mail wwoof@gmx. ch; www.dataway:ch/reini/wwoof/ Send 20 Swiss francs.

Turkey: WWOOF Turkey, Bahar Dölen, Buðday Ekolojik Yaþamý Destekleme Derneði, Buðday Association for Supporting Ecological Living, Lüleci Hendek Cad. 120/2, Keuledibi-Beyoðlu/Istanbul, Turkey 34425; tel +90 (0)212 252 5255; e-mail bahar@bugday.org; web: www.bugday.org

Uganda: WWOOF Uganda. P.O. Box 2001, Kampala, Uganda, East Africa; tel 256-346856; 251276; fax +251 273; e-mail bob–kasule@yahoo.com

If the prospective volunteer is interested in other countries (Ireland, France, Spain, Portugal, etc) there is at present no national WWOOF for these countries and farms are listed in the WWOOF Independents Listings. Look at the website (www.wwoof.org) for more details and also to check the up-to-date listings. There is a charge for the list of independents.

Rob Abblett was inspired by WWOOF Australia's international listings
The WWOOF list from Australia is without doubt the only book I would not leave England without. It includes some new addresses of potential volunteer work in countries which had previously been black holes for paid or unpaid work notably Bolivia, Chile, Paraguay, Peru and Uruguay (among others). I have recently come back from South America where I stayed on a WWOOF farm in Paraguay for two weeks, living and working with a Swiss German family on a large isolated plot of land, learning about their many tribulations as they struggled in vain to adapt from Swiss efficiency to Third World conditions. Afterwards, I became the first Wwoofer that a German woman host in Uruguay had ever had. She worked as a teacher in Montevideo and had integrated well into the country. She provided great food and wine for working on her large garden, picking strawberries, weeding and painting.

Religious Projects

Helping your fellow man or woman is a basic tenet of most of the world's major religions, and religious organisations are one of the largest sources of voluntary work worldwide. However, you don't have to be a missionary, or in many cases not even a religious person to be taken on. The fact that not all helpful people are driven by divine zeal is recognised by religious organisations, and some of them do not insist that you are a believer to volunteer with them. Nonetheless, it is undeniable, that whereas socially motivated, non-sectarian organisations offer their services free of prejudice to those in need, and refrain from imposing their beliefs and values on a culture different from their own; religious projects are much more likely to have a proselytising element. Of course, this part of the programme may be the thing that attracts the volunteer in the first place.

The other misconception about volunteering with religious organisations is that they are usually only interested in long-term volunteers who can spend a minimum of a year, and preferably two or three years on the project. While this is true in many cases, there are also many short-term possibilities lasting a few weeks or months as well.

In an article from *The Times* on work for good causes, Megan Mackeson describes working for Tearfund:

Because it is a Christian charity, we really support each other and Christian values are integral, but it is a challenging environment. I tend to throw myself into a job so I have to believe in what I do.

There are dozens of religious organisations in the UK that send volunteers abroad for short-term and longer term projects and the website www.medic-stravel.co.uk/NGOs/non–governmental–organisations.htm is a good starting point as it lists dozens of organisations that recruit volunteers for work overseas; religious ones are marked with a Christian cross symbol. There are far more religious organisations in the USA than the UK and some useful websites for religious projects there are:

Global PeaceWorks: www.globalpeaceoworks.org an organisation 'for all faiths and none but who have an interest in spirituality and religious expression' of all faiths to mingle as volunteers for various projects. The site also carries background information explaining some of the precepts of important world religions that volunteers might find themselves encountering (Hinduism, Buddhism etc) when working for a religious-based organisation.

Middlebury College: www.middlebury.edu/offices/ace/service/volopps. html.htm is a Vermont College's website with a volunteer section which includes a subsection of faith-based volunteer opportunities in the USA and worldwide.

Presbyterian Church USA: www.pcusa.org/one door is the online referral system of the Presbyterian Church in the United States through which prospective volunteers can find a wide variety of opportunities for short-term and longer-term with the PC in the United States and Worldwide.

ASSOCIATE MISSIONARIES OF THE ASSUMPTION
914 Main St; #5, Worcester, MA 0110, USA; tel/fax 508 767-1356; e-mail ama-usa@juno.com; www.AssumptionVolunteers.org.
A lay missionary association, Associate Missionaries of the Assumption (AMA) place volunteers with or nearby to their international religious communities. Volunteers typically help the local people through education and self-development programmes. Communities currently exist in Europe, Asia, Africa and the Americas. Approximately

15 volunteers a year are required for one or two years of service in the areas of parish ministry, health care, education, community development, and advocacy.

Volunteers are preferred to be Catholic, aged 23-40 who have a college degree and are fluent in the language of the country in which they intend to serve. Training consists of a discernment weekend and orientation in Massachusetts. Board and lodging and a monthly stipend are provided. The volunteer must obtain a visa for their stay as a lay missionary.

ASSUMPTION LAY VOLUNTEER PROGRAMME
23 Kensington Square, London W8 5HN; ☎020-7361 4752; fax 020-7361 4757; e-mail cburns@rayouth.freeserve.co.uk; www.alvp.org.uk
Assumption Lay Volunteers are individuals, from 21 years old, single or married who are willing to take up the challenge of living and working in a culture that is quite different from their own. The programme is for those whose faith calls them to share in the lives of the poor, the young and the marginalised.

There are opportunities to work alongside an Assumption community in the UK, Tanzania, Rwanda and the Philippines for a minimum of one year. Individuals interested do not have to have a professional qualification (although this would be an advantage) but they must have an openness to new and challenging experiences, be non-judgmental and have and ability to live in simple and sometimes basic conditions, plus a willingness to do anything.

BMS WORLD MISSION
PO Box 49, Baptist House, Didcot, Oxon OX11 8XA; ☎01235-517653; fax 01235-517601; e-mail short-term@bmsworldmission.org; www. bmsworldmission.org
BMS World Mission is a leading overseas Christian mission organisation alleviating suffering and injustice and improving the daily quality of life. BMS has three volunteer programmes which cover a variety of ages and skills:
Gap Year Programme: Action Teams of four young people to countries worldwide. New experiences, quality training, amazing people, challenging times, helping the needy, God at work, time of your life. Cost £3,400. Nine months (Sept-June) includes one month training, 6 months overseas, 2 months UK tour. Ages 18-25. Apply by March.
Summer Teams: Small Teams to a variety of locations including Brazil, India, Thailand and Spain to get involved with children's work, English teaching and church work. Generalist, practical and medical skills. Cost £800-£1,200. Two to five weeks July/Aug. Ages 18+. Apply by April.
Individual Volunteer Programme: Offers an opportunity to use your professional skills or experience on a short-term placement e.g. teaching, administrating, medical etc. Cost varies with location. Three months to two years. Ages 21 to post-retirement. Apply anytime.

CATHOLIC NETWORK OF VOLUNTEER SERVICE (CNVS)
6930 Carroll Avenue, Suite 506, Takoma Park, MD 20912-4423, USA; ☎ +1 301 270-0900; fax +1 301 270-0901; e-mail volunteer@cnvs.org; www. cnvs.org
CNVS is a resource centre of approximately 200 faith-based volunteer programmes. It publishes *RESPONSE Volunteer Opportunities Directory* (120 pages), which lists contact and other useful information about the member programmes and the full time volunteer opportunities they offer throughout the world. The indexes make this directory especially easy to use. Volunteer opportunities are from one week to one year or more

in length. Volunteers have a variety of skills and qualifications. People interested in volunteering can, if they desire, submit their profile (personal background information) online, which is then sent to the volunteer programmes. In this way, if any volunteer programmes see a potential match between the prospective volunteer and the needs of the programme, the programme(s) can contact the individual directly. To receive a free copy of the RESPONSE Volunteer opportunities Directory, contact CNVS or visit its website and view the directory online.

CHRISTIAN FOUNDATION FOR CHILDREN AND AGEING
1 Elmwood Avenue, Kansas City, KS 66103-3719, USA; ☎ +1 913 384-6500; (freephone USA 800-875 6564 fax +1 913 384-2211; e-mail volunteers@cfcausa.org; www.cfcausa.org
CFCA is a lay Catholic organisation that creates relationships between sponsors in the USA and children and ageing persons in 25 nations around the world. It works with poor and abandoned children and ageing people through person-to-person assistance programmes. Volunteers are a vital link in their service as they form part of a local mission team. Motivated by love, their goal is to embrace the poor and to serve, recognizing their dignity, and work with them towards self-sufficiency. At present, the Foundation has teams working in Central and South America, India, Africa and the Philippines.

Project Co-ordinators request long-term volunteers every year of varying skills and backgrounds, from agriculturists to child-care workers, nurses, building tradesmen, social workers etc. The Foundation cannot place medical doctors in a clinical or surgical setting, but there is a need for health care professionals who wish to provide more basic health care. Posts are for at least six months. Fluency in Spanish is required for Latin American placements.

Volunteers are responsible for travel, health insurance and personal expenses. Average cost for a nine to twelve-month period in Latin America or India would be $3,500. Room and board is provided at the project sites. Applicants need not be US citizens but all applicants must come to Kansas City for a two-day orientation, although this does not mean that a commitment to service has been made by either party. Due to travel expenses this may be difficult for applicants outside the USA. Volunteers need not be Catholic but must be comfortable living in Catholic or religious communities. The minimum age is 21 years.

Those interested should contact the Volunteer Co-ordinator at the above address.

COLUMBAN LAY MISSIONARIES
66 Newland Street, Silvertown, London E16 2HN; ☎020-7059-0253; www.columban.com/lm.htm
CLMP is for those who have a calling to share the lives of the poor and those on the margins of society. Missionaries are sent for three years to join the Columban Fathers in their worldwide Catholic ministry from Peru to Pakistan and from the Philippines to Fiji. At present, volunteers are needed in Chile and the Philippines.

Volunteers do parish work, women's and youth groups, adult literacy, health promotion, human rights, inter-faith dialogue and ecological work, working with marginalised groups. About 14 volunteers are taken on a year. Volunteers should be UK resident, aged 23-40 and in good health. They should also be Catholic. A six-month training course in the UK is followed by three years overseas. Volunteers expenses are all paid for plus an adequate allowance. National Insurance contributions are paid while overseas. A free newsletter is sent out 3 times a year to those who ask to go on the mailing list.

For further information, apply direct to the above address.

CROSSLINKS
251 Lewisham Way, London SE4 1XF; ☎020-8691 6111; fax 020-8694 8023; e-mail info@crosslinks.org; www.crosslinks.org
Crosslinks is a Christian Mission agency working in partnership with the church worldwide. It seeks to recruit people who are willing to use both their professional skills and spiritual gifts in Christian service in another culture.

The SMILE programme (Short Term Mission Involvement, Learning and Experience) sends volunteers to live and work alongside mission partners around the world. The work of volunteers can be anything from building to teaching, and from assisting in health centres to leading on youth camps. The actual placement will depend on the skills of the individuals and the requirements of the hosts which include Tanzania, Kenya, Poland, Ireland and the UK. There is also a programme, NEXT, for older volunteers aged 30-50+ on short-term missions overseas.

Programme lengths vary from a week for a summer leader to six months or longer for some African placements. Volunteers pay for their own flights and living costs while on placement. Minimum age 18 years. Apply to the SMILE Coordinator at the above address.

GLOBAL OUTREACH MISSION UK
108 Sweetbriar Lane, Exeter, Devon EX1 3AR; ☎01392-259673; fax 01392-491176; www.globaloutreachmission.org.
Global Outreach UK is a Christian evangelical missionary society with representatives in 39 countries. Christian camps, Bible courses, radio broadcasting and in particular establishing churches are all methods used to propagate the Gospel. Opportunities exist for volunteers as career and short-term missionaries, members of summer outreach teams and itinerant evangelists. A whole-hearted agreement with Outreach's Statement of Faith is required and volunteers must be over 18 years old. Volunteers must supply a doctor's certificate of good health and are responsible for raising their own funds.

A short-term missionary programme is designed for young graduates of Bible school, single or married couples, who require 'in service' training. The volunteers are attached to a local church for periods of 12 to 24 months and work with the pastor on all aspects of the church's programme.

Career missionaries are placed in churches financially unable to support a full time pastor, but able to provide accommodation and if possible, part salary, with the balance coming from interested churches and individuals.

For further details on volunteer requirements, financial information and other facts, contact the General Secretary at the above address.

ICYE-UK
Latin American House, Kingsgate Place, London NW6 4TA; tel/fax 020-7681 0983; e-mail info@icye.co.uk
ICYE is an international organisation established in 1949 and made up of autonomous national committees. The organisation aims to break down the barriers that exist between people of different cultures, faiths, ethnic groups and nationalities and raise awareness of social and environmental issues at home and abroad. Approximately 600 young people around the world take part every year. Participating countries are: Bolivia, Brazil, Columbia, Costa Rica, Honduras, Mexico, Ghana, Kenya, Nigeria, India, Japan, South Korea, Taiwan, New Zealand, Austria, Belgium, Denmark, Finland, France, Germany, Iceland, Italy, Spain, Sweden, Switzerland, Eastern Europe, and countries in the Middle East. For details of this year-long programme see *Professional and Longer-term Volunteering* at the end of the Worldwide section.

ICYE-UK also offers a short-term programme (two weeks to three months) to Costa

Rica, India, Nepal and Morocco, with no age limits.
Please contact the office for more information.

JESUIT VOLUNTEER COMMUNITY: BRITAIN
23 New Mount Street, Manchester M4 4DE; ☎0161-832 6888; fax 0161-832 6958; e-mail staff@jvc.u-net.com; www.jesuitvolunteers-uk.org
The Jesuit Volunteer Community offers young adults the opportunity for personal development through community living, whilst working in areas of social need alongside the marginalised. The JVC programmes focus on four values: spirituality, social justice, community and simple lifestyle.

Volunteers work full-time in a variety of placements and live together in small groups of 4-6 in Glasgow, Manchester, Liverpool or Birmingham. Current placements include work with the homeless, refugees and adults with learning difficulties. There are also opportunities to work in drug and alcohol rehab and advice centres. Each placement provides the necessary support and training. JVC provides a structured development programme that consists of a series of workshops/retreats during the course of the programme. Year programme is from September to July (ages 18-35). Summer programme: 3 weeks during August (ages 17-30). Deadline for postal applications is June.

Volunteers get accommodation, food allowance and pocket money. Foreign volunteers pay travel costs to and from the UK at the start and end of placements. Applications to Chris Leigh.

MENNONITE CENTRAL COMMITTEE
PO Box 500, Akron, Pennsylvania 17501-0500, USA; ☎+1 717 859-1151; fax +1 717 859-2171; e-mail mailbox@mcc.org; www.mcc.org
The Mennonite Central Committee is the relief and development agency of the North American Mennonite and Brethren in Christ churches. MCC has more than 800 personnel in 50 countries in Asia, Africa, Europe, Latin America and North America, usually in conjunction with other agencies to which they often second personnel.

MCC assignments include agricultural development, water conservation, health, formal and informal education, economic and technical projects, church-related programmes, relief administration, social services and peace-making. Language training is provided for work in non English-speaking areas. A small monthly allowance is paid, and all expenses, including round trip transportation, are met in full. Accommodation is also provided. North American assignments are two years in length; overseas assignments are three years.

Applicants must be members of a Christian church and committed to non-violent peace-making. Most applications come from North America and Europe, but applications are also accepted from Mennonite or Brethren in Christ church members from other continents.

Inquiries and applications should be sent to the Personnel Officer at the above address.

MISSION VOLUNTEERS USA & INTERNATIONAL
The Presbyterian Church (USA), 100 Witherspoon Street, Louisville, Kentucky 40202-1396,USA; www.pcusa.org/msr
The Mission Volunteers USA and Mission Volunteers International Programmes of the Presbyterian Church in the USA give participants a variety of opportunities to enter the world serving communities locally or globally. Various positions include teaching, health care, agricultural development, youth work, community service and more.

Volunteers must be active members of their church communities and be willing to live simple lifestyles. Room and board may be provided; volunteers may need to work with their church communities to raise funding. Service terms from three months to two years.

Further information can be obtained from the above address.

OPERATION MOBILISATION
Quinta, Weston Rhyn, Oswestry, Shropshire, SY10 07L; ☎01691-773388; fax 01691-778378; e-mail goglobal@uk.om.org; www.uk.om.org
Operation Mobilisation is an international mission organisation. It is now in more than 80 countries and has 3,000 workers who have joined for a year or longer. The main emphases of their work are evangelism with local churches and training of young Christians so that they are better equipped to share their faith. In addition, Operation Mobilisation has two ships, *Doulos* and *Logos II* which give similar evangelism and training opportunities to the land-based teams. The minimum age for the year programme is 17 years in the UK and 18 years abroad. There are opportunities for people with practical work experience and skills. Applicants of any nationality are welcome. Most are sponsored by their churches.

Short-term options comprise summer programmes, and many more opportunities are available on a year-round basis. These comprise an initial week of training, then volunteers/participants go out in teams in the country of their choice for one to eight weeks. The cost is dependent on duration and location.

For further information please contact the Personnel Department at the above address.

PERSONNEL PROGRAMME TEAM
Church Mission Society, 157 Waterloo Road, London SE1 8UU; ☎020-7928 8681; e-mail kathy.tyson@cms-uk.org; www.cms-uk.org
The Society sends mission partners to 26 countries in Africa and Asia. Such people go in response to requests from churches overseas for assistance in particular areas. A wide range of ages and occupations is represented by mission partners and all have a particular skill or occupation. There is a particular need for people to offer themselves for long service of six years or more although the minimum is two years' service. There are also some openings for short-term service; these too require a professional qualification or practical skill (see below).

All mission partners must be practising Christians though not necessarily Anglican. All should have technical or professional training and be qualified in their field. Mission partners receive an allowance related to the cost of living in the country they work in, fares are paid and there is a pension scheme. Visa and work permit requirements vary from country to country.

The Society also organises two programmes for young people aged 18 to 30. These are: Encounter for groups which last about five weeks; and Make a Difference Placements which are for individuals and enable young Christians to gain cross-cultural experience of mission through being placed in an appropriate location six to eighteen months. These placements are either overseas or in Britain and are task-based. Applicants are responsible for most of their own costs.

For further information about any of these schemes write to the Personnel Programme Team at the above address.

UNITED SOCIETY FOR THE PROPAGATION OF THE GOSPEL(USPG) Exchange Programme and The Methodist Church Experience Exchange Programme
Partnership House, 157 Waterloo Road, London SE1 8XA; ☎020-7486-5502; fax 020-7467-5283; e-mail eep@Methodistchurch.org.uk; www.uspg.org.uk
The Experience Exchange Programme (EEP) is run jointly by USPG and the Methodist

Church in the UK. It provides opportunities for all adults to spend 6-12 months living and working in Europe, Africa, Asia, or Latin America. Participants work alongside local people in church-based projects such as schools, community development programmes or hostels.

No specific skills are necessary although applicants should be flexible, adaptable and open to new ideas. Through living in another culture, participants learn to see the world and God's interaction with the world through others' eyes. Participants are strongly encouraged on their return to share what they have learned from their experience with church groups in the UK.

WEC INTERNATIONAL
Bulstrode, Gerrards Cross, Bucks SL9 8SZ; ☎01753-278103; e-mail info@uk. wec-int.org
WEC International seeks to evangelize the remaining unevangelized areas of the world in the shortest possible time. As well as spreading the Gospel, WEC volunteers also give practical help with medical, rehabilitation, education and community development projects. Small numbers of volunteers are needed to help full time WEC volunteers in over 60 countries of the world.

Those interested in summer service, practical projects or gap year openings go through the WEC Trek Programme where placements from three weeks to nine months can be arranged. Placements for one or two years are also available, particularly for those with specific skills or training such as teachers, nurses, doctors, mechanics, builders, secretaries etc.

All volunteers should be Christians. Volunteers pay their own travel costs and living expenses while on the programme. Board and lodging are provided in some situations.

Those interested should contact the above address.

WORLD EXCHANGE
St Colm's International House, 23 Inverleigh Terrace, Edinburgh EH3 5NS; ☎0131-315 4444; e-mail WE@StColm's.org; www.worldexchange.org.uk
World Exchange is organised by a number of British Churches acting together. It offers volunteer opportunities ranging from short-term visits, work camps and exchanges to one year placements. In the past volunteers have been placed in Asia, the Middle East, Africa and Central America.

Candidates can be of any age between 18 and 80. A small local allowance is paid and food and accommodation are provided.

World Exchange is always pleased to give information about working abroad as a volunteer. For details contact the address above.

WORLD HORIZONS
North Dock, Llanelli SA15 2LF, Wales SA15 2LU; ☎01554-750005; fax 01554-773304; e-mail gapyear@worldhorizons.co.uk; www.worldhorizons.org
World Horizons is a modern mission movement offering committed Christians the opportunity to be involved in expeditions and short term placements, as well as long-term in Europe, the Middle East, Asia, Africa, and the Americas as well as in the UK.

Catering, administrative, computing, building or mechanical skills are always helpful. Teaching English as a foreign language opportunities are also available as are supervising outdoor activities programmes for adults and teens. The minimum age for Europe is 16 and 18 for the rest of the world. Volunteers are responsible for raising funds to finance their trip. Accommodation is provided, but will need to be covered by the volunteer.

Write to Miriam Ashley at the above address.

WORLD SERVICE ENQUIRY

233 Marché Centre, 241-251 Ferndale Road, London SW9 1BJ; ☎0870-770 3274; fax 0870-770 7991; e-mail wse@cabroad.org.uk; www.wse.org.uk
World Service Enquiry is the information and advice activity of Christians Abroad for people of any faith or none. WSE provides expert and impartial advice about opportunities to work or volunteer in the Third World. The annual *Guide to Volunteering and Working Overseas* contains information about being involved in development issues, a list of volunteer agencies and basic information about working overseas. *Opportunities Abroad* is the UK's only monthly development job magazine available in a range of subscriptions. World Service Enquiry also provides personal advice and life coaching solutions for those seeking work in the development sector.

WORLD VISION

World Vision House, Opal Drive, Fox Milne, Milton Keynes, Buckinghamshire MK15 0ZR; ☎01908-841023; fax 01908-841001; e-mail studentchallenge@ worldvision.org.uk; www.worldvision.org.uk
World Vision, an international Christian relief and humanitarian aid agency dedicated to the relief of suffering and improvement in the quality of life of the world's poorest people. The charity has over 90 offices worldwide.
Student Challenge is World Vision's short-term summer programme for those aged 18-29 and provides young adults with hands on experience working overseas for six weeks in one of World Vision's long-term development programmes.
Applicants should be fully in sympathy with World Vision's Christian basis of faith.

YOUTH WITH A MISSION (YWAM)

13 Highfield Oval, Ambrose Lane, Harpenden, Herts AL5 4BX; ☎01582-463300; fax 01582-463305; e-mail enquiries@oval.com; www.ywam-England.com
YWAM is an international charitable organisation which is interdenominational in character and undertakes evangelical, training and relief ministries in about 100 countries. All tasks are undertaken by volunteers and are financially supported by their home church, fellowship, friends or family.
Volunteers are needed in whatever field they wish to offer their service, and they can serve from two weeks to a lifetime. Those wishing to serve for a long term must be willing to attend a basic training course with YWAM. Volunteers must be committed Christians with their own financial support (£300 per month is a rough average, depending on the location).
For more information contact YWAM at the above address.

Social Development and Community Schemes

Social Development and Community Schemes (sometimes called workcamps, although the sphere now embraces other projects too) are largely the product of a post-war era of the last century. After two World Wars, there was a huge amount of idealism invested in the idea that if the young people of all nations could mingle and cooperate on tasks together in other poorer countries there would never again be an international war. At the same time as helping their own world to be free of conflict, the youth who were working on social development schemes would be helping to rid the Third World of the twin evils of poverty and unemployment and aid the formation of active social communities engaged in promoting the common good worldwide.

It is worth quoting Dr. Justin Smith, Director of the Institute of Volunteering Research:

> Why should governments be interested in promoting volunteering, especially when some voluntary activities can be seen as a challenge to the authority of the state? There are two major benefits of volunteering. First, an economic one, volunteering makes an important economic contribution to society. Activities undertaken by volunteers would otherwise be funded by the state or by private capital. Volunteering adds to the overall economic output of a country and reduces the burden on government spending. But volunteering has a second and perhaps more important benefit. Volunteering helps in the building of strong and cohesive communities. It fosters trust between citizens and helps develop norms of solidarity and reciprocity,+ which are essential to stable communities. Moreover by helping to build this 'social capital' volunteering also plays a role in economic regeneration.

There are several large umbrella organisations for social development and community volunteering worldwide including SCI/IVS, Involvement Volunteers, International Cultural Youth Exchange (ICYE), Intenational Conference Volunteers, Global Vision, Global Citizens etc. Many of these represent smaller organisations that use these organisations as a central application point for volunteers. A useful website starting point is www.icvolunteers.org and click on their links page, or Other Volunteer Organizations pages. Also try the websites of the organisations mentioned above whose details are included in this section.

AIDCAMPS INTERNATIONAL
5, Simone Court, Dartmouth Road, London SE26 4RP; ☎020-8291-6181; fax 0870 130 3420; e-mail info@aidcamps.org; www.aidcamps.org.

AidCamps International is a registered charity offering volunteers the opportunity to participate in short-term voluntary work development aid projects overseas, run by local non-governmental organisations in the Third World.

AidCamps typically involve putting the finishing touches to needed community buildings, such as schools, health centres and son on, provided by the project. No skills or experience are needed and there is no 'hard hat' work involved.

In addition to the volunteer work, there are two and three-week AidCamps which give volunteers the chance to meet, live and work overseas with local people and experience their culture first hand, while providing a solution to a local problem, as requested by the locals.

AidCamps itineraries also include other local problem awareness visits, as well as trips to local and regional heritage sites, national parks, and cultural centres, so that volunteers can get a feel for both the richness of the area and the predicaments faced by its inhabitants.

In addition to volunteer work on three-week projects, camps provide volunteers with the opportunity to live overseas and meet with people of cultures very different from their own. Each AidCamp takes 10-15 volunteers who each pay a £550 participation fee. Half the fee goes directly into implementing the aid project; the other half is used to take care of the volunteers. The fee includes all ground transportation, accommodation and most meals. All ages of volunteers considered above 18 years old.

Applications to the above address.

AKTION SÜHNEZEICHEN FRIEDENDIENSTE (ASF, Action Reconciliation Service for Peace)
Augustr. 80, 10117 Berlin, Germany; ☎ +49 30-28395-184; fax +49 30-28395-135; e-mail asf@asf-ev.de; www.asf-ev-de

ASF operates two volunteer programmes: *Sommerlager* (workcamps) take place each summer many countries including: Czech Republic, France, Germany, Poland, Russia and The Netherlands. The work camp participants help with the maintenance of Jewish cemeteries and memorial centres, assist in social facilities, involve themselves in projects and support intercultural experiences. In addition historical and social issues are discussed. Age range is 16-70 years. Usually last two weeks.

The second programme is for long-term volunteers in thirteen countries including Belarus, Belgium, The United Kingdom, Israel, Norway, Russia, Ukraine and the United States. Long-term volunteers are usually aged 19-28 (older is possible) and committed to serve for 12 months starting March 1 or September 1. Projects include working with physically and mentally handicapped, elderly, poor and homeless, refugees, at memorial centres and museums, anti-racism initiatives and education work. Persons living outside Germany can only apply for the volunteer programme in Germany. Persons from Poland can apply for the programme in the UK as well as Germany.

About 300 volunteers are recruited annually for summer camps and 150 for long-term projects. Any nationality can apply for summer camps, the long-term option is restricted to nationals of the countries taking part in the scheme. Ideally, language ability of the country of placement is desired, but courses are available if needed. The cost of the volunteer contribution depends on the country of origin from 10 to 130 euros. Volunteers pay expenses to and from camp location.

Long-term volunteers pay 520 euros to subsidise their programme. In addition a monthly contribution of 100 euros is required to be provided by a support group. When the volunteer has a personal financial support group ASF will pay travel costs, insurance, retreats, guidance, room and board and pocket money.

Applications directly to ASF.

ALLIANCES ABROAD
Alliances Abroad Group, 1221 South Mopac Expressway, Suite 250, Austin, Texas 78746, USA; ☎ +1 888 622-7623; +1 512 457 8132; fax +1 512 457-8132; e-mail info@alliancesabroad.com; www.alliancesabroad.com

Alliances Abroad organises volunteer and internship placements worldwide in Argentina, China, Costa Rica, Ecuador, Hawaii, Mexico, Peru, Spain and South Africa. The volunteer programmes are individually designed for each participant according to their skills and areas of interest. Placements can be in any of the following fields: education, social services, veterinary medicine, planning and development, health care, recreation, music, theatre/arts, light construction/building, environment, business, journalism, reforestation, communications/public relations, and law.

About 200 volunteers a year are given placements of two weeks to one year. Minimum age 18. Volunteers stay with a host family; single room, full board provided free of charge. An application fee ($100) is required plus the cost of the individual programme (e.g. around $1000 for a month and $400 per extra month for Costa Rica).

For an application form contact the Program Director at the above address.

AMITY VOLUNTEERS TEACHERS ABROAD
3065 Rosecrans Place, Suite 104, San Diego, California 92110, USA ☎ +1 619 222 7000; fax +1 619 222 7016; e-mail avta@amity.org; www.amity.org
The Amity Volunteer Teachers Abroad (AVTA) Program offers native English-speakers the opportunity to serve as volunteer teaching assistants (interns) in language classrooms in Latin America, Africa and Europe. Countries participating in 2004 were Argentina, Brazil, the Dominican Republic, Mexico, Peru, Italy, Ghana and Senegal. AVTA participants work 20-25 classroom hours teaching all ages from pre-school to adult.

Host organisations abroad provide room and board with a host family, and organise meeting at the airport on arrival. For further details go to www.amity.org/avta_program. html.

ATD FOURTH WORLD
48 Addington Square, London SE5 7LB; ☎020-7703 3231; fax 020-7252 4276; e-mail atd@atd-uk.org; www.atd-uk.org
ATD Fourth World is an international organisation working in Europe, the USA, Canada, Asia, Africa, and Central and South America.

The movement is concerned with the 'Fourth World', a term referring to the part of any national population at the bottom of the social scale which is excluded from social, economic, and political life. Through long-term involvement with the most disadvantaged communities, the purpose of ATD Fourth World's work is to demonstrate the will and capacity of the very poorest individuals and families to fulfill their role as parents and citizens. Practical projects established with the poor include family centres, children's street libraries and learning clubs, youth clubs, literacy programmes, training workshops, family holidays and community programmes that reinforce co-operation between very disadvantaged families and the community they live in. Fourth World families are involved in the planning, implementation, and evaluation of these projects.

Full-time volunteers are part of an international voluntariat, whose members are full time workers from different professions and backgrounds who are concerned by the suffering of persistently disadvantaged families.

Applicants undergo a three-month training programme in their country of origin before entering the voluntariat. The minimum age for participation is 18. References are required and previous work experience is desirable, but no specific qualifications are needed.

Food, accommodation and pocket money are offered during the first year. General health insurance should be obtained by the volunteers themselves for the first three months, except for cover for accidents while at work. After the first year, minimum wage and National Insurance contributions are paid for by ATD Fourth World. Normal visa requirements apply.

ATD Fourth World also organises working weekends in the UK and summer work camps in the UK and France. They provide an opportunity to find out more about the organisation, to contribute practically to the development of ATD Fourth World and to discover how people can work together to change the situation of these families.

BRETHREN SERVICE
150 Route de Ferney, 1211 Geneva 2, Switzerland; ☎ +41-22 791 6330; e-mail bvs – gb@brethren.org; www.brethrenvolunteerservice.org
Brethren Service is an American based organisation, sponsored by the Church of the Brethren, whose primary activity relates to the exchange of personnel between America

and other countries. After a brief period of orientation volunteers are assigned to a project related to social work, community development, youth leadership in churches, etc. Most of those taking part in the scheme are American, but Brethren Service in Geneva does also send Europeans to projects in America.

Most volunteers are in their twenties, but the scheme is open to anyone aged from 19 years old, who is in good health. Although Brethren Service is a church sponsored agency, applicants need not be Christian in the orthodox sense, but they must be motivated primarily by humanitarian concern. The more skills the applicant has the better, although none are essential. However, most projects request persons with some training, experience or interest in 'social-type' work. A knowledge of foreign languages, for example, may increase the applicant's chances of being accepted. Volunteers going to the USA must pay for their own travel, but once there, room, board and pocket money are provided. The normal term of service is one year; two years if in Europe.

Those interested should write to the Co-ordinator at the above address for further details.

CANADA WORLD YOUTH/JEUNESSE CANADA MONDE
2330 Notre-Dame Ouest, Montréal, Québec, Canada H3J 1N4; ☎ +1 514 931-3526; fax +1 514 935-2621; e-mail cwy-jcm@cwy-jcm.org; www.cwy-jcm.org
Canada World Youth organises educational exchange programmes for about 1,000 young people annually aged 17-29, in Canada, Asia, Africa, Latin America, the Caribbean and Eastern Europe. Participants can work in the fields of social services, agriculture, community health, and information technology. Placements last from 5 to 7 months and recruitment takes place year round. The participant is matched with a counterpart from the other host country for the entire programme. Half of the programme is spent in Canada and the other half in the counterpart's country. Applicants must be Canadian nationals and be in good health (medical and dental examinations required). Participants must fundraise $1,500 to cover all expenses during the programme. Accommodation is provided with host families.

For further information visit the website.

THE CENTER FOR INTERIM PROGRAMS, LLC
195 Nassau Street, Suite #5, Princeton, NJ 08542, USA; ☎ +1 609 683-4300; fax +1 609 683-4309; e-mail Info@interimprograms.com; www.interimprograms.com. Second office in Cambridge, MA: P.O. Box 2647, Cambridge, MA 02238, USA.
The Center for INTERIM Programs organises placements on programmes worldwide for a cross-section of volunteers, from gap year students to recent graduates and from those considering career changes to someone on a sabbatical. Areas of work cover indoor and outdoor activities, urban, rural placements, work with children, academic/non-academic projects, social service programmes. Examples of programmes include: helping at an international film festival in Hawaii; volunteering at a Ghandi-style ashram in Bali; assisting at a professional sled dog kennel in Alaska; teaching in a village in Micronesia; construction work on a monastery in Ireland; sea turtle conservation in Greece.

Applicants pay a fee of US$1,900, which entitles them to consultation and information for a lifetime. Participants can take part in a variety of programmes organised in advance or as the year progresses. Individual programme costs range widely. The usual length of a programme is three months but many individuals weave 2-4 programmes together during a full year period. Although INTERIM does not find jobs for people, some programmes provide room and board, in exchange for work, in which case only transportation and miscellaneous costs need be considered.

For an information pack and application form contact the above address. Following receipt of application, an interview ideally takes place in person or by phone.

CIEE–International Volunteer Projects
7 Custom House Street, 3rd Floor, Portland, Maine 04101, USA ☎1-800-40-STUDY, +1-207-553-7600; fax +1-207-553-7699; e-mail info@ciee.org; www.ciee.org or www.councilexchanges.org
CIEE (Council for International Educational Exchanges) is a non-profit organisation that, in affiliation with co-operating organisations throughout Europe, sponsors International Volunteer Projects in 30 different countries. Projects are for young people in the USA. Participants have the chance to explore, in a cross-cultural setting, international perspectives on global issues such as environmental protection, cultural preservation and development, while working closely with 10-20 other volunteers from many countries. The minimum age for participants is 18.

The work, generally lasting for three weeks, involves manual labour or social service and is of great value to communities in need. There is a wide range of project possibilities including forest conservation in Eastern Europe, archaeological digs in Spain, and Park revitalisation in San Francisco. Participants' costs are minimal, being around $300 application fee plus transportation. The project host provides room and board.

For further information please contact Council at the above address. Please note CIEE in the USA is involved with placing American citizens only. For updated information on upcoming projects, visit their website.

CROSS-CULTURAL SOLUTIONS
2 Clinton Place, New Rochelle NY 10801, USA; ☎800 380-4777 (for the US and Canada) +1 914 632-0022 (outside the US and Canada); fax +1 914 632-8494; e-mail info@crossculturalsolutions.org; www.crossculturalsolutions.org. In the UK: Tower Point 44, North Road, Brighton BN1 1YR; ☎0845 458 2781/2782
Cross-Cultural Solutions offers unique short-term volunteer programmes that enable volunteers to work with local social service organisations in fields as diverse as health care, education, skills training, and arts/recreation. Volunteers may work in a variety of countries in Asia, Africa, Latin America and Eastern Europe.

Over 1,000 volunteers a year are assigned to projects that maximise their individual skills and interests. Activities can be as varied as teaching English to Chinese students, manning a health care post in eastern Ghana, training Indian women on how to develop small businesses or installing a recreational programme for Peruvian youth. Placements last from one week to six months. Volunteers contribute a programme fee which covers food, lodging, in-country transportation and professional in-country staff support. Visa fees, pocket money, airfare and other expenses are not included.

For more information on the volunteer opportunities available e-mail or telephone the above address.

THE DANEFORD TRUST
45-47 Blythe Street, London E2 6LN; ☎020-7729 1928; e-mail dfdtrust@aol.com
The Trust supports group and individual exchanges between young people in inner London, and young people in Africa, Asia and the Caribbean; the main placement areas overseas are Botswana, Zimbabwe, Namibia and Bangladesh.

The Trust helps about 20 individual participants a year. Applicants must live within the above areas and be aged between 17 and 28 years, keen to do much work them-selves and willing to maintain interest and do follow-up work in the wider community after placement. Any skills, such as typing, experience of working with children, driving licence etc. would be useful. Placements last between three months and a year. Accom-modation is provided, but most participants have to share full costs *(with help from the Trust)*.

Applications should be sent to Tony Stevens at the above address.

EDINBURGH GLOBAL PARTNERSHIPS
60 The Pleasance, Edinburgh EH8 9TJ; ☎0131-556 9497 (term-time); www. eusa.ed.ac.uk/societies/
Based at Edinburgh University and run entirely by students, EGP runs small-scale, long-term community development projects in Africa, Asia and Latin America.

Every summer EGP sends between 150 and 200 students to take part in projects in conjunction with communities for 4-6 weeks. The work includes construction, conserva-tion and teaching. A good knowledge of Spanish is essential for the placements in Latin America.

Applicants must be aged between 18-25. Details of the projects and application forms are available from November and the deadline is at the end of January. Enclose a stamped addressed envelope with all enquiries.

EIL: EXPERIMENT IN INTERNATIONAL LIVING
287 Worcester Road, Malvern WR14 1AB; freephone 0800-018 4015; fax 01684-562212; e-mail info@eiluk.org; www.eiluk.org
A charity based organisation offering a variety of ways to experience something of another culture. With partner offices in over 25 countries, there is a rich diversity of opportunity. As examples: a range of opportunities in the USA include College Programmes, Internships and Farmstays. We arrange Internships in Ghana or Spain, as well as volunteer programmes in Argentina, Thailand, Ecuador, Ghana, Guatemala, Kenya and Mexico. Also the European Voluntary Service programme (EVS): volunteer projects throughout Europe ranging from 3 to 12 months. Language courses and long-term study programmes can also be arranged either for individuals or for groups in countries including: Australia, Canada, France, Germany, Ireland, Italy, Mexico, Spain and the USA. Costs vary according to the type of programme and the length of stay: scholarships are available to appropriate applicants and some of the programmes are actually free.

EMMAUS INTERNATIONAL
183 bis, rue Vaillant-Couturier, 94140 Alfortville, France; ☎ +33-01 48 93 29 50; e-mail contact@emmaus-international.org; www.emmaus-international. org
The Emmaus movement started in Paris in 1949 and there are now some 340 Emmaus communities in 35 countries, mainly in Europe but also in Africa, Asia and North and South America. These communities try to provide a meaning in life for those without one - that meaning being to help others in need. Each community is autonomous and independent of race, sex, religion, politics, age etc. Living conditions are usually simple and the work hard.

One community accepts long-term volunteers: GIVE (Groupement International des Volontaires d'Emmaus, 21 Ave. de la Gare, 31750 Escalquens, France). Other Emmaus communities in Europe organise workcamps for volunteers during the summer. Volun-teers must usually speak English or the language of the country being visited, be over

18 years old and able to work at least two weeks. Accommodation and food are provided but volunteers pay all other costs.

Those interested in long term or summer voluntary positions should apply to the Secretary at the above address for more information on individual communities.

ENGLISH LANGUAGE TEACHING ASSISTANT PROGRAM (ELTAP)
University of Minnestota-Morris, Morris, Minnesota 56267; ☎ +1 320-589 6406; e-mail eltap@eltap.org; www.eltap.org
ELTAP is a placement programme open to undergraduates (12 semester hours), graduate students (3 semester hours) or as a non-credit option for other adults. Participants assist teachers and students in EFL and ESL classes, by bringing their native fluency in English to over 25 countries on all continents. Placements are 4-11 weeks throughout the year. Cost $300 placement fee, course fee and travel from the USA. Accommodation and board provided by the schools.

GAP ACTIVITY PROJECTS (GAP) Limited
Gap House, 44 Queen's Road, Reading, Berkshire RG1 4BB; ☎0118-9594914; fax 0118-9576634; e-mail volunteer@gap.org.uk; www.gap.org.uk
Gap Activity Projects, is the largest year out organisation for 17 to 19 year olds in the UK and Ireland. Founded in 1972, GAP sends an average of 1,500 volunteers from the UK and Ireland to 32 countries worldwide each year to carry out voluntary work placements.

Volunteers can choose between teaching English, classroom assistance, care work, medical projects, camps and outdoor education or environmental work and placements range from three to twelve months in length.

Although it is a non-profit organisation, GAP placements cost from £1,000. This includes the GAP fee, food, accommodation, visa, insurance, a living allowance and any courses that might be necessary, for example a teaching skills course.

In return, volunteers receive a full briefing and key information on the placement and country prior to departure. A support network, which includes a placement host, an in-country representative, a UK-based project manager and a 24-hour emergency telephone line. Finally, on return to the UK, volunteers are invited to join an Alumni Club and a Business partnership scheme which puts them in touch with leading graduate recruiters.

GAP CHALLENGE
Black Arrow House, 2 Chandos Road, London NW10 6NF; ☎020-8961 1122; fax 020-8961 1551; e-mail welcome@gap-challenge.co.uk; www.gap-challenge. co.uk
Gap Challenge is part of World Challenge Expeditions Ltd, which provides adventure and expedition training for groups of young people. It is a specialist in gap year placement abroad formerly called Fill the Gap. World Challenge started in 1988.

For approximately 450 young people a year Gap Challenge arranges: voluntary placements in developing countries; teaching placements in secondary or primary schools in India, Nepal, Malaysia, Tanzania, Zanzibar, Malawi, Belize and Peru; conservation placements in Malawi, Ecuador, Costa Rica and Malaysia; care and community work in India, South Africa, Belize, Malaysia and Peru; paid work in the tourist industry of Canada; paid work on stations and farms in Australia. The majority of placements are a minimum of three months, some last six and others a maximum of eight months.

Applicants must be between 18 and 25 years old and taking a year out between school and university. Those under 18 must submit a consent form signed by a parent or guardian.

All candidates must attend a two day selection course to demonstrate that they can work both independently and co-operatively. Informal interviews are held at this time from which a high percentage of candidates are selected. Those chosen then attend a compulsory two or three day skills training course where they meet past participants and receive an orientation specific to their destination country.

Fees range from £1,615 for a teaching placement in Manali, India, to £2,845 for a placement with a trekking agency in Nepal including a 21-day expedition. Prices exclude airfares and board and lodging.

For further details contact Diana Maisel, Gap Challenge Manager, at the above address.

Jessica Crisp taught at a primary school in Belize through Gap Challenge
I had wanted to go to a developing country where I could be useful to the community and preferably work with children. I did Spanish A-level and was keen to use it while I was away. I stayed with a young family in an adobe (mud) and tin house which the father, Tacio, had constructed himself. We did have electricity for lights and a telephone and a television, but no running water. My 'bathroom' was a large bucket of cold water in a small, stone outhouse. My class consisted of fifteen enthusiastic 8-10 year olds with lots of energy which was great for games and acting. Each weekend, my friend and a I travelled to a different part of Belize to explore the beautiful landscapes and find out more about the country.

GLOBAL CITIZENS NETWORK
130 North Howell Street, St Paul, Minnesota 55104, USA; ☎ +1 651 644-0960; e-mail eden@globalcitizens.org; www.globalcitizens.org.

GCN is a non-profit organisation that sends teams of volunteers to rural communities around the world including Belize, Guatemala, Kenya, Nepal, ST Vincent, the Yucatan, South Dakota and New Mexico. Projects are determined by the villages that GCN is in partnership with and are aimed at promoting cross-cultural understanding. The projects vary but have included building a health clinic, teaching in a primary school, developing eco-tourism or renovating a youth centre.

70-100 volunteers annually participate as part of a team (usually 8-10) members. A trained team leader accompanies all teams. Projects are initiated and directed by the host community. Volunteers pay a programme fee of $650 to $1950 for one to three weeks, which includes most in-country costs (food, lodging, transportation), a donation to the project in the village, training materials, medical/evacuation insurance (for trips outside the USA) and a portion of programme costs. Airfare is additional. No special qualifications are needed. Volunteers under 18 must be accompanied by an adult; e are not required to have special skills but some knowledge of Spanish would be helpful for Guatemala and the Yucatan. The minimum age is 18 unless accompanied by a parent or guardian. Trips last one, two or three weeks only all year round. Volunteers pay a contribution which ranges from US$550 to US$1600 depending on the programme. The cost of transportation to the programme is also at the volunteer's expense. Accommodation is provided.

GCN publishes a free quarterly newsletter, which is available on request. Applicants for trips should apply directly to the above address. Returned volunteers who are interested can also apply to be team leaders for other GCN trips. Potential team leaders have to be recommended by their own team leader and attend a training session in Minnesota. Team leaders can be any nationality and although the position is unpaid airfares and most in-country expenses will be paid.

> **Diana, from Colorado twice volunteered with Global Citizens Network in Mexico**
> *I learned that GCN is much more about building long-term relationships with communities, and not necessarily about the practical process of building. It was truly priceless to be allowed to be on the construction site in Mexico with a group of indigenous people. Tourists never get such an opportunity and we all believed that we truly made a difference in the lives of others.*

GLOBAL CROSSROAD
8738 Quarters Lake Road, Baton Rouge LA, 70809 USA;   ☎ +1 225 922 7854; fax +1 225 922 9114; e-mail info@globalcrossroad.com; www. globalcrossroad.com
Global Crossroad offers many exciting volunteering opportunities to international volunteers in countries including India, Nepal, Tibet, China, Sri Lanka, Thailand, Mongolia, Ghana, Cambodia and Costa Rica. Applicants can choose between different types of programme: volunteer, internship, mini-adventure. They also offer some paid teaching posts in China and Thailand.

Project prices are very competitive; for instance $800 for two weeks' volunteering in Ghana, which includes food and basic accommodation, but not flights.

Further details from the above website.

GLOBAL SERVICE CORPS
300 Broadway, Suite 28, San Francisco CA 99133, USA; ☎ +1 415-788 3666; fax +1 415-788 7324; e-mail gsc@earthisland.org; www.globalservicecorps.org
GSC is currently running programmes in Tanzania and Thailand and takes about 120 volunteers annually. In Tanzania, pre-med students, and healthcare professionals have the opportunity to work in health clinics and shadow doctors. Others interested in health can teach HIV/AIDS prevention to secondary school students. During summer GSC operates a summer camp to educate youth on HIV/AIDS in a casual, non-threatening environment. Environmental students and others can work on agricultural projects.

In Thailand, volunteers teach English to Thai students, or if interested in Buddhism, they can teach English to Thai monks and nuns. There are also opportunities for health-care students and professionals to work in local clinics.

Visas and work permits vary dependent on location and length of programmes. Length of programmes is usually 3 weeks to 3 months, but 6 months to a year is possible. Once accepted, GSV helps with documentation. Volunteers must be fluent in English and minimum age 18 (Thailand) or 20 (or junior status) for Tanzania. Upper age not an issue within reason; many volunteers are in their 60s. For an application and a current schedule of volunteers' fees go to the website or write to the above address.

GLOBAL VISION INTERNATIONAL
Nomansland, Wheathampstead,St Albans, Herts. AL4 8EJ; ☎01582-831300; e-mail info@gvi.co.uk; www.gvi.co.uk
GVI is a non-political, non-religious organisation, which specialises in providing overseas expeditions, research projects and independent voluntary work opportunities to the general public. Through its contacts with aid-reliant environmental organisations throughout the world, GVI volunteers fulfil a void in the fields of environmental research,

conservation, education and development.

Some of the projects volunteers can take part in through GVI include working with street children in Guatemala, social development schemes in Guatemala, Rainforest research expeditions in South America and pioneering wildlife research expeditions in South America. It has volunteer training centres in the UK, USA and South Africa. Expeditions start all year round and last 2 weeks to 12 weeks.

Details of programmes and volunteer contribution costs from the above address or website.

GLOBAL VOLUNTEERS
375E Little Canada Road, St. Paul, MN 55117, USA; ☎ +1 651 482-0915; fax +1 651 407-5163; toll free US 800 487-1074; e-mail @globalvolunteers. org; www.globalvolunteers.org

Global Volunteers is a non-profit US Corporation founded in 1984 with the goal of establishing a foundation for peace through mutual international understanding. The programme centres around one, two, or three-week volunteer work experience placements in rural communities in eighteen countries: China, Vietnam, Romania, Ghana, the Cook Islands, Ukraine, India, Ireland, Tanzania, Costa Rica, Jamaica, Mexico, Poland, Spain, Italy, Greece, Ecuador and the United States including Hawaii. About 1500 volunteers are engaged per year on these projects. At the request of local leaders and indigenous host organisations, Global Volunteers' teams live with and work alongside local people on human and economic development projects identified by the community as important to their long-term development. In this way, the volunteers' energy, creativity and labour are put to use and at the same time they gain a genuine, first-hand understanding of how the vast majority of the world's people live day-to-day.

Projects vary from site to site, and from one season to the next. Most volunteers work in one of three areas. There are voluntary opportunities in the area of education such as teaching English, providing training in business, maths or basic sciences in the classroom, or tutoring and caring for small children. Volunteers are also needed in the area of community infrastructure to help with the construction of community centres and health clinics, the establishment of portable water systems, repairing classrooms and roads, and building houses. Finally, volunteers are also required to share their professional services such as dentistry, assisting rural health-care providers and helping to establish small businesses. Sometimes volunteers are asked to simply assist with painting, planting or other beautification projects, for which specialised skills are not necessary. Everyone is welcome to apply, but minors must travel with a parent, guardian or chaperon. Team members must be in good physical and mental health. Most teams' placements last for 1-3 weeks; about 150 teams are recruited each year. Volunteers must pay for their own trip. Costs range from $500 to $2,395 excluding airfare. All trip-related costs are tax deductible to US tax-payers and cover ground transportation, on-site food and lodging, administrative fees, and all project related costs. Volunteers are provided with accommodation in the community where they work.

Those interested should contact Global Volunteers at the above address.

HABITAT FOR HUMANITY INTERNATIONAL
121 Habitat Street, Americus, GA 31709, USA; ☎ +1 912 924-6935 ext. 2489; e-mail hrstaffing@hfhi.org; www.habitat.org;

Habitat for Humanity International is a non-profit, poverty housing and homelessness oraganisation and aims to make decent shelter a matter of conscience and action. Established in 1976, HFHI works in partnership with communities and families in more than 80 countries.

For volunteer positions with HFHI, check the website or e-mail us. Full-time volunteer positions are available at international headquarters at the above address and overseas. Overseas positions usually require three years' commitment and professional work experience in the region of placement. Full-time volunteers get living expenses, housing and health insurance.

The Global Village department introduces concerned people to the hands-on building work a HFH affiliates around the world. Global Village teams work alongside homeowners and partners. These short-term missions last one to three weeks. See www. habititat.org/GV/ or e-mail gv@hfhi.org for more information.

To volunteer part or full-time in your local area, visit www.habitat.org/local/ for contact information in your own country.

HORIZON COSMOPOLITE
3011, Notre-Dame Ouest, Montréal (Québec), H4C 1N9 Canada; ☎ +1 514 935-8436; e-mail cosmopolite@sprint.ca; www.horizoncosmopolite.com
Horizon Cosmopolite arranges voluntary internships worldwide for example in Costa Rica, India, Guatemala, the Philippines, Nepal, Europe, Australia and Africa. Placements are offered in the following areas: community development, orphanage work with children, teaching, environment, medicinal plants; Horizon Cosmopolite also has workcamps worldwide and offers Spanish courses in Central/Latin America.

About 400 volunteers, mainly from Canada, are recruited annually and placements last from two weeks to one year. Minimum age 18. A knowledge of English and for some programmes, Spanish, is required. Inscription fee is $495 plus board and lodging from $120 per month up to $300 dependent on project. Air fares at the volunteer's expense.

There are over 1600 programmes on offer all of which can be found on the organisation's website.

Applications to the above address.

i-to-i INTERNATIONAL PROJECTS
Woodside House, 261 Low Lane, Leeds, LS18 5NY; ☎0870-333 2332; fax 0113-205 4620; e-mail uk@i-to-i.com; www.i-to-i.com; USA address: 190 E 9th Avenue, Denver Colorado 80203; ☎toll-free USA 800 985 4864; fax 303 765 5327; e-mail usca@i-to-i.com
i-to-i offers adventurous people of all ages exciting and rewarding volunteer projects in 15 countries in Latin America, Africa, Europe, Asia and Australia. For anyone who has the spirit to present the news on Ghanaian radio, monitor sea turtle hatchings in Costa Rica or teach English to Buddhist monks in Nepal, i-to-i has well researched placements with full in-country support and 24 hour back-up in the UK. Volunteers must be self-fundraising, although advice and support is also provided. Accommodation and food is included in most cases. Projects are available in a number of areas including: teaching, conservation, community work, media, advertising and health.

For further information and an application pack, contact the administrator on the above contacts.

ICA-UK
P.O. Box 171, Manchester M15 5BE; e-mail vsp@ica-uk.org.uk; www.ica-uk.org.uk
ICA-UK is a small, friendly charity with the motto 'Concerned with human development'. The volunteer programme of ICA-UK is a highly participatory programme for all those interested in volunteering overseas. Everyone is welcome: there are no formal skills or experience requirements.

There are four stages to the process: a volunteer orientation weekend, the volunteer foundation course (held in autumn), placement overseas and a debrief on return.

Recent volunteers have taken placements in Ghana, Guatemala, India, Mauritius, Mexico, Portugal, Tajikistan, Uganda and the USA.

INTERNATIONAL CONFERENCE VOLUNTEERS (ICV)
PO Box 755, 1211 Geneva 4, Switzerland; ☎ +41-22 800 14 36; fax +41-22 800 14 37; e-mail info@icvolunteers.org; www.icvolunteers.org

Based on experience gained with conferences in Geneva, Switzerland, ICV provides experienced logistical and organisational help to conference organisers and offers volunteer opportunities on an international level in Switzerland or elsewhere.

ICV works with approximately 300 active volunteers annually and maintains a database of over 1,000 volunteers. Volunteers can participate in the following areas: reception and information of delegates, communications, translation and interpretation, slide running, medical and social assistance, administration, information technology (IT), and transportation. Those under 18 must have a written authorisation from a parent or legal authority. Applicants of any nationality are welcome but knowledge of English is required. Volunteers are recruited for the length of the conference, usually 1-2 weeks, although for large events help may be needed before the actual conference (e.g. some of the AIDS conferences, volunteers assisted up to 6 months before, and during, the event).

Depending on the project, training, free admission, food and drinks on site, are provided; occasionally bus fares to the venue are also paid. Assistance with finding affordable housing and/or host families is available.

Those interested should visit the website and fill out a general information form which helps ICV to assess how they can best place the volunteer.

INTERNATIONAL CULTURAL YOUTH EXCHANGE (ICYE)
International Office of ICYE Federation, Grosse Hamburger Str. 30, 10115 Berlin, Germany; ☎ +49-30 28390550/51; fax +49-30 28390552; e-mail icye@icye.org; www.icye.org

ICYE is an international organisation composed of autonomous national committees in over 25 countries which offers young people over 16 years old the chance to live overseas for six months or one year. The volunteers are hosted by a family or in an alternative living situation and attend high school or perform voluntary service work in the community in which they are living. Only volunteers aged over 18 years perform voluntary service work. This work may include work with children or elderly people, involvement with rehabilitation, women's or disabled programmes, teaching, etc. ICYE is present in countries in Africa, Asia, Europe, Latin America, and the Pacific. Departure to the host countries mostly takes place in July/August of each year.

Age limits vary for different countries but no special skills are required. Volunteers should supply a health certificate. Usually volunteers pay a participation fee to the sending committee, which covers administration, travel and insurance costs.

Volunteers should apply through the ICYE National Committee in their country. Where ICYE does not have such a committee the nearest committee suffices. Further information can be obtained from the International Office, at the above address, from the ICYE National Committees and from the Website.

THE INTERNATIONAL PARTNERSHIP FOR SERVICE-LEARNING
815 Second Avenue, Suite 315, New York, New York 10017, USA; ☎ + 1 212 986-0989; fax +1 212 986-5039; e-mail info@ipsl.org; www.ipsl.org

The International Partnership conducts programmes combining studies with substantive community service in 12 nations including: Czech Republic; Guayaquil/Ecuador; Quito/

Ecuador; England; France; India; Israel; Jamaica; Mexico; Philippines; Russia; and Scotland; South Dakota (with Native Americans). The programmes last a summer (10 weeks), semester (3-4 months), or year. A three-week programme is available in India. Most participants are college/university undergraduates, but graduates and older participants are welcome. Participants may be of any nationality. An MA degree programme in International Service is also available.

About 250 volunteers a year take part in the programmes which involve: working with street children; assisting in primary schools in poor areas; community development; street clinics; work with the handicapped; recreation; adult literacy; women's projects; etc. Every effort is made to match participants to their service interests. The service is with existing, ongoing in-country agencies, is direct and substantive, usually 15-20 hours per week. Applicants should be minimum age 18, have the physical ability to engage in direct, hands-on volunteering, and for those travelling to Ecuador, France or Mexico, two years relevant language study is usually required. No other special skills are necessary but can help in placement.

Volunteers must be self-funding. Accommodation can be arranged (usually in home stays) at a cost.

Applications to the President at the above address.

INTERNATIONAL VOLUNTARY SERVICE (Northern Ireland)
34 Shaftesbury Square, Belfast BT2 7DB; tel 028 90 238147; fax 028 90 244356; e-mail colin@ivsni.org; website www.sciint.org

IVS-NI is the northern Irish branch of Service Civil International (SCI) and international network of organisations dedicated to the promotion of international understanding through the exchange of volunteers. About 100-150 incoming volunteers are placed in N. Ireland and 70-100 volunteers are sent abroad annually. IVS-NI is also a sending organisation for the European Voluntary Service Programme for 18-25s, which is European Union funded.

IVS-NI organises international workcamps lasting 2-3 weeks; also volunteer posts for 3 months to a year or longer. There is an Africa/Asia exchange of 6-8 weeks. In addition there are special programmes e.g. conflict resolution, training; study tours and so on.

Volunteers wishing to come to Northern Ireland from abroad should apply through a branch of SCI or a recognised partner in their own country. English is the working language on all camps. Applicants for the International Workcamps and longer posts, depending on the scheme, must be at least 18 years old; for the Asia/Africa programme at least 21 years old. Opportunities are available all year round but mainly from June to September. Volunteers pay for their own travel. Pocket money is provided on longer term schemes.

An International Workcamps brochure is available every mid-April for £3. For further details contact the above address.

INVOLVEMENT VOLUNTEERS ASSOCIATION INC
PO Box 218, Port Melbourne, Victoria 3207, Australia; ☎ +61 3 9646-9392; tel/fax+61 3 9646-5504; e-mail ivworldwide@volunteering.org.au; www. volunteering.org.au

IV volunteers from any country can participate as individual volunteers or groups of individual volunteers in Networked International Volunteering programmes as unpaid participants. The aim of Involvement Volunteering is to enable volunteers to assist non-profit projects related to the natural environment (at farms, national or zoological parks, animal reserves or historic places) or social service in the community (at homes, camps or schools for disadvantaged people, orphanages, village teaching of spoken English). Placements of 2-12 weeks are currently available in Argentina, Armenia, Australia, Austria,

Bangladesh, Belgium, Brazil, Cambodia, China, Denmark, Ecuador, Estonia, Fiji, Finland, Germany, Ghana, Greece, Guatemala, India, Israel, Italy, Japan, Kenya, Korea, Kosovo, Latvia, Lebanon, Macau, Mexico, Mongolia, Nepal, New Zealand, Papua New Guinea, Philippines, Peru, Poland, Russia, Sabah (Malaysia), Samoa, South Africa, Thailand, Togo, Turkey, UK, Ukraine, USA, Vietnam, and Zambia. Single Placement Programmes or Trip Programmes (as many placements as can be fitted in a 12 month period travelling the world) can provide valuable practical experience related to potential tertiary education, completed degree courses or completed careers (for early retirees). Some placements have food and accommodation provided while some can cost up to about £35 per week for food and accommodation, depending on the economy of the country and the host organisation.

Involvement Volunteers Inc is a registered not for profit organisation which charges a Lifetime's Registration Fee of approximately £100 of 150 euros. IV programme fees are from £160 to £262 (€238 to €388) up to £1,263 (€1870) for a programme of one to twenty-four Networked International Volunteering placements in one or up to 24 countries in a period of up to 12 months. IV associates and agents are there to support volunteers in many countries around the world.

Where appropriate IV volunteers are met on arrival at the airport and provided with support during their visit. Advice is given on banking, specially discounted internal travel, special trips, eco trips, discounted scuba diving courses, sea kayaking, snorkelling and sailing in suitable areas.

For further details, contact IVI at the above address.

JEUNESSE ET RECONSTRUCTION
10 rue de Trévise, 75009 Paris, France; ☎ +33 (0)1 47 70 15 88; fax +33 (0)1 48 00 92 18; www.voluntariat .org
Jeunesse et Reconstruction was created in 1948 with the aim of promoting international exchange between young people and intercultural relations through the organisation of voluntary work camps in France and abroad and longer-term voluntary service worldwide. The programme categories are summer work camps, mid-term and long-term volunteering, seminars and training, language courses and agricultural work in 63 countries. Jeunesse et Reconsruction sends volunteers to its partner organisations in different countries. Over 1000 volunteers are sent abroad and about 550 volunteers go to France. Workcamps involve activities related to social work, the environment, construction, building and renovating and agriculture.

Volunteers should be aged 18-35. No qualifications or previous experience are required. Short-term workcamps last 2-3 weeks, long-term 6-12 months. Food and accommodation are provided but all other expenses including travel and insurance are at the volunteer's expenses.

Contact the above organisation for further details.

LEAPNow: Lifelong Education Alternatives & Programmes
PO Box 1817, Sebastopol, CA 95473, USA; ☎ +1 707 829-1142; fax +1 707 829-1132; e-mail info@leapnow.org; www.leapnow.org
LEAPNow is a leading source for low-cost internships, volunteer positions, work exchanges, and experiential academic programmes. Their programmes are open to any nationality.

LEAPYear; for ages 17-20 is a nine-month programme that allows people to do voluntary work abroad while receiving a full year of college credit. It incorporates a semester of group travel, a 10-week internship, a month-long trek and a full curriculum of living skills and emotional literacy. For more information go to www.leapnow.org/leapyear.

Three-month Semester Programme: group semester programmes for ages 17 and upwards in Central America, South America, India/Bali, the South Pacific and Australia/ New Zealand/Fiji. For programmes costs and further details visit www.LEAPnow.org/ semesters

OPERATION CROSSROADS AFRICA
P.O. Box 5570 (34 Mt. Morris Park), New York, NY 10027, USA; ☎212 289-1949; fax 212 289-2526475; e-mail oca@igc.org; www.operationcrossro adsafrica.org

Founded in 1957, Operation Crossroads Africa sends people to work on community-initiated development projects in Africa and Brazil. Crossroads has projects in 10-12 African countries and Brazil, each summer. Over 10,000 people have participated in Crossroads since its inception, and it was the model for the Peace Corps (see separate entry).

200 volunteers are recruited annually onto four types of project: agriculture/refor- estation; construction/community development; community health/medical; education/ training (including women's development). Volunteers work 5-6 hours a day. Projects are six weeks long and are in rural villages. The work groups (8-10 volunteers per group) then travel for one week in the host country. All groups work with local counter- parts. The programmes run from mid-June to mid-August.

Volunteers are aged between 17 and 35. Knowledge of French is preferred for francophone countries and Portugese for Brazil and Guinea Bissau. Applicants of any nationality are welcomed. Participants must attend a 3 day orientation in New York prior to departure paying their own way to New York, participation fee ($3,500).

PEACE BRIGADES INTERNATIONAL – BRITISH SECTION
1b Waterloo Road, London N19 5NJ; ☎020-7281 5370; fax 020-7272 9243; e-mail pbiuk@gn.apc.org; www.peacebrigades.org

Peace Brigades International (PBI) is an international non-governmental organisation working for the non-violent transformation of conflict. For the last 20 years PBI has provided support to peace and justice activists whose lives and work are threatened by violence. The work is carried out by sending teams of international volunteers to provide international presence in Colombia, Indonesia and Mexico.

Volunteers receive training and are required to commit for a period of one year and be fluent in the language of the country of their interest. Minimum age is 25. For further information please send an A4 envelope with a 54p stamp on it to Susi Bascon at the above address.

PROJECT TRUST
The Hebridean Centre, Isle of Coll, Scotland, PA78 6TB; ☎018793-230444; fax 018793-230357; e-mail info@projecttrust.org.uk; www.projecttrust.org. uk

The Project Trust is an educational trust, which sends 200 school leavers overseas every year to over twenty countries around the world. At present these are: Botswana, Chile, China, Dominican Republic, Guyana, Honduras, China (Hong Kong), Japan, Malawi, Malaysia, Mauritania, Morocco, Namibia, Niger, South Africa, Sri Lanka, Thailand, Uganda, Vietnam. There is a wide variety of projects on offer, from teaching to development work, outward bound activities, and child and health care. Placements last for twelve months.

All volunteers attend a selection course on the Isle of Coll in the autumn before they go overseas. Week-long training courses take place on the Isle of Coll after final exams in the summer, and following a year overseas the volunteers assemble again on the Isle of Coll for a final farewell before dispersing to university or their future careers.

Volunteers raise £3,950 for the year which covers insurance travel costs, pocket money, meals (or a food allowance) and accommodation. Fundraising workshops are held throughout the country to help volunteers accumulate the necessary finance. Apply as early as possible to avoid disappointment.

RALEIGH INTERNATIONAL
Raleigh House, 27 Parsons Green Lane, London SW6 4HZ; ☎020-7371 8585; fax 020-7371 5116; e-mail info@raleigh.org.uk; www.raleigh.org.uk

Raleigh International is a youth development charity that carries out demanding environmental and community projects at home and abroad. During twelve weeks in remote areas volunteers, known as 'venturers', develop self-confidence and new skills which they are then encouraged to use on their return home. Currently, they are running expeditions to Chile, Costa Rica & Nicaragua, Belize, Namibia, Ghana and Borneo (Sabah). About 1,000 venturers every year go abroad, but a further 1-2,000 ex-venturers volunteer at home.

Venturers may find themselves helping with scientific research in tropical rain forests, building health centres and schools in remote villages, constructing bridges for the benefit of local communities or helping eye surgeons with cataract operations. All work is done with local venturers and volunteers. Applicants of all nationalities are welcome, but the ability to speak some English, as well as the ability to swim, is important. Voluntary staff, such as engineers, diving instructors, doctors and nurses, are also needed to run projects.

Venturers must be aged between 17 and 25, while skilled staff must be over 26. The length of placement is twelve weeks, and there are about ten expeditions throughout the year. Venturers have to raise their own funds, but many national fundraising events are arranged and they also receive plenty of local support. Venturers don't have to carry tents although they may find themselves sleeping under canvas in hammocks, or in cabins and other buildings depending on the project.

Those interested should contact the above address.

RETURNED VOLUNTEER ACTION (RVA)
1 Amwell Street, London EC1R 1TH; ☎020-7278 0804; fax 020-7278 7019; e-mail retvolac@lineone.net.

RVA is an independent membership organisation of and for serving overseas volunteers and development workers, and those interested or active in development work. RVA does not send volunteers to work abroad.

RVA's aims are: to press for improvements in overseas programmes, especially in training, support and project evaluation; to help returned workers evaluate their overseas experience and feed it into action in this country; to encourage those seeking placements overseas to examine their personal and political motivations and expectations. The membership database enables returned workers to be in touch on a cross-agency basis, and enables prospective volunteers to learn from their knowledge.

RVA is a small organisation and much of its work is done through its regular newsletter and its publications and training resources. RVA urges anyone considering working overseas to buy *Thinking About Volunteering* and *Volunteering and Overseas Development: A Guide to Opportunities*, which are available from RVA as a joint pack for £3.50 plus a 56p SAE. A full Resources List or Membership Form is available from the above address.

SERVICE CIVIL INTERNATIONAL/INTERNATIONAL VOLUNTARY SERVICE
Old Hall, East Bergholt, Colchester C07 6TQ; e-mail ivsgbn@ivsgbn.demon. co.uk; www.ivs-gb.org.uk

International Voluntary Service (IVS) is the British branch of Service Civil International (SCI), an international voluntary movement which was begun in 1920 by Pierre Ceresole, a Swiss pacifist, with the aim of furthering reconciliation between participants in the Great War of 1914-18. Its objectives are to promote peace, international co-operation and friendship through the means of voluntary work. The 'Service Civil' in its name describes its role as an alternative to military service; for example during the Second World War International Voluntary Service, the British branch of the organisation, was able to provide alternative service for conscientious objectors.

IVS sends volunteers to international workcamps and short-term projects in 25 countries and has partner organisations in 20 more. The camps span eastern and Western Europe including the former Soviet Union as well as Japan, North Africa, Turkey, the USA and Australia. Volunteers work for two to four weeks in an international team of ten to twenty people sharing domestic and social life as well as the work. The projects include: work with children, work with the disabled, solidarity work with people of other countries, and manual work, often connected with ecology or conservation. The projects are not holidays. The work can be hard and demands commitment.

Most workcamps are between June and September. Volunteers must pay for membership of IVS, a registration fee and their own travel costs. Free board and accommodation are provided on the project. For certain countries previous experience of voluntary work is required or preferred. English is the language of most projects, but other languages are an advantage. IVS is working towards equal opportunities, and welcomes applications from women, black people, disabled people, ethnic minorities, gays and lesbians. IVS UK can only accept applications from people with an address in Britain. The US branch of SCI is for volunteers living in the USA (IVS, 5474 Walnut Level Road, Crozet, VA 22932, USA; e-mail sciinfo@sci-ivs.org; www.sci-ivs.org.

Applications should be sent with a stamped, addressed envelope, for more information to the address above or to IVS North, 21 Otley Road, Headingley, Leeds LS6 3AA. £4 postage and packing is necessary for the listing of summer workcamps (available from April).

For further information about Service Civil International projects British applicants should contact the address in their country. Addresses can be found on the website at www.sciint.org.

Austria: SCI, Schottengasse 3a/1/4/59, 1010 Vienna.
Belgium: SCI, Rue Van Elewyck 35, B 1050, Brussels.
Belgium: VIA, Draakstraat 37, 2018 Antwerp.
Finland: KVT, Rauhanasema, Veturitori, 00520 Helsinki 52.
France: SCI, 2 rue Camille Flammarion, F-75018, Paris.
Germany: SCI, Blucherstrasse 14, 5300 Bonn 1.
Greece: SCI Hellas, Akadimias 78D & Kiafas 1, 10678 Athens.
Ireland: VSI, 30 Mountjoy Square, Dublin 1.
Italy: SCI, Via G Cardiano 135, I-00146 Roma.
Netherlands: VIA, MVB Bastiaansestraat 56, NL-1054 Sp Amsterdam.
Northern Ireland: IVS, 34 Shaftesbury Square, Belfast BT2 7DB.
Norway: ID, Nordahl Brunsgate 22, N-0165 Oslo.
Spain: SCI, Carirer del Carme 95, baixos 2a, E-08001 Barcelona.
Sweden: IAL, Tegelviksgatan 40, 11641 Stockholm.
Switzerland: SCI, Monbijoustrasse 32, P O Box 7855, Bern.
USA: SCI/IVS 5474 Walnut Level Road, Crozet, VA 22932..

Other organisations co-operating with Service Civil International:
Czech Republic: INEX, Senovazne namesti 24, C2 11647 Praha 1.
Denmark: MS, Studsgade 20, DK-8000, Arhaus C.
Hungary: Utilapu, Ulloi ut 103, F Szts, H-1091 Budapest.
Netherlands: SIW, Willemstaat 7, Utrecht.
Poland: OWA, ul. 3 Maja 46, V ptr., Ph 61728 Poznan.
Portugal: Instituto da Juventude, Avenida da Liberdade, 1200 Lisbon.
Turkey: Genctur, Zambak SOk 15/5, 80080 Istanbul.
Slovenia: MOST, Breg 12, PP279, Ljubljana.
USA: Volunteers for Peace, Tiffany Road, Belmont, Vermont O537O.

STUDENTS PARTNERSHIP WORLDWIDE (SPW)
17 Dean's Yard, Westminster, London SW1P 3PB; ☎020-7222 0138; fax 020-7233 0008; e-mail spwuk@gn.apc.org www.spw.org
SPW offers those aged 18-28 the opportunity to experience volunteering and living and working in partnership with young African and Asian volunteers while participating in health education, environment and school and community based programmes in rural areas of India, Nepal, Tanzania, Uganda, South Africa and Zambia. Overseas volunteers act as peer educators working with equal numbers of local volunteers and together they receive intensive in-country training before their placement begins. Volunteers help initiate small-scale, sustainable projects in their host communities and help a rural community to understand and assess its resources to find sustainable solutions to problems such as low crop yield, deforestation and water borne diseases.

A comprehensive four weeks' training in-country includes language learning, development theory, team-building skills and cross-cultural awareness. SPW works in partnership with local NGOs to ensure the sustainability and effectiveness of the programmes.

Volunteers should have 'A' levels or equivalent, need not be a student, and are asked to raise £3,300 towards the cost of their time overseas i.e. training, airfare, insurance, accommodation, living allowance, and contribution towards local participation. Fund raising advice is given.

Further details can be obtained from the above address.

TEACHING & PROJECTS ABROAD
Aldsworth Parade, Goring, Sussex BN12 4TX; ☎01903-708300; fax 01903-501026; e-mail info@teaching-abroad.co.uk; www.teaching-abroad.co.uk
Teaching & Projects Abroad offers placements in Bolivia, Chile, China, Ghana, India, Mexico, Mongolia, Nepal, Peru, Romania, Russia, South Africa, Sri Lanka, Thailand and Togo. Opportunities for volunteers to teach conversational English (no TEFL certificate required), take part in care work or conservation, or gain experience in medicine, veterinary medicine, journalism or business. Volunteers receive substantial UK and overseas support and are not isolated. Programme costs from £795 and includes accommodation, food, full medical and travel insurance and adminstration involving placement.

For more information contact Dr. Peter Slowe at the above address.

UNITED NATIONS ASSOCIATION(UNA)EXCHANGE
Temple of Peace, Cathays Park, Cardiff, CF10 3AP; ☎029-2022-3088; e-mail info@unaexchange.org; www.unaexchange.org
UNA exchange organises a wide range of international volunteer projects in over 50 countries worldwide. Projects are hosted by community based organisations and last between 2 weeks and 12 months. They include construction, renovation, environmental

and cultural projects, as well as work with young people, the elderly and people with special needs. The volunteer programme covers many countries in Europe, North America, North Africa and East Asia. There is also a specialised programme of challenging projects in Sub-Saharan Africa, Latin America and South East Asia. Volunteer projects aim to support community development initiatives, promote cultural exchange and provide an opportunity to gain a unique perspective on the host country.

Projects are open to any nationality volunteers aged from 18. There are also programmes for 14-17 year olds in Europe. Volunteers pay a registration fee of £50 (Wales) or £100 (overseas) and their own travel expenses. Food and lodging are provided at no extra cost. Check the website for project details or ask for an information pack by post.

VOLUNTEERS FOR PEACE INC
International Workcamps, 1034 Tiffany Road, Belmont VT 05730, USA; ☎ + 1 802 259-2759; fax + 1 802 259-2922; e-mail vfp@vfp.org; www.vfp.org
VFP offers over 2400 short-term voluntary service projects in 90 different countries. Although US-based VFP places volunteers from the USA, Canada and many other countries. There are several partner organisations in the UK from Cardiff to Edinburgh and most of them are listed in this book; they include UNA Exchange, Concordia, IVS, Youth Action for Peace, Quaker Voluntary Action and IVS Scotland.

These programmes are an opportunity to complete meaningful community service while living and interacting in an international environment. VFP places about 500 North American volunteers in foreign workcamps each year, plus about 500 foreign volunteers in US workcamps. Participants live and work with an international group for two to three weeks, providing a diverse cultural exchange with the other volunteers as well as the local hosts.

Work projects include: construction/renovation of low-income housing or community buildings, historic preservation, archaeology; environmental education, wildlife surveying, park maintenance, organic farming; social services, working with children, the elderly, physically or mentally handicapped, refugees, minority groups, drug/alcohol recovery, AIDS education; arts projects, festivals...

Most workcamps are for those aged at least 18; a few are for those aged at least 15. The main workcamp season is from May to September. A few camps operate year round. Volunteers provide their own transportation to the workcamp site and pay a US$200 registration fee per camp. Non-North American residents must apply through a partner organisation in their own country. In the UK this is: International Voluntary Service (IVS), Old Hall, East Bergholt, Colchester, Essex C07 5TQ; ☎01206-298215; fax 01206-29904.

WORLD YOUTH INTERNATIONAL (Aust.)Ltd.
18 Third Street, Brompton, South Australia 5007, Australia; ☎(08) 8340 1266; fax (08) 8340 3677; e-mail wyi@worldyouth.com.au; www.worldyouth. com.au
World Youth International was formed in 1988 to provide young people with new skills and to help them directionalise their lives. This led to World Youth International groups being created in other countries and the creation of exchange projects. Today WYI runs two programmes which are open to people from around the world: The Overseas Action Program for 18-30s and the Seniors Program for anyone over 50.

The Overseas Action Program is run in Nepal, Kenya and Brazil. Volunteers work alongside local people on community projects. Previous projects include: income-generating projects for orphanages and schools, reconstruction of temples, building playground equipment and agriculture. No specific skills or qualifications are essential but a working level of English is. Projects run twice a year and last three months. Volunteers pay a fee for the programme. The fee does not include the cost of airfare, visas, insurance, immunisations, pocket money and some food depending on the country. All accommodation is provided and ranges from host families to guest houses and camping.

To apply for the programme, contact the above address.

VOLUNTARY SERVICE OVERSEAS (VSO) YOUTH PROGRAMMES
VSO, 317 Putney Bridge Road, Putney, London SW15 2PN; ☎020-8780 7500; fax 020-8780 7300; e-mail enquiry@vso.org.uk; www.vso.org.uk
The **World Youth Programme** is aimed at young people giving them the chance to make a real difference to community projects in the UK and overseas. Nine volunteers from the UK are teamed up with the same number of volunteers from an exchange country in Asia or Africa. It provides volunteers with the unique opportunity to live and work with another young person from a developing country for six months, spending three months in the UK and three months overseas. Applicants should be aged 17-35. Volunteers are asked to fundraise £600. Millennium Awards initiatives are aimed at young people giving them the chance to make a real difference to community projects in the UK and overseas. It provides participants with the unique opportunity to live and work with another young person from a developing country for six months, spending 3 months in the UK and 3 months overseas working in a group. Applicants should be aged 17-25.

The **Youth for Development (YfD)** programme is aimed at young people aged 18 to 25 who are UK residents with at least one year of volunteering experience and/or community work. The 10 to 12 months placements give young volunteers the opportunity to gain work experience, develop their skills in an international setting, and make practical contributions to organisations overseas. YfD volunteers are asked to complete a global education project to promote international understanding and greater awareness of international development issues. YfD volunteers are also asked to raise at least £700 towards the cost of placement.

YOUTH ACTION FOR PEACE (YAP)
8 Golden Ridge, Freshwater, Isle of Wight, PO40 9LE; ☎08701-657927; fax 01983-756900; e-mail action@yap-uk.org; www.yap-uk.org.
Volunteers are needed to take part in voluntary work projects (workcamps) organised by YAP in the UK and through its sister organisations in 40 countries worldwide. The work undertaken may consist of tasks such as restoration, entertaining handicapped children or environmental work. Projects generally last 2-3 weeks each, and take place all year round.

Participants work about 35 hours per week with volunteers from different countries and locals. Food, accommodation and leisure activities are provided for camps in Europe, the USA and Japan. For camps in Africa, Asia, Latin America an entrance fee applies. No skills are required. Applicants must be 18 and over. Project database is at www.yap-uk.org.

Work with the Sick and Disabled

Many of the organisations featured in other sections of this book include work with the sick and disabled. It is worth mentioning as a field on its own however as it differs from other kinds of voluntary work in at least two major respects. All volunteer work is demanding, but work with the sick and disabled is mostly very challenging physically and emotionally. It can involve helping those who are either physically or mentally disabled who have special needs that are above and beyond what many dealings with other people entail, and if living on site, they may involve being available to help 24/7. This kind of work may also require large reserves of compassion and patience. Anyone who is intending to be, or who is already a nurse, is ideally suited and the experience gained from this kind of work could advance future job prospects in this and special needs fields.

In recognition of the unusual strains that this kind of volunteering can impose on the volunteer and the fact that it is not necessarily a nine to five job, most organisations provide free board and lodging, and sometimes pocket money, and even a long stay bonus. This differs from many other types of volunteer work where a contribution for board and lodging is often required.

There are some organisations devoted to disability work. For instance the Camphill organisation has over 100 communities worldwide where adults with mental disabililties live and work alongside able volunteers and are cared for under spiritual anthroposophy principles established by Rudolph Steiner. The other religious organisations in this book have programmes that involve caring for the sick and disabled in both rich and poor communities worldwide. All of the latter have a desperate need both for qualified medical, and therapeutic professionals and for general carers.

CAMPHILL SPECIAL SCHOOLS INC
1784 Fairview Road, Glenmore, PA, 19343, USA; ☎ +1 610 469 9236; e-mail BvrRn@aol.com; www.BeaverRun.org
Camphill Communities are part of the international Camphill Movement promoting social renewal through community living with children, youth or adults with developmental disabilities. Camphill is based on anthroposophy as developed by Rudolph Steiner.

There are various Camphill organisations throughout this book in Germany, Britain, the USA etc. and they can be applied to individually. Volunteers are an important part of Camphill establishments and they receive board lodging and pocket money.

Commitment should be for six months to a year if possible from September to July. Free health insurance and monthly pocket money are provided. For the USA a certificate of health and a visa for the USA are required. The latter is processed through Camphill on acceptance. Applicants should be proficient in English.

Useful publications about the Camphill organisation include *Village Life* and *Candle on the Hill* at $25 each. Other literature is available on request.

MOBILITY INTERNATIONAL USA (MIUSA)
PO Box 10767, Eugene, Oregon 97440, USA; ☎ +1 541 343-1284; fax +1 541 343-6812; e-mail info@miusa.org; www.miusa.org
MIUSA is a non-profit organisation that exists to increase the opportunities for educational

exchange for people with disabilities. MIUSA's programmes include organizing international educational exchange programmes, which include people with and without disabilities working together in the USA and overseas. Themes of the exchanges vary but the goals are to increase international understanding through contact between people, and to improve the lives of people with disabilities around the world by sharing information and strategies for human rights for all people. The exchange experiences last three to four weeks, and usually include a community service component and a stay with a family in the host country.

Persons with and without disabilities are encouraged to apply. Applicants must have an interest in human rights and international understanding. Fees and specific requirements vary depending on the programme.

MIUSA also serves as the USA National Clearing House on Disability and Exchange (NCDE) – a joint project with the US Department of State. Organisations and individuals with disabilities can contact MIUSA for information on international work, volunteer, study, and intern, programmes and providing accommodations.

For further information regarding MIUSA contact the Director at the above address. Enclose an International Reply coupon and a self-addressed envelope.

Professional and Longer-term Volunteering

AUSTRALIAN VOLUNTEERS INTERNATIONAL
71 Argyle Street, PO Box 350, Fitzroy, Victoria 3065, Australia; ☎ +61 3-9279 1788; fax +61 3-9419 4280; e-mail ozvol@ozvol.org.au; www.ozvol. org.au
Australian Volunteers International (AVI) is Australia's largest and most experienced international volunteer sending organisation. It provides opportunities for Australians to live, work and learn in partnership with developing communities in Asia, the Pacific, Africa, Latin America, the Middle East and in indigenous communities in Australia.

With a 50-year history, AVI has extensive experience and connections with governments, community organisations and individuals in several countries. Australian volunteers fill positions in every field of activity including education, health, IT, business and administration. Specialists are also recruited for positions in indigenous communities and organisations within Australia.

Volunteer assignments are usually one to two years. Volunteers must be at least 18 and an Australian (or New Zealand) citizen or permanent resident. Volunteers should normally also have a tertiary or trade qualification and relevant work experience.

In-country, AVI volunteers live under local conditions and receive either the equivalent of a local wage or a living allowance, which covers basic living costs. AVI also arranges accommodation, and provides airfares, visas and health problems.
Youth: AVI has a recent programme of short-term volunteer options for 18-25 year olds. The emphasis is on cross-cultural exchange and community development. No specific qualifications needed. Volunteers raise sponsorship to cover their costs.

AVI produces *Australain Volunteer* Magazine, an annual report and newsletter (for returned volunteers), and various promotional brochures outlining the magazine and its services. To obtain free copies e-mail ccr@ozvol.org.au.

Applications to your nearest AVI State Office:
National Office (Vic & Tas), address as above.

Sydney Office (NSW & ACT), Suite 46, Level 4, 8-24 Kippax Street, Surry Hills, NSW 2010; ☎+2-9211 1277; fax +2-9211-1234; nsw@ozvol.org.au.
Brisbane Office (Queensland), Yungaba, 182 Main Street, Kangaroo Point, QLD 4169; ☎+7-3891 1168; fax +7-3891 1314; qld@ozvol.org.au.
Adelaide Office (SA & NT), 19 Market Street (P.O. Box 536), Adelaide, SA 5001; ☎+8-8410 2770; fax +8-8410 2778; sa@ozvol.org.au.
Darwin Office (NT), 14 Shepherd Street, (P.O. Box 1538), Darwin NT 0801; ☎08-8941 9743; fax 08 8941 9768; nt@ozvol.org.au.
Perth Office (WA), (P.O. Box 8047 Subiaco East), Subiaco, WA 6008; ☎+8-9382 3503; fax +8-9388 2115; wa@ozvol.org.au.

BMS WORLD MISSION
PO Box 49, Baptist House, 129 Broadway, Didcot, Oxon OX11 8XA; ☎01235-517647; fax 01235-517601; e-mail shortterm@bmsworldmission.org; www.bmsworldmission.org.
The BMS has opportunities working in teams or individually, across Asia, Europe, Africa, Central and South America. Team. Opportunities include short-term team assignments as well as individual placements for three months to two years.

Individual volunteers with particular skills and offering between three months and two years can be placed in a variety of settings. Opportunities exist for school teaching, TEFL, youth and children's work, medical work, evangelism, finance and administration, IT and system support. For more information and an application form, write to the Volunteer Programme Coordinator at the above address.

BESO
164 Vauxhall Bridge Road, London SW1V 2RB; ☎020-7630 0644; fax 020-7630 0624; e-mail team@beso.org; www.beso.org
BESO is a development agency that offers professional expertise to organisations in less developed communities worldwide. Its advisers have responded to requests for assistance from governments and local authorities, media, educational and health institutions, and given technical and managerial advice to small businesses and local industries in more than 146 countries.

BESO men and women regularly undertake more than 550 assignments yearly, lasting between two weeks and four months per assignment. Through the advice and training given to clients, BESO has helped to strengthen economies by improving services and local infrastructure.

BESO assists clients who cannot afford commercial consultants. No fees are charged. Clients pay in-country costs and BESO usually meet travel expenses.

BESO is supported by DFID, British Industry, charitable trusts and individuals. It also collaborates with the World Bank, European Community and other multilateral aid organisations. The organisation has been in existence for 30 years and has sent more than 7,000 volunteers abroad.

For further information about BESO visit www.beso.org or contact them at the above address. contact Katie Latham at the above address.

BRITISH RED CROSS SOCIETY
National Headquarters, 9 Grosvenor Crescent, London SW1X 7EJ; ☎020-7235 5454; fax 020-7245 6315; e-mailinformation@redcross.org.uk; www.redcross.org.uk
The International Red Cross and Red Crescent Movement is the largest humanitarian aid network in the world, with approximately 120 million volunteers and 250,000 paid

staff worldwide. The British Red Cross is one of 175 National Societies which are all equal partners in the Federation of Red Cross and Red Crescent Societies (Federation) which has its headquarters in Geneva. When any National Society is faced with a development or relief need beyond its resources it will call upon the Federation to issue an appeal on its behalf. The Federation is separate from the International Committee of the Red Cross (ICRC) which carries out much of its work in war zones, providing humanitarian assistance to victims of conflict.

The British Red Cross recruits staff for both the Federation and the ICRC. It supports operations in Africa, Asia, Eastern Europe/Balkans and the Russian Federation and maintains a register for recruitment purposes. Selection days are held regularly to identify suitable candidates for the register and the professions invited to join include: medical/health staff, prostheticists, relief workers, logisticians, programme managers, water/sanitation engineers, disaster preparedness and development specialists, information/press officers, finance/accountancy staff, organisation experts and telecommunications specialists.

Candidates must be aged at least 25 and have the relevant professional experience and qualifications. Previous work experience in developing countries is required for most posts. Contracts vary in length from three months to two years. Salaries range from £17,500 to £30,500+ per annum. A local daily allowance, accommodation, transportation, and insurance are also provided. All staff attend a one-week residential induction course and detailed briefing prior to departure.

It is Red Cross policy for each National Society to recruit only nationals and residents from their country for international work. The British Red Cross therefore welcomes applications from British nationals and residents.

CATHOLIC INSTITUTE FOR INTERNATIONAL RELATIONS
Unit 3, Canonbury Yard, 190a New North Road, London N1 7BJ; ☎020-7354 0883; fax 020-7359 0017; e-mail ciir@ciir.org; www.ciir.org
Founded in 1940, CIIR is an independent charity, which works with people of any religious beliefs and none, to make a difference through an integrated approach to development. CIIR has its roots in radical Catholicism and has a close relationship with the progressive church in a number of countries.

International Co-operation for Development (ICD) is the overseas technical cooperation department of the Catholic Institute for International Relations, which recruits professionally qualified people with a minimum of two years' work experience to share their skills with communities in developing countries. ICD has development workers in Latin America, the Caribbean, Africa, the Middle East and South East Asia to implement programmes that challenge poverty and promote development.

ICD recruits development workers in response to requests from partners overseas. These partners are usually community organisations, peasant federations, women's groups, co-operatives, local development associations or government minstries. ICD development workers are employed in various capacities: as advisers in agricultural co-operatives, as health workers in urban and rural health care programmes, as trainers in peasant-run education programmes or as teacher trainers and university lecturers. ICD offers a minimum two-year contract, a salary based on local rates, a UK allowance, accommodation and essential household equipment, return flights, a pre-departure grant, comprehensive insurance cover, language training and extensive briefings.

Volunteers are needed to work in the London office. The Recruitment Officer at the above address can provide a current vacancy list.

CATHOLIC MEDICAL MISSION BOARD (CMMB)
10 West 17th Street, New York 10011-5765, USA; ☎ +1 212 242-7757; fax +1 212 242-0930; e-mail rdecostanzo@cmmb.org; www.cmmb.org
The Medical Volunteer Program of CMMB facilitates the placement of health care volunteers in independent medical missions in Latin America, the Caribbean, Africa and Asia. The Board reviews the licensed credentials, professional documents, CV, application form, letters of recommendation and physical examination of prospective US or Canadian licensed physicians, surgeons, nurses, dentists, lab technicians and other clinical/ancillary health providers who are seeking placement as volunteers.

Each mission/country has its own requirements. Most prefer one or more years service commitment although there are some short term possibilities (1-2 weeks to 1-3 months). Missions provide room and board. For long term volunteers assistance is also provided for travel, visas, medical licences. A modest stipend is offered as well. For all volunteers (and family members if applicable) emergency medevac insurance is provided.

Applicants should contact Rosemary DeCostanzo, Co-ordinator, Medical Volunteer Program at the above address/e-mail/fax/telephone number.

CHRISTIAN MEDICAL FELLOWSHIP
157 Waterloo Road, London SE1 8XN; ☎020-7928 4694; fax 020-7620 2453; e-mail healthserve@cmf.org.uk; www.healthservice.org
The Fellowship takes enquiries from Christian doctors and medical students, nurses, midwives and other healthcare professionals who are looking for work in developing countries and helps them with their search by means of a listing of about 40 medical missionary organisations with vacancies for professional medical staff to work in the developing world, for periods of two months and longer. There is a similar list for medical student electives of two to three months.

For further information contact the Health Serve team at the above address.

CONCERN WORLDWIDE
52-55 Camden Street, Dublin, Ireland; ☎ +353-1 4754162; fax +353-1 4754649; 47 Frederick Street, Belfast BT1 2LW, Northern Ireland; ☎028-90331 100; fax 028-90331 111; 248-250 Lavender Hill, London SW11 1LJ; ☎020-7738 1033; fax 020-7738 1032; Level 2, 80 Buchanan Street, Glasgow G1 3HA; ☎0141-2213610; fax 0141-2213708; e-mail info@concern.ie; www.concern.ie
Concern is a non-denominational organisation devoted to the relief, assistance and advancement of people in need in less developed areas of the world. It has over 154 international volunteers and staff working alongside 6,000 local staff on contracts lasting from six months to three years in 27 countries throughout Asia, Africa and Central America.

Volunteers are recruited from a broad skills base and include nurses, midwives, agriculturists, civil engineers, environmental health officers, foresters, teachers, social and community development workers, accountants, mechanics, administrators and logisticians. First-time volunteers commit for a two-year period, and food, accommodation, travel, monthly allowances, medicals and insurance are provided by Concern Worldwide. Volunteers must be aged at least 21, in good health and, in the majority of cases have a minimum of 18 months' post qualification experience.

For further information contact the Overseas Application Section at one of the addresses above.

CORD Christian Outreach Relief & Development
1 New Street, Leamington Spa, Warwickshire CV31 1HP; ☎01926-315301;

fax 01926; e-mail recruitment@cord.org.uk; www.cord.org.uk
CORD is a relief and development organisation currently operational in Albania, Afghanistan, Cambodia, Mozambique, Tanzania, Vietnam and Zambia. CORD is working in both the refugee and community development areas. In refugee camps CORD's expertise is in health care, community services and education. CORD's community development work focuses on rural integrated devlopment projects which generally involve assistance in health care, water and sanitation, agriculture, credit programmes and community care for the vulnerable.

CORD volunteers are committed Christians, over 21 years old, who have qualifications in one of the above fields, or who have managerial, financial and administrative skills which are needed to support these programmes. A remuneration package covers all costs and includes a monthly allowance based on position and responsibility. All applicants must have free right of entry into the UK. Cord is unable to process applications from outside western Europe. Details of current vacancies are on the CORD website.

CROSSLINKS
251 Lewisham Way, London SE4 1XF; ☎020-8691 6111; fax 020-8694 8023; e-mail smile@crosslinks.org; www.crosslinks.org
Crosslinks is an Anglican evangelical mission agency working in partnership with the church worldwide. It seeks to recruit people who are willing to use both their professional skills and spiritual gifts in Christian service in another culture.

Crosslinks placements can last anything from one week to two years. Volunteers will need to cover the cost of their journey to their placement overseas. Living expenses on the placement will be a minimum of £3 per day – actual cost depends on the individual country. There is no upper age limit on volunteers.

Enquiries should be made to the Programme Co-ordinator at the above address.

CUSO
2255 Carling Avenue, Suite 500, Ottawa, Ontario, Canada K2B 1A6; ☎ +1 613 829-7445; fax +1 613 829-7996; e-mail cuso.secretariat@cuso.ca; www.cuso.org
CUSO is a Canadian international development organisation which works in partnership with people to foster equality and freedom, safeguard their cultures and communities, and protect the environment. CUSO has partners in Africa, Asia, Latin America, the Caribbean and the South Pacific, as well as in Canada.

Only Canadian citizens and Canadian landed immigrants are recruited and placed. CUSO has 200+ volunteers at any one time working in 30 countries around the world sharing their skills. Applicants must be suitably qualified and in good health. Age limits depend on individual countries. Contracts are for two years. Salaries are modest by Canadian standards but are sufficient to cover living costs. CUSO also pays for travel to and from posting and medical, dental and disability insurance and cash benefits to assist with departure and resettlement costs. Couples and families can be accommodated on some postings depending on what facilities are available locally. CUSO provides an orientation prior to departure and immediately upon arrival overseas. Ongoing support is provided by field offices.

CUSO has seven offices throughout Canada which handle recruitment and selection. Applicants should send a copy of their résumé (and that of any adult who will accompany them) to the CUSO office nearest to them. Applicants residing outside Canada may send their résumé to the above address.

EIRENE, INTERNATIONAL CHRISTIAN SERVICE FOR PEACE
Engerser Strasse 74b, 56564 Neuwied, Germany; ☎ +49-2631 83790; fax +49-2631 31160; e-mail EIRENE-INT@eirene.org; www.eirene.org

Eirene organises three voluntary programmes which are complementary to each other: the north programme is operating in Europe and USA, the south programme in Nicaragua, Nigeria and Chad and the solidarity and learning programme in Africa, Latin America and Asia. In the north programme young and older volunteers, especially conscientious objectors, work together with minority groups such as migrant workers and handicapped people: in the south programme professionally qualified and experienced volunteers collaborate with projects in agriculture, irrigation, handicrafts, community development, co-operatives, health and vocational training: and in the solidarity and learning programme volunteers are invited to propose to Eirene a project in the Third World in which they want to collaborate. This scheme is financially and morally supported by basis groups in Europe: it provides a real link on the grassroot level between the Third World and Europe.

Approximately 30 volunteers are needed yearly; most of them are recruited from Germany. Those wishing to work in Europe and the USA must be at least 20 and those going to Africa or Latin America must be at least 21. All volunteers are expected to know the language of the country to which they are being sent, and to have some previous involvement in social and non-violent activities. In the north programme the minimum duration of service is one year, in the south programme it is from one to three years. Board, lodging, a monthly allowance, insurance and travel costs are all paid for, although volunteers are asked to find a support group to give some financial contribution as well as to support the service of the volunteer.

Applications should be made to the above address.

EMMS International (operating as Emmanuel Healthcare)
7 Washington Lane, Edinburgh EH11 2HA; ☎ 0131-313 3828; fax 0131-313 4662; e-mail info@emms.org; www.emms.org

Emmanuel Healthcare became the operating name in 2004, as a result of EMMS International and EHA (UK) merging. It supports programmes in India (slum project, hospitals and community health projects, AIDS hospice), Malawi (hospitals), Nepal (TB and leprosy clinic) and the Middle East (Nazareth Hospital) and helps to obtain volunteers for specialist work or general duties. In India and Malawi, qualified doctors and nurses are required, as are staff from other health-related disciplines. General help (IT people, business managers, carpenters, gardeners etc.) is also required. General help is welcomed in Nepal and Nazareth but medical or nursing staff cannot be taken due to licensing restrictions. Vacancies can occur at any time of year. Travel expenses are not paid. Simple accommodation is provided but food may not necessarily be included. For more information contact Emmanuel Healthcare.

To apply contact the following in writing directly:

Africa: Mr Mkeka Msowoya, Hospital Administrator, CCAP, Synod of Livingstonia, Ekwendeni Hospital, P.O. Box 19, Ekwendeni, Malawi; tel +265 339 222; 339 246 or fax 339 250; e-mail ekwehealth@sdnp.org.mw.

Africa: Dr Maureen Stevenson, Medical Superintendent, CCAP, Synod of Livingstonia, DGM Hospital, P.O. Box 5, Livingstonia, Malawi; tel +265 368207; e-mail ccaphealth@Malawi.net.

Africa: Dr Hans Rode, Medical Director, Mulanje Mission Hospital, CCAP, Synod of Blantyre, P.O. Box 45, Mulanje, Malawi; tel +265 1467044; e-mail mmh@Malawi.net.

India: Dr. Stephen Alfred, Lok Hospital, Pokharan Road No 2, Thane 400601, Maharashtra, India; 91 22 543 7799; e-mail Alfred@bom4.vsnl.net.in.

India: Dr Philip Varghese, Executive Director, Emmanuel Hospital Association, 88/92 Deepali Building, Nehru Place, New Delhi 110019 India; tel 91 11 6432055; e-mail vp@eha-health.org.

Israel: Mrs. Christine Farah, The Nazareth Hospital EMMS, P.O. Box 11, 16100 Nazareth, Israel; tel +9726 602 8817; fax +9724 656 1953; e-mail ChristineFarah@nazhosp.com.

FOOD FOR THE HUNGRY – INTERNATIONAL STAFF PROGRAMME

UK: 44 Copperfield Road, Bassett, Southampton, Hants. SO16 3NX; tel/fax 023-8090 2327; e-mail uk@fhi.net; www.uk.fhi.net

USA: 1224 E Washington Street, Phoenix, Arizona 85034, USA ☐+1 480 998-3100; fax +1 480 443 1420; e-mail hunger@fh.org; www.fh.org

Canada: #005-2580 Cedar Park Place, Abbotsford, BC V2T 3S5; ☐+1 604 853 4262; fax +1 604 853 4332; e-mail info@cfh.ca; www.cfh.ca

The International Staff Ministry of Food for the Hungry offers overseas opportunities for Christians who desire to help meet the literal and spiritual hunger of others. The programme offers invaluable experience that can open the door to a lifetime of cross-cultural ministry or employment. For people who are just beginning, as well as those with prior overseas experience. Food for the Hungry offers assignments of two to three years' commitment, as well as opportunities to serve as a career. Most overseas positions currently involve skills in agiculture/animal husbandry, primary health care/nutrition, engineering/water resources, physical or occupational therapy, community development or administrative logistics/office skills. Special linguistic knowledge or previous overseas experience not necessarily required. The minimum age is 18 years. Assistance will be given in raising the necessary support. Those interested in serving with Food for the Hungry must be able and willing to contribute actively to the physical and spiritual 'Vision of a Community' Contact the appropriate address above for further details.

GEEKCORPS

1121 Mass MOCA Way, North Adams, Massachusetts 01247, USA; ☎ 413-664 0030; fax 413-664 0032; www.geekcorps.org

Geekcorps has been set up by a group of Information Technology professionals to help small businesses in the developing world. Working principally in Ghana, they also offer voluntary attachments for IT specialists all over the world. Although it is based in the USA, you do not need to be an American citizen to apply. Most volunteers work for about three months.

GOAL

PO Box 19, Dun laoghaire, Co. Dublin, Ireland; ☎ +353-1 2809779; fax +353-1 2809215; e-mail info@goal.ie; www.goal.ie

GOAL is an international humanitarian organisation, dedicated to alleviating the suffering of the poorest of the poor in the developing world. It was founded in Ireland in 1977 by sports journalist John O'Shea who is the organisation's Chief Executive. GOAL works towards ensuring that the poorest and most vulnerable in our world and those affected by humanitarian crises have access to the fundamental needs and rights of life, ie. food, water, shelter, medical attention and primary education. It is non-denominational, non-governmental and non-political.

GOAL has responded to almost every natural and man-made disaster and catastrophe in the past 25 years and is operational in 20 countries in the developing world. In many other impoverished countries it provides financial support to indigenous and missionary organisations with similar philosophies. GOAL is currently operational in

Afghanistan, India, Philippines, East Timor, El Salvador, Honduras, Kosovo, Bosnia, Serbia, Angola, Uganda, Malawi, Sierra Leone, North Sudan, South Sudan, Ethiopia, Kenya, Mozambique, Congo and South Africa.

Since its inception, GOAL has sent over 900 volunteers to work in the developing world and employs over 2,700 local personnel on its current programmes. It has spent more than 150 million euros reaching those in greatest need and has managed this with low administrative costs. GOAL prioritises those affected by emergencies and also organises long term-projects.

Volunteer nurses, doctors, administrators and accountants are always in demand. Once a volunteer has been recruited, GOAL covers the relevant expenses including travel to the programme area and accommodation. Applicants must be over 23 and have two years' professional experience in their particular career.

HANDICAP INTERNATIONAL
14, Avenue Berthelot, 69361 Lyon, Cedex 07, France; ☎ +33 (0)4 78 69 79 79; fax +33 (0)4 78 69 79 94; e-mail handicap-international@infonie.fr; www. handicap-international.org

Handicap International is an emergency relief organisation that strives to intervene as rapidly as possible in favour of the handicapped and most vulnerable populations where and when armed conflict has destroyed existing systems of support and solidarity. Similar interventions are made in countries, which have severe economic problems, or where the areas of expertise particular to the organisation are needed. Areas of operation include eastern Europe, Africa and Asia, as well as France where the organisation is based. The organisation is currently involved in about 160 projects in about 60 countries.

Handicap International employs a range of professionals including specialist medics, agronomists, architects, engineers and educators, experts in techniques specific against landmines, technicians expert in the creation and fitting of prostheses, physical therapists, psychomotor therapists, psychologists and project managers and coordinators.

Further details from the above website.

HANDS AROUND THE WORLD
P.O. Box 25, Coleford, Gloucestershire GL16 7YL; tel/fax 01594-560223; e-mail info@handsaroundtheworld.org.uk; www.handsaroundtheworld

Hands Around the World is devoted to sending short-term volunteers to help in developing countries. It currently has volunteers in India, Brazil and Africa. Requirements vary depending on requests received and activities vary but are mostly, but not exclusively, group building and health projects.

50-60 volunteers with professional qualifications and unskilled volunteers are recruited annually. Health professionals including physiotherapists, occupational therapists, IT specialists, pharmacists, maintenance engineers and many others are needed. Group projects also accommodate people with no specific skills. Age limits are from 18 to 55 or 60 depending on health. Applicants need to have a reasonable level of fitness as some projects can be hard work in arduous conditions. Groups stay up to 4 weeks; skilled volunteers up to six months.

Hands Around the World pays air fares, visa costs and insurance. Volunteers are asked to fundraise to help cover project costs. Food costs are covered for groups. Volunteers pay their own personal expenses. Preparation and training is provided prior to the project.

Further details can be obtained from the above address.

HEALTH VOLUNTEERS OVERSEAS (HVO)
c/o 1900 L St. NW, Washington DC 20036, USA; ☎ +1 202 296-0928; fax +1 202 296-8018; e-mail info@hvousa.org; www.hvousa.org

HVO is a private non-profit organisation committed to improving health care in developing countries through training and education. HVO currently recruits 300 fully trained and qualified medical professionals per year to participate in programmes in the following specialities; anaesthesia, dentistry, nursing, oral and maxillo-facial surgery, orthopaedics, paediatrics, internal medicine and physical dermatology. Programme sites are in Africa, Asia, the Caribbean and South America.

Although each programme is different in goals and content, the principal concept remains the same – that volunteers should teach rather than provide service. Most programmes require Board Certified or Board Eligible physicians, dentists, oral surgeons or physical therapists, RNs and CRNAs. Volunteer requirements vary according to programme site. Usual length of placement is two to four weeks. Most sites provide housing for volunteers, but at other sites housing arrangements are made for the volunteers but the volunteers absorb the cost. A one month assignment costs a volunteer on average $3,000 (for transportation, room, board etc) in personal expense.

Those interested should contact the above address.

ICYE-UK
Latin American House, Kingsgate Place, London NW6 4TA; tel/fax 020-7681 0983; e-mail info@icye.co.uk

ICYE is an international organisation established in 1949 and made up of autonomous national committees. The organisation aims to break down the barriers that exist between people of different cultures, faiths, ethnic groups and nationalities and raise awareness of social and environmental issues at home and abroad. Approximately 600 young people around the world take part every year. Participating countries are: Bolivia, Brazil, Columbia, Costa Rica, Honduras, Mexico, Ghana, Kenya, Nigeria, India, Japan, South Korea, Taiwan, New Zealand, Austria, Belgium, Denmark, Finland, France, Germany, Iceland, Italy, Spain, Sweden, Switzerland, Eastern Europe, and countries in the Middle East.

The programme offers the opportunity for volunteers to spend a year working on one or more voluntary projects in their chosen country. The programme starts in July and lasts for 12 months. A limited number of 6-month placements are available starting in either July or January. Placements include: drug rehabilitation programmes, working with street children, human rights projects, and HIV programmes. Volunteers live either with a host family or on the project site. Volunteers have to be aged 18-30 and must have a commitment to intercultural learning and volunteering.

For the overseas programme the applicants have to raise money for the participation fee which covers travel, insurance, residential training, preparation, language course and seminars in the host country, pocket money and administration. Costs are £3,300 for a year and £2,900 for six months.

Some short-term projects are also available: (two weeks to three months) to Costa Rica, India, Nepal and Morocco, with no age limits.

Please contact the office for more information.

INTERNATIONAL HEALTH EXCHANGE (IHE)
IHE/REDR, 1 Great George Street, London SW1P 3AA; ☎ 020-7233 1100; e-mail info@ihe.org.uk

IHE specialises in helping to recruit and train health workers for NGOs in developing countries. IHE maintains a register of health professionals, publishes *The Health*

Exchange magazine and its *Jobs and Courses* supplement and runs 3-day and week-long information courses to prepare health professionals for work in developing countries.

For further information contact the Information Worker at the above address.

INTERNATIONAL SERVICE
Hunter House, 57 Goodramgate, York YO1 7FX; ☎01904-647799; fax 01904-652353; e-mail unais-uk@geo2.poptel.org.uk; www.internationalservice.org.uk

International Service works to promote self-reliance and long-term, sustainable development in West Africa, Latin America, and the West Bank and Gaza. IS provides skilled and experienced people to collaborate with locally organised initiatives, in response to requests for skills that are not available in the communities with which IS works. IS project workers pass on their skills to local people in a spirit of equality, respect, and professionalism, strengthening their efforts to improve their situation.

IS has about 60 volunteers working on a variety of different projects from outreach health programmes and art therapy schemes to agro-forestry and water engineering initiatives. Applicants should have at least two years' experience and are advised that placements are undertaken for a minimum of two years. Volunteers are paid a monthly allowance calculated in relation to the cost of living in the country in which they work, and is very adequate for a single person. Accommodation is also covered and there are a variety of grants paid during the period of service. Flights and insurance are also provided.

For further information contact the Recruitment Administrator at the above address or via e-mail.

MMA HEALTHSERVE
First Floor, 106/110 Watney Street, London E1W 2QE; ☎020-7790 1336; fax 020-7790 1384; e-mail info@healthserve.org; www.healthserve.org

The MMA acts as an agent channelling young doctors, nurses, dentists and paramedical workers to various mission and church organisations in many countries of the world. It does not have any voluntary work of its own overseas but recruits for most of the Protestant mission societies of the UK.

The conditions of service vary, according to the usual practice of the society concerned. Magazines, *Saving Health* and *Among All Nations* are published depicting medical mission work in the world, and listing present openings in the various Protestant mission and church hospitals.

Applicants should apply to the Secretary at the above address for information on openings.

MARYKNOLL MISSION ASSOCIATION OF THE FAITHFUL (MMAF)
PO Box 307, Maryknoll, NY 10545-0307; ☎ +1 914 762-6364; fax +1 914 762-7031; e-mail mmaf@maryknoll.org; www.maryknoll.org

Maryknoll is a Catholic missionary organisation dedicated to evangelising and joining forces and skills with the marginalised people in communities worldwide. Volunteers must share the vision and vocation of the organisation. About 130 volunteers work worldwide and have a variety of professions and skills including doctors and other health workers, educationalists for education and formation at grass roots level, social workers for community development and environmentalists for environmental issues. There are also pastoral ministries, justice and peace, human rights, vocational instruction fields among others.

Volunteers must have legal resident US status in order to qualify for missionary

visas. Language training is provided. The expected term of service is three and a half years. Volunteers receive a stipend and expenses and accommodation is provided.
    For further details contact the above address.

MEDAIR

1ˢᵗ Floor, 53a Endell Street, London WC2H 9AJ; tel 020-7836 1444; fax 020-7836 1144; e-mail united.kingdom@medair.org; www.medair.org; www.medair.org

Medair, founded in 1988 is a non-governmental, humanitarian Christian organisation. Based on Christian values, Medair's objective is to respond to crisis situations with emergency and rehabilitation programmes. Medair has representation in Canada, Germany, France, The Netherlands and Switzerland as well as the UK. More than 100 people work full time in the different projects on the field as well as in Europe, and more than 725 staff are employed locally in the different countries in which Medair operates.
    About 60 volunteers are recruited annually. The types of personnel recruited include logisticians, administrators, financial officers, office managers, water and sanitation engineers, medical doctors, midwives, nurses. All needed for overseas work, currently in Afghanistan, Congo, Angola, Sudan, Iran, Madagascar, Uganda and Zimbabwe for six months up to usually a year maximum. For the UK office, part-time project work, helping raise Medair's profile and recruit volunteers. Can be several hours or days per week.
    Volunteers must be fully qualified and able to speak English fluently (French useful for some countries). Ages 25-55, single or married without children for overseas positions. Volunteers get $100 per month plus all accommodation and expenses in the first year. This rises to $1000 per month after a year's service. UK office work is unpaid. Volunteers attend a compulsory Relief Orientation Course (ROC) before going overseas.
    Apply direct to the above address or online at www.medair.org.

> **After the Bam earthquake, Medair director Ivor Morgan learned there is a difference between need and want.**
> *One day, I talked to a newly widowed mother in Iran, standing by a tent in the ruins of her house. When asked what her greatest need was at that moment, she ignored the obvious list of water, food, blankets or heaters, and meekly said 'education' for her two surviving daughters. One of them was sitting on the ground behind her, books in hand, diligently studying.*

MÉDECINS DU MONDE UK

29th Floor, One Canada Square, London E14 5AA; ☎020-7516 9103; fax 020-7561 9104; e-mail info@medicinsdumonde.co.uk; www.medecinsdumonde.org (national headquarters France)

Médecins du Monde bring relief to the most vulnerable populations in the world and treats both physical wounds and psychologoical traumas. Médecins du Monde volunteers denounce obstacles threatening access to healthcare, violations to human rights and attacks on human dignity.
    MDM currently has 12 volunteers on international projects and 60 volunteers recruited for work in the UK on Project London. Apart from medical staff, the agency also recruits non-medical staff as support workers, logisticians, medical coordinators, project coordinators and advisors, human rights advisors and psychologists. Those applying for international projects need some language skills. International posts require commitments of 3, 6 or 12 months, and Project London 6 months.

Further information from the above address.

MÉDECINS SANS FRONTIÈRES
3rd Floor, 67-74 Saffron Hill, London EC1N 8QX; ☎020-7404 6600; fax 020-7404 4466; e-mail office@london.msf.org; www.uk.msf.org
Médecins Sans Frontières (MSF) is a leading non-governmental organisation for emergency medical aid. They provide independent medical relief to victims of war, disasters and epidemics in more than 80 countries. They strive to provide assistance to those who need it most, regardless of ethnic origin, religion or political affiliation.

MSF is a voluntary organisation. Each year, about 2,500 experienced doctors, nurses, logistics experts and engineers of all nationalities leave on field assignments. They work closely with thousands of national staff.

MSF recruits those with the following professional backgrounds: medical doctors, nurses, surgeons, midwives, anaesthetists, nutritionists, epidemiologists, bio-medical scientists, mental health professionals, water and sanitation engineers, construction engineers, logisticians with proven working knowledge of pumps and generators, vehicle mechanics, radio/communication equipment, simple water and sanitation systems, construction and financial controllers.

The selection process consists of interviews, tests and pre-departure training. The UK office can only process applications from people resident in the UK or Ireland. MSF has other offices worldwide. For details visit the website (www.msf.org).

MERCY SHIPS
PO Box 2020, Lindale, TX 75771-2020, USA; ☎ +800 424-7447; fax +800 882-0336; e-mail persgen@mercyships.org; www.mercyships.org
Mercy Ships is a non-profit Christian relief agency, operating ocean going ships which bring medical care, relief aid and the gospel to locations worldwide in order to attain long-term sustainable change in these places. Volunteer surgeons perform thousands of free operations to correct cleft palates, crossed eyes, removing tumors and cataracts. Medical and dental teams establish local clinics in outlaying villages to provide vaccinations, dental treatments, and basic medical care.

Over 1,000 volunteers are recruited each year: plastic surgeons, anaesthetists, nurses, dentists, cooks, seamen – officers and ordinary seamen, secretaries, hairdressers, engineers, mechanics, computer programmers and system analysts. Help is required all year round for short term periods (2 weeks to 3 months) and long-term placements – 2 years or more. Applicants must be minimum age 18, in good health with no medical restrictions, hold a driving licence (doctors and medical professionals), and in some cases have computer skills. Bi-linguists particularly needed. All volunteers must be self-funding but support can be given with fundraising. Accommodation is provided on ships but varies in onshore offices.

Applications to Human Resources International at the above address.

MERLIN – Medical Emergency Relief International
5-13 Trinity Street, London SE1 1DB; ☎020-7378-4888; fax 020-7378 4899; e-mail hq@merlin.co.uk; www.merlin.org.uk
Merlin is a humanitarian organisation set up in 1993 to provide medical relief in the first phase of international emergencies, when the local infrastructure has broken down and people are at their most desperate.

The need for volunteers is rising steadily. A range of professional and medical expertise is needed, but primarily it is for doctors, nurses and support staff which is people with logistics experience and/or administrative finance skills.

Volunteers of all nationalities can apply, but applicants need to attend an interview in the UK at their own expense. At least two years' post-registration experience is required for medical personnel. Previous overseas experence is not essential, but desirable.

Volunteers are constantly recruited on to a regsiter and positions are generally for 6-12 months. Travel expenses are paid for the second interview. A volunteer allowance is paid in the UK for work overseas and flights, visas, insurance and accommodation are all covered by MERLIN. Applications to the above address.

MISSION AVIATION FELLOWSHIP UK

1st Floor Castle House, Castle Hill Avenue, Folkestone, Kent CT20 2TN; ☎01303-850950; fax 01303-852800; e-mail Personnel@MAF-UK.org;www. maf-uk.org

Mission Aviation Fellowship UK is a charity that raises funds to enable MAF worldwide to fly light aircraft in the developing world to support church, mission, relief, and development agencies in their work. Serving with MAF overseas are pilots, aircraft engineers, avionics technicians, IT specialists, administrators, finance and management staff.

MAF also runs three-week overseas teams for supporters (ages 18-65) able to offer practical assistance to MAF programmes in the areas of renovation and maintenance etc. In addition there are some volunteering opportunities for one to six months available for those who are interested in long term work with MAF and want to try out life overseas.

MAF UK is recruiting suitably trained and experienced staff from the UK for the needs of MAF worldwide.

For a recruitment pack, please contact the Personnel Department at the above address. Note that only UK citizens or those legally resident in the UK can be employed by MAF.

PEACE CORPS OF THE UNITED STATES

1111 20th Street, NW, Washington, D.C. 20526, USA; ☎ +1 202 692-1800; e-mail webmaster@peacecorps.gov; www.peacecorps.gov

The Peace Corps was established by President J F Kennedy in 1961 since when over 150,000 Americans have offered their services abroad. The goals of the Peace Corps are to help promote world peace and friendship, assist developing countries to meet their needs for skilled personnel and to promote mutual understanding between people of the United States and those of developing countries. There are close to 7,000 Peace Corps volunteers and trainees in 77 nations in Latin America, Africa, Asia, the Pacific and Eastern Europe. Placements normally last for two years plus three months training time.

The Peace Corps is looking for people with practical experience. Specialists are needed in the areas of agriculture, business, engineering, forestry, fishing, health, maths and sciences and skilled trades such as masonry, carpentry, plumbing and education.

Volunteers must be US citizens and at least 18 years old. The volunteers receive a monthly allowance for rent, food, travel and medical costs, transportation to and from training sites and overseas placements and a readjustment allowance of US$225 per month, paid on completion of service.

Those interested should contact the above address.

PROJECT CONCERN INTERNATIONAL

3550 Afton Road, San Diego, CA 92123 USA; ☎ +1 619 279 9690; fax +1 619 694-0294; e-mail postmaster@projectconcern.org; www.projectconcern. org

Project Concern International (PCI) is an international health organisation that saves the lives of children by preventing disease and by providing access to clean water and nutritious food. Founded in 1961 by Jim Turpin, M.D. in San Diego, California, Project Concern now servces Romania, India, Honduras, Indonesia, Ghana, Zambia, Bolivia, Nicaragua, Guatemala, El Salvador, Nicaragua and Mexico City, reaching over 3 million people annually.

PCI is effective because our programs focus on training local volunteers to bring health care to their neighbours. Often, these volunteers provide the only health care a family will receive. Volunteers provide programme support in reproductive health education, maternal/child health care, water sanitation, capacity

TEARFUND
1OO Church Road, Teddington, Middlesex TW11 8QE; ☎020-8977 9144; fax 020-8943 3594; e-mail enquiry@tearfund.
Tearfund is an evangelical relief and development charity, working in partnership with Christians around the world to tackle the causes and effects of poverty and to bring Jesus Christ's message to the poor. Tearfund is currently active in the UK and in over 80 countries in Africa, Asia, South America and Eastern Europe.

One of the ways in which Tearfund supports its partners is by sending UK-based personnel for a variety of short to medium-term assignments in the UK and overseas. Applicants need to be committed Christians, with strong links with a home church.

For further information, please contact the Enquiry Team at the above address.

UNITED NATIONS VOLUNTEERS (UNV)
Headquarters mailing address: Postfach 260 111, D53153 Bonn, Germany; e-mail for information: information@unvolunteers.org; e-mail for volunteer applications enquiry@unvolunteers.org; web www.unvolunteers.org
United Nations Volunteers (UNV) programme is the UN organisation that supports human development globally by promoting volunteerism and mobilizing volunteers. It has initiatives in nearly 150 countries. UNV was created by the UN General Assembly in 1970 and is administered by the United Nations Development Programme (UNDP).

As part of its activities, UNV provides the opportunity for over 5,500 skilled and experienced professionals, 70 per cent of whom are from developing countries, to support peace, relief and development initiatives in over 140 countries. In addition, it engages thousands of other individuals in the work of the United Nations as online volunteers and manages the WorldVolunteerWeb, a global volunteering portal that serves as a knowledge resource base for campaigning, advocacy, information dissemination and networking.

Graduate qualifications and several years' working experience are preconditions for UN Volunteer assignments. Contracts are usually for two years, with shorter assignments for peace-building, electoral or emergency relief operations. Contracts are mostly for 2 years, with shorter assignments for humanitarian, Electoral and other missions. A monthly living allowance is provided to cover the UN Volunteers' expenses in the country of assignment.

VIATORES CHRISTI
38/39 Upper Gardiner Street, Dublin 1, Ireland; ☎ +352-1 8749346/8728027; fax +353-1 8745731; e-mail viatoreschristi@eircom.net
A lay missionary association founded in Dublin in 1960, Viatores Christi has its headquarters and training programme in Ireland. It recruits, trains and helps place volunteers overseas wherever there is need for them. Besides offering their own skills in such fields as medicine, teaching, carpentry, mechanical engineering, secretarial work,

etc. volunteers, as lay missionaries, should be prepared to participate actively in the work of the local Church.

Volunteers must undertake a part-time training course held at weekends in Ireland for a minimum period of nine months. To be assigned overseas they should be practising Catholics, at least 21, in good health and possess some professional qualification or skill. All assignments are for a minimum period of one year but most volunteers stay for at least two years.

Applications should be made to the Secretary at the above address.

building, food security, research, and funding development. PCI does not require a volunteer programme fee. Volunteer appointments are on a pro-bono basis.

VSO

317 Putney Bridge Road, London SW15 2PN; ☎020-8780 7500; e-mail enquiry@vso.org.uk; www.vso.org.uk

VSO is a registered charity, which works for economic and social justice by giving practical aid through a volunteer programme and so assisting individual development and the alleviation of poverty. It is committed to sharing skills with the peoples of developing countries. There are over 2000 volunteers in the field at any one time in 60 developing countries contributing to improvements in education, health and food production as well as in the use of appropriate technology, social development and the growth of business.

Historically VSO has provided volunteer teachers and about 40 per cent of its volunteers are working in educational posts; some of these are teacher training posts within community development projects and are not confined to the formal education sector.

Posts are usually for two years. Volunteers aged between 20 and 68 must all have qualifications and usually relevant work experience in their respective fields, although VSO does post some recent graduates if they have studied sciences or have a TEFL certificate and are prepared to teach.

VSO pays air fares, national insurance contributions, grants, and arranges language courses where necessary. Accommodation and salary, which is paid at the local rate for the job, are provided by the overseas employer.

For further details contact the Central Enquiries Unit on the above number.

WORLD SERVICE ENQUIRY

Room 237, Bon Marché Centre, 241-251 Ferndale Road, London SW9 8BJ; ☎0870 700 3274; fax 0870 770 7991; e-mail wse@cabroad.org.uk; www. wse.org.uk

World Service Enquiry is the information and advice activity of Christians Abroad, for people of any faith or none. WSE provides expert and impartial advice about opportunities to work or volunteer in the Third World. The annual *Guide to Volunteering and Working Overseas* contains information about being involved in development issues, a list of volunteer agencies and basic information about working overseas. *Opportunities Abroad* is the UK's only monthly job magazine available in a range of subscriptions. World Service Enquiry also provides personal advice and life coaching solutions for those seeking work in the development sector. Full details of all services are available in the guide or on the website.

Christians Abroad recruit qualified and experienced professionals and volunteers for teaching, health and administration posts on behalf of overseas partners. Current vacancies are advertised on the website www.cabroad.org.uk.

WORLDTEACH INC

Centre for International Development, Harvard University, 79 John F

Kennedy Street, MA 02139 Cambridge, USA; ☎ +1 617-495 5527; e-mail info@worldteach.org; www.worldteach.org
WorldTeach, a private, non-profit organisation based at the Harvard Institute for International Development, was formed in 1986 by a Harvard graduate with the purpose of contributing to education overseas and providing opportunities for North Americans and other speakers of English to gain experience in international development.

WorldTeach places volunteers as teachers of English as a foreign and second language in countries which request assistance. Currently, WorldTeach provides college graduates as teachers for one year contracts to Costa Rica, Ecuador, and Namibia. Six month opportunities are available in Yantai, China where volunteers teach adults and in Mexico and Honduras where volunteers teach English to nature guides. Additionally, undergraduate and graduate students can participate in the Shanghai Summmer Teaching Programme spending a summer teaching English and studying Chinese at a language camp for Chinese high school students.

Participants pay a programme fee, which covers the cost of international, round-trip airfare, health insurance, placement, training and support. Applications are accepted all year round on a rolling basis. Student loans can be deferred while volunteers teach. Limited, need-based financial aid is available and WorldTeach provides fund-raising ideas. Participants on the year long programmes must have a bachelor degree: no previous language or teaching experience is required.

The following organisations have been included in the various sub-sections of the *International Volunteering* chapter, but also require professional volunteers worldwide:

Alliances Abroad
BSES Expeditions
Catholic Network of Volunteer Service
Center for INTERIM Programs
Christian Foundation for Children & Ageing
Fundacion Golondrinas
Global Outreach UK
Habitat for Humanity International
LEAPNow
Mission Volunteers USA & International
Olympic Aid International
Personnel Programme Team
Scottish Churches World Exchange
Teaching & Projects Abroad
WEC International

See also *Worldwide, Religious Projects* section for longer-term commitments.

United Kingdom

Archaeology

ARBEIA ROMAN FORT & MUSEUM
Baring Street, South Shields, Tyne and Wear, NE33 2BB; ☎0191-454 4093; fax 0191-427 6862; www.twmuseums.org.uk
Archaeology and museum work includes excavation, site recording, drawing, finds processing, museum interpretation. No experience of archaeology necessary but volunteers must understand basic English. Minimum age 16. Volunteers wanted all year round and the usual period of work is two to four weeks. Accommodation can be arranged in local guest houses and camp sites at the volunteers' expense.

Useful publication *Guide to South Shields Roman Fort* available at the site for £1.95. Volunteers get a volunteer pack on arrival.

Applications to Elizabeth Elliott at the above address.

CASTELL HENLLYS TRAINING EXCAVATION
Dept., of Archaeology, University of York, York YO1 7EP; www.york.ac.uk/depts/arch/castellhenlys/web/
Castell Henllys is a Scheduled Ancient Monument and one of several Iron Age promontory forts in the Pembrokeshire Coast National Park. Archaeologists from York University have been excavating there for nearly 25 years exposing the details of daily life 2000 years ago layer by layer. A student training dig has been held on the site every year since 1981. Several thatched prehistoric buildings have been reconstructed there on their original foundations.

Approximately 70 volunteers are taken on annually to help excavate, record and survey the site. The minimum age is 16 years and minimum period usually two weeks and a maximum of four weeks in July/August. £160 per week is payable for training and food costs. Accommodation is on a campsite where tents can be hired. Local accommodation is also available and details are available on request.

For further details and an application form go to the website above.

COUNCIL FOR BRITISH ARCHAEOLOGY
Bowes Morrell House, 111 Walmgate, York YO1 9WA; ☎01904-671417; fax 01904-671384; e-mail info@britarch.ac.uk; www.britarch.ac.uk
The Council publishes *British Archaeology*, a bi-monthly full colour magazine, which includes an information section *CBA Briefing*, which carries announcements of forthcoming fieldwork opportunities on archaeological sites in Britain and costs £5 per issue (cheaper with an annual subscription).

SEDGEFORD HISTORICAL AND ARCHAEOLOGICAL RESEARCH PROJECT
Hawthorns, Sandy Lane, Docking, King's Lynn, Norfolk PE31 8NF; www.sharp.org.uk
About 60 volunteer archaeological and historical fieldworkers are needed for a long-

term investigation of an English parish, concentrating at present on Iron Age, Saxon and mediaeval periods. Volunteer fieldworkers pay £120 per week subsistence charge. Period of work is mid-June to late August. Hours are 8.30am-5pm, 6 days a week with Saturdays off. No professional qualifications needed.

Request for an application form with SAE to Christine Kelly, Project Adminstrator, at the above address.

SOUTH CADBURY ENVIRONS PROJECT
Simonburn Cottage, Sutton Montis, Yeovil, Somerset BA22 7HF; website www.southcadbury.org.uk

SCEP is an Archaeological Survey and excavation run jointly by the universities of Bristol and Oxford, in the landscape around the Iron Age hillfort of Cadbury Castle, Somerset.

Approximately 20 volunteers annually needed to assist with all the usual tasks on an excavation including geographical surveying, digging test pits, excavation (between March and October and November to February). washing finds and wet-sieving of soil. The November to February indoor season may not suit those susceptible to eyestrain.

Volunteers should stay a minimum of five days and there is no set maximum. There is limited accommodation available which costs between £5 (camping) and £12 (self-catering). No special skills are required, but volunteers interested in doing certified courses should go through the University of Bristol, Archaeology Field School website (see www.southcadbury.org.uk for links). You can also get a copy of the SCEP Fieldwork Report, 1998-2001 (£10) from the Centre for the Historic Environment, University of Bristol 43 Woodland Road, Bristol BS8 1UU.

Applications from volunteers should be sent to the Sutton Montis address.

UPPER NENE ARCHAEOLOGICAL SOCIETY
Toad Hall, 86 Main Road, Hackleton, Northampton NN7 2AD; ☎01604-870312; e-mail unas@friendship-taylor.freeserve.col.uk

The Society oversees the excavation of a Romano-British villa and underlying Iron Age settlement at Piddington, Northamptonshire. Volunteers are required to help with trowelling and a variety of excavation and post-excavation procedures. Volunteers may be of any nationality but must be able to speak English. The lower age limit is normally 16; no upper limit. Applicants should consider themselves physically capable of carrying buckets of soil, pushing wheelbarrows and kneeling to work.

Volunteers are required for a minimum of two weeks in August, but anyone within travelling distance is welcome to come and help on Sundays throughout the year. Pocket money is not provided, but volunteers must pay a specific contribution towards the everyday expense of running the excavation. Accommodation is a basic campsite, or bed and breakfast accommodation at reasonable rates can be arranged locally. This must be paid for by the volunteer.

Those interested should contact Mrs. D E Friendship-Taylor at the above address.

Arts and Music

BRITTEN-PEARS SCHOOL FOR ADVANCED MUSICAL STUDIES
Snape Maltings Concert Hall, Snape, Saxmundham, Suffolk IP17 1SP; ☎01728-687100; fax 01728-687120; e-mail enquiries@aldeburghfestivals.org

Aldeburgh Productions grew out of the Aldeburgh Festival founded in 1948 by Benjamin Britten, Peter Pears and Eric Crozier. Under the management of Aldeburgh Productions, the Britten-Pears School, set in the inspirational surroundings of Snape, Suffolk, has a distinguished tradition of training emerging professional musicians. Two interns are required to work on a voluntary basis in the Britten-Pears School for advanced musical studies, to support a small permanent administration team during the height of the season. Applicants should be students/recent graduates. Ideally one volunteer should work June and July and the second for August and September. This would be an invaluable opportunity to gain insight in the workings of an internationally renowned arts organisation. Duties will include driving the School car or minibus (if over 21), assisting with keeping files and databases in order and providing clerical support. Excellent secretarial and organisational skills are needed and a sound knowledge of English and knowledge of classical music is desirable. Accommodation provided in Aldeburgh and a living allowance for meals.

CHELTENHAM FESTIVAL OF LITERATURE
Town Hall, Imperial Square, Cheltenham, Glos. GL50 1QA; ☎01242-263494; fax 01242-256457; e-mail sarahsm@cheltenham.gov.uk
The Cheltenham Festival of Literature began in 1950 and is the largest and is one of Europe's largest and most popular. The wide range of events includes talks and lectures, poetry readings, novelists in conversation, creative writing workshops, exhibitions, discussions and a literary festival for children.

Festival volunteers (25) are needed to look after both the authors and the audience as well as helping with the setting up of events, front of house duties, looking after the office and assisting the sound crew. To work for 10 days from mid-late October (dates are slightly different each year). Hours are fairly long (10am-midnight). Applicants should be over 18, who have an interest in literature, arts administration or events management.

Volunteers are given free accommodation, food and drink. Free entry to all events is also provided. Overseas applicants welcome, but they must have a very high standard of written and spoken English.

Applications to Adam Pushkin, Festival Officer from June onwards to the above address.

HESSE STUDENT SCHEME
Aldeburgh Productions, Snape Maltings Concert Hall, Snape, Saxmundham, Suffolk IP17 1SP; ☎01728-687100; fax 01728-687120; e-mail assistant@aldeburgh. co.uk; www.Aldeburgh.co.uk
Volunteers to assist in the varied duties involved in the day-to-day running of the Aldeburgh Festival of Music and the Arts during June. Duties can include: programme selling, page turning, invigilating, exhibitions, assisting with stage moves and bus conducting on the coaches that run from Aldeburgh to all concert venues. In addition, students are also expected to devise, rehearse and perform in a concert of their own (one of the free events publicised in the Aldeburgh Festival booking brochure. In exchange, two groups of 12 students are awarded a grant which covers tickets to all the festival events together with bed and breakfast accommodation in Aldeburgh for each half of the Festival.

Applications are welcomed from anyone between ages 18 and 25 (on 1 June) irrespective of current course or occupation. Applications from overseas are particularly welcomed. A willingness to help, no matter how mundane the task, together with a passion for music are essential.

Further details and an application form from Jane Alexander at the above address by 30 April.

Child Care

BIRMINGHAM PHAB CAMPS
2 Lenchs Green, Edgbaston, Birmingham B5 7PX; ☎0121-440-5727; www. bhamphab.camps.org.uk.

This organisation runs holiday camps each summer for equal numbers of physically disabled and able-bodied young people, enabling the disabled young people to integrate with their able-bodied contemporaries. There are six camps a year, four of which cater for different age groups; Junior (7-10), Senior (11-13), Venture (14-16), and 18 plus. Two camps are run for severely (i.e. multiply-disabled) young people of various ages.

Many young people who are physically disabled have little opportunity to mix and form friendships with their peers and the camps are designed to remedy this isolation and overcome prejudice. There is a wide range of activities from swimming and discos to seaside and camping trips, in which all the young people take part. The camps are run entirely by unpaid volunteers, of whom 80 are needed each year. The volunteer will work at a camp for a week with a team including an experienced leader and a qualified nurse. The Camps are held at a variety of activity centres in the UK, which provide good accommodation.

Volunteers should be aged between 17 and 30, and speak English. Obviously the ability to communicate with young people is important. Skills in sport, music, art and so on are valuable, as is previous experience. Energy, dependability, a capacity for hard work and an ability to enthuse young people and win their confidence are essential.

A training day is held before the camps, where medical staff from special schools give advice on special needs, and the teams plan the camp programmes. Accommodation is provided, but expenses and pocket money are not. Transport from Birmingham to the camp and back is paid.

Volunteers should apply to the Volunteer Recruitment Officer at the above address.

BREAK
1, Montague Road, Sheringham, Norfolk NR26 8WN; ☎01263-822161; fax 01623-822181; e-mail office@break-charity.org; www.break-charity.org

BREAK provides holidays, short breaks and respite care for adults and children with physical and/or learning disabilities at two centres on the beautiful north Norfolk coast. Volunteers aged over 18 years, are needed to support Break's professional staff with caring for the centre's guests. Tasks will include helping individuals with a variety of special needs such as meals, dressing, toiletting, mobility and accompanying them on outings and other activities. Each week brings new and varied challenges, as every guest requires a differing level of support.

Placements are available for six weeks to six months. Accommodation, food and pocket money is provided, and UK travel expenses are paid. Volunteers must be able to understand and speak English to a level that enables them to communicate effectively with both staff and guests.

CALDECOTT FOUNDATION
Smeeth, Ashford, Kent TN25 6SP; ☎01303-815678; fax 01303-815677; e-mail care@caldecottfoundation.org

The Community provides therapeutic care and education for 68 children for 52 weeks a year. Children are admitted to Caldecott following placement disruption or family breakdown. Contact is maintained with home or family wherever possible.

The Caldecott school provides for both primary and secondary age children. The school endeavours to prepare children to return to mainstream education wherever possible. Volunteers are engaged to assist the residential and school staff in their care and education of the children.

There are no special skills required but the volunteers should enjoy being with children and have some ability in sports, music, arts and crafts, or possession of a driving licence would be an asset. Volunteers are usually taken on for between three months and a year. Travelling expenses and pocket money. Very limited accommodation.

Those interested should apply to Liz Flisher at the above address.

CAMPHILL LOCH ARTHUR COMMUNITY
Beeswing, Dumfries, DG2 8JQ; ☎01387-760618/760621; fax 01387-760618; e-mail admin@locharthur.org.uk
Loch Arthur Community began in November 1984, on an estate six miles from Dumfries, by the village of Beeswing. At present, it has over 500 acres of land, including farmland, a large loch, and forested areas. Seven households have been established, the smallest of which has a house community of nine people and the largest consists of 15. There are 70 people in the Community, including families with children, handicapped adults and other co-workers who join it for periods from a few weeks to several years.

Volunteers participate in activities such as farming (crops, dairy, beef, and sheep), gardening, estate work, creamery, bakery, weaving workshop, and housework, dependent on the needs of the Community at a given time. There are also people in Loch Arthur who require help with personal care (bathing, dressing, eating, etc).

No one receives wages in Loch Arthur, but all basic needs are seen to by the Community and everyone receives an amount of pocket money to suit their individual needs. There is a busy social and cultural life in the Community influenced by Christian festivals.

Applicants should apply directly to the above address.

CAMPHILL RUDOLF STEINER SCHOOLS
Murtle Estate, Bieldside, Aberdeen AB15 9EP; ☎01224-867 935; e-mail b.porter@crss.org.uk; www.camphillschools.org.uk
This is a residential school for children and adolescents in need of special care. Volunteers are needed to live-in and help care for the young people in a home and classroom setting. Volunteers are known as co-workers to emphasise the community aspect of life and the Camphill ethos, which is to allow every human being to reach their potential. The Murtle Estate is one of the original Camphill communities founded in the 1940s. At the time of press it is under threat from the proposed routing of the Aberdeen Western Peripheral Route, which cuts through farmland at the heart of the Murtle estate.

Volunteers from 80 countries commit themselves for one year to live in the Camphill Schools - joining with with the community life as fully as possible. Camphill Schools is a community with emphasis placed on Christian ideals, social responsibility and the development of the individual.

Applicants must be aged at least 19 and should be willing to live and fully involve themselves in the community activities with the children and young people. This is physically and mentally demanding work. Preference is given to applicants who plan to commit themselves to working for a year, although 6 months will also be considered. Free board and lodging and pocket money.

Certain medical conditions are acceptable but no one with a drug habit will be considered.

Contact the Co-worker recruitment group at the above address.

CHILDREN'S COUNTRY HOLIDAYS FUND (CCHF)
42-43 Lower Marsh, London SE1 7RG; ☎020-7928 6522; fax 020-7401 3961; e-mail cchf@dircon.co.uk; www.childrensholidays-cchf.org
CCHF is a registered charity that has been providing holidays for London children in need since 1884. One of the aspects of CCHF's work is to run residential summer activity holidays. These activity holidays provide a variety and balance of activities designed to meet the needs of all the children on them.

Volunteers (aged 18 upwards) are needed during the school summer holidays to work as Camp Supervisors, looking after small groups of children aged 8-12 under the guidance of an experienced camp leader. Relevant experience desirable although training will be given. Supervisors are responsible for the care and welfare of children in their group for the duration of the camp. A camp lasts for 7 days, on a variety of dates in July and August and are held in residential centres in the south of England.

Accommodation, board, insurance, travel and pocket money are provided. To ensure the safety of the children, applicants must have been residents of England or Wales for five years to enable police and social service checks to be made on them. Applications by May at the latest.

GREENHILL YMCA NATIONAL CENTRE
Donard Park, Newcastle, Co. Down BT33 0GR, Northern Ireland; ☎028-4372 3172; fax 028-4372 6009; e-mail greenhill@ymca-ireland.org
The Centre is an outdoor education centre which needs volunteers to act as domestic staff and cooks, instructors in outdoor pursuits such as canoeing, hill walking, archery, etc, and tutors in personal development. Around 14 volunteers are required for eight or nine weeks during summer and in winter two or three volunteers are needed. An interest in community relations would be an advantage.

Volunteers should be physically and mentally fit, aged 18 years or older and fluent in English. Volunteers for instructor positions will receive all relevant training. Board, lodging and pocket money are provided.

Applications should be made to the Programmes Manager at the above address.

INCLUDE (formerly Cities in Schools)
1, The Chambers, East Street, Reading, Berkshire RG1 4JD; ☎0118-952 7031; fax 0118-956 6004; e-mail include@cfbt.com; www.include.org.uk
Include helps children who have difficulties at school to build their confidence and self-image and to secure the inclusion of all young people in mainstream education and training. Volunteers are needed to help such children and young people in local projects. There is free training provided. The organisation's projects are usually small-scale but there are larger programmes run during vacations.

For further details and other contact addresses write to or e-mail the central office at the above address.

LEICESTER CHILDREN'S CENTRE
Quebec Road, Mablethorpe, Lincs. LN12 1QX; ☎01507-472444; e-mail helen@lanzetta.freeserve.co.uk; www.childrensholidaycentre.co.uk
This Centre provides summer holidays for groups of 30 girls and 30 boys from socially deprived backgrounds in the Leicester area. The two week-long camps are held from the beginning of May to the end of August each year. The centre requires about 15 volunteers to act as leaders organising, instructing, and supervising children aged seven to 11 on an outdoor activities programme. Energy, enthusiasm and a sense of humour are essential. Board, accommodation and a weekly wage are provided. Preference is

given to applicants able to work the entire season. Volunteers from overseas must be able to speak English and provide a no criminal record certificate from the appropriate authority in their home country. All volunteers are required to undergo an enhanced Criminal Record Bureau check. The minimum age is 18 years.

Write (enclosing a SAE) to H Eagle-Lanzetta, Centre Manager, at the above address from January or e-mail for an application form.

NANSEN HIGHLAND
Redcastle Station, Muir of Ord, Ross-shire IV6 7RX; ☎01463-871255; fax 01463-870258; e-mail Nansen@highlandhq.freeserve.co.uk; www. nansenhighland.co.uk

Nansen Highland is a charitable organisation offering training and support to young adults with a range of learning difficulties. Volunteers are required to deliver day training in life skills, social skills and vocational skills while working within a supportive staff team.

Nansen Highland requires volunteers to stay for a minimum of 3 months to enable continuity with the trainees. Experience with people with learning difficulties would be advantageous, but not essential. Good spoken English is essential and a police check result has to be provided prior to any commitment. Board and lodging may be available depending on demand. No travel expenses. All enquiries to the above adddress.

THE OK CLUB
Christian Holt House, Denmark Road, Kilburn, London NW6 5BP; ☎020-7624 6292; fax 020-7372 6598; e-mail enquiries@okclub.org.uk; www.okclub.org. uk

The OK Club carries out a range of Christian youth and children's work in Kilburn, northwest London. Activities include sports, creative arts, music, games, trips and holidays, mentoring, family work, schools work, church work. Volunteers are needed to help with this and also administration and office work. It is preferred that volunteers have some relevant work experience, are English-speaking and have skills in sports, arts, IT etc. Full-time volunteers should stay a year if possible; part-time any hours or days to suit. Full-time volunteers get accommodation and pocket money and food allowance. Part-time volunteers get accommodation at special cheap rate if needed.

Apply direct to the above address.

THE SHEILING COMMUNITY
The Sheiling School, Park Road, Thornbury, Bristol, BS35 1HW; ☎01454-412194; fax 01454-411860; e-mail mail@sheilingschool.org.uk; www. sheilingschool.org.uk

The Sheiling Community is part of the worldwide Camphill communities, which exist in 22 countries. About 30 Volunteers (known as co-workers) are needed annually to live and work with special needs people in the age ranges 7-16 and 16-19; living with them on a daily basis, working in a classroom and/or craft workshop. Volunteers should have a command of the English language, empathy/interest in those with special needs and an interest in community living. Volunteers should also be in good mental and physical health. Volunteers usually stay for a school year from mid-August until the following July. Board and lodging and weekly pocket money provided.

Applications to Ms Silke Woodward, Co-Workers the above address.

Conservation, the Environment & Heritage

ALICE TRUST
Waddesdon Manor, Aylesbury, Bucks. HP18 0JH; ☎01296-653307; fax 01296-653212; e-mail marian.ridgway@nationaltrust.org.uk
Waddesdon Manor, a National Trust property, is a magnificent French Renaissance-style chateau, home to the Rothschild Collection of superb 18th century French furniture and decorative arts. The gardens are considered to be one of the finest examples of Victorian flamboyance in Britain and contain a broad range of both formal and informal areas including a parterre, rose garden, large parkland with many mature trees, splendid walks and a rococo-style aviary.

Volunteer Gardeners are required in a diverse range of maintenance tasks, working alongside the team of professional gardeners. A limited number of full-time residential internships is available, normally for periods up to a maximum of six months. Rent-free accommodation and some assistance with food expenses may be available. No experience necessary, but commitment and reasonable fitness are required. Overseas, English-speaking applicants are considered. Early application is advised.

Other volunteer opportunities (non-residential) may be available for suitably qualified applicants within the Collection, gardens and aviary; contact the above address to find out more.

BERRINGTON HALL
Near Leominster, Herefordshire HR6 0DW; ☎01568-615721; e-mail yvonne. osborne@nationaltrust.co.uk; www.nationaltrust.org.uk
Berrington Hall is a National Trust Property which requires volunteer room stewards every day from April to October. Also needed are volunteer car park attendants to work on Bank Holidays. Volunteers must be aged at least 18. No accommodation is provided but travel costs are provided (up to 40 miles round trip) and those who offer 40 hours of service get a volunteer card entitling them to free entry to National Trust Properties in the UK and 10% discount in the shops. Overseas applicants are welcome.

Anyone interested should apply to the House Steward at the above address.

BTCV
Conservation Centre, Balby Road, Balby, Doncaster, DN4 0RH; tel 01302-572244; fax 01302-310167; e-mail information@btcv.org.uk; www.btcv.org. uk ☎01302-572244; fax 01302-310167; e-mail Information@btcv.org.uk; www.btcv.org.uk
BTCV is the country's leading charity protecting the environment through practical action. A network of over 160 offices allows some 130,000 volunteers of all ages and from all sections of the community to train and take part in a wide range of environmental projects, including tree-planting, repairing footpaths and dry stone walling, creating community gardens and involvement with recycling projects. Volunteers can give as much or as little time as they wish, ranging from one day to six months.

BTCV's UK and international programme of conservation working holidays enables thousands of volunteers between the ages of 16 and 75 to spend time in a spectacular setting, learning new skills and getting to know new people. Around 500 breaks take place throughout the UK each year, with costs starting at around £40 for a week inclusive of food, accommodation and training. BTCV also offers international destinations as diverse as Thailand, Iceland and the USA. International break prices range from £220-£1,450. No experience is needed for participation in BTCV's conservation projects – just energy and enthusiasm.

Contact the BTCV office for information about any of the above activities.

BTCV SCOTLAND

Balallan House, 24 Allan Park, Stirling, FK8 2QG; ☎01786-479697; fax 01786-465359; e-mail scotland@btcv.org.uk; www.btcv.org

BTCV Scotland is part of BTCV, the UK's largest charity dedicated to promoting all forms of practical conservation volunteering work. Every year, over 6,500 people – nearly all volunteers – are involved in activities run from local centres in Glasgow, Edinburgh, Stirling, Linlithgow, Aberdeen and Inverness.

BTCV Scotland is principally concerned with people. Through its services, it offers residential and local volunteering opportunities open to all, involves and supports local communities in effective environmental action to improve their own neighbourhoods and enables people to learn new skills applicable to real jobs in the environment. Training in tree-planting, dry stone dyking, fencing and habitat management is given. Long-term volunteers are recruited for several months while residential projects normally run for 7 to 14 days. Most volunteers are needed between March and October but some projects are undertaken during the winter.

A working knowledge of English is desirable. The minimum age of volunteers accepted is 16 years and volunteers must be aware that some tasks are physically demanding. Accommodation and food are provided at an average cost of £60 per project.

For more information contact BTCV Scotland at the above address for a programme.

CATHEDRAL CAMPS

16 Glebe Avenue, Flitwick, Bedfordshire MK45 1HS; ☎01525-716237; e-mail admin@cathedralcamps.org.uk; www.cathedralcamps.org.uk

Cathedral Camps invite young people to undertake maintenance and conservation work in Cathedrals and their environments, and major parish churches in Britain.

Volunteers join a group of 15-25 young people to work on these buildings of high architectural importance at different venues. Hours of work are normally 8.30am to 5.30pm, four and a half days a week. Camps take place from July to September and each one lasts for a week.

A contribution of £70 is requested towards the cost of the camp, board and lodging. The minimum age is 16 and most volunteers are aged 17-25: the upper age is 30. Applicants from outside the British Isles are welcome to apply.

For further details and an application form, contact Mrs Shelley Bent, Administrator, at the above address.

THE CENTRE FOR ALTERNATIVE TECHNOLOGY

Machynlleth, Powys SY20 9AZ; ☎01654-705950; fax 01654-702782; e-mail info@cat.org.uk; www.cat.org.uk

Established in 1974, the Centre for Alternative Technology is an internationally renowned display and education centre promoting practical ideas and information on technologies, which sustain rather than damage the environment.

The Centre runs a short term volunteer programme, from March to September inclusive, for stays of one or two weeks. There is also a long-term volunteer programme for individuals to help in specific work departments for 6 months. Short-term volunteers help with gardening, landscaping, site maintenance and preparation for courses. Long-term jobs for volunteers include the following departments: biology, engineering, gardening, information, media and site maintenance.

Applicants for the long-term programme should have relevant experience. Applicants for either programme can be of any nationality; long-term volunteers must be eligible for British state benefit payments, or be able to fund themselves. Accommodation for short-term is basic, youth hostel style, shared with other volunteers and with food and drinks provided. Other arrangements for long-term volunteers.

Applicants for the 60 short-term places and the 16 long-term places available annually should contact Rick Dance at the above address.

CONSERVATION VOLUNTEERS NORTHERN IRELAND
159 Ravenhill Road, Belfast BT6 0BP; ☎028-9064 5169; fax 028-9064 4409; e-mail cvni@btcv.org.uk; www.cvni.org.uk & www.btcv.org.uk

The Northern Ireland branch of the British Trust for Conservation Volunteers takes on some 200 people a year for week-long working holidays and a further 200 on weekend projects. Most of the projects involve conservation/environmental work. However, some are combined with special interest activities such as caving or canoeing. Volunteers aged 18 to 80 are needed year round but the majority are needed during the summer. Groups of ten to twelve participants carry out various conservation tasks including drystone walling, building kissing gates, footpath construction and repair, pond building, tree planting and woodland management. Sites for the work may be urban or rural – from the Mourne Mountains to the sand dunes of Portrush to Belfast's urban landscape. Costs around £35-£65 per week and £14 per weekend break which includes comfortable accommodation and meals.

Training programmes are offered all year round. Opportunities also exist for volunteers taking on specific areas of responsibility such as leading a group, educational work, or helping run our wildflower and tree nurseries. Places are available for anyone, who can commit 6 months of their time, at one of five offices in Northern Ireland.

THE CORNWALL WILDLIFE TRUST
Five Acres, Allet, Truro TR4 9DJ ☎01872-273939; fax 01872-225476; e-mail cwt@stgeorgeslooe.fsnet.co.uk and info@cornwt.demon.co.uk; www. cornwallwildlifetrust.org.uk

St. George's Island lies half a mile off the Cornish coast and comprises twenty-two and a half acres of rough grassland, scrub, woodland, beaches and cliffs. It is one mile in circumference and rises to 150 feet at its highest point. The island is open to day visitors, and their landing fees and other income generated go towards the island's conservation and upkeep. Volunteers on working holidays greatly assist the Island's conservation projects.

About 20-30 volunteers are taken on between Easter and October, usually for periods of one or two weeks, and they carry out tasks according to their enthusiasms, skills and abilities. This could include gardening, wood and track clearing, fencing, log-cutting, general conservation, general DIY and decorating. Volunteers live in a shared, self-catering chalet for which they buy their own food for the period. There is a charge of £5 for the boat from Looe. Volunteers are also required to meet and assist day visitors arriving by boat. As post is delivered and collected from the Island every two or three weeks, please allow at least three weeks for a reply to enquiries by post, or better still use our e-mail address.

FARMING AND WILDLIFE ADVISORY GROUP (FWAG)
National Agriculture Centre, Stoneleigh, Kenilworth, Warks. CV8 2RX; ☎024-7669 8702; fax 024-7669 6760; www.fwag.org.uk

FWAG is a registered national charity whose aim is to promote greater integration of landscape and nature conservation with modern farming through the provision of advice to landowners, farmers and other land managers.

FWAG groups are organised on a county basis and there are 115 farm conservation advisors who are employed by the Farming and Wildlife Advisory Group but who are directly responsible to the county-based FWAG groups.

There are both salaried and voluntary student placements. For a list of FWAG groups nationally and further details contact Jane Hampson, Personnel Officer, at the above address.

FESTINIOG RAILWAY COMPANY
Harbour Station, Porthmadog, Gwynedd, North Wales; ☎01766-516035; fax 01766-516006; e-mail tricia.doyle@festrail.co.uk; www.festrail.co.uk
Hundreds of volunteers are needed throughout the year to help in the operation and maintenance of a 150-year-old narrow gauge railway between Porthmadog and Blaenau Ffestiniog. The work done by individual volunteers depends on their skills many of which are built up over a period of regular commitment to the railway which provides on-the-job training. The railway is divided into departments: trains and stations operation, workshops for the maintenance of rolling stock and engines, civil engineering dealing with track and structures, buildings, parks and gardens, sales and catering and signals and telecommunications. Thus jobs range from selling tickets and souvenirs to the 'elite' task of driving the engines.

Railway enthusiasts and non-enthusiasts of any nationality may apply provided they speak a good standard of English. The minimum age is 16 years. Limited self-catering accommodation is provided for regular volunteers, for which a small charge is made; food is extra. Camping space and a list of local accommodation is also available.

Further information may be obtained from the Volunteer Resource Manager, Festiniog Railway Company.

Americans Janet Renard and Luke Olivieri were volunteers for the Festiniog Railway

Many of the volunteers are railroad/steam fanatics, but accepted us even though we didn't know the first thing about it. We elected to work in the Parks and Gardens section and spent a week weeding, planting, clearing etc. The work was hard and the evenings were busy too. We were taken to a pub one night, asked to dinner another, visited a Welsh male voice choir and went climbing in the area. Festiniog Railway depends completely on volunteers who come from all over, all ages, all professions. But they can always use more help, so we may well go back.

FOREST SCHOOL CAMPS
21 Dukes Avenue, London N10 2PS. ☎020 8444 8884; e-mail staffing@fsc.org.uk
Forest School Camps, a national organisation for young people, aims to give young people the opportunity to live in a rural camp for one or two weeks, learning to live in a community and learning about their surroundings. The numbers on camps vary but can be up to 65 children and 20 leaders. Some camps are mobile travelling by cycle, foot and canoe but cater for smaller groups.

Volunteers are needed to act as leaders and should be over 18 and preferably have been on one of the camps themselves. There are also Forest School Conservation Camps where volunteers undertake voluntary work. Volunteers contribute towards the expenses of food and need their own tent and sleeping bag.

For more information contact the General Secretary at the above address or for workcamp enquiries write to the Work Camps Secretary at the above address.

HAMMERWOOD PARK
Hammerwood, near East Grinstead, Sussex RH19 3QE; ☎01342-850594; fax 01342-850864; e-mail latrobe@antespam.co.uk.
Hammerwood Park is a grade I listed building built in 1792, open to the public and providing exclusive, limited accommodation. The restoration of the house and garden is a family project; the estate was derelict in 1982.

Usually 2 volunteers are taken on to help in all aspects of running an historic house and garden. Work is required 3-4 days per week. No wages are paid, but full board and accommodation are provided. Applicants must have the ability to deal with the public and be able to carry out tasks as they arise, even the mundane. The house has 101 wooden window frames, most of which are rotting, so help with painting is appreciated. Staff required from Easter to the end of September for a minimum period of one month. Suitable foreign applicants with a good level of English are welcome. An interview is desirable. Applications from January to David Pinnegar at the above address.

HEBRIDEAN WHALE & DOLPHIN TRUST
28 Main Street, Tobermory, Isle of Mull PA75 6NU; ☎01688-302620; fax 01688-302728; e-mail info@whaledolphintrust.co.uk; www.hwdt.co.uk
The Hebridean Whale & Dolphin Trust operates in Mull and on the Hebridean islands and is involved with research, education and conservation concerning Hebridean whales and dolphins and the marine environment. The Trust runs a small education/information centre and offices, which need voluntary assistance as does the schools/education programme. Volunteers assist with fundraising, office and administration work, educational and arts activities and working in the shop and Marine discovery

centre. An ability to work on one's own initiative is a distinct advantage. Help is given with finding accommodation costing £40-£60 a week.

Throughout the summer, a select band of volunteer assistants will join HWDT's Marine Outreach Project to conduct scientific research and educational outreach work on board our newly acquired 60-foot fully-equipped motor-sailor as it travels the stunning waters of Scotland's south western isles. All we're asking in return is a contribution of £150 per week to cover ALL expenses once on board the boat and, of course lots of enthusiasm and commitment to the aims of the project.

Application to the Volunteer Coordinator at the above address.

LAKELAND ARTS TRUST
Abbot Hall Art Gallery, Kendal, Cumbria LA9 5AL; ☎01539-722464; fax 01539-722494; e-mail education@abbothall.org.uk; www.abbothall.org.uk
Volunteer research assistants, reception staff, events helpers and coffee shop staff are needed to work in the Abbot Hall Art Gallery and the Museum of Lakeland Life. Hours are from 9am to 5pm Monday to Friday and weekends in July, August and September. Accommodation may be available free of charge.

Volunteers should be undergraduates or graduates wishing to gain museum experience. All applicants must be available for interview.

Enquiries should be addressed to Mrs Cherrie Trelogan, Deputy Director, at the above address.

LINCOLNSHIRE WILDLIFE TRUST
Banovallum House, Manor House Street, Horncastle, Lincolnshire LN9 5HF ☎01507-526667; fax 01507-525732; e-mail info@lincstrust.co.uk; www. lincstrust.org.uk
The Trust maintains several national nature reserves in Lincolnshire including Gibraltar Point and the newest, Deeping wetlands, was opened to the public in 2004. Volunteers are utilised for every aspect of its operations in Lincolnshire. For instance, at Gibraltar Point volunteers are included in site management, education and interpretation and running the Visitor Centre.

30-40 volunteers are engaged annually, some for set periods e.g. three months, others for e.g. one day per week. A volunteer residential placement is available on site for a minimum of three months with training and involvement for people seeking a career in nature conservation. Links with overseas organisations in Europe, USA and Japan mean that volunteers come from several different nations. Accommodation can be found for volunteers receiving training or in placements.

Applications direct to the above address/email.

LUNDY COMPANY
The Quay, Bideford, Devon EX39 2LY; tel 01237-470422; e-mail info@lundyisland.co.uk; www.lundy island.co.uk
Lundy is an island off the North Devon Coast owned by the National Trust since 1969 and managed by the Landmark in cooperation with the RSPB and English Nature. The island has 23 letting properties, a pub and a shop. Volunteers are needed to fill various positions available including conservation and farm work, and general island duties. The jobs are variable according to the time of year. Volunteers need no experience but must have lots of enthusiasm. Accommodation is provided free of charge and there is a reduced fare on boat trips. Volunteers are required from April to September for a minimum of a week. Applications should be sent to the Warden at the above address from January onwards.

THE MONKEY SANCTUARY
Murrayton, Nr. Looe, Cornwall PL13 1NZ; ☎01503-262532; e-mail info@monkeysanctuary.org; www.monkeysanctuary.org
The Monkey Sanctuary was established in 1964 and is home to a colony of Woolley and Capuchin monkeys. It was started as a refuge for ex-pet and ex-zoo woolley monkeys. The Monkey Sanctuary has a non-breeding policy, so it can use its funds to rescue monkeys in need.

Volunteers are required all of the year. First-time volunteers are booked in for two, three or four weeks. Volunteer jobs include preparing monkey food, cleaning enclso-sures, helping in the kiosk, and talking to visitors (summer only). Applicants must be fluent in English, in good health and over 18 years old. Accommodation and food can be supplied, but a contribution of £30-£35 is requested.

For further information contact the Volunteer Co-ordinator at the above address sending a SAE.

THE NATIONAL TRUST
Central Volunteering Team, Rowan, Kembrey Park, Swindon SN2 8YL; tel 0870 609 5383; fax 01793-496813; e-mail volunteers@nationaltrust.org.uk; www.nationaltrust.org.uk
Local Volunteering: The National Trust has 40,000 volunteers involved in its work, helping to get its properties open to the public. There are literally hundreds of ways to get involved from practical countryside conservation, to interacting with the public, and behind the scenes professional, technical and administrative support. *Working Holidays:* over 400 week-long and weekend residential conservation projects per year in beautiful locations owned by the National Trust. Costing from £70 for a week to £35 for a weekend including accommodation and meals. Participants must be over 18 for most holidays. For full details and a brochure call 0870 429 24 28, e-mail workingholidays@nationaltrust.org.uk or visit www.nationaltrust.org.uk/working holidays.

Long-term volunteering: full-time volunteering opportunities for 3-6 months are available at many National Trust properties (some include accommodation). These opportunities vary from assisting property managers to organising events, and offer the chance to gain work experience and enhance your CV. For further information call 0870 609 5383 or e-mail volunteers@nationaltrust.org.uk.

THE NATIONAL TRUST (Northern Ireland Region)
Northern Ireland Regional Office, Rowallane House, Saintfield, Ballynahinch, Co. Down, Northern Ireland BT24 7LH; ☎028-9751 0721; fax 028-9751 1242; www.ntni.org.uk/helping/volunteer-opps.htm
The National Trust in Northern Ireland offers hundreds of volunteers per year many opportunities for voluntary work, mainly of a practical nature, at National Trust properties (houses, gardens and countryside) in the area. Volunteers undertake a wide range of tasks on the Trust's behalf either on short-term group residential working holidays or longer-term (usually) individual volunteering. Work done by volunteers usually entails working with wardens on the coast and in the countryside, which can involve anything from butterfly surveys to building traditional dry stone walls. Other possibilities are gardening, forestry, tour-guiding and administration.

Volunteers must be over 16 years of age and in good health; the minimum age limit for those from overseas is 18 years.

You can fill in a form online at the above website. Opportunities also exist for long-term volunteers resident at particular properties.

THE NATIONAL TRUST FOR SCOTLAND (THISTLE CAMPS)
28 Charlotte Square, Edinburgh EH2 4ET; ☎0131-243 9470; fax 0131-243 9593; www.thistlecamps.org.uk
The National Trust for Scotland, founded in 1931 is Scotland's leading conservation organisation. In its care are over 100 properties and 180,000 acres of some of the finest countryside in Scotland.

Thistle Camps are residential voluntary projects organised by the Trust to help in the conservation and management of the properties in its care. Camps last one to four weeks and take place at locations all over Scotland, often in remote areas.

Work is always of a practical nature and can vary from upland footpath repair to drystone dyking and fencing to encourage woodland regeneration.

UK applicants must be aged at least 16. Non-UK citizens must be 18+ and understand English. All applicants must be reasonably fit. The cost is between £45 and £110 depending on the camp, with concession rates for students and the unwaged. Accommodation, food and transport from and to the pick-up and drop-off points is provided.

PILGRIM ADVENTURE
27 Oldbury Court, Fishponds, Bristol BS16 2HH; e-mail pilgrim.adventure@virgin.net; www.pilgrim-adventure.org.uk
Pilgrim Adventure is an ecumenical Christian organisation founded in 1987. They provide an annual programme of 'Pilgrim Journeys' on foot and by boat through Celtic Britain and Ireland.

A small number of volunteer team members are required to help lead all age groups of 10-25 people taking part in Pilgrim adventures annual programme of Pilgrim Journeys. Pilgrims stay in hostels, monasteries, tents and small hotels. Team members should be able to co-lead at least one Pilgrim Journey of a about 7 days each year, and take an active part in planning Pilgrim Journeys throughout the year. Training will be provided.

Applicants must have a sense of adventure and Christian commitment. Applications to Mr David Gleed at the above address.

ROYAL SOCIETY FOR THE PROTECTION OF BIRDS (RSPB)
The Lodge, Sandy, Bedfordshire SG19 2DL; ☎01767-680551; fax 01767-683262; e-mail Volunteers@rspb.org.uk; www.rspb.org.uk
Nationally, the RSPB has over 11,000 volunteers.

Local Volunteer Opportunities are available on over 150 reserves throughout the UK, via 13 regional and country offices and with over 200 youth and local groups. Applicants need not be bird experts. Volunteers of all ages required. For further information about volunteering in general, contact the Volunteer and Resource Co-ordinator at the above address and ask for the *Volunteering Information* brochure or visit the above website for a current list of volunteering opportunities.

Residential Volunteers are taken on 38 reserves throughout the UK. Accommodation is provided. Tasks/activities available include: management of reserves, work with visitors, research, survey and monitoring, species protection. Specialist skills are not always required. Volunteers must be over 16 (18 on some reserves), and must stay a minimum of one week. They must also have a genuine interest in and enthusiasm for conservation issues. Volunteers from overseas are welcome; a permit is ordinarily necessary as the work is unpaid, but applicants should check with their nearest British Embassy or High Commission before travelling. Overseas applicants must be over 18 and speak good conversational English. Further information can be found in the RSPB's free publication on residential volunteering, *You Can Do It,* available from the above address.

Applications should be made to the Residential Volunteering Development Officer, at the above address.

Mark Weston was an RSPB volunteer warden on Orkney

It was mid-July when I arrived at Egilsay on Saturday evening and was met by Andy Mitchell the warden, who took me to my accommodation. This was a bothy of a very high standard, with beautiful views of Rousay and Wyre, the two closest islands.

My first day was spent exploring the island, with its splendid machairs (fertile plains)- , lochs, rugged shoreline and amazing beach. There I found two llamas and a goat tucking into the abundant selection of wild plants and flowers that could be seen all over the Island. On the rocks, twenty or more grey and common seals were sunbathing, while eider ducks watched over their young along the shore. In the distance was Eday and to the north Westray, just two of the many islands surrounding Egilsay.

I had sent the warden an e-mail before arriving, giving him information about my skills and training and making it easy for him to plan our workload. It did not take long for my practical skills to be put to use fixing doors, windows, taps and fencing. On two occasions we visited Rousay where, after a strenuous but most enjoyable walk, we went looking for red-throated divers and hen harriers to monitor their breeding success, checked the cliffs to survey the kittiwake colonies, and then finished off with a little maintenance to the reserve information signs. At the end of the week we travelled to the Loch of Harray on Mainland Orkney, to help with some swan ringing. Nearly a hundred mute swans plus two whooper swans were herded into a pen by a line of canoes and passed to ringers for ringing, weighing, sexing and measuring.

My last night was a true taste of Orkney, an evening of jazz followed by a ceilidh on Wyre. The next day as I left Orkney, I knew I would return there as there was still so much to see. The wardens and residents had made me feel so welcome that I did not want to go. As the ship sailed out of Stromness, I reflected on the past two weeks. Then, as we passed The Old Man of Hoy, a pod of five killer whales surfaced in front of me. Perfect.

STRATHSPEY RAILWAY CO LTD
Aviemore Station, Dalfaler Road, Aviemore PH22 1PY; ☎01479-810725; fax 01479-811022; e-mail membership@strathspeyrailway.co.uk; www.strathspeyrailway.co.uk
Volunteers are needed to help run a small private railway in Scotland. Almost everyone you see working on the railway is a volunteer. Tasks include guard, ticket inspector, booking clerk, and also railway maintenance (including track, locomotives and rolling stock). No pay, but free, very basic accommodation in a sleeping car at Boat of Garten, (a hostel for members who work at Aviemore) is provided for £2.50 a night. The minimum age for volunteers is 16 and training is given on the job. A reasonable degree of fitness is required for some jobs. Membership required to take part in volunteer activities (ordinary membership £16 per annum).

Applications to the Commercial Manager at the above address.

TREES FOR LIFE
The Park, Findhorn Bay, Forres, IV36 3TZ; ☎01309-691292; 0845 458 3505 fax 01309-691155; e-mail trees@findhorn.org; www.treesforlife.org.uk
Trees for life is a Scottish charity dedicated to the restoration of the Caledonian Forest,

to a large, significant area of the central northern Highlands of Scotland. Much of the practical work is carried out by volunteers and includes tree-planting, removing redundant fencing, small tree nursery work and seed collecting.

About 300 volunteers are recruited annually for a week at a time. Volunteers should be reasonably fit as there is a lot of walking and physical work. There is also a 'gentle' week for those unable to maintain the pace of a normal work week. Stays are from Saturday to Saturday (8 days) and volunteers are taken to a remote location to work. Anyone can stay longer if they wish. Work takes place mid-March to beginning of June and beginning of September to end of October. Cost of £78 (£40 concessions) includes all food, accommodation and transport from Inverness.

Much information on the website. Applications to the above address.

WATERWAY RECOVERY GROUP
PO Box 114, Rickmansworth WD3 IZY; ☎01923-711114; fax 01923-897000; e-mail enquiries@wrg.org.uk; www.wrg.org.uk
Waterway Recovery Group was formed in 1970 to formalise voluntary restoration work by enthusiasts that had been carried out since the 1960s. The aim of the group is to be a co-ordinating force, not centred on any individual project, but backing up and assisting local restoration groups with publicity, the loan of tools and plant, technical advice, visiting work parties and Canal Camps.

Canal Camps can be joined by anyone aged 17 to 70 who has a week to spare helping to restore one of Britain's derelict canals. Jobs on the camps can include restoring industrial archaeology, demolishing old brickwork, bricklaying and pouring concrete, driving a dumper truck, clearing silt, helping to run a waterways festival, cooking for other volunteers, clearing vegetation and trees. The working day is roughly 9am to 5pm and volunteers pay about £42 towards the cost of food and basic accommodation. Volunteers also need to bring their own spending money for social activities. Camps take place almost year round from February to December.

Contact the above address for a *Canal Camps* brochure or browse the brochure on WRG's website.

WELSHPOOL & LLANFAIR RAILWAY
The Station, Pool Road, Llanfair, Caereinon, Welshpool, Powys SY21 OSF; ☎01938-810441; fax 01938-810861; e-mail info@wllr.org.uk; www.wllr. org.uk
The Welshpool and Llanfair Railway is a narrow gauge steam operated railway which needs volunteer maintenance staff at any time of year for varied duties from engine operation through trackwork to administration and the clearing of vegetation. The railway has a volunteer taskforce of about 200, about 25 of whom are active at a time. No pocket money is paid but accommodation is available at cheap rates. Volunteers should be at least 16 years old, fit and enthusiastic. Membership of the Welshpool & Llanfair Railway Preservation Society costs £17.50 per year.

Enquiries to The Deputy Manager, at the above address.

WHALE & DOLPHIN CONSERVATION SOCIETY (WDCS)
Moray Firth Wildlife Centre, Spey Bay, Moray, IV32 7PJ, Scotland; ☎0870 870 0027; fax 0870 870 0028; ☎ (wildlife centre) 01343-820339); e-mail info@wdcs.org; www.wdcs.org/wildlifecentre
The WDCS is a non-profit organisation that works for the protection of whales, dolphins and their environment worldwide. Volunteers are needed to help with the running of Moray Firth Wildlife Centre. Tasks include manning the exhibition centre, educating the

public about local wildlife, carrying out landbased shorewatches, vessel-based research and photo ID of whales, the organisation and promotion of events and helping with school visits. Volunteers should be fluent speakers and writers of English and have a background in biology/environment, or a strong interest in marine mammals. The minimum stay is a month but stays of four to six months are preferred. The centre will cover volunteers' expenses and accommodation is provided for those staying six months or longer.

Applications should be directed to the wildlife centre at the above address.

WILDFOWL AND WETLANDS TRUST (WWT)
Slimbridge, Gloucestershire GL2 7BT; ☎01453-891900 ext. 137; fax 01453-890827; e-mail sarah.aspden@wwt.org.uk; www.wwt.org.uk

The Wildfowl and Wetlands Trust is a registered charity that aims to conserve wetlands and their biodiversity through research, educational and habitat creation programmes for wetland birds. WWT operates 9 visitor centres around the UK. Volunteer opportunities exist at all centres (Slimbridge Headquarters, Arundel, Caerlaverock, Castle Espie, Llanelli, Martin Mere, Washington, Welney, The Wetland Centre in London).

At Slimbridge, volunteers are needed for the Grounds and Reserve, Visitor Services (membership, tower guiding, selling bird food, leading guided tours) and Education (making props for educational visits, face-painting), departments. Also required are volunteers for administrative activities (data inputting, filing) for all departments.

Benefits for volunteers include a training a social programme, discounts and the opportunity to learn lots about the unique environments of wetlands and wetland birds themselves. There is also a free hostel on-site that has limited places; this is for full-time grounds volunteers. Please contact Slimbridge and the above address for further details.

WILDLIFE TRUST OF SOUTH AND WEST WALES
The Welsh Wildlife Centre, Cilgerran, Cardigan, SA43 2TB; ☎01239-621212; fax 01239-613211; e-mail wildlife@wtww.co.uk

The Wildlife Trust of south and west Wales is the fourth largest wildlife trust in the UK, covering the area from Cardiff to Aberystwyth and southwest to the Pembrokeshire islands. With over 100 nature reserves the Trust welcomes volunteers who want to find out about the Welsh environment and how it can be protected and enhanced.

Volunteer assistant wardens are required for work on our reserves, including Skomer Island, a National Nature Reserve off the Welsh coast. Work involves meeting visitors, census work, general reserve maintenance, wildlife recording etc. Self-catering accommodation is available free of charge. Minimum age is 16 and volunteers should have an interest in natural history. Overseas applicants welcome. Volunteers can work also on a variety of reserves from a week to three months. Island volunteers will work a full week (seven days) for a maximum of two weeks between Easter and 31 October.

THE WORDSWORTH TRUST
Dove Cottage, Town End, Grasmere, Cumbria LA22 9SH; ☎015394-35544; fax 015394-35748; e-mail m.oskoui@wordsworth.org.uk; www.wordsworth.org.uk

The Wordsworth Trust is a registered charity responsible for maintaining Dove Cottage, the Wordsworth museum and the Wordsworth library. Volunteers are recruited to: work with the public in Dove Cottage, giving guided tours of the home of the poet William Wordsworth and working in the gift shop; perform reception duties in the museum; work with the collections in the library; or carry out administrative roles relating to marketing and information. Working for the Trust is an ideal opportunity for recent graduates seeking experience for careers in heritage or collections management.

Volunteers must have a high standard of spoken English and be able to meet their own costs. Placements are from 6 months to one year. Accommodation is provided.

Applications to Michelle Oskoui at the above address.

Religious Projects

L'ARCHE
10 Briggate, Silsden, Keighley, West Yorkshire; ☎01535-656186; fax 01535-656426; e-mail info@larche.org.uk; www.larche.org.uk
L'Arche Communities are places where people with and without learning disabilities live and work together as a family in a simple way. The lifestyle is non-competitive and based on the Christian belief that everyone, whether disabled or not, is of unique value. In the UK, L'Arche comprises a network of nine communities, most of which have several work projects including workshops for weaving, candlemaking and horticulture.

Volunteers are known as assistants and share life and work with people with learning disabilities in an ecumenical, Christian-based community. Any nationality may apply but visa requirements, where applicable, must be observed. Volunteers must be aged at least 18 and able to stay for six months or more. Three-month summer vacation work is also sometimes available. Assistants are given about £25 weekly pocket money and free board and lodging. Explanatory videos and tapes are available.

Anyone interested should apply to the above address.

CAREFORCE
35 Elm Road, New Malden, Surrey KT3 3HB; tel/fax 020-8942 3331; e-mail enquiry@careforce.co.uk; www.careforce.co.uk
Careforce places 100 Christians each year aged from 17 to 30 in tough places throughout the UK and Ireland. They serve both with outward looking churches where local resources are scarce and which are moving into their local communities in loving service and relevant outreach, and with Christian projects which serve the vulnerable in society including the homeless, the elderly, those with addiction or learning disabilities and physical disability and those with difficult family situations.

Placements begin in September and last for eleven/twelve months – some volunteers stay to do a second year. All volunteers are committed Christians and are in good health. Full board and lodging plus a small weekly allowance is provided together with full work and pastoral support given by the placement, the Careforce staff, and other volunteers. Applications from non-UK residents are accepted provided that they are recommended by their church pastor/leader – such volunteers are expected to pay their own travel costs to and from the UK and in most cases require a UK entry visa for the year.

Full details from the Director at the above address.

CHRISTIAN MOUNTAIN CENTRE
Pensarn Harbour, Llanbedr, Gwynedd LL45 2HS; ☎01341-241718; office@cmcpensarn.org.uk; www.cmcpensarn.org.uk
The Centre is a 50-bed outdoor pursuits centre set in a tidal estuary within the Snowdonia National Park. Volunteer helpers are needed to work 40 hours a week for a living allowance of £25-£70 per week plus full board and accommodation for three months

between 1 March and 30 October. Overseas applicants with a high standard of English welcome. Applicants are required to have a Christian faith. Apply to Mr. M Downey.

THE CORRYMEELA COMMUNITY
5, Drumaroan Road, Ballycastle, Co. Antrim, BT54 6QU, Northern Ireland; ☎028-20762 626; fax 028-20762 770; e-mail ballycastle@corrymeela.org; www.corrymeela.org
Corrymeela is an ecumenical Christian community working for reconciliation in Northern Ireland and the world at large. It runs an administrative centre in Belfast and a residential centre at Ballycastle on the North Antrim coast where people from all backgrounds can come together and meet in an easy relaxed atmosphere. It also has a retreat house at Knocklayde.

Opportunities exist at the Ballycastle centre and at Knocklayde for volunteer helpers on both a long and short-term basis. The commitment of the long-term volunteers is generally for 12 months commencing in September of each year, and the volunteers get a room and board plus a small weekly allowance. During the months of July and August, a number of additional volunteers are welcomed for periods of two to four weeks, to assist with family groups and projects or as summer staff helpers, assisting with recreation, arts and crafts, cooking, laundry etc. The lower age limit for all volunteers is 18 years.

Those interested in long-term volunteer work should contact the Volunteer Co-ordinator at the above address. In England, further information about Corrymeela is available from the Corrymeela Link, PO Box 4829, Earley, Reading, Berks. RG6 1XX; e-mail reading@corrymeela.org.

GRACE AND COMPASSION BENEDICTINES
St. Benedict's, 1 Manor Road, Kemp Town, Brighton BN2 5EA; ☎01273-680720; fax 01273-680527
An interdenomational charity running homes for the elderly and frail. The sisters are Roman Catholic. Volunteers are invited to join a life of prayer and care for a week or longer. Volunteers may also be interested in the lay community. Members can be of any age with a desire to share in the life of prayer and caring. You may join for a few months or longer. Board and lodging are provided and a small salary and there is free time and work. The care houses are in Heathfield, Brighton, Bognor, Bury St. Edmunds and Stroud. Why not come and see for yourself?

Teachers, nurses and doctors are also needed in the Charity's convents in India. Please write for further details.

THE GRAIL
125 Waxwell Lane, Pinner, Middlesex HA5 3ER; ☎020-8866 2195/0505; fax 020-8866 1408; e-mail grailcentre@compuserve.com
The Grail Centre in North London hosts courses, conferences and workshops. Subjects range across prayer, spirituality, arts and ecology and complementary therapies. Grail Volunteers help the resident community of women with domestic tasks, cooking, gardening, office duties and all aspects of hospitality. No special qualifications are required, but skills are appreciated.

Applicants should be at least 20 years old, in good health and with a functional grasp of English. It is also important that they can withstand a communal lifestyle and the constant pressure of visitors.

The minimum stay is three months though an occasional exception is made for students on a limited summer vacation. Board, lodging (single room), and necessary expenses are provided. Applicants should apply five to six months ahead of their intended date of arrival. Religious observance is not a requirement.

Apply by letter to the Volunteer Coordinator, include a photo and CV (résumé). UK applicants should enclose a SAE and overseas ones an international reply coupon. The Grail is not a vast organisation and accepts only about 15/20 volunteers annually.

LEE ABBEY COMMUNITY
Lee Abbey, Lynton, Devon EX35 6JJ; ☎01598-752621; e-mail relax@leeabbey. org.uk; www.leeabbey.org.uk
Lee Abbey is a centre for Christian retreats, conferences and holidays, run by a community working for the renewal and refreshment of the church. There is also a London branch with an international student hostel.

Volunteers over 18 years of age are needed to help care for guests. The minimum commitment is for a year. Volunteers should be committed Christians. Board, lodging and allowances are provided. Applicants should write to Personnel at Lee Abbey with information about themselves and their backgrounds and why they would like to join the community. Formal qualifications not necessary. Applicants from overseas must have a very good command of English.

LONDON CITY MISSION
175 Tower Bridge Road, London SE1 2AH; ☎020-7407 7585; fax 020-7403 6711; e-mail lcm.uk@btinternet.com; www.lcm.org.uk
LCM is based entirely in London and recruits volunteers to spread the Christian message through the work of 28 Christian centres in the City. About 30 volunteers are recruited at a time for a year and a further 30-50 for brief periods. Volunteers help with running activities for all ages at the centres and visiting around the district and helping in schools and open air outreach. Volunteers are mostly from the UK with some additional ones from within the European Union. Age limits are: year team (18-30), summer teams (16-30) and other opportunities 25+. Once on the team, volunteers get all their expenses and some pocket money. Accommodation is provided unless volunteers are very part-time, e.g. one day a week.

Applications to the above address.

LOSANG DRAGPA BUDDHIST CENTRE
Dobroyd Castle, Pexwood Road, Todmorden, West Yorks. OL14 7JJ; ☎01706-812247; fax 01706-818901; e-mail info@losangdragpa.com; www. losangdragpa.com
Losang Dragpa is a Buddhist College and Meditation centre based at Dobroyd Castle in the heart of the Yorkshire Pennines. The Centre is a registered charity dedicated to serving the community by providing a place of inner peace for everyone regardless of spiritual inclination. Volunteers are welcome to join the resident community in various development projects, which include restoring Dobroyd Castle to its former glory. The Centre offers Buddhist teachings, meditations, accommodation and food in exchange for 35 hours per week. Working visitors are permitted to stay for 1 week or 2 weeks (for international volunteers) during specific dates throughout the year.

Applicants must be at least 18 and able to speak a basic level of English. Interest in Buddhism is recommended. Losang particularly needs help from those with special-ised skills such as building, marketing, fundraising, decorating and landscaping. How-ever, skills are not essential as work can be found for any willing hands. Visit www. losangdragpa.com or contact reception for more information or to apply.

MADHYAMAKA CENTRE
Kilnwick Percy Hall, Pocklington, York YO42 1UF; ☎01759-304832 (Monday-Friday 10.30am-1pm & Sundays 2pm-5pm); fax 01759-305962; e-mail info@madhyamaka.org; www.madhyamaka.org

The Centre, established in 1979 is a residential Buddhist Centre with about 50 residents and room for many visitors. It is situated in an elegant Georgian mansion surrounded by spacious and peaceful grounds. As well as running evening classes, day courses and retreats the Centre welcomes volunteers who would like to come and work 35 hours a week in exchange for free dormitory accommodation and vegetarian food. On weekends and evenings, volunteers are free to explore the area and attend teachings and meditations if they wish.

The kind of work is generally building, decorating, gardening and housekeeping though it varies from week to week. Most volunteers stay one week and find the combination of being away from the daily rush of life amongst friendly people and stimulating conversation very relaxing. Special skills are not necessary.

MANJUSHRI MAHAYANA BUDDHIST CENTRE
Conishead Priory, Ulverston, Cumbria LA12 9QQ; ☎01229-584029; e-mail info@manjushri.org; www.manjushri.org

Manjushri Centre is a residential Buddhist community with about 100 residents, founded in 1977 to provide a peaceful and inspiring environment where people can learn about the Buddhist way of life and practice meditation.

Volunteers are needed for various duties including building, kitchen/garden help, and general household work/cleaning. Volunteers work 35 hours a week, Monday to Friday and are required for a minimum period of one week all year round except January. Minimum age 16. Overseas applicants with a reasonable standard of English are welcome. No smoking or drinking is allowed on the site. Accommodation and board are provided and volunteers are welcome to join in with the centre's activities such as meditation classes and courses. The weekend is free for relaxing at the Centre or to enjoy the beautiful local area.

Apply all year round to Working Visit Co-ordinator, at the above address. Applications essential.

QUAKER VOLUNTARY ACTION (QVA)
Friends Meeting House, 6 Mount Street, Manchester M2 5NS; tel/fax 0161-819 1634; e-mail mail@qva.org.uk

The aims of QVA are to promote co-operation and international understanding between people and to support communities.

Volunteer Opportunities in the UK: QVA organises volunteer projects lasting two to four weeks in Britain and Northern Ireland. They take place in the summer. Typical projects include playschemes, work with adults or children who have mental or physical disabilities, manual projects like decorating shelters for the homeless, youth work, community arts projects and more.

A volunteer team comprises eight to 15 people coming from all walks of life and nationalities. The age minimum for volunteers is 18 years. Volunteers with disabilities are welcome to apply. No special skills or qualifications are needed but motivation, enthusiasm and commitment to living and working with a group are.

Simple food and accommodation are provided but volunteers pay a small registration fee of depending on means.

Applications (from UK only) require a large SAE. Applicants outside the UK should apply through an organisation in their own country.

SCRIPTURE UNION
207-209 Queensway, Bletchley, Milton Keynes, Bucks MK2 2EB; ☎01908-856000; fax 01908-856111; e-mail team@scriptureunion.org.uk
Every year the 3,500-4000 volunteers are recruited to work on teams for Scripture Union Holidays and Missions. Volunteers work with children and young people developing relationships with them and teaching them of Jesus Christ. Most work in England and Wales with some overseas projects.

Volunteers are needed for: office work, activity supervisors, outdoor pursuits instructors, cooks, kitchen assistants, general holiday team members, crafts, creative arts, bible study, small group teaching. Skills and qualifications should be specific to role. Team members must be committed to Christ, enthusiastic, energetic, mature enough to be responsible for children, at least 17, willing to complete a Criminal Records Bureau application. Volunteers are needed all year round but overwhelmingly (90%) in summer. Board and lodging provided if on a residential holiday or mission.

Apply direct to the above address.

SONS OF DIVINE PROVIDENCE
13 Lower Teddington Road, Hampton Wick, Kingston-upon-Thames KT1 4EU; ☎020-8977 5130; fax 020-8977 0105; www.sonsofdivineprovidence.org
The Sons of Divine Providence provide services for people with learning difficulties and the elderly. There is also a school in Kenya where parishes are being developed. Volunteers are needed to befriend and support people with learning difficulties, shadowing and working with them at a horticultural centre where they are involved with landscaping and garden maintenance.

All applicants are interviewed and references checked. Criminal record checks are also carried out. For those working on the horticultural project it is best that they do not suffer from back problems. Help is needed all year round for periods of time dependent on the work being carried out. Travel expenses (bus fares, etc.) are provided.

The organisation produces several publications, *The Restless Apostle* (£4), *God's Bandit* (£1), *Half a pound of Providence* (£5.95), *Some call it Providence* (£4.50) and a quarterly booklet, *The Bridge*, all available from the above address.

Applications to the Recruitment Officer at the above address.

TARA BUDDHIST CENTRE
Ashe Hall, Ash Lane, Etwall, Derbyshire DE65 6HT; ☎01283-732338; fax 01283-733416; e-mail meditate@taracentre.org.uk; www.taracentre.org.uk
Tara Centre is a residential meditation centre situated in a large Jacobean mansion in 38 acres of wooded grounds. The Centre operates a 'working visitor' scheme whereby volunteers can help with all aspects of the centre's activities in exchange for full board and accommodation and any classes they wish to attend. As many as a 100 such fvolunteers are taken on annually. The work may include any of the following: DIY, joinery, building work, gardening, sewing, cooking, cleaning, plumbing, electrics, graphic display work and decorating. The usual period of stay is one week though people coming from abroad can stay longer. A basic knowledge of English is essential.

VINCENTIAN VOLUNTEERS
39 Marlsford Street, Liverpool, L6 6AX; ☎0151-261 0225; e-mail director@vincentvols.freeserve.co.uk; www.vincentianvolunteers.org
Vincentian Volunteers offer a year's programme (September to July) to young people aged 18-30 to serve the poor, whilst living in small Christian communities of three or four.

Training weekends are arranged six times per year. About 12 volunteers are taken on annually and work with the homeless, refugees, various groups suffering from some kind of disability, or living in marginalised aras. Applicants are accepted from anywhere but must pay their fare to and from the UK and be able to communicate in English. Board and lodging is provided as well as a small personal allowance.

Apply direct to the above address.

TIME FOR GOD
2, Chester House, Pages Lane, London N10 1PR; ☎020-8883 1504; fax 020-8365 2471; e-mail enquiry@timeforgod.org; www.timeforgod.org

This is a scheme which provides an opportunity for the applicant to serve for between nine months and one year in a range of placements. The scheme is sponsored by the Methodist, Anglican, Baptist, Catholic, Congregational, and United Reformed Churches, the National Council of YMCA's and the Church Army.

Every year some 150 volunteers are needed to care for children, the elderly, the homeless or the disabled in organisations such as the National Children's Home, YMCA, or to help with work of all kinds in local churches or community centres. Full board and lodging is provided during the placement. Volunteers receive weekly pocket money, and travel expenses are paid for the journey to the placement for an exploratory visit and on start of service. Volunteers are entitled to a week's holiday, with pocket money and fares home, for each three months of service (volunteers from overseas should be given fares for a reasonable journey in Britain). Christian applicants of any nationality or denomination are welcomed, provided that they speak fluent English and are between 17 and 25 (or between 18 and 25 for overseas applicants).

Those interested should visit the website above or write to the above address for more information.

Social and Community Schemes

BRAENDAM FAMILY HOUSE
Thornhill, Stirling FK8 3QH; ☎01786-850259; fax 01786-850738; e-mail info@braendam.org.uk; www.braendam.org.uk

Braendam Family House is a large, respite holiday home located in central Scotland for disadvantaged families from Scotland. Volunteers are needed for six month placements in the summer and winter seasons to support families, run activities, and do a share of the domestic work. Overseas applicants with a good standard of English and a UK working visa are welcome. Volunteers should be of minimum age 18, in good health and have patience and a sense of fun; those with a driving licence are preferred. All applicants need a police/criminal conviction check prior to starting and two references. Accommodation in a shared bedroom, travel expenses of up to £40, £32 per week spending money, and £40 to cover travel expenses during a five-day holiday after four months work, are provided.

Applications to the Manager at the above address.

CAMPHILL VILLAGE TRUST
29 Middlecave Road, Malton, North Yorkshire, YO17 7NE; ☎01653-693373; fax 01653-693363; e-mail coworker@camphill.org.uk; www.camphill.org.uk

One of the worldwide Camphill Villages that care for people with learning disabilities in a community setting. This takes the form of extended family households with work on the land, craft workshops and service industries. There are nine CVT communities in rural and urban areas of England and Scotland.

The CVT community takes on 25 to 40 volunteers annually to help in the house communities, working in the workshop, farm and gardens, serving in the cafeteria/catering/food processing and working alongside people with special needs. Volunteers should be at least 17. The work period is summer (June to September) but there are also positions for a year. The Community provides board, lodging and pocket money. A useful publication *Camphill Villages* is available from Botton Bookshop, Danby, Whitby, N Yorks Y021 2NH for £3.99 plus 50p postage and packing.

Applications to William Steffan, responsible for volunteers at the above address.

CSV
Full-time Volunteering Team, 5ᵗʰ Floor, Scala House, 36 Holloway Circus, Queensway, Birmingham B1 1EQ; tel 0800 374991; fax 0121-643 7582; e-mail volunteer@csv.org.uk; www.csv.org.uk/fulltimevolunteering
CSV invites anyone aged 16+ to experience the challenge and reward of helping those in need through full time, away from home, placements in the UK for between 4 and 12 months.

Placements are in a practical, social care setting and include: supporting people with disabilities to live independently in their own home, befriending young people leaving care, supporting a student with disabilities, or volunteering in a homeless hostel or at a residential home for elderly people or special needs children.

Volunteers are placed away from their home area according to their interests, experience and the needs of the project. Accommodation, full board, £29 weekly allowance, and all out-of-pocket expenses provided. Support is provided from both the project and CSV. No qualifications or previous experience are necessary.

Applications are welcomed from UK and other EU nationals.

EDINBURGH CYRENIAN TRUST
107a Ferry Road, Edinburgh EH6 4ET; ☎0131-555 3707; e-mail leslie@.org.uk
The Edinburgh Cyrenian Trust runs two communities for single, homeless men and women aged 18 to 30 years old; one in Edinburgh and another on a smallholding outside Edinburgh. Around 22 volunteers are needed each year to live with the residents and befriend them. Other tasks include performing various housekeeping and book-keeping tasks. Placements are for 6 months at a time.

Volunteers must be fluent in English, 18 to 30 years old, energetic and have initiative. Applicants with a full driving licence are preferred. Travel expenses to attend an interview are paid. Successful applicants receive one-way travel to the project, accommodation, pocket money and holiday and termination grants.

Applicants should apply to Steven Lynn or Leslie Dible at the above address.

GREAT GEORGE'S COMMUNITY CULTURAL PROJECT
The Blackie, Great George Street, Liverpool L1 5EW; ☎0151-709 4822; minicom/fax 0151-709 4822; e-mail staff@theblackie.org.uk
Great George's is a community-based alternative education and the arts centre which has been going for over 30 years. Volunteers over the age of 18 are always needed to try alternative education, arts, some sport, recreation and welfare in an inner-city context including youth work, craft and games; regular workshops with local youngsters,

staging exhibitions and events; and projects from cookery to contemporary and African dance, and from photography to fashion. Share cooking, cleaning administration, and some rebuilding work. Endless opportunities to learn and unlearn, to teach and to create. Wonderfully long hours. Stamina, a sense of humour and a sleeping bag required. Accommodation provided. Volunteers expected to stay for at least 4 weeks and to contribute towards food costs. Volunteers are welcome anytime but particularly over summer, winter and spring holiday periods.

For further information write to the duty office at the above address.

HOLY CROSS CENTRE
Holycross Church, The Crypt, Cromer Street, London WC1H 8JU; ☎020-7278 8687; fax 020-7278 8567; e-mail cmt@hcct.org.uk

The Centre is based in central London, Kings Cross area and is a social centre for people with mental health problems and addictions to drugs and or alcohol. The aims are to develop users social skills in a friendly and informal atmosphere, through peer support and volunteer/staff befriending.

Two full-time volunteers are needed for thirty-seven and a half hours per week for six months. Over 40 part-time volunteers to do at least 5 hours per week. Volunteers' duties involve mostly catering and befriending, but also arts and crafts, computers. Skills not as essential as a good attitude to users, but languages, catering experience, arts and crafts and computing skills all useful. A minimum commitment of six months is the expected minimum commitment.

Travel expenses are paid and meal provided on session. Full-time volunteers get free accommodation and £55/week allowance and meals.

Applications to M. Willett at the above address.

IONA COMMUNITY
Iona Abbey, Isle of Iona, Argyll PA76 6SN, Scotland; ☎01681-700404; fax 01681-700460; e-mail maciona@surfaid.org and staff@ionastaff.fsnet.co.uk; www.iona.org.uk

The Iona Community, an ecumenical Christian community, invites volunteers minimum age 18, to come for six to eighteen weeks to share in a ministry of welcome and hospitality. Members of the community are scattered throughout the world. Volunteers are not members but come to the historic island of Iona to share alongside guests in a weekly programme of work, worship and recreation, or assist at our Camas Adventure Centre on the Isle of Mull.

The food is mainly vegetarian (though all diets are catered for) and meal times are important times of contact with guests. Volunteers work as assistants in the kitchens, housekeeping, maintenance, shop, office, church and programme departments. They receive pocket money of £30 weekly and return travel expenses within the UK. Accommodation is shared with two or three others.

Applications are received throughout the year and invitations for voluntary places are sent out in January for the season, which runs from March to November. Contact the Staff Coordinator for further information.

LOTHLORIEN COMMUNITY (ROKPA TRUST)
Corsock, Castle Douglas, Kircudbrightshire DG7 3DR; ☎01644-440602 (office); e-mail lothlorien1@btopenworld.com

Lothlorien is a therapeutic community, where those who are experiencing mental health problems can develop their potential through living alongside people who are relatively well, in an atmosphere of friendship, acceptance and mutual support.

Lothlorien is situated in an isolated rural area in south west Scotland. The community comprises 13 people with mental health problems and 4 voluntary co-workers and 4 permanent staff. The four staff provide a continuity of support to the community, but are non-resident. The community has 17 acres of grounds which include organic vegetable gardens, woodland and outbuildings.

Lothlorien has links with the Samye Ling Tibetan Centre in Dumfries. Buddhist values are paramount, but the community is not a religious one and is open to all.

On a practical level volunteers, along with all community members, work in the vegetable gardens, do domestic tasks and maintenance in the house and grounds.

Volunteers are needed on a regular basis. Free room and board and pocket money (£35 per week) are provided plus a travel allowance of £100 to cover the cost of time off from the community. Minimum age: 21. Minimum stay: 6 months. Contact the project manager for more details.

RICHMOND FELLOWSHIP
80 Holloway Road, London, N7 8JG; ☎020-7697-3300; fax 020-7697-3301; e-mail kevin.tunnard@rfhq.org.uk; www.richmondfellowship.org.uk
The Richmond Fellowship provides residential care, counselling and support, as well as rehabilitation and work skills, to people recovering from emotional trauma, addiction and mental health problems. RFI runs a national network of more than 90 projects and work schemes, providing care for people irrespective of age, gender or religion.

RF has vacancies for volunteers who work alongside permanent staff. No formal qualifications are necessary as RFI values personal qualities and enthusiasm, but experience and/or qualifications in the social work, psychology, and nursing fields are sometimes an advantage. Volunteers will be expected to take part in the general running of the project, undertaking administrative and secretarial tasks, as well as assisting with food preparation, cleaning etc.

Applicants should be aged 22 or over and be able to speak fluent English. Volunteers are provided with board and lodging and a small stipend. Those interested should send a CV to the above address.

THE SIMON COMMUNITY
PO Box 1187, London NW5 4HW; ☎020-7485 6639; e-mail simoncommunity@ic24.net
The Simon Community is a small registered charity working and living with homeless people which aims to support primarily long-term rough sleepers, and others for whom no provision exists, with a philosophy of acceptance and tolerance. The Community operates three residential houses as well as participating in extensive outreach work in the city of London. Workers and residents share in the decision-making and running of the community.

Volunteers are required throughout the year and should be at least 19 years old, speak fluent English and be looking to stay for six months or more, though shorter periods are sometimes acceptable. Workers live in the project to which they are assigned; they receive full board and accommodation and £27 weekly pocket money. Every three months workers get two weeks' leave and a substantial amount of pocket money to ensure a good break. For long term workers there is a pattern of external training and internal training and support is provided for everyone throughout. Applicants attend a weekend following which their suitability as a worker is decided.

Apply to the address above.

Work With the Sick and Disabled

ASSOCIATION OF CAMPHILL COMMUNITIES
Gawain House, 56 Welham Road, Norton, Malton, N Yorks. YO17 9DP;
☎01653-694197; e-mail info@camphill.org.uk; www.camphill.org.uk
The Camphill Movement, which was founded in 1940, works to create communities in which vulnerable children and adults, many with learning disabilities, can live, learn and work with others in healthy social relationships based on mutual care and respect. Camphill is inspired by Rudolph Steiner and is based on the acceptance of the spiritual uniqueness of each human being, regardless of disability or religious or racial background.

The Association can supply more information on individual member communities but applications to work as volunteers should be sent to the individual centres. The addresses of current member communities are given below.

Botton Village, Danby, Whitby, North Yorks YO21 2NJ; ☎01287-660 871; fax 01287-660 888; e-mail botton@camphill.org.uk

Camphill Houses: Stourbridge, 19 South Road, Stourbridge, West Midlands DY8 3YA; ☎01384-441505; fax 01384-372122.

Cherry Orchards Community: Canford Lane, Westbury-on-Trym, Bristol BS9 3PE; ☎0117-950 3183; fax 0117-959 3665.

The Croft: Gawain House, 56 Welham Road, Norton, Malton, N Yorks. YO17 9DP; ☎01653-694197; fax 01653-600 001; e-mail andy@croftcvt.demon.co.uk

Camphill Devon Community: Hapstead Village, Buckfastleigh, Devon TQ11 0JN; ☎01364-642 631; fax 01364-644 188; e-mail devon@camphill.newnet.co.uk

Delrow: Hilfield Lane, Aldenham, Watford, Herts. WD2 8DJ; ☎01923-856006; fax 01923-858035; e-mail email@delrow.newnet.co.uk

Camphill Communities East Anglia: Thornage Hall, Thornage, Holt, Norfolk NR25 7QH; ☎01263-860 305; fax 01263-861 754; e-mail ccea@thornagehall.u-net.com

Grange Village: Newnham-on-Severn, Gloucs. GL14 1HJ; ☎01594-516 246; fax 01594-516 969.

The Hatch: St John's House, Kington Lane, Thornbury, Bristol BS35 1NA; ☎01454-413 010; fax 01454-414 705.

The Lantern Community: The Lantern Office, Folly Farm Lane, Ringwood, Hampshire BH24 2NN; ☎01425-479 926; fax 01425-471 841; e-mail LanternCom@aol.com;www.lanterncommunity.org.uk

Larchfield Community: Stokesley Road, Hemlington, Middlesborough, Cleveland TS8 9DY; ☎01642-593688; fax 01642-595778.

Camphill Milton Keynes Communities:, Japonica Lane, Willen Park South, Milton Keynes MK15 9JY; ☎01908-235 000; fax 01908-235 606; e-mail office@camphillmk.ndirect.co.uk

The Mount Camphill Community The Mount, Faircrouch Lane, Wadhurst, East Sussex TN5 6PT; ☎01892-782 025; fax 01892-782 917; e-mail themount@camphill.clara.net

Oaklands Park: Newnham on Severn, Gloucestershire GL14 1EF; ☎01594-516 551; fax 01594-516 821.

Orchard Leigh Camphill Community: Bath Road, Eastington, Stonehouse, Gloucestershire GL10 3AY; ☎01453-823 811; fax 01453-823 811.

Pennine Camphill Community: Boyne Hill, Chapelthorpe, Wakefield WF4 3JH; ☎01924-255281; fax 01924-240257; e-mail office@pennine.org.uk; www.pennine.org.uk

Camphill St Albans: 50 Carlisle Avenue, St Albans, Herts. AL3 5LX; ☎01727-811228; fax 01727-811909; e-mail mail@camphillstalbans.newnet.co.uk

Sheiling School: Ringwood, Horton Road, Ashley, Ringwood, Hants. BH24 2EB; ☎01425-478 680; fax 01425-478 680; e-mail sheilingco@aol.com

Sheiling School Thornbury: Thornbury Park, Bristol BS35 1HP; ☎01454-412 194; fax 01454-411 860; e-mail sheilingschool@thornbury.newnet.co.uk; www.home. newnet.co.uk/thornbury

Sturts Farm:, Three Cross Road, West Moors, Ferndown, Dorset BH22 0NF; ☎01202-875275; fax 01202-891623.

Taurus Crafts: Taurus Enterprises, The Old Park, Lydney, Gloucestershire GL15 6BU; ☎01594-844 841; fax 01594-845 636; e-mail enquire@taurus.newnet.co.uk

William Morris House: Eastington, Stonehouse, Gloucestershire GL10 3SH; ☎01453-824 025; fax 01453-824 025.

Coleg Elidyr: Rhandirmwyn, Llandovery, Carmarthenshire SA20 0NL; ☎01550-760 400; fax 01550-760 331.

Clanabogan Camphill Community: Omagh, Co. Tyrone BT78 1TJ; ☎02882-256111; fax 02882-256114.

Ballytobin Community: Callan, Co. Kilkenny; ☎056-25114; fax 056-25849; e-mail ballytobin@camphill.ie

Dunshane House: Brannickstown, Naas, Co. Kildare; ☎045-483 628; fax 045-483 833.

Duffcarrig Village Community: Duffcarrig, Gorey, Co. Wexford; ☎055-25911; fax 055-25910.

Beannachar: South Deeside Road, Banchory-Devenick, Aberdeen AB12 5YL; ☎01224-869 250; fax 01224-869 250; e-mail beannachar@talk21.com

Camphill Blair Drummond: Blair Drummond House, Cuthil Brae, Stirling FK9 4UT; ☎01786-841 573; fax 01786-841 188.

Corbenic: Torchry, Dunkeld, Perthshire PH8 0DY; ☎01350-723 206; fax 01350-723 300.

Loch Arthur Community: Beeswing, Dumfries DG2 8JQ; ☎01387-760 618; fax 01367-760 618.

Newton Dee Village: Bieldside, Aberdeen AB15 9DX; ☎01224-868 376; fax 01224-869 398.

Ochil Tower School: Auchterader, Perthshire PH3 1AD; ☎01764-662 416; fax 01764-662 416; e-mail OchilTowerSchool@csi.com; ourworld.compuserve.com/homepages/OchilTowerSchool

Camphill Rudolf Steiner Schools: Murtle House, Bieldside, Aberdeen AB15 9EP; ☎01224-867935; fax 01224-868 420; e-mail office@crss.org.uk

Simeon Care for the Elderly: Caranoc, Cairnlee Road, Bieldside, Aberdeen AB15 9BN; ☎01224-862 415; fax 01224-862 415.

BEANNACHAR
Beannachar, Banchory-Devenick, Aberdeen AB1 5YL; ☎01224-869138; e-mail beannachar@talk21.com; www.camphillscotland.org.uk
Every year the Beannachar Community takes on six to ten volunteers to live and work with young adults with special needs. Work is to be done in the kitchen, laundry, garden and on the farm; tasks also include making herbal medicines, woodwork and candles and weaving. Volunteers are also expected to participate in evening and weekend leisure activities. Volunteers need not be British, but they must speak fluent English and make a minimum commitment of twelve months. Board and lodging are provided, plus pocket money of £30.

Applications may be sent to Elisabeth Phethean, at the above address.

CARE-COTTAGE AND RURAL ENTERPRISES LTD
Care Regional Office North, 36D Newgate Street, Morpeth, Northumberland NE61 1BA; ☎06170-511157; fax 01670-511080; www.carefund.north@free. uk.com.
CARE provides care for adults with learning disabilities in communities in Devon, Kent, Lancashire, Leicestershire, Shrophshire, Northumberland, Sussex and Wiltshire.

Volunteers, aged 18 or over, live and work alongside residents and are expected to stay for a minimum of four weeks. Applicants must speak English and be personally interviewed at the Community they are assigned to. Accommodation is provided in single bedsits and meals are taken with the residents. Volunteers receive £25 per week pocket money and are expected to work up to 40 hours a week on a rota basis.

Those interested should apply to the Assistant Director of Fundraising at the above address.

CHURCHTOWN OUTDOOR ADVENTURE
Churchtown Farm, Lanlivery, Bodmin, Cornwall PL30 5BT; ☎01208-872148.
Churchtown Farm provides outdoor, environmental and adventurous training courses accessible to everyone, regardless of degree of special need. As well as the more traditional courses, in ecology and outdoor pursuits, a new development is the provision of personal development programmes which concentrate on personal growth, encouraging a positive image of self, and promoting self-confidence. In-service courses for teachers and carers can be organised and opportunities exist for team building and development courses, suitable for all staff groups. The Centre is attractively converted and well equipped with an indoor swimming pool, farm, nature reserve and pleasant grounds. Sailing and canoeing takes place on the nearby River Fowey and the Centre is only five miles from the coast. Help is available with care requirements and a qualified night staff is on call on site throughout the night.

Up to 16 volunteers are needed at a time to support the professional staff. Accommodation is in a shared house adjacent to the main Centre. Applications are invited from anyone who feels they have an empathy with special needs people. Whilst a background in environmental, outdoor or medical areas would be an advantage, volunteers are welcome regardless of academic qualifications. Currently an allowance of £25 per week is payable, provided that volunteers stay for longer than three weeks.

Those interested should apply to the Head of Care at the above address.

CURA DOMI-CARE AT HOME
Guardian House, Borough Road, Godalming, Surrey GU7 2AE; tel ☎ 01483-420055; fax 01483-4200538; e-mail curadomi@aol.com; www.curadomi. co.uk
Cura Domi is an organisation that arranges home care for the elderly nationwide. Assignments last two to three weeks or for much longer indefinite periods (i.e. live-in positions). Volunteers get £320-£420 per week, paid holiday for live-in positions and full board, lodging, and travel costs. Qualified moving and handling courses free to all carers plus 24 hour office support. No particular skills or qualifications are needed but a driving licence can be useful. Volunteers from abroad must speak fluent English. Work permits are required for non EU nationals.

Applications at any time to the above address.

THE DISAWAY TRUST
55 Tolworth Park Road, Surbiton, Surrey KT6 7RJ; ☎020-8390 2576; fax 020-8715 6336.

The Disaway Trust is a charity which provides group holidays for physically disabled people. The organisation is run by a Committee of volunteers and is entirely supported by voluntary help and contributions. Disaway relies on voluntary help to achieve its objective of providing disabled people with holidays. Each helper is asked to look after the needs of one holidaymaker during the holiday. This will include helping with, amongst other things, needs like washing, feeding, dressing and helping in the bathroom. Most holidays last for about a week. Inexperienced helpers will be allocated a holidaymaker needing minimal specialised care, and every effort is made to match helpers and holidaymakers with similar interests. Helpers have to be reasonably fit and strong, and every applicant is required to complete a medical form; acceptance is at the discretion of the Medical Officer. Minimum age limit for volunteers is 18 years.

Helpers are asked to pay approximately half of the cost of the holiday including a deposit of £100 to be submitted with the application form. Costs are given with holiday details. Many people enjoy this type of holiday, and previous helpers will vouch for their enjoyment of a fulfilling vacation in a friendly atmosphere. There is no limit to the number of helpers needed.

For an application form, please write to the above address.

FRIENDS FOR YOUNG DEAF PEOPLE
East Court Mansions, College Lane, East Grinstead, Sussex, RH19 3LT; ☎01342-323444; fax 01342-410232

Through its work FYD seeks to achieve social inclusion for all deaf children and young people through deaf and hearing integration. The aim is to improve communication skills and self esteem through early intervention family work, support and information for families and community projects focusing on sport, outdoor activity and the arts. FYD also aims to improve equal opportunities in education and employment through personal development training programmes and working with a trained peer supporter.

Volunteers are needed to do workshops with the deaf, especially children. To participate volunteers have to go on a weekend, residential training course which costs £60 they will then go on a list of supporters and asked to help with deaf workshops in their area geared towards social development of deaf children. Volunteers can progress their training level through courses and become more involved if they wish. Contact the above for application details.

HELP THE HANDICAPPED HOLIDAY FUND (3H FUND)
147a, Camden Road, Tunbridge Wells, Kent TN1 2RA; ☎01892-547474; fax 01892-524703; e-mail info@3hfund.org.uk; www.3hfund.org.uk

This charity arranges group holidays for physically disabled children and adults. Recent holidays have been to Majorca, Eastbourne, Norfolk, Norfolk Broads, Lake District, Blackpool. Each year around 100 volunteers are required. Volunteers may apply to assist with one or more holidays.

The success of the holidays depends on a full complement of volunteers. Half board hotel accommodation is provided and in return the helper looks after the guest in his/her care. School leavers, students and anyone in the age range 18 to 60 with a strong back, who is willing to give up a week of their time can really enjoy themselves in a happy and informal atmosphere whilst undertaking worthwhile voluntary work. Candidates for the Duke of Edinburgh Gold Award are particularly welcome.

The holidays will embrace a wide cross-section of disabilities many requiring considerable personal help particularly dressing, toiletting, eating and the pushing of wheelchairs. In consequence the work can prove particularly physically and mentally demanding and requires great patience and a strong sense of responsibility leavened with a sense of humour. Please note new helpers will not be given 'high care' guests to look after.

Those interested should apply to Margaret James, Charity Secretary at the above address.

HERTFORDSHIRE ACTION ON DISABILITY
The Woodside Centre, The Commons, Welwyn Garden City, Herts AL7 4DD; ☎01707-324581; fax 01707-371297.
For over 30 years the HAD has aimed to meet the needs of the disabled in Hertfordshire with services including counselling, equipment exhibitions and hire and driving instruction in a fully adapted car. The Organisation also has its own hotel at Clacton-on-Sea.

About 100 volunteers are needed annually to assist disabled people on holiday for two-week periods from February to December. Some UK travel expenses may be paid. Free return coach travel is provided to and from the Woodside Centre to Clacton. Volunteers also get free board and lodging. Further details (*HAD Client Services* and *Holiday Fact Sheets* 1-10) can be obtained by sending a 75p postage stamp to the above address. Ages 18-70 years.

HOLIDAY CARE
2nd Floor, Imperial Buildings, Victoria Road, Horley, Surrey RH6 7PZ; ☎01293-774535; fax 01293-784647; e-mail holiday.care@virgin.net
Holiday Care is a national charity that advises elderly, disabled people or anyone who has special needs or problems in finding a suitable holiday. It also runs 'Tourism for All' a scheme for low-cost holidays and runs a booking service for accessible accommodation in the UK. Information about volunteering can be obtained from the above address.

HOLIDAYS FOR DISABLED PEOPLE & YOUNG DISABLED ON HOLIDAY
c/o Flat 4, 62 Stuart Park, Corstorphine, Edinburgh EH12 8YE; ☎0131-339 8866; e-mail AliWalker1@aol.com
Holidays for Disabled People & Young Disabled on Holiday organises holidays in the UK and abroad for those with a physical disability aged between 18 and 35. 110 volunteers are required for at least a week each year, mainly over the summer months, to help with these holidays. No special qualifications are needed but volunteers should have a good sense of humour and be relatively fit. All nationalities are recruited. Helpers are asked to pay a small contribution towards the total cost of the holidays. Accommodation is provided.

Those interested should apply to the organisation at the above address.

INDEPENDENT LIVING ALTERNATIVES
Trafalgar House, Grenville Place, London NW7 3SA; ☎020-8906 9265; fax 020-8906 9265; e-mail enquiry@ILAnet.co.uk; www.ILAnet.co.uk
Independent Living Alternatives (ILA) is a non-profit making charity that promotes independence for people with physical disabilities. ILA provides physical support to people who want to live in their own homes and enables people to take full control of their lives and live spontaneously.

ILA needs full time volunteers, with four months to spare, to work as Personal Assistants (PAs) with people with physical disabilities in London. A placement is based on an atmosphere of interdependency and mutual respect, where both Service Users and Personal Assistants are equal.

Personal Assistants provide physical support such as helping someone to get dressed and have a bath and also practical assistance, such as cooking and housework. No experience is necessary as all training is provided. PAs must be over 18 and have an empathy with the philosophy of ILA.

Personal Assistants work on average four days a week and receive a living allowance for food, travel and leisure and free accommodation with no bills to pay while away from the work placement. PAs live in whilst working.

For further information and an application form contact Tracey Jannaway, Business Manager at the above address.

INDEPENDENT LIVING SCHEMES
Lewisham Social Care and Health, John Henry House, 299 Verdant Lane, Catford, London SE6 1TP; ☎020-8314 7239; fax 020-8314 3013; e-mail ken.smith@lewisham.gov.uk
Special projects known as Independent Living Schemes have been set up in Lewisham with the aim of enabling people with disabilities to lead the lifestyle of their choice. About 20 Volunteer helpers are wanted to assist with these schemes. Volunteers provide care for a severely disabled person; tasks include toiletting, bathing and administering suppositories. The volunteer helper would be expected to accompany that person on social, business and cultural activities. The helper also helps with the cooking, cleaning and shopping under the direction of the disabled person. Applicants may be of any nationality, although basic English and reading skills are essential. Applicants must be willing to enable severely disabled people to regain their civil rights.

Volunteer helpers are asked to spend six months on a scheme. There is a one month trial period, which means that a helper is not bound to stay. However, most volunteers do settle and stay with the scheme; some like it so much they sign on for a further six months.

Rent-free accommodation is provided for helpers in a fully furnished two or three bed-roomed flat to be shared with other helpers situated near the scheme. Heating and lighting bills as well as local telephone charges are met, and everyday household items like cleaning materials, light bulbs, bed linen etc., are supplied. A weekly allowance of £60, (£37 for food and £23 pocket money) is paid, and is payable for up to a fortnight's sickness. There are also monthly allowances for recreation (£7) and clothing (£8). A week's paid leave is given after a helper has been with the scheme for four months. Helpers get a Saver Return Rail Travel Warrant to any mainland UK destination, if required, or Travel Card if they decide to stay in London. Helpers' return fares to and from their home are covered at the beginning and end of their involvement with the scheme.

LEONARD CHESHIRE
Central Office, 30 Millbank, London SW1P 4QD; ☎020-7802 8200; fax 020-7802 8250; e-mail volunteers@lc-uk.org; www.Leonard-cheshire.org
Leonard Cheshire is the UK's leading charity providing support services for people with physical and learning disabilities. Many of the 80 residential Leonard Cheshire homes offer opportunities for volunteers, who assist with the day-to-day care and social activities of physically disabled residents.

Board, lodging and pocket money are provided. Period of work from 6-12 months. Volunteers must be able to speak good English. Enquiries to Volunteer Support Team at the above address.

LIFESTYLES INDEPENDENT LIVING PARTNERSHIP
Woodside Lodge, Lark Hill Road, Worcester WR5 2EF; ☎01905-350686; fax 01905-350684; e-mail worcslifesstyles@care4free.net
Volunteers are needed to enable people with a disability to lead as normal a life as possible in their own homes. Duties can include intimate personal care, cooking, housework, shopping and sharing leisure interests. Full time work in shifts can include weekends and sleeping over. Volunteers receive free accommodation plus an allowance of £60.23 per week. Accommodation is shared with with other volunteers, and all heating

and lighting bills are paid by social services.

Volunteers are required at all times of year. The normal minimum commitment expected is four months, but it may be possible to arrange placements during college vacations. Volunteers should be aged at least 18 and be reliable and caring.

Enquiries to the above address.

NCYPE (formerly St. Piers)
St Piers Lane, Lingfield, Surrey RH7 6PW; ☎01342-831234; fax 01342-834639; e-mail aboyce@ncype.org.uk; www.ncype.org.uk
NCYPE recruits 16-20 volunteers a year to work with children and young people with epilepsy and/or learning disabilities, in their residential setting. Help is needed all year round from 4 to 12 month periods. Volunteers should have no criminal convictions and a good standard of conversational English. Those with a history of back injury should consult their doctor before applying. Free full board and lodging, and £35 per week to cover out-of-pocket expenses provided.

For further information visit the website. Applications to the above address.

OTTO SCHIFF HOUSING ASSOCIATION
Central Office, The Bishops Avenue, London N2 0BG; ☎020-8209 0022; fax 020-8201 8089; e-mail pgusack@jcare.org
The Association provides sheltered accommodation, residential and nursing care to elderly Jewish refugees from Nazi persecution. The association has several large residential and nursing homes in northwest London in which care is provided. There are also two local, sheltered housing sites offering accommodation in warden controlled housing. The Association aims to provide high quality care to each person whilst enabling and promoting independence and individual rights.

A number of full time volunteers are recruited annually from mainly other European countries to provide personal support to residents in the residential homes. This support ranges from befriending and helping residents with daily activities to hospital and day centre escorting. The volunteers are provided with food, accommodation and a weekly personal allowance during their stay which is usually between six and twelve months.

Applicants are always very welcome and the Association is now a hosting member of the European Voluntary Service scheme and receives requests for places throughout the year from most European countries.

All enquiries should be made to Pauline Gusack, Volunteer Co-ordinator, at the above address or e-mail.

OXFORD CENTRE FOR ENABLEMENT
Windmill Road, Oxford OX3 7LD; ☎01865-227600; fax 01865-227294.
The Centre cares both for the assessment and management of clients with recent neurological disability as well as those with longer term disability.

Volunteers are needed at the centre to help with creative activities, gardening, table games, story groups, computers and cooking as well as outings. Also required are volunteers to help on the holidays, usually two per year. Carers have to be over 19. All nationalities welcome to apply but a clear grasp of English is essential as the centre's clients have communication problems. Volunteers who go on the holidays will be away a week, but helpers at the centre will be required on occasional days for an indefinite period.

On the holidays, accommodation and travel are paid for, but a small donation towards food costs is appreciated. No accommodation is available at the Centre.

Enquiries to Adele Stancliffe.

SHARE HOLIDAY VILLAGE

Discovery '80' Ltd. Smith's Strand, Lisnaskea, Co. Fermanagh BT92 OEQ, Northern Ireland; ☎028-6772 2122; fax 028-6772 1893; e-mail katie@sharevillage.org; www.sharevillage.org

Share is a registered charity that runs a residential centre, which through varied outdoor activities aims to encourage contact between disabled and able-bodied people. All ages from primary school children to senior citizens are welcomed at the Centre.

The Centre has a small permanent staff and relies heavily on volunteers – 200 are needed over the summer in one-week shifts, to assist disabled people as well as helping with domestic duties and outdoor activities. Full board and accommodation provided, and travel expenses are reimbursed.

Also needed are qualified outdoor activity instructors and a few volunteers with the relevant experience to assist them leading groups in sailing etc. Qualified instructors get £80-£120 weekly. The minimum age for general volunteers is 18 years. There is also a senior volunteer programme for those over 55. The minimum period of work is two weeks between April and October. Volunteers are also accepted for longer periods between 3-12 months to work in one area of the Centre's activities. Placements are available in arts programmes, working on the outdoor activity programme, or in the Centre's swimming pool complex, housekeeping, catering, or grounds maintenance teams. Volunteers accepted for long-term placements receive £50 per week pocket money, board and accommodation.

Applications should be sent at any time of year to the above address.

SPEYSIDE HANDICAPPED HOLIDAY TRUST

Badguish Outdoor Centre, Aviemore, Inverness-shire PH22 1QU; ☎01479-861285; e-mail info@badaguish.org

Volunteer care assistants are needed to work as part of a care team, providing care and activities for children and adults with special needs. Usually Mondays to Fridays, 5 days, £30 weekly pocket money. Meals are provided while on duty. Accommodation provided. Minimum age for volunteers and paid staff is 18 years.

STALLCOMBE HOUSE

Sanctuary Lane, Woodbury, Salterton, Nr. Exeter EX5 1EX; ☎01395-232373; fax 01395-233351; e-mail stallfarm@eclipse.co; www.stallcombehouse.co.uk

Stallcombe House is a residential farm community in East Devon for mentally disabled adults. Residents of the three households are involved in all aspects of the community, 55-acre farm and small organic horticultural area. Volunteers are needed annually to help care for the residents: cooking, cleaning and assisting the residents with their daily activities including personal hygiene, hobbies and outings. Placements are for 3-12 months. Other volunteers are needed seasonally to help with farm and garden work, and local volunteers who can work daily or less frequently on an on-going basis will be welcomed.

Residential care volunteers must want to work with people in a caring environment. All volunteers need a working knowledge of English and should be in good mental and physical health. Residential care workers receive accommodation and pocket money of £35 per week but assistance with travel expenses depends on the individual volunteer's circumstances.

Applicants should apply to Mr. C. Thistle, General Manager at the above address.

TOC H

The Stable Block, The Firs, High Street, Whitchurch, Bucks, HP22 4UJ; ☎01296-642020; fax 01296-640022; e-mail info@toch.org.uk; www.toch.

org.uk

Toc H runs short term residential projects throughout the year in Britain, usually from a weekend up to two weeks in length. Projects undertaken can include work with people with different disabilities or children in need; playschemes and camps; conservation and manual work; study and/or discussion sessions.

These projects provide those who take part with opportunities to learn more about themselves and the world. Whilst foreign applicants are welcome, a preference is held for those living in the EU. The Toc H programme is published twice yearly on the first Mondays in March and September. Whilst there is a minimum age limit of 16 years, there is no upper age limit. There is no closing date for applications but you are advised to apply early. Over 500 volunteers a year are recruited. Toc H does not offer any long-term paid employment opportunities or supervised placements.

Enquiries should be sent to the above address enclosing a stamped self-addressed envelope.

WINGED FELLOWSHIP TRUST
Shap Road, Kendal, Cumbria LA9 6NZ; ☎0845 345 1970; fax 020-7278 0370; e-mail admin@wft.org.uk; www.wft.org.uk

Every year some 4,000 helpers are needed in five holiday centres for physically disabled people located in Cornwall, Essex, Lancashire, Hampshire and Nottinghamshire. The purpose of the Trust is not only to provide holidays for severely physically disabled people, but also to enable the families who normally care for them at home to take perhaps their first worry-free holiday in years. Volunteers live in the centres and are given free board and lodging, during which time they not only take care of the physical needs of the guests but also provide companionship for them. Fares can be refunded. Overseas applicants with good English welcome.

WFT also provide holidays for blind and visually impaired people. Volunteer sighted guides always needed to help on these holidays too. All that is required of volunteers is that they be over 17 years. Those with nursing qualifications would be particularly welcome. The centres are in operation for 11 months of the year.

Those interested should apply to the above address.

WOODLARKS CAMP SITE TRUST
Woodlarks Camp Site, Tilford Road, Farnham, Surrey, GU10 3RN; ☎01252-716279; e-mail woodlarks@aol.com; www.woodlarks.org.uk

Woodlarks Camp Site Trust seeks to provide the physical and social setting for people of all ages with disabilities to expand their capabilities in an atmosphere of fun. This small-scale camping site and woodland activity area has facilities which include a heated outdoor swimming pool, an aerial runway across a valley, a trampoline, archery and more. The camp site is run entirely by volunteers and every summer about 500 helpers assist the same number of disabled people.

Camps are held weekly from May to September. Campers come mainly from special schools, clubs or organisations for people with specific disabilities; volunteers are normally taken on for the duration of one camp lasting one week, but some stay for more than one camp. Accommodation is provided in tents and a small fee is usually paid by helpers to cover the cost of food.

Those interested should contact the Honorary Secretary at the above address, enclosing a S.A.E. or an International Reply Coupon.

WORCESTERSHIRE LIFESTYLES
Woodside Lodge, Lark Hill Road, Worcester WR5 2EF; ☎01903-350686; fax

01905-350684; www.worcestershire-lifestyles.org.uk
An independent registered charity established in 1991 to assist people with disabilities to exercise freedom of choice, extend their horizons and make decisions about the lifestyle they wish to enjoy.

Volunteers act as the arms and legs of someone with a disability. Pocket money of £63.47 per week plus free accommodation. Commitment is five days per week and can include weekends and sleepovers. Volunteers are required for a minimum of four months all year round. Workers assist with personal care, household tasks and share leisure activities. Applicants should be over 18, honest, caring and adaptable. Training is provided. Overseas applicants with a good standard of English are welcome to apply.

Applications at any time to Niki Boho or Sophie Finney or e-mail niki@Worcestershire-lifestyles.org.uk.

YOUNG DISABLED ON HOLIDAY
Flat 4, 62 Stuart Park, Edinburgh EH12 8YE; ☎0131-339 8866.
As many as possible volunteers are needed for holidays for disabled people in the UK and abroad for one week throughout the summer. Each volunteer needs to help a disabled person on a one-to-one basis. Workers are expected to make a minimum contribution towards accommodation, food and trips. Preferred age group 18-35, though anyone up to the age of 40 would be considered. No previous experience required, just patience.

Overseas applicants welcome. Applications to Alison Walker at the above address.

Youth Activities

ADVENTURE PLUS
Hill Grove Farm, Dry Lane, Crawley OX8 5NA; ☎01993-703308; fax 01993-708433; e-mail enquiries@adventureplus.org.uk; www.adventureplus.org.uk
Adventure Plus is a Christian Trust which provides outdoor activity holidays and residentials for young people. Volunteers are needed for activity instruction, catering, dorm-leading, assisting with activities, music, art and crafts, drama and other general help. Help is needed from two days to three weeks. Those giving activity instruction must be qualified.

For more details and an application pack contact the Administrator at the above address.

BRATHAY EXPLORATION GROUP TRUST
Brathay Hall, Ambleside, Cumbria, LA22 OHP; ☎015394-33942; e-mail admin@brathayexploration.org.uk; www.brathayexploration.org.uk
The Group organises expeditions and leader training courses in the British Isles and overseas. Expedition members are aged from 15 to 26 years old. A variety of expeditions are organised by voluntary leaders each year, combining adventure with field study work, and volunteers are needed to participate. In some circumstances assistant leaders may be required and would have experience in the outdoors or scientific skills.

Around 100 physically fit volunteers are needed each year. To be considered for a place in an expedition leader team, applicants must be 20 to 60 years old and have expedition experience, or specific scientific or medical knowledge.

Applications should be sent to the above address.

THE OUTDOOR TRUST
30 West Street, Belford, Northumberland NE70 7QE; tel/fax 01668-213289; e-mail trust@outdoor.demon.co.uk; www.outdoortrust.co.uk

The Outdoor Trust is a registered charity, based in north Northumberland, providing outdoor-based training and development courses to people of all ages and abilities. Volunteers are asked to assist with the running of the courses as well as helping with the administration, domestic and repair work required to support all of the activities carried out by the Trust.

Volunteers are required for a minimum of one month, mainly during the summer season. Minimum age: 17. Applicants must be in good health, speak reasonable English, and have ability or be competent in one of the following activities: kayaking, canoeing, climbing, windsurfing or sailing. Accommodation and food is provided.

Applications to the personal department.

PESTALOZZI INTERNATIONAL VILLAGE TRUST
Sedlescombe, Battle, East Sussex TN33 0RR; ☎01424-87044; fax 01424-870655; e-mail office@pestalozzi.org.uk; www.pestalozzi.org.uk

The aim of the Trust is to provide educational opportunities in the UK for disadvantaged young people from developing countries in Asia and Africa who all live within the Village community (170 acre estate in a rural setting). The students aged from 16 years undertake the International Baccalaureate diploma course and work with the Pestalozzi Trust's Development Education Centre to promote development awareness and international understanding. Volunteers of different nationalities are engaged annually to help in many areas, dependent on the need at the time and the qualifications and interest of the volunteers. They may be involved in the Development Education Centre, with support education for the students, work on the estate, catering and domestic services, sports/recreational activities, funraising research. Volunteers must be at least 23. Placements can be of varying lengths but ideally between six and ten months. Food, single accommodation and some expenses are provided.

Those interested should send CV to Val Winslade, Trust Secretary.

TRIDENT TRANSNATIONAL
The Smokehouse, Smokehouse Yard, 44-46 St John Street, London EC1M 4DF; ☎020-7014 1420; fax 020-7336 8561; e-mail info.transnational@trid.demon. co.uk; www.trident-transnational.org

Trident Transnational is a charitable organisation providing non-English students and recent graduates aged 18-30 with high quality work experience placements in various UK business areas such as marketing/PR, office administration, IT, engineering, finance/accounting, hotel and catering, media etc. In most cases placements are unpaid, although most employers will pay a contribution towards work-related expenses such as lunch and travel.

After successful completion of the placement, candidates will be nominated for a Work Experience Certificate accredited by the University of Cambridge Local Examinations Syndicate (UCLES). Trident Transnational can organise enrolment on English language classes at the same time as placement.

Fees are £235. This includes being appointed to a personal advisor, the search for a suitable placement, advice on related matters etc.

Europe

Multi-National

THE ACROSS TRUST
Bridge House, 70-72 Bridge Road, East Molesey, Surrey KT8 9HF; ☎020-8783
1355; fax 020-8783 1622; e-mail brianm@across.org
The Trust is a registered charity that arranges weekly pilgrimages and holidays for
the sick and disabled (the unable) from March to November each year. These last 10
days. Places visited on pilgrimages include Lourdes, Rome, the Holy Land and Poland.
Places visited on holidays include Belgium, France, Spain, Switzerland, Austria, Ireland
and Holland. Transport is by 'jumbulance', a purpose-built jumbo ambulance, which
carries all the necessary facilities for the unable.

Each group consists of two to three nurses, a doctor (if necessary), a chaplain and
male and female helpers, all of whom volunteer their time and pay their own expenses
to care for the ten unable in the group. ACROSS gives priority to those with terminal
illness, with progressive diseases, those confined to bed or wheelchair, and people with
illnesses that make other forms of travel impossible or unsuitable. The group, with a
maximum of 24 or 44 persons, live together as a family throughout their holiday, with
everyone devoting themselves to the needs of the group 24 hours a day. The work of
caring for the unable, i.e. feeding, dressing, toiletting, etc. is shared among the group.

Volunteers need to be in good health and dedicated. Nurses and helpers pay the
same as the rest of the group. Accommodation is provided in Lourdes at the Trust's purpose-built homes. Once volunteers apply, they will be offered the available dates.

Enquiries for the appropriate application form (eg doctor, nurse, chaplain, lay helper)
should be sent to the Group Organisers at the above address.

APARE
25 Bd. Paul Pons, 84800 L'Isle-sur-la-Sorgue, France; ☎ +33 (0)490 85 51
15; fax +33(0)490 86 82 19; e-mail apare@apare-gec.org; www.apare-gec.
org
APARE organise voluntary workcamps dedicated to the restoration of historic buildings
and heritage sites in Provence and the Cévennes.

Volunteers of all ages and nationalities can spend two or three weeks from June to
October on one of the 25 work sites in southeastern France. Youth camps have a minimum age of 16, but there is no upper limit for other workcamps. Work includes restoring
a shepherd's shelter in the Provence Alps, or learning dry stone walling techniques in
the Vaucluse, restoring a Romanesque chapel or a mediaeval village in the Var, repav-
ing the streets of a Corsican village or restoring a fort on a deserted island in the Mediterranean. Technical advisors direct the volunteers' work and instruct them in traditional
building techniques such as lime facing and stone dressing.

The registration fee for work camps includes food and lodging, insurance and leisure expenses - 124 euros for the adult camps (3 weeks) and 91 euros (two weeks).
Teen camps cost 304 euros for three weeks.

Please order the programme from the above address.

ATD FOURTH WORLD
Summer Activities, 107 Ave Général Leclerc, 95480 Pierre Laye, France.
ATD Fourth World is an International organisation working with families who live in extreme poverty in city slums and deprived rural areas throughout the world. ATD Fourth World regards the existence of poverty as a denial of basic human rights and works towards the eradication of poverty, learning from the poorest and working in partnership with them. ATD organises European Workcamps and Street Workshops throughout the summer in France, Belgium, Spain, Switzerland and the UK.

Workcamp participants take part in manual work during the day while the evenings are reserved for discussions and exchange of ideas about the eradication of extreme poverty. There is a charge of £50 (or 76 euros) to cover accommodation and food. Street Workshops provide a concrete way to come together with the most underprivileged people through the sharing of skills (painting, crafts, computing, communication, sport, music, reading, etc.) to invent with them paths towards the participation of everybody in tomorrow's world. ATD summer activities are aimed at young people aged from 18 years old.

BOX-AID
11 Hill Top Lane, Saffron Walden, Essex CB11 4AS; ☎01799-523321; www. geocities.com/boxaidinfo.
Box-Aid makes, demonstrates and cooks with solar cookers and 'Wonderboxes' at Green Fairs in the UK, and also at Sunseed's desert technology centre in Spain. The latest solar cooker is the Anahat, which has a back-up for evenings. Box-Aid also works in co-operation with Compassion and other similar organisations in southern Africa, and sometimes shares volunteers with the Sunseed Trust.

Volunteers, of any nationality, would begin by experimenting with the cookers. If keen, they could then demonstrate them in the UK or spend from one to 24 weeks at the Spanish centre cooking food in them for other volunteers. After that they might be able to go to other countries where this fuel-saving type of cooking is needed. Board and lodging is provided in Spain, but not yet in the UK. No special qualifications are necessary; a driving licence is an advantage in Spain for those aged over 27. A knowledge of any extra languages is useful but not essential.

Applications can be sent, all the year round to Anna Pearce at the above address. Applicants may first like to read Anna Pearce's book *Simply Living* which will give them a much better idea of what would be needed from them in African countries.

BTCV (formerly British Trust for Conservation Volunteers)
36 St Mary's Street, Wallingford, Oxon. OX10 0EU; ☎01491-821600; fax 01491-839646; e-mail International@btcv.org.uk; www.btcv.org
BTCV is the UK's leading practical conservation charity for improving and protecting the environment. It aims to harness people's energies and talents to protect the environment by practical action. BTCV offers a programme of over 70 international working holidays each year lasting from one to three weeks throughout Europe, North America, Africa and Asia. These holidays offer people of all ages and backgrounds the chance to work with and get to know local people in places off the beaten tourist track and to make a real difference to protecting the environment.

Holidays offer a variety of sometimes unusual assignments e.g. turtle monitoring in Thailand, forest management in Japan and trail work in Canada. The working day is typically from 9am to 5.30pm and the evenings are free. Average costs are between £100 and £800 inclusive of accommodation, training and food. No experience necessary. For a copy of the International Brochure contact BTCV at the above address.

CONNECT YOUTH
Education and Training Group, The British Council, 10 Spring Gardens, London SW1A 2BN; ☎ +020-7389 4030; fax 020-7389 4033; e-mail connectyouth-enquiries@britishcouncil.org; www.connectyouthinternational.com

Connect Youth offers young people aged 18-25 the opportunity to volunteer to work in a variety of activities in the social, environmental and cultural fields. European Voluntary Service (EVS) can be long-term (6-12 months) or short-term (3 weeks to 6 months). There are no preconditions in terms of qualifications or social background and the main aims are to help young people develop a service that will benefit the community. Connect Youth provides details of sending organisations and host organisations in a range of different fields and which are responsible for recruiting young people and seeking suitable volunteer placements.

Volunteers must be legally resident in the European Union. There is no cost to the young person. The sending or hosting organisation and the EU co-fund the EVS experiences.

Initial enquiries should be made to Connect Youth who will send a list of approved UK sending organisations. The applicant should then contact the nearest one to them.

EUROPEAN VOLUNTARY SERVICE (EVS)
SOS Volunteer Helpdesk, Technical Assistance Office Socrates, Leonardo &

Youth Dept. Rue de Trèves, Trierstraat 59-61, 1040 Belgium Brussels; ☎ +32 2 233 02 99; fax +32 2 233 01 50; e-mail volunteers@socleoyouth.be; www. europa.eu.int/comm/youth/program/sos/
EVS is an action of the Youth programme initiated and managed by the European Commission. It allows young people with fewer opportunities and aged 18-25, to spend up to 12 months in voluntary Service projects in Europe, the CIS, Balkans, Southern Mediterranean rim, Latin America.

Approximately 7,000 volunteers are placed a year. Projects can be either short-term (3 weeks to 6 months) or long-term (6-12 months). Projects can be social, cultural, artistic, environmental etc. EVS looks for volunteers from backgrounds with the fewest opportunities. EVS pays the cost of travel and food and accommodation; insurance and pocket money are also provided.

To apply go to EVS homepage for application procedures, and consult the internet database for host projects under www.youth.cec.eu.int.

GROUPING OF THE EUROPEAN CAMPUSES
25 boulevard Paul Pons, 84800 L'Isle sur la Sorgue, France; ☎ +33-(0)4 90 27 21 20; fax +33-(0)4 90 86 82 19; e-mail gec@apare-gec.org; www.apare-gec.org
The Centre organises and recruits volunteers for the European Environment and Heritage Campuses. This extensive network of academic workshops is intended for all young people interested in these fields. As training projects, but also tools of action for the benefit of local initiatives for the protection of our heritage and environment, the campuses allow the participants to become part of multidisciplinary teams working voluntarily on research/action programmes in such fields as the Gdansk local environment plan in Poland and the programme for eco-tourism in the Zagori Natural Park in Greece. These truly practical academic workshops last thee to four weeks.

A new programme has been started for 18-25 year olds who want to volunteer for 6 months up to a year in Europe and the Mediterranean countries. Spheres of activity include environmental and heritage issues. Accommodation, transport and pocket money are provided.

To volunteer, applicants must have a university degree, with additional experience in environmental or heritage disciplines. Applicants must also speak several European languages. The groups of 15 are led by university tutors. The Campuses provide board and lodging but the volunteer has to pay his or her return fare. The determining factor in the choice of candidates will be their commitment to a multi-disciplinary, practical experience.

For more information on the Campuses please write to the above address.

INTEREXCHANGE
161 Sixth Avenue, New York, New York 10013, USA; ☎ +1 212 924-0446; fax +1 212 924-0575; e-mail info@interexchange.org; www.interexchange.org
InterExchange is a private, non-profit cultural exchange organisation which operates a variety of programmes for both US and non-US citizens. Its goals are to promote intercultural understanding through international work/training and educational opportunities. Over the past twenty years, thousands of people on these programmes: students, teachers and recent graduates, have experienced first-hand what it is like to live and work in another culture developing foreign language skills, acquiring tolerance and understanding of other cultures.

Placements can range from teaching posts in the Czech Republic, Hungary, Finland

and Poland, to farm work/hands-on horticulture in Norway, Finland and Switzerland. Language skills are always useful and in some cases essential but as long as volunteers have fluency in English a placement can be found for them. InterExchange prearranges necessary work and residence permits, all jobs, and in most cases housing. All positions are paid to provide the candidate with enough money to cover food, accommodation and in-country travel expenses. Prior to their departure participants receive detailed information about their placement, the visa process, language, and the appropriate or necessary items to pack. Programme fees range from US$200 to US$1,000.

Those interested should contact the Programme Manager at the above address.

INTERNATIONAL BOUWORDE-IBO
St. Annastraat 172, 6524 GT, Nijmegen, The Netherlands; ☎ +31 24 322-6074; fax +31 24 322-6076; e-mail info@bouworde.nl; www.bouworde.nl
Internationale Bouworde (or International Building Companions) gives volunteers the opportunity to assist in socially useful building projects in Europe. British participants will be integrated in international groups, especially in Belgium, Holland, Germany and Poland.

The workcamps last for two to three weeks. Volunteers work for 8 hours per day, 5 days per week. Camps take place between June and September. Bouworde in Belgium and Italy operate camps year round. The actual construction work provides the most important element of the camps, and volunteers are expected to treat it as such. It acts as a focus for the other aspects such as encounters with fellow participants and with the local population.

Volunteers should be aged 18+ years old and fit enough to be able to meet the physical demands of the camp. They must also be willing to adapt to foreign attitudes and lifestyles. Volunteers have to pay their own travel costs to and from Belgium and Holland. Volunteers participating in a camp in Germany or Poland will travel together with volunteers from Holland to the project. For part of this journey, organised and paid for by the Dutch branch of IBO, a contribution is asked. IBO pays the insurance and provides board and lodging. Apply, preferably by e-mail, or telephone, write or fax for an application form to the relevant address listed below.

IBO-Osterreichischer Bauorden: Gentzgasse 117/4/47, A-1180, Wien, Austria; ☎ +43 1 7749512; fax +43 1 177 4951222; e-mail bauorden@oebo.at; www.bauorden.at.

IBO-Bouworde: Tiensesteenweg 145, B-3200 Kessel-Lo, Belgium; ☎ 016 25 91 44; fax 016 25 91 60.

IBO-Internationaler Bauorden: Liebigstrasse 23, 67551 Worms-Horchheim, Germany; ☎ 06241-37900; fax 06241-37902; e-mail bauorden@t-online.de; www.home.t-onlin.de/homeibo-d/

IBO-Soci Costruttori: via Montebello 46A, 441000 Ferrara, Italy: ☎ 0+39 0532-245689; e-mail info@iboitalia.org; www.iboitalia.

IBO-Internationaler Bauorden: Sekretariat Schweiz, Bahnhofstr. 8, 9450 Altstalku; ☎ +41-71 755 1671; e-mail info@bayordeuich.

OCEAN YOUTH TRUST
Spur House, 1 The Spur, Alverstoke, Gosport, Hampshire PO12 2NA; ☎ 0870 241-2252; fax 0870 909-0230; e-mail oytsouth@aol.com; www.oyt.org.uk
The Ocean Youth Trust needs volunteers to act as First and Second Mates on its ocean sailing expeditions and voyages from March to October. The aim of the club is to provide young people aged 12-24 with the opportunity to take part in adventurous offshore sailing, and so to develop their sense of awareness and responsibility and their ability to work in a team. It has bases throughout the UK. Volunteers work for weekends, weeks

and occasionally longer voyages.

All Mates must be qualified to the appropriate RYA and OYT level. All volunteers must be fit and able to swim. Accommodation is provided, as are safety and foul weather equipment. First Mates are asked to make a contribution towards their upkeep, and other mates pay a daily rate towards the cost of food.

Applications should be made to the Fleet Manager at the above address. Volunteers are also required to help with tasks such as fundraising, recruitment, presentations and refit work on the vessels.

LA SABRANENQUE
Saint Victor la Coste, 30290 Laudun, France; ☎ +33 (0)4 66 50 05 05; e-mail info@sabranenque.com; www.sabranenque.com

La Sabranenque is a non-profit organisation working for the preservation of the rural habitat by restoring abandoned rural sites for present day use. Saint Victor la Coste serves as the headquarters for the organisation as the work projects are mainly in southern France, although there are three sites in Italy. Around 150 volunteers are needed for work which includes restoration of roofs, terraces, walls and paths, planting local tree species and the reconstruction of small houses. Techniques are learned on the job. Workcamps last a minimum of two or three weeks during the summer, and occasionally stays of two months or more are possible.

Volunteers must be at least 18 years old and in good health. No language skills or previous experience are required for summer workcamps, but non EC volunteers must obtain a French visa for their period of stay. Board and lodging are provided at a cost of about £200 per two-week project.

Applications to Marc Simon, the Programme Co-ordinator at the above address.

SUNSEED DESERT TECHNOLOGY
Apdo 9, 04270 Sorbas, Almeria, Spain; e-mail sunseedspain@arrakis.es; ; ☎ +34 950 525 770

Sunseed Desert Technology aims to develop, demonstrate and communicate accessible, low-tech methods of living sustainably in a semi-arid environment. It is a registered Spanish Association and a project of the registered UK charity The Sunseed Trust.

Short and long-term volunteers are required year round. Work includes gardening, dryland managements, appropriate technology, cooking including solar cooking, construction, publicity, education and more. Longer-term volunteers can carry out their own projects in these fields that may be suitable as university dissertation projects.

Beautiful environment, rural location in southeast Spain, opportunity to develop language skills, friendly community and delicious vegetarian food. Volunteers make a weekly contribution of between £49 and £98 depending on length of stay and hours worked, to cover all food and accommodation.

Volunteer staff posts also available throughout the year.

See website or contact the project directly for further details.

TUTMONDA ESPERANTISTA JUNULARA ORGANIZO – TEJO (World Organisation of Young Esperantists)
Nieuwe Binnenweg 176, NL-3015 BJ Rotterdam, Netherlands; ☎ +31-10 4361044; fax +31-10 4361751; e-mail oficejo@tejo.org: www.tejo.org

Esperanto is the international language invented by Zamenhof, a Polish oculist, in 1887. It now has more than a million speakers throughout the world.

In addition to arranging Esperanto courses for workcamps organised by other organisations, TEJO also coordinates the recruitment of volunteers for Esperanto workcamps in several European countries. These camps include work on building sites and enhancing the environment. No prior experience is needed; although most camps are limited to Esperanto speakers, a few camps may include Esperanto lessons for beginners. The camps are usually composed of people aged 16-30.

Enquiries should be sent to the above address enclosing an International Reply Coupon.

Belgium and The Netherlands

ANNÉE DIACONALE BELGE
Service Protestant de la Jeunesse, Rue de Champ de Mars, 5, 1050 Bruxelles, Belgium; ☎ +32 2-510 6161; fax +32 2-510 6164.
Part of the Service Protestant de la Jeunesse, or Protestant Youth Office, arranges for volunteers to spend between ten and 12 months in Christian or other institutions in Belgium. Around 15 volunteers a year are placed in children's homes, homes for the elderly and disabled etc. Volunteers receive free food, accommodation and laundry, their travelling expenses and pocket money of around £100 per month, most of the projects are available in the European Voluntary Service. Placements begin in September.

Participants should be aged between 18 and 25 and have a basic knowledge of French. Whatever their background all candidates' applications will be welcome. Possession of a driving licence and/or a teaching certificate would be advantageous.

Contact the Secretary at the above address for further details.

BELGIAN EVANGELICAL MISSION
137 Lyndhurst Avenue, Twickenham, Middlesex TW2 6BH; ☎020-8894 0912; e-mail bemuk@b-e-m.org
The Belgian Evangelical Mission conducts summer evangelistic campaigns in a number of towns and villages in both French and Dutch speaking Belgium. Around 60 volunteers from Britain are needed to join the international campaign teams which last from two to six weeks, during the summer.

Volunteers may be of any nationality provided they are Christians and can provide a home church recommendation. Summer evangelical team members pay £10 per day and a £5 deposit. All volunteers must pay for their own travel but accommodation is provided.

Those interested should apply to BEM at the above address.

UNIVERSALE ESPERANTO-ASOCIO
Nieuwe Binneweg 176, 3015 BJ Rotterdam, Netherlands; ☎ +31-10 4361 0444; fax +31-10 4361751; e-mail uea@inter.nl.net; www.uea.org
The Universale Esperanto-Asocio is the world organisation for the advancement of Esperanto. Its Head Office is situated in Rotterdam, where a staff of ten to twelve workers from various parts of the world, both paid and voluntary, are involved in day-to-day administration, accounts, mail order services, congress organisation, editing and production of books and magazines, and maintaining a library. The Association has another office in New York to deal with contacts with the UN. Thus the Association needs one or two volunteers from time to time to help with its work. The minimum period of service for volunteers is nine months, the maximum one year.

Volunteers *must speak Esperanto fluently* as this is the working language of the organisation. Other qualifications may be necessary depending on the specific vacancy. Applicants must be between 18 and 29 years of age. Free accommodation is provided, and insurance and a small living allowance are paid. Residents of EU countries do not need a visa or work permit.

Volunteers from other countries will need both. A period of six to twelve months should be allowed for the acquisition of these permits.

Applications should be made to the Director at the above address

Eastern Europe and Russia

AID TO RUSSIA & THE REPUBLICS (ARRC)
PO Box 200, Bromley, Kent BR1 1QF; ☎020-460 6046; fax 020-8466 1244; e-mail info@arrc.org.uk; www.arrc.org.uk
Aid to Russia and the Republics is a Christian charity, committed to improving the lives of disadvantaged children in the former Soviet Union.

Overseas Volunteering. Short-term voluntary opportunities are available for medical professionals (including physiotherapists, occupational therapists and psychologists), social workers, project managers, management consultants and accountants to assist and provide training for the charity's project partners in Russia and the republics of the former Soviet Union. Help is also needed from carpenters, mechanics and plumbers to work on either vocational training or assist the Charity's partners with building maintenance. Knowledge of the Russian language is helpful, but not always necessary. Volunteers must be in good health as overseas working conditions are poor. Placements are for at least 2 weeks and run during spring, summer and autumn. Accommodation is provided. Trips are usually self-funded, however where particular expertise is urgently required, this can be negotiable. A free monthly newsletter can be obtained from Aid to Russia and the Republics. Contact the Administrator at the above address for further information.

UK Volunteering. In the UK, volunteers are required all year round for various types of work including jobs in the office, representing ARRC at Christian exhibitions and selling Russian cards and gifts. ARRC is looking for expert advisors to help them improve their work and are keen to hear from financial experts, management consultants, fundraising advisors, database experts, data analysts and project management specialists. The offices are in Bromley, Kent, but location and amount of time given is flexible (some tasks can be done at home). Travel expenses to the offices are paid.

Although volunteers need not be Christians, it is essential they are respectful of others' beliefs.

A free bi-monthly newsletter and a free quarterly prayer letter can be obtained from Aid to Russia and the Republics. Contact the Administrative Assistant at the above address for further information.

ANGLO-POLISH UNIVERSITIES ASSOCIATION ASSISTED TEACHING PROJECT (APASS)
UK Northern Area, Secretariat: 93 Victoria Road, Leeds LS6 1DR.
Applications are invited for English language instructors in the summer language schools (language camps), held in education/leisure centres (4 weeks either in July or August; fifteen hours of instruction per week). A good command of written and spoken English is

expected. For legal reasons, the teaching is classed as voluntary but generous pocket money is offered. Free board and lodging, sporting/leisure activities and a 'grand tour' of 7 days with a choice of Warsaw, Zelazowa Wola (birthplace of Chopin), Krakow, Auschwitz, Tatra Mountains).

Teaching experience is welcome but not essential. Assisted travel available. For a comprehensive Info Pack, please send an A4, 45p stamped envelope plus postal order for £3.

Wayne Stimson found the APASS scheme very enjoyable
I had always wanted to teach English and, as a politics student, I also had an interest in the history and politics of the former Eastern Bloc states. I got the opportunity to combine these two when APASS arranged for me to spend seven weeks in a village near the Czech border called Dusniki Zdroj. Here I worked on two camps that gave children an activity-based holiday alongside English teaching. The children were mainly from the middle class, professional backgrounds and their English skills were often quite developed so teaching and general communication was not difficult. I tried to teach a little about the customs, culture and politics of the UK. I was treated very graciously by my hosts and found Polish people to be very warm and friendly.

ASSOCIATION FOR EDUCATIONAL, CULTURAL AND WORK EXCHANGE PROGRAMS (AIEP)
42 Yeznik Coghbatsi Str., Apt. 22, Yerevan 375002, Armenia; ☎ +374-2 584733; fax +374-2 529232; e-mail aiep@arminco.com; www.aiep.am
The Association for Educational, Cultural and Work Exchange Programs is a member of the Co-ordinating Committee of International Voluntary Service (CCIVS – see separate entry). The Association's programmes involve the annual participation of 25-50 volunteers from all over the world in the reconstruction of old monuments, temples and churches in Armenia and the improvement of the ecological atmosphere. Excursions, meetings and informal discussions are also organised. Placements last from 15-30 days from June to October. Minimum age of volunteers is 18. Accommodation and food are provided in youth camps.

The Association publishes a weekly newspaper, *Voice of Youth*. For further details contact the Co-ordinator of Exchange Programs at the above address.

BLUE WORLD/ADRIATIC DOLPHIN PROJECT
Zad Bone 11, Veli Losinj 51551, Croatia; ☎ +385 51 520276; fax +385 51 520275; e-mail adp@adp.hr; www.adp.hr
Blue World/ADP carries out research on bottlenose dolphins collecting data in the field and then analysing it. All aspects of the methodology will be taught to volunteers. ADP also raises awareness of the project through lectures and preparation of materials in 5 languages.

30-40 volunteers are accepted annually. Volunteers are involved in all aspects of research dependent on skills and motivation. Of particular interest to the project are students of biology/environmental sciences and geography. EU nationalities and US citizens (visa required). Volunteers must be English-speaking and conservation minded. Volunteers should be in good health and able to spend long hours under the sun up to 35 Celsius. Programmes last 12 days between June and September. Accommodation is provided, but no expenses.

Scientific papers and other information about volunteering free from the website.
Applications should be made direct to the above address.

BRITISH-ROMANIAN CONNECTIONS
P.O. Box 86, Birkenhead, Liverpool CH41 8FU; ☎0151-5123355; fax 0151-512 3355; e-mail brc@pascu-tulbure.freeserve.co.uk

BRC has two operations in Romania: Summer holiday English language camps (conversational English and games) and term-time Children's English Club providing conversational English as an extra curricular activity. About 1,000 volunteers are accepted annually. Usually British or Irish (should be native speakers of English). Minimum qualifications are good 'A' levels and a thorough knowledge of the English language. A degree is better and for the English Clubs, a TEFL qualification is preferred. No upper age restriction.

Summer language camps last 2-4 weeks July and August. Clubs minimum 3 months commitment (Sept-Dec, Jan-March, April-June). For the Clubs volunteers get accommodation and living allowance (for food). For further details contact the above address.

CENTRAL EUROPEAN TEACHING PROGRAM (CETP)
Beloit College, 700 College St., Beloit, WI 53511 USA; ☎608-363 2619; e-mail cetp@beloit.edu; www.beloit,edu/cetp

CETP arranges placements as English conservation teachers in elementary or high school or college state education establishments. Conversation teachers merely enhance oral fluency since local teachers teach formal grammar. Normal class hours are 7.45am to 2.10pm. Teachers have 18-22 class meetings per week; each class lasts 45 minutes. Year long programme that runs from September to June for graduates with overseas TEFL or teaching experience (TEFL Certificate not essential). The cost to the volunteer is about $3,500 which helps to maintain an extensive network of offices, full-time country co-ordinator, orientation, weekend opportunities for professional development, etc. Applicants are interviewed by telephone and the deadline for applications is normally 15th March but this can vary depending on the vacancy situation. Previous applicants have come from the USA, UK, Jamaica, Canada, Australia.

CHILDREN ON THE EDGE
A Project of The Body Shop Foundation
Watersmead, Littlehampton, West Sussex BN17 6LS; ☎01903-850906; fax 01903-859296; e-mail office@childrenontheedge.org; www.childrenonthe edge. org

Children on the Edge was founded in 1990 by Anita Roddick to alleviate the suffering of Romanian orphans in three orphanages in Halaucesti, North Eastern Romania. Today there are active projects in Romania, Albania, Kosovo and East Timor where their long-term commitment includes refurbishment, medical care and child development. There are no long-term placements available but there is opportunity to apply for short term work over the summer months on a playscheme in Romania. The deadline for applications for this scheme is usually the end of January each year. Forms are received from all over the world and are assessed and shortlisted. Accepted volunteers have to fund raise £1,200 for their two-week stay – this includes airfare, accommodation, food and art and play equipment needed for the children. Minimum age limit is 18.

To apply, or to obtain an information pack, contact Susan Handsford at the above address.

ECOLOGIA TRUST
The Park, Forres, Moray IV36 3TZ; ☎01309-690995; fax 01309-691009; e-mail info@ecologia.org.uk; www.ecologia.org.uk

Ecologia Trust arranges for people of all ages and gap year students, to work as volunteers at the Kitezh Children's Community in Russia (Kitezh Community, Kaluzhskaya oblast, Baryatino rayon, 249650 Russia). The community consists of ten families in a non-commercial partnership of foster families living as a community on common land. Each family has their own home built by the community and each family has three or four orphaned children in addition to their own. The community as a whole is responsible for the children and they have their own school where most of the adults are teachers as well as workers in the community. Kitzeh aims to create an alternative to state institutions which normally care for orphaned children.

Volunteers work in the kitchen, garden, the farm or help with whatever building work is in progress. They also speak English to the children and adults who are keen to learn English. Volunteers can stay for a few days up to a year, but most find that 1-2 months is the minimum time needed to settle in. Less than a month and you feel like a tourist visitor.

Application arrangements are made through Ecologia Trust. Total cost to volunteers includes organising fee £90; Invitation (3 month single entry) £145, Moscow-Kitezh Transfers with overnight Accommodation £125, 1 month in Kitezh £200 (2 months £300), additional months or short term visit (£60).

Sarah Moy volunteered at the friendly Kitezh community
Kitezh is so different from the rest of the world that it took a while to know where you could go, how to get involved in work/play with the children etc. I felt very much a part of the community and enjoyed sharing my talents (but would have liked to have taught more English). Apart from the obvious benefits of improving Russian and learning more about Russian culture and people, I gained much from the slower pace of life. I was very impressed by the idea of people who have made a career of genuinely caring and giving. I learnt more about a rural way of life and appreciated being reminded how many luxuries we have here. Altogether it was a fantastic experience.

EKO-CENTAR CAPUT INSULAE – BELI
Beli 4, 51559 Beli, Croatia; ☎ +385 51 840525; fax +385 51 840525; e-mail caput.insulae@ri.htnet.hr; www.caput-insulae.com

Eko-Centar is non-governmental and non-profit organisation working on integral protection of the Croatian natural and cultural heritage, particularly the tradition and the way of life of the people of the island Cres. The Eko-Centar runs a major conservation project, the Griffon Vulture Project, and a long-term project, Saving Small Marshes on the Island of Cres. It also participates in the international project, Clean up the World, organising the cleaning of beaches in the Ornithological Reserves on the island of Cres.

500 volunteers are recruited annually for a minimum of a week to a maximum of three months throughout the year. Activities include picking forest fruits and processing them for jam, juice, etc. (August-October), shearing, washing and processing wool (May and June), and cleaning ponds (only for groups in August). From September to November. Aid is also required with: in September and October, collecting firewood for the Eco centar in the forest Tramuntana; in November, picking olives and making olive oil; throughout the year maintaining the network of Eco-trails and restoring the Roman road, and cleaning the beaches in the ornithological reserve, cleaning canyons and illegal dump sites. For the Griffon Vulture project, volunteers work at the feeding place and recovery area for ailing birds near to the Eco-centre's building. Other projects include participation in building dry stone walls and terraced fields.

Volunteers should be aged a minimum of 16 and speak English. Accommodation is provided in dorms with access to four bathrooms, showers, and a large kitchen in the Eco-centar. Volunteers pay for all their other expenses.

Applications to the Project Co-ordinator at the above address.

INEX SLOVAKIA
Prazska 11, 81413 Bratislava, Slovakia; website www.inex.sk
Organises and hosts annual programme of international work camps with 300-400 volunteers per summer. Types of camp are many including environmental, social and those involving reconstruction. Camps last 2-3 weeks. Food, accommodation and some free time activities are provided by the host organisation, but volunteers pay their own travel costs, registration fee and insurance. Minimum age is 18 years.

Apply direct to Inex Slovakia in the first instance. They will provide details of their partner organisations abroad if relevant.

INTERNATIONAL EXCHANGE CENTER
2, Republic Square, 1010 Riga, Latvia; ☎ +371-7027476; fax +371-7830257; e-mail iec@iec.eunet.lv
The Center recruits volunteers of any nationality to work as counsellors in summer children's camps in Latvia, Russia, and the Ukraine. Placements usually last for between four and twelve weeks. A basic knowledge of a local language or Russian is required, and applicants should be aged between 18 and 35.

The Programme: includes Russian study of 10 hours per week for 4 weeks in universities in Moscow. During this time volunteers begin their 2-4 month work placement. Work placements are generally in the hospitality industry: bars, hotels and cafés. Other placements may be possible depending on skills and experience. Beginners can be accepted on the programme if they take a two-month study course (£495) before starting a placement. Extra 4-week blocks of study cost £245 (to be booked when applying). Programme deadline: 3 months before your earliest starting date. You can expect to earn £40-£140 per month or £65 average for state-owned enterprises. The cost of living is low in Russia.

UK applicants apply through International Student Exchange Centre, 35 Ivor Place, London NW1 6EA (☎020-7724 4493; fax 0207724-0849; e-mail isecinfo@btconnect.com).

JACOB'S WELL APPEAL
2 Ladygate, Beverley HU17 8BH; ☎01482-881162; fax 01482-865452; e-mail thejacobswell@aol.com; wwwthejacobswell.org
Jacob's Well Appeal is a registered charity offering volunteer work for between four weeks and three months in northern Romania. Jacob's Well have built their own rehabilitation unit to house young people preparing for the outside world, who have been brought up in a neuro-psychiatric hospital. Volunteers also help at a day centre for young people with disabilities who are living in the surrounding area.

The minimum age for volunteers is 18. Older applicants with relevant professional qualifications, such as physiotherapists, special needs teachers and nurses, are particularly welcome. Volunteers pay their own expenses.

For further information contact Dr. Beryl Beynon.

MOST
Breg 12-61000 Ljubljana, Slovenia; ☎ +386 61-142 58 067; fax +386 61-217208; e-mail most@mila.ljudmila.org; www.drustvo-most.si
MOST organises voluntary work in Slovenia, particularly in areas not adequately covered by the government such as ecology, care of the disabled and refugees. MOST also

organises workcamps mainly in summer, and an exchange scheme for local volunteers with organisations abroad. 200 Slovenian volunteers and 400 foreign volunteers are engaged per year.

There are opportunities for volunteers to participate in manual work such as building, painting or decorating. Ecologically-minded volunteers are needed to help with gardening and research work and also to find data and run campaigns. There are volunteer opportunities in the area of social work including work with mentally or physically disabled children, elderly people and refugees, and also to organise study sessions among marginalised groups. Applicants of all nationalities are welcome; there is no need for a visa or work permit. Volunteers must, however, be able to speak English and preferably have previous experience of voluntary work. The minimum age is 18.

Foreign volunteers usually join the summer workcamps, which last from two to four weeks, but there are also medium-term placements of six months and long-term placements of one year. Workcamp volunteers get food and accommodation free, while for the medium and long-term volunteers accommodation and pocket money are provided. On workcamps the accommodation is usually basic and communal.

Those interested in going from Britain, should contact the International Voluntary Service, British branch of Service Civil International who will forward the the application to the organisation in Slovenia.

NIGHTINGALES CHILDREN'S PROJECT
C/o Lin Davies, 33 Morgans Rise, Bishops Hull, Somerset TA1 5HW; tel 01823-289888; www.nightingaleschildrensproject.org.uk
Nightingales Children's Project places volunteers in a school and orphanage in Cernavoda, southeast Romania. About 120 volunteers are recruited throughout the year for one to three months to work and play with children aged between 2 and 13, some have HIV and some are special needs. Volunteers aged between 20 and 60, must be in good health and a caring, cheerful nature is advantageous. Food and accommodation are provided at a cost of £2.50 per day; volunteers must also pay for all their other expenses.

Applications to the UK Co-ordinator at the above address enclosing an A5 SAE.

PAHKLA CAMPHILL KULA
EE 79702 Prillimae, Rapla Maakond, Estonia; ☎ +372-48 34 449/430; fax +372-48 97 231; e-mail pahklack@hot.es
Pahkla Camphill Kula is a Camphill village of the international Camphill movement founded in Scotland in 1939 by Karl König. In Pahkla Camphill Kula people with needs live and work together with co-workers. Volunteers are always welcome and help in most areas of an extended family life as well as in the workshops (candle-making, weaving), and on the farm and in the creamery and gardens.

No formal qualifications are required but volunteers should be minimum age 20, physically fit, open-minded and willing. Volunteers are required all year round for a period of at least a year. Accommodation, food, and a small pocket money allowance are provided. Volunteers pay their own travel expenses.

Those interested should apply to the above address.

SERVICES FOR OPEN LEARNING
2 Bridge Chambers, The Strand, Barnstaple, Devon EX13 1HB; ☎01271-327319; fax 01271-376650; e-mail info@sol.org.uk; www.sol.org.uk
SOL is concerned with the recruitment of graduates, preferably with teaching or language degrees and TEFL qualification, to teach in schools in eastern central Europe especially

Hungary and Romania, but also Albania, Belarus, Bulgaria, Croatia, Czech Republic, Poland, Slovakia and Slovenia).

About 30 graduates are needed annually. Candidates must be native-speakers of English and available for interview in Britain (or eastern central Europe) in spring. As well as being certified fit to undertake the work by their doctor, volunteers must be prepared to stay a minimum of one academic year. Partial financial support (£120-£180 per month) local salaries, plus free independent accommodation, are provided for Romania and Belarus because of the additional expenses involved. Travel is at the teacher's expense.

Anyone interested should contact SOL at the above address.

SVEZHY VETER TRAVEL AGENCY
Karla Marxa 228A, Izhevsk 426057, Russia; tel/fax +7 (3412) 45 00 37; +7 (3412) 45 00 38; e-mail sv@sv-agency.udm.ru; www.sv-agency.udm,ru
On the website of the Svezhy Veter Travel Agency (www.sv-agency.udm.ru), you can find details of a scheme which recruits native English-speakers to go to the city of Izhevsk, several time zones east of Moscow, to teach mornings, plus an evening course at Secondary school 27 in exchange for free board and accommodation with local families. A TEFL certificate would be useful, as would the ability to speak some Russian in order to make the most of the opportunity of the many invitations you are likely to receive.

TEACHING & PROJECTS ABROAD
Aldsworth Parade, Goring, Sussex BN12 4TX; ☎01903-708300; fax 01903-501026; e-mail info@teaching-abroad.co.uk; www.teaching-abroad.co.uk
Teaching & Projects Abroad offers adventurous foreign travel with a chance to do a worthwhile job. Over 2000 places are available each year to teach conversational English (no TEFL required) or gain valuable work experience in medicine, conservation, journalism, business and many other professions. Placements all year last from one month upwards. Volunteers are needed in Bolivia, Chile, China, Ghana, India, Mexico, Mongolia, Nepal, Peru, Romania, Russia, South Africa, Sri Lanka, Thailand and Togo.

For further information on Teaching & Projects Abroad, contact Dr. Peter Slowe at the above address.

ZAVOD VOLUNTARIAT
Service Civil International, Slovenia, Breg 12, SI-1000 Ljubljana, Slovenia; ☎+386-1-2717620; fax +386-1-2417626; e-mail placement@zavod-voluntariat.sl; www.zavod-voluntariat.si
Voluntariat is a non-profit and non-governmental organisation which co-ordinates voluntary work and international work camps in Slovenia. Voluntariat aims to promote social justice, sustainable development and solidarity through voluntary service. Voluntariat organises between 15 and 20 work camps in Slovenia every year. Most work camps are held from June to September and last two or three weeks. The main topics of the work camps are ecology, Bosnian refugees, children and handicapped people. Most work camps do not require any special skills. Accommodation and food are provided. Applications should be made through the applicant's own country branch of Service Civil International. Long and medium-term voluntary work: projects of LTV and MTV are based mostly in Ljubljana and they include: refugee projects, projects for youngsters from deprived backgrounds and projects for elderly people. Voluntariat also offers long and medium-term voluntary work abroad.

Ireland

CONSERVATION VOLUNTEERS IRELAND
The Steward's House, Rathfarnham Castle, Dublin 14, Ireland; ☎ +353-1 4952878; fax 01-492879; e-mail inp@cvi.ie; www.cvi.ie
CVI coordinates and promotes volunteer environmental work nationwide through its affiliations with many local conservation organisations. There is an annual membership fee which gives members details of and access to a wide range of projects lasting a weekend or longer.

Volunteers pay a contribution towards costs which start at about 25 euros for a weekend.

GROUNDWORK — IRISH WILDLIFE TRUST VOLUNTEERS
Garden Level, 21 Northumberland Road, Dublin 4, Ireland ☎ +353-1 6604530; fax +353-1 676 8601; e-mail groundwork@iwt.ie; www.groundwork.ie
Groundwork is a special section of The Irish Wildlife Trust dedicated to organising voluntary conservation projects. It was started in 1981 to tackle the rhododendron infestation of the Killarney Oak Woods. The *ponticum* species of rhododrendron (introduced into Ireland in the nineteenth century) has a tendency to become so dense that it blocks 98 per cent of light reaching the woodland floors thus preventing any regeneration at that level. Summer camps to control the problem are now established in both the Killarney and Glenveagh National Parks. Volunteers pay about 25.50 euros per week to cover food and accommodation.

For more information on workcamps and booking details visit the website above.

PILGRIM ADVENTURE
27 Oldbury Court Road, Fishponds, Bristol BS16 2HH; ☎0117-9655454; e-mail pilgrim.adventure@virgin.net; www.pilgrim-adventure.org.uk
Pilgrim Adventure is an ecumenical Christian organisation based in Bristol, which organises 'pilgrim journeys' to the remoter parts of Ireland and the UK.

A small number of volunteer team members are required to help lead all age groups of 10-25 and assist with worship and camp/hostel chores. Applicants must be have a Christian commitment, be at least 18 years old, have an interest in, and experience of hillwalking. Full board and accommodation are provided on trips. Team members should be available to help lead pilgrim journeys for at least seven consecutive days each year and assist with pilgrim planning throughout the year

For further details, please contact David Gleed at the above address.

THE SIMON COMMUNITY OF IRELAND
St Andrews House, 28-30 Exchequer Street, Dublin 2, Ireland; ☎ +353-1 671 1606; fax +351-1 671 1098; e-mail info@simoncommunity.com; www.simoncommunity.com
The Simon Community is a voluntary organisation which provides accommodation, food and companionship for homeless people. Full-time volunteers are involved in running the emergency shelters and long stay community houses for homeless people in projects throughout Ireland.

All nationalities are welcome and no formal or special qualifications are required. Personal qualities such as compassion, sensitivity, and adaptability are most important. Fluency in English and the ability to communicate are essential. Accommodation and a weekly pocket money allowance are provided. Volunteers are expected to stay for a minimum of six months; two weeks holiday, with an allowance, are given after every three months of a stay. The minimum age is 18.

Further information can be obtained from the Recruitment Co-ordinator at the above address.

VOLUNTARY SERVICE INTERNATIONAL (VSI)
30 Mountjoy Square, Dublin 1, Ireland; ☎ +353-1 855 1011; fax +353-1 855 1012; e-mail info@vsi.ie; www.vsi.ie
VSI is the Irish branch of Service Civil International (SCI – see separate entry). Each year VSI organises placements for 350-450 volunteers on 30 different voluntary work projects in Ireland such as: tree-planting in the Macroom area; working in a special school for children with severe learning difficulties; assisting an information service and community programmes for elderly, young people and children. VSI also exchanges 250 Irish volunteers with SCI branches and partner organisations worldwide in Australia, North Africa, the Middle East, the USA and throughout Europe. Placements last from two to three weeks from June to October. Volunteers minimum age 18, should have a good standard of English. Food, accommodation and insurance are provided but volunteers must pay all their other expenses.

For those in Ireland a *VSI International Volunteer Projects* book (published each April) can be obtained from the above address at a cost of £4, similar books are produced in most European countries.

Applications should be made through your local SCI branch or partner workcamp organisation, see the SCI main entry for address details.

VOLUNTEERING IRELAND
Coleraine House, Coleraine Street, Dublin 7, Ireland; ☎ +353-1 8722622; fax +353-1 872 2623; e-mail info@volunteeringireland.com; www. volunteeringireland.com
Volunteeing Ireland is the national resource for volunteering in the Republic of Ireland, promoting, supporting and facilitating voluntary action of all kinds. Over 1,000 volunteers are recruited annually to do anything that interests them, from working with animals and people (whether young, old, with extra support needs etc), to working on a particular issue (homelessness, the environment etc.) Placements can be from a couple of hours on a Time Limited Commitment project (TLC©), or as a regular commitment for a year or longer. Qualifications, skills and experience vary from project to project.

For further information and a free factsheet, *Residential Volunteering Opportunities in Ireland...useful contacts*, contact the Manager at the above address.

France

AMIS DE CHEVREAUX-CHATEL
rue du Château, 39190 Chevreaux, France; ☎ +33-3 84 85 95 77; fax +33-3 84 85 95 77; e-mail accjura@free.fr; www.accjura.free.fr
An international workcamp involving the restoration of the Castle of Chevreaux, is organised during the last three weeks of July and the first three weeks of August. Work involves clearing, reconstruction of ruins, stoneworking, carpentry or archaeology.

Volunteers are expected to work about six hours a day. After work: local recreation facilities including a swimming pool. At the weekends there are discovery tours of the landscapes of the Jura, horse-riding etc. Volunteers are unpaid and will be lodged on site (under tents) with camp beds. All sanitary and kitchen equipment is provided. Ages: 18-25. No special qualifications required, but must be motivated.

For further details contact Jacques Genest, President of the Association at the above address.

ASSOCIATION ALPES DE LUMIÈRE
Prieure de Salagon, Mane, 04300-Forcalquier, France; ☎ +33-492 75 22 01; fax +33 4 92 75 46 10; e-mail adl–chantier@wanadoo.fr; www.alpes–de – lumiere.asso.fr

The Association organises several camps around Provence lasting about three weeks between June and September dedicated to the restoration of historic buildings, and the development of historic sites. These sites become recreational and cultural centres. Food and basic accommodation, but not pocket money are provided for the volunteers. The emphasis of the camps is also on enriching the participants' awareness of the culture and customs of the area. The working day begins at 7.30am and ends at 1.30pm; the afternoons are free. Participants work a 30-hour week under the direction of a specialist and a group leader.

Applicants of all nationalities will be accepted for the 150 places available each year. The minimum age is 18 years, and applicants must be fit and not subject to any allergies.

Enquiries should be sent to Laurence Michel at the above address.

ASSOCIATION   CHANTIERS-HISTOIRE   ET   ARCHITECTURE MÉDIÉVALES(CHAM)
5 et 7, rue Guilleminot, 75014 Paris, France; ☎ +33-1 43 35 15 51; fax +33-1 43 20 46 82; e-mail cham@cham.asso.fr

CHAM is dedicated to the conservation and restoration of medieval buildings around France. 600 volunteers per year are needed to work in July and August for a minimum of ten days on the restoration of monuments, châteaux, bridges and abbeys.

Applicants should be enthusiastic and have a very good knowledge of French; they must also be over 16 years of age. No pocket money is provided and applicants must pay, not only for their travel expenses, but also a contribution of 33 euros, plus about 10 euros per day for their board and lodging.

Those interested should apply to direct to the above address.

ASSOCIATION DE RECHERCHES ET ETUDES D'HISTOIRE RURALE
Maison du Patrimoine, 21190 Saint-Romain, France; ☎ +33 3 80 21 28 50; e-mail st-romain.arehr@libertysurf.sr

This association is conducting a long term research project on the archaeological, ethnolological and historical development of Saint-Romain village and its area.

Approximately 140 volunteers per year are needed to work during July and August for a fortnight or longer. The work consists of digging and restoration. No qualifications or experience are needed but a knowledge of French is useful. The minimum age is 18. There is a small daily charge for board and accommodation. Also a registration fee which includes insurance cover. Accommodation is at the Association's Centre or on a nearby campsite.

Applicants should write to Serge Grappin, the Director, at the above address, or e-mail.

ASSOCIATION LE MAT
Le Viel Audon, 07120 Balazuc, France; ☎ +33-4 75 37 73 80; fax +33 (0)4 75 37 77 90; www.vielaudon.free.fr
Le Mat undertakes restoration, reconstruction and environmental activities at the village of Viel Audon in the Ardèche region of France during July/August. Around 300 volunteers are needed each summer to assist with this work, although only groups of 50 people can be catered for at any one time. Volunteers can choose their daily task from those offered as long as they work at least five hours per day for a minimum of ten days.

Volunteers should be 17 to 25 years old. To be sure that young foreigner volunteers have a good holiday, they should at least understand and talk French at a basic level needed for daily life. Camping areas are provided and some beds are available but volunteers must pay for food (about 8 euros daily), 6 euros for insurance and a joining fee of around 10 euros.

Those interested should contact the Co-ordinator at the above address for more information.

BARDOU
34390 Olargues, France; ☎ +33-4 67 97 72 43.
Bardou is a beautifully restored 16th century hamlet owned by Klaus and Jean Erhardt. A couple of volunteer helpers are made welcome yearly from Easter to October to help with spring-cleaning, gardening and maintenance such as painting and to help keep the stone houses clean. The hamlet attracts many visitors during the year especially musicians, orchestras, actors and so on who are performing in the region. 20 hours participation weekly is asked with tasks. The minimum stay is one month. Volunteers are able to go to any of the cultural events locally. Shorter stays or those outside the project months cost starting at 8 euros per person/night in individual houses. Enquiries should be sent to Klaus and Jean Erhardt, enclosing an international reply coupon.

CHANTIERS DE JEUNES: PROVENCE/CÔTE D'AZUR
La Ferme Giaume, 7 Ave. Pierre de Coubertin, 06150 Cannes la Bocca, France; ☎ +33-4 93 47 89 69; fax +33-4 93 48 12 01; e-mail cjpca@club – internet. fr; www.cjpca.fr.st
This non-profit association provides voluntary activity holidays for 13 to 17-year olds. These workcamps take place on the islands of St Marguerite, just off Cannes; also in the country and in the Alpes Maritimes. There are a variety of camps throughout the year but mainly in summer, lasting two to 15 days. There are 15 participants at a time on each camp. Volunteers spend five hours a day working on the restoration of historic buildings. In the afternoons, and also evenings the volunteers can choose from a range of activities including sports. The camps are based on communal life and the participants prepare the meals on a rota basis and help with the general domestic shores. Applicants of all nationalities are welcome and a knowledge of French is a great asset. Cost available on application.

Please contact Celine Sauger at the above address for further details.

CHÂTEAU DE SAINT-AUGUSTIN
Château sur Allier, 03320 Lurcy-Levis, France; ☎ +33-4 70 66 42 01; fax +33-4 70 66 41 34; e-mail malaure@inforic.com
A couple of voluntary assistants are needed to give general help in a 35-hectare safari park based around an 18th century château. In the winter months work may include teaching cookery and restoration of old paintings. No wages are paid, but board and lodging is provided. The period of work is by arrangement. Applicants must love animals

and nature and preferably hold international driving licences: the positions would be ideal for those who wish to perfect their French.

Enquiries to Mme de Montesquieu at the above address.

CLUB DU VIEUX MANOIR
Ancienne Abbaye du Moncel, 60700 Pontpoint, France; ☎ +33 (0)3 44 72 33 98; fax +33 (0)3 44 70 13 14; e-mail clubduvieuxmanoir@free.fr
This non-profit making association is dedicated to the rescue and restoration of endangered monuments and historical sites. Each year 4,000 volunteers contribute to the preservation of France's heritage and at the same time acquire manual and technical skills as well as some knowledge of archaeology and history. Apart from working on a site, club members may take part in research, publication or committee work. There are three permanent sites: at Guise in the province of Aisne, at Argy in Indre and at Pontjoint in Oise.

Volunteers are invited to arrive at any time provided they come equipped with sleeping bag and camp cooking utensils. Special arrangements can be made for groups of scouts, factory employees and children from holiday camps. There are several summer vacation sites throughout the country at which the minimum length of stay is 15 days. Participants must pay 80 francs per day for their board and lodging, which may entail accommodation in the monument itself.

All volunteers must be very fit. Initial membership in the Club de Vieux Manoir costs 13.72 euros. The minimum age is normally 15; however, at the centre for specialised courses in restoration at the Chateau d'Argy, the minimum age is 17. All nationalities may participate.

Further details may be obtained by sending a stamped self-addressed envelope to Therese Beckelynck, *Animatrice Permanente*, at the above address.

CNRS – UMR 6566
Université de Rennes 1, Campus de Beaulieu, 74205 CS, Laboratoire d'Anthropologie (bât. 24-25), Campus de Beaulieu, 35042 Rennes cedex, France; ☎ +33 (0)2 23 23 56 26; fax +33 (0)2 23 23 69 34); www.ens. univ-rennes1.fr/dea-archeo/.
This organisation places about 100 volunteers annually at various prehistoric or proto-historic excavation sites in France in Brittany, the Charente, Poitou, and the Loire Valley. Placements are for a minimum of two weeks between June and September. Volunteers must be at least 18, be in good health – a recent tetanus jab is required, and be students of archaeology. Board and lodging is provided at a cost.

Applications with IRC enclosed to Jean Laurent Monnier, Director of Research at the above address.

COLLÈGE CÉVENOL (INTERNATIONAL WORKCAMP)
Le Chambon-sur-Lignon 434000, Haute Loire, France; ☎ +33-4 71 59 72 52; fax +33-4 71 65 87 38; e-mail contact@cevenol.org; www.cevenol.org
This workcamp lasts 17 days in July each year at the College Cevenol International in the Massif Central (Auvergne). The surrounding country is wooded and mountainous and provides an invigorating setting for the camp activities.

The present school at Chambon-sur-Lignon has been partly built by workcamps held at the site, and in fact it is this construction work, landscaping and maintenance with forms the work done in the summer. The camps also offer daily language classes (two hours) for foreigners run by the Collège Cévenol. In the evenings discussion groups meet or those who wish to can use the time for relaxation. Some outings are organised in the area. It will suit those who like a bracing experience, and mixing with young people of all nationalities.

Volunteers should be aged between 16 and 30 years, and in good health. Accommodation is provided at the school itself, food is provided, and all other facilities. The camp is free of charge in exchange for their work campers are given board and lodging. Campers are expected to join in all group activities. All nationalities are welcome. The volunteers may go, at a very reduced price, on the Discovery trip of France organised by the College at the end of the Workcamp.

Application forms can be obtained from Monsieur le Directeur du Collège Cévenol, Camp International de Travail, at the above address.

COTRAVAUX
11 Rue de Clichy, 75009 Paris, France; ☎ +33 (0)1 48 74 79 20; fax +33 (0)1 48 74 14 01; e-mail informations@cotravaux.org; www.cotravaux.org
Cotravaux is a co-ordinating body for voluntary work organisations in France. It aims to develop the services provided by workcamps, and to find new workcamp opportunities. The kind of work done by the individual organisations covers a wide range of projects, in cities or villages all over France, like the renovation of monuments, environmental protection, social action etc. All the projects involve young people from many countries. Most workcamps take place during the summer vacations, from the end of June to October. A few workcamps of shorter duration are open during the Easter and Christmas vacations. Usually camps last two to three weeks but there are also long-term stays available (6 to 12 months) During the summer, teams can succeed each other at the same work site. The organisations which are members of Cotravaux are: Concordia, Neige et Merveilles, Service Civil International, Jeunesse et Reconstruction, Alpes de Lumière, Compagnons Bâtisseurs, Union REMPART, UNAREC, Fédération Unie des Auberges de Jeunesse (FUAJ), Solidarités Jeunesses, Action Urgence International (AUI), Espaces-Chantiers Environnement Local (ECHEL).

Conditions for participation, type of accommodation provided, and expenses paid, obviously vary from organisation to organisation. Volunteers should apply to the individual organisations for information: their addresses can be obtained from Cotravaux at the above address.

Note that most French organisations have partners in other countries which can receive applications. Cotravaux can give you a list of such organisations in your country.

ETUDES ET CHANTIERS (UNAREC)
33 rue Campagne Première, 75014 Paris, France; ☎ +33 (0)1 453 89626; fax +33 (0)1 432 28636; e-mail unarec@wanadoo.fr; www.unarec.org
UNAREC is involved in both short-term conservation projects during the school holidays and long-term projects for professional training throughout the year. UNAREC also organises short-term volunteer exchanges with 30 countries.

About 800 volunteers every year are needed for both short and long term projects, to help with conservation and building work, to lead groups and to take part in international exchanges. Applicants can be of any nationality. Those applying for posts as group leaders need an international driving licence and knowledge of French. Those aged 14 can volunteer for teenage workcamps, for which camp fees have to be paid. Those over 18 years of age can apply to join adult workcamps, for which there are no camp fees. Projects last for two to three weeks. Accommodation and insurance are provided but not pocket money. European volunteers must bring an E111 form. For workcamps in France there is an application fee of 115 euros; 145 euros for workcamps abroad.

For further information please contact Francois Ribaud at the following address:

Délégué international, 3 rue des petits gras, 63000 Clermont-Ferrand, France; ☎+33 (0)4 73 31 98 04; fax +33 (0)4 73 31 98 09.

GROUPE ARCHEOLOGIQUE DU MESMONTOIS
Rue Gaudot, F-21410 Mâlain, France; e-mail malain-gam@hotmail.com
The organisation undertakes archaeological digs and restoration work near Dijon, France. About 40 volunteers are needed to help with tasks, which include sketching and photographing the finds, model making and restoration. The digs last from one to four weeks and are held during July.

Volunteers skilled in any of the above areas are especially welcome but no qualifications or skills are obligatory. The minimum age of volunteers accepted is 17 years. Volunteers pay about 15 euros per week towards the board and lodging provided.

Those interested should apply to M. Roussel at the above address.

JEUNESSE ET RECONSTRUCTION
10 rue de Trévise, 75009 Paris, France; ☎ +33 (0)1 47 70 15 88; fax +33 (0)1 48 00 92 18; www.voluntariat .org
Jeunesse et Reconstruction was created in 1948 with the aim of promoting international exchange between young people and intercultural relations through the organisation of voluntary work camps in France and abroad and longer-term voluntary service worldwide. The programme categories are summer work camps, mid-term and long-term volunteering, seminars and training, language courses and agricultural work in 63 countries. Jeunesse et Reconstruction sends volunteers to its partner organisations in different countries. Over 1000 volunteers are sent abroad and about 550 volunteers work in France. French workcamps involve activities related to social work, the environment, construction, building and renovating and agriculture.

Volunteers should be aged 18-35. No qualifications or previous experience are required. Short-term workcamps last 2-3 weeks, long-term 6-12 months. Food and accommodation are provided but all other expenses including travel and insurance are at the volunteer's expenses.

Contact the above organisation for further details.

MINISTÈRE DE LA CULTURE
Sous-Direction de l'Archeologie, 4 Rue d'Aboukir, 75002 Paris, France; ☎ +33 (0)1 40 15 77 81; e-mail chantiers-de-fouilles.DAPPA@culture.gouv.fr; www. culture.gouv.fr
The Ministry compiles an annual list of archaeological excavations requiring volunteers in France. The list is drawn up during spring for that summer season. Around 10,000 volunteers are needed in total, as assistants in all aspects of archaeological excavations for periods of two weeks to one month. The minimum age of volunteers accepted is usually 18 years. No special skills are needed for most teams but some leaders may require experienced volunteers. Accommodation in houses or at campsites is provided.

Write to the Information Scientist of Excavations to receive a copy of the list or look up the website for updated information from 15 April to 1 September.

MUSEUM NATIONAL D'HISTOIRE NATURELLE
Institut de Paléontologie Humaine, 1 Rue René Panhard, 75013 Paris, France; e-mail iph@mnhn.fr
Professor Henry de Lumley, Director of the Institut de Paléontologie Humaine, organises archaeological excavations in France each year from April to August. Volunteers are required to assist with these excavations and they should be prepared to stay for the

duration of the camp, which is between two weeks and one month. There is a camping site but volunteers must provide their own tents, etc. They must also pay their own travelling expenses although expenses will be paid while at the camp.

Further information can be obtained from Henry de Lumley at the above address.

NEIGE ET MERVEILLES
Hameau de la Minière de Vallauria, 06430 Saint Dalmas de Tende, France; ☎ +33 (0)4 93 04 62 40; e-mail doc@neige-merveilles.com; www.neige-merveilles.com
Neige et Merveilles is an international work camp involved with the reconstruction of a mountain hamlet near the Italian border, one and a half hours north of Nice.

Volunteers should be minimum age 18 and the camps generally last two or three weeks and inscription costs 70 euros. Longer volunteer stays are also possible for two to six months from March to November for which the inscription is the same. Apart from construction work tasks include working in the kitchen, childcare, services and cleaning. The camp is run by a specialist *animateur*. About 30-50 volunteers are taken on annually from 15th April to 15th October. There are also opportunities to learn French and to explore the region while on the camp.

SERVICE ARCHÉOLOGIQUE D'ARRAS
77 rue Baudimont, 62000 Arras, France; tel/fax +33-3 21 71 42 62.
This organisation carries out archeological research on the Roman and Medieval town of Arras. About 15 volunteers per year help with the excavations, and with the washing and cataloguing of the archaeological finds.

No special skills and/or qualifications are required. The minimum age limit is 18 years, the maximum is 35. The minimum period for which volunteers are normally recruited is 15 days between July and August. No expenses are paid, and pocket money is not provided. Volunteers will be provided with accommodation. There is a small inscription fee payable in cash on arrival for volunteers from abroad.

Those interested should apply to the above address.

SERVICE ARCHÉOLOGIQUE DU MUSÉE DE DOUAI
191 rue Saint Albin, 59500 Douai, France; ☎ +33 (0)3 27 71 38 90; fax +33 (0)3 27 71 38 93; e-mail arkeos@wanadoo.fr
Volunteers are needed to assist with archaeological digging and history research in the neighbourhood of Douai in northern France, during summer. A minimum of 15 days is recommended during the excavation season, which is generally from 10 July to the beginning of September. Previous relevant experience is an advantage. A knowledge of French is extremely helpful, but English will suffice. The minimum age for volunteers is 18 years. Board and accommodation are provided.

For further details contact Pierre Demolon, Director of Archaeological Services at the above address.

SERVICE REGIONAL DE L'ARCHÉOLOGIE
6 rue de la Manufacture, 45000 Orléans, France; ☎ +33-2 38 78 85 41; fax +33-2 38 78 12 95.
Diggers and draughtsmen/women to work on an archaeological dig in Orleans or one of the other digs in central France. Volunteers should have relevant experience: some knowledge of French is desirable. Eight-hour day, five-day week. No salary, but board and lodging are provided free. The minimum period of work is two weeks between June and September. Applications should be sent in April to the above address.

SERVICE RÉGIONAL DE L'ARCHÉOLOGIE
6 Rue de Chapitre, 35044 Rennes Cedex, France; ☎ +33 (0)2 99 84 59 00; e-mail SRA@bretagne.culture.fr
The Service Régional de l'Archéologie organises archaeological excavations in Brittany. Volunteers (10-30 per site) are needed to take part in various excavations throughout Brittany between April and September. Seven-hour day, five or five and a half days a week. Board and accommodation, often on a campsite is usually provided free of charge, but on some sites there is a charge for administration and insurance. The minimum period of work is two weeks and the minimum age 18. No previous experience is necessary, but a basic knowledge of French is required.

For further information on the sites apply to the above address enclosing an International Reply Coupon.

SOLIDARITÉS JEUNESSES
10 rue du 8 mai 1945, 75010 Paris; ☎ +33 (0)1 48 00 09 05; fax +33 (0)1 42 46 49 32; e-mail workcamp@solidaritesjeunesses.org; www.solidaritesjeunesses. org
SJ organises international workcamps in France and cooperates with more than 70 organisations in around 55 countries. They exchange volunteers with these organisations. Volunteers are placed on workcamps, projects linked to the environment, renovation, construction or social work. Volunteers are placed in groups of up to 15 people of different nationalities. SJ receives about 1,300 volunteers annually and sends about 700 abroad.

Workcamps (short or long-term) are open to anyone. Volunteers work for five or six hours a day and spend the rest of the time on leisure activities. As well as manual and social work volunteers can also work in SJ offices or local centres.

The camps usually last three weeks and most are during summer though there is a year round programme of projects. Volunteers are typically aged 18-30, but there exist workcamps for 15-18 year-olds, and there is no upper age limit. There is a registration fee which is payable in advance to cover food, accommodation and insurance and the budget for leisure activities. Pocket money and travel costs are at the volunteers' expense. Volunteers who are interested can go on training schemes for those who wish to work in developing countries or conflict zones. There are also regular seminars and leader training sessions.

Volunteers from abroad usually apply to a partner organisation in their own country and not to SJ in France. In the UK these include YAP UK (☎01983-752557 and Concordia (☎01273-422218).

UNION REMPART (Pour la Rehabilitation Et l'entretien des Monuments et du Patrimonie Artistique)
1 Rue des Guillemites, 75004 Paris, France; ☎ +33-1 42 71 96 55; fax +33-1 47 71 73 00; e-mail monpert@rempart.com; www.rempart.com
Over 150 workcamps are operated by REMPART in every part of France. About 4,000 volunteers are employed each year to restore and maintain châteaux, churches, villages and the old quarters of cities which are of unique historical or cultural value. REMPART strives to revivify rather than merely preserve ancient buildings and sites. Another of their aims is to remain sensitive to the temperament and requirements of the local community. Volunteers are accepted for weekend workcamps and for spring and summer vacation projects; the usual minimum length of stay is 15 days.

Participants must pay about 7 euros per day for food and accommodation in cabins or tents. For people whose tastes, studies or professional aspirations have prompted an interest in archaeology, architecture or the history of art and ecology, the association organises courses which provide an opportunity to learn the practical techniques of restoration.

Volunteers of all nationalities are welcome, although knowledge of some French would be an asset. The minimum age is generally 13, but is set at 16 or 18 for more difficult jobs. There is no upper age limit.

Applications and enquiries should be sent to the above address.

Germany, Switzerland and Austria

CAMPHILL AM BODENSEE
Heimsonderschule und Hof Brachenreuthe, 88662 Germany; ☎ +49 (0)7551 8007-0; fax +49 7551 8007-50; e-mail brachenreuthe@t-online.de; www. brachenreuthe.de
The Heimsonderschule Brachenreuthe is a boarding school for about 75 mentally disabled children (ages 4-17) operating in a village-like framework in common with other Camphill villages. The children, staff and their families, the teachers and trainees all live and work together. The work and life there is based on the anthroposophical teachings of Rudolph Steiner.

Volunteers should be minimum age 19, in good health and with a working knowledge of the German language. Volunteers help with caring for the children (dressing, washing, feeding and organising leisure activities) as well as helping with the housework. A stay of at least six months is preferred though shorter and longer periods are also possible at any time of year except summer (July and August) when the school is closed. A good time to start is from the end of August. continuing to the end of July the following year. Volunteers receive monthly pocket money plus board, accommodation and social security.

EU nationals should apply in writing and state the length of their availability.

FRIEDENSDORF INTERNATIONAL (Peace Village International)
Aktion Friedensdorf e.V., Lanterstrasse 21, 46539 Dinslaken, Germany; ☎ +49 (0)2 06 44 97 40; fax +49 (0)2 06 44 97 49 99; e-mail info@friedensdorf. de; www.friedensdorf.de
Peace Village International takes up wounded children from war and crisis areas for medical treatment in European hospitals. After the appropriate medical treatment, the children live in the Peace Village institution in Oberhausen for rehabilitation until they return to their native countries and to their families.

Volunteers are required all year round to take care of the children in the Peace Village. Duties include alll kinds of day care occupations, such as helping them during meals, toiletting, changing clothes etc. Applicants of all nationalities are welcome. Basic knowledge of German is necessary. Experience as a social worker is desirable. The minimum placement is three months. Accommodation and board are provided. Other costs have to be borne by the applicants (such as travel costs, health insurance and so on). The minimum age is 18 years and the volunteer must be in good health and free from infectious illness.

Applications should be sent to Nadine Schulz at the above address.

GRUPPO VOLONTARI DELLA SVIZZERA ITALIANA
CP 12, 6517 Arbedo, Switzerland; ☎ +41 (0)79 3540161 (NATEL); 091-8574520 (office); fax 071-6829272; e-mail Fmari@vtx.ch; www.adonet.org
The GVSI is a voluntary group consisting of adults and young people from the Italian part of Switzerland as well as foreign volunteers, which organises relief programmes in crisis-struck areas and work camps and activities for the handicapped.

Volunteers are provided with accommodation in a house in one of the villages and help with normal tasks within the community such as helping the aged, cutting wood and working in the stables and orchards. Participants also share daily tasks such as cleaning and cooking. Most volunteers stay in workcamps run from the end of June until September; they must be at least 18 years of age, adaptable hardworking, and must pay their own travel costs.

For more information on GVSI write to the above address.

IJGD (Internationale Jugendgemeinschaftsdienste Bundesverein eV – Gesellschaft fur Internationale und Politische Bildnung)
Kaiserstr. 43, 53113, Bonn 1, Germany; ☎ +49 228-2280 00; fax +49 228-2280024; www.ijgd.de
IJGD organises a number of international work camps and workshops in Germany that last between two and four weeks. The projects include renovating educational centres, assisting with city recreational activities and conservation work. They take place around Easter and from June to the end of September.

Around 1,800 volunteers take part in these projects every year. Participants should be aged between 16 and 26, and able to do physical work. Food, accommodation and insurance are provided but participants must cover their own travel expenses.

Those interested should contact the IJGD at the above address.

INVOLVEMENT VOLUNTEERS – DEUTSCHLAND
Volksdorfer Strasse 32, 22081 Hamburg, Germany; ☎ +49-40 41269450; e-mail ivgermany@volunteering.org.au
Involvement Volunteers enables people to participate in voluntary activities related to conservation, environmental research, archaeology, history or social welfare. Individual placements or Team Task placements run for 2-12 weeks, some with free accommodation and food, others costing up to £34 per week. Volunteers need to understand and speak some English. Individual placements and/or Team Tasks are available in Germany; in addition, German applicants are placed in Australia, California, Fiji, Hawaii, India, New Zealand, Thailand and the Lebanon.

Involvement Volunteers – Deutschland is a non profit organisation which charges a fee of approximately £200 to cover administration costs. For volunteers coming to Germany, this fee includes travel and visa advice, arrival advice for suitable accommodation and transport from the airport, and a communication base for the visit.

For further information please contact the above address.

LANDDIENST-ZENTRALSTELLE
Mühlegasse 13, Postfach 728, 8025 Zürich, Switzerland; ☎ +41 (0)1 261 44 88; fax +41 (0)1 261 44 32; e-mail admin@landdienst.ch; www.landdienst.ch
The Landdienst-Zentralestelle was started over 50 years ago to enable farmers in Switzerland to receive volunteer helpers from Switzerland and abroad to help with busy times like harvests. Every year thousands of young Swiss help on farms throughout Switzerland. The annual total of volunteers from abroad is about 600.

Volunteers should be aged at least 17 and the upper limit is around 25 (but may be flexible). A basic knowledge of German, French or Italian is necessary. It is easier to place volunteers in the German-speaking areas. There is an inscription fee. Volunteers make their own travel arrangements. The farmers provide board and lodging and a daily allowance. Sundays are free. The minimum period of work is three weeks and the maximum two months anytime from March to October.

Further details can be obtained from the above address.

MARKUS GEMEINSCHAFT e.V.
Hauptstrasse 1, 06577 Hautaroda, Germany; ☎ +49 (0)34673-736910; fax +49 (0)34673-736930; e-mail verein@gutshof-hauteroda; www.gutshof-hauteroda.de

Markus Gemeinshaft is part of the worldwide Camphill Communities for the handicapped. 15-20 volunteers are taken on annually to help with farm work, gardening, housework with handicapped people. If skilled they can work in the bakery and marketing and guest-house. No other skills or qualifications are insisted upon but a driving licence and knowledge of German are welcome as is an openness towards handicapped people and biological farming. Applicants must be in good physical and mental health with no infectious diseases. Length of stay is normally 3 months at any time of year. Longer stays require a work permit for those resident outside the EU. Garden and farm work is usually in summer only. Volunteers get free board and lodging and about €75 pocket money. They need to arrange their own health insurance.

Applications direct to the above address.

NORDDEUTSCHE JUDEND IM INTERNATIONALEN GEMEIN-SCHAFTSDIENST) NIG e.V.
Gerberbruch 13A, 18055 Rostock, Germany; ☎ +49-381 4922914; fax +49-381 4922914; e-mail NigeV@aol.com

NIG was started by the students of Rostock University in 1990 for the purpose of supporting important and urgent work for environmental and nature protection, maintenance of monuments and social projects in north-eastern Germany, in cases where local financial, material and personal means are not sufficient. Another aim is to bring together young people from all over the world and offer the chance to learn about different countries and people, their problems and to co-operate. NIG has exchange partners with 40 organisations worldwide.

About 400 volunteers are placed in Germany annually. Camps include archaeology, agriculture, cultural projects, construction, environmental projects, renovation, teenage camps, work with children, mentally and physically disabled and study programmes. The camp-language is English but German is needed for those working in children's summer camps. Camps last about three weeks and food and accommodation are provided.

A full list of camps is published annually and is available from the above address.

OPEN HOUSES NETWORK
Goetheplatz 9B, D-99423 Weimar, Germany; ☎ +49 (0)3643 50 23 90; fax +49 (0)3643 85 11 17; e-mail info@openhouses.de

Open Houses Network is a non-profit organisation working in the field of the preservation and restoration of historic monuments in Eastern Germany. About 100 volunteers are recruited each year to help with all kinds of work on the construction sites as well as managing other volunteer groups.

Volunteers are needed from 2 weeks to 6 months, primarily from May to October but positions can be found all year round. Applicants should have a basic knowledge of

English or German. Accommodation and food are provided free of charge.
Applications to the above address.

PRO INTERNATIONAL
Bahnhofstr. 26A, 35037 Marburg/Lahn, Germany; ☎ +49 (0)6421-65277; fax +49 (0)6421-64407; e-mail pro-international@lahn.net; www.pro-international.de
This organisation seeks to rebuild broken relationships between individuals and peoples by the promotion and encouragement of contact between young people from all over the world. To this end, workcamps, seminars and holiday courses are organised in Germany. About 400 volunteers per year participate in these workcamps. Volunteers may work as child-minders or manual workers, while others take part in activities connected with handicapped children, or the environment.

What actually happens in a work camp is dependent largely on the individual volunteer. Applicants of all nationalities are welcome as the camps are intended to be international. It is advisable, however, that applicants should have knowledge of English (or German for camps working with children). Volunteers must be aged between 16 and 26, although child-minders must be aged over 18. Camps are held at Easter and between June and October and the length of time for which volunteers are normally required is two to three weeks. The participation fee is €65, but meals and accommodation are free of charge. The Easter and summer programmes are published in November.

Applicants should contact a cooperating organisation in their own country, in the UK this is Concordia. Alternatively, send an international reply coupon to the above address.

WWOOF AUSTRIA
Einödhofweg 48, 8042 Graz, Austria; tel/fax 0316-464951; ☎ +43 8463-82270; e-mail wwoof.welcome@telering.at; www.wwoof.welcome.at.tf
WWOOF is a worldwide organisation of organic farms which take volunteer workers. Volunteers at WWOOF Austria are required to take part in a cultural exchange where you live and help a farming family, learning about organic farming methods in the process. WWOOF work is available on more than 120 farms. Movement between farms is possible. Board and accommodation will be provided, but not wages. Applicants from outside the European Union must secure their own travel insurance and pay for their own travel. In Austria they are covered by an insurance against accidents. A year's membership for WWOOF Austria costs approximately €20 plus two international reply coupons from your post office. Membership includes a list of Austrian organic farmers looking for work-for-keep helpers.

For more information contact Hildegard Gottlieb at the above address.

Scandinavia

APØG - work on organic farms in Norway
Elias Hofgaardsgt. 43, 2318 Hamar, Norway; ☎ +47 62 53 36 16; fax +47 62 53 36 17; e-mail biodynfo@frisurf.no; www.oikos.no
The aim of APØG is to establish contact between organic farmers in need of helping hands and youth seeking work or experience on an organic farm. Young people are

given the chance of gaining experience of running an organic farm and through active participation learn about the ideology of organic agriculture. At present 39 farms are registered with APØG and volunteers participate in all types of farm work such as attending to sheep, haymaking, maintenance, restoration of mountain pasture, preparation of herbs, vegetables, smoking meat, handmilking, making cheese, felling trees and making fences. Work varies from farm to farm and is dependent on the season in which the volunteer is working. Similarly the skills required depend on each individual farm. Placements can be for any length of time from two weeks to one year. Some farms provide food, accommodation and pocket money, others just provide board and lodging.

A booklet in which the details of the 39 farms are listed is available at the above address for £10. Applications should be made direct to the owner of the farm at which you wish to work. Non-EU nationals should obtain a Norwegian work permit from the Norwegian Embassy in their country. EU nationals can obtain a permit after arrival in Norway. You can get more information by e-mail or telephone.

ATLANTIS YOUTH EXCHANGE
Kirgegata 32, 0153 Oslo, Norway; tel/fax +47 22 47 71 79; e-mail post@atlantis-u.no; www.atlantis-u.no
Atlantis is a non-profit foundation for international youth exchange, recruiting about 400 young people each year to work in Norway on the Working Guest Programme. Working Guests stay with Norwegian families, and although much of the work is agricultural, volunteers may also be involved with the day-to-day running of the household and helping with the children. The programme is quite energetic and there are opportunities for travel to Northern Norway. The minimum stay is four weeks, the maximum is normally three months. Families tend to prefer that the Working Guests stay for at least eight weeks.

Volunteers do not require any special skills, but farm experience is an advantage. Most Norwegians speak English so knowledge of Norwegian is not compulsory though, of course, it is an advantage. The volunteer should be aged 18 to 30 and will require a medical certificate and references. Board and lodging are provided, and pocket money of Kr700 a week is paid for the standard 35-hour working week.

Further details and application forms may be obtained from the above address. There is a registration fee of £100-£200. UK applicants may also apply through Concordia and Americans to Interexchange (161 Sixth Avenue, New York, NY 10013; ☎+1 212 924-0446).

> **Robert Olsen spent a summer as a farm worker on the Atlantis Working Guest scheme**
> *The work consisted of picking fruit and weeds (the fruit tasted bitter). The working day started at 8am and continued till 4pm, when we stopped for the main meal of the day. After that we were free to swim in the sea, borrow a bike to go into town or whatever. I was made to feel very much at home in somebody else's home. The farmer and his daughter were members of a folk dance music band, which was great to listen to. Now and then they entrusted me to look after the house while they went off to play at festivals. Such holidays as these are perhaps the most economical and most memorable possible.*

DANISH DIACONAL YEAR
Diakoni-Året, c/o Dialcouisse Stiftelsen, Peter Bangs Vej 1, 2000 Frederikesberg, Denmark; ☎ +45 3838 4126; fax +45 3887 1492; e-mail dialconiaaret@dialc ouisseu.dk; www.diakoniaaret.dk
Offers young people aged 18-25 to work for nine months as volunteers in Denmark.

Situations include social placements, placements dealing with children and youth, or care placements with handicapped and elderly people. Volunteers receive pocket money, board and lodging.

For more information contact Anne Marie Boile Nielsen, Volunteer co-ordinator at the above address.

FORENINGEN STAFFANSGARDEN
Furugatan 1, 82060 Delsbo, Sweden; ☎ +46 (0)653-16850; fax +46(0)653-10968; e-mail info@staffangarden.com; www.staffansgarden.com
Foreningen Staffansgarden is an anthroposophical Camphill community for mentally disabled adults in Sweden. Between five and ten volunteers work in the community every year. A volunteer can help in many ways, including working in the bakery and the garden, weaving, farming, cooking and cleaning or merely by participating in daily life with the handicapped adults.

Applicants of all nationalities are welcome as long as they have a genuine desire to live communally with other people. The minimum age limit is 19 years and the minimum length of placement is six months, although it would be preferred if volunteers stayed for one year. Applications should be made to Matti Remes at the above address.

HOGGANVIK LANDSBY
5583 Vikedal, Norway; ☎ +47-52 760111; e-mail hogganvik@camphill.no
Hogganvik is one of the Camphill communities located in Norway. It is an integrated community with adults with special needs. Work and free time are combined. Activities include: forestry, gardening, farming (bio-dynamic), woodwork, housework, care of the handicapped. In the summer volunteers can swim, fish, and walk in the mountains. In the winter there is the possibility of skiing.

Volunteers are welcome all year round; in the summer from a few weeks and at other times a year is preferable. Six to eight people are taken on annually. No special qualifications are required but volunteers require a willingness to live a different life-style with many different types of people and a willingness to learn Norwegian. Pocket money, board and lodging, and expenses for exceptional needs are provided.

Applications to the above address.

KANSAINVÄLINEN VAPAAEHTOISTYÖ RY (KVT: Finnish Branch of Service Civil International)
Rauhanasema, Veturitori, 00520 Helsinki, Finland; ☎ +358-9 144408/144418; e-mail kvt@kvtfinland.org; www.kvtfinland.org
KVT aims to promote world peace, cultural understanding, sustainable development and care for the environment. For this KVT and SCI organise voluntary work camps for people over 18 years, aiming to bring people with different backgrounds to work and live together, and in this way to reduce causes of war. KVT has been the Finnish branch since 1981.

KVT sends and receives about 200 volunteers. Globally, SCI exchanges thousands of volunteers every year. International work camps are 2-4 weeks long and the minimum age is 18. A basic knowledge of English is necessary and some camps may need special qualifications. Board and lodging are always provided by the host organisation, and insurance by SCI. Travel expenses and pocket money are not paid.

Non-Finnish volunteers should apply through SCI in their own country (check: www.sciint.org). For the UK see IVS Colchester in this book.

KRISTOFFERTUNET
Hans Collins vei 5, 7053 Ranheim, Norway; ☎ +47 7382 6850; fax +47

7382-6851; e-mai: adm@kristoffertunet.no; www.kristoffertunet.no
Kristoffertunet is an urban community project with adults in need of special care. At the moment there are 30 people living in the community, including volunteers and co-workers with their families. The community consists of three big houses, and work in the houses, the garden, the farm, the weavery, and a pottery workshop. Each house dines together and their are community gatherings for festivals and cultural events. The volunteers take an active part in the shaping of life at Kristoffertunet.

About six volunteers are accepted per year. It is preferred volunteers stay a year but shorter or longer is possible. If not from the EU, volunteers must have a work permit valid for one year and speak English. Volunteers should be motivated to learn Norwegian and experience from/interested in handicrafts, gardening, drama, bio-dynamic farming etc, and must be over 18 years old. Board and lodging are free and pocket money is provided.

Applications direct to the above address.

MELLEMFOLKELIGT SAMVIRKE (MS)
Borgergade 14, 1300 Copenhagen, Denmark; e-mail msworkcamp@ms.dk; www.mstravels.dk
Besides arranging for the volunteering of about 800 Danes in international workcamps abroad every year, MS also organises international workcamps in Denmark and Greenland which are open to foreign volunteers. The main objective of these workcamps is to promote the open and positive cultural meeting between the volunteers and the local inhabitants. The workcamps provide an excellent opportunity for young people from all over the world to live and work together with the locals.

Camps in Denmark consist of an extensive range of projects such as environmental camps, nature conservation work/study camps, social camps etc. Many camps in Denmark are open to disabled persons. In Greenland, the camps are organized in small settlements where the volunteers renovate buildings and carry out tasks with local inhabitants.

The minimum age limit for participation is 18 (20 in Greenland) and the volunteers must be willing to spend two to three weeks in a camp during July and August. Food, accommodation and insurance are provided but the volunteers must pay their own travelling expenses.

Applications from British people should be made through UNA-IYS in Cardiff, or IVS.

SOLBORG VILLAGE
Solborg, 3520 Jevnater, Norway; ☎ +47 32132480; fax +47 32132020; e-mail solborg@camphill.no; www.solborg.com
Solborg is a member of the worldwide community of Camphill villages where mentally disabled adults live together with co-workers helping run the community doing indoor and outdoor tasks where ever needed. About 30 volunteers a year are accepted by the Village Trust of Norway across Norwegian Camphill communities; Solborg can accept short-term volunteers in summer at any time. Solborg volunteers help with workshops, cooking and cleaning in the houses and weaving, woodwork and forestry work. Applicants from non-European Union nations should apply at least 6 months before they wish to start work. Help with arranging visas can be given. Applicants should stay 3 months to a year, and be in good mental and physical health. Full board and lodging are provided plus $150 per month pocket money and medical insurance.
Apply direct to the above address.

STIFTELSEN STJÄRNSUND
770 71 Stjärnsund, Sweden; ☎ +46 (0)225 800 01; fax +46 (0)225 800 05;

e-mail fridhempost@hotmail.com; www.frid.nu
Stiftelsen Stjärnsund is a centre for spiritual development that aims to bring a holistic view into everyday life. It is a non-profit organisation, politically and religiously independent. The centre is rurally situated in the beautiful village of Stjärnsund, 2 hours by train from Stockholm. The centre runs courses in body awareness, Tai Chi, meditation, music, self realisation etc. The centre has Bed & Breakfast, a garden cultivating vegetables and a vegetarian lunch-restaurant.

The volunteer working guests take part in the daily life of the centre. Normally, tasks involve helping in the kitchen, cleaning and work in the garden cultivating vegetables. For the first week the voluntary guest work 20 hours and pay about £35. After that an agreement can be made to stay a shorter or longer period to work 30 hours a week with free board and lodging.

THE SWALLOWS IN DENMARK
Osterbrogade 49, 2100 Copenhagen O, Denmark; ☎ +45-35261747; fax +45-35381746; e-mail svalerne@svalerne.dk; www.svalerne.dk
The Swallows in Denmark is a non profit organisation which provides financial support for grass roots organisations in Bangladesh and Tamil Nadu, India by collecting and selling second hand goods and by selling sustainably produced handicrafts from developing countries. During the summer, the Swallows sometimes conduct workcamps for international volunteers to assist with collecting and selling second hand goods. There are no camps planned for 2005 but they hope to organise them again soon. The work involves collecting, sorting and selling paper, books, clothes, furniture, electronics and household goods.

The camp is both a summer income generating activity and an international get-together for people, aimed at increasing understanding on cultural diversities by bringing together people from different nationalities. Volunteers have to cover their own travel costs and daily spending money. Food and accommodation are provided by the Swallows. The Swallows in Denmark is part of the Emmaus International Community founded by Abbé Pierre.

Spain, Portugal, Italy and Cyprus

AGAPE CENTRO ECUMENICO
10060 Prali, Turin, Italy; ☎ +39 (0)1 21 80 75 14; e-mail office@agapecentr oecumenico.org; www.agapecentroecumenico.org
Agape is an ecumenical conference centre in the Italian Alps for national and international meetings about (political movement, theology, feminism, gay and lesbianism issues) for adults and children. It was built by an international group of volunteers between 1947 and 1951 as an act of reconciliation after the war, and is sponsored by the World Council of Churches. Each summer more than 15 volunteers (Italians and foreigners) help the permanent staff to run the centre which is especially active over the summer. Volunteers are expected to give 6-7 hours a day, six days a week. Stays of 3-5 weeks are usual during the period June to September. Shorter times may be possible at other times of year e.g. Christmas and Easter. The jobs to be done include working in the kitchen and laundry, cleaning, running the coffee bar, babysitting and general maintenance work. Applicants must be aged at least 18 and would find knowledge of Italian and

other languages an advantage. Free board and lodging (hostel type) are provided, but participants must cover their own travel costs to and from the centre.

For further details contact the Secretary at the above address.

ASSOCIAZONE CULTURALE LINGUISTA EDUCATIONAL (ACLE)
via Roma 54, 18038 San Remo, Italy; tel/fax +39-0184 506070; e-mail info@acle.org;www.acle.org

ACLE is looking for volunteers to work on the restoration of several once derelict medieval houses in a small mountain village called Baiardo. Situated on a hill top 23km from the bustling coastal town of Sanremo, Baiardo is the perfect place to work and relax. The houses are being renovated with a view to running Italian culture courses and as a retreat for those who need it most. The town is idyllic with winding cobbled streets and unparalleled views across the French Alps. The houses have a rustic charm and are set on 2000-year-old foundations.

Volunteers are required year round, but particularly in spring and autumn. Basic accommodation is provided. There are beds, fully functioning bathrooms and kitchens. You'll need your own work clothes and sleeping bag. The work can be physically demanding and may include landscaping, digging, plaster/paint stripping, clearing rubble, shifting furniture and cleaning. Volunteers are responsible for their flights, food and medical insurance. E-mail for further details.

ACLE also recruits Theatrino actors and English camp tutors – see the website for more information.

CENTRO CAMUNO DI STUDI PREISTORICI
Via G. Marconi 7, 25044 Capo di Ponte (Brescia), Italy; ☎ +39 364-42091; fax +39 364-42572; e-mail info@ccsp.it and ccspreist@tin.it; web www.ccsp. it and www.harkarkom.com

The Centro is a research institute concentrating on the study of prehistory and tribal art, mainly in Asia and Africa and run by a non-profit making cultural association. Up to ten volunteers and apprentices a year are accepted to participate in the exploration of sites, to help with laboratory work, research, mapping, graphics, editing, translation, bibliographical work and computerising data both for local research and for expeditions abroad. Fieldwork in the Alpine area takes place mostly in the summer, but the centre operates throughout the year.

Volunteers are taken on for an initial period of three months. Board and accommodation are not provided but assistance is given in finding basic accommodation are available at a modest cost; limited places are available in a shared house, and assistance can be given in finding alternatives. A few scholarships are available; candidates are selected after the initial trial period of three months. Volunteers must be aged over 18 and be deeply interested in archaeology, tribal art, anthropology or the history of religions, but formal qualifications are not necessary. Knowledge of languages, of computer programmes and/or editorial work are welcome.

Those interested should contact the above address for further details.

DEYA ARCHAEOLOGICAL MUSEUM AND RESEARCH CENTRE
Deya, Mallorca, Balleares, Spain; ☎ +34 971-639001; fax +34 971 634152.

DAMARC has been excavating in Mallorca for over thirty-five years. Volunteers join a team of specialists and other participants from the USA and various European countries for two-week sessions. Participants work together in the field and laboratory and live together in the Research Centre.

Accommodation is provided in dormitories of six to eight bunk beds. Meals are home-cooked and participants help in preparation and household chores on a rotational basis. Volunteers must be students of archaeology or mature persons with an interest in expanding their learning and experience in prehistory, especially that of the Balearic Islands. DAMARC is not able to pay for the volunteer's travel costs or room and board. Volunteers pay £450 to participate in any of the two-week excavations, covering room, board and tuition. Participants should have medical and travel insurance for Spain. Volunteers must also be physically fit.

Those interested should contact Earthwatch in the UK (www.uk.earthwatch.org), or the USA (☎800 776 0188), for application details. Graduate students working for credits can apply to DEYA direct.

ENGLISHTOWN
Eduardo Dato, 3, 1ˢᵗ Floor, 28010 Madrid, Spain; ☎ +34 915914840; fax +91 44 58782; www.vaughanvillage.com
Englishtown is a unique project set up in an abandoned Spanish village, which has been transformed into a village 'stocked' with native English-speaking volunteers who live together with an equal number of Spanish people for an intensive week of activities, sports, games and group dynamics. The English native volunteers exchange conversation for room and board. All they have to do is cover their travel expenses to Madrid and arrive with a helpful spirit to chat and exchange stories with the Spaniards for the duration of the programme. Aside from helping the Spaniards make a 'quantum leap' in their English communication skills, Englishtown offers the change to learn about Spanish culture and make lifelong friends. Since its inception in 2001, over 50 programmes have attracted over 1600 English-speaking volunteers and Spaniards. Demand is so great that a second venue has been opened. A cross-section of English speakers so far has included retired Irish farmers, Canadian civil servants, a Los Angeles firewoman and Australian business people.

ESPAÇO T ASSOCIATION FOR SUPPORT AND COMMUNITY INTEGRATION
Avenida de França, 256, Centro Comercial Capitolio, salas 5, 12, 22 e 23, 4050-276 Porto, Portugal; ☎ +351 (0)2 830 24 32 or +351 (0)2 830 55 93; e-mail espacot@espacot.pt; www.espacot.pt
Espaço cares for people with multiple problems: physical, psychological and social, providing them with artistic activities including photography, drama, painting, sculpture, physical education, dance, Tai Chi and so on.

About 50 volunteers are taken on annually to help with these cultural activities. At present volunteers are taken on as needed at any time and for variable periods. There are no funds to pay or house volunteers and so they must be able to fund themselves. Applicants should speak Portuguese, Spanish or Italian and have some artistic experience. They must have no criminal record, and be in possession of a national passport/identity card and references.

Enquiries should be addressed to the President, at the above address.

INSTITUTO DE LA JUVENTUD 'SERVICIO VOLUNTARIO INTERNACIONAL'
José Ortega y Gasset 71, 28006 Madrid, Spain; fax +34 91 309 30 66.
This organisation arranges summer workcamps in Spain which involve archaeological excavations, the reconstruction of monuments, the preservation of the countryside, building work, nature studies and community work. About 800 volunteers take part in the camps each year which last from two to three weeks. There are no restrictions or

special skills required. Board and lodging are provided.

Those interested should apply to the address above, or if possible to an affiliated organisation in their own country. Internationale Begegnung in Gemeinschaftsdiensten e V, 7252 Weil der Stadt Marklingen, Haupstrasse 64, Germany; Concordia, 28 Rue du Pont Neuf, 775001 Paris, France; United Nations Association (Wales), Welsh Centre for International Affairs, Temple of Peace, Cathays Park, Cardiff CF1 3AP.

LIPU – ITALIAN LEAGUE FOR THE PROTECTION OF BIRDS
via Trento, 49-43100 Parma, Italy; ☎ +39 (0)521 273043; fax +39 (0)521 273419; e-mail info@lipu.it; www.lipu.it

LIPU is a member of the worldwide association Birdlife International. Its national head office is in Parma and there are 100 divisions throughout Italy which recruit volunteers. Paid staff work in the head office and in the 50 LIPU infrastructures (among oasis and recovery centres).

About 350-400 volunteers are engaged annually to work on the camps in areas of conservation, research and data collection, surveillance of nesting sites of endangered species, fire surveillance, environmental education, animal recovery in specialised centres, management of protected areas. A further 1,000 volunteers work as counsellors, check clerks, voluntary guards, division activists and as managers of oasis locations. Placements last from one week to one month during the periods April to October but the situation is being reviewed to include a wider range of possibilities, and potential overseas programmes with other member organisations are also being looked into.

Skills required by the volunteer depend on the type of work for which they volunteer. Volunteers must speak a language known to the camp tutor, English is generally fine although a knowledge of Italian would be advantageous. Minimum age 18. In some cases volunteers have their board and accommodation provided, in others they must be self-funding.

Applications to the Promotion Office: Silvia Ferrario (☎ +39 (0)2 2900 4366; fax +39 (0)2 653367; e-mail silviaferrario@lipu.it).

M.E.E.R.   E.V.   (MAMIFEROS   ENCUENTROS   EDUCACIÓN RECONOCIMIENTO)
Germany: Weichselstr. 20, 10247 Berlin, Germany; tel/fax +49-(0)30 82706265; e-mail meer@infocanarias.com; www.m-e-e-r.org

The M.E.E.R. project was founded in 1997 by the environmental engineer Korina Gutsche and biologist Fabian Ritter. It is dedicated to combining whale watching tourism on La Gomera (Canary Islands), with scientific research and education. Three volunteers are required every two weeks throughout the spring (February-June) to assist with: cetacean research aboard whale watching vessels; data inputing; analysing data; cataloguing photo-ID shots of cetaceans; getting involved with public work (events,etc).

A knowledge of English or German is essential and Spanish is very useful. Those with experience in behavioural research and photography are particularly welcome. Volunteers must be in good health and able to swim, a team spirit is vital. Minimum age 18. Accommodation provided.

For further details e-mail meer@infocanarias.com.

PROYECTO AMBIENTAL TENERIFE
c/o 59 St Martins Lane, Covent Garden, London WC2N; e-mail edb@huron. ac.uk; www.interbook.personal/net/delfinc/

Proyecto Ambiental Tenerife organises whale and dolphin conservation and research projects in the Canary Islands at a cost of £95 which includes half board accommodation, project transfers, all training, and funds the projects. There are also projects based in

Tenerife with satellite programmes in La Gomera and El Hierro for which a surcharge is payable. For qualified divers there is a marine habitat survey in Tenerife for which again a surcharge is payable. About 150 volunteers from all over Europe participate in these projects per year. A positive attitude is most essential, and a knowledge of European languages is particularly useful.

For further information on the projects available visit the website or send an SAE (33p stamp) to Proyecto Ambiental Tenerife at the above address. There is also an office in Tenerife (Calle Jose Antonio 13, Arafo, Tenerige; tel/fax 922 510535).

Turkey, Greece and Malta

ARCHELON – Sea Turtle Protection Society of Greece
Solomou 57, GR-10432 Athens, Greece; tel/fax +30 210 5231342; e-mail stps@archelon.gr; www.archelon.gr

The Sea Turtle Protection of Greece (STPS) is a non-profit organisation that runs sea turtle conservation projects in Greece with the assistance of an international contingent of volunteers. Summer field work lasting from early May through to late October is conducted on Zakynthos, Crete and Peloponnesus where the Mediterranean's most important loggerhead nesting beaches are found. At the Sea Rescue Centre, volunteers will have the opportunity to assist our staff in daily treatment of sea turtles that suffer from accidental and deliberate injuries.

350-400 volunteers are engaged annually and receive on-site training and supervision by field leaders and/or experienced project members. They must be prepared to participate in any aspect of the project. Duties are allocated by the field leaders, according to the needs of the project, and include working throughout the night or long hours during the day in the heat. Placements last for a minimum of 4 weeks. There is a greater need for volunteers during the beginning (early May to June) and the end (September to late October) of the projects.

Participants in the projects must be at least 18, able to communicate in English and carry a health insurance policy. Volunteers must be prepared to live a communal life, living and working in both populated and secluded areas, sometimes as members of small teams (5 to 10 persons) and under uncomfortable conditions. Although relevant experience is not necessary, the ability to live and co-operate with people of different cultures and backgrounds is essential. Those with artistic skills, experience in construction or with inflatable boats and/or car drivers or motorbike riders are especially useful. Applicants wanting to carry out research must inform the STPS in advance.

Volunteers stay on designated free camp sites with outdoor basic sanitary and cooking facilities provided; volunteers must bring their own camping gear (sleeping bag, tent, etc). Travel and expenses must be paid by the volunteer and an estimated £6 per day is required to cover basic food needs. A participation fee of 100 euros, (£60/$65), which also covers an 'STPS Volunteer' T-shirt and a one year subscription as an STPS supporter entitling the holder to the STPS newsletter *Turtle Tracks* three times a year, is required; members of STPS Volunteer Club do not need to pay the participation fee.

Applications to the Programme Co-ordinator at the above address; successful applicants will be informed within a month of receipt of their application.

CONSERVATION KORONI
Poste Restante, Koroni 24004, Messinias, Greece; ☎ +30-977 529224; fax +30-725 22779.
Conservation Koroni recruits about 40-50 volunteers annually to help catalogue the numerous species of flora and fauna indigenous to Messinia on the Southern coast of Greece. Volunteers also help with cleaning and monitoring local beaches which are the nesting grounds for loggerhead sea turtles during the summer months.

Volunteers are required for a minimum period of one month between May and October. Minimum age 18. A basic level of health and fitness is required for beach work. A driving licence would be useful, but all that is essentially required is a keen interest in environmental issues and general conservation. Applicants of any nationality are welcome but all participants must be able to communicate in English. Accommodation is provided – usually two to a room in an apartment or house. There is a charge of £100 per month for accommodation.

Applications to the President at the above address.

CONSERVATION VOLUNTEERS GREECE (CVG)
Omirou 15, Kifissia 14562, Athens, Greece; ☎ +30-10 62 31 120; fax +30 10 80 11 489; e-mail cvgpeep@otenet.gr; www.cvgpeep.gr
CVG is a non-profit, non-governmental organisation promoting conservation work and intercultural exchanges between young people from all over the world. Volunteers are invited to participate in international workcamps in remote areas of Greece, whose projects have a strong emphasis on Greek culture. CVG is a member of the Alliance of Voluntary Service Organisations.

Approximately 160 volunteers, aged between 18 and 30, are recruited annually to help with construction and environmental work, animal care, and archaeological projects. Placements are from 15 to 20 days throughout July and August. Volunteers must be able to speak English fluently. Basic accommodation is provided but all other costs are at the volunteer's expense. Travel information to the camps is provided.

Applications should be made to the partner organisation in the country of the applicant's residence; for a list of partner organisations contact the above address or visit www.alliance-network.org.

DIMITRIS PERROTIS COLLEGE OF AGRICULTURAL STUDIES (DPCAS)
The American Farm School, Summer Internship Program (SIIP), PO Box 23 GR. 551 02, Thessaloniki, Greece; ☎ +30-31 471 803; fax +30-31 475 192; e-mail vvergos@afs.edu.gr
The DPCAS in Thessaloniki, Greece, accept students already enrolled in university level programmes in agriculture (or related subjects) an 8 week programme in English during June/July. The programme fuses practical, hands-on experience, classroom and fieldwork, and an introduction to the dynamic and varied world of Greek agriculture. Furthermore, the programme offers a unique introduction to the culture and customs of one of the world's most hospitable countries, Greece. Five weeks of paid supervised agricultural work assignments are carried out in various farm departments. Free accommodation is provided but the cost of prepared meals is deducted from the stipend. Evenings are devoted to learning about the Greek language, culture and dance. Excursions to Mt. Olympus, Meteora and other sites of northern Greece are part of the programme, and participants are encouraged to explore the nearby beautiful beaches of Halkididi and Katerina on their free weekends.

Further information is available from Dr Evangelos Vergos, Dean of the Dimitris

Perrotis College of Agricultural Studies at the above address and contact information. Applications are due by 30 March. Successful applicants will pay a registration fee of US$500 and roundtrip transportation to/from Thessaloniki.

GENÇTUR-International Voluntary Workcamps
Istiklal Cad. Zambak Sok. 15/A Kat: 5 Taksim 34435 Istanbul, Turkey; ☎ +90-212 249 25 15; fax +90-212 249 25 54; e-mail workcamps.in@genctur.com; www.genctur.com
Gençtur organises international voluntary workcamps in small villages and towns involving mainly manual work such as constructing schools, village centres, health care houses, teachers' lodgings, digging water trenches, landscaping projects, environmental development projects etc. Gençtur encourages the participants to have contact with the locals for cultural exchange and uses all occasions to create an international, intercultural atmosphere. The language of the Camp is English. Camps last two weeks with free board and lodging and are organised between June and October. The joining fee is £40. An optional three days' sightseeing in Istanbul is also organised at extra cost. Those interested should apply to the above address, or the partner workcamp organisation in their home country. For further details please send a SAE and an International Reply coupon.

Mary Jelliffe worked in Turkey on a Gençtur workcamp
My workcamp commenced in August. It consisted of digging an irrigation canal from the nearby hills to the village and was located in Central Anatolia. I was told that our camp was the most easterly, since the majority are in Western Turkey. Conditions in our remote village were fairly primitive. We lived in a half-built school-room sleeping on the floor and sharing the daily duties of collecting water and sweeping out the scorpions from under the sleeping bags. The Turkish volunteers were a great asset to the camp: through them we could have far more contact with the villagers and learn more about Turkish culture in general. In fact, I later stayed in Istanbul and Izmir with two of the women volunteers I'd met on the camp.

GREEK DANCES THEATRE
8 Scholiou Street, Plaka, 10558 Athens, Greece; ☎ +30-210 324 4395; fax +30-210 324 4395; e-mail mail@grdance.org; www.grdance.org
The Dora Stratou theatre in Athens is an institution centred around Greek dance. It is both a theatre and a dance company. The theatre, founded in 1953 has 2500 complete traditional Greek costumes, jewellery and other objects and accessories collected from all regions. Its troupe of dancers put on daily displays of dancing and have their own purpose built theatre near the Acropolis.

Volunteers are need for all aspects of theatre and administration all year round for periods of a month or longer. No accommodation or pocket money. Please contact the above address for further information.

GREEK SUMMER-AMERICAN FARM SCHOOL
1133 Broadway, Suite 1625; NY, New York 10010, USA; ☎ +1 212-463 8434; fax +1 212-463 8208; e-mail nyoffice@amerfarm.org; www.afs.edu.gr/
American office of the American Farm School in northern Greece. Summer programme. Provides 6-weeks service to the community. Participants live in rural Greek village and complete a much-needed work project for the village. This usually comprises an outdoor construction project. Applicants of any nationality. Must be at least 18 years old and have

medical certificate of good health signed by a physician. Participant pays a programme fee and air fare. Accommodation is provided on the project. Apply direct to the above address or *Dimitris Perrotis College of Agricultural Studies*, also in this section.

MALTA YOUTH HOSTELS ASSOCIATION
MYHA Head Office, 17 Triq Tal-Borg, Pawla PLA 06, Malta; ☎ +356-21693957 (only 4pm-5pm Mon.Tues.Wed); e-mail myha@keyworld.net
MYHA Short-Term Camp: gives people the opportunity to learn about the country while spending some of their time doing voluntary work. This involves spending a minimum of 3 hours a day doing office work, building, decorating and administration work in Malta's youth hostels and youth and charitable institutions. Age limits 16-30. To apply send three international reply coupons or $2. Applications to be received three months before camp starts. Temporary, free accommodation to those needing social assistance.

NOAH'S ARK ANIMAL SHELTER
PO Box 241, Agia Triada, Akrotiri, Chania TK73100, Crete, Greece; e-mail noahsark@chania.zzn.com; www.chaniascape.net/noahsark.htm
Noah's Ark Animal Shelter, located on the island of Crete, cares for about 700 stray animals comprising about 550 dogs, 100 cats, 12 donkeys and all kinds of birds. Noah's Ark operates on donations from animal lovers, occasional grants from foreign animal associations, and donated food from hotels and tavernas in the summertime. All animals are vaccinated, neutered and tattooed on arrival. Re-homing is done wherever possible to private homes and animal welfare associations in Germany, Sweden, Switzerland, etc. and some in Crete.

About 80 volunteers, aged 18 to 50, are recruited annually including some qualified veterinarians. Duties include nursing, feeding, cleaning, manual work around the grounds, waste food collection, and assistance with rescues. The work is very hot and tiring, sometimes strenuous, and can be emotionally upsetting due to the circumstances in which some of the animals may be found. Volunteers work approximately 8 hours a day, five days per week. Placements last anything from one week to one year; it is advisable to spend a few weeks at the Shelter before planning a long-term stay. More volunteers are required in the winter as most come in the summer – winters can be very wet and windy, summers very hot.

Applicants of any nationality are welcome but must be able to communicate in either English, German or Greek. Those with or without experience with animals are required. Accommodation is available in holiday villas at a daily rate; for long-term volunteers (three months or more) the Shelter tries to provide accommodation.

Applications to Silke Wrobel at the above address.

SKYROS HOLISTIC HOLIDAYS
92 Prince of Wales Road, London NW5 3NE; ☎020-7267 4424; fax 020-7284 3063; e-mail connect@skyros.com
Skyros runs a holistic holiday community on Skyros island in Greece. About 8 volunteers, aged 21-35, are recruited annually to help with site maintenance and work as mechanics, handymen, chefs and nurses (the last two must be qualified). Volunteers are recruited for periods of three months from May to July and August to October. Postgraduates, qualified registered nurses, trained and qualified chefs, or musicians, and fluent Greek speakers are needed. Applicants must be in good health. Accommodation in bamboo huts, full board, £55 per week, and free tuition on courses are provided.

Applications to The Personnel Manager at the above address.

United States of America

Conservation, the Environment, Heritage

AMERICAN HIKING SOCIETY VOLUNTEER PROGRAMME
P.O. Box, 20160, Washington DC 20041-2160, USA; ☎ +1 301 565 6704; fax +1 301 565 6714; e-mail info@americanhiking.org; www.americanhiking. org
AHSVP publishes the *AHS Hiker's Information Center*, the online resource for volunteer opportunities. The *Hiker's Information Center* is an extensive database of volunteer opportunities, trail descriptions, local trail clubs, National Trails Day events and Horse Trails Caucus members around the USA. For more information contact the Membership & Marketing Manager at the above address or visit the website.

APPALACHIAN MOUNTAIN CLUB-Volunteer Trail Opportunities
PO Box 298, Gorham, NH 03581, USA; ☎ +1 603-4662721; fax +1 603-466 2720; e-mail tmrobinson@outdoors.org; www.outdoors.org
The Appalachian Mountain Club is a non-profit-making recreation and conservation group which is responsible for over 1,400 miles of trail in the north-east of the United States, including over 350 miles of the Appalachian National Scenic Trail. Every summer the club sponsors three unique weekly volunteer based camps in NH, MA and ME. They are open to individuals, families and other groups. Volunteers work in teams and are given training and tools to enable them to undertake all types of trail, shelter and other work. Over 500 volunteers participate annually.

Volunteers must be at least 16 years old, in good health, willing to learn and work hard with others and have backpacking experience. All volunteers must have their own accident insurance. Room and board are provided at a cost of US$55 upwards or more, per week, to the volunteer.

For further information contact the North Country Volunteer Co-ordinator at the above address.

APPALACHIAN TRAIL CONFERENCE
Volunteer Trail Crew Program, P O Box 10, Newport, VA 24128, USA; ☎ +1 540 544-7388; fax +1 540-544-6880; e-mail crews@appalachian trail.org; www.appalachiantrail.org
The ATC coordinates the management and maintenance of the Appalachian Trail which is a footpath conceived in about 1921, of more than 2,160 miles, which winds through fourteen states from Maine to Georgia in the eastern United States.

Each year over 400 volunteers help with trail construction and rehabilitation. Good physical fitness is essential and an ability to work hard, sometimes under adverse weather conditions. Periods of work range from one to six weeks from May to October. Accommodations (tents in the field) and meals are provided for volunteers. Enjoy the camaraderie with people of all ages, from all walks of life, from all over the country and from around the world.

Applicants can be anyone age 18 or older. Please be sure to check with the American Embassy office nearest you, about the likelihood of obtaining a tourist visa before submitting an application for the crew program. Once you have discussed the situation with the embassy and received an affirmation that you may receive a tourist visa, you may submit your crew program application. Upon request, ATC will send you a confirmation letter (if you have been selected) that you may present at the embassy.

For further information contact the above address

ARCOSANTI
HC 74, Box 4136, Mayer, Arizona 86333, United States of America; ☎ +1 520 632-7135; fax +1 520 632-6229; e-mail arcosanti@aol.com; www. arcosanti.org/

Arcosanti is a prototype city based on ecological urban design using the principles of architect Paolo Soleri which combine architecture and ecology and utilise solar energy. Student volunteers are invited to take part in a five-week Arcosanti Workshop. The first week is an intensive introduction to 'arcology' (architecture and ecology), and the remaining weeks are a hands on experience involving construction, recycling, site maintenance and cultural events and their preparation.

About 10-20 students take part in each workshop of which there are ten throughout the year. The capacity for each workshop is 50 so more volunteers are needed. Volunteers must be aged at least 18. Relevant experience in architecture and practical skills such as carpentry, building construction, model making, welding, ceramics, landscaping, agriculture etc. is helpful, but not a pre-requisite. The cost is $450 for the seminar, plus $87.50 per week to cover board and lodging. After the five week workshop volunteers may be considered for additional resident volunteer work for which accommodation will be provided free but volunteers pay for their own meals.

Applications to be sent to the above address.

CAPE PERPETUA INTERPRETIVE CENTER
PO Box 274, Yachats, OR 97498, USA; ☎ +1 541 547-3289; fax +1 541 547-4616; e-mail arand@fs.fed.us; www.orcoast.com/capeperpetua

The Cape Perpetua Interpretive Center whose scenic area spans 2700 acres along the central Oregon coast, is managed by the USDA Forest Services. A wide variety of volunteer opportunities are available although the Center particularly needs: interpretive naturalists – this involves helping with guided nature walks and with school group field trips in the autumn and spring for one or two days a week; living history and living interpretation participants (involves dressing in a costume and becoming that character for a 15-30 minute programme) and Cape Perpetua hosts. Other projects at the Center requiring volunteers include: landscaping, construction, carpentry, maintenance, exhibit work and design, interpretive materials, organisation, photography, writing, funding development, computer skills, and marketing. Placements are from June to September; training takes place between March and April.

Volunteers must be able to communicate well in English, adapt to situations, be flexible and self-motivated, and be able to work with limited supervision. Some knowledge of the environment and ecosystems is also required. As the Center is located in a remote area with hilly terrain it is recommended that applicants are mobile. At times rigorous walking or maintenance is required. Accommodation and a $5 per day reimbursement for lunch are provided.

Applications to the above address.

CARETTA RESEARCH PROJECT
PO Box 9841, Savannah, GA 31412-9841, USA; ☎ +1 912 447-8655; fax +1 912 447-8656; e-mail WassawCRP@aol.com

The Caretta Research Project is a hands-on research and conservation project involving the threatened loggerhead sea turtles that nest on Wassaw National Wildlife Refuge, Georgia, USA. The work is variable depending on time of season and turtle activity. Mid-May through to mid-August is egg-laying season and participants spend each night patrolling 6 miles of beach looking for nesting female turtles. The turtles are then tagged, all related data is recorded, and the nests are protected either by relocation into a hatchery or by screening so racoons cannot raid them. Late July through to September is hatching season and participants monitor nests and escort emerging hatchlings down the beach and into the surf. The work is hard but rewarding.

Approximately 95 volunteers are recruited annually to take part in all aspects of the project's work. The placements last one week, from Saturday to Saturday throughout mid-May to mid-September; some have signed up for three week placements but one week is the normal duration. Participants must be at least 16 years old (the oldest so far was 78) and in good health as they may be expected to walk long distances. A positive mental attitude is of particular importance: the project requires upbeat, adaptable people who can cheerfully endure close quarters, rain storms, insects, and the heat and humidity of a week in the subtropics without air conditioning. Previous volunteers have come from all over the USA, Canada and Europe. The cost of the placement is $550 per person per week and covers full training, transportation to and from the island, all food and basic but comfortable housing.

Applications to the above address from 2 January and the Centre advises that most years, 75% of places were filled in the first 2 days of booking.

CLINIC FOR THE REHABILITATION OF WILDLIFE
PO Box 150 Sanibel, Florida 33957, USA; ☎ + 1 239 472 3644; fax +1 472 8544; e-mail crowclinic@aol.com; website www.crowclinic.org

CROW clinic which comprises a fully-equipped wildlife hospital in a twelve and a half acre sanctuary, relies almost entirely on volunteers for all funding, transport of patients, rescues, event coordination and the majority of grounds and clinic work. In large part due to volunteers, CROW is able to receive and treat over 3,600 wildlife patients annually.

CROW has about 150 volunteers who work at cleaning and cage maintenance, diet preparation for patients, baby bird care, releases and occasional rescues, possibly infant mammal care, assisting clinic staff with treatments, autopsies, clerical and administration work and so on. Volunteers should be able to tolerate physical labour in often hot and humid conditions and be able to stay for a minimum of 4 weeks. Volunteers have to pay for their own meals but housing is provided, as are washer/dryer services and linens. Students and non-students welcome.

Applications to the Volunteer Co-ordinator at the above address.

COLONIAL NATIONAL HISTORICAL PARK
PO Box 210, Yorktown, Va 23690, USA; ☎ + 1 757 898-2414; fax +1 757 898-6346; e-mail Chris–Bryce@nps.gov; www.nps.gov/colo

The Colonial National Historical Park recruits about 60 volunteers a year mainly in the Historical Interpretation and Preservation area, staffing the information desk, giving visitors a brief overview of what they can do on their visit, staffing two historic houses, and giving walking tours of the battlefield and town. Placements last from three months to one year all year round. Volunteers must be at least 18, have good English language skills, obtain their own medical insurance and pay their own travel expenses. A driving licence would be useful towards acquiring a state driving licence as housing is provided at a location one mile from the place of work. In addition to housing the volunteer receives a stipend.

Applications to the Volunteer Co-ordinator at the above address.

THE COLORADO TRAIL FOUNDATION
710 10th Street, #210, Golden, CO 80401-5843, USA; ☎ +1 303-384-3729 x 113; fax +1 303-384-3743; e-mail ctf@coloradotrail.org; www.coloradotrail. org

The Colorado Trail Foundation (CTF) provides and maintains a non-motorised 500-mile trail between Denver and Durango, Colorado. Each year, the CTF offers weeklong and weekend volunteer trail crews to maintain the Trail. Crew dates begin in mid-June and end in early August. Volunteers must be 16 years or older and in good physical health. Volunteers need to bring their own tent, sleeping bag and personal items; CTF provides food and trail tools. The registration fee is $50 for weeklong crews and $25 for weekend crews. Trail crew registration information and schedules, as well as other volunteer opportunities, are listed on the website www.coloradotrail.org.

> **American Rhiannon Mercer on getting down and dirty maintaining the Colorado Trail**
>
> *In summer 2004, I volunteered with a Colorado Trail Foundation backpack crew for a week set inside the beautiful Collegiate Peaks Wilderness outside of Leadville, Colorado. This turned out to be a fun crew full of laughs and the grunts of hard labour needed to complete a large turnpike and culvert project. We began on Saturday loading up the packhorses and our own backs in intermittent rain. From the parking area, camp was four miles south along the Trail. On reaching the campsite we discovered that the poles for the kitchen tent were 'missing' but with an axe and a handsaw, we got that tent upright in no time. We were not so lucky with the 'missing' dehydrated green beans for which no remedy presented itself. After a tour of the worksite and a tool safety demonstration, the crew scattered into the hills for day hikes. I headed for Rainbow Lake arriving to a terrific hailstorm combined with a gorgeous alpine view.*
>
> *Starting Monday, the initial work involved clearing out an immense quantity of smelly muck from the waterlogged and damaged trail. Tons of dirt were required to replace the tread and build the turnpike. We entertained ourselves with ridiculous stunts, even when there were still hours of work to do; for instance four competitors, of whom I was one, raced to haul two buckets of dirt down to the work site, empty them and race back. The next stage of work involved rocks, needed in all sizes, which had to be rolled to their new home from faraway places. Then logs had to be cut and peeled to act as a stabilizer for the turnpike. In the end, I have to say, the completed project was a beauty to behold.*
>
> *It's experiences like this one that have kept me returning to volunteer with the Colorado Trail Foundation four times. A week spent getting dirty, eating heartily and soaking in the wilderness of the Rockies among great company from the US and overseas is hard to beat.*

D ACRES OF NEW HAMPSHIRE
P O Box 98, Rumney, New Hampshire 03266, USA; ☎ +1 603 786 2366; e-mail dacres@cyberportal.net; www.dacres.org

D Acres is a small-scale organic farm based over 150 acres in the White Mountain region of New Hampshire. The project is run as a cooperative farm and provides a resource base for active participants to live communally and contribute time and energy to maintain the vibrancy of the project. The land consists of mixed forest and five acres of meadows and gardens. Over 100 species of plants have been introduced to the farm from fruit and medicinal herbs to ornamental flowers. Animals are also kept and participate in work activities on the farm.

Volunteers participate in a work-trade scheme through which they provide their skills for 26 hours per week and contribute $15 per week for board and lodging. Food is provided in the form of organic produce and all members of the community participate in the preparation of meals and help with housekeeping in the main central building. Use of the telephone and internet is also included, as is use of the library, workshop and facilities of the site including acres of New Hampshire and the great outdoors. Free-time, outside the 26 hours can be used for personal projects. A minimum of six weeks is requested. This scheme will appeal to those interested in living a simple rural life and working towards sustainability. A number of internships and apprenticeships are also offered. See the website for further details.

EXOTIC FELINE BREEDING COMPOUND INC
HCR 1, Box 84, Rosamond, California 93560, USA; ☎ +1 661 256 3793; fax +1 661 256 6867; e-mail info@cathouse-fcc.net; www.cathouse-fcc.org
The Feline Conservation Center is a non-profit organisation dedicated to the conservation and propagation of scores of the world's rarest and most endangered species of big cats. In addition to a breeding programme, the Center also carries out research and education, and is entirely funded through public donations. Mindful of public opinion about caged animals, the Center is proud of its new regime of habitat enrichment in line with best practice, which says that animal compounds should be as much like natural habitats as possible and that animals should be active and stimulated.

Volunteers are always needed. Those wanting to work as interns (keepers) are unpaid, but housing is provided at cost. Applicants should have studied, or being studying relevant subjects, or be experienced in the field. International applications are welcomed.

For further details contact the general manager at the above address.

FARM SANCTUARY
P.O. Box 150, Watkins Glen, NY 14891, USA; ☎ +1 607 583-4512; fax +1 607 583-4349; e-mail educate@farmsanctuary.org; www.farmsanctuary.org
Farm Sanctuary is a non-profit farm animal protection organisation which investigates and prosecutes farm animal abusers, passes legislation banning cruel farming practices, and operates the largest shelters in the USA for victims of 'food animal' production. Interns volunteer to help operate the shelters, conduct educational programmes, and initiate campaigns to stop farm animal suffering. All interns are responsible for a specific job for 40 hours per week (and shelter emergencies as needed). In addition to an assigned schedule there are special educational opportunities (stockyard investigations, animal adoptions, etc.) that interns are welcome to participate in.

The minimum commitment period for interns is one month; two to three month stays are preferred. Accommodation is provided at the New York or California farm shelters in shared bedrooms with shared bathroom and kitchen facilities. Upon acceptance at one of the shelters a $150 deposit needs to be paid (refundable on completion of intern contract).

For an application form contact the Education/Intern Co-ordinator at the above address or apply online at www.farmsanctuary.org.

FLORIDA PARK SERVICE
3900 Commonwealth Boulevard, MS 535, Tallahassee, FL 32399, USA; ☎ +1 850 245-30908; fax + 1 850 245-3091-3947; e-mail Phillip.Werndl@dep. state.fl.us: www.floridastateparks.org/volunteer
The Florida Park Service recruits volunteers to assist with running the state parks in Florida. About 5,000 volunteers help every year in park operation, wildlife research, outdoor skills, botanical research, restoration of ecological damage. Placements last from 2-16 weeks all year round. Volunteers must be able to communicate in English. Accommodation is sometimes provided dependent on where the volunteer is placed.

Applications to, and further details from, the above address.

FOUR CORNERS SCHOOL OF OUTDOOR EDUCATION
PO Box 1029, Monticello, Utah 84535, USA; ☎ +1 435 587-2156; fax +1 435 587-2193; e-mail fcs@fourcornersschool.org; www.sw-adventures.org
The Four Corners School, a non-profit organisation located in Monticello, Utah and has a mission to educate people of all ages and backgrounds about the need to preserve the natural and cultural treasures primarily in the American Southwest and also around the world. Its programmes consist of Canyon Country Youth Corps, The Bioregional Outdoor Education Project, and Southwest Ed-Ventures. Southwest Ed-Ventures offers adventure and travel vacations with a purpose. Fees in part, support the other two programmes. Up to 200 people a year take part in activities, such as assisting at archaeological sites by documenting and mapping. Participants also help with various other research and education projects. No special qualifications are needed as instruction is given by trip experts. Participants under 14 must be accompanied by an adult. Participants stay for 4-9 days, and there is a wide range of activities from spring to autumn. Accommodation is in tents (which can be rented). Participants pay a fee that covers the cost of specialist instruction, food, transportation, camp gear, supplies, travel from a start location, and permits. Travel costs to Utah must also be paid.

Applicants of all nationalities should contact Janet Ross at the above address.

KALANI OCEANSIDE RETREAT
RR 2 Box 4500, Beach Road, Pahoa, Hawaii 96778; ☎ +808 965-7828 (business); + 1 800 800-6886 (registration); fax +808 965-0527; e-mail volunteer@kalani.com; www.kalani.com/volunteer.htm
Kalani Oceanside Retreat is a non-profit organisation centred on an educational celebration of Hawaii culture, nature and wellness. Kalani is located on the big island, on twenty acres of pristine land, surrounded by tropical forest and the Pacific Ocean. The retreat centre operates with the assistance of approximately 45 volunteers who help to provide services to the guests of the retreat, in the kitchen, housekeeping and grounds/ maintenance departments. Two volunteer programmes are offered: Resident Volunteer (three month, 30 hours per week) and Volunteer Scholars (one month, 20 hours per week). Participants receive mainly vegetarian meals, shared lodging, and a week-long vacation (three month program only). The cost of the program is $1200 (about £655) for three months and $900 for one month. Volunteers must be at least 18 years old and in good health; experience in one of the volunteer areas is preferred.

Application forms can be downloaded from the website

KOKEE RESOURCE CONSERVATION PROGRAM
P.O. Box 100, Kekaha, Hawaii 96752, USA; ☎ +1 808 335 9975; fax +1 808 335 6131; e-mail kokee@aloha.net; www.aloha.net/rep
The Kokee Resource Conservation Program is dedicated to the preservation of the

Hawaiian forests. It is a volunteer-driven project focused on the removal of invasive species from predominantly native forests which will naturally reseed once the threats are removed.

Volunteers are taken to the wet montane forests and the mesic montane forests to remove Kahili ginger and strawberry guava. Environmental education of youth often runs concurrently with invasive species removal. A small amount of work is done in our nursey in an effort to grow native plants for outplanting at selected locations.

About 100 volunteers are taken on a year, many of whom are regulars. Any nationality welcome if eligible for US visa.. Volunteers come all year round but winter is cold in the mountains. Volunteers stay for two to four weeks and must be able to hike several miles carrying a 35lb backback. Accommodation is provided for a small fee and volunteers buy their own food and are self-catering at their own expense.

Send applications to Ellen Coulombe, Programme. specialist.Natural History Museum is located amid the splendour of Kaua'i's canyons and mountain rainforests and is a museum of the flora and fauna as well as Hawaiian culture. Volunteers are needed as hike guides (must be trained), basket making instructors, lei and wreath making, grounds maintenance, restoration of historic civilian conservation corps camps: tasks such as painting, glazing, carpentry and children's activities.

A large number of volunteers are needed at the time of the two annual festivals the Banana Poka RoundUp (usually last Sunday in May) and *Eo E Emalini i Alakai* (second Saturday in October). A driving licence is useful as is good health (nearest hospital 17 miles). Usual stay is less than one month, but longer possible. Rustic accommodation is provided for $2-$7 per night plus 4 hours work per day.

Apply direct to the above address.

LUBBOCK LAKE LANDMARK
The Museum of Texas Tech University, Lubbock, Texas 79409-3191, USA; ☎ +1 806 742-2481 museum office; +1 806 742-1117 Landmark office; fax +1 806 742-1136; e-mail lubbock.lake@ttu.edu; www.ttu.edu/museum/lll/LLLhtml

The Lubbock Lake National Historic and State Archaeological Landmark is an archaeological preserve on the outskirts of Lubbock, Texas. Located in a bend of an ancient valley, Yellowhouse Draw, the preserve contains a well-stratified, concurrent cultural, faunal, and geological record that spans the past 12,000 years. Over 100 archaeological activity areas have been excavated from five major stratigraphic units, representing all of the major time periods of North American archaeology. The programme is aimed at the excavation and interpretation of data and requires the assistance of 50 volunteers a year.

Volunteers must be able to read, write, and speak English and are required to act as field and laboratory crew members during the excavations, collection workers for the care of the collections in the museum, or as leaders on tour programmes.

The minimum age for prospective volunteers is 18 years, and the period of participation is from six weeks to three months between June and August. Volunteers must pay for their own travelling and incidental expenses but receive free board and lodging in the field camp.

For further details contact Dr Eileen Johnson, Director of the Lubbock Lake Landmark, at the above address.

MODOC NATIONAL FOREST
Heritage Resource Management, 800 West 12th Street, Alturas, CA 96101, United States of America; ☎ +1 530 233-8731; fax +1 530 233-8709; e-mail

ggates@fs.fed.us; www.r5.fs.fed.us/modoc

The United States Forest Service of the US Department of Agriculture can place international volunteers/trainees to work in Heritage Resource Management (Archaeology) on National Forests across the USA. Volunteers/trainees with or without archaeological experience are accepted. Accommodation is provided free and the volunteer/trainee will receive a weekly stipend of about US$120. Duties include assisting with historic and prehistoric archaeological excavations, archaeological inventory (field walking to locate and record sites), archival research, and other aspects of Heritage Resource Management. Duty stations are often in rural or remote locations.

Contact Gerald R Gates, Heritage Resource Program Manager, at the above address.

NATIONAL PARK SERVICE

Fort Necessity National Battlefield, 1 Washington Parkway, Farmington, Pennsylvania 15437, USA; ☎ +1 724 329-5512; fax +1 724 329-8682; e-mail carney–rigg@nps.gov; www.nps.gov/fone

The National Park Service operates a national park and the historic Fort Necessity facility important in the French and Indian Wars of 1754, referred to as the Seven Years War in Europe. Volunteers are recruited as the contact people at the visitor centre, they research and develop material for talks, guided tours and the living history department. About 10 volunteers are taken on every year to work as one of the following: librarian, photographer, artist, curatorial assistant, resource management worker, tour guide, living history interpreter, and administration helper.

Volunteer applicants must be able to communicate in English and have a background in the study of history. French students are particularly welcome. Help is needed all year round for as long as the volunteer can spare. Accommodation may be provided but volunteers have to support themselves financially. A 'J' Visa is required to work for the Federal Government.

Applications to the Park Ranger at the above address.

NORTH EAST WORKERS ON ORGANIC FARMS (NEWOOF USA)

New England Small Farm Institute, P.O. Box 608, Belchertown, MA 01007, USA; tel +1 413 323 4531; e-mail programs@small farm.org

Part of WWOOF that supplies a list of farms in the north east of the USA only. Most of the farms on the Newoof list offer full season apprenticeships only and can send a list of other US farms apprenticeship programs. List costs $10. Applicants have to be US residents.

OHIO STATE PARKS

1952 Belcher Drive C-3, Columbus, OH 43224-1386, USA; ☎ +1 614 265-6561; e-mail jim.henahan@dnr.state.oh.us; www.ohiostateparks.org

Ohio State Parks operates 74 parks in Ohio. The parks are varied from three acres to 200,000 acres in size; some featuring historic sites, others are based around natural features such as lakes, beaches, etc. Volunteers perform a wide variety of services from leading nature or history tours, greeting campers, participating in environmental research, clearing and maintaining a variety of hiking, biking and horse-riding trails, performing office administrative support, etc.

There are currently some 6,000 volunteers working for the Ohio State Parks, a number which varies each year and by season. Volunteers normally work two to three months in the spring, summer, or autumn seasons but schedules are flexible to fit travel requirements. Applicants must be fluent in English, be in good health, have an interest in the environment and the ability to work well with people. Accommodation is provided on campsites or in hostel-style housing. Volunteers must cover all other expenses.

Applications to the Volunteer Programme at the above address.

SOUTHEASTERN WILLING WORKERS ON ORGANIC FARMS (SEWWOOF)
P.O. Box 134, Bonlee, North Carolina 27213 USA; e-mail sewwoof@crosswinds. net
SEWWOOF is a correspondence service putting farms in the southeast USA in contact with apprentices through a farm list which it publishes. Applicants wanting apprenticeships pay a fee of $6 for a list of farmers and contact the farmers direct.

STUDENT CONSERVATION ASSOCIATION
PO Box 550, 689 River Road, Charlestown, NH 03603, USA; ☎ +1 603 543-1700; fax +1 603 543-1828; e-mail internships@sca-inc.org or cwc-program@sca-inc.org; www.sca-inc.org
SCA offers expense paid internships to college students and adults through its Resource Assistant Programme, and summer volunteer opportunities to high school students through the Conservation Work Crew Programme.

Resource Assistants (RAs) work across the USA, including Alaska and Hawaii as members of resource staff through the National Park Service, Bureau of Land Management, US Forest Service, US Fish and Wildlife Service, and other state and private organisations. Positions include, but are not limited to, archaeology, backcountry patrol, recreation and ranger management, geology, ecology, hydrology, environmental education, trail maintenance, visitor services, and forestry. Participants receive room and board, and a weekly living allowance. International participants will need to arrange for, and cover the cost of, travel to the USA, although up to $300 may be available for travel within the USA, a $20 application fee also needs to be paid. Positions are available year round and there is no application deadline. A list of current available positions can be found at www.sca-inc.org/vol/raca/racanow.htm. To request an application form visit the website or contact SCA by telephone, fax, or e-mail.

Conservation Work Crew (CWC) members work for 4-5 weeks throughout the summer months in a crew of 6-10 high school students, aged between 16-19, and supervised by one or two SCA crew leaders with experience in back country living and first aid. CWC participants work on various trail maintenance and trail construction projects at sites throughout the USA. Participants will need to arrange and cover the cost of travel to the USA. An application packet for this program will be available in January for Summer positions. For more information contact SCA by e-mail, telephone, fax, or post.

US DEPARTMENT OF AGRICULTURE-FOREST SERVICE (USDA)
1400 Independence Avenue S.W., Washington DC, 20250-0003; ☎ +1 202 205 8333; e-mail fsjobs@fs.fed.us; www; www.fs.fed.us/fsjobs/volunteers. html.
Volunteers for the Forest Service have been organised formally since 1972. Typical volunteer jobs include maintaining trails, campground hosting, wildlife conservation and timber management. They are also required to help with recreation, range activities, office work, interpretation and the visitor information services. There are almost no restrictions on the type of volunteers required and the organisation attempts to tailor jobs to match the volunteers' skills. Volunteers must, however, be able to speak English, and be in good physical condition although the organisation tries to accommodate disabled applicants.

The length of time for which volunteers are required varies, but the longer the commitment (preferably between six and eight weeks) a person can make, the better the chance of obtaining a placement. Volunteers are mostly required on a seasonal basis although there are some limited year-round opportunities. Food and incidental expenses may be reimbursed, and lodging is provided for long-term full time volunteers only.

Those interested should contact the above address for details of the regional Forest Service offices.

WWOOF HAWAII
World Wide Opportunities on Organic Farms, 4429 Carlson Road, Nelson, British Columbia, Canada VIL 6X3; tel/fax 1 250 354 4417; e-mail wwoofcan@shaw. ca; www.wwoofhawaii.org.
US youths and hundreds of people from all over the world go 'wwoofing' every summer. Farm hosts are available on the Hawaiian islands. Volunteer experiences range from small homesteads to large farms. Duties include general work, milking goats etc. Pocket money is not usually provided, but board and lodging are provided free of charge. Opportunities may be available all year round. Minimum age is sixteen. If not a US citizen, only EEA nationals with valid tourist visas need apply. Applications available on line. Otherwise send full name, mailing address and registration fee. Hawaii membership is $15 plus postage. Cash or cheques made payable to John Vanden Heuvel. WWOOF will then send you a booklet detailing host farms.

WWOOF USA
309 Cedar Street, #5C, Santa Cruz, CA 95060, USA; tel +1 831 425-3276; e-mail info@wwoofusa.org; www.wwoofusa.org
Publishes an organic host farm directory with hosts in all 50 states, including Alaska and Hawaii. Also go to website www.wwoofhawaii.org for details of Hawaii hosts.

Office, Lobbying & Political Work

THE EUROPEAN UNION INTERNSHIP PROGRAM
Delegation of the European Commission, 2300 M Street NW, Third Floor, Washington, DC 20037-1434, USA; ☎ +1 202 862-9500; fax +1 202 429-1766; www.eurunion.org/delegati/ppa/interns.htm
The Delegation of the European Commission offers a variety of internship positions at its office in Washington, DC. Internships are intended to provide students and recent graduates with the opportunity to acquire considerable knowledge of the European Union, its institutions, activities, laws, statistics and relations with the USA.

Internships are offered exclusively on a voluntary (unpaid) basis. A working knowledge of French is useful but not essential. Preference is given to candidates available on a full time basis, i.e. 25-40 hours a week, Monday to Friday. Internships are offered three times a year in keeping with the 'semester calendar' from: September to December (application deadline June 15); January to May (application deadline October 15); June to August (application deadline February 15).

Applications to the above address must contain a résumé, a recent transcript, an application form and a cover letter stating the reasons for pursuing an internship with the European Union.

LEGACY INTERNATIONAL
1020 Legacy Drive, Bedford, VA 24523, USA; ☎ +1 540 297-5982; fax +1 540 297-1860; e-mail Staff@legacyintl.org; www.globalyouthvillage.org

Legacy International operates a Global Youth Village. Every summer this Village runs workshops in which about 100 young people (aged 14-18) and staff from around the world participate. The aim of the workshops is to encourage people to gain different perspectives on development issues, prejudice, peace building, and community action, challenging young people and staff to put cross-cultural theory and skills into practical action. The issues addressed in the workshops included: war and peace, distribution of the world's resources, prejudice, and the effects of social pressures. Cultural programming and co-operative living help participants learn to respect differences and discover similarities that transcend cultural, religious, political, and language barriers. About 25 volunteer staff are recruited annually for four to five weeks from from July to August. Accommodation is provided.

For further information contact Leila Baz, Staff Director at the above address, or visit the website to learn more about the volunteer opportunities available, and apply online.

PEACE ACTION EDUCATION FUND
1100 Wayne Avenue, Suite 1020, Silver Spring, MD 20910; ☎ +1 301-565 4050 ext. 302; fax +1 301 565 0850; e-mail bfitzgerald@peace-action.org; wwwpeace-action.org

Peace Action Education Fund and Peace Action work together towards making economic justice a reality. Peace Action is the largest grassroots peace organisation in the USA with over 100,000 members and 100 local and state affiliates. The Peace Action Education Fund conducts the non-lobbying programmes needed to achieve its aims. The Fund recruits two interns each semester and during the summer to help with the work of both organisations. Programmes which volunteers may find themselves working on include: nuclear abolition – attending a conference and protest in New Mexico; halting weapons trafficking and promoting human rights; lifting the sanctions on Iraq; promoting a lasting peace in Yugoslavia.

Applications with covering letter, résumé, references, and writing sample to the Intern Co-ordinator at the above address. Application forms can be downloaded (www. peace-action.org/intern).

TREES FOR LIFE (USA)
3006 W. St. Louis, Wichita, Kansas 67203-5129 USA; ☎ +1 316 945 6929; fax +1 316-945 0909; e-mail info@treesforlife.org; www.treesforlife.org
Trees for Life is a non-profit, movement that helps plant trees in developing countries. These trees provide a low-cost, self reliant source of food for many people and protect the environment. Volunteers in the villages are trained by Trees for Life to provide essential support for programmes that respond to the needs of their communities. Since the inception of Trees for Life, more than three million people have helped plants tens of millions of fruit trees in countries like India, Guatemala and Brazil. Trees for Life also teaches school children in the USA about the environment, through The Trees for Life Adventure. This programme has provided 2 million students with seeds and instructions for the trees.

Anyone who would like to volunteer at the Trees for Life office can follow 45 volunteers who have worked there over the past nine years. Full-time volunteers usually live and serve at the Kansas international office and live in the Tree House, a community-living residence at the office and they receive simple room, board and a stipend. Past volunteers have been referred by Brethren Volunteer Service or Mennonite Voluntary Service and some have come on their own. Internships are also offered at Trees for Life.

For further information about volunteering contact Jeffrey Faus at the above address.

Social, Cultural & Community Schemes

ALDERSON HOSPITALITY HOUSE
PO Box 579, Alderson, WV 24910, USA; ☎ +1 304 445-2980; e-mail omcO1283@wvnet.edu; www.hospitalityhouse.home.att.net
The Alderson Hospitality House provides hospitality to people visiting the federal prison for women in Alderson, West Virginia. The small community in the House believes in the importance of visiting prisoners and strives to encourage visitors by meeting their needs. Volunteers are required to help with general housekeeping duties, gardening and the maintenance of the large guest house and its 11 guest rooms. The volunteers are responsible for making the house welcoming and attractive to guests.

Volunteers are required for short and long-term periods (3 months to 1 year). Board and lodging are provided, along with a small monthly stipend. Applicants must speak English, and a knowledge of Spanish would be helpful; a sense of humour and a warm, outgoing personality are also essential. It is preferable that applicants should be good at house repairs, cooking, listening and playing with children. A driving licence would also be helpful.

Applications should be made to John or Hillary Benish at the above address.

AMITY INSTITUTE INTERN TEACHER PROJECT
3065 Rosecrans Place, Suite 104, San Diego, California 92110, USA; ☎ +1 619-222-7000; fax +1 619 222 7016; e-mail interns@amity.org; www.amity. org

The Intern Teacher Program provides volunteer teaching assistants from over 40 countries to serve as living models of language and culture at primary, secondary and post secondary levels. Interns offer a native perspective on their language, culture and country, enabling students to better understand and appreciate the languages they study.

Volunteer interns should be aged 20-30 and in possession of a degree or studying. The minimum stay is 3 months. Interns work up to 20 hours per week including a maximum of 3 hours of admin work. Volunteers may also teach independently if mutually agreed by the host school, the intern and Amity. Volunteer interns must be compensated by the host school at the standard rate for additional hours (up to a maximum of 10 hours per week). Free board and lodging is provided by a host family.

Costs to the volunteer include $50 Amity processing fee, health insurance coverage with Amity's provider $210 per three month period. Personal spending money of $150 per month for the length of assignment.

For further details, contact the above address or e-mail.

ANNUNCIATION HOUSE
815 Myrtle Avenue, El Paso, Texas 79901, USA; ☎915-533-4675; fax 915-351-1343; e-mail volunteercoordinator@annunciationhouse.us; www. annunciationhouse.org.

Annunciation House sponsors three large houses of hospitality, for the homeless poor, intended in particular for the those without documentation, who are largely immigrants from Mexico and refugees from Central America. The hospitality offered in the houses includes everything to do with food, shelter, clothing, social needs and networking with immigration asylum counsellors. Annuniciation House is an independent organisation supported by individual contributions and donations and by an all volunteer staff. Working for the organisation is a way of life that requires a complete commitment and openness to doing whatever needs to be done.

Volunteers are needed as hospitality shelter staff, for social services, work with Hispanics (especially Central and South Americans and Mexicans), immigration/refugee services, basic health care, border education and research, office and computer work, accounting and bookkeeping, building maintenance and construction trades, community development and Christian-based communities. Annunciation House is located at the border between El Paso, Texas and Juarez, Mexico.

Volunteers must make a minimum commitment of one year. Shorter term and special skills (e.g. research interns, construction trades, building maintenance, computer, accounting etc) are handled on a case by case basis. There is a ten-week Summer Internship Programme available. At any one time there are 15 full time volunteers serving at the houses operated by the organisation.

Volunteers should be aged at least 20 and single, or married without dependants, and willing to participate in community prayer and spiritual reflection, and to respect others' faith backgrounds.. A college education and Spanish are helpful. International volunteers must be able to speak English and should arrange the required B1 or B2 visa that allows them to do voluntary work in the USA.

Volunteers receive only room and board. Laundry facilities are provided. Minor medical expenses are covered at a local clinic. Volunteer accommodation is in the hospitality houses. There is a transportation allowance of $300 towards the home journey after one year's complete service.

A week-long volunteer training programme is provided on site, plus ongoing training while in service. Volunteers meet regularly for staff discussions, prayers and reflection.

Application should be completed at least three weeks prior to proposed arrival date. Intakes are in January, April, June, August and November; for the ten-week internship.

Applications to the Volunteer Coordinator at the above address.

BENEDICTINE LAY VOLUNTEERS
Mother of God Monastery, 110 S.E. Avenue, Watertown, SD 57201 USA; ☎ +1 605 882-6631; fax +1 605 882-6658; watertownbenedictines.org
Sponsored by the Mother of God Benedictine Monastery this programme provides volunteers with the opportunity to live in a monastic setting and serve American people. Volunteers provide the community with whatever skills they have – teaching children, cooking, gardening, recreation/camp services, service to the elderly.

Approximately two one year placements are available yearly to single people who are at least 21 years old, in good health and who speak English. Board, lodging, and local transportation are provided. Depending on the site, short-term placements of from two weeks to two months are also possible in June and July.

Apply to the Director at the above address for further information.

BRETHREN VOLUNTEER SERVICE
1451 Dundee Avenue, Elgin, Illinois 60120, USA; ☎ +1 800 323 8039 (toll free in N America); fax +1 847 742-0278; e-mail bvs–gb@brethren.org; www.brethrenvolunteerservice.org
The goals of the BVS programme are making peace, advocating social justice, meeting human needs and maintaining the integrity of the environment. Volunteers serve in community-based organisations or national offices working on grass-roots needs as well as on systemic structural changes leading towards these goals. Projects include counselling delinquent youth, community development work, care of the elderly and people with AIDS, office work and refugee work. Volunteers serve a minimum of one year in the USA. There are also overseas projects (see *Worldwide* section).

Volunteers must be at least 18 and in good health. Specific requirements may apply to some placements. The volunteers' experience begins with three weeks of orientation in preparation for service. Participants receive living expenses and $60.00 per month stipend, as well as medical and accidental death insurance.

Contact the Recruitment Officer at the above address for further information.

BUDDHIST ALLIANCE FOR SOCIAL ENGAGEMENT (BASE)
P.O. Box 4650 Berkeley, California 94704, USA; ☎ +1 510- 655-6169; fax +1 510 655 1369; e-mail bpf@bpf.org; www.bpf.org./base/html
BASE is a Buddhist Peace Fellowship programme started in 1995 around the San Francisco Bay area. BASE provides a community-based structure that combines Buddhist practice with social action and service in the community. Participants can be full or part-time and should be practising Buddhism as the programme includes Buddhist practice

and retreat and ongoing training sessions are integral. The participant volunteers his or her services in the community including prisons (advocacy, administration, teaching, prison meditation), or working on the Buddhist magazine *Turning Wheel*.

A Volunteer Application Form can be downloaded from the website. The minimum commitment to the programme is six months.

CAFÉ 458 AND COMMUNITY OF HOSPITALITY, ATLANTA, GEORGIA, USA; ☎ +1 404 525-3276; fax 404-681 1592; e-mail reuter@samhouse.org; www. samhouse.org

Café 458 is special kind of bistro whose clients are homeless people. It is a non-profit organisation that takes on volunteer waiting staff with a difference. The organisation uses chic décor and good food to attract clients whom it then gets to talk about their problems in a pleasant surroundings and encourages them to set and reach achievable goals in their lives whether it be getting their glasses mended or weaning off addictions to drugs and alcohol, to getting a job and then works with them intensively.

Volunteer positions are flexible and involve a range of duties,- which can include guest counselling, administration, kitchen work including cooking, volunteer coordination and restaurant management. The project is proud of its success and the fact that only 10% of their clients relapse compared with 90% national average. Volunteers live in, in a faith-based community and receive room and board, transportation, health insurance, use of Community vehicles and a monthly stipend.

Apply to the Volunteer Coordinator at the above address.

INTERMOUNTAIN PLANNED PARENTHOOD
721 N 29th ST W, Billings, MT 59101, USA; ☎ +1 406 248-3636; fax +1 406 254-9330; e-mail impp@ppfa.org; www.impp.org

InterMountain Planned Parenthood (IMPP) is the largest provider of reproductive health care, advocacy and education in Montana. Volunteers aid in the operation of programmes in five clinics across the state as well as from their homes.

More than 30 volunteers are recruited annually in IMPP clinics in the areas of development, education, administration and internships. The length of placement depends on the position, individual commitment, and requirements of the IMPP. For most positions, outside experience, training and qualifications are subject to the position but on-the-job training can usually be arranged. Internship requirements are determined by the educational facility and IMPP. Individuals must express an interest in reproductive health care. Volunteers should be at least 18 years old. All nationalities are welcome but a knowledge of English is preferable. All positions are unpaid although out-of-pocket expenses may be reimbursed. Accommodation is provided in nearly all five clinic locations for volunteers with special needs.

Applications to the Volunteer Co-ordinator at the above address.

JESUIT VOLUNTEER CORPS: SOUTHWEST
P.O. Box 40039, San Francisco, CA 94140-0039; USA; ☎415-522-1599; e-mail jvc@JesuitVolunteers.org; www.jesuitvolunteers.org

The Jesuit Volunteer Corps is a service organisation which offers women and men an opportunity to work full time for justice and peace. Jesuit Volunteers work in the USA by serving the poor directly and working for structural change. The challenge for the volunteer is to integrate Christian faith by working and living among the poor and those on the margins of society by living simply and in community with other Jesuit Volunteers and by examining the causes of social injustice. Since 1956 Volunteers have worked in collaboration with Jesuits whose spirituality they incorporate in their work, community lives, and prayer. The JVC seeks to develop persons whose year or more of service challenges them to live always conscious of the poor, devoted to the promotion of justice and service of faith.

Applicants should be 21 years or older, or have a college education and have a firm Christian outlook, be in good physical condition, adaptable and have a good sense of humour. A one year commitment beginning in August is expected; room and board are provided, plus a small monthly stipend.

Applications should be made to the above address.

JUBILEE PARTNERS
P.O. Box 68, Comer, GA 30629, USA; ☎ +1 706-783 5131; fax +1 706-783 5134; www.jubilee.partners.org
Jubilee Partners is a Christian service community in Comer, Georgia, dedicated to serving the poor and oppressed. The primary ministry is resettling newly arrived refugees in the USA. JP also campaigns to abolish the death penalty and is involved in various peacemaking activities. Volunteers' jobs include teaching English as a second language to refugees, childcare, gardening, maintenance and grounds upkeep, cleaning and cooking, construction, auto repair. Most volunteers do a variety of tasks. Applicants should be over 19, in good health, able to speak good English and able to obtain an visitor's visa to the United States on their own behalf. Volunteers should also be able to come for a complete term of January through May, June through August or September through December. There are ten volunteers per term. Dormitory style housing, food and pocket money ($15 per week) provided. Volunteers must also be prepared to participate in the spiritual life of the community. Apply direct.

KOINONIA PARTNERS Inc
1324 Georgia Highway, South Americus, GA 31719, USA; ☎ +1 229-924 0391; +1 229-924 6504; e-mail volunteer@koinoniapartners.org; www.koinoniapartners.org
Koinonia is a Greek word meaning fellowship and is a 600 acre farm community founded in 1924, in southwest Georgia, dedicated to living out the teachings of Christianity and is committed to peace and non-violence and unity for all people. The farm has over 100 acres of pecan trees, and corn, peanuts and sweet potatoes and sells products through mail order and serves the community with an outreach centre.

About 300 volunteers are engaged annually to performs a variety of tasks both indoor and outdoors including, farming/gardening, office/computer, youth program helper, maintenance, food services, librarian/archivist, baking and shipping mail order products. All skill levels are valued. Driving licence useful. Volunteers should be at least 18 years old.

The usual length of stay is one to three months with possible extension. A working visa is required if staying longer than 3 months; usually a B1 or B2 (volunteer worker or religious worker). Volunteers are needed year round but especially in autumn and winter. Room and free noon meal on weekdays. Pocket money of $25 per week and $50 per month stipend for other expenses.

KOHL CHILDREN'S MUSEUM OF GREATER CHICAGO
165 Green Bay Road, Wilmette, IL 60091, USA; ☎ +1 847-512 1312; fax +1 847-512 1356; e-mail info@kohlchildren'smuseum.org; www.kohlchildensmuseum.org
The Kohl Children's Museum is a small, children's museum in the Northern suburbs of Chicago. It exhibits hands-on, creative environments which encourage discovery,

exploration and self-esteem for children 0-8 years and their families. The museum also organises a variety of educational programmes.

About 150-200 volunteers are recruited annually all year round for periods of at least two months. Volunteers are needed as Exhibit Guides working with the public, assisting with special activities for visitors and helping with special events on and off site. Also Discovery Guides, which involves managing events planned in advance with a different theme every month. Special training is provided. Also Support Volunteers providing clerical and administrative support to various departments of the museum. Volunteers should be able to commit to a minimum of 40 hours per year.

For further details contact Marc Perry, Manager of Volunteer Services at the above address.

LUTHERAN VOLUNTEER CORPS
1226 Vermont Ave, NW Washington, DC 20005 USA; ☎ + 1 202 387-3222; fax + 1 202 667-0037; e-mail staff@lvchome.org; www.lvchome.org
The Lutheran Volunteer Corps (LVC) places full time volunteers in urban ministries and social service agencies for one year of service. Volunteers serve in many ways, including working with at-risk youth, assisting refugees, organising tutoring programmes, rehabilitating low-income housing, and caring for people with AIDS.

Since its beginning 20 years ago, more than 1,000 people have joined the LVC. Full-time volunteers are recruited and placed in eight urban areas – Washington, DC; Baltimore; Maryland; Chicago; Illinois; Minneapolis/St. Paul, Minnesota; Milwaukee, Wisconsin; Seattle and Tacoma, Washington; and Wilmington, Delaware.

Volunteers commit to exploring their spirituality while working for social justice, living in a community, and simplifying their lifestyles. They live with four to seven other volunteers in racially mixed, low-income neighbourhoods near their places of employment.

Non-US citizens need to obtain their own work permit. Volunteers must be at least 21 years old and without dependants. LVC is open to persons from all faith backgrounds. Skills needed vary depending on the placement agency, but for all volunteers, flexibility, dependability, commitment, and a sense of humour are essential. Volunteers serve for one year with an option to renew. The application process begins February 1st and runs throughout the summer; the programme begins at the end of August. Volunteers receive room and board plus $85 per month personal allowance. Travel to the placement, health insurance and two weeks of vacation are also provided.

Those interested should contact the LVC office at the above address.

MENDENHALL MINISTRIES, MISSISSIPPI
P.O. Box 368, Mendenhall, MS 39114, USA ☎ + 1 601-847-3421; fax 601 847 3754; e-mail develop@mbc-tmm.org; www.mbc-tmm.org
Mendenhall Ministries is an integrated community development operation located in rural Mississippi. The project includes a thrift clothing store, cooperative health centre, adult education centre, cooperative farm, community law office, community recreation centre. The project is church-based and volunteers are welcome to help in all departments year round and for any length of service. Short-term volunteers also welcome.

For further details of volunteering opportunities, contact Bea Ross, Volunteer Coordinator, Development Office at the above address.

ST ELIZABETH SHELTER
804 Alarid Street, Santa Fe, New Mexico 87501, USA; ☎ + 1 505 982-6611.
St Elizabeth Shelter began in 1986 as an interfaith effort to address homelessness in Santa Fe and Northern New Mexico. Its long-term vision is to abolish homelessness.

The Shelter currently operates a 32-bed emergency shelter, a 3 to 9 month transitional support programme that offers assistance with rent, food, and counselling to shelter guests who are trying to make the transition into stable housing and employment, and a transitional housing programme that offers affordable housing, case management, and counselling to homeless individuals and families in 17 apartments for families, and 28 for individuals.

Hundreds of volunteers and 5-10 interns per year are required to work full time handling the emergency shelter's daily operations. The placement provides a unique and challenging opportunity to learn firsthand how a homeless shelter is run and to make a meaningful contribution to solving one of society's most vexing social problems. Duties include supervision of shelter operations, volunteer co-ordination, delivery of donated items and facility maintenance, admitting new guests, crisis management, conflict resolution, and assisting with case management services. Placements are available from three months to one year; a one year commitment is preferable.

Applicants for the internship must have at least two years of college education; Spanish language ability and inter-cultural experience is a plus. A private furnished apartment above the shelter, a weekly stipend, and a food allowance are provided. Those who stay for nine months or more are eligible for health insurance and an exit stipend upon completion of their placement.

For an application pack, contact Hank Hughes.

Summer & All Year Camps

ALDERSGATE CAMP & RETREAT CENTER
P.O. Box 367, Brantingham, NY 13312, USA; ☎ +1 315 348 8833; fax +1 315 348 4279; e-mail info@aldersgateny.org; www.aldersgateny.org
Aldersgate camp is a Christian summer camp that takes on 120 volunteer staff for the summer camps from June to the end of August. These include cooks, bakers, crafts teachers, plumbers, electricians, cleaners, medical professionals, handypersons, gardeners, receptionists. Volunteers are especially needed to serve as counsellors and sports and activities instructors. A volunteer programme also operates for the rest of the year to maintain the site for the summer camps. These are usually organised groups that arrive for one or two weeks from September to June.

Full board and lodging provided. About 30 paid posts are also offered.

Application forms can be completed online.

CAMP AMERICA
37Aa Queen's Gate, London SW7 5HR ☎020-7581-7373; e-mail brochure@campamerica.co.uk; website www.campamerica.co.uk
Camp America is the leading summer camp programme in the world, offering 40 years of experience placing people from Europe, Asia, Africa, Australiasia and South America on American summer camps. Camp America is looking to recruit skilled people for a variety of job choices available all over the USA, from *Camp Counsellor* roles, to *Campower* or *Resort America* positions. Camp America takes pride in evaluating your background, training and main skill areas to help find the right placement for you. There are dozens of different roles on camps/resorts to match every aptitude.

Camp Counsellor; this position consists of working with children and/or teaching sports activities, music, arts, drama and dance etc. Experience in sport coaching,

religious counselling, teaching, childcare, health care and lifeguard is preferable. Applicants must be available to leave the UK between 1 May and 27 June for a minimum of 9 weeks.

Campower; typical job roles involve assisting in kitchen/laundry duties, administration and general camp maintenance. This supportive role represents an ideal camp alternative for those not wishing to work directly with children. Experience in administrative roles, maintenance work, health care and catering is preferable. Suitable for students who do not have direct childcare experience. Applicants must be available to leave the UK between 1 May and 27 June for a minimum of nine weeks.

Resort America; similar to the Campower position, duties mainly consist of providing catering and administration support at holiday resorts and hotels. Experience in leisure and hospitality management, food and beverages supervision and entertainment is a plus. The application process for this programme closes in February. Ideal for students with availability to leave the UK between 1 May and 27 June for a minimum of twelve weeks.

All programmes offer individuals free return flights from London and other selected international airports to New York, along with transfer to your camp/resort. Free accommodation and meals and up to 10 weeks of travel time after camp or resort duties. Pocket money, which ranges from $600 to $1100 (dependant on age and experience). Resort America offers up to $2,200 based on number of weeks worked.

Camp America welcomes on-line applications, please visit the website www.campamerica.co.uk To request an application packet please email brochure@campamerica.co.uk or call 020 7581 7373

YMCA TROUT LODGE & CAMP LAKEWOOD
13528 State Highway AA, Potosi, Missouri 63664, USA ☎ +1 573 438 2154 ext 278; e-mail ozarkhr@@ymcalouis.org; www.ymcaofthe Ozarks.org
Trout Lodge is a non-profit family holiday and conference centre located about an hour and a half from St. Louis. It is a unique YMCA branch set amongst 5,500 acres of woodland on the shores of a private lake. The Lodge has 60 rooms for guests, 19 loft suites, 20 cabins for families and conference rooms for up to 300 people. There is a wide range of outdoor and indoor sporting activities on site including horse riding at the Triangle Y Horse Ranch. Moor than 40,000 visitors stay each year.

The YMCA puts Christian principles into practice through its programmes, facilities and natural surroundings that strengthen family life and foster health and physical fitness through teaching of outdoor skills. It also promotes intercultural understanding and educates for stewardship of the earth and its fragile resources.

Opportunties for volunteers with their own RV (Recreational Vehicle) exist all year round and include helping with guest services, nature and outdoor skills program, team building, food service, maintenance, carpentry, water-based activities, and equestrian activities. Registered nurses are also welcomed as volunteers. Volunteers get three meals a day in the guest dining room and facilities (electricity, water etc) and access to all the activities enjoyed by guests. Volunteers are expected to stay for three to twelve weeks. Internships also available. Interns get accommodation provided and full board.

For more information contact Jessica Clay at YMCA of the Ozarks at the above address and telephone number.

Work with the Sick and Disabled

L'ARCHE MOBILE
152 Mobile, 151A South Ann Street, Mobile, Alabama 36604, USA; ☎ +1 251 438-2094; fax +1 438-2094; e-mail larchmob@hotmail.com; www.larchusa.org
L'Arche is an International Federation of Communities in which people with a mental disability and those who help them live, work and share their lives together. L'Arche was started in 1964 and there are now over 127 communities in over 30 countries. 12-14 Assistants are needed, annually, at the Mobile community, which consists of four homes and a work/day programme for disabled people.

Duties of assistants include sharing with the manual labour of keeping a home together; cooking, cleaning, yardwork, repairs, etc. Assistants also help people with self-care and community living skills, as well. Shared prayer is a regular part of the life of the Community, although no one is required to participate. Assistants work in the homes from the rising hour to 10pm, with a three-hour break in the afternoon (at the weekend, only a two-hour break is possible).

Applicants need no special qualifications or professional experience, but they should be aged 16 to 70 and in reasonably good health. Assistants generally work for three months to a year. Board and lodging are provided. Most assistants have private bedrooms, but otherwise share all the living conditions of the handicapped people. No pocket money is provided, but Medical Insurance is provided after one month of the three-month trial period is completed. Three weeks vacation are given for the first year; one month per year thereafter.

Those interested should apply, at any time of the year, to Dennis O'Keefe at the above address.

CAMPHILL SOLTANE
224 Nantmeal Road, Glenmoore, PA 19343, USA; ☎ +1 610-469 0933; fax +1 610 469-1054; e-mail info@camphillsoltane.org; www.camphillsoltane.org
   Camphill Soltane provides a transition to adulthood for young people with developmental disabilities, ages 18-25. 12-15 volunteers come each year to live and work in this Camphill Community of 80 people, participating in a wide range of artistic, educational and recreational activities.
   Volunteer co-workers may participate in or lead a variety of workshops and other activities, including: biodynamic gardening, painting, drama, pottery, hiking, camping, academic classes, cultural outings etc. Volunteers also take part in household chores. Camphill Soltane will facilitate volunteer worker visas for international applicants who are accepted. Minimum age is 20. Volunteer stay is for a year from the end of August to the end of the following July. Applicants pay all travel costs. Soltane provides a small monthly stipend, health insurance (after 3 months) and vacation funds. Room and board are provided. Volunteers live in a community house with a private room.
   Applications available online through the website.

CAMPHILL SPECIAL SCHOOL
1784 Fairview Road, Glenmore, PA, 19343, USA; ☎ +1 610 469 9236; e-mail BRVolunteer@aol.com; www.beaverrun.org
Camphill Special School is a large, residential school for children with special needs. Children live in family-style homes and attend school on campus. A variety of therapies is offered as well as an extensive pre-vocational programme for older students. Volunteers participate in all aspects of life from assisting students in the home to helping in the classroom, sharing in recreational activites, as well as other tasks such as cooking, cleaning and land maintenance. The pre-vocational programme includes working at

the barn (horses, sheep, goats and chickens), woodwork, weaving, food co-op and life skills. 35-40 volunteers accepted annually. Free board and lodging are provided as well as medical insurance, and monthly pocked money of $140.

For further information go to www. Beaverrun.org or call 610-469 9236.

CAMPHILL VILLAGE KIMBERTON HILLS
PO Box 1045, Kimberton, PA 19442, USA; ☎ +1 610 935-3963; e-mail information@camphillkimberton.org

Kimberton Hill is a community, where international volunteers share life and work with adults with development disabilities. The Camphill movement was founded by Karl Koenig and is inspired by Rudolf Steiner's Anthroposophy.

Short and long-term volunteers are needed to help with home making, land work, in the craft workshops, bakery and the coffee shop. Volunteers with a specific interest in maintenance work, dairy farming, and care of the elderly are also needed. Short-term volunteers are accepted for a minimum of a year beginning by September 1st. Room and board, a small stipend, and health insurance (when needed) are provided. A knowledge of English is essential, plus lots of good will and enthusiasm. Help will be given to overseas volunteers in obtaining the necessary visa.

Applicants should write to the above address.

CAMPHILL VILLAGE
Camphill Road, Copake, NY 12516, United States; ☎ +1 518 329-4851; fax +1 518 329-0377; e-mail cvvolunteer@taconic.net; www.camphill.org

There are several Camphill centres in the USA and many more worldwide. Camphill village in Copake comprises a community of 240 people about 102 of whose adults have learning disabilities. The village is about 100 miles north of New York City, located in 800 acres of woodland and farmland. It has a dairy farm, gardens, craft and gift shops, bakery etc. and 20 family residences in which life is shared by 5-5 adults with disabilities and 2-4 co-workers and families, often with children. Co-workers live as full-time volunteers, participating fully in village community life. Board and accommodation are provided, plus medical insurance, $100 monthly pocket money and $600 at the end of a 12-month stay towards a three-week vacation.

A one-year commitment is preferred. However, shorter time periods may be arranged. It is best to apply six months prior to arrival. Volunteers must pay their own air fares. Volunteers should have good social skills, and if possible, practical skills in crafts, arts, household/cooking, gardening or farming.

Pamphlets about the Camphill communities worldwide and the other Camphill communities in the United States and further details about volunteering from the above address

CATHOLIC WORKER FARM OF SHEEP RANCH
P O Box 53, Sheep Ranch, California 95250, USA; ☎ +1 209-728-2193; web www.catholicworker.org

The Catholic Worker Farm in Sheep Ranch is one of many Catholic Worker cells and is part of the Catholic Worker Movement started in 1933 in New York. The main tenets of the Movement are direct service to the poor, voluntary poverty, communal living and non-violent resistance to war and injustice with an emphasis on the connectedness of people with their environment. The Catholic Worker is one of earliest back-to-the-land movements in the USA. There are no organisational ties to the Roman Catholic hierarchy and Catholic Worker communities do not depend on it for support. Each CW community is run solely by the people who comprise it. In most cases, the people need not be Roman Catholic.

The farm is situated in 80 acres in the Ponderosa Pine belt of the western slope of the Sierra Nevada at about 3,000 feet elevation. In 1980 the farm began selling handmade beeswax candles in Bay Area churches. This has evolved into a viable cottage industry the proceeds of which go towards maintaining the daily existence of the farm's people and help towards providing hospitality and room and board for volunteers. Among other activities the farm provides retreats for people living with HIV and AIDS. Volunteers help with these retreats by assisting with meals and by providing companionship to the guests. The farm has a large garden, apple orchard, chickens and goats, which volunteers can also help with. Volunteers should be open and accepting of people of all sexual orientations; volunteers do not need to be Catholic. The farm provides a unique opportunity to serve others while living a simple farm life. If interested the contact is joarthurro@yahoo.com, or write to the above address. Other opportunities to participate in Catholic Worker cells are listed on their website given above.

CENTRE FOR PURPOSEFUL LIVING (CPL)
3983 Old Greensboro Road, Winston-Salem North Carolina 27101, USA; ☎ +1 336 761-8745; fax +1 336 722-7822; e-mail inquiry@ufhg.org; www.ufhg. org
The Center for Purposeful Living offers a service learning opportunity called *Soul-Centred Education for a Lifetime* that builds on common sense, clear thinking, interpersonal and leadership skills, freedom from barriers, and a clear sense of life purpose. The focus is on what works. Take a year to know yourself. This programme is an outgrowth of the organisation's acclaimed all volunteer project (Human Service Alliance) that for 14 years, provided free, hands on care for the terminally ill. The full-time programme requires a full year commitment with a minimum of 45 hours per week of applied service learning. CPL offers scholarships to full-time and part-time students including free room and board (full-time only). All of the faculty and administrative staff of the CPL serve without financial compensation. CPL is an all-volunteer university. Short-term internships are available.

Those interested in volunteering should contact the above address.

EMMANUEL HOUSE – HOME FOR THE ELDERLY
475 Evergreen, Ann Arbor, MI 48103, USA; ☎ +1 734 669-8825; e-mail EmmanuelHse@Juno.com
Emmanuel House is staffed completely by volunteers. There are no paid staff, and residents are charged no fees. Volunteers care for the residents, the house and grounds, etc. No special skills are needed as all training is provided. Live-in volunteers are welcome to stay from two weeks up to two years.

Applications to the Administrator at the above address.

GOULD FARM
100 Gould Road, Monterey, Massachusetts 01245, USA;; ☎ +1 413-528 1804; fax +1 413-528-50513-5027; e-mail events@gouldfarm.org; www. gouldfarm.org
Gould farm is a working farm that provides residential care and treatment for adults with mental illness. Gould farm provides challenging opportunities for volunteers and student interns from around the world. Mature individuals with experience in any of a variety of disciplines are encouraged to apply. Internships are also available to college leavers or those applying through religious foundations.

Volunteer commitments are usually from nine to twelve months in length. All positions are live-in and full-time requiring 40 hours work per week. Applications are accepted year round for 10-12 rotating positions. Greatest need is usually in May and September.

Areas in which work is available include residential support, maintenance and forestry work, gardening and farming, cooking and restaurant work and administration.

Volunteers should contact the Human Resources Manager at the above address.

INNISFREE VILLAGE
5505 Walnut Level Road, Crozet, VA 22932, USA; ☎ +1 434 823-5400; fax +1 434 823-5027; e-mail innisfreevillage@prodigy.net; www.innisfree village. org

Volunteers are needed to join the life-sharing community living and working with adults with mental disabilities. Volunteers are house parents, sharing cooking, cleaning and personal care. They also participate in the weavery, woodshop, garden, bakery or community centre kitchen.

Applicants should be at least 21, possess an interest in living with people with disabilities, have patience, common sense, ability to empathise and a sense of humour. Interest in community process and living are also essential.

Board and lodging are provided as are medical expenses and $215 a month pocket money. Volunteers are required to stay for a year including 15 days' paid vacation. They also accumulate $45 a month for severance. Anyone interested should write or e-mail to the above addresses for further information.

KAIROS DWELLING
2945 Gull Road, Kalamazoo, Michigan 49048 USA; ☎ +1 269-381 3688; fax +1 269 388 8016; fax +1 434 823-5027; e-mail kairosdwelling@aol.com; www.innisfree village.org

Kairos dwelling is a home for the terminally ill. Volunteers are needed to join the small permanent staff of four. Should have a personal interest in the field and with a loving and compassionate presence and strong inter-personal skills. Period of stay two months to a year with a minimum of 40 hours commitment per week. Volunteers get free board and lodging, on the job training and support and the opportunity to attend seminars/workshops. Applications are accepted continuously.

SPROUT
893 Amsterdam Avenue, New York, NY 10025, USA; ☎ +1 212-222-9575; toll free 888-222-9575; fax 212-222-9768; e-mail leadership@gosprout.org, www.gosprout.org

Sprout is a private, non-profit organisation dedicated to helping individuals with developmental disabilities both physical and mental, to grow through challenging and safe travel experiences. Based in New York City, programmes are available to suitable clients throughout the United States. Sprout helps over 1800 people with special needs every year.

Participants have the opportunity to experience age-appropriate, recreational and leisure activities in a small group setting. By offering these experiences, Sprout hopes to enhance the mobility, self-confidence and socialisation of their participants. And through community-based activities, Sprout strives to break down some of the barriers that exist between participants and the general public.

The majority of the people who participate in the vacations organised by Sprout are adults with developmental disabilities, most of them with learning difficulties. Participants range from the moderate to high-functioning levels with some participants requiring more assistance than others. All participants can travel within the typical group size of 10 participants and 3 leaders.

Sprout is always looking for volunteers to be Trip Leaders on 170 trips to 50 destinations around the USA and the Caribbean. Sprout runs trips year round but the busiest season is during June to September. Volunteers come from all over the world and many backgrounds and are usually wanting the improve their leadership skills. Volunteers get all expenses related to the organised trip from NY and back. All activities, meals and accommodation are included.

For more details call 001-212-222-9575 or contact the address/e-mail above.

THE WINANT-CLAYTON VOLUNTEERS

St. Margaret's House, 21 Old Ford Road, Bethnal Green, London E2 9PL; ☎020-8983 3834; e-mail wcva@dircon.co.uk; www.wcva.dircon.co.uk

This Association organises an annual exchange between the United Kingdom and the eastern states of the United States of America for a small group of volunteers. Selected volunteers work on community projects which include visiting housebound people, working with children of all ages, psychiatric rehabilitation/HIV/AIDS and the elderly. The exchange lasts for about ten weeks, the last two weeks being free for individual travel, between June and September.

In order to be selected to travel to the United States, volunteers must be resident in the UK or Eire and over 18 years old. Volunteers must have some experience of community or group work, an interest in people, a sense of humour, flexibility, stamina and a satisfactory way of dealing with stress.

The Association provides pocket money and accommodation for the two months of work. No other expenses are paid except bursaries may be paid for candidates from Ireland or the East End of London. Interviews are held each February.

Please contact the Co-ordinator at the above address for application details.

Canada

CAMPHILL COMMUNITIES ONTARIO
7841, 4th line, Angus, Ontario, LOM IBI, Canada; ☎ +1 705-424 5363; fax +1 705-424 1854.
Camphill Communities Ontario consists of two residential places for special needs adults. (1)Rural Camphill Nottawasaga: volunteers live on 300 acres of woodland fields and gardens with 27 handicapped adults. Volunteers support care needs, house communities, craftworkshops and and land workshops. (2) Urban Sophia Creek: volunteers live in downtown Barrie and share life with special needs adults and support them in urban skills. 8-10 volunteers are accepted annually. Volunteers with training in work with the mentally handicapped can take the more responsible positions. Non-trained volunteers support trained staff. All applicants must obtain a Canadian work visa to enter Canada. Volunteers must be at least turning 20 during their year at Camphill. A year is preferred but there is a 3-month summer stint (June to September) mainly for garden work. Private room, board and pocket money provided.

Apply direct to the above address.

FRONTIERS FOUNDATION
419 Coxwell Avenue, Toronto, Ontario, Canada, M4L 3B9; ☎ +1 416 690-3930; fax +1 416 690-3934; e-mail frontiersfoundation@on.aibn.com; www.frontiersfoundation.ca
The Foundation organises workcamps, which take place mainly during the summer months. These projects are organised with the cooperation of requesting communities (native or non-native) on low incomes: these can involve native communities in isolated northern areas. Under the leadership of one of their number, the volunteers live together as a group, and work with the local people on the construction either of housing or community buildings. Volunteers with skills relevant to the construction process are preferred and those with previous social service or child experience for the recreational/educational projects. Volunteers work in teams of 2-8 people.

All applicants must be over 18, and produce a doctor's certificate which states that they are capable of performing manual work in an isolated area. The minimum period of work is 12 weeks. All living and travel expenses inside Canada are paid, and, in addition, pocket money is provided for those who serve for longer than the minimum period. Up to 18 months is possible.

Applicants should write to the above address.

Sarah King did a lot of freetime activities on a Frontiers community project.
One of the great benefits about being a guest worker was that our activities became a focal point for the community. We played volleyball, helped break in wild horses, watched bears, made wild berry pies and rose-hip jelly, went camping, hunting, fishing and swimming, baked porcupine packed in clay, ate a delicacy of sweet and sour beaver tail, and all took up jogging around a local basketball park.

MAISON EMMANUEL
1561 Chemin Beaulne, Val-Morin, Québec, Canada JOT 2RO; ☎ +1 819 322-7014; fax +1 819 322-6930; e-mail contact@maisonemmanuel.org; www.

maisonemmanuel.org
Maison Emmanuel is a life sharing community with intellectually disabled adults and children. Volunteers help with workshops and in the school, assisting with pottery, woodwork, weaving, candlemaking, farming and gardening. About 30 volunteers are recruited annually for a minimum stay of one year from mid-August to the following July. French language skills are advantageous but not essential. $175 to $275 per month pocket money depending on experience; also board and lodging, and a travel allowance are provided.

Applications to the above address.

CRITTER CARE WILDLIFE SOCIETY
481-216 Street, Langley, British Columbia BC V2Z 1R5, Canada; ☎ +1 604-530 2064; fax +1 604-532 2009; www.crittercarewildlife.org
Critter Care Willdlife Society is located on three acres in Campbell Valley Regional Park not far from Vancouver. Critter Care provides short and long-term care to native mammal species, and through rehabilittion and public education helps prevent the suffering of injured and orphaned wildlife. About 75-80% of the work at the animal shelter is with baby animals and it is very busy from mid-March to September. Spring, summer and very early autumn bring the majority of admissions. Winters are spent caring for animals too young to be released in the autumn and which have to be wintered in the centre. There also seem to be more injured animals in winter.

The centre offers volunteer internships to interested and motivated individuals. Interns are involved in all aspects of running the shelter including feeding, food preparation, cleaning, laundry, administering treatment, participating in building projects, painting and so on, with two days off per week but not consecutively. The minimum period is eight weeks; most interns want to stay long enough to see the creatures (raccoons, squirrels, skunks) they have weaned released. Volunteers are provided with basic accommodation and most of their food. No meat is provided but volunteers can purchase their own.

Applications to Gail Martin by e-mail or fax, or fill in an application form on line.

ORES-FOUNDATION FOR MARINE ENVIRONMENT RESEARCH
P.O.Box 756, 4502 Solothurn, Switzerland; tel/fax +41 32 623 63 54; www.ores.org
ORES works on the feeding, breeding and population ecology of St. Lawrence whales in Eastern Canada and have developed and introduced minimally intrusive research methods that are labour intensive. Volunteers are actively involved in the ongoing research work on whales such as beluga, sperm, minke, humpback, blue etc. in their natural environment. This type of situated learning includes theory and lectures given by experienced staff making the experience thoroughly involving for volunteers.

No particular skills are needed bar basic English language ability and the ability to work from a boat. Volunteers carry out observation and data gathering, weather permitting, by small research teams from open, inflatable boats. Tracking and plotting whales using Global Positioning System equipment, photo-indentification, echo-graph etc. Helpful but not essential skills include photography, computer, carpentry, boating. Accommodation is provided in tents on a fully laid out and equipped camping site. Volunteer programmes last two weeks, or internships of six weeks, or long-term (twelve weeks). Programmes run from the beginning of July to the end of September. Fees range from 1,400-5,900 Swiss francs.

Apply direct to the address above.

Mexico, Central & South America

General Opportunities

AMERISPAN UNLIMITED
117 South 17th Street, Suite 1401, Philadelphia, PA 19103, USA; ☎ +1 215 751-1100 or freephone in USA: 800 879-6640; fax +1 215 751-1986; e-mail info@amerispan.com; www.amerispan.com/volunteers_intern/
Amerispan represents 150+ local organisations in Latin America and Spain, and offers total immersion cultural programmes creating a full understanding of language, culture and life in the host country by combining language classes with homestay and volunteer work. Programmes throughout Latin America include healthcare, education, ESL teaching, environmental, social work, student service co-ordinating. Participants work in clinics, orphanages, national parks, animal refuges, radio stations, schools, law firms, etc. Specially designed professional internships are also organised for volunteers with matching interests, skills, education and/or experience, either to learn or to share knowledge in bussinness, law, computers, marketing and tourism etc.

About 200 volunteers are recruited annually for periods of 4-12 weeks (minimum commitment 4 weeks) all year round. Advice on necessary entrance visas will be given. Spanish or Portuguese speaking requirements vary but a minimum of high beginner level required and level of placement is dependent on level of Spanish. Spanish lessons provided throughout project. Applicants must be minimum age 18. Generally participants are completely self-funding and shared accommodations with kitchen facilities is provided with a $45-$95 cost per week for accommodation (top cost indicates meals provided). Prices of programmes vary depending on the country and the length of stay from $185-$195 weekly. Many volunteer packages include language classes and a local homestay. There is an Amerispan registration fee of $350.

For more information consult the Amerispan website.

AMIZADE
920 William Pitt Union, University of Pittsburgh, Pittsburgh, PA 15260, United States of America; fax +1 412-648-1492; e-mail volunteer@amizade.org; www. amizade.org
Amizade is a non-profit organisation dedicated to promoting volunteerism and providing community service in locations throughout the world. The organisation collaborates with community-based organisations around the world.

Amizade short term volunteer programmes (1-3 weeks) offer a mix of community service and recreation which provide volunteers with the opportunity to participate first hand in the culture of the region where they are working. Past projects have included building a vocational training centre for street children on the Amazon, building on additional rooms to a health clinic in the Bolivian Andes, and doing historic preservation and environmental clean-ups in the Greater Yellowstone area. Volunteers do not need any special skills just a willingness to help. Programme sites include Navajo Indian Reservation, USA; Brazilian Amazon; Bolivian Andes; Greater Yellowstone region, USA; Korrawinga Aboriginal Community, Australia; and Appalachia, USA.

Further details from the above address.

BOSPAS FRUIT FOREST FARM

C/o Piet Sabbe, Oficina de Correo, Ibarra, Ecuador; e-mail bospasforest@gardener. com; www.ecuativer.com/bospas

Belgian Piet Sabbe and his Ecuadorian wife Gabriela Peralta own and manage a 15 hectares farm growing a variety of crops and trees, organically and sustainably on the western slopes of the Andes near the village of El Limonal. The owners are members of a farmer organisation and they involve the local community in their activities.

About 40/50 volunteers are taken on annually all year round to learn about farm work on a tropical fruit farm and have a kind of apprenticeship in rural living. Volunteers carry out tree planting, grafting fruit trees, how to swing a machete and harvest bamboo, bananas and pineapples. Currently, trail building is an important activity in and around the farm. Occasionally, volunteers are asked to give visitors a guided tour of the farm. A minimum stay of four weeks is requested but shorter periods are possible. Volunteers are lodged in a dormitory-style attic, but should bring their own sleeping bag and mosquito net. Three meals a day are provided and plenty of fruit and fruit juices. There is a volunteer contribution of $190 for four weeks. For a stay of three weeks or less the contribution is $12 per day.

Contact by e-mail or regular post for more information.

BUNAC VOLUNTEER COSTA RICA

Volunteering Department, BUNAC, 16 Bowling Green Lane, London EC1R OQH; ☎ 020-7251 3472; fax 020-7251 0215; e-mail volunteer@bunac.org. uk; web www.bunac.org

Bunac offers three or six month placements in this beautiful and diverse Central American country. Typical projects are in rural areas and include working with agricultural organisations, working on environmental projects in the rain forest, on small business development or teaching English. Applicants must be able to communicate confidently in Spanish.

Volunteers should be aged 18-32. The cost for 3 months is £425 and for 6 months £525. This covers programme literature, placement, 1 day arrival orientation and arrival accommodation in San Jose. The cost does not include flights and insurance and a local payment towards accommodation during placement.

To apply, download an application from Bunac's website (www.bunac.org), and send it completed and with a registration fee and any other documents specified by Bunac's Volunteering Department. All applicants are invited to attend an interview.

BUNAC VOLUNTEER PERU

Volunteering Department, BUNAC, 16 Bowling Green Lane, London EC1R OQH; ☎ 020-7251 3472; fax 020-7251 0215; e-mail volunteer@bunac.org. uk; web www.bunac.org

Bunac offers 2 or 3 month placements in this fascinating South American country. All applicants are placed at Flores de Villa, a vibrant community centre on the outskirts of Lima. Volunteers are needed to get involved with such tasks as health education, teaching and building projects.

Applicants must be able to communicate confidently in Spanish and be at least 18. The cost for two months is £695, 3 months £895 this covers programme literature, placement, 3-day arrival orientation and arrival accommodation in Lima and all accommodation during placement. Additional costs are flights and insurance.

CACTUS
No 4 Clarence House, 30-31 North Street, Brighton BN1 1EB; ☎0845-130 4775; fax 01273-775868; e-mail sarah@cactuslanguage.com; www.cactuslanguage.com

Cactus is a company which organises language-learning holidays in countries worldwide. It also operates a combined volunteering and language learning programme in several Latin American countries: Guatemala, Peru and Costa Rica. Volunteers can choose between social work (orphanages, street children etc.), education (classroom assistant, English teacher, assisting with crafts, sports etc.); healthcare (working in clinics, with handicapped children etc) and environment (turtle hatcheries) maintaining tracks in cloud forest, orchid gardens, canopy tours.

All volunteers must complete a language course of at least 4 weeks immediately prior to their placement. Course and minimum commitment is 8 weeks. It is hoped to extend the scheme to Mexico, Bolivia and Ecuador. Skills and qualifications required depend on the placement; some require none others, e.g. medical, education, childcare, wildlife require qualification or experience in the requested area of work. Minimum age is 21 years. Placements can be extended if wished, once in the country of choice. Airport transfer arranged. Meals provided during language course and may be included during the volunteer placement. Accommodation with host family or local lodging; may be shared during placement. Cost of programme to volunteer is from £989 (Guatemala) to £1,329 (Costa Rica).

Applications to the above address.

CALEDONIA LANGUAGES ABROAD
The Clockhouse, Bonnington Mill, 72 Newhaven Road, Edinburgh EH6 5QG; ☎0131-621 7721/2; fax 0131-621 7723; e-mail courses@caledonianlanguages.co.uk; www.caledonialanguages.co.uk

Caledonia Languages Abroad organise volunteer placements in Bolivia, Brazil, Cuba, Peru and Costa Rica. Participants must take a language course in the country first and usually require at least an intermediate level of the appropriate language before commencing the placement.

About 15 volunteers annually are recruited to teach English, or perform community or tourism work. Placements are from four weeks to 6 months all year round. Applicants pay for all expenses for the duration of the language course and volunteer work: airfares, placement fee, subsistence, accommodation.

As well as offering Spanish courses in Spain and Latin America Caledonia offers courses in the following languages in their respective countries: French, Italian, German, Portuguese and Russian.

Applications to the above address.

Keri Craig from Scotland describes learning Spanish and volunteering with Caledonia Languages
What an utterly amazing time I had in Costa Rica at the language academy and doing my volunteer work! The moment I arrived I was welcomed into my family, they couldn't do enough for me, and while I was there I became very

close with them. Everyone at school was friendly and so helpful, whether it was organising extra classes or booking hotels at the weekend. My teacher, Gaby was wonderful and my Spanish improved no end. Considering my Spanish was very basic it was very pleasing to develop it so quickly – it is a big advantage being immersed in the culture. The dance classes at school were also a great favourite.

For my volunteer work I decided to do four weeks at the Aldea Infantil SOS in Tres Rios (about an hour on the bus from school). It is an independent orphanage in a beautiful location and very different to what I had been expecting. The set-up involved seven to eight children living in each of the ten houses, it was almost like a village with an 'aunt' who looked after the day-to-day care and welfare of 'her' children. Half the children attended the local school in the morning, half in the afternoon and I had different groups on different days. I was left very much to my own devices, I could choose to teach English or merely play games and interact with the children. I also chose the hours I worked (9am-2pm, Monday to Thursday). The experience there was amazing. I made some close friendships with some of the children, and it was especially rewarding when even the more 'difficult' children came to hug me.

They are definitely appreciative of volunteers there and I will definitely be returning to Costa Rica one day though I have so many friends there now, that I shall be able to do it independently. I am however very grateful for the great service provided by Caledonia Languages and for being introduced to such a fantastic country.

CARIBBEAN VOLUNTEER EXPEDITIONS
Box 388, Corning, New York 14830, USA; ☎+1 607 962-7846; e-mail ahershcve@aol.com; www.cvexp.org
Caribbean Volunteer Expeditions takes on between 20 and 80 volunteers a year to document, measure and photograph historic buildings in the Caribbean. The tasks normally take one or two weeks at any time of year. Volunteers pay their own way.

For further details contact the above address.

CASA DE LOS AMIGOS-Service & education project
Ignacio Mariscal 132, Colonia Tabacalera, 06030 Mexico; ☎+52-55 5705-0521/705-0646; fax +52-55 5705 0771; e-mail convive@casadadelosamigos. org; www.casadelosamigos.org
The Casa de los Amigos is a Quaker service centre and guesthouse based in Mexico City. Established in 1956, the Casa provides hospitality to people from around the world, many of whom are working on issues of social concern in Latin America. Since its foundation the Casa has maintained a variety of service projects including workcamps in rural Mexico, aiding Central American refugees, post earthquake reconstruction, among other projects. Out of the Casa's service component has come the opportunity for volunteers to work in a variety of social service organisations in Mexico City.

Volunteers can apply for full time service work with Mexican social service organisations for a period of 2 months or more. The work is intense and challenging and includes assisting groups that focus on community centres, people with HIV/AIDS, street children, human rights, women's issues, and the environment. Basic Spanish is a requirement and technical skills are helpful but not essential. The program requests a donation of US$50 to cover administrative costs. The volunteer should also budget for an additional US$300-$400 per month for food, accommodation and other living expenses.

For details and application forms contact Christophe Grigi, the Program Coordinator, at the above address.

CASA GUATEMALA
UK contact: 30 Church Road, Upton, Wirral, CH49 6JZ; ☎**0151-606-0729;**
www.casa-guatemala.org
Casa Guatemala is a children's home situated in the Rio Dulce area of Guatemala, Central America. About 200 skilled and unskilled volunteers a year are recruited for a variety of positions including: administrative director, volunteer coordinator, dentist, agronomist/farm administrator, toddler care, bar/restaurant manager, shop manager, English teachers, doctor, nurse etc. The orphanage owns and runs a nearby hotel and shop which exist purely to fund the orphanage.

Volunteers stay a week to a year depending on the position. Accommodation is provided. Volunteers working at the orphanage are asked to make a one-off payment of US$180 towards running costs. Meals are provided in a main dining-room. Volunteers working at the hotel only do not pay anything. Volunteers live in a communal house so it is important to be able to get on with people of different countries, backgrounds, languages and cultures.

Details of individual posts can be obtained by contacting Casa Guatemala's UK contacts by e-mail (pete_rachel@lineone.net) or by telephoning the above number.

CASA RIO BLANCO - Rainforest Reserve
Apdo. 241-7210, Guapiles, Pococi, Costa Rica; tel/fax +506 382-0957.
Volunteers are invited to take part in volunteer projects ranging from research to hands on projects. These have included building bat houses, gardening, developing educational materials, research, map trails, trail clearing and community service. Projects can be tailored to suit the interests of volunteers. Volunteers who speak Spanish can work in local schools. Volunteers should be aged at least 18 and be available for at least four weeks at any time of year. Volunteers pay a monthly charge of $600 for room, board and laundry. Accommodation is in a cabin with hot water and shared bathrooms.

Anyone interested should write to the above address enclosing three international reply coupons.

CENTRO LINGUISTICO LATINOAMRICANO DE COSTA RICA
Apdo. 425-4005, San Antonio de Belén, Heredia, Costa Rica; ☎**506-443-5571; fax 506-441-0261; e-mail cellcr@sol.racsa.co.cr; www.Spanish.co.cr**
The Centro Linguistico Latinoamericano offers students who enrol in the Spanish immersion programme at the school in Costa Rica the opportunity to participate in many different volunteer projects such as in medical clinics, public school teacher training in ESL and computers, home building, orphanages, pregnant minors, etc. In 1999 ten volunteers were given placements but there are plans to increase this number. Applicants of all nationalities are welcome. Volunteers must be 18 or over, in reasonable health (people with special needs are accommodated) and enrolled in the school for at least two weeks of Spanish classes prior to voluntary work.

Volunteer programmes are ongoing therefore participants can stay as long as they wish although a special visa is required after 90 days. A one time $25 registration fee, a school enrolment and homestay fee ($17 per day which covers most meals), air fare and miscellaneous expenses must all be paid by the volunteer. School tuition costs $345 per week and covers homestay, three meals a day and laundry service. Sometimes a nominal fee is charged by particular volunteer programmes.

Applications to the above address.

CHRISTIANS FOR PEACE IN EL SALVADOR
122 De Witt Drive, Boston, MA 02120; ☎617 445 5112; fax 413-723 4047; e-mail crispaz@igc.org; www.crispaz.org
Christians for Peace places volunteers with parishes, co-operatives, NGOs and other church-based organisations in El Salvador. About 13 volunteers are recruited annually to participate in pastoral work in the fields of human rights, agriculture, women's advocacy, water procurement, special, popular and health education, youth work, and labour issues. Short and long-term programmes are organised lasting either 3 months or one year. Minimum age of participants is 18. Accommodation is provided but living expenses have to be paid by the volunteer.

For further details visit the website or contact the above address.

CORPORACION PARA EL DESAROLLO DEL APRENDIZATE (CDA)
Grajales 2561, Santiago, Chile; ☎+562-689 16 33; fax +562-689 16 33; e-mail cdachile@terra.cl; www.cdachile.cl
CDA is a foundation for the treatment and stimulation of 5-18 year olds with neuro-cognitive deficit, from deprived backgrounds who also attend the normal school system. The family also receives attention.

Volunteers are invited to work with the staff in the CDA centres in Chile to provide assistance to the staff working with children and young people, in the preparation of didactic materials, in fund raising and organisational activities, and other suitable activities appropriate to the skills listed on their CV. A good level of basic Spanish is preferable as the work staff do not speak English. Minimum age is 18, (this can include those whose eighteenth birthday falls just after arrival in Chile). High altitude area so may not suitable for those with a heart condition. Minimum period of work is usually 4 months. Volunteers have to start either mid-March and finish mid-July, or start mid-August and finish mid-December to fit in school terms.

Volunteers should be self-funding as regards travel and living expenses. In the case of centres at Santiago and Illapel accommodation is provided; elsewhere help will be given with finding accommodation.

Applications should be sent to Helena Todd Malfroy, Virginia Opazo 47, Santiago, Chile (e-mail todd@rdc.cl).

CUBA SOLIDARITY CAMPAIGN
c/o Red Rose Club, 129 Seven Sisters Road, London N7 7QG; ☎020-7263 6452; fax 020-7561 0191; e-mail office@cuba-solidarity.org.uk; www.cuba-solidarity.org.uk
The Campaign organises and selects volunteers for the twice yearly (July and December) international work brigades to Cuba. The brigades last for three weeks. One third of the time is spent working on either agricultural or construction projects alongside Cubans. Another third of the time is spent on a wide range of visits to schools, hospitals, farms, etc. in order to find out about life in Cuba. The rest is free time either in Havana, on the beach, or at the brigade centre.

The total cost is approximately £800 and includes all flights, accommodation, visa and food. Contact Cuba Solidarity Campaign for an application form and further information. The closing dates are 2 months before departure.

ECUADOR VOLUNTEER
Reina Victoria 1325 y Lizardo Garcia, Quito-Ecuador; tel/fax +593-2-2564-488; e-mail info@ecuadorvolunteer.com; www.ecuadorvolunteer.com
EV offers volunteer positions throughout the country in a variety of fields from ecological

studies to community work. They also provide the necessary training and Spanish instruction that the volunteers will need prior to starting their work.

Projects include: scientific research aimed at the conservation of rain forests, various ecological projects working in the rain forests of Ecuador; community positions working with poor children and orphans, elderly, homeless, single mothers and people with AIDS; medical positions i.e. professional positions for doctors, nurses and people with medical qualifications, to work with the Department of Health in Quito.

Minimum length of stay is a month for ecological work and two months for community and medical work.

Volunteers study at the school for a week to two months before they start work. They can also continue their Spanish Instruction while working.

Applications to the above address.

EXPLORATIONS IN TRAVEL INC
2458 River Road, Guilford, VT 05301, USA; ☎ +1 802 257-0152; fax +1 802 257-2784; e-mail explore@volunteertravel.com;   www.volunteertravel. com.

Explorations in Travel Inc arranges individual volunteer placements in Belize, Costa Rica, Ecuador, Guatemala and Puerto Rico. Placement sites include schools, animal shelters, sanctuaries and rehabs, conservation organisations, rainforests and sustainable tourism projects.

40-50 volunteers are recruited annually. Some placements require a foundation in the Spanish language. Volunteers should be at least 18 years old, flexible, self-motivated and enthusiastic. Placement durations vary, with one month being average. Accommodation and meals provided at a small cost.

Applications to the above address.

FUNDACION GOLONDRINAS
Isabel La Catolica 1559, Casilla 1211, attn Maria-Eliza Manteca, Quito, Ecuador; ☎ +593-2 2226602 (office Quito); +593-6 2648679; e-mail manteca@uio. satnet.net; www.ecuadorexplorer.com/golondrinas

The Foundation Golondrinas works both in the conservation of highland cloudforest (the Cerro Golondrinas Cloudforest Conservation Project) and in the implementation of permaculture/agroforestry in deforested areas under agriculture.

The project was established in 1992 on the western slopes of the Andes in the north of the country and is seeking to conserve this area with its exceptionally rich biodiversity and high levels of endemism. Fundacion Golondrinas has been implementing small scale activities in several parts of the area; i.e. tree nurseries and three demonstration sites where permaculture and agroforestry techniques are applied in order to teach local farmers sustainable productive methods.

The majority of volunteers (about 100 annually) are short term. A commitment of at least a month is required. It is important that candidates have a basic knowledge of Spanish, be in good physical shape and be prepared to work and live in primitive conditions. A contribution is required for food and accommodation on the project site: US$280 for a month; US$240 (plus tax) for a minimum of three months. The type of work is mainly manual labour such as planting trees, cutting weeds, maintenance in the tree nursery and minor building and carpentry tasks. The main location is Guallupe.

Four long-term volunteers are also needed for a minimum of a year to further develop eight acres agro-forestry, permaculture demonstration site *(centro productivo y educativo agroforestal)*. Tree nursery, bamboo, fruit and nut trees, nitrogen fixing trees, alley cropping, tree planting. And/or scientists or students (as part of their studies for which credit is granted or as a practice for their career) to assist and carry out research on sustainable agriculture, forest resource management, flora and fauna. Room and board are provided. No salary. Location: Guallupe and the Golondrinas Reserve. Bilingual Spanish necessary. Candidates with agro-forestry/permaculture certificate or degrees and wide knowledge in an environmental science preferred.

For more information visit the website. Applications to the above address.

FUNDACION JATUN SACHA
Eugenio de Santillan N34 248 y Maurian, Casilla 1712867, Quito, Ecuador; ☎ +593 2 243 2240; fax +593 2 245 3583; e-mail volunteer@jatunsacha. org; www.jatunsacha.org
Jatun Sacha is a non-profit organisation whose main purpose is conservation in Ecuador. The organisation has nine biological reserves where about 800 volunteers annually, are accepted to participate in activities such as reforestation, environmental education, agroforestry, light construction, organic farming, light construction, personal projects etc.

Volunteers stay from 14 days to 6 months all year round. For stays of up to 180 days a tourist visa is sufficient. Volunteers must be in excellent health with medical certification to that effect. There is a $35 application fee and continental reserve fee of $350 per month; and for the Galapagos a $50 application fee and a volunteer fee of $660 per month. All expenses including accommodation are borne by the volunteer.

Applications direct to the above address.

GENESIS II CLOUD FOREST
Apdo 655, 7050 Cartago, Costa Rica, Central America; e-mail volunteer@genesis-two.com; www.genesis-two.com/volunteer
This organisation is responsible for preserving a cloud forest in the mountains of Costa Rica (altitude 2,360 metres) for bird-watching, recreation and academic research. Volunteers are needed to help with the system of trails which are continuously being expanded and improved and other related work. Tasks include trail work, gardening, reforestation, transplanting and fence construction. Volunteers work for six hours per day, five days per week.

Around five volunteers are needed annually for a minimum period of one month. Volunteers must pay a donation to the project of US$150 per week which covers cooking, sleeping and laundry facilities. Volunteers of all nationalities are welcome and a knowledge of Spanish is useful and preference is given to people experienced in construction or ecological work. Since conditions are rugged and work takes place at high altitudes, applicants should be in good physical condition with all senses intact. Accommodation is provided.

For more details contact the Co-owner at the above address. Applicants should note that competition for places is very tough, with many places filled by March and most places filled by May. Enclose five international reply coupons with any correspondence.

GLOBAL EXCHANGE - Mexico Programme
2017 Mission Street, Suite 303, San Francisco, CA 94110, USA; ☎ +1 415 255-7296; fax +1 415 255-7498; e-mail mexico@globalexchange.org; www. globalexchange.org/campaigns/mexico
Global Exchange is a non-profit education, research, and action centre forging closer ties between North Americans and grassroots groups working for human rights, peace, and democracy around the world. Global Exchange's Mexico programme works in

close collaboration with Mexican human rights organisations and NGOs to monitor human rights abuses, to influence media coverage of events in Mexico, and to educate and pressure US policy makers on Mexican issues. For more information visit Global Exchange's website.

Short-term: (3 weeks to six months) volunteers are required for crucial human rights observation in the state of Chiapas. Internships (unpaid) are also available at the San Francisco, CA, USA office. Applicants for human rights obserbation must be: be fluent and highly articulate in Spanish and English; have prior experience with community organising, peacemaking work, international relations and/or public relations; and demonstrate an extensive working knowledge of Mexico's history and current events. Applicants for internships should check www.globalexchange.org/getinvolved/ for current openings.

Apply with résumé, cover letter, and three letters of recommendation that specifically address your qualifications for this position, to the above address. Also include emergency contacts and a copy of your passport.

GREEN REEF ENVIRONMENTAL INSTITUTE
100 Coconut Drive, San Pedro Town, Ambergris Caye, Belize; ☎ +501-226-2833 or +501-606-3786; e-mail greenreef@btl.net; www.greenreefbelize.com
Green Reef is a private, non-profit organisation dedicated to the promotion of sustainable use and conservation of Belize's marine and coastal resources. It works in the areas of environmental education, marine research, protected areas management and advocacy.

About 20 volunteers are needed annually to help with turtle monitoring, proposal writing, graphic designing and coral reef monitoring. The minimum stay is 4 months. Volunteers must be self-funding as regards food, transport and rent. Accommodation available at the Bacalar Chico Field Station. Volunteers so far have come via the Peace, Corps, various university groups from the USA and independently.

For more information contact the above address.

INSTITUTE FOR CENTRAL AMERICAN DEVELOPMENT STUDIES (ICADS)
Apto. 300-2050, San Pedro Montes de Oca, San José, Costa Rica; ☎ +506 225-0508; fax +506 234-1337; e-mail icads@netbox.com. www.icadscr.com
ICADS organises four study abroad programmes which incorporate volunteer work into students' studies: a month long intensive Spanish programme that gives volunteers the opportunity to work in various orphanages, health clinics and human rights organisations; two semester programmes – one that focuses on environmental issues and research, the other which allows volunteers to work for two months in various organisations in Costa Rica and Nicaragua; the fourth programme is a condensed, non-credit version of the semester internship programme.

About 300 volunteers are recruited annually all year round except December. Basic language skills in Spanish are very useful. Students pay a programme fee which varies according to which internship they undertake. The fee covers tuition, travel to and from the work site, board and lodging. Donations are also given to the organisations at which the students volunteer.

For more details of the programmes and their costs visit the ICADS website or contact the above address.

LATIN LINK: Step/Stride Programmes
175 Tower Bridge Road, London SE1 2AB; ☎ 020-7939 9000; fax 020-7939 9015; e-mail step.uk@latinlink.org; or stride.uk@latinlink.org; www.latinlink.

org and www.stepteams.org
Latin Link is a long-term mission which has recognised the need for short-term opportunities both in terms of the benefits to those going and those hosting in Latin America.

Latin Link's Step programme provides volunteers with an opportunity to carry out construction in teams of ten to twelve people in Latin American countries including Argentina, Bolivia, Brazil, Ecuador, Mexico, Cuba and Peru. Most projects are community based in both rural and urban areas.

Projects in the past have included building or extending schools, churches, clinics and community centres. In addition to the building work however, volunteers are strongly encouraged to get actively involved in the life of the church and community. Teams leave in March for four to six months or over the summer months for seven weeks. Volunteers joining the Spring teams are asked to raise a contribution of £2,450 towards the cost of the trip while Summer volunteers raise £1,850. Any extra money raised goes directly to the projects to pay for building materials.

Latin Link's other programme is Stride, which gives volunteers the opportunity to do individual placements in Latin America using any specific skills they have. Opportunities include among other things, school and TEFL teaching, children's work, church work, agricultural work and prison work.

Volunteers are required to stay a minimum of six months or eight if they have no prior knowledge of Spanish or Portuguese, and up to a total of two years. The cost of the programme is about £2000 plus approximately £450 per month. As with STEP the cost includes flights, insurance, training, debriefing, food and accommodation.

Latin Link is looking for committed Christians to work alongside the church in Latin America. Applicants for the Stride programme should have a level of maturity which reflects the individual nature of the projects. Those interested in staying for a longer period of time should contact Daniel Kirk on 020-7939 9005; e-mail daniell@latinlink.org or write to the above address.

MAR DE JADE
Mar de Jade, PMB 078-344. 827 Union Pacific, Laredo, TX 78045-9452; tel/ fax 322-222 1171, USA; e-mail info@mardejade.com; www.mardejade.com
Mar de Jade, a tropical, ocean-front retreat centre in a beautiful unspoiled fishing village near Puerto Vallarta on the Pacific Coast of Mexico, offers unique volunteer opportunities in a 21-day work/study programme. Volunteers work in a farmers' health clinic, in local construction, in cottage industries, or teaching. No prior knowledge of Spanish is required. Most volunteers study Spanish and practise their Spanish while working. Classes are taught in small groups by native speakers. In their free time, volunteers relax and enjoy great swimming, kayaking, hiking, boating, horseback riding and meditation. The programme is offered from April 16th to November 1st to people of all ages. The cost for the 21-day programme is US$1310 (subject to change on a yearly basis), and includes shared room, board, 12 hours of Spanish per week and 15 hours of community work. A longer resident programme is available at a reduced weekly cost.

For more information, contact Mar de Jade at the above address.

MELIDA ANAYA MONTES (MAM) LANGUAGE SCHOOL
Boulevard Universitario, Casa No. 4, Colonia El Roble, San Salvador, El Salvador; tel/fax 503-226-2623; e-mail cis@netcomsa.com; www.cis-elsalvador.org
Takes on two to eight volunteer teachers. No experience needed. Interested in issues of social justice since CIS-MAM works with members of the Salvadorian opposition. The minimum stay is 2 months. To teach 3 days a week 5.15pm-7pm. Volunteers must be entirely self-funding. Help is given with finding but not paying for accommodation.

Apply to Jennie Busch, Volunteer Co-ordinator.

NICARAGUA SOLIDARITY CAMPAIGN

129, Seven Sisters Road, London N7 7QG; ☎020-7272 9619; fax 020-7272 5476; e-mail nsc@nicaraguasc.or.uk; www.nicaraguasc.org.uk
The Nicaragua Solidarity Campaign (NSC) organises work/ study tours to work with fair trade procedures in Nicaragua. There are two brigades per year in the summer, each lasting for one month. The groups work for two weeks and spend the third week on a programme of talks and visits to organisations in Managua and around the area where the brigade is working. The programme can be varied according to the interests of the group.

Volunteers must be fit, adaptable and prepared to get involved in the work of NSC in Britain on their return from Nicaragua. The total cost including air fares, living expenses and transport in Nicaragua is approximately £1,100.

For further details contact the above address.

PITHEKOS

Via Savona 26, 20144 Milano, Italy; ☎ +39(0)2 89405267; fax +39 (0)2 700594457; e-mail asspithekos@tiscalinet.it
Pithekos is an ecology and conservation association, was started in 1999 during the organisation of a voluntary field work project with the local university in Veracruz state, Mexico. The project dealt mainly with collecting data on Howler Monkeys and also vegetation and insects censuses. The Howler Monkey project was suspended for 2004 but should continue in 2005. It is a conservation project directly involving local people. About 10 volunteers are needed to help with research by observing animals and data collection. A knowledge of Spanish is required. The minimum period is about 9 weeks from the beginning of July. Volunteers have to pay a fee to participate which funds the organisation's researches and some volunteer expenses.

Pithekos also has a conservation project running in Sulawesi, Indonesia assessing the coral reef, for which paying volunteers are also needed.

Applications direct to Pithekos.

EL PORVENIR

2508 - 42nd Street, Sacramento, CA 95817; ☎ +1 303-520-0093; fax +1 916 227 5068; e-mail jemerritt@elporvenir.org; www.elporvenir.org
El Porvenir means 'the future'. El Porvenir, founded 1990, is a small, non-profit organisation dedicated to sustainable development in Nicaragua. The priorities are to construct water, sanitation and reforestation projects.

70 volunteers per year are needed for 8-15 days, work experience trips (6 per year), participating in construction of water, sanitation or reforestation in Nicaragua. Volunteers join local families in the construction of hand-dug wells, spring capture/gravity flow systems and latrines and *lavanderos* (washing facilities) and reforestation. Work is all manual.

Volunteers can be any nationality and each group is accompanied by a bilingual North-american staff member of El Porvenir. No experience needed as all tasks can be learnt on site. Must be in good health and over 18 years. Groups start usually Jan, Feb, Mar, June, July, August and November. The charge to volunteers is $800-$950 plus they must arrange their own round trip to Nicaragua. The fee covers all board and lodging.

Contact Elisabeth Merritt, Co-Director, for more information.

RAINFOREST CONCERN
27 Lansdowne Crescent, London W11 2NS; ☎020-7229 2093; fax 020-7221 4094; e-mail info@rainforestconcern.org
Rainforest Concern is a British registered charity established with the objective of conserving threatened rainforests and the biodiversity they contain. Volunteers are needed for rainforest projects in Ecuador, and for turtle protection in Costa Rica and Panama.

In Ecuador, Rainforest Concern is creating a continuous corridor of protected rainforest to link the cloud forests of the Andes with the mangroves of the Pacific Ocean. In so doing a secure environment will be provided for the many rare and endangered plant and animal species which depend on these forests for their survival. Depending on the time of year and the work required at a particular period, volunteers assist with scientific research: species auditing/surveying to compile flora and fauna lists, trail maintenance, reforestation, socio-economic work with local communities, teaching English and conservation issues to schools. Accommodation and full board are included and for costs and availability, please see contact details for individual projects on the website.

In Costa Rica, Rainforest Concern manages 2,000 acres of lowland rainforest backing onto a 6km stretch of beach, which is protected in the interests of the leatherback turtle. Populations of the leatherback turtle are critically threatened by poachers who collect the eggs for selling. Between March and August, volunteers are invited to participate in turtle protection programmes in Costa Rica, and now also in Panama, protecting the beach from poachers, monitoring and tagging turtles and clearing trails.

Applicants should be at least 18 years old, in reasonable health and have a serious commitment to conservation. Apply to the above address or via the website.

RECIFE VOLUNTARIO-VOLUNTEER CENTRE OF RECIFE
Av. Visconde de Suassuna 255, Boa Vista, CEP 50.050-540 Recife, Pernambuco, Brazil; ☎ +55 (81) 3221 7151; tel/fax +55 (810 3221-6911; e-mail recife@voluntario.org.br; www.voluntario.org.br
Recife Voluntario works with about 30 institutions in Recife and its suburbs. It aims to promote volunteerism in a region which is home to 3.5 million inhabitants. It runs courses for volunteers and offers a centralised placement service to institutions and projects in social, environmental and cultural spheres. The range of jobs open to volunteers is wide and includes administrative, technical, artistic, teaching, care of retired or sick etc. and they can find themselves working with every type of person from street children to the retired and sick.

For stays of under 6 months no work permit is required. However the volunteer should apply for a volunteer work permit for this period if the host institution requires it. Obtaining the permit is the volunteer's own responsibility.

No special skills or qualifications are essential but preference in selection will go to those with expertise in IT, psychology, management etc. A basic knowledge of Portuguese is absolutely essential. Applicants should also be over 18 and open-minded. Some institutions provide accommodation and pocket money/stipend.

Applications should be addressed at any time, by e-mail if possible to the above address.

EL SANTUARIO DE LA LUZ
Cobano de Punturenas, Costa Rica; fax +1 506 642-0089; e-mail akialba@hotmail.com
El Santuario is a retreat centre, a sanctuary for people and animals living in the rainforest of Costa Rica. Volunteer projects in the local community include: teaching English or

any special skills the appplicant may have; planting/reforestation; creating paths and an educational trail with labelled trees and fauna with a description of their use; gardening with herbs and weeding. Minimum stay of one month at any time of year, volunteers are especially needed from May to July (planting season). Applicants must be strong, healthy individuals, not afraid of hard work and nature, able to deal with the sun; knowledge of Spanish is useful but not essential. Volunteers pay a participation fee of $150 per week which covers food, accommodation and materials needed for the projects.

Applications to the Director at the above address.

SEA TURTLE RESTORATION PROJECT
PO Box 400, Forest Knolls, CA 94933, USA; ☎ +1 415 488-0370; fax +1 415 488-0372; e-mail info@seaturtles.org; www.seaturtles.org & www. tortugamarina.org

The Sea Turtle Restoration Project works to protect sea turtle populations in ways that both meet the sea turtles' ecological needs as well as the needs of local communities. The project encompasses grassroots action, multimedia campaigns, litigation, environmental education and hands-on conservation in Punta Banco, Costa Rica, in co-operation with PRETOMA the Costa Rican organisation advocating for sea turtles.

Nearly 70 volunteers are recruited annually to carry out nesting beach patrol, sea turtle hatchery work and educational activities with local children. Placements last at least two weeks (longer if requested) during the period mid-August to mid-January. Volunteers must be able to speak Spanish if they cannot speak English. The cost of a two-week stay ranges from $500-$700, which covers board and lodging.

Details of the project and related publications can be found on the websites. Volunteers can e-mail the Office Manager at info@seaturtles.org or the Costa Rica office at info@tortugamarina.org. Applications should be sent to the Office Manager who will forward the information to the Costa Rica project site or e-mailed direct to rarauz@sol. racsa.co.cr.

TASK BRASIL - The Abandoned Street Kids of Brazil Trust
PO Box 4901, London SE16 3PP; ☎020-7394 1177; fax 020-7394 7713; e-mail info@taskbrasil.org.uk; www.taskbrasil.org.uk

TASK BRASIL is a UK registered charity set up to operate a network of services for street children in Brazil. Through its Project Daiana for street children, it runs the Casa Jimmy home for children up to 6 years old, and pregnant girls. There is also a Street Approach Project which works with children and adolescents directly on the streets of Rio de Janeiro, assessing their immediate needs and referring them to care, shelters or back to their own families.

A maximum of two to four volunteers are recruited at any one time to work 40 hours per week for stays of one month to a year all year round. Volunteers, minimum age 21, help care for children and run workshops for adolescents, hence any skills particularly in music, computing, TEFL, crafts and sports are very useful. A knowledge of Portuguese, Spanish, or Italian is desirable. Placements cost from £1,200-£2,500 depending on length of stay. Board and lodging are provided.

For an application form and more information contact the above address.

THIRD WORLD OPPORTUNITIES
1363 Somermont Drive, El Cajon, CA 92021, USA; ☎ +1 619 449-9381; e-mail pgray@ucsd.edu; www.ecsd.org(programs)

Third World Opportunities works with the Rancho San Juan Bosco Home for Boys in Tecate, Mexico providing various work projects during spring and summer months. These are six-day events. Cost of the week is $225, which covers room, board and building materials, but does not include cost of transportation in getting there. Transportation information about transport can be provided. Knowledge of Spanish is helpful but not mandatory for volunteers.

For further information contact M. Laurel Gray, Project Co-ordinator, at the above address.

VOLUNTARIOS DE OCCIDENTE

Montalvo 4 - 18 y Cevallos, Oficina 310, Ambato, Ecuador; e-mail voccidente@hotmail.com; www.geocities.com/vdovolun/vdovolunteer.htm

VDO is a small independent organisation that recruits volunteers to teach English and other subjects such as information technology and sports in primary schools based in the rural area around the industrial centre of Ambato. It is a poor area, and without volunteers to teach them, the children would have no chance to learn English, which is a prerequisite for accessing secondary education.

Volunteers are needed for the four school terms of the year. The normal commitment is for two months. For positions other than those teaching English such as special courses, painting, construction, social work, community work etc., the minimum time can be one month. The maximum time allowed by the immigration authorities without a visa is six months. You can ask for a visa that will let you stay up to one year. Fees to the volunteer from VDO are: confirmation fee $95, fees if lodged in VDO home, per month $175; fees is living with a recommended affiliated local family in basic conditions, $225 a month ($400 for two months); better accommodation costs $275/$500.

For further details contact Gonzalo Alarcon and Maria Teresa Lopez at the above e-mail or postal address.

> **Andrew Kitching taught English to Ecuadorian primary school children**
> *I taught English, computing and sports in two primary schools to children from three to eleven years old. Every morning, when the volunteers arrived at the schools, we were bombarded with hugs, toothless grins, flowers, fruit and shouts of 'Good morning teacher.' It's a pleasant way to start the day, and the reason behind it is simple: classes are fun, and they provide the children with something seriously lacking around here; opportunity.*
>
> *Living and working in a relatively poor community is not mentally or physically easy; but I've come out of it with good friends, good memories, and a lot to think about.*

VOLUNTEER BOLIVIA
Mail address: Casilla 2411, Cochabamba, Bolivia; street address: Calle Ecuador 342, Cochabamba, Bolivia; fax 591 4 4526028; www.volunteerbolivia.org
Volunteer Bolivia offers a Spanish language immersion experience, volunteer positions and homestays in Cochabamba, Bolivia. Volunteers work with a wide range of humanitarian organisations to give them a chance to make a difference.

About 50-60 international volunteers are recruited annually to work in micro-enterprises, environmental organisations, literacy centres, children's services, education and health. Volunteers should stay for a minimum of one month and there is no maximum limit subject to the Bolivian government provided a courtesy visa if necessary. Volunteers who do not speak Spanish will be able to learn in the program's language classes. Volunteers are accepted all year round and help will be given finding accommodation with Bolivian families. Volunteers live and work in Bolivia at their own expense. Tours and travel arrangements can be made for individuals and groups.

Further details on the website.

YOUTH CHALLENGE INTERNATIONAL
305-20 Maud, Toronto, Ontario M5V 2M5, Canada; ☎ +1 -416-504 3370; fax +1 416-504-3376; e-mail generalinfo@yci.org; www.yci.org
Youth Challenge International combines community development, health work and conservation work in dynamic projects carried out by teams of volunteers aged 18-30 years. Projects last from five weeks to three months in Costa Rica, Guyana, Vanuatu and Tanzania and Ethiopia and provide opportunities for young people to build their skills and leadership capabilities on grassroots development projects. Areas of priority include HIV/AIDS, Community Infrastructure, Youth Skills Building, Women's Networking and Capacity building..

Participants who do not hold a Canadian passport are responsible for the cost of the flight to the host country as well as obtaining visas and other required travel documents. Participation fees start at about $2,735. Details and costs of the programmes are available on their website.

Professional and Longer-term Volunteering

AMAZON-AFRICA AID ORGANISATION
P.O.Box 7776, Ann Arbour, MI 48107, USA; ☎ +1 734 769 5778; fax +1 734 769 5779; e-mail info@amazonafrica.org; www.amazonafrica.org
Amazon-Africa Aid Organisation is a non-profit organisation which sends volunteer physicians, gynaecologists, dentists and family practitioners to work at its medical clinic in the Amazon. It also provides support to health, education and welfare organisations along the Brazilian Amazon.

The minimum volunteer stay is a month and volunteers are needed year round. Room and board are provided but all other personal expenses are borne by the volunteer.

For a volunteer pack, contact the above address.

THE CHOL-CHOL FOUNDATION
Rengalil, Camino Temuco-Imperial Km 16, Casilla 45, Temuco, Chile; tel/fax +56 45-6140074; e-mail info@cholchol.org; www.cholchol.org
The Chol-Chol Foundation works with women from indigenous communities of the Ninth region of Chile, delivering integral education for those with limited resources in order to create opportunities for self-sufficient development. Its activities stem from this goal in the fields of agriculture, health, commercialisation, micro-enterprises, etc. About 5 to 10 volunteers, minimim age 21 are recruited annually. Fluency in Spanish and a university degree are essential; a driving licence is preferable. Placements vary according to any given time, they last from three months to a year.

For further information, contact Johanna Perez, the volunteers' program coordinator.

CONCERN AMERICA
P.O. Box 1790, Santa Ana, CA 92702, USA; ☎ +714-953-8575; fax +1 714 953 1242; e-mail concamerica@earthlink.net
Concern America is an international development and refugee organisation. Through the work of professionally trained volunteers, Concern America assists impoverished communities and refugees in developing countries in their efforts to improve living conditions. At present there are volunteers in Brazil, El Salvador, Guatemala, Honduras and Mexico in the Americas and Guinea and Mozambique in Africa. Concern America programmes emphasise training of community members to impart skills and knowledge,which will remain long after the volunteers have gone. Round trip transportation, health insurance, and room and board provided as well as a small monthly stipend (approx. $350 per month). A repatriation allowance of $50 per month of service first year; $100 a month second year and $150 per month in the third year. Qualifications: degree/experience in public health, medicine, nutrition, nursing, agriculture, community development, education and appropriate technology. Minimum commitment is two years and minimum age is 21.

GALAPAGOS NATIONAL PARK'S VOLUNTEER PROGRAMME
Avenida Charles Darwin S/N, Puerto Ayora, Isla Santa Cruz, Galapagos, Ecuador; ☎ +593 5 526511; fax +593 5 520497; e-mail velasqu 1@spng.org.ec; www. galapagospark.org
Ecological organisation that operates in the Galapagos islands of Ecuador. Offers

professionals the opportunity to work as volunteers in the monitoring of native and endemic threatened species, environmental education activities and marine and coastal cleaning campaigns.

25-30 volunteers are engaged annually. Skills required can be anything from a computer programmer's to a biologist's. For details of the latest requirements visit the website. Period of commitment is three months to a year. Volunteers must be self-funding and pay their own living expenses. Accommodation may be available but can become full. Volunteers may also be sent to other islands where the organisation does not have a volunteer house. Good health is essential and fieldwork is very demanding.

For application details visit the website.

HCJB UK
131 Grattan Road, Bradford, West Yorkshire BD1 2HS; ☎01274-721 810; fax 01274-514960; e-mail info@hcjb.org.uk; www.hcjb.org

HCJB undertakes media and medical ministries in Ecuador, South America, and the United Kingdom and elsewhere. Around 50 volunteers are needed each year to help with various projects. Audio and broadcasting engineers, announcers, scriptwriters and other volunteers with experience in communications are needed for media ministries; doctors wishing to do their medical electives, nurses and laboratory technicians are required for the medical ministries in Ecuador, and youth workers, printers, secretaries, office helpers, etc. are needed for each. Placements vary from one to three months or longer, all year round.

All volunteers are welcome but they must be committed Christians and in agreement with this organisation's Statement of Faith. Only medical volunteers must speak Spanish but it is an advantage to speak Spanish if wishing to serve in Ecuador. Volunteers must raise their own financial support and accommodation on a rental basis is provided. No visas are required for periods of less than three months.

For more details contact the Director of Personnel at the above address.

IRISH MISSIONARY UNION
IMU, St Paul's Retreat, Mount Argus, Lower Kimmage Road, Dublin 6W, Ireland; ☎ +353-1 4923325/4923326.

The IMU was founded to promote co-operation between missionary, mission-sending and mission-aid organisations, thereby helping them to make the best and most efficient use of their personnel and other resources. Its principal aim is to assist the Bishops in the task of spreading the Gospel and therefore the IMU works in close collaboration with the Irish Hierarchy. It also acts as a liaison between missionary bodies and national or international organisations involved in evangelization and development.

The IMU recruits volunteers to work in the following areas in African and Latin American countries: medicine, education, trade, agriculture and pastoral and community development. Qualified and experienced doctors, nurses, laboratory technicians, teachers, paramedics, builders, plumbers and social workers are all needed. It is essential that all volunteers should derive their motivation from Christian values, and be in good health and at least 21 years of age. The minimum length of placement is two years. A monthly allowance, accommodation, resettlement allowance, insurance and return air fare are all provided.

Those interested should contact the Judith Lenehan at the above address at any time of the year.

LOS MEDICOS VOLADORES
PO Box 445, Los Gatos, CA 95031-0445; ☎ +800 585 4568 in CA only,

otherwise +1 408-356 9054; www.flyingdocs.org
Los Medicos Voladores organises medical, dental and optometrical teams to remote villages in northern Mexico and Baja. Up to six volunteers are flown in small aircraft to different areas for four-day stints, once a month, to provide professional health care services to rural inhabitants of Mexico. Volunteers who are health care professionals, pilots, those bilingual in Spanish and educators are especially welcome.

Volunteers are lodged locally, sometimes in private homes. There is a volunteer's annual membership fee of $35 and $200 for travel costs. Living expenses are also borne by the volunteers.

QUEEN LOUISE HOME FOR CHILDREN/LUTHERAN SOCIAL SERVICES
PO Box 866, Frederiksted, St. Croix, US Virgin Islands 00841.
The Home provides temporary care for abused, abandoned, neglected and developmentally retarded children, regardless of race, religion or national origin, while permanent placement plans for them are processed. The Virgin Islands Department of Human Services relies heavily upon the Home to meet a large part of the evergrowing need for institutional childcare. The Home takes in approximately twelve volunteers annually to work as cottage parents. Cottage parents serve as caretakers for twelve hour shifts for eight to ten children, aged between three and twelve. Responsibilities include caring for each child's emotional, physical, educational and spiritual needs; developing creative, social, educational, recreational and cultural programmes for them; and maintaining the cottages, grounds, clothes and vehicles. Applicants may either be married with no dependants or two single people who work as a team. They must have experience with children, be flexibile, patient and be culturally adaptable, as well as professional and objective in judgement and attitude. They must be team workers and willing to work under supervision.

Applicants of any nationality are welcome, but they must have had two years of college training (preferably in child development but this is not essential). They must possess a strong personal Christian commitment and have had experience of childcare in or out of a job setting. A valid driving licence is essential. The Home is wheelchair-accessible, but disabled applicants should note that the role of cottage parent demands a high level of energy and physical capabilities. Cottage parents are contracted for one year.

The Queen Louise Home is part of the Americorp programme and volunteers are eligible for the same benefits of other participants in their programme. Eligibility is limited to US citizens only.

Enquiries should be sent to the Director at the above address.

Israel, Palestinian-Governed Territories & Egypt

THE CHURCH'S MINISTRY AMONG JEWISH PEOPLE
30c Clarence Road, St Albans, Herts AL1 4JJ; ☎01727-833114; fax 01727-848312; e-mail enquiries@cmj.org.uk; www.cmj.org.uk/
Every year CMJ needs volunteers to work in its two centres in Israel for periods of three to 12 months. The work usually consists of the preparation and serving of meals for guests, housework and part-time reception work. No special skills are required and volunteers may be of any nationality provided they are over 18 years old and in good health. A stay of six months is preferred, but occasionally, short-term posts are available.

Volunteers must pay for their own travel expenses and medical insurance (approximately £80) and a contribution towards board and lodging of about £35 per week is encouraged, possibly paid by the volunteer's home church. Visas are arranged in Israel.

Further details can be obtained from the Volunteer Promoter at the above address.

EMMS International (operating as Emmanuel Healthcare)
7 Washington Lane, Edinburgh EH11 2HA; ☎0131-313 3828; fax 0131-313 4662; e-mail info@emms.org; www.emms.org
Emmanuel Healthcare became the operating name in 2004, as a result of EMMS International and EHA (UK) merging. It supports programmes in India (slum project, hospitals and community health projects, AIDS hospice), Malawi (hospitals), Nepal (TB and leprosy clinic) and the Middle East (Nazareth Hospital) and helps to obtain volunteers. General help is welcomed in Nazareth but medical or nursing staff cannot be taken due to licensing restrictions. Vacancies can occur at any time of year. Travel expenses are not paid. Simple accommodation is provided but food may not necessarily be included. For more information contact Emmanuel Healthcare, and to apply contact the following person in writing :
Israel: Mrs. Christine Farah, The Nazareth Hospital EMMS, P.O. Box 11, 16100 Nazareth, Israel; tel +9726 602 8817; fax +9724 656 1953; e-mail ChristineFarah@nazhosp.com.

THE FOUR HOMES OF MERCY
PO Box 19185, Jerusalem 91191; ☎ +972 2-6282076; fax +972 2-6274871; e-mail homes4@bezeqint.net
The Four Homes of Mercy is an independent charity, non-profitable and non-governmental. The aim of the Society is to develop new methods and social recreational programmes which enable the profoundly disabled people to be as independent as possible. The four homes are located in Bethany, West Bank, Palestine. The four homes are: The Old Age Home for Men and Women, the Crippled Teenage Home, the Crippled Children's Home and St. Mary's Maternity. The first three homes are located in Bethany and St. Mary's is located in Beit Jala, a twin town to Bethlehem, also in the West Bank, Palestine.

Volunteers participate in various activities dependent on their skills and field of interest such as painting, white-washing, playing with and feeding residents, gardening, sewing, nursing, helping in the kitchen, teaching patients English, playing music, occupational and physiotherapy (if suitably qualified).

Placements last from one month to two years. Previous volunteers, aged between 25 and 60, have come from America, Britain, the Netherlands and Sweden. English is widely spoken although knowledge of Arabic would be advantageous. Health insurance is advisable. Accommodation is provided when available and pocket money of $50 per month provided. For those boarding at the homes meals are provided. All other expenses must be covered by the volunteer.

Applications preferably through an organisation or church which can recommend the applicant. Note that because of the very unstable situation between Israel and Palestine recruiting may be subject to interruption. However, the Four Homes are hoping for better days and more volunteers.

FRIENDS OF BIRZEIT UNIVERSITY (FoBZU)
1, Gough Square, London EC4A 3DE; ☎020-7373 8414; fax 020-7835 2088; e-mail fobzu@fobzu.org; www.fobzu.org
Birzeit University is a Palestinian university, 26 kilometres north of Jerusalem in the Occupied West Bank. Every year the University holds international workcamps which offer volunteers the opportunity to experience the local situation at first hand and to contribute to improving the local conditions of life. Tasks include helping farmers with their harvest, building basic sanitation facilities in refugee camps and other community work. A wide range of visits, meetings and cultural events are also arranged. The placements last 14-15 days. Minimum age of volunteers is 18. Accommodation is provided but other expenses must be covered by the volunteer.

Applications to the Co-ordinator at the above address.

FRIENDS OF ISRAEL EDUCATIONAL FOUNDATION
P.O. Box 7545, London NW2 2QZ; ☎020-7435 6803; fax 020-7794 0291; e-mail info@foi-asg.org; www.foi-asg.org
FOIEF runs the Bridge in Britain Scheme, which is a school leaver award scheme. Twelve travel awards are granted competitively each year. Each Bridge group spends six months working in Israel. Travel to and from Israel and basic living expenses are provided, but not pocket money. The Foundation also offers placements in Israel for young artists, farmers and horticulturists/botanists. All awards are offered to permanent UK residents only.

Further details from the Director at the above address.

INTERNS FOR PEACE (IFP)
475 Riverside Drive, Room 240, New York, New York 10115-0109, USA; ☎+1 212 870-2226; fax +1 212 870-2911.
Interns for Peace (IFP), established in 1976 in Israel, was the first and remains the only programme with the purpose of training community development and peace workers in Israel, and now in Palestinian Gaza/West Bank, Jordan and Egypt, initiating co-operative inter-communal action that unites all people. About a dozen interns (community peace workers) organised placements for thousands of Jews and Arabs in the fields of business, athletic, cultural, educational, women's, and community development projects. Intern graduates and former participants in IFP activities become lifetime advocates of co-existence, if not full time professionals. IFP is also developing pilot projects to improve ethnic relations worldwide.

Applicants should be: dedicated to Israel, humanity, and to a peaceful Middle East; proficient in advanced Hebrew or Arabic; resident in the Middle East for six months prior to IFP placement; have a college education and prior work experience outside a university setting; work well with people, especially children and young people. Volunteers must pay for their own travel expenses to and from the Middle East, visas and travel insurance. During the placement interns are funded by the IFP but are expected to help receive scholarship funds to cover this cost. Minimum commitment one year.

For further details and an application form contact the North American Executive Director at the above address. Applications must be accompanied by a CV and 500-word essay explaining why the applicant is interested in working for IFP, what they have to offer and what they expect to gain from the experience.

ISRAEL ANTIQUITIES AUTHORITY
PO Box 586, 91004 Jerusalem, Israel; ☎ +972-2 620 4622; fax +972-2 628 9066; www.antiquities.co.il
A number of archaeological excavations in Israel conducted by the Israel Antiquities Authority, universities and research institutes from Israel and abroad, accept volunteers every year, usually during May, June, July and the first half of August. A detailed list is available on the internet website of the Israel Ministry of Foreign Affairs given above.

The minimum age is usually 18 years old and the minimum participation period usually two weeks. Volunteers must be willing and able to do any work connected with the excavation for long hours in hot weather. Accommodation and food are provided by the expedition but full or part payment may be asked.

THE JERUSALEM PRINCESS BASMA CENTRE FOR DISABLED CHILDREN
East Jerusalem, Via Israel, POB 19764, Jerusalem 91197, Israel; ☎ +972-2 6283058/6264536; fax +972-2 6274449.
The Centre is a non-governmental, charitable organisation which cares for physically disabled children up to 15 years. Volunteers may be involved in activities such as: recreational therapy, hydrotherapy, assisting in kindergarten classes, or helping with general maintenance – painting or gardening. Opportunities are also available for professionals in the fields of physiotherapy, hydrotherapy and occupational therapy. 10 to 15 volunteers are recruited throughout the year, ranging between 1 and 5 at any one time. Minimum period of stay is 3 months but a longer commitment period is preferred.

Volunteers must be covered by their own health insurance and be entirely self-funding. Pocket money of $50 per month is only paid to professionals. Board and lodging in single/double rooms at the Centre are provided to all volunteers free of charge. Male volunteers cannot be accommodated on site due to traditional restrictions – children's mothers sleep at the Centre – however, alternative arrangements can be made.

Applications must either be made through formal organisations – churches, schools, etc. or direct applications from individuals must be accompanied by references.

KIBBUTZ PROGRAM CENTER
Volunteer Department, Takam-Artzi, 18 Frishman Street, corner of Ben Yehuda, Tel Aviv 61030, Israel; Postal address: PO Box 3167, Tel Aviv, Israel; ☎ +972-3 527 8874; +972-3 524 6156; fax +972-3 523 9966; e-mail kpc@vollentir.co.il; www.kibbutz.org.net.il
This organisation accepts visitors, both as individuals and groups, as volunteers in the kibbutz for a minimum period of two months and maximum six months. While staying in the kibbutz the volunteers are part of the kibbutz population and enjoy a great part of the kibbutz social and material benefits. A basic knowledge of English is necessary for

participation, and the age limits are 18-38 years. A working visitor on a kibbutz works an eight hour day, six days a week. Apart from Saturday, which is usually the day of rest, the visitor receives three extra days per month. As a rule, working visitors must be prepared to do any kind of work allotted to them by the work manager. No volunteer is forced to stay at a workplace against his/her will. If a volunteer stays for 4 to 6 months then they usually get to choose their place of work. The volunteers can always request to be reassigned to a different branch of work and – if possible – the volunteer leader will allow the volunteer to move after a certain period of time.

The kind of work involved is of a very diversified nature, and depends on the type of kibbutz that the volunteer is sent to. It is still mainly agricultural, but increasingly tends to be industrial as well. As the kibbutz is a self-supporting community, with its own services, many volunteers also go into essential services. The kibbutz provides rooms (for two to three persons), meals in the dining hall, laundry service, work clothes, medical care, entertainment and pocket money. The volunteers are entitled to use the facilities on the kibbutz particularly for sports and swimming. Travel expenses are not paid.

The best way to ensure a place on a kibbutz is by applying through the Kibbutz Program Centre by the address above via e-mail, fax or telephone. You can also contact the Kibbutz Representative in your own country. In the UK this is 1, Accommodation Road, Golders Green, London NW11 8EP; ☎020-7458 9235; for the USA: 27 West 20th Street, New York, NY 10011; ☎+1 212 255 1338.

KIBBUTZ REPRESENTATIVES
16 Accommodation Road, Golders Green, London NW11 8EP; ☎020-8458 9235; fax 020-8455 7930; e-mail enquiries@kibbutz.org.uk
Each year working holidays on kibbutzim in Israel are organised for about 3,000 people aged 18-45 and in good health. The work may involve physical labour in the fields, orchards, fishponds, cowsheds and gardens; or work in the kitchens, laundry, general services or factory. Applicants must pay for their own travelling expenses and insurance for their stay lasting from two to three months with the option of extending it up to a year. A special work visa is needed and this will be arranged at the Kibbutz Representatives office. They will then receive free board and accommodation, leisure and entertainment facilities and occasional excursions, plus a small amount of pocket money.

All nationalities are welcome, except those which do not hold diplomatic relations with Israel. One can arrange to travel either as an individual or with a group of around ten people, which will be organized by Kibbutz Representatives. Prospective participants are all interviewed by Kibbutz Representatives and kibbutz life is fully explained. Kibbutz Representatives is the only official organisation which represents all the kibbutzim in Israel.

Enquiries to the above address.

MARTIN (SZUSZ) DEPARTMENT OF LAND OF ISRAEL STUDIES & ARCHAEOLOGY
Bar Ilan University, Ramat-Gan, Israel 52900; ☎ +972 3-5318299/350; fax +972 3-5351233; e-mail maeira@mail.biu.ac.il; www.dig-gath.org (Tel es-Safi/ Gath Archaeological Project website)
The Tell es-Safi/Gath Archaeological Project is a long-term archaeological venture studying the site of Tell es- Safi in central Israel (half way between Jerusalem and Ashkelon), one of the largest ancient sites in Israel. It was settled from the proto-historic through modern periods and is identified as the Gath of the Philistines mentioned in biblical texts and claimed to be the home of Goliath. Excavations have revealed extensive and impressive Bronze and Iron Ages remains. Volunteers are invited to apply

for participation (minimum two weeks). Room and board are provided but volunteers have to fund both the cost of this and travel to Israel. An accredited academic field school is also run, in which students can receive university credits. Dates for 2005 are 10 July to 5 August.

For additional information and application forms, contact the above.

NES AMMIM (ECUMENICAL CHRISTIAN VILLAGE)
in the UK: c/o Revd Peter Jennings, The Methodist Manse, 68 Melbourn Road, Royston, Herts. SG8 7DG; ☎01763-230210; e-mail pjennings@royston1999. freeserve.co.uk
The ecumenical Christian village of Nes Ammim is home and study centre for the development of mutual respect, tolerance and understanding. Situated in the Western Galilee, surrounded by Jewish communal settlements and Arab towns with Muslim, Druze and Christian populations, Nes Ammim offers a place of cross cultural learning: to experience Jewish life in the State of Israel; to live as an ecumenical community in the diaspora; to witness the development of Jewish-Arab coexistence and cooperation.

Twelve volunteers are recruited annually for a twelve month period to work in areas of horticulture, carpentry, hotel and hostel work. Volunteers must be aged between 20 and 40. German or Dutch language skills and a knowledge of continental European Reformation and post-Reformation theology are useful but not essential. Shared accommodation, pocket money and health care insurance are provided. Volunteers pay for their own air fare.

Those interested should apply to the above address. For more information on Nes Ammim, e-mail nesam–cc@netvision.net.il.

NEVE SHALOM/WAHAT AL-SALAM
Doar Na Shimshon, 99761 Israel; ☎ +972-2 9912222; fax +972-2 9912098; e-mail rita@nswas.com; www.nswas.com
NS/WAS is a Jewish/Palestinian village with educational institutions intended to contribute to understanding and tolerance between these two peoples. The Community also has a guesthouse. Volunteers assist in the nursery, kindergarten, school and guesthouse doing simple, unskilled work. There are five to six volunteers working at NS/WAS at any one time. It is preferred that applicants speak fluent English. Volunteers must be aged between 19 and 30. Volunteers are expected to stay at least six months and preferably twelve months at any time of year. Pocket money and accommodation are provided free.

Anyone interested should contact Rita Boulos, the Volunteer Recruiter at the above address.

OTZMA
111 Eighth Avenue, Suite 11E, New York, New York 10011, USA; ☎212-284-6721; e-mail otzma@ujc.org; www.otzma.org
OTZMA is a 10-month volunteer leadership development program for Jewish adults, ages 20-26 (college graduates preferred). OTZMA provides its participants with the opportunity to live and work with Israelis on kibbutzim, immigration absorption centres, and areas of urban renewal. OTZMA also includes an intensive educational programme, hiking trips throughout the country, and the unique experience of an Israeli adoptive family. Upon return to North America, OTZMA graduates are expected to apply their skills and knowledge to serve their local Jewish communities. Applicants pay their own airfare and a fee to cover the programme costs.

Interested applicants should contact OTZMA office via e-mail or phone.

OXFAM-QUÉBEC
Middle East Regional Office, PO Box 20560, Jerusalem, Israel; tel/fax +972-2656 8923/3; e-mail oxfamqot@palnet.com; www.oxfam.qc.ca
Oxfam-Québec has been active in the Middle East since 1989. In order to strengthen civil society and ensure a long-term developmental impact. Oxfam Québec works in partnership with local non-governmental organisations and institutions. This support is manifested through technical and financial assistance, as well as the management of large-scale bilateral and multi-lateral projects. In the Middle East, Oxfam-Québec emphasises initiatives involving women, refugees and youth.

Oxfam-Québec has placed more than 50 volunteers and youth interns in Palestine and Lebanon. Approximately five volunteers are recruited a year for positions with local partner organisations, working on health, community and human rights projects.

Applicants must be of Canadian nationality and in good health. Other criteria vary with placements. A commitment of one or two years is usual. Volunteers receive accommodation, a monthly installation allowance, medical, dental, life and disability insurance, return airfare, visa costs, tuition fees for children, storage expenses and a re-integration grant. Pre-departure briefing in Canada, and an in country orientation upon arrival in the Middle East are also organized.

For the latest information on volunteer vacancies visit the website.

RELIGIOUS KIBBUTZ MOVEMENT
7 Dubnov Street, Tel Aviv, Israel; ☎ +972-3 6072777; e-mail kdati@virtual.co.il; www.virtualjerusalem.com/clients/kibzdati
The Movement accepts a limited number of volunteers to work on its kibbutzim which are situated in many parts of Israel, including the Beit Sh'ean Valley, Ashdod, Ashkelon, and the Jerusalem and Tel Aviv areas. It should be noted however that only Jewish young people who are ready to follow an orthodox way of life are taken on as volunteers by the Movement. The minimum period of stay is two months. The volunteer works at least eight and a half hours each day, most of the work being seasonal and agricultural. The Movement also runs four Kibbutz-Ulpan programmes (five months in duration), which combine formal instruction in Hebrew with voluntary work in a Kibbutz. These programmes take place throughout the year.

Volunteers must be at least 18 years of age, and in good health. No special qualifications are needed, but people with diplomas in life-saving are appreciated. All nationalities are welcome. Accommodation and food are provided, and moderate pocket money is paid. Expenses are not paid, including those arising from travel. A tourist visa is required but no work permit is needed.

Applications should be sent to: Bnei Akiva, 2 Hallswell Road, London, NW11 0DJ or to Kibbutz Representatives, 16 Accommodation Road, London NW11 8EP.

UNIPAL - A Universities' Trust for Educational Exchange with Palestinians BCM
Unipal, London WC1N 3XX; unipal1@hotmail.com; www.unipal.org.
Unipal recruits volunteers to teach English to Palestinian refugee children living in camps in Palestine in the West Bank and Gaza, and camps in Lebanon. Cost £500 includes flights, food, accommodation and insurance. The minimum age is 20. The posts last 5 weeks (July/August). Send a 42p SAE for details. Application should be by the end of February. Interviews are held in March.

WIND SAND & STARS
6 Tyndale Terrace, London N1 2AT; ☎020-7359 7551; fax 020-7359 4936; e-mail office@windsandstars.co.uk; www.windsandstars.co.uk

Expedition members are needed to participate in a 4-week summer expedition to the desert and high mountain areas of Sinai in Egypt. Participants will have the opportunity to work on a number of community based projects directly with the local Bedouin. They will travel and live with the local people learning about their culture and way of life. Participants will also have the opportunity to learn about leadership and remote survival skills and pursue their own research and study in their own areas of interest. There will also be time to explore the beautiful environment of Sinai, trekking through the high mountain regions and camel trekking through the sandstone desert visiting ancient and historical sites along the way.

Enquiries to the above address.

Africa

General Opportunities

AFRICA AND ASIA VENTURE
10 Market Place, Devizes, Wilts. SN10 1HT; ☎01380-729009; fax 01380-720060; e-mail av@aventure.co.uk; www.aventure.co.uk
Africa and Asia Venture is essentially a gap year organisation aimed at adventurous students who want to spend part of their year out gaining work experience with youth in Kenya, Uganda, Tanzania, Botswana and Malawi in Africa and also in the Indian Himalayas and Nepal in Asia and Mexico in the Americas. Projects include teaching in secondary and primary schools, conservation and community projects. About 490 students participate annually. Age range is 18-24. Placements last four months starting in September, October, January or May. The basic participation fee is £2590 which covers placement, orientation course on arrival, in-country back-up, living allowance and accommodation, a donation towards a deserving child or school equipment, a safari and comprehensive health and personal effects insurance.

Contact the above address for an application form.

AFRICAN CONSERVATION EXPERIENCE
P.O. Box 28, Ottery St. Mary, Devon, EX11 1ZN; ☎0870-241 5816; fax 0870 241 5816; e-mail info@conservationafrica.net; www.conservationafrica.net
ACE organises conservation work placements on game reserves in southern Africa inluding game capture, monitoring and census, wildlife veterinary work, wildlife rehabilitation, behavioural studies and conservation on horseback. About 200 volunteer placements are made annually. Placements last 4-12 weeks and the minimum age is 17 years. Volunteers pay a fee, which covers flights and
board and lodging. Fund raising guidance provided by ACE. An enthusiasm for conservation is essential. Further details and a brochure pack available from the above address.

ASSOCIATION DES CHANTIERS DES JEUNES (ACJ)
B.P. 171, Salé Medina, 11005 Morocco; tel/fax +212 3785; e-mail acj.ong. maroc@caramail.com
Founded in 1967, ACJ is a not-for-profit organisation that works to safeguard the environment, incorporates youth into the social and cultural life of the area, development of the rural regions, restoration of monuments, to institute peace and cooperation between people without distinction of their religion, race or colour.

ACJ places about 400 volunteers annually. The types of work done by volunteers include assisting with children's activities, restoration of monuments, maintenance work etc. There are also courses in ceramics, and other Moroccan handicrafts and language. Volunteers should be over 18. Workcamps last from one to three weeks and participants are from many countries. Volunteers pay a participation fee which covers board and lodging. There are about 90 volunteers per camp.

Apply direct to ACJ at the above address.

ARIDE ISLAND NATURE RESERVE
c/o Island Conservation Society UK, Hazeley Brook, Keele Road, Keele, Staffordshire, ST5 5AL; ☎01782-751605; e-mail rob@lucking.idps.co.uk

Aride Island is an internationally important nature reserve in the Seychelles (off the east coast of Africa) owned by the Royal Society of Wildlife Trusts. The island requires two volunteers for each three-month period to assist the island manager in scientific monitoring, research, habitat/species management and tourist guiding. Specialists such as mechanics, carpenters, solar electricians etc. may be required from time to time.

Volunteers should have a degree or equivalent in environmental/biological sciences, or other technical skills (see above). Applicants should be fit and have good health as nearest medical post is one hour away by boat. A contribution of £400 is required towards expenses. Basic accommodation is provided. Fact sheets are available from the above e-mail address.

Apply direct to the above address. Specific queries can be answered by e-mail.

AZAFADY
Studio 7, 1A Beethoven Street, London W10 4LG; ☎020-8960 6629; fax 020-8962 0126; e-mail mark@azafady.org; www.madagascar.co.uk

Azafady is a charity working on environmental, humanitarian and sustainable development projects in Madagascar (a large island off southern east Africa) since 1995. They have bases in London, Miami and Madagascar.

Volunteers with Azafady are involved in grass roots conservation and development work with an award-winning team of dynamic, young staff researching lemur, turtle and bird monitoring, forest management, GPS and other data collection, projects that improve well-being, generate income or aid food security. Voluntary worker visas are supplied by the Malagasy Council in London, UK. Volunteers should be in good physical and mental health. Projects last 10 weeks, or long-term volunteers, running their own projects can stay up to a year. Volunteers have to bring their own tents. The minimum volunteer donation is £2,000 of which £500 is the initial deposit to secure a placement. It is hoped that the money will be raised from sponsorship and Azafady can advise on this. The funds cover in-country project linked travel, meals and safe water, accommodation when not in tents, back-up, in-country training, in-country language classes. Groups of 10-15 for the ten week projects.

For more information and an application form apply to the London HQ.

The Centre for Alternative Development Strategies (CADS)
Sierra Leone: 61 Sackville Street, PMB 1290, Freetown, Sierra Leone; ☎ +11 232 22 224839; fax +11 232 22 22224439; e-mail development@cads-sierraleone.org; www.cads-sierraleone.org; in the US: CADS, 1361 S. Irving Street, Denver, Colorado 80219, USA; ☎ +303 937 3798; fax +303 937 3798; e-mail cadsintlprograms@aol.com

CADS runs international volunteer exchange programmes in Sierra Leone and Liberia that work on projects emphasising cooperation, where volunteers from all over the world can work together in sharing resources, ideas and solutions. Volunteers pay a registration fee of US$750 or the equivalent a month in advance of arrival. This covers registration certificates, reading materials and an audio-visual documentary on Sierra Leone or Liberia sent prior to arrival. Volunteer fees are paid in cash in US dollars or equivalent on arrival in Freetown. There are two durations of stay: short term: the minimum stay is one week and the maximum four weeks and costs US$4,895; longer term is for five to 12 weeks and costs US$7,950.

The CADS range of activities covers reconciliation, reconstruction and rehabilitation programmes, community based projects, agricultural projects, earth rescue programmes, overseas exchanges and academic guidance programmes.

For further information contact one of the above addresses.

CHANTIERS SOCIAUX MAROCAINS
BP 456 Rabat, Morocco; ☎212 7 29 71 84; fax 212 7 69 89 50; e-mail csm@wanadoo.net.ma
CSM organises English courses for Moroccan youths from 15-18 years of age. The courses are organised for young adults from modest or poor families in Rabat, Marrakech and Fez, who that do not have the financial resources to afford private schools.

Fifteen placements are offered to volunteers willing to introduce the English language to Moroccan youths giving them the opportunity to discover a new language and for older students to overcome any difficulties they have encountered while learning the language. As well as this academic aim these programmes are also considered a useful forum for both volunteers and Morrocans to build exchange experiences and knowledge and build long-term understanding of each other's cultures. It is believed that by promoting contact between young individuals from different countries leads to a greater level of cultural respect, which is fundamental for a peaceful future.

Programmes take place in July/August and last four weeks. Each volunteer has a class of 25-30 students. Lessons take place four hours each morning Monday to Friday. Free board and accommodation is provided with a host family. All other expenses are borne by the volunteers.

Applications from the UK can be made through ICYE in London (020-7681 0983).

CHARITY YOUTH TRAVEL ORGANISATION FOR WORKING EXPERIENCE ABROAD (CYTOFWEA)
P.O. Box MA 30, HO. V/R Ghana; ☎233-91-27008; e-mail cytotwena 001@yahoo.com
An NGO, non-political and non-profit organisation which arranges voluntary work in Ghana and overseas in a cross-cultural environment. Arranges placements in Ghana in health, early childhood development, education (teaching at all levels of schooling), forestry, conservation, fisheries, environmental protection, tourism, agro-forestry, agriculture etc. Participants should be a specialist in their preferred field of voluntary work and other skills may also be of advantage. Must be in good health. Minimum age is 18. Minimum stay is 3 months. Teachers are required during the school year term time. Accommodation is provided. A week's orientation is given before starting. Volunteers are self-funded.

Apply direct to Sylvanus Nuku Ameko, Co-ordinator, at the above address.

THE FUTURE IN OUR HANDS-TANZANIA
P.O. Box 147, Bunda, Tanzania
The Future in Our Hands organisation carries out activities in relation to voluntary work including programmes in environment conservation and development. Six volunteers are accepted annually to help with teaching management of non-governmental organisations, environment conservation, education, health, poverty alleviation, research. Volunteers require education/and or experience in the field of activity they choose to apply for. Volunteers stay five weeks to six months. Once in Tanzania, one week is spent planning the work programme to cover the entire period of stay. Volunteers are required all year

round. The volunteer coordinator can arrange all accommodation by arrangement. Apply to the above box number address.

GREENFORCE – Africa, Amazon, Borneo, Fiji, Bahamas
11-15 Betterton Street, Covent Garden, London WC2H 9BP; ☎020-7470 8888; fax 020-7470 8889; e-mail Greenforce@btinternet.com; www.greenforce.org

Greenforce is an international non-profit organisation. Greenforce is invited by the host country government to undertake base line biodiversity studies in previously unsurveyed areas. This information may be needed prior to setting up a new National Park or setting up new areas for tourism. Greenforce also undertake conservation education programmes. When they leave an area all the equipment is donated to that region and the local staff are all suitably trained. Greenforce primarily work in remote tropical regions of outstanding natural beauty and run land and marine projects.

Greenforce need volunteers to work for 10 weeks in any of their project locations. No experience is necessary, as Greenforce provides full training. If an overseas volunteer cannot attend the UK Training Weekend they will receive the Greenforce Distance Learning Packs and Video. On marine projects Greenforce provides free dive training up to and including BSAC Sports Diver. On arrival in the host country all volunteers attend training lectures at the host country university prior to going to the field. Volunteers contribute around £2,550 towards their project. This covers food, accommodation, visa, medical insurance, in-country travel, training etc. Volunteer numbers are restricted to four per member of staff.

One volunteer per expedition is chosen to stay on as a Greenforce trainee. The trainee then assists the staff on the next expedition. Greenforce pay all food, accommodation and travel costs for trainees. Paid staff positions are offered first to ex-trainees. All staff qualify for funding to pay the fees for a UK MSc of their choice. Therefore Greenforce can be either an amazing 10 weeks in a beautiful location or the start of a career in conservation. Call for the latest brochure or view their website.

KENYA VOLUNTARY DEVELOPMENT ASSOCIATION (KVDA)
Box 48902, Nairobi, Kenya; ☎+254-2 225379/247393; fax +254-2 225379.

KVDA places about 270 volunteers on six workcamps throughout Kenya every year. 45 volunteers are required for each of six community-based projects such as building schools, hospitals, bridges and any other community supported projects dependent on the need at the time. Help is needed in April, July, August and December. Minimum age 17. Participation on the camps costs US$200 to cover board and lodging expenses. Other fees, e.g airfare to and from Kenya, to be met by the volunteer.

Applications to the Director at the above address.

MADVENTURER
Adamson House, 65 Westgate Road, Newcastle upon Tyne NE1 1SG; ☎0191-261 19961; e-mail team@madventurer.com; www.madventurer.com

Madventurer is the brainchild of a one-time gap year teacher in Ghana. It supports a trust, the Mottey African Development (MAD) Foundation, set up to support a wide range of development projects in rural Africa. The fund is used to pay for project materials, scholarships and grants to help local people set up businesses.

Paying volunteers participate in expeditions which are project work combined with adventurous travel. Madventurers spend 4-5 weeks working on a community project and 21-77 days adventure travelling. Mad projects are currently run in Tanzania, Ghana, Uganda and Kenya. These are building projects, teaching and coaching opportunities, medical placements and environmental projects. Madventurers needs builders (can be without previous experience), medics (from pre-med up to elective stage), qualified sports coaches, conservationists and teachers.

Costs to the volunteer range from £890 plus a group kitty of £475 for a 4-5 week project without adventure travel, up to £1,530 for a 4-5 week project with 54 day walking safari. Charges do not include flights, insurance or visas. There are also two-week projects for those who cannot take more time off. All volunteer costs include a £200 contribution to project materials.

For more details and an information pack, contact the Mad team at the above address.

NIGERIAN CONSERVATION FOUNDATION (NCF)

Lekki Conservation Centre, Km 19, Lagos-Epe Expressway, PO Box 74638, Victoria Island, Lagos, Nigeria, West Africa; ☎ +234-1 2642498; fax +234-1 2642497; e-mail ncf@hyperia.com; www.ncf-nigeria.org

NCF promotes conservation through the management of protected areas, advocacy, research and education. Volunteers not only assist in these areas but with publications, communications and fund-raising too. The period for which the volunteer stays and time of year is flexible. Command of English is essential; knowledge of a Nigerian language and/or French is a distinct advantage. Volunteers must be in good health. A monthly allowance adequate for sustenance is provided but volunteers must pay their own accommodation costs.

NCF produces a variety of publications a list of which can be found on their website. Applications to the Principal Manager – Education Unit at the above address.

OPERATION CROSSROADS AFRICA

34 Mount Morris Park, New York, N.Y. 10027; ☎ +1 212 289-1949; fax +1 212 289-2526; e-mail oca@igc.apc.org; www.igc.org/oca

Founded in 1957, Operation Crossroads Africa sends people to work on community-initiated development projects in Africa and Brazil. Crossroads has projects in 10-15 African countries and Brazil, each summer. Over 10,000 people have participated in Crossroads since its inception, and it was the model for the Peace Corps (see separate entry).

200 volunteers are recruited annually onto four types of project: agriculture/reforestation; construction/community development; community health/medical; education/training (including women's development). Volunteers work 5-6 hours a day. Projects are six weeks long and are in rural villages. The work groups (8-10 volunteers per group) then travel for one week in the host country. All groups work with local counterparts. The programmes run from mid-June to mid-August.

Volunteers are aged between 17 and 35. Knowledge of French is preferred for francophone countries and Portugese for Brazil and Guinea Bissau. Applicants of any nationality are welcomed. Participants must attend a 3 day orientation in New York prior to departure paying their own way to New York, participation fee ($3,500).

PCEA TUMUTUMU HOSPITAL

Private Bag, Karatina, Kenya; ☎ +254 171-72026; fax +254 171-72656; e-mail Tumutumu@AfricaOnline.co.ke

PCEA Tumutumu Hospital is a 203 bed general hospital situated in the central highlands of Kenya, two hours drive north of Nairobi. The hospital has out-patient, medical, surgical, obstetric, paediatric, community health, and nurse training departments.

Usually 20 medical students on electives, plus up to around 6 other volunteers are needed annually; health professionals are also required for a minimum period of one year. Fluency in English as well as respect for the Christian tradition of the hospital is imperative. No smoking or alcohol is allowed in the hospital compound, including the student accommodation block. A housing and maintenance allowance is provided to long-term volunteers. All other volunteers get board and lodging at minimal expense.

Applications to the Medical Superintendent at the above address.

ST DAVID'S (AFRICA) TRUST
Beaufort Chambers, Beaufort Street, Crickhowell, Powys NP8 1AA; tel/fax 01873-812453; e-mail info@africarust.gi; www.africatrust.gi
St David's Africa Trust is registered as a charity by the Charity Commissioners in Gibraltar and arranges educational/working visits to Africa (Ghana). Tropical field workers are needed for three and six month programmes in Ghana, West Africa directed by Dr. Kwansah-Filson DVM for a few pre-university, post university and older volunteers. Teaching in schools, an orphanage and in SOS Villages across Ghana. The in-country two week induction course covers language, health and street-cred training. Interviews and pre-departure UK briefings for volunteers and their families.

SAVE THE EARTH NETWORK
P.O. Box CT 3635, Cantonments-Accra, Ghana, West Africa; ☎ +233-21 667791; fax +233-21 231485; e-mail sten@gppo.africaonline.com.gh
SEN is an organisation which promotes sustainable development in Ghana. Volunteers from around the world are needed to work on SEN programmes in the area of community development projects in education, agriculture, health, environmental conservation and welfare, alongside staff and volunteers from the local community in Ghana.

21-28 volunteers are recruited annually to do a variety of jobs including teaching English and Maths in schools, to orphans and the homeless, street children etc., assisting in HIV/AIDS prevention work, community farming and forestry, rainforest conservation work etc.

No special qualification, skill or previous experience is required and there is no age limit. Good health is essential and a visa is required for people who are not citizens of any West African country. Length of stay varies from a month to a year and volunteers are required any time. Volunteers must pay their own expenses. Room and board is arranged with local host families. The cost of participation is US$250 for four weeks. Payment is made in cash, in Ghana after arrival. There is a 25% discount for those who stay longer than 8 weeks. Volunteers work four/five days per week and two or more hours per day.

Apply direct to the above address.

SUDAN VOLUNTEER PROGRAMME (SVP)
34 Estelle Road, London NW3 2JY; tel/fax 020-7485 8619; e-mail davidsvp@blueyonder.co.uk; www.svp-uk.com
SVP annually recruits about 40 graduates and undergraduates who are native English speakers to teach English in schools and universities in Northern Sudan. National and regional accents are not a problem. A TEFL certificate or knowledge of Arabic is helpful but not essential. Volunteers must be in good health.

Placements last at least 6 months. Volunteers are not required from April to June. Accommodation and about US$100 per month in Sudanese currency is provided.

Application form, newsletter and annual report available from the above address. .

TSAVO CONSERVATION TRUST
Postal address: P.O. Box 48019, Nairobi, Kenya; physical address:(10th Floor, Fedha Towers, Standard Street, Nairobi); ☎ +254-(0)20-331191 or 222075;

fax +254-(0)20-330698 or 216528; e-mail discoverycentre@originsafaris.info; www.originsafaris.info/community-volunteer.com
The Tsavo Conservation Trust is an emerging conservation initiative in the wilds of East Africa which is seeking volunteers to participate in a variety of conservation and community projects. Volunteers contribute US$191 each per week to cover participation costs. For instance, at present Tsavo is recruiting volunteers to supervise and assist in the construction of a Primary school building (www.savannahcamps.com/tdc/typicalprimarysch.html). Volunteers should be competent, but not necessarily qualified.

For further details visit www.originsafaris.info/community-volunteer.com.

UGANDA VOLUNTEERS FOR PEACE (UVP)
P.O. Box 3312 Kampala, Uganda; ☎ +256-77 402201; fax +256-41 349203; e-mail uvpeace@yahoo.com
UVP works towards peace, development and much needed solidarity in Uganda. It organises international work camps in January, March, April, June, August, October and December for 3 week periods. Age limits 15-35 years. Languages required: English, Swahili and French. Accommodation is provided free. There is a particpation fee of US$200 and international membership costs US$100 per year.

Further details from the above address.

UNITED CHILDREN'S FUND INC
PO Box 20341, Boulder, CO 80308-3341, USA; ☎ +1 303 469-4339; toll-free in and to N. America 1-800-615-5229; e-mail United@unchildren.org; www.unchildren.org
United Children's Fund places about 12-20 volunteers annually on projects in Uganda, East Africa. These projects involve: health care, working in village clinics, teaching in local village schools, assisting teachers, school construction, working with women's groups on income generating projects, women's rights issues, village workshops regarding all aspects of improving village life. Volunteers do not need special skills and may work on projects where they feel they can make the biggest difference. Minimum age 18. Placements last one or two months, the average stay is one month at any time of year. Applicants pay a programme fee which ranges from US$1,850 (for a month); $2,950 (2 months). This covers all food, lodging and transportation plus local fees when in Uganda.

For further details on the conditions in Uganda and the volunteer projects available visit the website. Applications to the Executive Director at the above address.

VILLAGE EDUCATION PROJECT - Kilimanjaro
Mint Cottage, Prospect Road, Sevenoaks, Kent TN13 3UA; ☎01732-459799; e-mail info@kiliproject.org; www.kiliproject.org
Organises volunteers to work in village primary schools improving the buildings, teaching materials and teaching English as a foreign language. Only native English-speakers considered. TEFL qualification is an advantage, but not a requirement. Stays of 8-9 months, usually January onwards to coincide with new school year. Accommodation is provided in the village. Volunteers pay for all their own expenses.

Education to 'A' level standard for teaching English to primary school pupils and helping with extra curricular activities and giving assistance with basic computer training.

Professionally trained volunteers give assistance to local teachers to increase their knowledge, confidence and classroom performance.

Further information on the website www.kiliproject.org, or apply direct to the above address.

WWOOF/FIOH
Working Abroad Programme Ghana, P.O. Box TF 154, Trade Fair Centre, Accra, Ghana, West Africa; ☎ +233-21 716091; fax +233-21 716091; e-mail ncscomm@ghana.com

This umbrella organisation includes WWOOF Working on Organic Farms and The Future in Our Hands. Volunteers can work on organic farms, summer workcamps, teaching in nursery kindergarten and acquire drumming and dancing, tie-dye and batik making skills. Environmental activities include tree planting. There is also a Christian outreach programme (on bicyles), or technical work at the Bicycle institute (bicycle repairs and maintenance). Volunteers need entry permit visas. Visa extensions if necessary can be arranged by the organisation. Upper age limit of volunteers is 50. Period is 1-6 months. Accommodation is provided free. Volunteer teachers go through an orientation so as to be able to teach effectively.

For further details and an application form apply direct to Ebenezer Nortey-Mensah enclosing three international reply coupons.

YOUTH CHALLENGE INTERNATIONAL
305-20 Maud, Toronto, Ontario M5V 2M5, Canada; ☎ +1 -416-504 3370; fax +1 416-504-3376; e-mail generalinfo@yci.org; www.yci.org

Youth Challenge International combines community development, health work and conservation work in dynamic projects carried out by teams of volunteers aged 18-30 years. Projects last from five weeks to three months in Tanzania and Ethiopia as well as South America, and provide opportunities for young people to build their skills and leadership capabilities on grassroots development projects. Areas of priority include HIV/AIDS, Community Infrastructure, Youth Skills Building, Women's Networking and Capacity building..

Participants who do not hold a Canadian passport are responsible for the cost of the flight to the host country as well as obtaining visas and other required travel documents. Participation fees start at about $2,735. Details and costs of the programmes are available on their website.

Professional and Longer-Term Volunteering

ACTION PARTNERS
Bawtry Hall, Bawtry, Doncaster DN10 6JH; ☎01302-710750; fax 01302-719399; e-mail info@actionpartners.org.uk; www.actionpartners.org.uk

Action Partners is a Christian organisation working with the church in the UK and abroad including Africa. Professionals can be placed for one year and upwards. Medical or other electives can be arranged for a shorter time. Action Partners operates in Cameroon, Chad, Egypt, Nigeria and elsewhere. Opportunities exist in agriculture, church work, education and health. Volunteers are given training and assistance in raising their prayer and financial support through their home churches and other concerned individuals and groups. Accommodation is provided and allowances are paid from the total support cost.

Enquiries and applications to Lois Fenton-Smith at the above address.

AFRICA INLAND MISSION
2 Vorley Road, Archway, London N19 5HE; ☎020-7281 1184; fax 020-7281 4479; e-mail enquiry@aim-eur.org; www.aim.eur.org

Africa Inland Mission is a Christian organisation that sends volunteers with a strong Christian commitment to teach in rural secondary schools in East Africa (mainly Kenya, Uganda and Tanzania). Periodically, there are also opportunities for qualified teachers, secretaries and medical doctors. Usually 30-50 volunteers are taken on annually. The age limits are 18-70 years and good health is essential. Vacancies arise all year round, but for teaching applicants the deadline for applications is the end of March. Volunteers raise all their own finances and though accommodation is usually provided, rent may have to be paid. The costs for 12 months range from £4,000 to £5,500 depending on the country. Africa Inland Mission produces a quarterly magazine. A-levels or above for teaching in rural schools.

Applicants should apply directly to the Assistant Personnel Director at the above address.

BAW KU YOUTH VOCATIONAL TRAINING CENTRE
PO Box 27, Bawku, Uer., Ghana; ☎+233-743 22627; fax +233-743 22627.

The Baw Ku Vocational Training Centre offers vocational courses to young people in the areas of carpentry, masonry, dressmaking, secretarial/typing skills and auto mechanic courses in order to create job opportunities for the youth in Ghana, in particular the female population. About four volunteers including an English teacher, are recruited each year to help run these courses for a minimum stay of 2 years. Volunteers should be English-speaking (as all subjects are taught in English), aged between 18 and 55 and in good health. Applicants should be suitably qualified to be able to teach the courses both practically and theoretically. Accommodation is provided but for all expenses volunteers should be self-funding.

Applications to the Director at the above address.

BUNAC VOLUNTEER SOUTH AFRICA
Volunteering Department, BUNAC, 16 Bowling Green Lane, London EC1R OQH; ☎ 020-7251 3472; fax 020-7251 0215; e-mail volunteer@bunac.org.uk; web www.bunac.org

Bunac offers a fantastic opportunity to get involved in one of the many volunteer projects based around the beautiful city of Cape Town. Group departures are followed by a one-week orientation and an eight-week placement. Typical placements include working in a township crèche, working as a classroom assistant in a primary school, working on a community farm which provides education and training projects for marginalized youths, and working at a centre which provides care and support for young children with HIV and AIDS. Accommodation and meals are provided during the placement in addition to full in country support.

CONCERN AMERICA
P.O. Box 1790, Santa Ana, CA 92702, USA; ☎ +714-953-8575; fax +1 714 953 1242; e-mail concamerica@earthlink.net

Concern America is an international development and refugee organisation. Through the work of professionally trained volunteers, Concern America assists impoverished communities and refugees in developing countries in their efforts to improve living conditions. At present there are volunteers in Mozambique and Guinea in Africa; also in Brazil, El Salvador, Guatemala, Honduras and Mexico in the Americas. Concern America programmes emphasise training of community members to impart skills and knowledge,which will remain long after the volunteers have gone. Round trip transportation, health insurance, and room and board provided as well as a small monthly stipend (approx. $350 per month). A repatriation allowance of $50 per month of service first year; $100 a month second year and $150 per month in the third year. Qualifications: degree/experience in public health, medicine, nutrition, nursing, agriculture, community development, education and appropriate technology. Minimum commitment is two years and minimum age is 21.

FOCUS, Inc.
c/o Marilyn T Miller, MD, 1855 West Taylor Street, Chicago, IL 60612, USA; ☎ +1 312 996-7445; fax +1 413-7895; e-mail marimill@uic.edu
FOCUS recruits ophthalmologists as short-term volunteers for eye clinics in Nigeria where they provide medical and surgical eye care services. Around 15 volunteers are needed for placements of three weeks or longer, all year round.

Applicants must be certified ophthalmologists and need to obtain a Nigerian visa. Usually a US medical licence is required but this would be waived for UK ophthalmologists. Board, lodging, laundry services and transportation within Nigeria are provided but volunteers pay for their own international travel.

IRISH MISSIONARY UNION
IMU, Orwell Park, Rathgar, Dublin 6, Ireland; ☎ +353-1 4965433/4971770; fax +353-1 4965029.
The IMU was founded to promote co-operation between missionary, mission-sending and mission-aid organisations, thereby helping them to make the best and most efficient use of their personnel and other resources. Its principal aim is to assist the Bishops in the task of spreading the Gospel and therefore the IMU works in close collaboration with the Irish Hierarchy. It also acts as a liaison between missionary bodies and national or international organisations involved in evangelization and development.

The IMU recruits volunteers to work in the following areas in African and Latin American countries: medicine, education, trade, agriculture and pastoral and community development. Qualified and experienced doctors, nurses, laboratory technicians, teachers, paramedics, builders, plumbers and social workers are all needed. It is essential that all volunteers should derive their motivation from Christian values, and be in good health and at least 21 years of age. The minimum length of placement is two years. A monthly allowance, accommodation, resettlement allowance, insurance and return air fare are all provided.

Those interested should contact the Judith Lenehan at the above address at any time of the year.

ONE WORLD VOLUNTEER INSTITUTE
Den reisende Høgskole, Hornsjø, 2636 Øyer, Norway; ☎ +47-6126 4444; fax +47-6126 4017; e-mail oneworld@online.no; www.oneworldvolunteers.org
The One World Volunteer Institute runs two programmes involving a Solidarity Worker Team and a One World Communication Team. The former is in cooperation with the NGO 'Humana People to People', and is a 14 month programme including a six month preparation which is theoretical and practical. The volunteer learns leadership and problem solving, and languages (where appropriate). The participants also study about what they are going to do and where they are going. After the educational part, the second period is to work on a development aid project in one of the following locations: Angola, Mozambique, Zambia, Namibia or South Africa; following this the participant does two months of information work including presentations and exhibitions to promote

the work that they have been doing. Placements last 10 or 14 months.

The One World Communication Team is about creating development through information and cooperation. This team produces articles and films and photographs, and uses the internet to tell of the positive events happening in the developing world, thus creating a better understanding about different countries. The course consists of travel to different continents. Placements last 13 months.

Between 100 and 150 volunteers are recruited annually and this number is set to increase to over 200. A solidarity worker can expect to work as a teacher, work in construction or agriculture, educate people about AIDS, arrange activities for AIDS sufferers, assist Child Aid programmes, help with sales of second-hand clothing, or work in Human Resource management. No formal qualifications are required but an applicant needs to be self-motivated, hard working, flexible and ready to meet lots of new challenges. Minimum age 18.

In Norway the participant pays an enrolment fee of £140 and a course fee of £1,650 which covers all boarding expenses in Norway and part of the cost of training. There are limited scholarships available for up to 50% of the course fee and there also exists a system, called NetUp, for raising the money to pay the course fee. In Africa, accommodation is provided and the participant receives an allowance to cover food, travel, medical and out-of-pocket expenses.

For a free information pack contact the above address. Write to the President of FOCUS at the above address for more details.

PA SANTIGIE CONTEH FARMER'S ASSOCIATION (PASCOFAAS)
PMB 686 Freetown, Republic of Sierra Leone, West Africa; ☎ +232-22 228568; fax +232-22 224439; e-mail cbau@Sierratel.SL
PASCOFAAS is centred around Makarie and over 20 neighbouring villages in the Bombali district, and was founded in 1982 to promote increased agricultural productivity for food production and income generation in order to improve the living conditions of its approximately 2,000 members with special attention to women, children and young people.

Activities undertaken include agriculture, the planting of rice and trees, construction of houses, roads and so on. Opportunities open to volunteers include secretarial work in the head office, agricultural and construction work and training local people in different skills.

All nationalities may apply as long as they speak English. They are required all year round for periods of two weeks to two years. Up to 20 international volunteers are taken on at a time. Preference will be given to volunteers who are willing to help programmes either financially or with materials. The minimum age is 17. Expenses and pocket money are not paid but accommodation is provided.

The Association also supplies information to anyone interested in farming in rural areas of Sierra Leone. For further details about this or the voluntary work, contact Andrew Conteh, the Director, at the above address.

PCEA TUMUTUMU HOSPITAL
Private Bag, Karatina, Kenya; ☎ +254-171 72026; fax +254-171 72656; e-mail Tumutumu@AfricaOnline.co.ke
PCEA Tumutumu Hospital is a 203 bed general hospital situated in the central highlands of Kenya, two hours drive north of Nairobi. The hospital has out-patient, medical, surgical, obstetric, paediatric, community health, and nurse training departments.

Usually 20 medical students on electives, plus up to around 6 other volunteers (e.g. accounts and computer specialists, architects and surveyors) are needed annually; health professionals are also required for a minimum period of one year. Fluency in English as well as respect for the Christian tradition of the hospital is imperative. No smoking or alcohol is allowed in the hospital compound, including the student accommodation block. A housing and maintenance allowance is provided to long-term volunteers. All others receive board and lodging at minimal expense.

Applications to the Medical Superintendent at the above address.

RURAL UPGRADE SUPPORT ORGANISATION (RUSO)
c/o University of Ghana, PMB L21, Legon, Accra, Ghana; ☎ +233 21 513149; e-mail benxzola@africanus.net
RUSO is a non-political, non sectarian and non-governmental organisation that employs volunteer humanitarian action to empower local communities and contribute grass-roots solutions to rural challenges of providing healthcare, education and small scale business management, cultural exchange and social development. It is a unique service organisation registered in Ghana on September 6th 1999 to help the rural people from different cultures gain a new understanding of each other in the spirit of sharing ideas by working together toward a common goal.

About 35 foreign volunteers (usually active and retired professionals, and students) work side-by-side with the permanent staff of RUSO in the fields mentioned above. Accommodation is provided but no expenses. Refer to the www.interconnection.org/rap/ for details of volunteer costs. Apply direct or through the website.

LALMBA ASSOCIATION
7685 Quartz Street, Arvado, CO 80007, USA; ☎ +1 303 420-1810; fax +1 303 467-1232; e-mail lalmba@aol.com; www.lalmba.org
The Lalmba Association operates medical clinics and other health programmes plus care for orphaned children in Eritrea, Ethiopia and Kenya. Ten volunteers are needed annually to staff these projects. Most opportunities are for medical staff, (physicians, nurses, and midwives), but occasionally volunteers with managerial or administrative skills are needed to act as project directors. All placements are for one to two years with preference given to 2-year applicants.

Applicants should be at least 25 years old, qualified in either the USA or certain European countries, and have some experience in their field. Round trip transportation, board, lodging, health and life insurance and pocket money are provided.

Contact the Medical Director, Marty Downey at the above address for more information.

> **Marc Seidman M.D. on volunteering through Lalmba Association**
> *In America, I always felt that if I weren't a doctor, someone else would take my place and care for my patients. In Ethiopa, I knew this wasn't so. The people had no one else to turn to. People would come to the clinic on the verge of death from TB and we'd start them on treatment. Day by day, we'd watch them gain weight, strength, and hope. We'd watch them literally gain back their lives. Now THAT is job satisfaction.*

SKILLSHARE INTERNATIONAL
126 New Walk, Leicester LE1 7JA; ☎0116-254 1862; fax 0116-2542614; e-mail info@skillshare.org; www.skillshare.org
Skillshare International is an international development organisation working for sustainable development in partnership with the people and communities of African countries and also India. Skillshare International places, within its local partner

organisations in Botswana, Lesotho, Mozambique, Namibia, South Africa, Swaziland, Tanzania and Uganda, skilled professional, called development workers, and health trainers, who share and develop skills, facilitate organisational effectiveness and organisational growth. Development workers and health trainers are recruited from around the world to work in agriculture, rural development, community development, education, engineering, environmental conservation, healthcare, HIV and AIDS, income generation and vocational training. Placements can be short-term, but most are long-term lasting up to three years. Skillshare International supports development workers with flights, national insurance, medical cover, accommodation and a modest living allowance.

For more information, visit www.skillshare.org or telephone the above number.

TANZED
80 Edleston Road, Crewe, Cheshire, CW2 7HD; ☎01270-509994; e-mail nicolapugh1@hotmail.com; www.tanzed.org; also P.O. Box 848 Morogoro, Tanzania

Tanzed is a small charitable programme at primary school level in rural Tanzania which sends 12-24 teachers per year. Applicants must have a UK passport, have a degree, a teaching qualification and a suitable attitude towards developmental education. Volunteers stay for one year with the possibility of extending.

Normal school hours are 7.30am-3pm. Volunteer teachers work alongside Tanzanian teachers to help improve the standard of English-teaching for both pupils and teachers. Volunteers make a donation of £2000 to cover all costs and receive monthly expenses equivalent to a local teacher's salary. Accommodation is provided by the local community.

Applications are welcomed throughout the year with departure dates in September and January. Applications are available on the website or from the office.

TETE YOUTH ORGANISATION (TEYO)
P.O. Box 378, Soroti-Uganda.

The Teyo organisation trains young locals in technical and vocational skills as well as in management and natural environmental protection. They recruit two volunteers a year with technical/vocational skills such as carpentry and joinery, tailoring and garment cutting, brick-laying and concrete practice, and environmental and management skills.

Two volunteers are recruited. Married couples are welcome. Applicants should be aged 35-55, able to stay for six months to a year and qualified in one of the above skills and able to teach it to others. Volunteers have to fund themselves and there is no accommodation provided.

Apply in writing to the above address.

VISIONS IN ACTION
2710 Ontario Road, NW, Washington, DC 20009, USA; ☎ +1 202 625-7402; fax +1 202 588-9344; e-mail visions@visionsinaction.org; www.visionsinaction. org

Visions in A ction is an international non-profit organisation founded in 1988 out of the conviction that there is much that individuals can learn from, and contribute to, the developing world by working as part of a community of volunteers committed to achieving social justice in an urban setting. Visions volunteers work side-by-side with host country nationals, allowing a genuine understanding of the country's needs to emerge. The Development Volunteer programme aims to work towards social and economic justice in the developing world by providing overseas volunteer opportunities with non-profit organisations, working as partners in the development process.

60-80 volunteers per year work in indigenous or expatriate organisations as development journalists, community workers, project managers, low-income housing facilitators and healthcare assistants, etc. Placements are available in the following sectors: agriculture, appropriate technology, children, communications/journalism, education, environment/natural resources, food/nutrition, family planning, health, housing, human rights/law, mental or physical disabilities, natural science, refugees/relief, small business, social science, women and youth in South Africa, Uganda, Tanzania, and Mexico. Programmes last for one year or six months. Applicants may be of any nationality, but they must have a college degree or equivalent work experience. Programmes begin at various times in the year. The average cost of participating in a program is $5,000. Volunteers must pay for all their costs. The programme fee includes housing, medical insurance, work visas, and stipends.

Those interested should apply at the above address.

VOLUNTEER GHANA
Volunteering Department, BUNAC, 16 Bowling Green Lane, London EC1R OQH; ☎ 020-7251 3472; fax 020-7251 0215; e-mail volunteer@bunac.org. uk; web www.bunac.org

Bunac recruits a varying number of volunteers yearly to teach English in a Ghanaian school for up to a year. Travel time is available during or after the teaching placement. Volunteers should be aged 18 and over and previous classroom experience is desirable. Volunteers pay a total of about £1,500 which includes the return flight, comprehensive insurance, 5-day orientation period and accommodation on arrival, all programme literature plus full support services both during the application procedure and throughout the placement.

Volunteers either stay in rented accommodation or home stay (volunteers pay local rates for food and accommodation), which gives them the chance to become fully immersed in Ghanaian culture. Back up support and advice provided by BUNAC in the UK and the host organisation, Student & Youth Travel Organisation SYTO in Accra. Applications are accepted year-round. Group flights depart every month.

To apply, download an application from Bunac's website (www.bunac.org), and send it completed and with a registration fee and any other documents specified by Bunac's Volunteering Department. All applicants are invited to attend an interview.

Asia

General Opportunities

ASIAN RURAL INSTITUTE
442-1 Tsukinokisawa, Nishinasuno-machi, Nasu-gun, Tochigi-ken 329-2707 Japan; ☎ +81 (0)287-36-3111 510 549 3708; fax +81 (0)287-37-5833; e-mail ari@nasu-net.or.jp; www.ari.edu
ARI is a non-profit, Christian organisation that provides leadership training for rural leaders in organic farming methods and sustainable agriculture as well as in community leadership. About 25-30 trainee leaders are recruited annually from villages around Asia to spend nearly a year on the programme, which aims to teach self-sufficiency based on farming and forming a just and peaceful community with a Christian ethos.
ARI accepts volunteers to support the leadership trainees on their programme. Volunteers have to stay for a minimum of three and a maximum of twelve months. Volunteers in the past have come from the USA, South Korea, Canada, Germany and the United Kingdom. Volunteers work alongside the leadership trainees which means doing farm work and helping prepare meals etc in a communal community.orming a just , usually for three weeks. Volunteers should be 21 and over, in

AMERICAN-EURASIAN RESEARCH INSTITUTE (AERI)
577 San Clemente Street, Ventura, California 93001, USA; tel/fax 805-653-2607, e-mail jkimball@csen.org or 1607 Walnut Street, Berkeley, California USA 94709; ☎ +1 510 549 3708; fax 510 849 3137; www.csen.org
AERI is a non-profit education research organisation that sponsors scholarly exchanges and research expeditions related to history, archaeology, petroglyphics and ethnography projects in Kazakhstan, Mongolia and Russia; also in America and Canada.

About 25-30 volunteers are recruited annually, usually for three weeks. Volunteers should be 21 and over, in good health and able to withstand difficult living conditions and interface with international cultures. No special skills are needed. The cost to volunteers varies depending on the project from about $1100 to $1400 for three weeks and includes board and accommodation. Projects include a survey of desert-steppe zone of the Middle Gobi, Mongolia and excavations in the southern Don region north of the Black Sea in Russia.

For more details and an application form go to the 'Fieldwork Opportunities' section of the website www.csen.org.

BANGLADESH WORK CAMPS ASSOCIATION (BWCA)
289/2 Workcamp Road, North Shajahanpur, Dhaka-1217, Bangladesh; ☎ +880-2 -9358206/9356814; fax +880-2-956 5506/5483; e-mail bwca@bangla.net; www.mybwca.org
Bangladesh Work Camps Association (BWCA) promotes international solidarity and peace through organising community development which takes the form of national/

international workcamps for volunteers in rural and urban areas of Bangladesh. The projects organised include environmental and health education, literacy, sanitation, afforestation, community work, development and construction, etc. Volunteers work 30 hours a week on placements which last from 1 to 6 weeks from October to February. A RTYP (Round The Year Program) is also available to medium-term volunteers staying for a minimum period of three months. At least 30 volunteers a year are recruited onto one of the three international workcamps and 20 volunteers through RTYP.

Volunteers ages 18-35, must be able to speak English, be adaptable to any situation and be team-spirited. Accommodation and simple local food is provided but volunteers must pay all other expenses including insurance and travel.

Applications to BWCA three months in advance of scheduled Camp/Programme date. Applications must come through a BWCA partner organisation in the applicant's country. If this is not possible individual, direct applications may be accepted and should be accompanied by a payment of US$25. Apply in the first instance for the address of the nearest partner organisation.

THE BATEMANS TRUST
Stocks Lane Farm, Steventon, Abingdon, Oxon. OX13 6SS; ☎01235-832077; fax 01235-832077; e-mail info@batemanstrust.org; www.batemanstrust.org
The Trust runs a charity which supports a boarding home in Chennai (Madras), India, for under-privileged children of Anglo-Indian origin from poor or destitute homes. It provides for all their needs, education, food, clothing, medical care and provides extra-curricular activities such as sports, arts, music. The charity also supports them when they leave the boarding home at 16, by providing accommodation in its hostels and funding for further education or training up to the age of 22.

Approximately 4 long-term and 4 shorter-term volunteers are needed. Should be qualified teachers or TEFL teachers to run an extra tuition programme for children with special needs. Also needed are volunteers with skills such as music or needlework for shorter placements. Nurses and those with medical training are also suitable for social education classes and help with medical programmes. Volunteers should be fit and healthy and over 22 years. The minimum period for teachers is 6 weeks. 4 months is preferred and for short-term specialists the term is 2 weeks.

Volunteers pay their own flights and bring their own spending money. Short-term volunteers are asked to pay £25 per week towards food and accommodation. Long-term volunteers are asked to raise £500 and all their food and accommodation is included. An Indian tourist visa is sufficient.

Apply in writing sending a CV and letter/send an SAE for further information.

BHARAT SEVAK SAMAJ
Nehru Seva Kendra, Gurgaon By-pass Road, Mehrauli, New Delhi 30, India; ☎ +91 11 66644761,6642215.
The Samaj was founded by Shri Jawahar Lal Nehru, the first Prime Minister of India, as a non-political national platform for mobilising people's spare time, energy and resources for development and reconstruction. It has a network of branches all over the country, with a membership of over 750,000, 10,000 members working on projects, and about 20 foreign volunteers helping each year. Any person who offers his services for a minimum of two hours a week can become a member of the Samaj.

Its normal programme includes the organisation of urban community centres in slum areas, night shelters, child welfare centres, nursery schools, training camps for national reconstruction work, family planning camps and clinics, and publicity centres. The work also encompasses relief and reconstruction work after natural calamities, such as famine, drought, cyclones and earthquakes as well as the construction of houses for the Schedule Caste (lower caste) and tribes and low cost latrines in villages.

Both skilled and unskilled workers are welcomed. Foreign volunteers, who can serve for between 15 days and three months, should be prepared to live in simple accommodation and respect local customs and traditions. They must finance their own stay, and it is preferred that they speak English.

Applicants should contact the General Secretary at the above address for further details; IRCs should accompany all letters.

CENTRE FOR CO-ORDINATION OF VOLUNTARY WORKS AND RESEARCH (CECOWOR)
9 Raja Desing Nagar, Desurpattai Road, Gingee Villupuram, Dt. 604 202, Tamil Nadu, India; tel/fax +91-4145 22747.
Founded in 1989, CECOWOR is an organisation which works towards the liberation and upliftment of the underprivileged sections of Indian society such as women, tribals, and casteless dalit people. It initiates various development programmes in the fields of education, environment, children, women's development, human resource development, vocational and self-employment training, human rights, etc. Every year four workcamps in January, April, September/October and November, each lasting a month, are run and further opportunities are available for those wishing to work on voluntary projects for longer periods (six weeks or more). Volunteers work in any of the areas listed above which interest them.

Applicants should be aged between 17 and 70, in reasonably good health with an open mind to explore a different culture. All costs for the programmes and workcamps must be met by the volunteer and a US$50 non-refundable registration fee must be paid prior to departure. Workcamps cost US$150 for the month-long duration, other programmes cost US$200 per month, these fees cover board and dormitory-style lodging.

Applications to the Director at the above address.

CULTURAL DESTINATION NEPAL
GPO Box # 11535, Dhapasi, Kathmandu, Nepal; ☎ +977-1 437 7623; +977-1 437 7696; fax +977 1 437 7696; e-mail cdnnepal@wlink.com.np; info@volunteernepal.org.np; -www.volunteernepal.org.np
Cultural Destination Nepal runs a programme 'Volunteer Nepal!' which is designed for people who wish to visit Nepal and contribute their time and skills to benefit the community as well as learn about Nepalese culture and customs by living as a member of a Nepali family and carrying out voluntary work (usually placements in schools teaching children). About 75 volunteers are recruited annually.

The programme is from two to four months and costs 650 euros. This covers two weeks orientation (pre-service training), homestay, cultural orientation tour (sightseeing), cross-cultural orientation (social behaviours), hiking, lectures on different topics, cultural activities, food and accommodation during the programme, trekking, jungle safari, white water rafting, etc. A non-refundable application fee of 50 euros is also required. Additionally, air fare to and from Nepal, visa fee, insurance, entrance fees, and other personal expenses must be met by the volunteer. The programme starts five times a year in February, April, June, August and October but other dates can be arranged upon request.

Applicants should be aged 18-65, have at least a high school diploma or A-level equivalent, be able to communicate in English, be flexible, physically fit and willing to immerse themselves in another culture. For teaching no previous experience is needed but for other projects relevant experience is required.

Applications to arrive two and a half months prior to programme commencement date at the above address.

DAKSHINAYAN
F-1169, Ground Floor, Chittaranjan Park, New Delhi-110019, India; tel/fax +91-11 6276645; e-mail dakshinayan@vsnl.com; www.dakshinayan.org

Dakshinayan is a non-profit, non-religious organisation which promotes international and intercultural solidarity and a better understanding of the myth and reality of 'third world poverty' through its Development Education Programme.

Under this programme self-supporting volunteers are placed on grassroots development projects throughout north India. This provides them with an opportunity to observe and experience the culture of rural India; study the problems of disadvantaged communities and participate in development efforts.

The programme is open to both skilled and unskilled participants minimum age 18. Participants have to cover all their expenses (travel, food, accommodation and other personal expenses). On the projects they have to contribute US$250 a month for food and accommodation in order not to be a burden on the project's resources. Dakshinayan charges a nominal fee of US$50 towards administration expenses. Volunteers should stay a minimum of one month up to a maximum of six months at any time of year.

Applications should be sent to Siddharth Sanyal, at the above address.

Economist Geoffroy Groleau from Montreal found his way to Dakshinayan via the internet

The application process is simple and can be conducted fully over the internet. The registration fee which must be provided before setting out for the project is the primary source of revenues for Dakshinayan. So there I was in March, stepping on to a train from New Delhi heading to Jharkhand. The project provides an opportunity to acquire a better understanding of the myths and realities surrounding poverty in the developing world, and specifically about the realities of rural India. The tribal people of these villages do not need or want fancy houses or televisions, but simply an education for their children and basic healthcare in order to improve the life they have been leading in relative isolation for centuries. It was interesting for me to see that they lead a quiet and simple life based on the rhythm of harvests and seasons, in marked contrast to most Westerners. The primary role for volunteers is to teach English for a few hours every day to the kids attending the three Dakshinayan-run-schools. I should also mention the numerous, unforgettable football games with enthusiastic kids at the end of another sunny afternoon.

Volunteers should be aware that Dakshinayan is an Indian NGO, fully run by local people, which in my view is a positive aspect, but it also means that volunteers have to adapt to Indian ways.

DORE (Devoted Organisation for Reforming Environment)
196-b Khari Bazar, Ranikhet 263645, Dish, Almora (Uttaranchal), India; ☎ +91 5966-20458.

DORE recruits 15-25 volunteers a year to help in the areas of natural resource management, child health and education, socio-economic development of rural villages, introduction of appropriate technology, and eco-tourism in India. Volunteers can stay from one to six months but preferably in the summer. No special skills or qualifications are required but practice in very basic Hindi conversations is advisable for the comfort of the volunteer. All expenses (accommodation, food, airfares, etc.) must be met by the volunteer.

Applications to the Secretary at the above address.

FOUNDATION TO ENCOURAGE THE POTENTIAL OF DISABLED PERSONS
195/197 Ban Tanawan, Moo 8, Tambon Sanpheeseu, Amphur Muang, Chiang Mai 50300; ☎ +66 53 852172; fax +66-53 240935; e-mail assis@loxinfo. co.th; www.infothai.com/disabled
The Chiang Mai Disabled Centre is Thailand's first Disabled Centre. The Centre builds and distributes free, mobility aids to needy disabled persons including steel and PVC wheelchairs, walkers and crutches. It also provides free classes in English and computing to disabled persons.

About six to eight volunteers are taken on annually to build wheelchairs, provide physical therapy, fund raise and to teach English and computing. Volunteers are expected to stay for three months and it helps to have an interest in Thai language and culture. Volunteers pay all their own expenses and find their own accommodation.

Applications should be send direct to the above address.

EARTHCARE
GPO Box 11546, Hong Kong, China; ☎ +852-25780434; fax +852-25780522; e-mail care@earth.org.hk; www.earth.org.hk
Earthcare, a local Chinese charity, aims to promote the concepts of benevolence and compassion in traditional Chinese teaching to establish a green lifestyle, environmental conservation, humane education and the protection of animals. About 150-200 volunteers are recruited annually to help in the following areas: fundraising, computer/ data processing/maintenance, administration, clerical work, campaigning, animal care/treatment, publishing/printing, photography and filming, multimedia design and application, public relations and education. Campaigns include: banning bear farming and advocating herbal alternatives to animal derived remedies in Chinese medicines.

Minimum period of voluntary work is two weeks at any time of year. Applicants must be able to speak English, any knowledge of Cantonese would be a bonus. Very simple accommodation can be provided but all other expenses must be met by the volunteer.

Applications to the above address.

GLOBAL ACTION NEPAL
Baldwins, Eastlands Lane, Cowfold, West Sussex RH13 8AY; ☎01403-864704; e-mail info@gannepal.org
Volunteers are taken for six months to work with GAN in poor Nepalese communities. GAN runs programmes for people of all ages and all nationalities between November and April. Volunteers are engaged in a wide range of fields, most specifically, working with children's clubs in activities as diverse as drama, dance and debating, and in developing the English skills of Nepalese teachers. GAN works in areas where volunteers can be of most long-term benefit to Nepal where sustainability is fundamental to the projects' existence.

Basic cost to the volunteer is £1,650 (excluding flights), which includes are full three-week training programme once in Nepal, as well as visa costs, insurance, full board and lodging and transport in-country.

Enquiries by e-mail to enquiries@gannepal.org or phone 0800 5877138 for further information.

GOODWILL GROUP
2nd Floor Ruam Rudee Building III, 51/2 Soi Ruam Rudee, Ploenchit Road, Lumpini, Phatumwan, Bangkok 10330 Thailand; ☎ +66 2-656 8493; fax +66 2-255-4176; e-mail goodwill@goodwillbangkok.com; www.goodwillbangkok.

com
Language school that accepts about 20 part-time volunteer English teachers. Experience of teaching helpful, but not essential. Commitment is the key qualification. Minimum period of 6 months. A minimum of 3 hours a week (more if wished). Note that volunteers have to find their own accommodation.

Contact Kurt Heck for more details

HIMALAYAN EDUCATION LIFELINE PROGRAMME (HELP)
Mansard House, 30 Kingsdown Park, Whitstable, Kent CT5 2DF; ☎01227-263055; www.help-education.org
HELP supports Himalayan schools and orphanages with financial and human resources and so enables young people from poor communities in the Himalayas to improve their employment opportunities through education and in so doing enhance not only their own standard of living, but also that of their extended families and of the wider communities they come from.

Volunteer teachers are needed to teach English in local schools. Volunteers should be able to stay at least two months and will need to meet all their own expenses. The school will provide accommodation either at the school or with a host family and all meals are provided. Costs to the volunteer are £100 registration fee to HELP, £70 monthly for full board and accommodation (£50 if sharing), a minimum donation to the project for two months £300 or £400 for a longer assignment. Other tasks needing volunteers are school nursing and caring for young orphans.

Those with teaching ability and qualifications are ideal, but anyone with usable skills is considered. Normally the minimum age is 20 years and the usual length of stay is two to six months. Schools volunteers are needed from March to December and orphanage volunteers all year round.

For further details and application go to the website above.

INDIA DEVELOPMENT GROUP (UK)
68 Downlands Road, Purley, Surrey CR8 4JF; ☎020-8668 3161; fax 020-8660 8541; e-mail idguk@clara.co.uk; www.idguk.org
IDG (UK) works in India to alleviate poverty and improve the employment situation and quality of life in rural and backward areas of India and to arrest the migration of the rural poor to city slums by offering training in appropriate technology, primary health care and social forestry at the Schumacher Institute in Lucknow, northern India.

Five to ten volunteers are taken on annually in India to help with the above programmes for six months at a time, preferably November to March/April. IDG can arrange reasonably priced accommodation at the organisation's boarding house or with a family. Volunteers should be 20-45 years old and should be capable of withstanding the rigours of the Indian climate and the health and hygiene situation. Knowledge of English is essential and UK and other nationalities will need a visa.

The UK office also needs some volunteer office staff.

INDIAN VOLUNTEERS FOR COMMUNITY SERVICE
12 Eastleigh Avenue, Harrow, Middlesex HA2 0UF; ☎020-8864 4740; fax 020-8930 8338; e-mail enquiries@ivcs.org.uk; www. ivcs.org.uk
IVCS offers a learning opportunity to anyone over the age of 18 who is keen to go to India and learn about Indian culture and rural development work through their 'DRIVE' scheme. Each year, between September and March, people are sent to a rural project in North India for three weeks' acclimatisation and then on to other projects including assisting in primary school, painting murals, making teaching aids, teaching

conversational English classes and writing articles for a twice yearly research journal (*International Journal of Rural Studies*), where they may stay for longer periods of time (3 weeks to 6 months), provided that they are able to make themselves useful. Project Visitors as they are called, must pay all their own expenses, including airfares, personal and sightseeing expenses and basic board and lodging in the projects.

No skills are required. Project Visitors are going primarily to learn, to have a unique and rewarding experience and to see a different way of life. For more details, contact the General Secretary at the above address.

INSIGHT NEPAL
PO Box 489, Male Patan, Pokhara, Kaski, Nepal; ☎ +977-61 30266; e-mail insight@mos.com.np; www.insightnepal.org
Insight Nepal's 'Placement for Volunteer Service Work' is a programme which arranges work places for volunteers interested in teaching English in schools, or to help community development projects in the semi urban and urban areas of Nepal. Participants pass through four different phases of the programme: orientation, placement, village excursion and a recreational tour. Each placement lasts three months and 60 volunteers are taken on a year. Volunteers must be aged 21 to 65 years with at least A-level education (High School Diploma US). The programme runs all year round. Meals and accommodation will be provided. The programme costs US$40 application fee plus US$800 programme fee which covers all four phases of the programme.

Further details from the above address.

INTERSERVE
325 Kennington Road, London SE11 4QH; ☎020-7735 8227; fax 020-7587 5362; e-mail enquiries@isewi.org; www. interserveonline.org.uk
Each year 60-80 volunteers participate in the On Track Programme in Pakistan, India, Nepal, the Middle East and Central Asia. Generally volunteers become involved in medical, educational and technical projects, which last from three months to a year. This is a self-financing scheme. Volunteers must be committed Christians who have a desire to share their faith as well as their skills.

Further information may be obtained from the On Track Co-ordinator at the above address.

JAFFE PUNNOOSE FOUNDATION
Kunnuparambil Buildings, Kurichy, Kottayam 686 549, Kerala, India; ☎ +91-481 2320041; fax +91-481 2430470;e-mail jaffeint@sify.com; www. jaffeinternational.com
Voluntary positions are available to young and experienced teachers interested in teaching at English medium high schools, hotel management colleges, teacher education colleges, language schools, vocational training institutes etc. in Kerala state, southern India. Positions are available from July to March every year and duration ranges from two weeks to three months.

No salary is offered but volunteers will be provided with free transportation from the nearest airport and free homestay with English-speaking native families. Assistance will also be given for visiting places of interest in Kerala.

Volunteers should be motivated to share and experience the life and culture of the people of Kerala through living and working with them.

For more information contact the above address or fax enquiries.

JAN JAGARITI EDUCATIONAL SOCIETY
M-186, Mangolpuri, Delhi 110083, India; ☎27921979/27868766; e-mail jjes@vsnl.com

JAN Jagariti Educational Society (JJES) is a non-governmental organisation dedicated to the development concerns of disadvantaged people living in the slums and resettlement colonies of the northwest district of the Capital District of Delhi for more than two decades. JJES caters to the developmental needs of about 300,000 people by undertaking needed interventions in the sectors of health, education, environment, capacity building, income generation, gender through cooperation with like-minded national and international organisations. The JJES has developed a Perspective Plan for a decade after working with local people. JJES is anxious to receive volunteers for mutual learning.

Contact Dharmbir Singh for further details.

JOINT ASSISTANCE CENTRE
G 17/3 DLF City Qutab Enclave, Phase I, Gurgaon, Haryana, 122002 India; ☎ +91-124 352141; fax +91-124 351308; e-mail nkjain@jac.unv.ernet.in; address in the USA: Joint Assistance Centre Inc. P.O. Box 6082, San Pablo, California 94806, USA; ☎ +1-510 464-1100; fax +1-603 297 3521; e-mail jacusa@juno.com; www.jacusa.org

The JAC is a voluntary group concerned with disaster preparedness. Volunteers from abroad can help by participating in workcamps held all over India and in Nepal. Jobs undertaken include: office and library work, editing, developing useful training resource materials. Workcamp projects may involve road repair, construction of community centres, replanting forests and conservation projects, etc. About 100 volunteers are needed each year, all year round although workcamps are held intermittently. Placements vary from four to 1-4 weeks (short-term) or long-term projects for upwards of 3 months.

Volunteers must be aged at least 18 and English-speaking. Very basic accommodation with elementary facilities is provided and volunteers are asked to contribute about £150 for the first month and about £80 a month subsequently towards the cost of their stay. Internship/study for a minimum of 3 months is charged £350 and includes supervision, placement and travel to first project and £80 per month subsequently. Fees include basic accommodation and simple vegetarian meals while on a project but exclude travel and incidentals. An initial processing fee/registration of £35 is payable along with application.

For further information contact JAC at the above addresses. enclosing four international reply coupons.

KAREN HILLTRIBES TRUST
Midgley House, Spring Lane, Heslington, York YO10 SDX; ☎01904-411891; fax 01904-430580; e-mail enquiries@karenhilltribes.org.uk; www.karenhilltribes.org.uk

Karen Hilltribes Trust is operating in the Mae Hong son province of northwest Thailand to help the people develop their own social, educational and economic infrastructure. 40-50 volunteers are engaged annually to teach in schools and help with installing water systems and undertaking research. Volunteers should be English-speakers and eligible for a non-immigrant/tourist visa for Thailand depending on length of commitment. Length of stay will depend on the job undertaken. 6-9 month teaching placements are available from October to March/July; 8 week placements in July/August for undergraduates. Other placements can be arranged depending on the skills offered. 2 teams to install water systems in July/August are usually committed well in advance. Volunteers are asked to make a financial contribution towards the work they are involved with and to cover their costs including accommodation with a Karen family.

Applications to Fiona Crocker at the above address.

KOREAN INTERNATIONAL VOLUNTEER ASSOCIATION (KIVA)
11th Floor Sekwang B/D, 202 Sejong-ro, Chongro-gu, Seoul, South Korea 110-050; e-mail info@kiva.or.kr; volunteer@kiva.or.kr; www.kiva.or.uk
KIVA organises international voluntary work placements throughout Korea. One of these placements requires about four native English speakers to teach children English in an orphanage in Seoul. The aim of the orphanage programme is to act not only as a learning experience for the children but for the volunteer as well, as knowledge of the respective different cultures is exchanged between teacher and child. Placements last a minimum of four weeks. Volunteers need to be emotionally stable and have a good sense of humour. Simple board and lodging is provided but volunteers need to fund their own airfares and other expenses.

Applications four weeks in advance of programme commencement to the above address.

LANKA JATIKA SARVODAYA SHRAMADANA SANGAMAYA (Inc)
98 Rawatawatta Road, Moratuwa, Republic of Sri Lanka; ☎ +94-1 647159/+94-1 655255; fax +94-1 656512; e-mail volunteer@itmin.com/sarvish@itmin.com
The ideals on which this organisation is based are contained in its name: 'Sarvodaya' means the awakening of all, and 'Shramadana' means the sharing of labour. For over 40 years the movement has sought to improve the quality of life of those who live in the most deprived areas of Sri Lanka, placing as much stress on the spiritual and cultural elements of life as on purely material development. Construction work is undertaken in 8,000 villages around the country. Sarvodaya organises work camps for study groups, student intern programmes and undergraduates. Individual volunteers are also welcomed. Volunteers are placed to help with social development activities in remote areas and other related social welfare activities according to their interests.

Volunteers should be aged at least 21 and in good health. They should get the recommendation of a recognised organisation/institution in their respective countries. The usual period of service is three to six months but it depends on the visa extensions given by the authorities concerned. No expenses are paid. Limited accommodation is available in dormitories. Volunteers are recruited according to the availability of vacancies.

Those interested should write to the Senior Executive Sarvodaya International Unit.

LITTLE CHILDREN OF THE WORLD INC
361 County Road 475, Etowah, TN 37331, USA; tel/fax +1 423 263-2303; e-mail lcotw@tds.net; www.littlechildren.org
Little Children of the World (LCW) is a non-profit Christian agency dedicated to helping develop caring communities for children at risk, especially those who are victims of poverty, neglect, or abuse. LCW has ongoing child service programmes covering health care, housing assistance, education (formal and informal), livelihood opportunities, and Christian values formation, in eleven communities on the Negros Island in central Philippines. The total programme is distinctive in being family-centred, community based, participatory and holistic.

About 30 volunteers are recruited annually year round for periods of at least one month but most stay for three months and six months to a year placements are also possible. Volunteers can employ whatever talents, training and experience that they bring with them. Especially needed are health workers, teachers in informal education, agriculturists, accountants, and house construction volunteers. Research opportunities are also available, in particular involving street children and children with disabilities. Additionally, those with skills in handicrafts and marketing are wanted. LCW looks for people with imagination, ingenuity and a sincere commitment to serving the least fortunate and a willingness to work in partnership with people of a different race and culture. Knowledge of English is adequate for most purposes and a driver's licence would be useful. Minimum age 18. Volunteers meet all their own expenses and accommodation can be provided in a fully furnished Mission House equipped with kitchen, bath, cable, TV and VCR. A contribution towards utility and lodging costs is requested. Volunteers can enter on a tourist visa which can be renewed as often as needed for about $15.

LCW distributes a free quarterly newsletter, *Jericho Street Echoes* to all on its mailing list, and to others on request.

Applications to the Volunteer Service Director at the above address.

NEW HOPE RURAL COMMUNITY TRUST
PO Box 176, Ashford, Kent TN24 9WD; ☎01233-611281; e-mail uknewhope@hotmail.com; www.newhopeindia.org.
New Hope Rural Community Trust is a registered charity run by volunteers. Its main objective is to relieve poverty and sickness and in particular to support the work of the New Hope Rural Leprosy Trust in Orissa State, India, by assisting with the provision of equipment and facilities required by the Trust to function. About 4-5 volunteers a year are recruited to work on and observe the various programmes run by New Hope in India. Areas of work include: a leprosy eradication programme, working with disabled children, and community health and educational programmes. Volunteers are needed to help with nursing, working with people with learning problems, health care, educational work, computing, teaching and using management skills. Applicants should have relevant skills in the area for which they volunteer. Help is needed all year round for periods of 2-3 months. Accommodation and traditional Indian meals are provided but a contribution towards the cost is appreciated. All expenses are to be met by the volunteer.

Volunteers are also expected to raise much needed funds towards any of the programs mentioned to help in ongoing work of New Hope India. Further information on any programme can be found on the website or by writing to the above address. Volunteers can take the funds raised to India and spend it on the project they want to help.

NEW INTERNATIONAL FRIENDSHIP CLUB NEPAL (NIFC-Nepal)
PO Box 11276, Maharajgunj, Kathmandu, Nepal; ☎ +977-1 427406/429176; fax +977-1 429176; e-mail nifc@mos.com.np; www.geocities.com/nifnepal
Friendship Club Nepal is a small Nepali-run NGO organising regular workcamps to assist rural communities. A long-term project in Chitwan district will establish a co-operative farm demonstrating improved farming methods. Volunteers are required to participate in both research and physical workcamps. Research work usually involves investigating and writing a report on the development situation (health, education, environment or agriculture etc.) in a rural area. A physical workcamp might involve constructing steps to a village, helping build a school or planting trees. Teachers are also needed for schools.

Volunteers should be aged between 17 and 65. Proficiency in English is essential and relevant experience or background knowledge preferable. Volunteers must be flexible, sensitive to cultural differences and able to work in a group and take the initiative in organising work. Working hours are approximately 36 hours, a six day week. Work-camps last 15 days, medium-term placements 2-6 months. No wages or fare paid but basic Nepali style board and lodging provided. Work camp fee US$150; medium-term volunteers should contribute US$150 per month. Registration fee US$30. Volunteers should arrange their own travel, visa and insurance.

Recruitment throughout the year; preferably apply at least 2 months in advance of intended departure date enclosing CV.

NON FORMAL EDUCATION OFFICE, NUA KLONG
Nua Klong District NFE Center, Moo 4/6, Tambol Nua Klong, Amphoe Nua Klong 81130 Thailand; ☎ +66 07563 6488; e-mail volunteerthailand@yahoo.com; www.volunteerthailand.com
English language school that requires about four volunteer teachers a year. Volunteers must be graduates and native English-speakers and willing to live in developing world conditions. Period of work is a minimum of three weeks. There is no maximum length of stay dependent on financial resources for self support and within Thai immigration restrictions. Volunteers need only a holiday visa appropriate to their nationality.

Volunteers are typically expected to work three to six hours a day depending on location. Accredited classes are 30 classroom hours so the teacher can arrange his her own schedule within reason. It is possible to arrange free housing or homestay. The NFE will assist in finding and transportation arrangements to accommodation in bunga-lows, which are low cost.

Applications to the above address.

PEOPLE'S WELFARE COMMITTEE
GPO Box 12137, Kathmandu, Nepal; ☎ +977-1 356841; fax +977-1-356841; e-mail jbardewa@wlink.com.np
The People's Welfare Committee is a non-government, non-profit, social organisation. Its main aim is to provide education, agricultural knowledge, cultural exchange, health and sanitation to people in Nepal. Volunteers working 3-5 hours a day, can be involved in all the above programmes.

Volunteers are required all year round and should be minimum age 16. A knowledge of English and good health are required. Accommodation is provided but applicants must pay for all their other expenses.

For more information send an IRC to the above address.

PERSONAL OVERSEAS DEVELOPMENT
Gap Year Programmes and Career Breaks, 7 Rosbury House, Lytton Grove, Putney, London SW15 2EY; ☎ 020-8246 5811; e-mail info@thepodsite.co.uk; www.thepodsite.co.uk
Personal Overseas Development coordinates career breaks, time off and gap years for people wishing to volunteer their time and skills where it is needed. They arrange placements for people wanting to do something worthwhile in their year out, or a break from work. In Thailand, they organise teaching English in schools for 3-5 months (£750-£1,1650) on stunning tropical islands in the south, or in the hill tribe areas of the north of the country. Alternatively, you can work in one of two animal rescue centres: one which tries to rehabilitate captive wild animals about 115 miles from Bangkok and the other which looks after rescued dogs (about 300 of them) on the island of Koh Samui . The work period is from two weeks to six months and costs £350-£1990. Costs do not include flights, visas or food. Accommodation is provided.

Further details can be obtained from the above address.

RURAL COMMUNITY DEVELOPMENT PROGRAMME - NEPAL
Kalanki-14, Kathmandhu, Nepal; ☎ +977-1-278305; fax +977-1-415679; e-mail rcdpn@mail.com.np; www.rcdpnepaul.com

RCDPN takes between 150 and 200 volunteers a year as teachers in schools and orphanages, working with local communities in forestry and conservation and work at a hospital. For teaching work volunteers should have excellent English writing and speaking skills, for the hospital they should be medical students. Period of work from 2 weeks to 5 months maximum. Participation cost to volunteer is $200 registration, $225 language and culture orientation and $40-$50 per week for board and lodging. Applicants should pay this amount to the office in Nepal.

Applications should be addressed to the National Co-ordinator at the above address.

RURAL ORGANISATION FOR SOCIAL ELEVATION (ROSE)
SAC Kanda, PO Kanda District Bageshwar, 263631, K.S.S., Uttaranchal, India; ☎ 91 5963 241081; e-mail jlverma_rosekanda@yahoo.co.in

Kanda is a small village on Himalaya in northern Uttaranchal. Pradesh. The objective of ROSE is to improve the plight of the poorest people through education, rural development and the raising of social awareness. This is done through ROSE's school for pupils aged five to 12 years. ROSE is funded locally and from donations and visitor resources. The types of activities which volunteers from abroad can take part in include: helping teach English in the school, administrative duties, cultural activities, visiting women's community groups, working on an organic agriculture farm, trekking and walking, planting trees, writing project reports, local path making, construction and environmental work.

It is preferred that volunteers come in organised groups for two week workcamps and work five hours daily, six days a week for a minimum of two weeks. The administration fee is 2000 rupees and 300 rupees a day for full board. Concessions are given to groups and long-term volunteers.

Further details from Jeevan Lal Verma, Director at the above address.

RURAL RECONSTRUCTION NEPAL
G.P.O. Box 8130, Lazimpat, Kathmandhu, Nepal; ☎ +977 1 415418; fax +977 1 418296; e-mail rrn@rrn.org.np; www.rrh.org.np

RRN implements integrated rural development programmes and works in the forefront of policy advocacy in Nepal. About 25 volunteers per year are accepted to assist in project implementation, information management and fund-raising activities. For volunteers based in the communities a fair understanding of the Nepali language is needed. Volunteers should be in good health and capable of living in a stringent climate. Volunteers have to be self supporting and pay for their accommodation which is arranged by RRN. They are also expected to stay a year or longer. A work station and communication facility are provided.

For more details contact Sarbaraj Khadka, at the above address.

SAMASEVAYA
National Secretariat, Anuradhapura Road, Talawa NCP, Sri Lanka; ☎ +94-25 2276266; +94-25 76266; samasev@sltnet.lk.

Samasevaya works towards peace through organising development programmes in self-reliance education, environmental conservation, children's development, women's development, nutrition and health. About 10 volunteers a year are recruited to assist with the work on these projects. Minimum age 18 and volunteers must be in good health and prepared to work in rural areas. Placements are available all year round and normally last one month but this period can be extended. Simple accommodation is provided and volunteers are requested to pay US$90 per month for their food; all other expenses, including entry visa (visas can be extended once in Thailand if necessary) must be met by the volunteer also.

Applications to the National Secretary at the above address.

SAVE THE WORLD
P.O.Box 5947, Kathmandhu, Thamel, Nepal; ☎ +977 1 222939; fax +977 1 420718; e-mail savetheworldnepal@hotmail.com
STW works to raise public awareness for peace, human rights and sustainable development activities. Detailed information is provided on the website. 6-8 volunteers are taken on annually to work in the areas of education, health and environment related social organisation. Volunteers are normally recruited for three months and are provided with food and lodging.

Apply direct to the above address.

SHIN SHIZEN JUKU (New Nature School)
Tsurui-mura, Akan-gun, Hokkaido 085-12, Japan; ☎ +81 154 64-2821.
SSJ runs three operations needing staff and volunteers. The first is for English teachers who are needed to help teach English to both adults and children. The contract is for six months and there is pay of 30,000 yen to 50,000 yen per month.

Volunteers are needed for a second operation in a small village, Ueno SSJ near Nara and Kyoto to help with an English coffee shop and manual work.

Volunteers are needed any time of year and usually stay two or three months, or longer if they wish. There are usually several volunteers staying at a time. A knowledge of Japanese is a great help, but not essential. An international driver's licence is necessary. Applicants should be loving, responsible, honest and enthusiastic to teach English to Japanese people. For voluntary work, a tourist visa is sufficient. Food and accommodation only are provided in return for work.

Anyone interested should contact Hiroshi Mine, Manager, at the above address.

SOCIETY FOR THE PROMOTION OF HUMAN RIGHTS (SPHR)
Post Office: Amjhupi, Post Code 7101, District Meherpur, Bangladesh; ☎ (880) 0791-62703
SPHR is devoted to promoting human rights mobilizing popular support and raising consciousness through volunteers in Bangladesh. About 150 volunteers are accepted annually to assist with this work which includes mediation and abritrating. There are no age restrictions. Volunteers get pocket money but all other expenses including accommodation are borne by the volunteers.

Apply direct.

STUDENT ACTION INDIA
c/o Voluntary Services Unite, UCL, 25 Gordon Street, London WC1H OAY; ☎ 07071-225866; 07071-225866; e-mail info@studentactionindia.org.uk; www.studentactionindia.org.uk
Student Action India (SAI) is a development, non-governmental, non-profit organisation. Their aim is to engage young people in global issues through their Development in Action project. This includes a volunteer placement scheme in India, an annual magazine and quarterly newsletter. Volunteers produce a personal project, which serves as a resource for SAI and their Indian partner organisations. SAI undertake talks and presentations

in the UK.

Volunteers work on a range of projects, including non-formal teaching, office-based work, environmental projects, GPS schemes, women's income generation projects and a school for deaf and blind children. No special skills required. No specific skills or upper age limit but must show an interest in learning about global issues and have realistic expectations of volunteering. Placements are for two months (Jul-Sept) or 5 months (Sept-Feb). Interviews, training and feedback must be attended in the UK.

Application forms available from the coordinator at the above address.

TABITHA FOUNDATION USA
P.O. Box 272, Jamestown IN 46147, USA; www.tabitha-usa.org

Tabitha Foundation is a US benevolent trust founded in 2003 to support mission and aid efforts in the areas of health care, education, sanitation, small businesses and co-operatives. Tabitha projects always involve the instruction of indigenous trainers who, by example and teaching, work to restore control to communities themselves and guide the work towards self-sustainability. The goal is to create a healthy, viable community to allow human beings to realise their full potential. All the members on the board of the Tabitha foundation are unpaid volunteers.

Volunteers are needed to provide labour and funding to build homes for homeless Cambodian families. Trips are organised several times a year. Building teams are inter-national as Tabitha has representatives in Canada, the UK and Australia. Volunteers work under the direction of Khmer builders to construct a small house. Trips last about ten days and from the USA cost about $2,500 which covers flights, food and accom-modation and in-country travel.

Further details from the above website.

TEACHING & PROJECTS ABROAD
Gerrard House, Rustington, West Sussex BN16 1AW; ☎01903-859911; fax 01903-785779; e-mail info@teaching-abroad.co.uk; www.teaching-abroad. co.uk

With Teaching & Projects Abroad you can take part in adventurous foreign travel with a chance to do a worthwhile job. Over 2,000 places are available each year to teach conversational English (no TEFL required) or gain valuable work experience in medicine, conservation, journalism, business and many other professions.

Placements are available throughout the year and last from a month upwards. Vol-unteers are needed in Asia (India, Nepal, China and Thailand) and also Bolivia, Chile, Guatemala and Ghana, Mexico, Mongolia, Papua New Guinea, Peru, Romania, Russia, South Africa, Togo and Ukraine.

For further information on Teaching Abroad or Business Abroad, contact Dr Peter Slowe at the above address.

UNITED CAMBODIAN COMMUNITY DEVELOPMENT (UCC)
Sovansakor St., Kampot Town, Kampot Province, Cambodia; ☎+855 33 932 499; e-mail 01294-2257@mobitel.com.kh;1903-859911; www. unitedcambodian.org

UCC is a small, independent NGO working in the Kampot province of southern Cambodia carrying out projects aimed at helping to rebuild a country that has been devastated by decades of destruction caused by wars, and hardship under the ruthless Pol Pot regime of the 1970s. UCC started in 1992 and its projects include a vocational school for war-wounded amputees and permanently disabled people and an agricultural training centre/farm that is working to re-integrate a Khmer Rouge community with their

neighbours. UCC also has programmes covering child development and well digging.
Both skilled and unskilled volunteers are accepted. Skills needed include medical and technical and construction skills. A volunteer donation is required and this is divided into a cost per week that decreases the longer you stay. You can contact UCC direct for further information. There is also a contact office in the USA: UCC, c/o USF School of Law, Center for Law & Global Justice, 2130 Fulton Street, San Francisco CA 94117-1080, USA; tel/fax 415-422-5922; e-mail lverson@usfca.edu.

VISWADARSANAM CENTRE FOR HUMANITY AND NATURE
Feny Land, Nariyapuram Pin 689 513, Pathanamthitta District, Kerala, South India; ☎ 00 91 468 235 0543; fax 2322264; e-mail viswadarsanam@yahoo. com

Viswadarsanam is a voluntary environmental organisation based at a centre set amidst lush green vegetation where the aim is to promote a holistic and natural way of life. Activities include: running a development centre, preparing newsletters, books, information sheets and audio visuals, conducting guided educative wilderness trips, nature walks and trekking for interested groups. Interests of the organisation extend into rural development, cottage industry, art and cultural heritage, flora and fauna and travel and tourism.

Volunteers are needed to commit as much time as they can to the project (usually one to three months). Work includes administration and planning of long and short-term projects such as nature projects and holistic health. Volunteers also help with international correspondence, computer work, preparing newsletters, booklets, leaflets and handbooks. Volunteers also get involved in alternative lifestyle projects including herbal medicine, yoga, meditation and Kerala cooking. There is also an opportunity to teach local students. Volunteers get food and basic (not necessarily single) accommodation for which there is a charge from £100 (for 15 days) to £430 (for three months).

Further details and an application form are available from the above address.

VOLUNTARY WORK OPPORTUNITIES IN NEPAL
**GPO Box 11969, Kathmandu, Nepal; fax +977 1 416144;
e-mail vwop2000@hotmail.com**

VWOP is a voluntary programme which liaises between international volunteers and the schools/organisations which provide voluntary jobs and opportunities in urban and remote areas of Nepal, including teaching in schools, being involved in environmental, health, agriculture and research programmes. Volunteers may also arrange and implement their own ideas/programmes/activities, which directly help the local community. We also help those who intend to invest in education, livestock, health, the environment, research etc. in rural areas of Nepal.

Qualifications and experience are not essential except for environmental and health programmes. Volunteers who wish to can have first hand experience of living and working with local village people. Volunteers are invited to participate in cultural activities and will have the opportunity to explore other parts of Nepal where they can engage in trekking, white water rafting, sightseeing etc.

Volunteers stay with a local family during placement sharing their home, food and amenities. Volunteers pay some amount for food accommodation and organisation fee. Fees are US$20 (application), US$50 (administration) and US$50 per month (host family).

Application forms from VWOP above.

VOLUNTEERS FOR ENGLISH IN SRI LANKA

58a Coverton Road, Tooting, London SW17 0QN; ☎020-86823986; e-mail info@vesl.org; www.vesl.org

VESL is a non-profit organisation that was established to provide the students of rural schools with the chance to gain learning and confidence levels in spoken English and to promote cultural understanding. VESL sends up to twenty volunteers to Sri Lanka during the summer to work alongside local teachers in a four-week summer programme (mid-July to mid-August) teaching English to children and adults in five different rural communities across the country. Two to four hours teaching a day, Monday to Friday. A TEFL or other teaching qualification would be useful but is not essential. Volunteers need to raise under £1,000 for flights, food, accommodation, insurance, training, back-up and support.

Further details and an application form from the above address.

> **Sophie Harrison enjoyed her volunteer stint with VESL for which she is now operations manager.**
> *This summer I went with four other volunteers to live and work in the north and east of the country (Sri Lanka). We taught English classes to several thousand children in five rural schools: a Sinhala school in Marassana, a Muslim school near Trincomalee, a Tamil school near Batticola, a Sinhala school in Matale District and lastly a Tamil School in Point Pedro. It was difficult, and interesting, and entertaining work. The most striking thing, though, was the response of the children. They are enthusiastic to the point of being terrifying. Everywhere we went the shortage of teachers and resources was counterbalanced by the passion and energy of the students. Everywhere we went, we were asked to come back – spoken English, indeed English full-stop, is a skill that everyone wants to acquire but in several of the schools they had no English teachers at all; and at others the language is rarely spoken and is seen as a real option only for the privileged.*

> **Mags Fearon also enjoyed her VESL experience**
> *It was challenging, fascinating, interesting and fun – my summer with VESL gave me amazing insight into what life is like in the most isolated communities on a most beautiful island. I have never taught such enthusiastic students in my life (or eaten such unbelievably hot food). Best of all was the sense that I was making a measurable difference to people's lives. It is not often you get the opportunity to do something so worthwhile.*

WILD ANIMAL RESCUE FOUNDATION OF THAILAND (WAR)

65/1 3rd Floor Pridi Banomyong Building, Sukhumvit 55, Wattana, Bangkok 10110, Thailand; tel/fax 662 712 0778, 712 9525; e-mail volunteer@warthai. org;www.warthai.org

WAR has been operating in Thailand for over a decade and is involved in many conservation projects dealing with all native species including gibbons, bears and tigers. It recruits paying volunteers to help with its projects which are devoted to the care of wild animals in need. 80-100 volunteers are accepted annually to help with the work of looking after abused and maltreated wild animals.

The following four projects accept volunteers:

Phuket Gibbon Rehabilitation Project on the island of that name of the south coast of Thailand. The aim of the project is the rehabilitation of gibbons that have been confiscated from captivity, so they can be returned to their habitat. Volunteers work an eight hours day six days a week. Tasks include preparation of food, cage maintenance and observation and data collection. There is also the possibility of being asked to do some English teaching at the local primary school. Accommodation is provided in bungalow type buildings near the sanctuary and meals are available at local restaurants. All expenses including health insurance are borne by the volunteer.

Wild Animal Rescue and Education Centre – Baan Talae Nork is a 250-acre area of virgin mountainous rainforest secured by WAR from the Thai royal forestry department for the creation of a visitors' educational centre. It is 80kms from Ranong. The sanctuary is home to all wild species common to Thailand and is also used for the overspill of Gibbons from the Gibbon Rehabilitation project. The project also includes the education of local people, particularly children to help end illegal hunting and abuse of animals by humans. The hours of work and tasks are similar as for the Gibbon project and additionally volunteers will be included in the education programmes. Accommodation in local-style huts, self-catering with food easily obtainable from the local markets.

Monkey Hospital and Lopburi Zoo – Lopburi' Lopburi is known as the Monkey City, owing to the large number of macaques that inhabit the old quarter. More than 1,000 monkeys have been coexisting together with humans in the city and environs. Each year, a number of monkeys are injured by traffic, electrocuted and attacked by other monkeys. The monkey hospital at the zoo about 3 hours' drive from Bangkok is run by the Thai military with support from WAR. Additionally, there is a wild animal rescue centre that looks after animals from inside and outside the zoo. Volunteers work the same hours as for the other projects and help the zoo veterinarians, and with building and maintaining cages and feeding the animals. The sick and blind animals need a great deal of care.

Sea Turtle Conservation Project – Ranong begun in 2003, runs from December to March only and works in conjunction with WAR to redress the decline in all four species of sea turtle found off Thailand. The aim of the programme is to first define sea turtle status in the area and to establish a long-term, sea turtle conservation programme and promote awareness of marine turtles amongst the local people.

Volunteers are needed to monitor the beaches along this coastline and on the adjacent islands particularly during the nesting and breeding season and to work with local communities to mark and record the location of all nests and turtles seen along the Baan Talae Nork coastline. Accommodation is in good, local style huts at the Wild Animal Rescue and Education Centre, 400 metres from the beach. The huts are self-catering using food from local markets.

All the projects above can be accessed through WAR. The donations required by volunteers range from $1020 for the first three weeks for a short-term volunteer up to $3250 for 12 months (long-term volunteer). Any additional weeks beyond the three-week, eight-week and twelve-month periods are charged at $105 per week. An airport pick up, orientation at the WAR office in Bangkok, a night's accommodation in Bangkok and on-site accommodation. Not included are onward transport from Bangkok, personal expenses including insurance. Further information from the WAR office or website above.

Professional and Longer-term Volunteering

AMITY VOLUNTEER TEACHERS ABROAD (AVTA)
3065 Rosecrans Place, Suite 104, Sand Diego, California 92110, USA; ☎ +1 619 222 7000; fax +1 619 222 7016; e-mail avta@amity.org;www.amity. org
Amity is a non-profit international teaching exchange organisation, which promotes international friendship and cultural understanding. Amity provides voluntary teaching opportunities in China. Posts are in post-secondary schools for 12-16 hours per week. Transportation, benefits, housing and a small stipend are paid by the cooperating denominations for each volunteer. Volunteers should be graduates but not necessarily an experience teacher or Mandarin speaker and able to commit to two years' service.

Contact the Volunteer Coordinator, AVTA, at the above address.

EMMANUEL HOSPITAL ASSOCIATION
808/92 Deepali Building, Nehru Place, North Delhi – 19, India; ☎ +91 11 6432055/6461487; fax +91 11 6432055/6461487; e-mail eha@giasd101. vsnl.net.in; www.eha.org.uk
Emmanuel House Association (EHA) is a federation of 18 hospitals and 25 community health and development projects providing affordable and appropriate health care services to the poor and marginalised segment of the population in North, Central and Northeast India. The 18 EHA hospitals provide curative services to its catchment areas at a subsidised rate and treatment is usually free of cost for patients who are unable to pay. The 25 EHA community health and development projects provide preventive services, integrating health with development and trains local people as health care givers to make it sustainable, it also mobilises the community to further help themselves by organising them into self-help groups through micro enterprise programmes. Sanitation, adult literacy and income generation are also integrated into these health programmes.

The Association recruits: trained doctors – obstetricians/gynaecologists, surgeons, opthalmologists, physicians, ENT specialists, orthopaedics, plastic surgeons; nurses; dentists; health workers; technical professionals e.g. engineers, IT specialists, architects, builders, evaluators; those with educational qualifications – literacy experts, school teachers, trainers; professional videographers, photography technicians, creative writers; business experts – microenterprise and credit scheme professionals, financial managers, and accountants. Relevant qualifications are required of the individual roles. Knowledge of English is essential, any other language (Hindi, Marathi) skills very desirable and in some cases necessary. A stipend is paid to cover basic board and lodging for volunteers when in India; any other expenses (airfare, insurance, etc.) to be met by the volunteer. Placements from 6 months to two years arranged all year round.

Applications to Dr Alletta Bell, Co-ordinator for Overseas Personnel, at the above address or e-mail Dr Bell at 75201.3443@compuserve.com.

INTERNATIONAL CHINA CONCERN (ICC)
PO Box 20, Morpeth, NE61 3YP, UK; ☎ +44 01670-505622; e-mail uk@intlchinaconcern.org; www.intlchinaconcern.org.8
ICC is a China-based charitable organisation involved in projects in China's government orphanages. By bringing care and improvement of conditions ICC aims to make a difference to the lives of China's orphans. ICC is a bridge between China and the West to channel finances and people resources to help.

Twenty to thirty volunteers are recruited annually to perform one of the following roles: administration assistant (correspondence), accounts assistant (book-keeping), physical or occupational therapy co-ordinator, special education teacher, special needs nursing carer. Knowledge of Mandarin Chinese is helpful but not essential. Volunteers are required from 6 months to two years and must be self-supporting.

For more information please visit the website.

INTERNATIONAL NEPAL FELLOWSHIP (INF)
69 Wentworth Road, Harborne, Birmingham B17 9SS; ☎ 0121-427 8833; fax 0121-428 3110; e-mail ukoffice@inf.org.uk; www.inf.org.np
INF is an evangelical Christian mission working in Nepal and the Himalayan Region. INF is a bridge builder, working with individuals, communities and the government of Nepal to improve the health and develop the health services of the people of western Nepal.

Volunteers work in the following areas: health, technical, administration and support services, training and education. Placements are from three months although the usual period of recruitment is two and a half years. Applicants must be at least 21 years old, be committed Christians, and have a degree or equivalent qualification plus two years' experience. Volunteers must be self-financing.

Applications are accepted all year round at the above address or for those applying outside Europe contact the International Headquarters, INF, PO Box 5, Pokhara, Nepal; ☎ +977-6120111; e-mail recruit@inf.org.np

INTERNATIONAL OFFICE FOR ASIA-YMCA OF THE USA
101 N. Wacker Drive, Chicago, IL 60606, USA; e-mail STERLING@YMCAUSA. ORG; for look under Y-world at www.YMCA.NET
Volunteers are required to teach conversational English in community-based YMCAs throughout Taiwan. The OSCY program is more than a language program, it is a cultural learning opportunity for both the teacher and the student. Approximately 20-25 people are placed annually. Due to visa restrictions, teachers must be US or Canadian citizens.

In Taiwan, teachers are expected to work a thirty-hour week, with up to 15 of these spent in the classroom. Applicants must speak English fluently, be flexible in adjusting to new situations and be interested in participating in extra-curricular activities that strengthen personal relationships and a sense of community. The length of placement for teaching in Taiwan is one year. Applicants must have a four-year degree. Teaching experience and training are desirable.

The deadline is April 15 for the autumn placement. Accommodation is provided in addition to a return airfare (to the USA), monthly allowance, health insurance, paid vacation and financial bonuses.

Write to the Taiwan OSCY Program Administrator at the above address for brochures and application forms.

THE LEPROSY MISSION
Goldhay Way, Orton Goldhay, Peterborough PE2 5GZ; ☎01733-370505; fax 01733-404886; e-mail post@tlmew.org.uk; www.leprosymission.org.uk
The Leprosy Mission, a Christian charity, offers opportunities for volunteers (3-6 months), medical electives (6-8 weeks) and short-term professionals (3-9 months) to serve overseas. Placements are required to raise airfares, insurance and medical costs, with board and lodging during the assignment provided by The Leprosy Mission.
Free board and lodging is offered at the centre, but all other costs must be met by the volunteer.

The Leprosy Mission also offers a new Internship programme (for 1 to 2 years) with an allowance to cover living expenses. The intern will meet all other costs.

Applications should be made to the National Director at the above address.

THE NEO-HUMANIST FOUNDATION – Ananda Marga Project
45 Mu 2 Paksong Village, Patho District, Chumporn 86180, Thailand; ☎ +66-229 6886; e-mail anandashyama@hotmail.com.
The Neo-Humanist Foundation operates worldwide in Africa, North and South America, Canada, Europe and Asia. The Ananda Shyama Project, a home for disadvantaged children, is based in 8 beautiful acres of rainforest in Southern Thailand. Up to 3 volunteers at a time are required to help with children or to work in the garden. Volunteers with a knowledge of organic farming would be particularly welcome. (the project is trying to establish a 4 acre organic farm to supply all the project's needs). The placement is for 6 months to a year.
Volunteers need to be fit (for garden work) - knowledge of Thai herbs would be useful but not essential. Accommodation and vegetarian food are provided as well as medical care for accidents or illness acquired while working on the project. There is also the opportunity to participate in yoga, meditation, swimming, trekking and rafting. Please note that food is strictly vegetarian - no meat, fish or eggs. No smoking, drugs or alcohol are allowed.
Applications and further information on the Project to the Chairman Volunteer at the above address.

VIA (formerly Volunteers in Asia)
PO Box 20266, Stanford, CA 94309, USA; ☎ +1 650 723-3228; fax +1 650 725-1805; e-mail info@viaprograms.org; www.viaprograms.org
For over 40 years, VIA has been working with partner Asian organisations and institutions to provide native English speakers to teach English and work as English resource persons. Volunteers might teach at the middle school or college level, or work with local non-profit organisations assisting with their translation and editing needs. Current programmes run in China, Indonesia and Vietnam.

Between 30 and 40 volunteers are recruited annually for placements lasting one to two years. Applicants must be native English-speakers, hold a US passport or reside in the USA hold a college degree, be mature and responsible. Volunteer's participant fee covers round-trip airfare from the San Francisco area to Asia, basic health insurance, visa, cross-cultural training, in-country orientation, and home office and in-field support. See website for current costs. One and two-year volunteers receive housing and a monthly living stipend from their hosting institution.

Applications are due in early February. In person interviews are required, and mandatory training sessions in California take place in spring and just before summer departure. Exact dates are on the website. Applicants must fund their own travel costs to California.

Australia and New Zealand

General Opportunities

AUSTRALIAN KOALA FOUNDATION
Level 1, 40 Charlotte Street, Brisbane, QLD 4000, Australia; ☎ +61-7 3229 7233; fax +61-7 3221 0337; e-mail research@savethekoala.com; www. savethekoala.com akfkoala@gil.com.au; www.akfkoala.gil.com.au

The Australian Koala Foundation (AKF) is a non-profit, non-government funded, conservation organisation whose central aim is the conservation of Australia's unique koala and the preservation of its diminishing habitat. Founded in 1986, the AKF now has international offices in Washington DC, USA and Tokyo, Japan. From simple beginnings, the AKF is now a major conservation voice for the future of wild koalas in both domestic and international forums.

The major scientific research project, the *Koala Habitat Atlas*, is the spearhead that encapsulates the prime objective of the AKF – conservation of the koala and its habitat. Using GIS and satellite imaging technology to identify, map and rank koala habitat, the *Koala Habitat Atlas* provides land-use planners with this vital information in a practical format. Volunteers can assist in fieldwork expeditions which contribute to the *Koala Habitat Atlas*. Field trips are usually two weeks in duration and occur four times a year. Costs begin at AU$1,000 per week, depending on location. Volunteers can also assist with general office duties, especially during the major public awareness and fundraising campaign – Save the Koala – held in July each year. Applicants should advise the AKF of any specialist areas of expertise or interest they may have. Minimum age 18.

Volunteers for office duties are generally required from March to October each year but contact Lorraine O'Keefe, General Manager, Administration and Finance, at GPO Box 2659, Brisbane, QLD 4001, Australia, to discuss the voluntary opportunities available. Also check out the website for upcoming fieldtrips.

CONSERVATION VOLUNTEERS AUSTRALIA (CVA)
PO Box 423, Ballarat, Victoria 3353, Australia; ☎ +61-3 5333 1483; fax +61-3 5333 2166; e-mail info@conservationvolunters.com.au; www. conservationvolunteers.com.au

Conservation Volunteers Australia is Australia's largest practical conservation organisation. CVA welcomes everyone who is enthusiastic about the outdoors and hands-on conservation. CVA offers a unique and exciting Australian conservation experience. Projects include endangered flora/fauna surveys, habitat restoration, bush track construction, heritage projects, seed collection, wildlife surveys, research projects. Locations include National Parks, World Heritage Areas, remote/outback areas, coastal and river environments, farms and urban projects. The six-week Conservation Experience package costs about 1,000 Australian dollars (25 Australian dollars per day). This includes all food, accommodation and project-related travel plus a *Nomads Adventure Card*. Cost does not include fare to Australia. Projects start every Friday from CVA offices in all State and Territory capitals, plus regional centres. For a list of addresses of the 24 CVA offices around Australia, see the website.

Volunteers must be aged 15+; no experience necessary as training is given. For more information e-mail or write to CVA, or book online via the website.

NEW ZEALAND TRUST FOR CONSERVATION VOLUNTEERS (NZTCV)
343 SH17, RD3, Albany, Auckland, New Zealand; tel/fax 09 415 9336; e-mail conservol@clear.net.nz; www.conservationvolunteers.org.nz

The New Zealand Trust for Conservation Volunteers is the main organisation in New Zealand that organises volunteer projects (currently 120 of them) that help to restore New Zealand's ecosystems to their natural beauty by mobilising volunteers for this purpose. Projects listed on the website cover a range of conservation/environmental activities and many of these are continuous. Projects take place over days, or can last several months such as the volunteer hut wardens needed for the Central Whirinake Forest Park, near the Bay of Plenty (North Island) from November to February annually. Work includes planting, weeding, track maintenance, wildlife, marine and pest managemtn. Projects last from one day to six months. Some projects provide accommodation in return for work.

Projects are organised regionally and a list of regional offices' addresses can be found on the website www.conservation volunteers.org.nz. In 2005 a volunteer training programme is going to be set up. No further details at time of press.

WWOOF
P.O. Box 1172, Nelson, New Zealand; tel/fax 03 5449890; e-mail wwoof@wwoof.co.nz; www.wwoof.co.nz

Volunteer farm labourers for unpaid work on organic properties including orchards, nurseries, farms etc. in New Zealand. It must be stressed that these positions are unpaid and that participants must pay for their own travel expenses; they do however, receive free food and accommodation. Positions are available at any time of year. WWOOF runs 650 farms around New Zealand.

Applicants must be aged over 16 and should not be from countries whose nationals need special invitations to enter New Zealand. For further information write to Jane and Andrew Strange at the above address enclosing £12 membership fee.

Professional and Longer-term Volunteering

AUSTRALIAN VOLUNTEERS INTERNATIONAL
71 Argyle Street, PO Box 350, Fitzroy, Victoria 3065, Australia; ☎ +61 3-9279 1788; fax +61 3-9419 4280; e-mail ozvol@ozvol.org.au; www.ozvol. org.au

Australian Volunteers International (AVI) is Australia's largest and most experienced international volunteer sending organisation. It provides opportunities for Australians to live, work and learn in partnership with developing communities in Asia, the Pacific, Africa, Latin America, the Middle East and in indigenous communities in Australia.

With a 50-year history, AVI has extensive experience and connections with governments, community organisations and individuals in several countries. Australian volunteers fill positions in every field of activity including education, health, IT, business and administration. Specialists are also recruited for positions in indigenous communities and organisations within Australia.

Volunteer assignments are usually one to two years. Volunteers must be at least 18 and an Australian (or New Zealand) citizen or permanent resident. Volunteers should normally also have a tertiary or trade qualification and relevant work experience.

In-country, AVI volunteers live under local conditions and receive either the equivalent of a local wage or a living allowance, which covers basic living costs. AVI also arranges accommodation, and provides airfares, visas and health problems.

Youth: AVI has a recent programme of short-term volunteer options for 18-25 year olds. The emphasis is on cross-cultural exchange and community development. No specific qualifications needed. Volunteers raise sponsorship to cover their costs.

AVI produces *Australain Volunteer* Magazine, an annual report and newsletter (for returned volunteers), and various promotional brochures outlining the magazine and its services. To obtain free copies e-mail ccr@ozvol.org.au.

Applications to your nearest AVI State Office:

National Office (Vic & Tas), address as above.

Sydney Office (NSW & ACT), Suite 46, Level 4, 8-24 Kippax Street, Surry Hills, NSW 2010; ☎+2-9211 1277; fax +2-9211-1234; nsw@ozvol.org.au.

Brisbane Office (Queensland), Yungaba, 182 Main Street, Kangaroo Point, QLD 4169; ☎+7-3891 1168; fax +7-3891 1314; qld@ozvol.org.au.

Adelaide Office (SA & NT), 19 Market Street (P.O. Box 536), Adelaide, SA 5001; ☎+8-8410 2770; fax +8-8410 2778; sa@ozvol.org.au.

Darwin Office (NT), 14 Shepherd Street, (P.O. Box 1538), Darwin NT 0801; ☎08-8941 9743; fax 08 8941 9768; nt@ozvol.org.au.

Perth Office (WA), (P.O. Box 8047 Subiaco East), Subiaco, WA 6008; ☎+8-9382 3503; fax +8-9388 2115; wa@ozvol.org.au.

PART TWO

NON-RESIDENTIAL WORK

UNITED KINGDOM

THE UNITED STATES OF AMERICA

Non-Residential Work

The majority of organisations featured in this part of the book offer voluntary work, which serves to complement existing statutory services rather than to replace or compete with them.

One of the volunteer's greatest assets is that they are doing whatever their chosen task may be because they want to, not because it is their job. It can make all the difference to a prisoner or a sick person to know that whoever is dealing with them is there because they genuinely desire to help. Volunteers can visit an old person or go shopping with someone with learning difficulties, that would be prohibitively expensive were they doing so as paid professionals.

Another advantage possessed by the voluntary sector is that it can react to events in a far quicker manner than the statutory authorities, which may have to drag a new idea through levels of bureaucracy before it can take a new course of action. The most conspicuous example of this involves AIDS: the Terrence Higgins Trust, a charity, was using volunteers to take positive action to help sufferers from AIDS long before the Social Services had adjusted to its existence.

Volunteers are also, of course, able to involve themselves in activities that most people would accept are not the responsibility of the state; examples in this book range from promoting vegetarianism to campaigning against nuclear weapons. People can also pursue their own interests through voluntary work; cat lovers can assist the Cats Protection League in rescuing stray, unwanted and neglected cats and help raise funds for the League, or those with equine interests can help the Riding for the Disabled Association. In the USA section of this chapter there is notably scope for those wishing to pursue their interest in the arts (among other interests) either by volunteering to work for a non-profit theatre or perhaps assisting with poetry readings for a non-profit arts project.

The work listed in this chapter may often be pursued on a full time basis, but since few of us are lucky enough to have no other commitments, the majority of opportunities described below are more of a part-time nature. Some of these part-time duties involve several hours a week; others merely require a degree of regularity or consistency. Some may continue for several years; others may last only for a weekend, or for a couple of weeks during the summer.

In attempting to categorise the different types of voluntary work available in the UK section of this chapter, it has not been possible to draw distinct dividing lines, although it is to be hoped that the classification system used will act as a useful guide. There are obvious overlaps, for instance between the section on *Disease and Disability* and the sections of *Children* and *The Elderly*. At the beginning of several sections, an attempt is made to cross-refer readers to other relevant sections, but it is assumed that the general areas of overlap will be easily deduced from a glance at the table of contents. It should also be mentioned that several sections, notably *National/Local Volunteer Organisations, Community Projects* and *Fund Raising and Office Work* describe organisations that cut across the general classifications system.

United Kingdom

National and Local Volunteer Organisations

Unbeknown to a large part of the general public, the UK's voluntary resources are carefully monitored by several complex and overlapping networks of official and semi-official organisations. At the national level, these organisations are concerned with collecting and interpreting data, and producing new plans and programmes in response to both national and local needs. The local offices are in charge of implementing these plans, and acting as recruitment and referral agencies on behalf of the prospective volunteers, and of the local bodies that require volunteers.

As far as individual applicants are concerned, the national offices that are described below are of little practical value, other than as a source of information and referral to the appropriate local office. Local branches – whatever title they adopt – act more or less in the same way as labour exchanges. However, they vary a great deal in their policies, and some are more actively involved in recruitment than others. All can at least offer information on local volunteer needs, and can refer enquiries to the appropriate local organisations.

The people who run local volunteer bureaux should be in touch with all nearby organisations and institutions concerned with voluntary work, and be aware of the type of help that they need. For example, a conservation group may need people with a knowledge of architecture, an old people's home may want car drivers with their own cars, or a youth club may require a bricklayer to help build a new clubhouse.

There is normally a short informal interview before a volunteer is sent on to an agency. This is to make sure that the volunteer will be used in a situation where his or her interests and abilities will be put to the greatest use, and to tell him or her what exactly their job will entail. There is a big difference between vaguely wanting to 'do something useful', and being prepared, for example, to give up every Monday evening for an indefinite period in order to drive people to and from a hospital. Of course not all voluntary work involves a regular commitment of time, but there are many cases, especially those which concern befriending people, where some degree of regularity is essential.

NATIONAL ASSOCIATIONS

CSV RETIRED AND SENIOR VOLUNTEER PROGRAMME (RSVP)
237 Pentonville Road, London N1 9NJ; ☎020-7643 1385; fax 020-7833 8434; e-mail dmurphy@csv.org.uk; www.csv-rsvp.org.uk

RSVP covers England, Scotland and Wales and has 8,000 volunteers over the age of 50 engaged in volunteering in schools, hospitals, health centres, running visiting schemes for frail older people, transport projects in rural areas, environmental and cultural projects. The Organisation is volunteer-led and managed by local groups across the UK who wish to engage older volunteers in their activities.

Some of the tasks done by senior volunteers: assisting with numeracy and literacy in schools, mentoring young people, visiting/telephoning, befriending frail or disabled people, running after school clubs, older people's clubs, gardening and DIY projects, clearing pathways, helping in libraries and museums, organising publicity and fundraising.

Volunteers should be over 50 (no upper limit) and out of pocket expenses are paid. Most volunteers continue until ill health intervenes. RSVP publishes *Focus*, a monthly magazine for all organisers and *Newslines*, a glossy magazine published 2/3 times annually depending on funding.

NATIONAL YOUTH AGENCY
Eastgate House, 19-23 Humberstone Road, Leicester LE5 3GJ; ☎0116 2427350 e-mail nya@nya.org.uk; www.nya.org.uk
The National Youth Agency aims to advance youth work to promote young people's personal and social development, and their voice, influence and place in society. The website contains details of a range of publications and a list of volunteer agencies in the UK. *Volunteer Action!*, a free annual magazine celebrating young people's volunteering and community action. This includes an extensive listings section giving details of a range of organisations, which involve young people as volunteers.

NORTHERN IRELAND VOLUNTEER DEVELOPMENT AGENCY
4th Floor, 58 Howard Street, Belfast, BT1 6PG; ☎02890-236100; www. volunteering-ni.org
Can offer advice how to find work local to you in Northern Ireland.

VOLUNTEER DEVELOPMENT SCOTLAND (VDS)
Stirling Enterprise Park, Stirling FK7 7RP; ☎01786-479593; fax 01786-449285; e-mail vds@vds.org.uk; www.vds.org.uk
VDS is the representative voice for volunteering in Scotland. It promotes equality of opportunity, high standards of achievement and new initiatives, to expand the range and effectiveness of volunteer action and active citizenship. It can also provide a useful starting point for those interested in voluntary work in Scotland, by operating a referral service to other agencies and organisations using volunteers.

WALES COUNCIL FOR VOLUNTARY ACTION
Baltic House, Mount Stuart Square, Cardiff CF10 5FH: ☎029-2043-1700; www.wcva.org.uk
A good starting point to discover opportunities in your local Welsh area.

LOCAL VOLUNTEER BUREAUX AND COUNCILS

Prospective volunteers are recommended to consult one of their local volunteer associations or councils for advice on voluntary work opportunities within their area. Not all local associations are actively involved in recruiting volunteers, but all should be prepared to at least refer applicants to an appropriate local recruiting body.

A few of the more active local volunteer bureaux and councils are described below, but it must be emphasised that these are only included as examples, and their activities are typical of many such bureaux up and down the country. Volunteering England, (Regent's Wharf, 8 All Saints Street, London N1 9RL; ☎020-771520 8900; e-mail volunteering@volunteeringengland.org; www. volunteering.org.uk) and should be able to advise you of your nearest bureau or council.

COUNCIL FOR VOLUNTARY SERVICE - Rochdale Volunteer Development Agency
156/158 Drake Street, Rochdale, Greater Manchester OL16 1PX; ☎01706-631291.
The Council for Voluntary Service for Rochdale Metropolitan Borough supports the work of over 400 local organisations involved in voluntary activities with disabled, elderly, young or disadvantaged people, etc. It also represents the interests of the voluntary sector with the local authority and seeks to develop new initiatives in voluntary work. CVS Rochdale provides a duplicating, typing and DTP service for member organisations, along with IT training.

Rochdale Volunteer Development Agency has over 200 volunteer vacancies on its register. They interview prospective volunteers and refer them on to organisations where they are needed. They also give essential advice to organisations on the effective management of their volunteers. For more details telephone 01706-630111.

DENBIGHSHIRE VOLUNTARY SERVICES COUNCIL
Station Road, Ruthin, Denbighshire, North Wales LL15 1BP; ☎01824-702441; e-mail gaynor@vvbxdenbighshire.freeserve.co.uk
DVSC collects information about the opportunities available for volunteers within the area of Denbighshire. Potential volunteers are provided with advice and information before being referred to appropriate organisations. Volunteers are recruited to help support vulnerable people, holiday play projects, and/or undertake environmental/conservation work, clerical work, driving etc.

Those interested should contact the Volunteer Bureau Organiser at the above address.

GWENT VOLUNTEER BUREAU
8 Pentonville, Newport, S Wales; ☎01633-213229; lynn.clubb@gavowales. org.uk
This Bureau recruits, places and provides support for volunteers in Gwent. There are around 200 mostly non-residential positions offered each year. The minimum age for volunteers is usually about 15 years. Special or useful skills such as having a driving licence may be required for some jobs, but are not necessary for most. The length of

time for which volunteers are required varies widely.

Those interested should contact Gwent Volunteer Bureau at the above address.

THE INDEPENDENT ADVICE CENTRE
16 Market Place, Wantage, Oxon OX12 8AE; ☎01235-765348; fax 01235-763862; e-mail help@advicecentreonline.com; ww0w.wantage.com/advice
The Independent Advice Centre provides, free and confidential advice on a range of topics including debts, benefits and employment. Our trained advisors are all volunteers as are the drivers who transport the elderly and infirm to shops etc. A Directory of local voluntary work is held. For further information contact the Office Manager at the above address.

TUNBRIDGE WELLS VSU - YOUTH IN ACTION
The Jukebox, c/o Tunbridge Wells Girls Grammar School, Southfield Road, Tunbridge Wells, Kent TN4 9UJ; ☎01892-531584; wendy@vsuinkent.org; www.vsuinkent.org.
VSU recruits volunteers aged between 14 and 25 in the West Kent area and aims to give them the opportunity to initiate, organize and implement projects, playschemes, and activities with the elderly, disabled, children, conservation, fund raising, etc.

Those interested should contact the above address for further information.

VOLUNTARY ACTION LEICESTER
The Leicester Active Community Centre, 9 Newarke Street, Leicester, LE1 5SN; ☎0116-2553333; fax 0116-257 5059
The Volunteer Centre recruits for both statutory and voluntary organisations in the Leicester City area. Opportunities are available during the daytime, evenings and weekend and are both long and short-term. As with other Volunteer Bureaux there is a variety of voluntary openings available covering a wide range of subjects and activities. These can be viewed on the internet by visiting www.do-it.org.uk. This is a national site detailing voluntary opportunities from all over the UK. The site offers prospective volunteers a variety of roles and the opportunity to register online and request copies of the information from the organisation who posted it on to the website.

Many roles ask for particular skills and experiences such as having interpersonal skills, patience, IT skills and the ability to keep confidences etc. these vary and depend on the role. Most voluntary opportunities are for those 18 and over. Organisations recruiting volunteers are encouraged to pay out of pocket expenses and offer training.

VOLUNTEER CENTRE TAMESIDE
95-97 Penny Meadow, Ashton-under-Lyne, Lancashire OL6 6EP; ☎0161-339 2345; e-mail office@tamesidevb.org.uk. www.tamesidevb.org.uk.
The Volunteer Centre Tameside provides hundreds of volunteering opportunities for hundreds of people locally. They recruit volunteers, provide meeting rooms for groups, offices and other resources for voluntary and community organisations in Tameside. For further information contact the Centre.

VOLUNTEERING ENGLAND
Regent's Wharf, 8 All Saints Street, London N1 9RL and New Oxford House, 16 Waterloo Street, Birmingham B2 5UG; ☎0121-633 4555; fax 0121-633 4043; e-mail info@navb.org.uk
Volunteering England is the result of a merger of the National Centre for Volunteering and the Consortium for Opportunities for Volunteering in 2004 and is a democratic membership network of self-determining local volunteer bureaux. It is not a headquarters

organisation with local volunteer bureaux branches.

The aim is to provide an advice service to volunteer bureaux on organisational and management issues and on issues relating to volunteer development. The organisation encourages communication and the exchange of information, experiences and skills between volunteer bureaux. Regional Development Groups facilitate this work at regional level.

Volunteering England helps volunteer bureaux to help volunteers by promoting volunteer work to individuals seeking volunteer opportunities. VE also provides training for new VB managers and organises training for VB staff through its annual National Conference.

VOLUNTARY SERVICE BUREAU
34 Shaftesbury Square, Belfast, BT2 7DB, Northern Ireland; ☎028-90 200850; fax 028-90 200860; e-mail info@vsb.org.uk; www.vsb.org.uk
As the Volunteer Bureau for Belfast, VSB provides the support mechanisms to enable individuals to access voluntary opportunities, matching volunteers to voluntary placements, and maximising mutual benefits. Promoting the importance of active participation and citizenship, VSB provides support each year for 3,000 volunteers and 600 organisations whose work involves volunteers. Support includes advice, information, training and good practice standards. To complement general volunteering opportunities a number of specialist volunteering programmes have also been developed including: Millennium Volunteers, Young Citizens in Action, Retired and Senior Volunteer Programme.

In addition to the Bureau function and in a response to identified need VSB has developed a number of volunteer-led practical services which include: Befriending, Transport, Home Security, Environmental/Painting and Decorating.

VSB also provides advice, information and assessment services to a number of external charitable trusts, designed to help those in need throughout Northern Ireland.

VOLUNTEER LINK-UP (West Oxfordshire)
Methodist Church, 10 Wesley Walk, Witney, Oxon OX28 6ZJ; fax 01993-776277; e-mail westoxonvb@freeuk.com; www.westoxfordshrvb@care4free.net
The Volunteer Link-Up is a volunteer bureau offering free advice and support to anyone exploring opportunities for voluntary work. The bureau has 200 registered volunteers and recruits approximately 80 new volunteers per year. There are a wide range of local (West Oxfordshire) opportunities for volunteering as well as information provided on national and international voluntary placements. Duties can include: driving, visiting and shopping for elderly and disabled people, practical tasks such as clerical, computing and committee work, and working in day centres and with groups for disabled, elderly people and those with mental health problems. Many other opportunities of work can be found in addition to these such as in conservation. All that is required from the applicant is a desire to volunteer. In some cases work-related expenses may be paid.

Contact the Manager at the above address.

OTHER NATIONWIDE ORGANISATIONS

The organisations listed and described above, whether at the national or local level, are all inter-related through official and semi-official networks. The entries below refer to organisations and schemes that are nationwide in their scope and also cover such a wide spectrum of voluntary work opportunities that they defy classification elsewhere. Other national bodies that are more specific in their activities and volunteer needs will be found under the other divisions of this chapter.

BRITISH ASSOCIATION OF SETTLEMENTS AND SOCIAL ACTION CENTRES (Bassac)
1st Floor, Winchester House,11 Cranmer Road, London SW9 6EJ; ☎020-7735 1075; fax 020-7735 0840; e-mail info@bassac.org.uk; www.bassac.org.uk
Bassac is a support organisation for multi-purpose community centres around the UK. These centres are always looking for volunteers for all kinds of voluntary work including looking after the mentally and physically handicapped and the elderly so contact them for volunteering opportunities. Details can be found on the Bassac website.

CHRISTIAN VOCATIONS
St. James House, Trinity Road, Dudley, West Midlands DY1 1JB; ☎01384-233511; fax 01384-233032; e-mail info@ChristianVocations.org: www.ChristianVocations.org
Christian Vocations publishes *Mission Matters* annually giving information about current long-term opportunities of interest to Christians and the *Short term Service Directory* which contains short term positions in the UK and abroad at a cost of £5 plus £2 postage and packing. CV also offers and advisory service. Details on request.

EIL CULTURAL & EDUCATIONAL TRAVEL
287 Worcester Road, Malvern Link, Worcs. WR14 1AB; ☎01684-562577; fax 01684-562212; e-mail info@eiluk.org; www.eiluk.org
EIL exists to promote understanding between people of different cultures and countries throughout the world. It believes that people learn to live together by living together. To this end, it has a network of families across 45 countries who are interested in hosting visitors from other countries. It operates a variety of programmes for both individuals and groups. Within the operation the following opportunities for volunteering exist: hosting visitors to the UK, co-ordinating and organising host communities, providing administrative support in the Malvern Office, working as a tour leader with visiting groups during the summer, meeting groups at the airport and carrying out orientation, assisting on a European Voluntary Service Programme.

The requirements and the period for which volunteers are recruited depend upon the particular job. All volunteers receive expenses. Tour leaders stay and eat with the group throughout the tour and will also receive some payment.

Further information can be obtained from the above address.

FSU
Central Office: 207 Old Marylebone Road, London NW1 5QP; ☎020-7402 5175; fax 020-7724 1829; e-mail centraloffice@fsu.org.uk; www.fsu.org.uk
FSU provides family support services in some of the UK's most disadvantaged areas. The family centres offer a full range of community-based, needs-led, and culturally sensitive, services for socially excluded families and children. These services include parenting skills, family case work, counselling, children's groups and playschemes and many others.

The main areas of volunteering are at a local level and include sitting on management committees offering advice and professional experience, assisting with fundraising and working directly with service users in providing practical help.

FEDERATION OF CITY FARMS & COMMUNITY GARDENS (FCFCG)

The Green House, Hereford Street, Bedminster, Bristol BS3 4NA; ☎0117-923 1800; e-mail admin@farmgarden.org.uk; www.farmgarden.org.uk

FCFCG is the national organisation which supports and advises those who wish to set up and operate community managed farms and gardens in city areas. A list of city farms which you can become involved with either on a volunteer basis or as a full time worker can be obtained by sending an A4 SAE to the above address or via e-mail.

LEAGUE OF JEWISH WOMEN

4th Floor, 24-32 Stephenson Way, London NW1 2JW; ☎020-7387 7688; fax 020-7387 2110; e-mail office@league ofjewishwomen.org.uk; www. leagueofjewishwomen.org.uk

The League of Jewish Women is the leading national Jewish Women's Voluntary Service organisation in the UK. It provides all types of service to the whole community regardless of race, colour or religion. Membership is over 4,000 and almost 75% of these actually carry out voluntary work such as working with the young, in hospitals, for the physically and mentally disabled, the elderly, and with and for other organisations including the WRVS, the Red Cross, Adult Literacy, Relate, and the Council of Christians and Jews.

Membership is open to all Jewish women resident in the UK who are over 15 for a minimal annual subscription. There are groups throughout the UK which meet regularly. No special skills are required, all are welcome and expenses are paid where necessary.

Applications for membership should be made to the General Secretary at the above address and will be forwarded to the relevant Group Secretary.

REACH

89 Albert Embankment, London SE1 7TP; ☎020-7582 6543; e-mail mail@reach-online.org.uk; www.reach-online.org.uk

REACH finds part-time, expenses-only roles for people who now have time to give and who want to offer their managerial or professional career experience for the benefit of nearby voluntary organisations. This placement service is available throughout the UK to both volunteers and charitable organisations needing their expertise, free of charge. There are no age limits.

For further information contact Sue Evans, the Director, at the above address.

VICTIM SUPPORT

National Office, Cranmer House, 39 Brixton Road, London SW9 6DZ; ☎020-7735 9166; fax 020-7582 5712; www.victimsupport.org

Victim Support is the national charity for people affected by crime. It is an independent organisation, offering a free and confidential service, whether or not a crime has been reported. Trained staff and volunteers offer information and support to victims and witnesses at local branches, the criminal court-based Witness Services and the Victim Supportline (0845 30 30 900). The organisation also promotes victims' and witnesses' rights in all aspects of criminal justice and social policy by lobbying the government to introduce policies that take into account the needs and rights of victims and witnesses.

Scheme volunteers are community based and support people who have suffered crimes in their area. Witness Service volunteers are based in Crown or Magistrates' Courts. Supportline volunteers are London based. Applicants should be understanding, good listeners, get on well with people of all ages, cultures and backgrounds and be a minimum of age 18. Full training is given and out-of-pocket expenses are paid.

For further information contact the Information Officer, Lesley Malone, on 020-7896

3730 or info@victimssupport.org.uk.

WOMEN'S ROYAL VOLUNTARY SERVICE (WRVS)
Milton Hill House, Milton Hill, Steventon, Abingdon, Oxon. OX13 6AD; ☎01235-442951; fax 01235-861166; e-mail enquiries@wrvs.org.uk; www. wrvs.org.uk

The Women's Royal Voluntary Service (WRVS) is one of Britain's largest active volunteering organisations. Throughout England, Scotland, and Wales, 100,000 volunteers, (13% of them men) men focus on the needs of elderly and in particular helping them practically to maintain their independence and stay in their own homes.

In local communities WRVS provides Meals on Wheels, Books on Wheels, social transport and clubs for the elderly, and Good Neighbours schemes.

WRVS supports the emergency services by setting up rest centres and providing refreshments for the rescuers during disasters such as fire, flood, and bomb scares. In hospitals WRVS runs shops and cafés and provides guiding and information services. In 2001 their services allowed WRVS to give back £4.5 million to hospitals.

WRVS welcomes everybody aged over 14 and needs people with a range of skills and experience. Training is given to all volunteers and people from all sections of the community are encouraged to get involved.

To volunteer anywhere in Britain telephone 0845 601 4670.

Advice and Counselling

Below are listed several organisations that need help from volunteers to offer the general public advice and support with their problems. To offer direct help the volunteer needs more than a sympathetic ear and a liking for the sound of their own voice; they need to be mature enough to cope with serious problems, intelligent enough to offer appropriate advice, and discreet enough to respect their clients' confidence. Of course, no organisation will place a volunteer in a position of responsibility without giving them due preparation: for example RELATE gives its advisors full training, and in exchange expects them to give a regular commitment of their time for at least five years.

Those who are not willing to become so deeply involved can still be of use by helping with the administration and office work involved with running such large national organisations. Obviously those who know how to type or have experience of office procedure can be of the greatest use here, but there may still be scope for those whose main qualification is enthusiasm.

BLACKLINERS
Unit 46, Eurolink Business Centre, London SW2 1BZ; ☎020-7738 5274 (helpline); 020-7738 7468 (administration); fax 020-7738 7945; e-mail bliners@aol.com; www.blackliners.org

Blackliners is a black-led voluntary organisation providing services to people of African, Asian and Caribbean extraction living with or affected by HIV/AIDS, and providing information to these communities on HIV/AIDS and sexual health. Among the services they offer are a telephone helpline, counselling, a domiciliary/home care service, housing and advocacy service, volunteer service, a health advisory and secondary prevention service targeted at African communities, a health advisory and primary prevention service targeted at young black people, a drop-in service at Hammersmith, training/workshops, and *Newsline*, a quarterly newsletter.

An open day is run on every first Monday of each month. Those interested should contact the Volunteer Coordinator at the above address.

CARA
95 Sirdar Road, London W11 4EQ; ☎020-7792 8299; fax 020 7792 8004; e-mail mail@caratrust.freeserve.co.uk
By building community among those affected by HIV/AIDS, CARA provides practical, emotional and spiritual support to people from any faith tradition or none. Volunteers are involved in providing, befriending and practical help. Volunteers also staff our drop-in centre and help with office administration. Meals provided twice a week are cooked by volunteers. Those with experience of helping or caring and an interest in spirituality can also train as one of CARA's Pastoral Visitors. Essential characteristics are flexibility and a willingness to be enriched by CARA's diverse community.

CITIZENS ADVICE BUREAUX
National Association of Citizens Advice Bureau, Myddelton House, 115/123 Pentonville Road, London N1 9LZ; www.citizensadvice.org.uk
The CAB Service is independent and provides free, confidential and impartial advice to everybody, regardless of race, sex, disability, sexuality or nationality. It is the largest advice-giving network in the UK, with over 2,000 outlets and 22,000 volunteers. They help people deal with nearly six million problems every year, in bureaux, by phone and e-mail, at each outreach sessions in places like GP surgeries and courts, even in people's homes.

C A Bureaux also make a record of every enquiry brought to them. They use this evidence to highlight the effects that policies and practices have on people, and to suggest where improvements can be made to the policies and services of national and local government and businesses. The CAB aim to stop problems at their source, using the direct experience of the communities that CAB serves.

As regards volunteering, CAB utilises all kinds of people. No specific qualifications are needed before you start. Training and support are available every step of the way. There are many ways to get involved: train to be an advisor, or help keep the bureau running as an administrator, be a trustee board member, social policy coordinator, use your language skills, receptionist, fundraising and public relations.

For further details contact your local CAB direct or visit www.citizensadvice.org.uk

CRUSE BEREAVEMENT CARE
Cruse House, 126 Sheen Road, Richmond, Surrey TW9 1UR; ☎020-8939 9530; fax 020-8940 7638; helpline 0870 1671677; e-mail info@crusebereav ementcare.org.uk; www.crusebereavementcare.org.uk
Cruse Bereavement Care is the largest bereavement charity in the UK with over 150 local branches. It offers help to people bereaved by death, in any way, whatever their age, nationality, or belief. Cruse's help includes a free counselling service for bereaved people, opportunities for contact with others through bereavement support groups and advice or information on practical matters. It is personal and confidential help, backed by a wide range of publications. There is also a quarterly magazine for bereaved people (subscription £10 per annum) and a journal, *Bereavement Care*, for those working with the dying and the bereaved (subscription £17 per year).

Cruse also arranges training courses for those who work either in a professional or lay capacity with the bereaved.

For a Cruse Mail Order Catalogue or leaflets on Cruse services please contact by above details.

DEPRESSION ALLIANCE
35 Westminster Bridge Road, London SE1 7JB; ☎020-7633 0557; fax 020-7633 0559; e-mail information@depressionalliance.org; www.despressionalliance.org
Depression Alliance employs volunteers to help fund its offices in London, Cardiff and Edinburgh. Volunteers are required all year round and priority is given to those who have experienced depression. Applicants must be fluent in English. Travel and additional out-of-pocket expenses are paid.

Applications to the Volunteer Support Officer at the above address.

FAMILY PLANNING ASSOCIATION
2-12 Pentonville Road, London N1 9FP; ☎020-7837 5432; fax 020-7837 3042; www.fpa.org.uk
FPA is a charity whose role is to promote sexual health and family planning through information, research, education and training and publicity. Expenses and training are provided.

The FPA welcomes volunteers who would like to work in any of the four centres in the UK, which are in London, Glasgow, Cardiff and Belfast.

Further details from the above address.

THE FOUNDATION FOR THE STUDY OF INFANT DEATHS (FSID)
Artillery House, 11-19 Artillery Row, London, SW1 PIRT; ☎020-7222 8001; e-mail rhea.varma@sids.org.uk; www.sids.org.uk/fsid/
The Foundation funds research into why cot death occurs and helps the families devastated by the tragedy. It also informs and educates health professionals and the public about cot death and gives advice to parents on how they can reduce the risk.

About 10-15 volunteers are needed annually to work in the London office of the Foundation, working in the information and media, appeals and general administration departments. Duties would include creating spreadsheets, data entry, filing, photocopying, stuffing envelopes, and working with various departments on a project to working with various departments on a project to project basis. Help is needed all year round for flexible lengths of time. For those working at least 2 hours a day, up to £4 will be paid towards travel expenses; if over 5 hours work a day is being carried out, a further £3 towards lunch will be paid. Applicants should be resident in the UK.

Applications to the Volunteer Co-ordinator at the above address.

FWA (THE FAMILY WELFARE ASSOCIATION)
501-505 Kingsland Road, Dalston, London E8 4AU; ☎020-7254 6251; e-mail fwa.headofficefwa.org.uk; www.fwas.org.uk
FWA is a national charity that offers emotional and practical support to families and individuals living in poverty. Volunteers are needed both to offer assistance to social workers in local projects and also to take part in fundraising activities. Volunteers are also needed to staff the FWA telephone information and helpline. Expenses are paid.

Further information from the above address.

LONDON LESBIAN AND GAY SWITCHBOARD
PO Box 7324 London N1 9QS; ☎020-7837 7324; e-mail admin@llgs.org.uk; www.llgs.org.uk
London Lesbian and Gay Switchboard provides a 24-hour telephone information, advice and support service for gay men and women. As well as having detailed information on clubs, pubs, discos, befriending and counselling organisations in London and UK (including information on specialist groups such as disabled and married gays); they also operate an accommodation service for those gay people seeking somewhere to live as well as those wishing to let, within the Greater London Area. They have a need for many volunteers to answer the telephone lines, produce publicity, carry out fund raising, administration and training.

Volunteers are of either sex and are welcomed on the basis of being lesbian or gay and willing to undertake a short, supervised training aimed at expanding their knowledge of the London gay scene, AIDS and the law. Travelling expenses are reimbursed for unemployed volunteers.

Application packs can be requested by telephoning the Volunteer Recruitment Hotline on 020-7837 7606.

MARRIAGE & RELATIONSHIP COUNSELLING SERVICES
24 Gratfton Street, Dublin 2, Ireland; ☎ +351-1 8720341; fax +353 1 6716730; e-mail mrcs@eircom.net
Marriage and Relationship Counselling Services, a non-denominational organisation in existence since 1962, offers relationship counselling, separation and divorce counselling, psychosexual therapy, mediation, and Teen Between – a service for adolescents experiencing the break-up of their parents' relationship.

The Irish Institute of Couple Counselling (MRCS' training and education department) provides courses in relationship skills, pre-marriage preparation and basic counselling skills.

Many of the professionals within the organisation provide their services voluntarily which means no clients are refused counselling through inability to pay.

For futher details contact the Chief Executive, Elizabeth Everett, at the above address.

RELATE
Little Church Street, Rugby, Warwickshire CV21 3AP; ☎01788-573241; e-mail enquiries@relate.org.uk; www.relate.org.uk
Men and women who would like to volunteer as relationship counsellors are required to undertake a selection and training programme and commit at least seven hours a week of their time, for forty weeks a year. RELATE looks for an informal commitment from their volunteers for five years. Volunteers are normally over the age of 25. Out-of-pocket expenses are paid, some RELATE centres pay counsellors who work substantially more than the basic voluntary commitment.

Local RELATE centres are always happy to hear from interested people and are listed under 'RELATE' or 'Marriage Guidance'.

Arts and Music

BIRMINGHAM FILM AND TV FESTIVAL
9 Margaret Street, Birmingham B3 3BS; ☎0121-212 0777; fax 0121-212 0666; e-mail info@film-tv-festival.org.uk; www.film-tv-festival.org.uk.

The Birmingham Film and TV Festival is one of the UK's leading moving image festivals. It screens the best of international cinema and has developed specialisms in South Asian cinema and locally-produced work. The festival needs three to four volunteers as festival assistants, technical assistant, press and marketing assistant and runner. All positions are unpaid, although reasonable travel expenses will be met. To work initially 3-5 days per week, then 6-7 days per week during the festival build-up, and the festival itself. No accommodation.

Volunteers should be studying or have studied a media oriented degree, or have some experience in film and TV. The posts involve long hours, so applicants should be enthusiastic and not afraid of working hard. However, the work is very rewarding, provides the opportunity to work and learn at the same time and gain good contacts for the future. Suggested minimum period of work is two months between July and September (but long-term volunteers are welcome). An interview is necessary.

Apply from Feb/March to Ms Yen Yau, Deputy Director.

BROADSTAIRS FOLK WEEK
Pierremont Hall, Broadstairs, Kent CT10 1JH; ☎01843-604080; fax 01843-866048; e-mail info@folkweek.demon.co.uk; www.broadstairsfolkweek.com

The Broadstairs Folk Week Trust, a registered charity, organises events throughout the year and an annual festival. 2005 will be the festival's 40th year. The whole town and its promenade, jetty, bandstand, taverns, halls, churches and streets becomes the venue for international music, song and dance.

About 120 volunteers are needed as door stewards, shop staff, PA and sound technicians, drivers, campsite stewards and collectors. Volunteers are also needed to handle publicity and liaise with international personnel. Posts are unpaid but staff receive a season ticket for access to all events. Free camping is available. Volunteers work four hours a day. Minimum period of work is three days between 8th and 15th August. Overseas applicants with good English are considered. Applications from March to Jane de Rose.

GLOBE EDUCATION
Shakespeare's Globe, International Shakespeare's Globe Centre, New Globe Walk, London SE1 9DT; ☎020-7902-1400; fax 020-7902 1401; e-mail alex@shakespearesglobe.com; www.shakespeares-globe.org

The Globe Theatre and International Centre need 30 volunteer administration staff for work placements. Hours by arrangement. Duties include stewarding, front of house, special projects, lecture programme workshops etc. usual theatre hours. Volunteer staff are required all year and the minimum period is 3 months. Apply at any time to Alexandra Massey, Courses Administrator.

PROUD GALLERIES
5 Buckingham Street, London WC2N 6BP; ☎020-7839 4942; fax 020-7839 4947; e-mail kate@proud.co.uk; www.proud.co.uk

Proud Galleries Group was launched in 1998 by Alex Proud to bring affordable, high quality photography to a mainstream market. Based upon a formula of exhibiting accessible shows around popular themes such as music, fashion, film and sport, Proud Galleries instantly took the photography world by storm. A series of landmark shows including *Destroy: The Sex Pistols, Rankin's Nudes, The Rock 'n' Roll Years, Underexposed and Rebel Life: Bob Marley,* attracted blanket media coverage and full-house, star-studded opening nights. With up to 10,000 paying customers per show, the galleries soon became one the most popular, private, photographic galleries in Europe. The Group of galleries includes Proud Camden Moss and Proud Brighton.

Voluntary work experience at Proud is offered all year round. A minimum of 4 weeks is expected and applicants should be over 18 with fluent English. Qualifications preferred but not essential. Duties include: helping with the running of the gallery, organising/planning launch nights, hanging and wrapping of prints, customer service, research for future exhibitions, maintaining press books etc. Possibility of more responsability if staying longer. Ideal for anyone interested in learning more about the industry.

Children and Youth

Voluntary work with young people can mean far more than working with those who are from disadvantaged backgrounds or suffer from some physical disability. For example, the hundreds of thousands of members of the Guide Association depend upon the assistance of thousands of adult volunteers to keep the movement going, not only to act as leaders but also to provide transport, deal with paperwork and so on.

Indeed, many of the opportunities in this section are to do with helping young people to make constructive use of their time, which can also be of great assistance to hard-pressed mothers, who have their offspring taken off their hands for a while. Not listed here, however, are the untold number of children's play schemes operated by local authorities during the school holidays which keep children aged up to thirteen occupied during the week while their parents are at work. These play schemes are normally staffed by paid workers but additional assistance from volunteers will normally be greatly appreciated, whether it is offered on a regular or irregular basis. People with artistic, musical or sporting abilities will normally be especially appreciated. For further information contact the Recreation Department of your local authority, which will be co-ordinating play schemes in the area.

The subject of child abuse has been made much of in recent years and continues to be the subject of media focus and attention. Any prospective volunteer applying for a job which involves direct contact with children should be prepared to undergo a thorough vetting by the prospective employer before being accepted. For example the Social Services departments around the UK will have candidates' names run through the police computer to check for a criminal record. If the volunteers are from abroad they will be asked to provide a Certificate of Good Conduct. Generally speaking, students and others working for short periods during their holidays or for work experience will not be subject to such checks.

Other voluntary opportunities connected with child care and youth work will be found under *The Sick and Disabled, Hospitals,* and *Education.*

ARMY CADET FORCE ASSOCIATION
E Block, Duke of York's Headquarters, London SW3 4RR; ☎020-7730 9733; fax 020-7730 8264; e-mail e-mail@armycadets.com; www.armycadets.com
The ACF is a national Voluntary Youth Organisation committed to developing confidence, self-discipline, self-respect and health in 13-18 year olds so that they can gain employment and take their place in society as responsible, contributing young citizens. It achieves this through a challenging structured programme of military, adventurous, sporting and citizenship training. Adult volunteers are needed to conduct this training. They should be in good health, aged between 18 and 55 and British citizens. Training is given to them at the Cadet Training Centre in Surrey.

Those interested should contact the General Secretary at the above address.

BARNARDO'S
Tanners Lane, Barkingside, Ilford, Essex 1G6 1QG; ☎020-8550 8822; fax 020-8550 8848; www.barnados.org.uk.
Barnardo's, the UK's biggest children's charity, works with 90,000 children, young people and families a year. It no longer runs orphanages. Over 300 projects provide a range of services from under fives day care, to work with young people with severe physical and learning disabilities. Volunteers are needed for our child care work, fund raising activities and retail shops.

Please note that Barnado's is unable to provide accommodation or financial support for volunteers from overseas, unless they are sponsored by an international agency. You can find out more about volunteering and Barnado's by visiting our website, or you can contact the Regional Corporate Volunteer Development Managers:

London, East Anglia, South East: Tanner's Lane, Barkingside, Ilford, Essex IG6 1QG; ☎020-8498 7077; fax 020-8551 8267; e-mail celya.maxted@barnados.org.uk.

Midlands (East): The Sherwood Project, 2 Clinton Avenue, Sherwood Rise, Nottingham NG5 1AW; ☎0115-969 1177; fax 0115-985 8616; e-mail eileen.burwood@barnados. org.uk.

Midlands (West): Brooklands, Great Cornbow, Halesowen, West Midlands B63 3AB; ☎0121-550 5271/6; fax 0121-550 2594; e-mail michael.baker@barnados.org.uk.

North East: Orchard House, Fenwick Terrace, Jesmond, Newcastle upon Tyne NE2 2JQ; ☎0191-240 4800; fax 0191-280 4801; e-mail lana.kirkup@barnados.org.uk.

North West: 7 Lineside Close, Liverpool L25 2UD; ☎0151-488 1100; fax 0151-488 1101; e-mail rachel.hodges@barnados.org.uk.

Northern Ireland: 542-544 Upper Newtownards Road, Belfast BT4 3HE; ☎028-9067 2366; fax 028-9067 2399; e-mail: Hrrecruit.NI@barnados.org.uk.

Scotland: 235 Corstorphine Road, Edinburgh EH12 7AR; ☎0131-334 9893; fax 0131-316 4008; e-mail volunteer.scotland@barnados.org.uk.

South West: Unit 19, Easton Business Centre, Felix Road, Easton, Bristol BS5 OHE; ☎0117 941 5841; fax 0117 941 5341; e-mail Pauline.twomey@barnados.org.uk

Wales: 11-15 Columbus Walk, Brigantine Place, Atlantic Wharf, Cardiff CF1 5BZ; ☎029-2049 3387; fax 029-2048 9802; e-mailmatthew.hunt@barnados.org.uk.

Yorkshire: Four Gables, Clarence Road, Horsforth, Leeds LS18 4LB; ☎0113-393 3223; fax 0113-258 0098; e-mail jo.hunt@barnados.org.uk.

BRISTOL ASSOCIATION FOR NEIGHBOURHOOD DAYCARE LTD (BAND)
81 St Nicholas Road, St Pauls, Bristol BS2 9JJ; ☎0117-954 2128; fax 0117 954 1694; admin@BANDLtd.org.uk; www.BANDLtd.org.uk
BAND was formed in January 1978 with three member groups. These groups arose in response to the Finer Joint Action Committee Report (1976) which recognised that one

of the most fundamental needs of a working single parent was a facility for school age children during holidays, and after school. Such a facility would enable parents to work full time and the family unit to become stable and financially independent. BAND currently has 180 member groups. Volunteers are needed to help the above groups carry out their aim.

For further information contact the above address.

CHALCS
Unit 5, Technorth, 9 Harrogate Road, Leeds LS7 3NB; ☎0113-262 3892; fax 0113-2959596.
CHALCS runs a Thursday evening literacy/numeracy scheme (term time) located in Leeds for underachieving children aged 6-11. Children are taught by volunteer tutors, supported by a qualified teacher. There is a pool of 20 volunteers, but CHALCS always needs more as there are always children waiting for our help.

Applications to Sim Sobers at the above address.

CHILDREN NORTH EAST
89 Denhill Park, Newcastle upon Tyne NE15 6QE1; tel 0191-256 2444; fax 0191-256 2446; e-mail enquiries@children-ne.org
The organisation was founded in 1891 and its main concern is to support children, families, and young people in difficulty or need in Northumberland, Tyne and Wear and Durham. It runs eight Family Link Schemes with more than 200 trained volunteer parents who befriend families in their own homes, a Family Centre, a safe babysitting service, a youth enquiry service, a community-based childcare project, a development project looking at the role of fathers and a playbus/toy library which visits isolated villages in the Tynedale area of Northumberland.

Any volunteers interested in helping with these activities should apply to the Director at the above address.

THE CHILDREN'S SOCIETY
Edward Rudolf House, Margery Street, London WC1X OJL; ☎0845 300 1128; www.childrensociety.org.uk
The Children's Society is a voluntary organisation of the Church of England and has been campaigning for children's rights since 1881. Today, the Children's Society has grown into one of Britain's most innovative charities with over 100 projects.

The Children's Society is supported by parishes throughout the country whose care and financial help make a genuine difference to the lives of the country's most vulnerable children. The Children's Society's work includes: reaching out to child runaways afraid and in danger on the streets; helping children and families living in some of Britain's most deprived areas, make a better life for themselves by taking an active part in regenerating their communities; supporting children experiencing problems at school to help them avoid the downward spiral into truancy or exclusion; working with 15 and 16-year-olds on remand to get them out of prison and help them face up to the consequences of their behaviour and turn away from a life of crime.

To find out how to get involved with the Children's Society fundraising or projects, contact the above address.

CONTACT A FAMILY
209-211 City Road, London EC1V 1JN; ☎020-7608 8700; fax 020-7608 8701; e-mail info@cafamily.org.uk; www.cafamily.org.uk
Contact a Family is a national charity for any parent or professional involved with

or caring for a child with special needs. It brings families with a special needs child together through local mutual support and self-help groups. It advises parents who wish to start a group in their neighbourhood for parents of children with disabilities and offers nationwide support to families where the child has a rare syndrome or disability. They do not offer financial support. Contact a Family's team of parent advisors are an excellent first point of contact for information or contacts.

For more information and volunteering contact the above address.

DEAF EDUCATION THROUGH LISTENING AND TALKING (DELTA)
PO Box 20, Haverhill, Suffolk CB9 7BD; tel/fax 01440-783689; e-mail ann. brighton@deafeducation.org.uk; www.deafeducation.org.uk
Delta is a nationwide support group of teachers and parents of deaf children. DELTA provides support, information and advice to guide parents in helping their children develop normal speech and to live independently within a hearing society. Volunteers are always needed. There are regional branches, which hold regular meetings and conferences. DELTA also runs courses for parents and families including summer schools for parents with hearing-impaired children. While the children enjoy themselves, their parents attend lectures, workshops and discussion groups. Volunteers can assist with childcare and some out of pocket expenses will be reimbursed.

For further information contact Wendy Barnes at the above address.

DUKE OF EDINBURGH'S AWARD
Gulliver House, Madeira Walk, Windsor, Berkshire SL4 1EU; ☎01753-727400; e-mail info@theaward.org; www.theaward.org
The Award is a programme of adventurous, cultural and practical activities undertaken voluntarily by young people; it is now operating in over 50 countries. All participants are required to complete a Service Section which is intended to encourage them to realise that as members of a community they have a responsibility to others and that their help is needed. This Service Section involves practical work in one of the following fields (after some initial training): first aid; coastguard service or mountain rescue; work with the WRVS; or care of the mentally handicapped. For the Gold Award this participant must give practical service over a minimum period of 12 months, as well as reaching the required standard in the course of instruction and the service to which it is related. The scheme relies on an estimated 50,000 adults in the UK, who assist as leaders, organisers, instructors, fund raisers and committee members.

The Award programme is open to all young people between the ages of 14 and 25. Adults who help as instructors and assessors must be suitably experienced or qualified persons nominated by the appropriate bodies.

Applications should be made to the Operations Officer at the above address, who will pass them on to the appropriate Volunteer and Training Manager.

ENDEAVOUR TRAINING
Sheepbridge Centre, Sheepbridge Lane, Chesterfield S41 9RX; ☎01246-454957; fax 01246-261865; e-mail info@endeavour.org.uk; www.endeavour. org.uk
Endeavour is a National Development Training Organisation and Educational Charity which aims to provide a range of opportunities for young people (normally 14 to 26 years old) to fulfil their full potential.

Endeavour consists of two different, yet complementary parts, The Endeavour Training Service and Endeavour's Voluntary and Community Service, the latter involves volunteer staff who support the full time Endeavour Workers on Youth Projects such as

'Up2Us' in the organisation and the delivery of development training activities.

The Voluntary and Community Services Long Term Work: runs training programmes for volunteers on a national basis; supports local groups which meet to have fun, receive and give training, and provide a service to the community; organises expeditions and work projects at home and abroad, offering service and adventure, through The Endeavour John Hunt Exploration Group (JHEG); takes part in and organises National events, conferences, and expeditions.

Endeavour's Youth Projects (such as Project Endeavour) provide opportunities for young people, through innovative   youth projects based in clearly defined geographical boundaries throughout the country. The project work meets the personal and social needs of young people (14 to 19 year olds) who are disadvantaged or 'at risk'.

Endeavour's youth projects of long term personal/social skills development, are wholly dependent on the continued suppport of trusted and trained volunteers. The role of the volunteers enables the full time workers of Endeavour to cascade the effectiveness of the work to a much wider population. This is done through a peer education element within the programme.

Endeavour has always striven to recognise and credit the work undertaken by its volunteers. In the past this has been done by the use of in-house certification as well as the use of accredited certification from national bodies.

Expenses may be paid to volunteers supporting the voluntary programme of activities and projects.

Applicants should contact Endeavours Voluntary and Community Services Team, at the above address.

FRIENDS FOR YOUNG DEAF PEOPLE (FYD)
120a Abbey Street, Nuneaton, Warwickshire CV11 5BX; ☎02476-641017; fax 02476-641517; e-mail fyd.egho@charity.vfree.com
FYD aims to promote an active partnership between deaf and hearing people which will enable young deaf people to develop themselves and become active members of society.

Volunteers are needed all year round to work on projects and there is also a training programme. Reasonable travel expenses or agreed expenses will be paid.

For further details, please contact the above address.

GINGERBREAD: The Association for One Parent Families
First Floor, 7 Sovereign Close, Sovereign Court, London E1W 3HW; e-mail office@gingerbread.org.uk; www.gingerbread.org.uk
Gingerbread was founded in 1970 by a woman who was experiencing difficulties in keeping a home together for her sons and herself. The authorities told her that the boys should be taken into care whilst she found a home, which would not only have been far more expensive for the state, but would also have broken up the family. The organisation grew as a result of the initial publicity, and there are now more than 260 self-help groups operating throughout England and Wales, with a separate organisation covering Scotland.

Although the organisation runs largely on a self-help basis, volunteers are also needed, especially to assist with childcare. This ranges from baby sitting for individuals to running full and part-time holiday play schemes and after school care for 5-11 year olds. Help may also be needed by lone parents who are ill and therefore unable to take their children to school, go shopping, or perform household jobs.

Those interested should contact the national office at the above address, who will put them in touch with their local branch.

GREAT ORMOND STREET HOSPITAL CHILDREN'S CHARITY (GOSHCC)
40-41 Queen Square, London WC1N 3AJ; ☎020-7916 5678; fax 020-7831 1938; www.gosh.org
GOSHCC Trust needs volunteer helpers who are aged a minimum of 18 years and are able to offer a commitment of one day per week for at least six months.

For further details, please contact the Voluntary Services Co-ordinator at the above address.

GIRL GUIDING UK
17-19 Buckingham Palace Road, London SW1W 0PT; ☎020-7834 6242; fax 020-7828 8317; e-mail joinus@girlguiding.org.uk; www.girlguiding.org.uk
Girl Guiding UK is part of a worldwide movement with over ten million members that enables girls and young women to fulfil their potential and take an active and responsible role in society. It works through a distinctive, stimulating and enjoyable programme delivered by trained volunteer leaders.

Girl Guiding UK welcomes volunteers aged 18+ to help Leaders, whether at Unit meetings, on camping trips, in the County office or at events. Young or old, male or female are all welcome to join us in creating a stimulating and safe environment in which Rainbows (girls aged 5-7), Brownies (girls aged 7-10, Guides (girlls aged 10-14) and Senior Section (girls and young women aged 14-25) can learn and play. Volunteering with a group of girls may require the commitment of two hours a week during term-time and a week in July and August. Those who are able to volunteer with a Unit for more than 6 months may wish to become a Unit leader and help to bring guiding to the many girls who are waiting to join throughout the UK. You would then be required to take part in Girlguiding UK's Leadership Qualification. If you are looking for full-time volunteering experience, you could consider volunteering at one of the Training and Activity Centres around the UK as a House Assistant or Trainer.

For further information about Guiding in your area contact Guiding Support Services at the above address.

LEARNING WITHOUT WALLS
St Martin's Youth & Community Centre, Gooch Street, Highgate, Birmingham B5 7HE; ☎0121-622 5066; fax 0121-666 6111; e-mail withoutwalls@hotmail.com
Without Walls offers support, information and guidance to young people (16-25 years) who are homeless, in isolated housing and/or housing crisis in the Birmingham area. The Centre has showers, laundry facilities, and somewhere to prepare and eat food. About 30 volunteers are needed at any one time to work on a group/individual basis supporting young people. Duties include aiding with: fundraising, one-to-one work and support/guidance, group work, DIY, sport and leisure activities, budgeting, administration, outreach work, developing possibilities for other volunteers. Volunteers can stay as long as they wish. Travel to and from the centre and any other expenses incurred through volunteering are paid.

Applications all year round to the Project Manager at the above address.

LONDON CITY YMCA
8 Errol Street, London EC1Y 8SE; ☎020-7614 5000; fax 020-7628 4080; e-mail andy@;lcity.co.uk; www.londoncityY.org
The London YMCA offers opportunities for volunteers to assist with work with homeless young people (in the hostel) and with young people on local estates (detached youth work), also with mentoring young people and with general reception/administrative duties.

About 12 volunteers a year are recruited to work for a minimum period of one year (six months for reception/administration roles). Applicants should be at least 18. Previous experience of working with disadvantaged young people, IT skills, a driving licence, and language skills are all very useful and the ability to speak English is essential. Travel expenses (within reason) and two meals a day are provided. Under exceptional circumstances (e.g. full time, experienced volunteer) accommodation may be available.

Applications all year round to the Chief Executive at the above address.

NATIONAL ASSOCIATION OF CHILD CONTACT CENTRES (NACCC)
Minerva House, Spaniel Row, Nottingham NG1 6EP; ☎0845 4500 280; fax 0845-4500 420; e-mail contact@naccc.org.uk; www.naccc.org.uk
NACCC promotes safe child contact within a national framework of child contact centres. The centres are neutral meeting places where children of separated families can enjoy contact with one (or both) parents, and sometimes other family members, in a comfortable and safe environment when there is no viable alternative. The Contact Centres aim to provide short-term help and support towards establishing meaningful contact between child and visiting parent. Centres are staffed by volunteers whose role it is to make contact an enjoyable experience for both child and parent. Full training and ongoing support is given to the volunteer.

There are over 300 member Centres throughout England, Northern Ireland and Wales. Some Centres offer supported contact whilst others can also provide supervised or assessed contact. In addition they can act as a handover point.

For further information contact the National Administrator at the above address.

NATIONAL ASSOCIATION OF TOY & LEISURE LIBRARIES (PLAY MATTERS)
68 Churchway, London NW1 1LT; ☎020-7387 9592; fax 020-7383 2714; e-mail admin@playmatters.co.uk; www.natll.org.uk
The National Association of Toy & Leisure Libraries is the parent body for over 1,000 toy libraries in the United Kingdom; it is a registered charity. The first toy libraries were set up by parents to loan toys to children with physical and/or mental handicaps. Now a growing number of toy libraries (over 50%) are open to all children in the community. Many toy libraries are run wholly by volunteers; those which have a paid organiser are also dependent on voluntary help. There are toy libraries in many venues, such as schools – nursery, infants' and junior - attached to public libraries and some loan to groups such as childminders and play groups. Increasingly, toy libraries are seen as an essential part of the Government's national childcare strategy. They offer a befriending, supportive service to parents and carers. Leisure libraries also offer a similar service to people who are mentally and/or physically handicapped and to their carers.

Each toy/leisure library is autonomous and the need for voluntary help can vary from one to another. Anyone wishing to offer their services should contact NATLL who will put them in touch with the nearest toy/leisure library. If there is not a toy/leisure library in your area, help and advice is available to anyone wanting to start one. Please contact the above address. A SAE would be appreciated.

THE NATIONAL AUTISTIC SOCIETY
Head Office: 393 City Road, London EC1V 1NG; ☎020-7833 2299. Volunteering Network: Castle Heights, 72 Maid Marian Way, Nottingham, NG1 6BJ; ☎0115-911 3369; e-mail volunteers@nas.org.uk
The NAS runs befriending schemes, which match trained volunteers with children, teenagers, adults or families affected by autism. This requires a long-term commitment, normally of one year. Locations of schemes are listed on the NAS website. Between

them, the people involved decide how often the befriender will visit and what kind of things they will do together, but as a guideline visits are normally weekly for 2 or 3 hours. Befrienders could take a child out to a park, go shopping along with the family to provide an extra pair of hands or visit a cinema or gallery with an adult. Contact the Volunteering Network for more information.

NATIONAL PLAYBUS ASSOCIATION/MOBILE PROJECTS ASSOCIATION
Brunswick Court, Brunswick Square, Bristol BS2 8PE; ☎0117-9166581; fax 0117-9166588; e-mail playbus@playbus.org.uk; www.playbus.org.uk
The Association exists to promote the use of playbuses and adapted vehicles as mobile community resources, and to act as a national umbrella organisation to promote good practice in mobile community work. Mobile play and educational schemes visit isolated areas, both rural and urban. These include playgroups for the under fives, holiday playschemes and afterschool work, youth club work, exhibition and welfare rights work, education and health projects and work with the elderly. The Association provides information, publications and support services to the 250 projects operating in the United Kingdom.

Anyone interested in helping with one in their area or seeking advice on how to organise one should contact the headquarters at the above address.

OFF THE RECORD
27 Murray Place, Stirling, FK8 1DQ; ☎01786-450518; e-mail off-the-record@aberlour.org.uk
Off the Record provides information, advice and counselling for the under 25s and is open four afternoons a week. New Volunteers are always needed for the centre and for a variety of groups run by Off the Record. Please telephone for further details.

RATHBONE TRAINING
Head Office, 4th Floor, Churchgate House, 56 Oxford Street, Manchester M1 6EU; helpline 0800-917 6790; e-mail advice@rathbonetraining.co.uk
Founded at the beginning of the century by Elfrida Rathbone, to benefit educationally deprived people, Rathbone is now a national charity with centres throughout Britain. Their aim is to improve opportunities for people who have limited access to services; many of whom have learning difficulties and other special needs. The range of services provided include: training and employment, residential and independent living centres; work with families and children, vocational education projects and a special education helpline. In addition, Rathbone produces a range of publications and reports, commissions research and where possible seeks to influence the policies of central and local government insofar as these affect people who have been denied the opportunity to realise their full potential.

Volunteers are seen as having a unique contribution to make and are needed all year round, to give one-to-one support in social and communication skills and literacy and numeracy. Only a few hours a week are needed, but a regular commitment is important.

Volunteers are also needed to answer the national special education helpline which gives advice to parents of children with learning difficulties. Telephone workers and research and administration workers needed. Full training is provided and can give good office experience.

Contact the Robert Marshall, on the above number to discuss any volunteering opportunity.

SAILORS' FAMILIES SOCIETY
Newland, Hull HU6 7RJ; ☎01482-342331; e-mail info@sailors-families.org.

uk; www.sailors-families.org.uk

The Society cares for the children of deceased, disabled, and distressed seafarers nationwide. The Family Support Scheme provides monthly grants, school clothing allowance, special needs grants and educational support for individual children. There is also a holiday scheme for the provision of a one-week caravan holiday each year.

The Society has a number of fundraising committees in various parts of the country staffed by volunteers. A fundraising pack is available to help volunteers raise funds for the Society. Those interested in helping should contact the Fundraising Manager at the above address.

SCOUT ASSOCIATION
Gilwell Park, Chingford, London E4 7QW; ☎020-8433 7100; fax 020-8433 7103; e-mail info.centre@scout.org.uk; www.scouts.org.uk

The Scout Association aims to prepare young people to take a constructive place in society by providing interesting and enjoyable activities under voluntary adult leadership. Scouting began in 1907 based upon Lord Baden-Powell's ideas and book, *Scouting for Boys*. The Movement quickly spread and the world Scout population is now 28 million in 216 countries and territories. In the UK there are some 550,000 members including Beaver Scouts (boys and girls aged six to eight years, Cub Scouts (boys and girls aged eight to ten and a half), Explorer Scouts young men and young women (14-18) and Scout Network young men and young women (18-25). All offer a progressive training scheme which encourages personal development as well as collective and individual achievement. There is an emphasis upon outdoor activities. Scouting in the UK is committed to offering its services to young people in minority communities and in remote and inner-city areas.

Long-term voluntary opportunities are available with Scout Groups throughout the country and there is the possibility of occasional paid jobs at activity centres during the summer. Similar opportunities are also available in some other countries, notably the USA and Switzerland, for suitably qualified and experienced adults.

Further information can be obtained from the above address.

ST BASIL'S
Heath Mill Lane, Deritend, Birmingham B9 4AX; ☎0121-772 2483; e-mail stbasil@stbasil.freeserve.co.uk; www.stbasils.org.uk

St Basil's works with young people to enable them to find and keep a home, to develop their confidence, skills and opportunities and to prevent homelessness. St. Basil's is the foremost agency in the West Midlands working with youth who are homeless or at risk of becoming homeless with projects across Birmingham along with resettlement and advice centres.

Volunteers are needed to assist staff with various duties, which will assist young people in their learning and development of independent life skills. Applications are welcome from volunteers for various tasks as all projects have different and changing requirements. An example of some duties: fundraising, administration, teaching, gardening, cooking and DIY tasks. For further enquiries or applications, please contact St. Basil's Human Resources Team at the above address.

TEAM-UP WITH THE PRINCE'S TRUST
18 Park Square East, London NW1 4LH; ☎020-7543 1234; fax 020-7543 1367; www.princes-trust.org.uk

The Prince's Trust is a personal development programme for 16-25 year olds are student's in a gap year or taking time out after graduating or reviewing your options, you can Team-up with The Princes Trust. The Trust has been running successfully throughout the UK since 1990.

Team is a 12-week training course which helps young people make the most of their talents and can help develop skills, confidence and motivation which are all needed to find and sustain a job. During the programme participants work in a team of up to 15 other 16-25-year-olds with different skills and backgrounds. You will:

○ Benefit from two weeks' work experience.
○ Achieve a nationally recognised qualification.
○ Enjoy a residential action-packed team building week.
○ Take part in challenging projects, which you choose.

Programmes take place in 300 different locations around the UK, which means there is no problem finding a team close to where you live.

For further information call free on 0800 842 842 or visit www.princes-trust.org.uk.

TOPS DAY NURSERIES
104 & 106 Herbert Avenue, Parkstone, Poole, Dorset BH12 4HU; tel/fax 01202-716130; ☎01202-382165 (out of hours); e-mail tops@ndirect.co.uk
TOPS Day Nurseries recruits about 10 volunteers each year all year round to help with childcare. They offer parents a high standard of childcare with flexible hours to suit their family needs. Volunteers must undergo police and social checks before they start work. No expenses are paid.

Applications to Cheryl Hadland at the above address.

UK YOUTH
2nd4 Floor, Kirby House, 20/24 Kirby Street, London EC1N 8TS; ☎020-7242 4045; fax 020-7242 4125; e-mail info@ukyouth.org; www.ukyouth.org
UK Youth provides a range of services to provide and support quality youth work throughout the UK. There are over 40,000 youth workers including part-time workers and volunteers, involved in over 6,000 affiliated groups. Volunteers are welcome, whether they bring a specific practical skill or simply enjoy working creatively with young people.

Prospective volunteers should contact their local youth club or Local Association – details of local associations are on the website www.ukyouth.org.

Community Projects

Community projects can take many forms and have many functions: they may exist to run a drop-in centre for local unemployed people or elderly people, to provide a local base for arts and crafts, or to run a toddlers playgroup. What they all have in common is that they are all run by the community for the community. Sometimes local authorities may provide some funds or premises to assist a community project, but most depend for their existence on the time and energy of volunteers.

Many community projects exist in towns and cities up and down the country but they need not be solely in urban areas: for example, residents of country villages isolated by reductions in bus services may now legally pool their resources and share car journeys, on an organised basis. The best community projects depend on an individual spotting some local need, then setting out to meet it.

BARKING & DAGENHAM BEFRIENDERS

102 North Street, Barking, Essex IG11 8LA; ☎020-8507 9660; fax 020-8507 8009; e-mail bardag.befrienders@virgin.net

Barking and Dagenham Befrienders recruits and trains volunteers in the Greater London area to befriend young people, aged 10-18 and those who are vulnerable, on a one-to-one basis. The young people are referred by the local authority – social services, education, youth service, and the criminal justice system – police, courts, youth justice team. A pool of 40 volunteers currently work for the organisation and more are always needed to keep the numbers up.

Volunteers commit 4 hours a week, which can involve taking the young person out, filling in paperwork and contacting them on the telephone. There is also a club which meets twice a week (one for the younger people, the other for the older ones) to aid interaction between befriender and befriended and to assist young people with social skills. Applicants minimum age 18 must be willing to make a one year commitment to the scheme. Out-of-pocket expenses, travel and mileage, and lunch is provided on days of work.

Applications to the Project at the above address.

COMMUNITY MATTERS

12-20 Baron Street, Islington, London N1 9LL; ☎020-7837 7887; fax 020-7278 9253; e-mail communitymatters@communitymatters.org.uk; www.communitymatters.org.uk

Community Matters exists to provide advice and information to local community organisations on running voluntary organisations, managing community centres, identifying and meeting community needs, working with statutory authorities and other voluntary organisations, etc. Help is needed from volunteers who are able to conduct research, do general clerical work or provide legal advice.

Some volunteers give regular help perhaps once a week, others just occasionally to help with specific jobs such as mailings. Expenses are covered where necessary.

Applications should be sent to the Adminstration Officer at the above address, who can also advise on the addresses of community organisations around the country.

FREE FORM ARTS TRUST

274 Richmond Road, Hackney, London E8 3QW; ☎020-7249 3394; fax 020-7249 8499; e-mail contact@freeform.org.uk; www.freeform.org.uk

Free Form is a registered charity which uniquely combines the skills of artists and architects on large scale projects which involve local communities; demonstrating the art of urban regeneration and improving the environment both socially and physically. Work may be either interior or exterior and examples include mosaic wall panels, landscaping, street furniture and planting. Free Form is organised as a practice, with artists and architects working together in teams, with the involvement of local communities throughout the design process. In addition, 15-20 trainees and a number of volunteers are annually offered skills training through the Trust's projects, enabling many of them to move on to further education or enter directly into full employment. Anyone who is interested in finding out more should write to the above address.

HACKNEY INDEPENDENT LIVING TEAM (HILT)

Richmond House, 1a Westgate Street, London E8 3RL; ☎020-8985 5511 (extension 222.227); fax 020-8533 2029; e-mail volunteers@hilt.org.uk; www.hilt.org.uk

HILT supports adults with a learning difficulty in Hackney to live in the community as independently as possible, and to continue to develop their independence and personal identity.

Four to twelve months placements are available for full-time volunteers to provide support on all projects and activities of HILT such as sports, leisure and social activities, arranging and participating in holidays with service users, accessing education and training opportunities, offering support in personal development. Applications are also encouraged from local part-time volunteers.

Applicants must: have a commitment to enabling people with learning difficulties to have as much control over their lives as possible and to providing a service which reflects the cultural, racial and religious needs of service users; be dedicated to the promotion of anti-discriminatory practice; have a willingness to understand the emotional needs of service users; and attend regular supervision to communicate issues, ideas and suggestions. Minimum age 18.

Full-time volunteers are provided with an allowance of £55 per week, free accommodation and London travel cards are provided. Part-time volunteers can claim expenses. Applications to the Volunteer Coordinator at the above address.

SNAC (SPECIAL NEEDS ACTION FOR CAREERS)
Unit 2, Beasleys Yard, 126 High Street, Uxbridge, Middx UB8 1JT; tel/fax 01895-258737; e-mail uxbridgesnac2004@yahoo.co.uk

SNAC recruits as many volunteers as it can (some work only 1 or 2 days a week) to assist special needs clients with severe learning difficulties. The work is located in the London Borough of Hillingdon (specifically Uxbridge) and involves assisting clients to learn basic skills, taking clients to and from work placements, helping with arts and crafts and making simple gifts, helping to arrange functions and attending training courses.

Volunteers can work for as much time as they can spare for as long as they want to do so. Their help is required all year round sometimes at short notice. Minimum age 19. Applicants should be in good health with a caring attitude. Previous experience would be an advantage and a driving licence very useful. Training is provided at no charge and travel costs for attending work placements with clients will be reimbursed. Those interested in helping should contact the Unit Co-ordinator at the above address.

Conservation, the Environment
& Heritage

Since the first edition of this book was published over 20 years ago, public interest in environmental matters has increased hugely. Concern for the environment was once regarded by many as the preserve of cranks: now it has become a selling point in car advertising and politics.

The organisations in this section share the goal of preserving the environment against the ravages of progress or preserving the past in museums. They have different objectives, and use voluntary help in many different ways: for example, the Henry Doubleday Research Association needs knowledgeable guides for its organic gardens in Coventry and Kent while the London Wildlife Trust needs voluntary assistance for hands-on conservation work and promotion of wildlife issues throughout the Greater London area.

Those who find that voluntary work for our environment whets their appetite for more can consult *Green Volunteers,* which is available from Vacation Work (www.vacationwork.co.uk) at £10.99.

ALEXANDER FLEMING LABORATORY MUSEUM

St.Mary's Hospital, Praed Street, London W2 1NY; ☎020-7886 6528; fax 020-7886 6739; e-mail Kevin.Brown@st-marys.nhs.uk; www.st-marys.org.uk/about/fleming–museum.htm

Volunteer Guides are needed all year round to conduct visitors around the Alexander Fleming, Laboratory Museum, which is based on a reconstruction of the laboratory in which Fleming discovered penicillin. The job includes making a short presentation and retail duties in a small museum shop. Full training will be supplied. Knowledge of subject matter is not required. Hours from 10am-1pm from Monday to Thursday. Minimum age is 16. The museum lacks disabled access.

Applications to Kevin Brown, Trust Archivist and Museum Curator.

THE BARN OWL TRUST

Waterleat, Ashburton, Devon TQ13 7HU; ☎01364-653026; fax 01364-654392 (phone first); e-mail info@barnowltrust.org.uk; www.barnowltrust.org.uk

The Barn Owl Trust operates mostly in southwest England and uses volunteers for a range of tasks. Opportunities for office-based voluntary work include word processing, filing, data entry and telephoning. Outdoor volunteers construct and erect nesting boxes and carry out survey work.

The Trust has recently purchased 25 acres of land in order to create good Barn Owl habitat. Volunteers can help with survey work, research and practical tasks.

Volunteers can be taken on for various periods and at any time of year. Some contribution towards expenses can be arranged.

The Trust publishes a range of free leaflets, runs a free information and advice service and produces educational materials. For further information, contact David Ramsden at the above address.

BBOWT

The Berkshire, Buckinghamshire and Oxfordshire Wildlife Trust The Lodge, 1 Armstrong Road, Littlemore, Oxford OX4 4XT; ☎01865-775476; e-mail gemmaswann@bbowt.cix.co.uk; www.bbowt.org.uk

BBOWT is one of 47 county-based Wildlife Trusts in the UK concerned with all aspects of local wildlife protection. BBOWT's objective is to protect the future of wildlife and to create a greater appreciation of and involvement in wildlife and wildlife sites and to generate more opportunities for all to enjoy our wildlife heritage and develop a better understanding of the environment as a whole.

As an integral part of its aims, BBOWT encourages active participation by volunteers. Volunteer work falls into three areas:

Practical conservation work which comprises roving, mid-week teams who carry out work on a variety of sites, regular work parties on nature reserves. Other work involves species recording and habitat monitoring. No experience is necessary though specific skills will be utilised.

Sales and fundraising and public relations and education volunteers, help with stalls at events. Office administration which includes filing, computing and data base work in a busy membership office.

Anyone interested in any of the above should contact BBOWT at the above address.

BEALE PARK
The Child-Beale Trust, Lower Basildon, Reading, Berkshire RG8 9NH; ☎0118-984 5172; fax 0118-984 5171; e-mail administration@bealepark.co.uk; www.bealepark.co.uk

Beale Park is a charity dedicated to the conservation of the land it owns and rare breeds of animals and birds. It is open to the public in the form of a park of 300 acres which includes ancient water meadows and 45 acres of woodland. Animals graze the meadows while birds are housed in spacious bird enclosures which are part of a captive breeding programme. Peacocks, golden pheasants, owls are amongst the birds kept and llamas and highland cattle are amongst the free grazing animals.

20-30 volunteers per year work at Beale Park helping with animal and bird care and maintenance, the gardens, grounds, organic farm, education (environmental) and administration. Volunteers can be taken on for a few days, weeks or all year. Expenses and pocket money are paid but accommodation is not readily available.

Anyone interested should contact the Beale Park office at the above address.

BRIDPORT MUSEUM
The Coach House, Gundry Lane, Bridport, Dorset, DT6 3RJ; ☎01303-458703; fax 01303-458704; e-mail curator-bridportmuseum@btconnect.com

The Bridport Museum is a local museum, with a local history centre, store and fifteen collections. Volunteers are required to help with a variety of behind the scenes work, including documentation, storage and research. The work would suit those who have an interest in local history and museums as well as those who are looking for experience in the museum sector.

Applicants should be at least 18 years old and able to commit to regular hours. A preliminary interview will be held with all those interested. Please contact the Curator at the above address.

BRITISH ASSOCIATION OF FRIENDS OF MUSEUMS (BAFM)
Fonthill Cottage, Lewannick, Launceston, Cornwall; ☎0870 2248904; e-mail secretary@bafm.org.uk; www.bafm.org.uk

BAFM is an umbrella organisation which acts as a national forum for Friends and volunteers who support museums in the UK. It shares news, provides help and advice on good practice, holds regional meetings and produces a number of publications including a handbook on setting up and running a Friends organisation (cost £5). There is also a charter and handbook for Heritage Volunteer Managers and Administrators (cost £6.80). BAFM is run by a Council who are members of particular Friends' organisations.

For further information contact the Secretary at the above address.

BRITISH NATURALISTS' ASSOCIATION
1 Bracken Mews, Chingford, London E4 7UT; www.bna-naturalists.org

The Association was founded in 1905 (as the British Empire Naturalists' Association) in order to bring nature lovers in all parts of the UK and from overseas into contact with each other. It encourages and supports schemes and legislation for the protection of the country's natural resources, and organises meetings, field weeks, lectures and exhibitions to extend and popularise the study of nature. The Association does not supplement the activities of local and regional bodies, some 50 of which are at present affiliated to it.

Volunteers who wish to offer practical help on such projects as clearing a village pond should join their local branch, if possible. These are at present operative in the following areas: Buckinghamshire, Dorset, Essex, Hampshire, Hertfordshire, Kent, Lancashire, London, Greater Manchester, and Devon.

The subscription rate for members is variable: £15 or £12 for senior citizens. It includes two issues of the Association's Journal *Country Side*, and the *British Naturalist*, which provides details of branch activities.

Applications for membership should be sent to the Hon. Membership Secretary at the above address.

CANTERBURY OAST TRUST
South of England Rare Breeds Centre, Highlands Farm, Woodchurch, Ashford, Kent TN26 3RJ; ☎01233-861493
The Trust offers work for volunteers throughout the year at the Centre, which is a commercial tourist attraction run by a charity for adults with learning disabilities. There are a variety of volunteering opportunities ranging over general farm work, arts and crafts, horticulture, gift shop and gardening and restaurant work.

Applicants can be of any nationality but should speak good English and will have to provide references. They must be capable of working alongside disabled people. The minimum age is 16 and good health is essential. Disabled applicants can also apply, although individual cases have to be discussed. Volunteers are required all year round, but demand peaks in summer when the minimum stay is a month. No accommodation is provided and volunteers need their own transport. Limited travel expenses may be paid. Enquiries and applications should be sent to the Volunteer Co-ordinator.

CLEVELAND IRONSTONE MINING MUSEUM
Deepdale, Skinningrove, Saltburn, Cleveland TS13 4AP; ☎01287-642877; fax 01287-642970; e-mail visits@ironstonemuseum.co.uk
The 8Mining Museum preserves and interprets the ironstone mining heritage of Cleveland and North Yorkshire. This is a unique, award-winning, small, independent museum run by volunteers on a day-to-day basis: six museum guides, two receptionists, and two collection care staff. No accommodation. The museum is open from Monday to Saturday. Minimum period of work is 4 hours per week. Positions are available from July to October. Applicants should be interested in local history and heritage. Minimum age: 16.
Apply to the Museum Manager at the above address.

CPRE (Council for the Protection of Rural England)
128 Southwark Street, London SE1 OSW; ☎020 7976 6433; fax 020-7976 6373; e-mail info@cpre.org.uk; www.cpre.org.uk
CPRE fights for a living and beautiful countryside. It is active locally, nationally and internationally. As a registered charity, CPRE relies upon volunteers for the achievements of its objectives. Membership is open to all.
Enquiries to the above address.

THE EARTH CENTRE
Denaby Main, Doncaster DN12 4EA; ☎01709-512000; fax 01709-512010; e-mail info@earthcentre.org.uk; www.earthcentre.org.uk
The Earth Centre aims to inspire practical action by individuals and organisations consistent with sustainable development, which is done through its visitor centre built on the site of a former colliery which once had strong links with the local community.

Volunteers are needed to work as gardeners, and in the exhibitions, galleries, marketing and activities. Training is provided and is on-going and a reimbursement of travel expenses is given plus a meal allowance.

Applications should be sent to the Volunteer Manager.

EAST SUSSEX COUNTY COUNCIL
County Hall, St. Anne's Crescent, Lewes, East Sussex BN7 1UE; ☎01273-482670; fax 01273-479536; e-mail cathy.abel@eastsussex.gov.uk; www.eastsussex.gov.uk

East Sussex County Council has a Voluntary Ranger Service which is active every Wednesday. Volunteers take part in a range of different practical conservation tasks including coppicing, hedge-laying, bridge and stile building, tree planting, path clearance, pond creation etc. Anyone can apply and training will be given. Due to the nature of the work volunteers should be reasonably fit and able-bodied. No expenses are provided by the County Council..

Apply direct to the above address.

HENRY DOUBLEDAY RESEARCH ASSOCIATION
Ryton Organic Gardens, Coventry CV8 3LG; ☎024-7630 3517; fax 024-7663 9229; e-mail enquiry@hdra.org.uk; www.hdra.org.uk

The Gardens, which are open to the public, need volunteer guides each year. At present, these are needed in Ryton Organic Gardens, and in Yalding Organic Gardens in Kent. These organic and environmentally friendly gardens are designed to educate and give pleasure. There are also opportunities for volunteers in the organic cafe/shop and also to help in the office. Volunteers are also required in HDRA's Heritage Seed Library. Applicants of all nationalities are welcome, but some knowledge of gardening, conservation, organic growing and the environment is an advantage. Volunteers are welcome to work on a part-time basis, all the year round.

Those interested should apply to the Chief Executive at the above address.

IRONBRIDGE GORGE MUSEUM
The Wharfage, Ironbridge, Telford, Shropshire TF8 7AW; ☎01952-433522; fax 01952-432204; www.vtel.co.uk/igmt

The Ironbridge Gorge Museum is widely regarded as one of Britain's premier museums. Set amongst the beautiful Shropshire countryside, it is an independent educational charity providing enjoyment to hundreds of thousands of visitors each year. The Museum was founded in 1967 with the aims of conserving, restoring and interpreting the unique heritage of the Severn valley around Ironbridge.

Approximately 30 local volunteers help at the Museum complex every year. Volunteers are required to help with a huge variety of activities in all the different sections of the Museum. Most opportunities for volunteers are with the Blists Hill Victorian Town, where demonstrators, clad in Victorian style costume, are required to work in exhibits, explaining to visitors about the site, and its shops, businesses and houses. The opportunity also exists for volunteers to learn and use traditional skills within the exhibits, and there is an opportunity to research and present street activity of the period (c1900). Good communication skills, the ability to work unsupervised, and a good command of English language are all essential requirements.

Volunteers are also required to assist with general site maintenance and with the making and repair and maintenance of the period style clothes worn at the Victorian Town. Volunteers must be graduates or undergraduates with an interest in social and industrial history, and must have a tendency towards neatness, patience and accuracy.

At the Coalport China Museum volunteer demonstrators are needed to work in a ceramic workshop making and painting porcelain flowers. The possibility also exists for work with historic printing and manufacturing equipment. In the pottery workshop, volunteers can have the opportunity to make, decorate and fire earthenware items, or help with school parties. Good communication skills and an ability to speak English are essential.

Voluntary researchers are needed at the Long Warehouse, Coalbrookdale where a variety of research, cataloguing and interesting projects are always waiting to be undertaken. A knowledge of library and archive procedures would be a distinct advantage, as well as an interest in history. Volunteers are also required to assist with documentation; therefore the ability to type and to do a repetitive job is essential along with a good command of English.

At the Jackfield Tile Museum demonstrators are required in the Tile Works, explaining and practising the art of decoration and glazing. There would be opportunities to work as a guide or with school parties.

Volunteers are requested to work a minimum of two weeks, maximum of four. Accommodation is not provided. Luncheon vouchers are supplied for volunteers working 9.45am-5.15pm (a full day). Training, costume, equipment and supervision are all provided as appropriate.

For an application form contact Lorraine Ford at Blists Hill Victorian Town, Legges Way, Madeley, Telford TF7 5DU; e-mail lorraine@friends2000.fsnet.co.uk.

KENTWELL HALL
Long Melford, Sudbury, Suffolk CO10 9BA; ☎01787-310207; fax 01787-379318

A privately owned Tudor mansion, situated in park and farmland, approximately 1.5 miles from the historic town of Long Melford, famous for its annual recreation of Tudor life which takes place during June and July and in which up to 1,500 schoolchildren visit on weekdays and the public at weekends.

Volunteer Tudors (700) needed for historical re-creations. Duties consist of demonstrating 16th century life and activities to visiting schoolchildren and the public. The re-creations run for 7 days a week for 4 weeks; most volunteers stay one or two weeks during June and July. Take 16th century skills or learn them there. All ages and nationalities welcome. Applications to Dan Champion, Tudor Recreation Volunteers, at the above address.

All, meals, evening entertainment and space on campsite provided for volunteers only. Applicants can be of any age; interest in the 16th century would be helpful. For these positions applications must be made in January or February.

> **James Donnan put on a Tudor mantle at Kentwell and acquired new skills**
> *From the moment I walked through the gates, I knew Kentwell was a special place. Not only was the fine Tudor house impressive, but the tranquil setting immediately put me at ease. I knew it was the right place to take a break from the modern world and experience life at a gentler pace.*
>
> The magic of Kentwell re-enactments is in bringing history to life in an engaging and entertaining way. This is not about being an anonymous player in a massive battle display, it is about presenting the reality of everyday Tudor life.
>
> Where else do you have the opportunity to learn new skills and gain knowledge from so many likeminded people. I tried my hand at everything from baking bread in a wood-fired oven to driving a horse-drawn cart; all very different from my everyday high-tech life. Whatever the task, there are enthusiastic people at your side showing you what to do. Above all, it's the people who make Kentwell

> special. I now have an army of genuine friends across the country. You rarely get all this out of a week on the costas.

THE LONDON AQUARIUM
County Hall, Westminster Bridge Road, London SE1 7PB; ☎020-7967 8010; fax 020-7967 8029
The London Museum claims to be the UK's largest. Volunteers are needed to study a specialised field of the housed waterlife and provide information on this to the public. Any applicants with a proven interest in biology are welcome at any time. Applications with CV to Human Resources at the above address.

LONDON CANAL MUSEUM
12/13 New Wharf Road, Kings Cross, London N1 9RT; ☎020-7713 0836; fax 020-7689 6679; e-mail volunteering@canalmuseum.org.uk; www.canalmuseum. org.uk
Small, local history museum requires long-term volunteers for a half or full day per week for visitor reception, gift shop and general tasks. Opening hours are Tues-Sun 10am-4.30pm. Local travel expenses are reimbursed. Apply to Jeanette, volunteer co-ordinator.

LONDON WILDLIFE TRUST
Harling House, 47-51 Great Suffolk Street, London SE1 0BS; ☎020-7261 0447; fax 020-7261 0538; e-mail enquiries@wildlondon.org.uk; www. wildlondon.org.uk
The Trust was founded in 1981. It is an independent voluntary organisation with charitable status which operates throughout the Greater London area and is affiliated to the national partnership of Wildlife Trusts. The Trust has the following aims and objectives; to positively promote an interest in wildlife and raise awareness of the Trust among the public to encourage them to support the work of the Trust as members or supporters, to protect identified sites of wildlife interest, to promote positive management of those sites, thereby conserving or enhancing the wildlife interest of those sites and to encourage local community involvement and volunteer support.

Approximately 600 volunteers per year help the Trust with practical conservation work, wardening, educational activities, publicity, campaigning, local group work, monitoring and surveying wildlife and visitors to reserves. Volunteers of any nationality will be accepted but fluent English is essential. It would also be useful if volunteers have had previous experience in any of the above areas, especially in ecological surveying. Volunteers must also be reasonably fit. The length of time for which volunteers are recruited is dependent on the project. Lunch and travel expenses are available.

Those interested should contact The Support Services Officer at the above address.

LUDLOW MUSEUM
Ludlow Museum Resource Centre, Parkway, Ludlow, Shropshire SY8 2PG; ☎01584-813666; fax 01584-813601; e-mail ludlowmuseum@shropshire-cc.gov.uk; www.shropshireonline/llmrc.nsf
The Museum covers the geology and history of the area around Ludlow. It is a small place attracting mainly tourists visiting this beautiful region of Britain. 2 or 3 voluntary museum workers are needed from June to August. To work either 9am-5pm Mon-Fri, or part-time at least 3 days a week. Applicants should have an interest in museums and need to have good oral and written English. Apply to Ms K Andrew, County Curator of Natural History, at Ludlow Museum office.

MARINE CONSERVATION SOCIETY
Unit 3, Wolf Business Park, Alton Road, Ross-on-Wye, Herefordshire HR9 5NB; ☎01989-566017; fax 01989-567815; e-mail info@mcsuk.org; www.mcsuk. org

The Marine Conservation Society is the only environmental organisation which works exclusively to safeguard the marine environment across the whole range of conservation issues. The Society is a registered charity with an expanding membership, which encourages members to take part in projects to help provide a sound research base for campaigns.

Volunteers assist with beach surveys and clean-ups, measuring the impact of human activity and waste by surveying and recording pollution. Surveys of marine life are also undertaken at the Society's head office and involve assisting with the day to day operation of projects and campaigns. Volunteer divers are also needed to help with underwater surveys of coastal areas. Volunteers may also be needed to assist at shows and exhibitions. Applicants of any nationality may apply and no special qualifications are needed, except for the diving-related activities. The length of time for which volunteers are recruited depends on the task, but volunteers are usually required between May and October every year. Applicants should note that no accommodation is provided for volunteers, and no expenses are paid.

For further information contact the Society at the above address.

MID-HANTS RAILWAY (WATERCRESS LINE)
Railway Station, Alresford, Hampshire SO49JG; ☎01962-733810; fax 01962-735448; e-mail watercressline@compuserve.com; www.watercressline.co.uk

A preserved steam railway running trains between Alresford and Alton. Part-time and full-time volunteers are needed. Tourism students are particularly welcome to apply, and there is the possibility of unpaid work for those studying engineering. The period of work is for a minimum of two months May to September. Applications should be addressed to Volunteer Recruitment at the above address.

MUSEUM OF CANNOCK CHASE
Cannock Chase Council, Valley Road, Hednesford, Cannock, Staffordshire WS12 5TD; ☎01543-877666; fax 01543-428272; e-mail museum@cannockchasedec. gov.uk

A small but busy museum situated on an ex-colliery site telling the history of coal mining and domestic life in the local area. Volunteer museum attendants are required to work variable hours 2-3 days per week including weekends. These positions are intended to offer unpaid work experience but there is the possibility of some paid hours if work becomes available. A variety of tasks will be involved including reception work, working with school and adult groups, tourist information, greeting the public and working in the museum stores and library. Applicants should be 18 or more with a good basic education and preferably with some knowledge or interest in museums or history. Must have an interest in working with children, experience of public speaking, a good telephone manner, be willing to work with the public and be of smart appearance. Staff are required from May/June to September. Overseas applicants are welcome but must have a good standard of English.

Applications should be sent to Ms Lee Smith at the above address no later than April.

NATIONAL SEAL SANCTUARY
Gweek, Helston, Cornwall TR12 6UG; ☎01326-221790/221361; fax 01326-221790/221210; www.sealsanctuary.co.uk

The National Seal Sanctuary recruits about 24-50 volunteers a year to assist with the daily running of the animal care department. This involves preparing feeds, helping with feeds and assisting in the hospital during the winter: feeding pups, preparing treatments, assisting with rescues. Volunteers care for donkeys, ponies, goats, and carry out pool cleaning. There are also some research opportunities for university students.

Applicants, minimum age 18p, must speak English fluently and be physically fit and free from back problems as the work is demanding. Work can last from two weeks to six months all year round. No expenses are paid and a local bed and breakfast costs about £12 per night.

Applications to the Work Placements Co-ordinator at the above address.

NORTH YORK MOORS NATIONAL PARK AUTHORITY
The Old Vicarage, Bondgate, Helmsley, York YO62 5BP; ☎01439-770657; fax 01439-770691; e-mail general@northyorkmoors-npa.gov.uk; www.northyorkmoors-npa.gov.uk

The North York Moors National Park covers 554 square miles in North Yorkshire. Between Easter and October of each year, 200 volunteers act as voluntary rangers throughout the park. Tasks include providing information to visitors, patrolling the park and carrying out both conservation work and improvements to the public rights-of-way network. Weekend and day-long training sessions for prospective rangers are held during winter. Voluntary rangers are required to work a minimum of 12 sessions each lasting for six hours between 10am and 5pm during the opening season.

The National Park also offers a range of additional volunteering activities through its Volunteer Service. Individuals and groups have the opportunity to become involved in a wide range of conservation work. Regular work tasks are held each Tuesday throughout the year and fortnightly Saturdays and Sundays. Areas for volunteer involvement with this national park are constantly expanding. For more details on the North York Moors National Park Volunteer Service or to register please contact the Volunteers and New Deal Co-ordinator at the above address.

Volunteers should be between 18 and 65 years old, able to get on well with people and reasonably fit. Applicants with knowledge of the area and driving licences are preferred. No accommodation is available but a mileage allowance is paid.

Applicants should apply to the Head of Park Services at the above address.

NORTH YORKSHIRE MOORS RAILWAY
Pickering Station, Pickering, North Yorkshire YO18 7AJ. www.northyorkshire moorsrailway.com

Volunteers needed for all aspects of the operation and maintenance of a busy 18-mile stretch of steam railway running from Grosmont (near Whitby) to Pickering. Work includes train operations, sales, catering, engineering (both civil and mechanical). Volunteer work is available all year round for both skilled and unskilled people minimum age 16 who are reasonably fit. Basic accommodation is available.

Applicants should contact John Bruce, Volunteer Liaison Officer, North York Moors Historical Railway Trust care of the above address or fill out an application on the website.

PEAK PARK COUNTRYSIDE VOLUNTEERS
Peak National Park Office, Aldern House, Baslow Road, Bakewell DE45 1AE;

☎01629-816290; fax 01629-816291; e-mail ppcv@peakdistrict-npa.gov.uk
Each year thousands of volunteers help to protect the wildlife habitats and areas of outstanding natural beauty in the Peak District National Park over weekends, bank holidays and during school and college holidays around the year. Types of work to be done include building and repairing footpaths, stiles, steps, footbridges, fencing, walling, hedgelaying and tree planting, pond clearance and collecting litter.

No specific requirements are expected of volunteers except that they be between 14 and 65 years old. No accommodation is available so applications from local volunteers are preferred; but tools, materials, training and drinks are provided. Individuals outside the UK should not apply until they are in the country and have accommodation arranged.

Those interested should contact the Volunteers Organiser at the above address.

TREE COUNCIL
71 Newcomen Street, London SE1 IYT; ☎020-7407 9992; fax 020-7407 9908; e-mail info@treecouncil.org.uk; www.treecouncil.org.uk
The Tree Council promotes and co-ordinates the Tree Warden Scheme, which was launched in September 1990. The Scheme is a national initiative to enable people to play an active role in conserving and enhancing their local trees and woods. Between 7,500 and 8,000 volunteers per year act as tree wardens and gather information about their local trees, give advice on tree matters, protect threatened trees and encourage local projects to do with trees and woods. Trees are a precious part of the national heritage and action must be taken now if future generations are to enjoy the beauty and variety of British landscapes. To be most effective, this action should be taken by people on the spot; the people who know their own localities intimately and have most to gain from the protection and enhancement of their immediate environment. The Tree Council is working closely with local authorities and voluntary organisations to set up schemes in town and country throughout the British Isles.

Anyone can volunteer to become a Tree Warden as long as they are enthusiastic about trees; volunteers are needed all the year round. Tree Wardening can often happily be combined with other activities such as taking the children to school, exercising dogs and family walks. Some wardens have demanding jobs; others are unemployed or retired.

Applications to the above address will be forwarded to the relevant local organisations, or write for a list of these organisations.

WILDLIFE TRUST OF SOUTH AND WEST WALES
Fountain Road, Tondu, Bridgend CF32 OEH; ☎01656-724100; fax 01656-726980
The Wildlife Trust of South and West Wales (WTSWW) manages near 100 nature reserves to protect and enhance both habitat and species. It also carries out habitat and species surveys, educational activities and administration including membership database, management, volunteer management, fundraising, and profile-raising events.

Volunteers are taken on for either a fixed term placement or for on-going work. Volunteers have to arrange their own accommodation. WTSWW will pay travelling expenses from the volunteer's place of residence to work as agreed with the Finance Department prior to acceptance. Volunteers are needed all year round for a very varied programme of work including coppicing, leaflet distribution, woodlands management, insect and bird surveys, scrub removal, leading children's activities etc.

Apply direct to address above.

WIRKSWORTH HERITAGE CENTRE
Crown Yard, Wirksworth, Derbyshire, DE4 4ET; ☎01629-825225; e-mail heritage@crownyard.fsnet.co.uk

The 'Wirksworth Story' in a former silk mill offers a mock lead mine, information about local customs and social history. Family friendly. General Museum Assistant who must be able to communicate confidently with the public and pro-active and enthusiastic to help with all aspects of running a small business. Working hours to be arranged. Minimum period of work is a month. Positions are available all year. No accommodation.

Applications to Mrs. Vaughan at the above address.

Education

For one reason or another large numbers of people in Britain manage to slip through the state education system without managing to learn basic skills: it is estimated that there are two million adults who can barely read, and half a million who are totally illiterate. There are many more who do not reach their full potential in the education system, and volunteers can provide invaluable help in amending this situation by offering their assistance as tutors.

There is also a large number of immigrants living in ethnic minority communities around Britain who have little or no knowledge of English, which can lead to immense problems in coping with day-to-day life. Volunteers are greatly needed to act as language teachers with them: the job requires patience and a sympathetic approach, but no formal qualifications.

This section also includes details of ways in which volunteers can help other organisations whose aims are educational, although not necessarily to do with fundamentals such as literacy or speaking English.

THE AFRICA CENTRE
38 King Street, Covent Garden, London WC2E 8JT; ☎020-7836 1973; fax 020-7836 1975; e-mail info@africacentre.org.uk: www.africacentre.org.uk

The Africa Centre functions as an education centre, which gives information about Africa and its culture. The Centre requires 10 volunteers per year to work mainly as administrative and secretarial assistants in its office, but also as Programme assistants, who will help in the running of a variety of activities from Film Festivals to workshops on African culture, researchers for radio programme and conference organisers.

Volunteers, of any nationality, are required all the year round and can work for up to twelve months. Volunteers can be of any age. Previous experience and CV needed. Although the Centre does not provide accommodation for its volunteers, it will pay for any travel expenses.

Applications should be made to the Director, Adotey Bing, at the above address.

COMMISSION FOR RACIAL EQUALITY
St Dunstan's House, 201-211 Borough High Street, London SE1 1GZ; tel; ☎020-7939 0000; fax 020-7939 0001; e-mail info@cre.gov.uk; www.cre. gov.uk

The Commission for Racial Equality was set up under the 1976 Race Relations Act. It receives an annual grant from the Home Office, but works independently of Government.

The CRE is run by commissioners appointed by the Home Secretary and has support from all the main political parties. The CRE has three main aims: to work towards the elimination of racial discrimination and to promote equality of opportunity; to encourage good relations between people from different racial backgrounds; to monitor the way the Race Relations Act is working and recommend ways in which it can be improved. The CRE is the only Government-appointed body with statutory power to enforce the Race Relations Act.

There are over 100 Racial Equality Councils in the UK, many of which can use voluntary help in such areas as running projects and assisting with general administrative duties of the organisation as well as with publicity.

The needs of Councils vary from area to area; prospective volunteers should contact their local Councils directly, either by finding their address from the phone book or through the Customer Services Manager at the above address.

GLOSA Education Organisation (GEO)
PO Box 18, Richmond, Surrey TW9 2AU; www.glosa.org

GLOSA's aim is the organisation of 1,000 international Latin and Greek language roots into an expressive and euphonious International Auxiliary Language (IAL). GEO aims to publicise this language, to provide information about it among the public, pupils and educationalists and promote the teaching of GLOSA as a second language in schools worldwide.

GLOSA is already taught as a second language in the USA, Asia, and Africa and there are now more than 100 volunteers in different countries helping with the above aims. Volunteers mainly working from home, are urgently neededed worldwide to help publicise GLOSA via the writing of articles for journals and newspapers. Voluntary translators are needed to translate many GLOSA publications, especially the central vocabulary, as are people to teach GLOSA either in their school etc via letters and cassettes or small groups/individuals in their own town. Applicants of all nationalities accepted. Knowledge of GLOSA is preferable, but motivation is the main qualification as GLOSA can be mastered in just a few days. Volunteers are needed all the time, and can help for as long or short a time as they want. Funds are limited but paper/ink expenses can sometimes be paid. Free literature about GLOSA is provided.

Those interested should write to Wendy Ashby at the above address.

THE HORNSBY INTERNATIONAL DYSLEXIA CENTRE
Wye Street, London SW11; ☎020-7223 1144; fax 020-7924 1112; e-mail dyslexia@hornsby.co.uk; www.hornsby.co.uk

The Hornsby International Dyslexia Centre is a charity designed to assist people with dyslexia. Activities include after school learning clubs, holiday programmes and teacher training courses and conferences.

Volunteers are needed for work with children in the after school club and the holiday programmes. They should be literate, enjoy working with children and have sympathy with learning difficulties. The centre prefers the age range of volunteers to be 15-20 years. If volunteering from school, references from the school would be needed. The Centre can pay various expenses, and valuable experience and references can be obtained by volunteering.

Those interested should contact Dr. Ruth Hawson, Head of Centre, at the above address.

Elderly People

Improved medical knowledge and nutrition have steadily increased life expectancy over the last one hundred years or so and like other highly developed countries, Britain now has a rapidly growing number of octogenerians. Parallel with this has been an increase in the average age of the population as products of the post World War Two 'baby boom' grow older without having replaced themselves with equal numbers of children. The result of these factors is growing pressure on the stretched resources of the social services to cope with the frailties of an increasingly large proportion of the population, and the activities of the voluntary organisations described below are becoming more and more needed. Although the state can take care of an old person's physical needs, volunteers can be of invaluable assistance in helping their mental well-being.

It can make an immense difference to the life of an elderly person if they are visited by a volunteer, even if it is for only an hour a week. There are many simple practical jobs which a volunteer can do to improve the quality of life of an old person, from shopping, gardening or going to the library, to simply changing a light bulb, but the most important job that the volunteer can do is simply to provide companionship, whether the old person lives alone or in a home or hospital: this is a job at which the young are particularly successful. For many housebound people the volunteer may be their only visitor, someone to talk to over a cup of tea, and someone who is there because they care, not because they are just doing their job.

There are many ways of entering this field of voluntary work: Age Concern, the British Red Cross and the WRVS are the principal national organisations, which are active on a local scale. If none of the opportunities listed in this section appeal, you can simply phone up the administrator in charge of a local old people's home and ask if you can help in any way.

Apart from the entries below, other voluntary work concerning elderly people is discussed in the sections on The Sick and Disabled and Hospitals.

ABBEYFIELD SOCIETY
Abbeyfield House, 53 Victoria Street, St Albans, Herts AL1 3UW; ☎01727-857536; fax 01727-846168; e-mail post@abbeyfield.com; www.abbeyfield.com

The Abbeyfield is one of the largest UK-wide providers of housing with care for older people in the voluntary sector. Founded in 1956 Abbeyfield has now grown to include over 500 member societies throughout the United Kingdom with around 800 houses providing accommodation for 8,500 residents and involving more than 10,000 volunteers.

Abbeyfield provides two types of housing. Over 700 supported sheltered houses where residents can make their own home and enjoy the company of others whilst receiving the support they need from dedicated staff and volunteers. Care in over 80 registered care homes across England, Scotland and Wales. A number of Abbeyfield homes also provide special care for more advanced dementia, nursing care or day care.

Abbeyfield societies need a wide range of skills from volunteers in order to function effectively. Executive committees usually have a solicitor, an accountant and a doctor to liaise with the medical profession and advise on medical matters generally. People with property development experience, such as estate agents or chartered surveyors are valuable. A committee would also need several members who are available during the day to be responsible for the day-to-day operational administration of the houses. Besides these voluntary committee members, whose responsabilities require fairly specific amounts of time, there is always a need for volunteers whose time cannot be given on such a regular basis. These contributions may take the form of visiting, taking residents on outings, gardening, handiwork, organising events or coffee mornings, or deputising for the housekeeper on their days off.

Those interested should contact the above address for the address of their nearest local society.

AGE CONCERN ENGLAND
Astral House, 1268 London Road, London SW16 4ER; ☎020-8765 7200; fax 020-8765 7211; e-mail ace@ace.org.uk; www.ageconcern.org.uk
The Age Concern movement is a federation of over 400 independent charities which exists to promote the well-being of older people, helping to make later life a fulfilling and productive time. Through the provision of services, it provides the bit of help some older people need to continue living their independent lives. For those seeking new opportunities and active lives, Age Concern promotes the role of older people as citizens, enabling them to influence decisions that affect them, and to contribute their experience and skills to the communities and to society as a whole. It also campaigns with and on behalf of older people to influence policy on the things that matter to them.

The hundreds of regional and local Age Concern organisations rely upon thousands of volunteers to provide a wide and varying range of services and opportunities appropriate to the needs of older people in their area. These can include running day centres, lunch clubs, transport schemes, home visiting, and providing practical advice and assistance, and can extend to the provision of intensive care for mentally and physically frail elderly people in some areas. The time and skills of volunteers are highly valued; everyone should have something to offer their local Age Concern organisation.

Details of the nearest Age Concern Group can be discovered from the telephone directory.

COUNSEL AND CARE
Twyman House, 16 Bonny Street, London NW1 9PG; ☎020-7241 8555; advice line 10am-12.30pm and 2pm-4pm local rate number 0845-300 7585; e-mail advice@counselandcare.org.uk; www.counselandcare.org.uk
Counsel and Care is a registered charity providing a nationwide service for older people, their carers, and relatives.

The organisation runs a free advisory service and provides advice on a wide range of issues such as welfare benefits, accommodation, residential care, community care, and hospital discharge, backed up by a series of well-researched and regularly updated fact sheets.

C&C administer a number of trust funds for single payments and advise on other charities who may be able to provide financial assistance.

Volunteers are needed to carry out a wide variety of activities, from responding to requests for information to assisting in project work, depending on individual interests.

C&C offer a free advisory service, particularly concerning care, for those of pensionable age who are facing problems, and provide advice on finding and paying for care in a registered home.

Enquiries to the above address.

HELP THE AGED
207-221 Pentonville Road, London N1 9UZ; ☎020-7278 1114; fax 020-7278 1116; www.helptheaged.org.uk

Help the Aged offers a variety of opportunities for voluntary work:

Help the Aged Shops: There are over 378 shops in the UK and they are always looking for people who can spare a morning, afternoon or a full day each week to help in their local one. You can become involved in all aspects of retail work with full training provided.

Fundraising Events: Help the Aged organises many fundraising events across the country each year and we are always grateful for volunteers to help both before and on the event day.

*Local Committees.*Help the Aged committees are groups of volunteers in a county or region who organise high profile fundraising events and agree with Help the Aged, on how the money raised will be spent on local projects working with older people. Volunteers can be involved with their local committee by helping with the practical side of organising an event, being a secretary or a treasurer or even setting up a new committee for your area.

*Other opportunities.*These occur year round and include research work, home-based secretarial and clerical work and helping with administration at Head Office or one of the three Regional offices.

For further information please contact the Volunteer Co-ordinator at the above address.

JEWISH CARE
Stuart Young House, 221 Golders Green Road, London NW11 9DQ; ☎020-8922 2405; e-mail volunteer@jcare.org; www. jewishcare.org

Jewish Care is the largest Jewish social services organisation in the United Kingdom providing a comprehensive range of services for members of the Jewish community in London and south east England. Volunteers play an indispensable role in Jewish Care; it can only offer the wide range and quality of services because of the contribution which each volunteer makes.

As well as looking after older people, Jewish Care also looks after people who have a physical disability, or Alzheimer's disease, or a mental health problem or who are visually impaired. However, Jewish Care's largest area of work is with elderly people for whom it provides a wide range of services. These include: five community centres which provide a vibrant and stimulating range of activities for independent older people and a network of services for their frailer members; teams of home care workers and voluntary visitors who enable people to live in their homes for as long as possible; seventeen residential homes where people who are unable to live in their homes will find a warm and caring Jewish environment.

Volunteers are needed to assist in Jewish Care by providing activities in the community centres and befriending in the residential homes and by visiting elderly frail clients who are still able to live in their own homes. Other ways of helping include driving, escorting, and shopping.

For further information about current vacancies, call the Volunteers Department on 020-8922 2405.

Fund Raising and Office Work

Fund raising has always been one of the most important activities of any charity or voluntary body, but in the past it has tended to suffer from a less than glamorous image; people have tended to associate it with rattling collection boxes in the high street on damp Saturday afternoons. This has in recent years changed with the help of the media: both one-off events like Live Aid or annual appeals like the BBC's Children in Need or ITV's 'Telethon' have added a veneer of show-business to this essential activity. Such media-generated appeals are not, however, covered in this section, as the regular ones tend to be seasonal in their operation and they generate their own publicity at the appropriate time.

There is hardly an organisation in this book that would turn down an offer of either money or administrative help from a volunteer. The organisations in this section have many different specific objectives, but all have in common the fact that their greatest need for voluntary help is with raising money and doing office work.

It must be stressed that the list of organisations requiring this type of help is almost endless, and the few entries below are merely given as examples. If a volunteer wishes to help a specific organisation, then he or she should find the address of the local branch from the phone book and offer their services. Alternatively, many organisations advertise in local and national newspapers for help with a specific project; for example the British Legion appeal for poppy sellers in early autumn. Most good causes have some established machinery for fund raising, such as flag days or jumble sales, but they should also welcome new ideas, such as an offer from a school to organise a sponsored swim. The most dramatic fund raising schemes, such as wind surfing around Britain or running across the Himalayas, are normally the result of individual enterprise, someone feeling that he or she has some special way of attracting the attention of the public. It is always advisable to contact the relevant organisation before arranging any project, as it may be possible to link it with some publicity material such as leaflets or T-shirts to increase its impact.

Clerical and administrative work are equally essential in any organisation whether commercially or voluntarily run. The examples of office work included below range from routine filing and letter-writing/e-mailing to organising complete surveys and investigative research studies. Although it may seem mundane, it is work that must be done if the organisation's overall aims are to be successful.

ACTION AGAINST HUNGER UK
Unit 7B, Larnaca Works, Grange Walk, London SE1 3EW; ☎020-7394 6300; fax 020-7237 9960; e-mail info@aahuk.org; www.aahuk.org

Action Against Hunger is part of an international network that has been at the forefront of the fight against famine and bringing relief to disaster areas for over 20 years. AAH brings assistance either during an emergency situation or after the event through rehabilitation and sustainable development programmes. In 2004 countries where they were active included Cambodia, Malawi, Zimbabwe and Tadjikistan.

Volunteers are constantly needed at UK head office in the departments of human resources, finance, communications and fundraising. Work includes filing, management of donations, maintenance of databases, follow-up of donations, maintaining photographic library, researching/collecting/managing information on companies, assisting at festivals, outdoor collections, general administrative office duties. Work is unpaid but travel expenses are paid within London.

Applications direct to the above address.

ACTION AID
Hamlyn House, MacDonald Road, Archway, London N19 5PG; ☎020-7561 7561 or Chataway House, Leach Road, Chard, Somerset TA21 1FR; ☎01460-238000; e-mail HRenquiries@actionaid.org.uk; www.actionaid.org

This charity aims to improve the quality of life in some of the poorest parts of the world. Although Action Aid does not operate an overseas voluntary programme, volunteers are required all year round at the London office. UK Volunteers are also needed at Action Aid's Chard office in Somerset to do administrative work. Applicants can be of any nationality, but they must speak English. Pocket money is not provided, but Action Aid will pay for reasonable travel expenses and lunch.

Those interested for work in London should apply to H R Department, and for work at the Chard office should contact Merle Wright.

AKLOWA
Takeley House, Brewers End, Takeley, Bishops Stortford, Herts; ☎01279-871062; fax 01279-871256.

Aklowa is a charitable organisation established in 1977 with the overall aim of promoting understanding of African culture and society through the study and participation in the music, dance and the arts of Africa, all in the setting of an 'African Traditional Heritage Village'. A voluntary receptionist and volunteers with secretarial skills are needed to help at Aklowa.

Applications to the above address.

ANTI-SLAVERY INTERNATIONAL
Thomas Clarkson House, The Stableyard, Broomgrove Road, London SW9 9TL; ☎020-7501 8290; e-mail antislavery@antislavery.org; www.antislavery.org

Anti-Slavery International works to eliminate all forms of slavery in the world today, including debt bondage, forced labour, forced marriage, the worst forms of child labour, human trafficking and traditional slavery. It conducts research, campaigns, presses governments to implement national and international laws against slavery and supports local organisations' initiatives to release victims of slavery by exposing current cases. Based in London, volunteers carry out a range of tasks from basic administration and office duties including photocopying and data entry as well as work on specific projects such as media related work, fundraising or research projects. Good references are essential. The minimum period for volunteering is three months and volunteers are reimbursed for lunch and travel expenses within the London area. Anyone interested in volunteering should visit www.antislavery.org/support/volunteer/volunteer/htm

ASTHMA UK
Providence House, Providence Place, Islington, London; ☎020-7226 2260; fax 020-7704 0740; www.asthma.org.uk

Asthma UK is the new name of The National Asthma Campaign. Asthma UK is the charity dedicated to improving the health and well-being of people with asthma. In the UK this means building and sharing expertise about asthma. Volunteers are needed to help in the London office with distribution of materials, data entry and filing. Volunteers of all nationalities are accepted. The office has no disabled access. Travel expenses are paid. Applications to volunteer@asthma.org.uk or to Kate Taylor at the above address.

THE BALMORE TRUST
Viewfield, Balmore, Torrance, Glasgow G64 4AE; ☎01360-620 742.
The Balmore Trust is a small grant-giving Trust funded largely by its shop, The Coach House Charity Craft Shop, which is run by volunteers. Related activities include a branch of Tools for Self-Reliance and occasional activity in 'material aid' both in Glasgow and also in the shipment of hospital and educational supplies to parts of the Third World.

Volunteers are needed to work in the shop, to help with work servicing the shop (especially baking), to refurbish tools for export to developing countries and also to help with the collection and distribution of goods as 'material aid'. Applicants of all nationalities will be accepted, but accommodation and expenses cannot be provided except in special circumstances.

Those interested should contact Rosalind Jarvis at the above address.

BOOK AID INTERNATIONAL
39-41 Coldharbour Lane, London SE5 9NR; ☎020-7733 3577; fax 020-7978 8006; e-mail info@bookaid.org; www.bookaid.org
Book Aid international is the major UK support for libraries in sub-saharan Africa, working with partners that give the widest possible access to books and information. Carefully selected materials, both donated and purchased are made available to organisations in about 40 developing countries. Whilst the majority of volunteers work in the library/warehouse helping to process the books, there are a number of volunteers who assist in other departments or on specific projects. Book aid also needs volunteers to help collect and deliver book donations to London. Please note that volunteers are not sent overseas.

For further information on the volunteer programme, please contact the volunteer coordinator at the above address.

BRAINWAVE
Huntworth Gate, Bridgwater, Somerset TA6 6LQ; ☎01278-429089; fax 01278-429622; e-mail brainwavetherapy@hotmail.com; www.brainwave.org. uk
Brainwave was set up in 1982 to provide therapy to children and adults suffering from brain injury. The charity runs programmes to teach families how to deliver exercises in their own homes, moreover, a broad range of therapies are offered at the Brainwave Centre including riding for the disabled, an external therapy area, sensory garden, music therapy and multi-sensory room, all geared to stimulating various functions including mobility, co-ordination, communication and most importantly, the Centre backs up its therapies with a programme of ongoing advice and support via home visits, with videos being used to monitor and demonstrate progress.

Volunteers are required to help fundraise, collecting money in supermarkets, public houses, on the streets, and house to house. Applicants should be in good health, have a pleasant telephone manner, be patient and hospitable. A driving licence is particularly useful. A mileage allowance is paid but all other expenses must be met by the volunteer.

Applications all year round to the Community Fundraising Manager at the above address.

BRITISH HEART FOUNDATION APPEAL
14 Fitzhardinge Street, London W1H 6DH; ☎020-7935 0185; fax 020-7488 5820;.
Volunteers are always needed to help with fundraising events throughout the United Kingdom. Enquiries should be made to the nearest Regional Office which is listed in all telephone directories.

CANCER RESEARCH UK
P.O. Box 123, Lincoln's Inn Fields, London WC2A 3PX; ☎020-7242 0200; e-mail volunteering@cancer.org.uk; www.cancerresearchuk.org
Cancer Research UK is the world's largest independent organisation dedicated to cancer research. Formed in February 2002 as a result of a merger between the UK's two leading cancer research organisations, the Cancer Research Campaign and Imperial Cancer Research Fund. With a team of 3,000 scientists, research doctors and nurses, Cancer Research UK is building on the strengths of both charities.

Volunteers support Cancer Research UK in many different ways. With a chain of nearly 700 shops across the UK, the charity relies on volunteers to help run the stores effectively, processing stock, serving customers, displaying merchandise, helping with accounts and administration. Volunteer drivers are also needed to collect stock donations locally.

There are also nearly 1,400 fundraising groups and committees across the country organising events that range from coffee mornings to society balls and they always need extra help. Or some people choose to organise a one-off fundraising event, involving family and friends in raising money for research into cancer, or support the work of the Organisation by helping at its offices or events.

For further information about volunteering opportunities call 020-7009 8675 or e-mail the above address.

CARE INTERNATIONAL UK
10-13 Rushworth Street, London SE1 ORB; ☎0207-9349 334; fax 0207 934 0543; e-mail info@ciuk.org; www.careinternational.org.uk
CARE International combats hunger, sickness and poverty by providing relief during emergencies and by assisting the world's poorest people to improve their social and economic well-being. It seeks to promote fundamental and lasting change by building strong communities and acting in partnership with local people, donors, and other stakeholders. CI is non-sectarian and non-political in its work.

CARE International UK operates in 65 countries but voluntary positions are only available within the London office. Volunteers are used whenever there is a requirement such as during fund-raising campaigns etc.

Volunteers are normally recruited for periods of one to four weeks, all year round. No special skills are required and volunteers may be of any nationality. Reasonable travel expenses within London and lunch are provided.

Those interested should contact the Personnel Officer at the above address.

THE CAT SURVIVAL TRUST
The Centre, Codicote Road, Welwyn, Hertfordshire AL6 9TU; ☎01438716873; fax 01438-717535; e-mail cattrust@aol.com; www.catsurvivaltrust.org
The CST is a charity registered in 1976 and is the only organisation that works to conserve endangered species of wild cat in their native habitat. This is achieved by conserving the remaining wild habitat of the species. The Trust has purchased a wildlife reserve in Argentina, which contains five species of wild cats.

The work of the Trust is all carried out by volunteers. There are no paid staff. Applicants should be aged 17-70 (older possible) and able to spare a minimum of two weeks. The office needs computer operators, filing clerks and a librarian. Also needed are fundraisers, and maintenance workers for the Trust's headquarters. A very small number of volunteers who are qualified biologists, zoologists, botanists etc. work for the trust in Argentina entirely at their own expense.

Volunteers staying overnight or longer at the Welwyn headquarters can stay in caravans at the Centre or bring their own caravan. Basic food is supplied free from the farm shop on site.

Further details and an application form from the above address.

CATS PROTECTION
17 Kings Road, Horsham, West Sussex RH13 5PN; ☎01403-221900; fax 01403-218414; e-mail cpl@cats.org.uk; www.cats.org.uk
The objects of the Charity are to rescue stray, unwanted and neglected cats, to provide information on the care of cats and kittens, and to encourage the neutering of all cats not required for breeding. The practical work of the Charity and fund raising are carried out by voluntary workers through a system of over 260 local branches and groups, with some 50,000 members.

For further information those interested should contact the above address.

CHANGE
Bon Marché Centre, Room 222, 241-251 Ferndale Road, London SW9 8BJ; ☎020-7733 6525; fax 020-7733 9923; e-mail change@sister.com
CHANGE researches and publishes reports on the condition and status of women all over the world and organises exhibitions, international meetings, training workshops, book stalls, and other events.

Volunteers are always needed to help with all aspects of this work; basic administration, data entry, media work, organising meetings, human rights day events, exhibitions, book stalls, Parliamentary lobbying and research. The duration of particular projects can vary from one month to one year. Volunteers of any nationality with skills in any of the above areas are welcome.

DIAL UK
St Catherine's, Tickhill Road, Balby, Doncaster, South Yorkshire DN4 8QN; ☎01302-310123; fax 01302-310404; e-mail enquiries@dialuk.org.uk; www. dialuk.org.uk
Dial UK is the co-ordinator of the DIAL network of disability information and advice services. DIAL groups are run by people with direct experience of disability. They give free, independent, impartial advice to disabled people, carers and professionals. DIAL centres are independent organisations with their own management committees, staff and volunteers.

Dial UK provides a number of services to DIAL advice centres, including a reference information service, training and management support.

Volunteers work within the DIAL network, engaged in a variety of functions including writing, clerical work, information officers and disability advice workers. Applicants may be of any nationality provided that they are resident in the UK, good English is essential and volunteers must have direct experience of disability. Volunteers are required to work full and part-time all year round. Lunch and local travelling expenses are normally paid.

Those interested should contact Dial UK at the above address and will receive details of a local advice centre where they may be able to work.

DIAN FOSSEY GORILLA FUND
110 Gloucester Avenue, Primrose Hill, London NW1 8HX; ☎020-7483 2681; e-mail dan@dianfossey.net; www.gorillas.org
Dian Fossey was sent to Africa in the 1960's by the Anglo-American archaeologist Louis Leakey to undertake a study of the last remaining mountain gorillas. She founded the Karisoke Research Centre over a quarter of a century ago and pioneered the way animals are studied in the wild. Her researches were constantly impeded by the activities of poachers who are high on the list of factors that threaten the survival of the mountain gorillas. Dian Fossey herself died in mysterious circumstances at the Karisoke Centre in 1985. Her life and work were the subject of the cinema film *Gorillas in the Mist*, which starred Sigourney Weaver who is also honourary president of the Fund.

The high profile of the Dian Fossey Gorilla Fund helps in its efforts to protect the last few hundred mountain gorillas in Central Africa but the effort needs to be constant and sustained. About 75 volunteers work annually in the UK in office administration and fund-raising activities. The Fund will pay travel expenses.

DIRECTORY OF SOCIAL CHANGE
24 Stephenson Way, London NW1 2DP; ☎020-7391 4800; e-mail info@dsc. org.uk; www.dsc.org.uk
The Directory of Social Change researches and publishes reference guides and handbooks. It also provides practical training courses, runs conferences, organises charity fairs, encourages voluntary groups to network and share information, campaigns to promote the interests of the voluntary sector.

A volunteer or possibly more is/are needed to do extremely variable work related to the above for usually a minimum of six months and probably not more than a year. Expenses (travel and food) paid.

Apply to Jill Lincolnl at the above address.

ENVIRONMENTAL INVESTIGATION AGENCY
1st Floor, 62-63 Upper Street, London N1 ONY; ☎020-7354 7690; fax 020 7354 7961; e-mail info@eia-international.org; www.eia-international.org
EIA, founded in 1984, is an independent not-for-profit campaigning organisation working to protect the natural environment and the species that inhabit it. The EIA has a small but dedicated team of staff and volunteers. Dubbed the 'Animal Detectives' by the press, EIA has built up a reputation for in-depth research and undercover investigations. EIA teams gather unique film footage, interviews and information from across the world, often at considerable personal risk. The results of EIA's research are used for their campaigns and to brief other conservation and animal welfare organisations, as well as governments and intergovernmental organisations. EIA works through international conventions to develop workable and effective solutions to environmental abuses, and to implement changes, which will protect exploited species.

Volunteers are often required mainly to help in EIA's London office. Duties may include opening the post, supporting the fundraising officer, undertaking research campaigns computer input onto a database, replying to queries from members, and accounts. Applicants are required for from a few hours on occasional days to full time for several months. Travel expenses from within the London area are reimbursed, and a contribution is made towards lunch costs. Applicants should note that there is no wheelchair access to the office.

Those interested should contact the Volunteer Co-ordinator at the above address.

FARM AFRICA
9/10 Southampton Place, London WC1A 2EA; ☎020-7430 0440; fax 020-7430 0460; e-mail farmafrica@farmafrica.org.uk; www.farmafrica.org.uk
FARM Africa aims at reducing poverty by enabling marginalised African farmers and herders to make sustainable improvements to their well-being through more effective management of their renewable natural resources.

Volunteers are required to work in the UK performing administration in the fundraising department of FARM. Duties include updating the database, filing and typing. Applicants must be computer literate and native English speakers. Help is needed for just one day a week. Travel within London and lunch are provided.

Applications to the Fundraising Administrator at the above address.

THE HAEMOPHILIA SOCIETY
Chesterfield House, 385 Euston Road, London NW1 3AU; ☎020-7380 0600; fax 020-7387 8220; e-mail info@haemophilia.org.uk; www.haemophilia.org.uk
The Society was established in 1950 to serve the needs of people with haemophilia and similar blood disorders. The Society represents the interests of people with haemophilia by providing help, information and advice to them and their families. Volunteers serve the Society at all levels (the Board of Trustees, Chairman and Vice-Chairman are all volunteers) and all its 23 local Groups are run by volunteers. Volunteers of all nationalities are welcome to serve the Society in any way they can whenever they can spare the time.

For a complete and up-to-date contact list for local groups please write to the above address.

HARVEST HELP
3-4 Old Bakery Row, Wellington, Telford TF1 1PS; ☎01952-260699; fax 01952-247158; e-mail susan@harvesthelp.org; www.harvesthelp.org
Harvest Help is a UK-based charity working with poor farmers in Zambia and Malawi to help them feed their families, earn and living and work towards self-reliance. The UK office in Telford often requires administrative support from volunteers. Usually 5/6 volunteers are accepted a year. Some of these are part-time and others come for work experience placements over the summer. We also welcome occasional volunteers. Volunteers duties include: part-time administration, part-time communications assistant, occasional volunteers for collating resource material and stuffing envelopes. Volunteers usually need basic administration skills and familiarity with computers. Age immaterial. Travel expenses paid.

HEADWAY: Brain Injury Association
4 King Edward Court, King Edward Street, Nottingham NG1 1EW; ☎0115-924 0800; fax 0115-958 4446; e-mail information@headway.org.uk; www.headway.org.uk
HEADWAY exists to promote understanding of all aspects of brain injury and to provide information, support and services to people with brain injury, their families and carers. Headway relies on donations to fund its important work.

Headway has over 100 local groups around the UK, many of which run Headway House Centres. These provide activities, and therapeutic facilities for people with a brain injury. Volunteer opportunities are often available from central office. Volunteers are always welcome to contact Central Office; placements will vary according to local need. Out-of-pocket expenses will be reimbursed.

HEALTHPROM
Star House, 104-108 Grafton Road, London NW5 4BD; ☎020-7284 1620; fax 020-7284 1881; e-mail healthprom@healthprom.org; www.healthprom.org
Healthprom works in partnerships to improve healthcare for the most vulnerable in Eastern Europe and Central Asia.

Needs volunteers for some interesting ongoing opportunities in administrative, research, communications and fundraising areas. Excellent experience to be gained by committed and reliable volunteers with an interest in international development work. Local travel and lunch expenses paid. Applications to Tanya Buynoskaya, Business Manager, including CV to the above address.

HERITAGE CERAMICS
Unit B18, Charles House, Bridge Road, Southall, Middlesex UB2 4BD; ☎020-8843 9281; fax 020-8813 8387; e-mail info@heritageceramics.org; www.heritageceramics.org
Heritage Ceramics, founded in 1984, is a small collective of artists who work in the area of ceramics and pottery with the aim of exploring and producing work with themes that spring from the African experience. The UK based organisation provides basic and advanced training in all aspects of ceramics and pottery, as well as providing input in arts and crafts education in schools through outreach workshops.

Six volunteers work with Heritage every year mainly contributing to and assisting in administrative management, but also in technical/practical operations in the workshop. Applicants may be of any nationality and no special qualifications are necessary apart from a basic command of the English language. Volunteers usually work for one year on a full or part-time basis. In most cases Heritage pays for travel and subsistence.

For further information contact Mr Tony Ogogo at the above address.

INDEX ON CENSORSHIP
Writers and Scholars Educational Trust, 33 Islington High Street, London N1 9LH; ☎020-7278 2313; fax 020-7278 1878; e-mail Natasha@indexoncensorship.org: www.indexoncensorship.org
The Trust is a charity that publishes manuscripts that have been banned and gives details of writing that has been censored anywhere in the world. There is a constant need for help in the office both with research and general clerical work. Volunteers are needed to work on a regular basis even if only for half a day per week.

For further details contact the editor at the above address.

JEWISH CHILD'S DAY
Fifth Floor, 707 High Road, London N12 0BT; ☎020-8446 8804; fax 020-8446 7370; e-mail info@jewishchildsday.co.uk; www.jewishchildsday.co.uk
This organisation needs occasional clerical help with its fund raising for a wide variety of children's organisations in Israel, the UK, France, Yugoslavia, Morocco and Tunisia.

Applications should be sent to the Director at the above address.

KIDS' CLUBS NETWORK
Bellerive House, 3 Muirfield Crescent, London E14 9SZ; ☎020-7512 2112; fax 020-7512 2010; e-mail chris.taylor@kidsclubs.org.uk; www.kidsclub.com
Kid's Club Network is the only national UK charity which supports and promotes school age children before and after school and during school holidays. Volunteers have the opportunity to help at an administrative level or the organisation can put them in touch with clubs that are members of Kids' Clubs Network.

Volunteers can help in the London office assisting with general administrative duties including photocopying, word processing, mailouts and filing, as well as helping with the preparation for training events and seminars. Applicants may be of any nationality but they should speak fluent English. The London office is accessible to wheelchair users. All volunteers must abide by an Equal Opportunities policy. Volunteers will be expected to work for Kids' Club Network on a fairly flexible basis; the office needs help all year round. Expenses will be paid subject to negotiation with the volunteer.

Those interested should contact The Administrator at the above address.

KURDISH CULTURAL CENTRE

14 Stannary Street, London SE11 4AA; ☎020-7735 0918; fax 020-7582 8894; e-mail admin@kcclondon.org; www.kcclondon.org

The Centre gives assistance to Kurdish refugeees and asylum seekers in the UK, promotes Kurdish culture and is involved in relief work in Kurdistan.

Approximately 100 volunteers of all nationalities work for the Centre every year, helping with office work, translation, relief work, and work with refugees in London. Help is needed all the year round and volunteers are welcome to work with the Centre as much as possible. Travel and lunch expenses are paid.

Those interested should apply to Sarbest Kirkuky at the above address.

LIVE MUSIC NOW!

4 Lower Belgrave Street, London SW1W OLJ; ☎020-7730 2205; fax 020-7730 3641; www.livemusicnow.org.

Live Music Now is dedicated to enabling people with special needs who have limited access to music to experience and participate in live musical performances of the highest quality. There are over 300 of the finest young professional musicians taking part, performing almost 2,400 concerts and workshops annually throughout the UK. Volunteers are needed for a variety of different tasks. For more information please contact Alice Wilkinson at the above address.

MEDAIR

Willow House, 17-23 Willow Place, London SW1P 1JH; ☎020-7802 5533; fax 020-7802 5501; info@medair.org.uk; www.medair.org.

Medair is an international Christian, humanitarian organisation that sends qualified, professional personnel including doctors and engineers to areas if the world in crisis. About 600 volunteers work in the field, and others are employed in the UK office and offices in other European countries. Volunteers in the UK office work part-time on project work, helping to raise Medair's profile and recruit volunteers. Work can be for several hours or days per week. Volunteers are needed all year round and work is unpaid.

For further information contact the above address.

NATIONAL SOCIETY FOR THE PREVENTION OF CRUELTY TO CHILDREN (NSPCC) WESTON HOUSE

42 Curtain Road, London EC2A 3NH; ☎020-7825 2500; fax 020-7825 2525; e-mail infounit@nspcc.org.uk; www.nspcc@org.uk

Although the society's active work is conducted only by professionally qualified staff, volunteers are always needed to start fund-raising groups or join in existing groups. The society has around 2,000 fund-raising groups that raise money through organising events, flag days, and house to house collections. Many individuals and groups of people help by running their own fun activities in aid of the Society.

Those willing to help should contact the Community Appeals Dept. at the above address.

OCKENDEN INTERNATIONAL
Constitution Hill, Woking, Surrey GU22 7UU; ☎01483-772012; fax 01483-750774; e-mail oi@ockenden.org.uk; www.ockenden.org.uk
Ockenden International runs projects overseas targeted especially at care of Vietnamese and Cambodian refugees. Occasionally, there are vacancies in their offices abroad, but there are far more vacancies in the UK office for volunteers/interns. The average period is for 3-6 months. Areas may include policy, media, publications and fund raising. Current opportunities are displayed on the website.

Further details are also available from the Personnel Officer at the above address.

ONE VILLAGE
Charlbury, Oxford OX7 3SQ; ☎01608-811811; fax 01608-811911; e-mail progress@onevillage.co.uk; www.onevillage.org.uk
One Village works with craft producers' co-operatives in Africa, Asia, South America, and sells their products in the UK. There are opportunities for volunteers in One Village shops in the UK, particularly in Woodstock near Oxford; these take the form of both long-term commitments and temporary holiday-time jobs. There are other posts that can sometimes be filled by volunteers. The length of time for which volunteers are recruited varies. Expenses are sometimes paid.

Applicants, of any nationality, should contact Roy Scott at the above address.

OXFAM (GB)
Oxfam House, 274 Banbury Road, Oxford OX2 7DZ; ☎01865-311311; e-mail givetime@oxfam.org.uk; www.oxfam.org.uk
OXFAM (GB) volunteers work in Great Britain to help OXFAM carry out its purpose of working with others to overcome poverty and suffering. As well as raising funds, this involves campaigning and educating the public in order to help tackle the causes of poverty. OXFAM is committed to an Equal Opportunities Policy and welcomes offers of help from people of all backgrounds and abilities.

OXFAM does not send volunteers overseas but thousands of volunteers are involved in OXFAM's work throughout Great Britain. Some help organise fund-raising events, others are involved in campaigning and educational work. In the regional offices, help with clerical and administrative work is often needed too. People with special skills such as book-keeping, design and typing can often put their talents to use with OXFAM, but there are lots of opportunities for people without any particular qualifications. There are a number of volunteer placement opportunities throughout the country offering the opportunity to develop skills and experience in fund-raising, volunteer recruitment and support, campaigning, retailing, IT and administration.

In the Oxford headquarters over 100 volunteers work with over 500 staff on a range of duties from routine packing to research projects. Oxfam cannot provide accommodation or pocket money, but does reimburse travel and lunch expenses, dependent on the number of hours worked.

For further information, look up your local OXFAM office or shop in the telephone book, or for work in Oxford or more information on graduate/student placements contact F&IS Human Resources at the above address, or visit the website.

PLAN UK
5/6 Underhill Street, Camden, London NW1 7HS; ☎020-7482 9777; fax 020-7482 9778; e-mail mail@plan-international.org.uk; www.plan-international.org.uk
PLAN International is a long-term development agency helping over a million children,

their families and communities in over 40 countries around the world. The areas covered include Asia, the Far East, Africa and South America, and the majority of fund-raising is done through child sponsorship.

Volunteers are needed in the small and friendly London Office to help support the work of about 54 paid staff. There is a base of over 30 daytime volunteers. The volunteer work includes a wide range of basic administrative tasks, including computer work and processing the communications from the children. Every effort is made to match the skills of the volunteers to the work available, and applicants of any nationality are welcome. Full training is given on all tasks. The usual minimum commitment is one day per week. Those interested should contact Dora Anyi, Human Resources, at the above address.

POPULATION CONCERN
Studio 325, Highgate Studios, 53-79 Highgate Road, London NW5 1TL; ☎020-7241 8500; fax 020-7267 6788; e-mail info@populationconcern.org.uk; www.populationconcern.org.uk
Population Concern raises funds for overseas population and development programmes, provides an information service and campaigns on population and related issues in schools and amongst the public. Projects are being undertaken in many developing countries in Africa, the Caribbean and Asia, but volunteers are only required in the London office. Volunteers may work on a regular basis or just for short intensive periods, all year round. The work available depends on the applicant's interests and skills but includes such areas of work as information, education, fund-raising and occasional project work.

Special skills such as typing, word processing and artwork designing are desirable but not essential. Students or recent graduates in Demography and related disciplines are very welcome. Payment of travelling expenses is negotiable but accommodation is not provided.

Those interested should apply to the Information Officer at the above address.

PSYCHIATRY RESEARCH TRUST
De Crespigny Park, Denmark Hill, London SE5 8AF; ☎020-7703 6217; fax 020-7703 5796; e-mail s.refault@iop.kcl.ac.uk; www.iop.kcl.ac.uk/home/depts/prt/prt.htm
The Trust raises funds for research into mental illness, brain disease and mental disability at the Institute of Psychiatry. Approximately 50 volunteers around the country are engaged by the Trust as fundraisers who work from home organising activities that will generate contributions for the trust. There are no restrictions on the type of volunteer required by the Trust.

For further information please contact Sandra Refault at the above address.

ROYAL NATIONAL LIFEBOAT INSTITUTION
West Quay Road, Poole, Dorset BH15 1HZ; ☎01202-663000; e-mail info@rnli.org.uk; www.lifeboats.org.uk
The operator of the lifeboat service throughout the United Kingdom and the Republic of Ireland, the RNLI is supported entirely by voluntary contributions. It is impossible to estimate the number of volunteers who assist the service; most of the crews of the lifeboats run from the 230 lifeboat stations are unpaid, and there are also some 1,500 fund-raising branches around the UK.

There is an important distinction between these two forms of voluntary work; while anyone who is willing to help with fund-raising will be welcomed, only those who pass a medical, can swim, meet age requirements and live in the vicinity of a lifeboat station can be accepted as crew members.

It is preferred that those interested should apply to their local branch of the RNLI, but if there is any difficulty about obtaining the relevant address, please contact the Public Relations Department at the above address.

SAVE THE CHILDREN UK
1 St. John's Lane, London EC1M 4AR; ☎0845 606 4027 (volunteer action line); fax 020-7703 2278; www.savethechildren.org.uk
Save the Children is the UK's largest international children's charity working to create a better future for children. In a world where children are denied basic human rights, Save the Children champions the right of all children to childhood. Behind their work are thousands of volunteers, raising vital funds and telling people about what the charity does. If you would like to find out more about becoming a volunteer in the UK call the action line on 0845 606402.

SAVE THE RHINO INTERNATIONAL
16 Winchester Walk, London, SE1 9AQ; ☎020-7357 7474; fax 020-7357 9666; e-mail info@savetherhino.org; www.savetherhino.org
A London-based charity raising funds for projects protecting rhinos and other endangered wildlife in Africa and Asia, through conservation challenges, marathons and donations.

Office volunteers are occasionally needed to carry out general office work including data entry, managing mailings, leafleting and money collections. Volunteers work 10am-6pm with lunch and travel expenses provided. Must be over 18 with some office and financial administration experience. Volunteers are required all year round for a minimum of two weeks. Foreign applicants with good written and spoken English are welcome.

Applications to Nicky Springthorpe at the above address.

THE SOCIETY FOR MUCOPOLYSACCHARIDE DISEASES
46 Woodside Road, Amersham, Bucks HP6 6AJ; ☎01494-434156; fax 01494-434252; e-mail mps@mpssociety.co.uk; www.mpssociety.co.uk
This organisation offers support to those suffering from Mucopolysaccharide (MPS) diseases and their families, carers and professionals. Mucopolysaccharide is the umbrella name for a range of rare metabolic diseases which are passed on genetically. Some sufferers may be less affected than others, but for many the diseases cause severe disabilities, mental and physical, in some cases leading to death in childhood.

About 150 volunteers a year are needed to help raise funds to support research into MPS diseases. Duties include administration and caring for affected children and their siblings at Society events. Most volunteers are required for no more than 3-7 days at a time. Applicants should be minimum age 18 and prepared to undergo a police check. Knowledge of languages desirable. Local travel to conferences and Family Days is paid but not for those working in the office. Accommodation is only provided at conferences.

The Society produces several information booklets on MPS each costing £1. For further information on the Society and MPS diseases or to volunteer your services contact the Director at the above address.

ST. JAMES'S HOUSE
15-20 Bruges Place, Baynes Street, London NW1 0TF; ☎020-7428 5999; fax 020-428 5996; e-mailstjameshouse@btclick.com
St. James's House provides work experience and training opportunities for people

with mental health problems in London. Training within St. James's House comprises computing/admin skills or workshop activities. The workshop is rehabilitative in nature and may involve training individuals in paper recycling, furniture restoration, card making, and the production of soft furnishings.

Volunteers may work directly with clients, help out with training, administration, fund-raising, audits, and mental health projects in collaboration with other organisations. There are no restrictions on the type of volunteer required other than people living legally within the UK, able to communicate effectively in English. Travelling expenses are paid for people living outside of the borough and a small subsistence payment is awarded to volunteers.

Those interested should contact St. James's House at the above address.

SOIL ASSOCIATION
Bristol House, 40-56 Victoria Street, Bristol BS1 6BY; ☎0117-929 0661; fax 0117-925 2504; e-mail p.demolou@douaisis-agglo.com; www.soilassociation. org
The Soil Association exists to research, develop and promote sustainable relationships between the soil, plants, animals, people and the biosphere, in order to produce healthy food and other products while protecting and enhancing the environment. Volunteers are welcomed to assist with general office administration as well as being involved in specific projects (when available). Office and keyboard skills will be useful to provide support for teams. Potential volunteers are asked to forward their CVs along with details of their availability to Helen Robinson via e-mail to hrobinson@soilassociation.org, or the above postal address.

SURVIVAL INTERNATIONAL
6 Charterhouse Buildings, London EC1M 7ET; ☎020-7687 8700; fax 020-7687 8701; e-mail info@survival-international.org; www.survival-international. org
Survival International is a worldwide organisation supporting tribal peoples. It stands for their right to decide their own future and helps them to protect their lives, lands and human rights. Survival works for threatened tribal peoples in the Americas, Africa, Asia and Australasia. Survival lobbies international organisations, governments and multi-national companies, works to raise awareness of the situation of tribal peoples and supports practical realistic field projects with the aim of assisting the survival and self-determination of tribal peoples.

Volunteers are required in the London office to assist with clerical and secretarial work, library duties, visual aid materials and fund-raising activities. Those interested should contact the London office.

THE TIBETAN COMMUNITY IN BRITAIN/THE TIBETAN REFUGEE CHARITABLE TRUST
c/o 1 Cultworth Street, London NW8; ☎020-8683 43199.
The Tibetan Community in Britain is the association of all Tibetans living in the United Kingdom, formed in 1970 to establish a formal organisation to instil co-operation and mutual help among its members. It also seeks to inform the people and government of Britain of the plight and suffering of the Tibetan people under the Chinese occupation and to preserve and promote Tibetan culture within and beyond the Community. Anyone interested in the struggle of Tibetans to regain their independence and preserve their unique culture is welcome to become involved. The Community organises public events in the UK and sends donations to the Tibetan administration in India towards their various projects for Tibetan refugees and in particular, provision for Tibetan children's education.

The Tibetan community in Britain would greatly welcome the involvement of anyone who subscribes to its objectives and especially those who can offer skills in publicity and fundraising work. Those interested should contact the secretary, Mr. Chonpel Tsering, at the above address or call the above number (evenings).

TOURISM CONCERN
Stapleton House, 277-281, Holloway Road, London N7 8HN; ☎020-7133 3330; fax 020-7133 3331; e-mail info@tourismconcern.org.uk; www.tourismconcern.org.uk

Tourism Concern campaigns for ethical and fairly traded tourism. The UK London office accepts about 15 volunteers a year to carry out general office work and to maintain the database and library. Must do one full day a week minimum. Volunteers often stay for years. Fares within London and lunch provided. Applications should be addressed to Francesca Leadlay.

UGANDA SOCIETY FOR DISABLED CHILDREN (USDC)
68 Adrian Road, Abbots Langley, Herts. WV5 OAQ; ☎01923-263102; fax 01923-267838; e-mail ugandasoc@aol.com; www.charitynet.org/usdc

USDC is a development agency established in 1985 specifically to operate in Uganda. Its mission is to provide resources and opportunities for children with disabilities to achieve their potential and lead fulfilling lives.

The focus of its activities is on the individual child living at home with his/her parents and other family members, who are the principal carers. It follows a community-based approach, using local and appropriate resources. Promoting public awareness of disability issues and challenging negative attitudes are also accorded high priority. It collaborates with the Government of Uganda and other partners to strengthen service provision through professional, technical and material support.

One full-time employee is based in the UK. There are opportunities for volunteers to become involved in publicity and fundraising activities elsewhere; for example distributing leaflets to family, friends and colleagues; collecting on Children's Day; helping on stalls at local events; preparing envelopes for a mailing; organising a small fundraising event.

In Uganda thirty national staff are headed by an Executive Director. Placements may be considered on a case by case basis for professionals with appropriate skills and experience and the necessary financial support.

Please contact the Executive Director for further information.

WAR ON WANT
37-39 Great Guildford Street, London SE1 OES; ☎020-7620 1111; fax 020-7261 9291; e-mail drudkin@waronwant.org; www.waronwant.org

This organisation undertakes development and relief work to alleviate famine in the Third World. A national network of groups throughout the United Kingdom raise funds and campaign in their local areas. Volunteers are required for office and administrative work in the head office in London. Work continues all year round and volunteers give whatever time they can.

Any special skills that volunteers have will be utilized but none are essential. All volunteers are welcome but there is no access for disabled people at the London office. London office volunteers have their travelling expenses within London paid and receive a lunch allowance per day.

Those interested in wishing to work in the London office should contact David Rudkin at the above address.

WOMANKIND (Worldwide)
2nd Floor, 32-37 Cowper Street, London EC2A 4AP; ☎020-7588 6096; e-mail info@womankind.org.uk; www.womankind.org.uk
This is a small development charity dedicated to helping women in developing countries to help themselves to overcome poverty, ill-health and disadvantage. Volunteers are not recruited for overseas work. Five or six volunteers at any one time are needed in London to help with office work, fundraising, events and sometimes, research. What the volunteer actually does depends very much on what skills the applicant has and the time she or he can offer. Volunteers are needed all the year round, but the length of time for which they are recruited depends on the individual. Travel and lunch expenses are paid.

Those interested should contact the above address.

THE WOMEN'S ENVIRONMENTAL NETWORK (WEN)
P.O. Box 30626, London E1 1TZ; ☎020-7481 9004; e-mail info@wen.org.uk; www.wen.org.uk
WEN is dedicated to informing and educating and empowering women and men who care about the environment.

WEN is run almost entirely by volunteers who are involved in a whole range of activities such as research, campaigns, administration, and many other areas. WEN welcomes enthusiastic volunteers from all nationalities. Volunteers are required all year round and the length of volunteer recruitment varies. Travel expenses and lunch expenses are paid.

Those interested send in CV with a covering letter to WEN.

WOMEN'S THERAPY CENTRE
10 Manor Gardens, London N7 6JS; ☎020-7263 6200; fax 020-7281 7879; enquiries@womenstherapycentre.co.uk; www.womenstherapycentre.co.uk
The Centre was founded by Luise Eichenbaum and Susie Orbach to provide a psychotherapeutic service for women by women, and to develop and promote an understanding of women's psychology. Several volunteers work at the Centre within the areas of administration, advice and information, although limited space restricts the number of volunteers the Centre can take. Vacancies occasionally arise to undertake specific pieces of fund-raising research. Female only applicants of any nationality of minimum age 18 years will be considered. Enthusiasm and a commitment to women's issues are essential. Travel and lunch expenses will be provided.

If interested, please contact Ann Byrne at the above address.

WORLD VISION UK
World Vision House, Opal Drive, Fox Milne, Milton Keynes MK25 0ZR; ☎01908-841005; fax 01908-841014; e-mail rachel.oxborough@worldvision.org.uk; www.worldvision.org.uk
World Vision UK offers office work in Milton Keynes only. About 30 volunteers help out in any one year doing clerical and administration work. Volunteers can be taken on at any time and for any period. Expenses are paid. Most volunteers live in Milton Keynes.

WWF-UK
Panda House, Weyside Park, Godalming, Surrey GU7 1XR; ☎01483-426444; fax 01483-426409; e-mail wwf-uk-sc@wwfnet.org; www.wwf-uk.org
WWF fundraises and campaigns partly through a network of around 300 voluntary supporters' groups in the UK. Scientific research could be carried out by volunteers who can finance themselves and with appropriate degrees. Volunteers can also assist with

fundraising in the UK. Accommodation cannot be offered.

Volunteers within the UK should write to the above address to obtain a list of regional WWF groups; international volunteers can apply to WWF International, 1196 Gland, Switzerland.

WRITERS IN PRISON COMMITTEE OF INTERNATIONAL PEN

9-10 Charterhouse Buildings, Goswell Road, London EC1M 7AT; ☎020-7253 3226; fax 020-7253 5711; e-mail intpen@gn.apc.org

This organisation researches and campaigns on behalf of writers, journalists, publishers, poets, editors, etc. who have been arrested, killed or attacked because of their views. It deals with all cases in all countries. Volunteers of all nationalities are needed to help with photocopying, filing and general correspondence. Other tasks might be open to volunteers according to their skills.

Volunteers should have typing skills, and knowledge of languages other than English, French or Spanish would be useful. The office is situated up eight flights of stairs and there is no lift which makes it unsuitable for disabled applicants. Volunteers should be able to make a commitment of one day per week for at least two months. Help is needed all year round. Local travel costs are paid.

Applications should be made to Sara Whyatt at the above address

Hospitals

There is much that volunteers can do in a practical way to make a patient's stay in hospital more comfortable, and support the hard-pressed professional staff with patient care. It must be stressed, however, that the range of activities a volunteer can do is strictly limited, as they must not encroach upon the professional's preserve, and in many cases the number of hours a volunteer can help will be limited.

For example, it is permitted to drive a patient's relatives to and from hospital, but driving an out-patient home would encroach on the work of the ambulance service so may not be permitted. Nearly all of the work involving hospitals is concerned with direct contact with the patients and their families. The range of services provided by volunteers includes running shops, canteens, libraries and telephone lines, befriending and escorting patients, and arranging outings, flower arranging, hairdressing and writing letters for them. They may also be of help in preparing the homes of patients for their return.

The majority of hospitals either have their voluntary work organised by a Friends organisation (see the entry for the National Association of Hospital and Community Friends below) or employ their own Voluntary Services Co-ordinator; the voluntary services of the remaining hospitals may be run by another organisation such as the Red Cross or the WRVS. However, the incessant commercial pressure on the NHS trusts to exact the best financial advantage from any aspect of healthcare means that that the services traditionally provided by volunteers are increasingly likely to be contracted to professional profit-makers. Trolleys and tea-bars are being replaced by well-known retail outlets located within hospital premises and paying market rents. The Friends organisations contribute their profits towards improving patient facilities and this can include the purchase of medical equipment. The NHS trusts now have to balance such contributions against the profits from contracting out. The Friends organisations have thus received a serious challenge to their virtual monopoly of service providing.

A simple telephone call to a local hospital should enable you to find out who to contact if you wish to offer your services there. The individual hospitals listed below are given only as examples of the needs of hospitals up and down the country.

Other work involving hospitals and hospital patients will be found in the sections on *Sick and Disabled People*, *Mental Health*, *Children and Youth* and *Elderly People*.

NATIONAL ASSOCIATION OF HOSPITAL & COMMUNITY FRIENDS
11-13 Cavendish Square, London W1G OAN; e-mail info@hc-friends.org. uk;www.hc-friends.org.uk
Friends are a range of independent healthcare charities operating all over the UK involving some 60,000 active volunteers in 800 organisations giving 20 million hours and raising £36 million each year. Although most are based in hospitals, 40% of Friends organisations undertake some form of community based activity, perhaps attached to a nursing home, GP practice, prison court, day-centre, specialist unit, or directly in people's homes.

Friends volunteers work to meet local needs identified in partnership with healthcare professionals, including undertaking fundraising for equipment or buildings, providing services such as visiting or befriending, running libraries and hospital radio, shops/trolleys and tea bars, carer support schemes, lunch clubs and day centres, drop-in centres, transport services, guiding services and much more.

For further details contact the above address.

NATIONAL BLOOD SERVICE
Southampton Centre, Coxford Road, Southhampton SO16 5AF; ☎02380-296700; fax 02380-296783; www.blood.co.uk.
The National Blood Service needs volunteers to help prepare and serve refreshments to blood donors at various venues across the South Region. Travel expenses are paid. Please contact the Collection Planning Department at the above address.

ST PANCRAS HOSPITAL VOLUNTARY SERVICES DEPARTMENT
4 St. Pancras Way, London NW1; ☎020-7530 3339.
The range of jobs for volunteers at St Pancras Hospital is very varied: chatting to patients, writing letters, helping with arts, crafts and pottery, doing the shopping for patients, accompanying wheelchair patients to parks or on other outings and other activities run by the Activities Organiser, helping with the trolley ship and entertainment afternoons. There is a well organised voluntary programme for the large number of helpers under the direction of a full time Voluntary Help Organiser. The patients at St. Pancras are primarily geriatrics, but there are also psychiatric and tropical diseases wards and two Day Hospitals (Psychiatric and Elderly). Volunteers are also needed from time to time in these areas to assist in groups. Many of the patients have been in hospital for a long time and are in particular need of contact with ordinary people leading ordinary lives. Personal attention to lonely patients, whether in the capacity of listener or entertainer, is invaluable.

Volunteers are provided with overalls and free meals, but no accommodation. All volunteers must commit themselves to three hours per week for at least eight weeks. Volunteers of any nationality over 18 years of age can bring pleasure to a person in hospital. The most important requirement is the possession of a cheerful and relaxed personality.

Applications may be submitted to the Voluntary Services Manager at the Hospital.

UNIVERSITY COLLEGE LONDON HOSPITALS NHS TRUST
Voluntary Services Department, Private Patients Wing, Huntley Street, London WC1E 6AU; ☎020-7380 9828; www.uclh.org

The Department co-ordinates a wide variety of patient-orientated activities in several hospitals within the Trust. It is always looking for responsible and reliable people to join its regular team of just under 200 people who offer their time and support for the well-being of patients.

Volunteers do not need any special skills, other than good spoken English and a genuine interest in people. Volunteers are offered meal vouchers and local travelling expenses but not accommodation.

Enquiries should be made to the Voluntary Services manager at the above address.

Pressure Groups

Most charities and voluntary organisations would like to improve public knowledge of and interest in their chosen area, whether it is research into heart disease or care for the mentally handicapped. Pressure groups go further than this and are working for long-term defined changes not just in public perception, but in real terms.

Those groups listed in this chapter have many different objectives, from campaigning for nuclear disarmament to fighting for the human rights of prisoners of conscience abroad. Clearly, a prospective volunteer is required to share the views of the organisation he or she would like to help. Organisations that are protesting against specific local developments, such as the extension of a motorway, or the closing of a village school, have not been included because such groups normally receive full coverage in the local media.#

ALCOHOL CONCERN
Waterbridge House, 32-36 Loman Street, London SE1 OEE; ☎020-7928 7377; e-mail contact@alcoholconcern.org.uk; www.alcoholconcern.org.uk

There are many local alcohol advice agencies which train and use volunteers as alcohol counsellors to give individual help to those who come to them with problems. Alcohol Concern operates a scheme called VACTS (Volunteer Alcohol Counsellors Training Scheme) which is a national initiative set up to ensure minimum standards in the training and on-going supervision of volunteer counsellors. Local alcohol agencies whose courses meet the agreed minimum standards are granted official recognition and any counsellors who undertake the recognized course of training and supervision are eligible for formal accreditation.

For further details on the scheme and information on which agencies train volunteers to the VACTS standard, contact Ewa Cwirko-Godycka at the above address.

AMNESTY INTERNATIONAL
UK Section, 99-119 Rosebery Avenue, London EC1R 4RE; ☎020-7814 6200; fax 020-7833 1510; e-mail information@amnesty.org.uk; www.amnesty.org. uk
Amnesty International is a worldwide voluntary movement of people who campaign for human rights. It is independent of any government, political idealogy, economic interest or religion. Its mission is promoting general awareness of human rights and opposing specific abuses of human rights.

Volunteers are needed to do routine clerical work: envelope stuffing, typing, wrapping parcels etc. Travelling expenses are reimbursed for office helpers and commercial luncheon vouchers are provided.

Enquiries should be sent to the Volunteer Coordinator, Amnesty International UK, at the above address.

ANIMAL AID
The Old Chapel, Bradford Street, Tonbridge, Kent TN9 1AW; ☎01732-364546; fax 01732-366533; e-mail info@animalaid.org.uk; www.animalaid.org.uk
This UK based organisation campaigns against all animal abuse (including vivisection, factory farming, the fur trade and animals in circuses), and promotes living without cruelty as an alternative. Volunteers are needed occasionally to assist with general office duties at Tonbridge including computer data entry, amending letters, packing up letters and parcels. Applicants may be of any nationality and travel expenses are paid.

Applications should be made to Mary Shephard at the above address.

CAMPAIGN AGAINST ARMS TRADE
11 Goodwin Street, Finsbury Park, London N4 3HQ; ☎020-7281 0297; fax 020-7281 4369; e-mail enquiries@caat.org.co.uk; www.caat.org.uk
CAAT is the UK's only focused, single issue, grassroots campaign devoted to ending the international arms trade. It operates in the UK and has many volunteers in its London office undertaking research, administrative, press, fundraising and campaign work. Tasks are varied and can include writing briefings, data entry, organising events and lots of envelope stuffing. CAAT refunds travel expenses and provides a vegetarian lunch. Anyone interested in volunteering should contact Kathryn Busby, using the contact details above.

CAMPAIGN FOR NUCLEAR DISARMAMENT (CND)
162 Holloway Road, London N7 8DQ; ☎020-7700 2393; fax 020-7700-2357; e-mail cnd@gn.apc.uk; www.cnduk.org
The aim of CND is to persuade the Government to abandon nuclear weapons, and all foreign policy based on their use. The membership of 25,000 is distributed among about 150 local groups which collect signatures for petitions against nuclear warfare, hold meetings, and recruit people to join in nationally organised marches and demonstrations, and help organise them. Specific weapons recently campaigned against include Trident, Britain's nuclear weapons system and French nuclear testing in the Pacific. Membership is optional: any supporter is welcome to join in the activities of the organisation.

Those interested should apply to the organisation at the above address to find out the address of their local group. There is also a youth CND section at the same address (see under *Youth & Student Campaign for Nuclear Disarmament* below).

CHILD POVERTY ACTION GROUP (CPAG)
94 White Lion Street, London N1 9PF; ☎020-7837 7979; e-mail staff@cpag. demon.co.uk
CPAG works to draw attention to the problems of the impoverished and to provide these people with advice concerning their rights. They accomplish this by publishing research pamphlets, such as *The Welfare Benefits Handbook*. Volunteers are needed to carry out the clerical work of sending out the literature. Travelling expenses are paid and an allowance is given for lunch.

Enquiries may be addressed to CPAG at the above address.

FARMERS' WORLD NETWORK
The Arthur Rank Centre, National Agriculture Centre, Stoneleigh Park, Warks. CV8 2LZ; ☎024-7669 6969 ext. 420; fax 024-7641 4808; e-mail adrian@fwn. org.uk; www.fwn.org.uk
The Farmers' World Network is a group of farmers and people with agricultural connections which seeks to promote awareness among the United Kingdom farming community of the problems of developing countries and the relationship between European and Third World agriculture. Volunteers are also needed to carry out basic administration in the office at the above address or carry out research assignments, possibly from home.

Volunteers need a knowledge of agriculture or food production but no other restrictions apply.

Those interested should contact the Executive Director at the above address.

THE FAWCETT SOCIETY
1-3 Berry Street, London EC1V OAA; tel 020-7253 2598 ext. 202; e-mail info@fawcettsociety.org.uk; www.fawcettsociety.org.uk
The Fawcett Society is the UK's campaign for equality between men and women. Established in 1866, it has its roots in the Suffragette movement. Today it is a modern and vibrant campaigning organisation with thousands of individual members and a network of local groups and partnership organisations.

Fawcett has an all-year round intern and volunteering programme, offering short and longer-term placements, full or part-time. Interns/volunteers are assigned to particular projects/campaigns or task areas; work includes assisting policy work and research as well as general administrative tasks. There are usually three to four interns working at Fawcett at any one time. Travel within Greater London is reimbursed and a fixed daily lunch allowance is paid.

More information and an application form can be downloaded from the website. Applications should be made at least two months in advance.

FRIENDS OF THE EARTH
26-28 Underwood Street, London W1 1JQ; ☎020-7490 1555; fax 020-7490 0881; e-mail info@foe.co.uk; www.foe.co.uk
For over 20 years FOE has led the way in putting forward positive solutions to many of the environmental problems which threaten this planet. FOE campaigns locally, nationally and internationally in order to get politicians, industry and individuals to take action to protect the environment. It is one of the UK's leading environmental pressure groups and campaigns on more issues than any other environmental organisation.

FOE is committed to empowering local communities and individuals to get actively involved in the debate to protect the environment. We strongly believe that pressure for change is most effective when people have access to the facts and we devote considerable resources to research, information and education activities and to publishing and distributing innovative environmental materials.

FOE employs over 100 staff, based mainly at the national office in north London. There are also small regional offices in: Belfast, Birmingham, Bristol, Cambridge, Cardiff, Leeds, Brighton, Liverpool, and Luton.

Volunteering opportuunities. Volunteers play a vital role in the success of the organisation. There are usually about 40 volunteers helping at the London office, about 15 in the regional offices and over 2,300 people working on a voluntary basis in local network groups throughout England, Wales and Northern Ireland.

The London and Regional Offices need anyone interested in pursuing a career in environmental campaigning or administration within the voluntary/environmental sector, volunteering at FOE offers an opportunity to gain valuable work experience. Volunteers carry out a variety of administrative support work from helping with mailouts and sorting incoming post to assisting with research and information gathering work. For further details and an application form send a SAE to the Volunteer Coordinator at the London address.

Volunteering in your local area. anyone living outside reasonable travelling distance from London or the regional offices can get involved with FOE through local groups.

FOE has a network of around 250 local voluntary groups. As a member of a local group there are opportunities to get involved with a range of activities: organising fund-raising events, and helping to distribute leaflets and newsletters. Local groups meet on average one evening a month. For further details please register on the website.

GREEN ALLIANCE
40 Buckingham Palace Road, London SW1W 0RE; ☎020-7233 7433; fax 020-7233 9033; e-mail ga@green-alliance.org.uk; www.green-alliance.org.uk
Green Alliance is an environmental charity working to promote sustainable development by ensuring that the environment is at the heart of decision-making. It works with senior people in government, parliament, business and the environmental movement to encourage new ideas, dialogue and constructive solutions. A London-based environmental policy organisation; Its central aim is to raise the prominence of the environment on the agendas of the key policy-making institutions of the UK and in so doing to help improve their environmental performance across the board in Britain and throughout the world.

Volunteers are needed to assist with several tasks from administrating to policy research in the London office. Applicants can be of any nationality but they must have a work permit and be able to speak English; specialist office skills would also be useful. Long-term volunteers prepared to commit to work one or two days a week for six months preferred.

Please apply to R. Butterworth at the above address.

GREENPEACE
Canonbury Villas, London N1 2PN; ☎020-7865 8100; fax 020-7865 8200/8201; e-mail info@uk.greenpeace.org; www.greenpeace.org.uk
The UK-based administrative office of the international environmental pressure group engages volunteers to help with fund-raising and routine office work every year. Volunteers are required all the year round. Travel expenses will be reimbursed.

Those interested should contact Human Resources, at the above address.

LIBERTY (NATIONAL COUNCIL FOR CIVIL LIBERTIES)
21 Tabard Street, London SE1 4LA; ☎020-7403 3888; e-mail info@liberty-human-rights.org.uk; www.liberty-human-rights.org.uk
Liberty is a pressure group which works to defend and extend civil liberties throughout the UK. Volunteers at the London office help prepare publications, assist with research or perform routine administrative tasks/ volunteer lawyers assist with legal casework. A luncheon allowance is provided for volunteers and travelling expenses are paid inside London.

Enquiries should be sent to the Office Manager at the above address.

MINORITY RIGHTS GROUP INTERNATIONAL (MRG)
379 Brixton Road, London SW9 7DE; ☎020-7978 9498; fax 020-7738 6265; e-mail minority.rights@mrgmail.org; www.minorityrights.org
MRG International is an NGO working to secure the rights of ethnic, religious and linguistic minorities and indigenous peoples worldwide. Its activities are focused on international advocacy, training, publishing and outreach. Although space restrictions mean that MRG is able to accept only a small number of volunteers, it is happy to consider applications from individuals who wish to apply. Members from ethnic minority communities and refugees are especially welcome. Work is likely to involve the following: assistance to members of staff, helping with mailing and reception duties. Travelling expenses within London are paid. Enquiries to the above address.

PRISONERS ABROAD
89-93 Fonthill Road, Finsbury Park, London N4 3JH; ☎020-7561 6820; e-mail info@prisonersabroad.org.uk; www.prisonersabroad.org.uk
This charity works for the welfare of British prisoners in foreign jails. The specific work done for individual prisoners varies enormously; liaising with foreign and British lawyers, and prisons and other authorities, writing personally to prisoners and organising penpals, providing funds for prisoners to buy essentials like blankets and medicines, etc. Volunteers are needed all year round to help with all office activities; typing and other clerical work, answering telephone and postal queries, word processing and writing letters to prisoners. Volunteers normally help for a minimum of three months on a regular basis.

Good communication skills are important and languages are an advantage but not essential. Travelling expenses and a lunch allowance are paid.

Volunteers should e-mail: volunteer@prisonersabroad,org.uk.

RAIL FUTURE (Railway Development Society)
Room 107, The Colourworks, Dalston, London, E8 3DP; ☎020-7249, 5533; fax 020-7254 6777; e-mail info@railfuture.org.uk; www.railfuture.org.uk
The RDS was formed in 1978 by an amalgamation of earlier societies. It is a national pressure group, with a network of local branches, fighting for the improvement of Britain's railway system as a vital environmental issue. It maintains regular contact with Railtrack, the Rail Franchising Director, Train Operating Companies, freight customers, ministers, MPs and local authorities. It produces reports, leaflets, a quarterly journal and branch newsletters.

It requires over 100 volunteers a year to help with its activities. Involvement can be at a national or local level. There are no restrictions on applicants and no special qualifications are required.

Enquiries to the above address.

SURVIVAL INTERNATIONAL
6 Charterhouse Buildings, London EC1M 7ET; ☎020-7687 8700; fax 020-7687 8701; e-mail info@survival-international.org; www.survival-international.org
Survival International is a worldwide organisation supporting tribal peoples, standing for their right to decide their own future and helps them protect their lives, lands and human rights. Survival works for threatened tribal peoples in the Americas, Africa, Asia and Australasia. Survival lobbies international organisations, governments and multi-national companies, works to raise awareness of the situation of tribal peoples and supports practical realistic field projects with the aim of assisting the survival and self-determination of tribal peoples.

Volunteers are required in the London office to assist with clerical and secretarial work, library duties, visual aid materials and fundraising activities. A commitment of anything from half a day to five days per week for a minimum of three months is required.

Those interested should contact the London office.

SUZY LAMPLUGH TRUST
P.O. Box 17818, London, SW14 8WW; ☎020-8876 0305; fax 020-8876 0891; e-mail info@suzylamplugh.org; www.suzylamplugh.org
The Suzy Lamplugh Trust charity is the leading authority on personal safety. The Trust works alongside government, educational establishment, public bodies and the business sector and is dedicated to improving personal safety through research, campaigning, training, consultancy, practical support, educational resources and partnership initiatives.

Their office in East Sheen, London takes on volunteers to help with administration, database, IT, graphics, accounts, packing of resources (leaflets, books and alarms), and telephone answering. It is hoped volunteers will stay as long as possible for continuity.

Contact the address above for more details.

TOOLS FOR SELF RELIANCE
Ringwood Road, Netley Marsh, Southampton SO40 7GY; ☎023-8086 9697; e-mail info@tfsr.org; www.tfsr.org
Tools for Self Reliance aims to empower artisans working in developing countries so that they can better participate in the development of themselves and their communities. To achieve this work TFSR work with local partner organisations to provide hand tools and skills training, and by raising awareness in the UK of the causes of poverty. Volunteers are needed to help with all aspects of this work: refurbishing and packing tools, office work, building maintenance, gardening and general site work at the Head Office in Netley Marsh. TFSR also has a network of local voluntary groups throughout the UK.

THE VEGETARIAN SOCIETY
Parkdale, Dunham Road, Altringham, Cheshire WA14 4QG; ☎0161-925 2000; fax 0161-926 9182; e-mail info@vegsoc.org; www.vegsoc.org
The Vegetarian Society is a registered educational charity, promoting understanding and respect for vegetarian lifestyles. Volunteers are needed from time to time to help at headquarters. Tasks include photocopying, stuffing envelopes and data entry. Jobs tend to arise at short notice so the Society keeps a list of volunteers' addresses so they can contact them when needed. Those interested should contact the local network co-ordinator at the above address.

WORLD DEVELOPMENT MOVEMENT
25 Beehive Place, Brixton SW9 7QR; ☎020-7737 6215; fax 020-7274 8232;

e-mail wdm@wdm.org.uk; www.wdm.org.uk
The World Development Movement (WDM) is dedicated to tackling the root causes of poverty. WDM works together with people in the Third World WDM successfully changes the policies of governments and business that keep people poor. WDM is a democratic network of members, groups and campaigners. Volunteers are needed in the London office. Volunteer vacancies are advertised on the web page www.wdm.org.uk/vacancy/index.htm. Volunteers work as an integral part of the team in an atmosphere of respect and equality, performing a range of duties across several WDM departments. No accommodation is provided but travel expenses to and from the office and a lunch allowance are paid. Apply to the volunteers Coordinator.

YOUTH & STUDENT CAMPAIGN FOR NUCLEAR DISARMAMENT (Y+SCND)
162 Holloway Road, London N7 8DQ; ☎020-7607 3616; fax 020-7700 2357; e-mail info@youthstudentcnd.org.uk; www.youthstudentcnd.org.uk
Y+SCND campaigns for nuclear disarmament worldwide and on related issues such as nuclear power, and the USA's plans for a Missile Defence System. Volunteers in the London office are involved in organising and co-ordinating peace camps and actions, sending Y+SCND members to festivals over the summer to do campaigning work and producing the Y+SCND magazine *Now!* New members and activists are always welcome. Volunteers are always needed in the office to do organisational and administration work, and all over the country to join or establish local groups to further the aims of Y+CND.
Contact the office if interested in getting involved. There are also separate national offices for Scotland (15 Barrland Street, Glasgow G41 1QH) and Wales (Nantgaredig, Cynghordy, Dyfed SA20 OLR).

Prisons and Probation

There is a strong historical link between volunteers and prisons: indeed, the statutory Probation Service itself was begun when the authorities realised how successful voluntary involvement had been in reintegrating prisoners into society. The special value of volunteers in this work lies in the fact that they are not a formal part of 'the system', and so offenders often respond more readily and openly to them than they would to paid and officially appointed officers.

By visiting a convicted prisoner, a volunteer can be of use either by simply providing companionship, or by maintaining a link with the prisoner's family, as a period of imprisonment can prove a strain on marriages. The need for the help of a volunteer does not end with the release of an offender; the support of a known and trusted volunteer can be of great help in finding a job and somewhere to live. This is especially valuable in time of high unemployment, as ex-prisoners will experience more difficulty than most people in finding work. The organisations listed below show the many ways in which a volunteer can be of use to a prisoner both before and after release.

LONDON PROBATION AREA
71/73 Great Peter Street, London SW1P 2BN; ☎020-7222 5656; fax 020-7222 0473; www.probation-london.org.uk

The Service undertakes a wide range of activities with voluntary helpers within Greater London Area. These relate to most aspects of the Probation and Prison Service's work and would entail, for example, one-to-one contact with clients, group work, adventure activities, or practical help on a regular or single task basis.

Applicants should be at least 18 years old and under most circumstances it would be helpful if they could offer their services for at least 12 months. The personal qualities needed are sound common sense, tolerance and kindness. Applicants must also be prepared to work closely with supervising Probation Officers.

Those interested should, in the first instance, contact, Partnership Support Unit, Mitre House, 223/237 Borough High Street, London SE1 1JD; ☎020-7740 8500.

NATIONAL ASSOCIATION FOR THE CARE AND RESETTLEMENT OF OFFENDERS (NACRO)
169 Clapham Road, London SW9 OPU; ☎020-7582 6500; www.nacro.org. uk

NACRO runs housing, employment, youth training, education and advice projects for offenders and others; provides research, information and training services for people concerned about crime and offenders; and contributes to the development of crime policy and the prevention of crime. Over 1,000 staff work on about 100 projects and other services throughout England and Wales.

Opportunities for voluntary work are limited to a small number of projects providing education for unemployed adults and activities for young people, which are organised on a local basis. NACRO aims to be an equal opportunities employer and to eliminate unfair discrimination against anyone in its selection process.

NACRO produces a free leaflet, *Voluntary Work with Offenders*. For a copy or more information, contact NACRO's National Publications & Information Department at the above address.

NATIONAL ASSOCIATION OF PRISON VISITORS
32 Newnham Avenue, Bedford, MK41 9PT; ☎01234-359763; e-mail info@napv.org.uk; www.napv.org.uk

In the UK prison visitors are officially appointed. Normally they make an appointment to see the governor of the prison nearest them. If this interview passes satisfactorily they are accepted for a probationary period of three months. After this they must be appointed by the Home Office. It is important that people in prison (and in other penal institutions) should not lose contact with the outside world. Prison staff and visiting probation officers have a part to play, but the prison visitor has a unique contribution to offer, working alongside this team rather than as a member of it. Although appointed by the Home Office and subject to the regulations of the prisons, he or she is a volunteer, not an 'official' and this independent status has an appeal to the prisoner. The main role of the visitor is to establish a one-to-one, impartial, non-authoritarian relationship with the prisoner. There are 1400 visitors in the UK and 8-10% of prisoners have prison visitors. The Association wishes to expand its activities and new recruits will be welcome. Prison visitors should not be confused with Voluntary Associates, who work in co-operation with the Probation and After-Care Service.

Visitors must be at least 21 and not over 70, and are normally expected to retire at 75. To be of value, visits must be made at frequent intervals, normally weekly or fort-nightly, early in the evening, and at weekends. Both men and women are taken on, and women visitors can visit men's prisons. Visitors usually visit their nearest prison.

Those interested should apply to the Governor of their nearest prison.

THE NEW BRIDGE
27a Medway Street, London SW1P 2BD; ☎020-7976 0779; fax 020-7976 0767; www.thenewbrige.org.uk
The New Bridge operates a nationwide befriending scheme for people who are in prison, parenting classes for young offenders in institutions in the South West, Feltham and Manchester and a Foreign Nationals initiative to help ameliorate the isolation of foreign prisoners held in British prisons. Some 250 volunteers lend their time to the organisation, of whom the majority are involved in the befriending scheme. This entails the volunteer keeping in touch with the prisoner through letters and visits while he or she is in prison and offering encouragement in starting a new life on their release. Volunteers should be aged at least 21, be good listeners, non-judgmental, mature in outlook and have an ability to cope. For parenting classes, experience of parenting, group work, working with offenders, or teaching is required, and for work with foreign nationals, fluency in at least one other language besides English is desirable. Expenses may be reclaimed, and those interested should write to the above address.

PRISON ADVICE AND CARE TRUST (PACT)
Lincoln House, 1-3 Brixton Road, London, SW9 6DE; ☎020-7582 1313; fax 020-7735 6077; e-mail info@pact.uk.net; www.imprisonment.org.uk
Pact is one of the leading charities working with prisoners and prisoners' families to reduce the damage prison inflicts and to support prisoners and their families back into the community. Its current projects include: a drop-in and Freephone Telephone Support, Advice and Information for prisoners' families, Visitor Centre management at various prisons, supervised play for children visiting prisons and campaigning for more children's facilities, visits for the most isolated prisoners, support for women with mental health needs on their first night in custody, nationwide volunteer recruitment, training and development, cheap, overnight hostel accommodation for families visiting prisoners in London, development of services for prisoners and prisoners' families in the Southwest.

The charity recruits, trains and supports volunteers to help in the Visitors' Centres, the play projects in prinson, working on the telephone helpline, office, administration, supporting the work of the first night in custody project at Holloway prison and visiting prisoners. The minimum age is 21 years.

SOVA
Chichester House, 37 Brixton Road, London SW9 6DZ; ☎020-7793 0404; fax 020-7735 4410; e-mail mail@sova.org.uk; www.sova.org.uk
SOVA recruits and trains volunteers to work with offenders and young people at risk across England and Wales. About 2,000 volunteers are deployed at any one time. The types of work volunteers are involved in include teaching basic skills, helping offenders with a range of practical problems, housing, benefits, employment, substance abuse etc. and befriending young offenders (10-17 year-olds)/young people who are disadvantaged.

To be eligible volunteers need to have a minimum of two hours available each week during the daytime (9am to 5pm) for at least one year, aged over 17 and if an ex-offender themselves to have been out of prison for at least one year. Volunteers are needed all year round and receive expenses.

Anyone interested should contact the above address.

Problems, Emergencies and Housing

During the 1990s, the sight of the homeless person bedding down for the night in a cardboard box amongst many others became all too familiar an image and it is a phenomenon still with us. There are many people trapped by poverty, who find it hard to cope and resort to living on the streets. The following organisations illustrate how the individual can help to alleviate homelessness and the problems that accompany it.

Many of the organisations listed below deal with individuals who are facing a rapid succession of linked problems, such as bereavement, poverty, homelessness, unemployment and hopelessness. Without some assistance many such cases may end up with suicide, alcohol or drug abuse, or crime. Sometimes a friendly voice, interested enough to listen to them can make all the difference; for many, it is not so simple. It is significant that the suicide rate has dropped since the Samaritans began operating. In other cases skilled help is needed, to liaise with council housing departments, for example.

Some of the organisations listed under *Sick and Disabled People*, *Children and Youth*, *Elderly People* and *Prisons and Probation* also contain provisions for dealing with crises within their respective areas of activity.

ACTION ON HOMESLESSNESS
12/14 Duke Street, Trowbridge, Wiltshire BA14 8EA; ☎01225-776606; e-mail midcalf@cableinet.co.uk
Based in Trowbridge AOH provides a variety of services to clients that are homeless, vulnerably housed or socially excluded. Volunteers are needed who can offer at least one day a week to work within a day-centre or with AOH housing/training projects. For more details, please call the above number.

HOLY CROSS CENTRE
Holycross Church, The Crypt, Cromer Street, London WC1H 8JU; tel/fax 020-7278 8687; e-mail cmt@hcct.org.uk; www.hcct.org.uk
This centre in the Kings Cross area of London is social centre for people with mental health issues and drug/alcohol problems. About 40 part-time volunteers are needed to run the Centre, catering and befriending clients and offering peer support in a friendly and informal atmosphere, with the possibility of teaching arts and crafts and computing. Volunteers work five hours per week and the minimum commitment is three months. In return volunteers get travel expenses and a meal for each session. Training and support are given.

Apply to M. Willett, Centre Management Team, at the above address.

HOMELINK
45-47 Blythe Street, London E2 6LN; ☎020-7729 7573; fax 020-7729 7589;

e-mail Homelink@dial.pipex.com
HomeLink is a rent-in-advance scheme that assists non-priority single homeless people into tenancies in the private-rented sector, primarily in East and North London. HomeLink has a team of Tenancy Sustainability Volunteers who offer support to clients. Volunteers may be assigned to clients whilst they look for accommodation to offer· support and encouragement; to clients who are moving in to new homes and need support in setting up home; to existing clients experiencing difficulties. The main role of HomeLink's volunteers being to support, encourage and empower clients as they make the transition from homelessness to having settled, independent accommodation. There are limited opportunities for property sourcing and office volunteers.

Experience of similar kind of work not required as training given. Applicants will need really good communication skills and empathy with clients and a good standard of English. Out of pocket expenses including travel are paid and financial help with childcare. Some of the tenants are refugees and volunteers with appropriate languages are very welcome. As a rule volunteers spend around 2-4 hours a week with clients.

HOUSING JUSTICE
209 Old Marylebone Road, London NW1 5QT; ☎020-7723 7273; fax 020-7723 5943; e-mail info@housingjustice.org.uk; www.housingjustice.org.uk
Housing Justice has ten Housing Advice Centres (HACs) across the country. The HACs help anyone with a housing problem, including landlord and tenant issues, threatened homelessness and homelessness. Each HAC has its own opening hours and different range of services. Volunteers are needed to work in the advice centres, to do administrative work and help with projects.

Those interested should apply to the above address or to their local HAC.

SALVATION ARMY
101 Newington Causeway, London SE1 6BN; ☎020-7367 4871; fax 020-7367 4712; e-mail thq@salvationarmy.org.uk; www.salvationarmy.org.uk
The Salvation Army performs a greater variety and volume of social service than any other voluntary organisation in the world. It has 25,000 Officers in 84 countries who have dedicated their lives to the service of God in the Army; but their work is made even more effective by the support of individuals who give voluntary help in hostels, homes and centres. In Britain alone the Army has nearly 1,000 centres of worship, evangelism, and community activity, as well as 125 social centres, all of which operate varying programmes for helping others.

There now exists in Britain a nationwide network of homes, hostels and other centres caring for people in physical and moral need. Although much of the work is done by officers, volunteers can provide valuable ancillary services.

For further details contact the Personnel Secretary, Social Services, at the above address.

THE SAMARITANS
The Upper Mill, Kingston Road, Ewell KY17 2AF; ☎020-8394 8300; fax 020-8394 8301; www.samaritans.org
The Samaritans is a registered charity, founded in 1953. The Samaritans' service is available 24 hours to provide confidential and emotional support for people who are experiencing feelings of distress or despair, including those which may lead to suicide.

Volunteers do not need any formal qualifications or previous experience to be a Samaritan. But a natural ability to listen and remain open-minded are essential. You also need to be over 18 and available for a three to four hour shift, including some night work.

You can apply either by contacting us through the website, the Volunteer Recruitment number (08705 627282), or by contacting your local samaritans branch. If selected, you will get full training and support as a volunteer.

If you don't think being a listening volunteer is for you but would like to help in other ways, please do contact us.

SHELTER, National Campaign for the Homeless
88 Old Street, London EC1V 9HU; ☎020-7505 2000; e-mail info@shelter.org.uk; www.shelter.org.uk

Shelter helps provide a housing aid service and aims to improve housing conditions all over the country, as well as offering telephone advice direct to London's homeless people. Volunteers work in the national headquarters and in the regional offices around the country. The type of work that they do relates to skills; for example, some may have office experience which is always useful, while others may have a specialized knowledge of housing or campaigning. But enthusiasm and conscientiousness are also valued. In addition, many people help to finance the organisation with fund raising events. All are welcome to join local groups or become members of the campaign.

The commitment of time to Shelter depends on the volunteer. Some volunteers have helped for years, while others only do so for a week or two. Travel expenses are reimbursed.

Applicants should contact the supporter helpdesk on the telephone number above for an information pack.

WOMEN'S AID FEDERATION OF ENGLAND (WAFE)
P.O. Box 391, Bristol, BS99 7WS; ☎0117-944 4411 admin; 08457-023468 (helpline 24 hrs); fax 0117-924 1703; e-mailinfo@womensaid.org.uk; www.womensaid.org.uk

Women's aid provides advice, information and temporary refuge for women and their children threatened by emotional or physical abuse, including violence, harassment or sexual abuse. Through 204 autonomous local groups it provides information, advice and refuge. The National office provides a helpline service, as well as information and publications to both the general public and local groups. It also lobbies on issues concerned with domestic violence and related legal issues.

The Head Office does not handle volunteers for local branches. For this, contact your nearest branch through the telephone directory or visit the website.

WOMEN'S AID LTD
Everton House, 47 Oid Cabra Road, Dublin 7, Ireland; ☎+353 18684721; fax; +353 18684722; freephone helpline: 1800-341 900 (access in Ireland only); e-mail info@womensaid.ie ; www.womensaid.ie

Women's Aid is an organisation which provides advice and support to women and children suffering physical, emotional, sexual and financial abuse in their own homes. Women's Aid also provides training to other groups who come into contact with women and children who are suffering from domestic violence.

The aims of Women's Aid include providing education and awareness to groups in order to increase levels of awareness about the issue, lobbying government and state agencies on social and legal reform and initiating research and compiling statistics on the extent of domestic violence in Ireland. Volunteers can assist with work in areas such as the crisis helpline, fundraising activities and charity shop work.

There are no special requirements, but the ability to show empathy, concern and a non-judgmental attitude is essential for all voluntary work with Women's Aid. Workers on the helpline are required to undergo the helpline training.

Sick and Disabled People

The National Health Service is unable to provide full support for all those who have chronic illnesses or permanent disabilities. The organisations in this section are able to help fill this gap because they have specialised knowledge of these conditions and can provide appropriate support.

Volunteers can help these organisations in a wide variety of ways, whether directly, perhaps by helping with swimming therapy, or indirectly, such as by walking puppies for future training as guide dogs for the blind. In cases such as Arthritis Care (below) there is a particular need for volunteers with the relevant disabilities or injuries. In other cases, able-bodied volunteers prove more useful.

Other sections dealing specifically with the sick and disabled include *Hospitals*, *Children and Youth* and *The Elderly*.

ARTHRITIS CARE
18 Stephenson Way, London NW1 2HD; ☎020-7380 6500; fax 020-7380 6605; www.arthritiscare.org.uk

Arthritis Care is the largest UK-wide voluntary organisation working with and for all people with arthritis. It aims to empower people to take control of their arthritis, their lives and their organisation. It has groups nationwide and 70,000 supporters. AC offer The Source, a helpline service for young people with arthritis by telephone letter and e-mail. Freephone 0808 808 2000 weekdays 10am-2pm. It also offers a range of self-management and personal development training courses for people with arthritis of all ages to enable people to be in charge of their arthritis. AC also runs four hotels in the UK and produces a range of publications including a bi-monthly magazine. For more information about Arthritis Care call the information line 0845 600 6868.

Thousands of volunteers support the organisation nationwide by helping to run local branches and groups, delivering training courses, providing telephone support and promoting Arthritis Care and its work. For more information contact your local branch; details are on the website.

BIRMINGHAM TAPES FOR THE HANDICAPPED ASSOCIATION
20 Middleton Hall Road, Kings Norton, Birmingham B30 1BY; ☎0121-628 3656; fax 0871-242 8647; e-mail d.demaine@tiscali.co.uk

The Association sends a monthly tape-recorded sound magazine to handicapped people around the country.

Those interested in helping should contact Mr Derek L Hunt, Honorary Secretary, at the above address.

BRISTOL CANCER HELP CENTRE
Grove House, Cornwallis Grove, Clifton, Bristol BS8 4PG; ☎0117-980 9500; e-mail info@bristolcancerhelp.org; www.bristolcancerhelp.org

Opened in 1980, the Centre offers programmes which complement orthodox medical treatment for cancer patients. The patient receives medical supervision and counselling on nutrition, lifestyle and relaxation and meditation methods, as treatment is based on the principle that the whole person rather than just the disease should be treated. Approximately 20 volunteers are needed all year round to assist with the Centre's shop and busy helpline, gardening, fund raising and clerical duties. Ideally volunteers work for a half or full day per week on an on-going basis.

Volunteers should be reliable, over 17 years old, and have a caring but humorous personality. A driving licence is an advantage but not essential. Only in special circumstances will travelling expenses be paid, but lunch is free.

Those interested should contact the Volunteer Coordinator at the above address.

BRITISH LIMBLESS EX-SERVICEMEN'S ASSOCIATION (BLESMA)
185-187 High Road, Chadwell Heath, Romford, Essex RM6 6NA; ☎020-8590 1124; fax 020-8599 2932; e-mail blesma185@btconnect.com; www.blesma. org

BLESMA operates two residential homes and a welfare service to make sure that limb-less ex-servicemen and women (including spouses) do not suffer hardship. The Association operates a regular Welfare Visiting Service through its branches across the country. Organized social activities are arranged and a general information and advice service is provided.

The Association needs some 50 volunteers to help branches with welfare visits throughout the country. The amount of time given is up to individual volunteers. Possession of a driving licence would be advantageous and out of pocket expenses will be paid.

For further details contact the General Secretary at the above address.

THE BRITISH RETINITIS PIGMENTOSA SOCIETY (BRPS)
P.O. Box 350, Buckingham, MK18 1GZ; ☎01280-821334; (office); 01280-860363 (helpline); fax 01280-815900; e-mail info@brps.org.uk; www.brps. org.uk

The Society was formed in 1975 and it aims to give relief to sufferers of RP in any way which may help them to live with, or overcome, their handicap, and to raise funds for scientific research to provide treatments leading to a cure for retinitis pigmentosa It is a membership organisation run by volunteers with over thirty-five branches throughout the UK.

For further details of how volunteers can help with this please contact the Honorary Secretary at the above address.

COPE FOUNDATION
Bonnington, Montenotte, Cork, Eire; ☎+353-214 507131; fax +353-21 4507580; e-mail hoadmin@cope-foundation.ie; www.cope-foundation.ie.

The Foundation operates a number of services for people with a mental handicap in Cork city and County, including care units, schools, training centres, hostels and sheltered workshops. Voluntary help is needed in all of these areas, especially during the school holidays.

For further details contact the Head of Human Resources at the above address.

CYSTIC FIBROSIS TRUST
11 London Road, Bromley, Kent BR1 1BHY; ☎020-8464 7211; fax 020-8313 0472; e-mail enquiries@cftrust.org.uk; www.cftrust.org.uk

The Trust is a registered charity with branches throughout Britain which give support to patients and their families. Volunteers are generally already familiar with cystic fibrosis and its problems, due to prior experience of the disease; however, outside volunteers within the local community are welcome.

Enquiries may be sent to the above address.

DARWIN NURSERIES & FARM SHOP
Newmarket Road, Cambridge; ☎01223-293911.
Darwin Nurseries is a horticultural project for adults with learning disabilities, offering the opportunity for people to be involved in all aspects of growing plants and selling them to the public. Volunteers do not need any special qualifications but it would be helpful if applicants enjoyed working outside.

Applications to the above address.

DEAFBLIND UK
The National Centre for Deafblindness, Cygnet Road, Hampton, Peterborough PE7 8FD; tel ☎01733-358100; fax 01733-358356; e-mail info@deafblind. org.uk; www.deafblind.org.uk
Deafblind is the association of deafblind and dual sensory impaired people. It represents, supports and provides comprehensive services for its deafblind members, their carers and professionals who work with them.

Deafblind Uk's volunteer befriender scheme offers people the chance to make a real difference in their community by offering friendship to a local deafblind person. In exchange for some of their spare time and compassion, volunteer befrienders will have the satisfaction of knowing that their efforts have made a real difference.

Volunteers are like a 'good neighbour' and may be asked to help by visiting a deafblind person in their home for a chat, help write a letter or read mail and a newspaper. They may be asked to take a deafblind person out and about, shopping, visiting friends, or visit a club or run an errand.

Anyone interested in helping deafblind people and have time to spare should contact Lisa Bloodworth, Volunteers Co-ordinator.

DISABILITY SPORT ENGLAND
N17 Studios, Unit 4G, 784-788 High Road, Tottenham, London N17 ODA; ☎020-7490 4919; www.euroyellowpages.com/dse/dispengl.htm
Disability Sport England is the leading National Event Agency providing opportunities, in a variety of sports for people with a disability. The organisation has a strong membership base with ten regions around the country. Each of these co-ordinates qualifying events for our national competitions and fundraising events to support their work. Such events always require volunteers.

About 7,000 volunteers are recruited annually to help in the areas of field management, fundraising, public relations and general office duties. The work may be in a local club, within a region or in one of Disability Sport England's offices. A minimum commitment of one week is required all year round. An understanding of the needs of the disabled community within sport is necessary. Travel and out-of-pocket expenses may be paid.

An information pack is available at a cost of £2.50 from the above address.

DRUGSCOPE
Waterbridge House, 32-36 Loman Street, London SE1 OEE; ☎020-7928 1211; fax 020-7922 1771 e-mail info@drugscope.org.uk; www.drugscope.org.uk
Drugscope is a membership based organisation with over 1,000 members and is the national co-ordinating body for the drug abuse treatment field. Anyone interested in volunteer work in the area of combatting drug abuse may be able to obtain addresses of local agencies which may need volunteer helpers.

EATING DISORDERS ASSOCIATION
First Floor, Wensum House, 103 Prince of Wales Road, Norwich NR1 1DW;

☎0870 770 3256 (admin); 0845 634-1414 (adult helpline); e-mail info@edauk.com; www.edauk.com
The Eating Disorders Association (EDA) is a national charity offering support and information to people in eating distress along with their families, friends and professionals involved in the treatment of eating disorders.

Volunteers are needed nationwide to offer support in the form of self-help groups, or postal, telephone or e-mail support. Regional training days are provided. For further information about the Self Help Network contact Rachel Hogg - SHN Contacts Coordinator 0870-770 3256, ext 236; shn@edauk.com.

Volunteers are also needed for the helpline, based in Norwich. Full training is given to volunteers selected.

For further information about volunteering for the helpline in Norwich, please contact Sheila Hamner, Helpline Manager 0870 770 3256 0870 770 3256.

THE GUIDE DOGS FOR THE BLIND ASSOCIATION
Hillfields, Burghfield Common, Reading RG7 3YG; ☎0118-9838392; fax 0118-9838290; www.guidedogs.org.uk
Opportunities for helping with The Guide Dogs for the Blind Association include fundraising, puppy walking, boarding dogs, driving, and helping at the guide dog Centres. For more information about Guide Dogs and its activities, visit the website or telephone the above number.

HERTFORDSHIRE ACTION ON DISABILITY
Woodside Centre, The Commons, Welwyn Garden City, Herts. AL7 4DD; ☎01707-324581; fax 01707-371297; e-mail herts – action@dial.pipex.com
For over 40 years HAD has aimed to meet the needs of disabled people in Hertfordshire with services including counselling, equipment, accessible transport, exhibition and sales and driving assessments and instruction in a fully adapted car.

HAD also has its own hotel in Clacton-on-Sea allowing disabled people to go on holiday with volunteer help during the year. Helpers work on a rota basis, aiding the mobility of guests, to give companionship and assist them in dressing, transferring from wheelchair to bed/bath/toilet, pushing guests in wheelchairs to shops, church, the seafront etc. and escorting them on outings in the hotel minibus.

Volunteers, at the rate of six per fortnight, are needed annually to assist. Free return transport is provided to and from the Woodside Centre to Clacton. Volunteers also get free board and lodging. Ages are 18-70 years. Enquiries with a SAE to the above address.

KITH AND KIDS
c/o The Irish Centre, Pretoria Road, London N17 8DX; ☎020-8801 7432; fax 020-8885 3035; e-mail projects@kithandkids.org.uk; www.kithandkids.org.uk
Kith and Kids is a self-help organisation which provides support for the families of children with a physical or learning disability. Volunteers are needed to take part in social training schemes working on a two-to-one basis with learning disabled children and young people, helping them with everyday skills and helping to integrate them into the community. Volunteers must be aged a minimum of 16 years. No experience is necessary, but lots of enthusiasm is essential. Volunteers work a minimum of two consecutive weeks during August or a week at Christmas and Easter from 9.30am to 5pm daily. Lunch and travel expenses within the Greater London Area are provided. There is also a preparatory three-day training course before each project. There is no accommodation so volunteers should be based locally. Kith and Kids also organises a

one-week camping holiday in August with accommodation for volunteers provided.

For further details contact the volunteer organiser at the above address.

LONDON EAST AIDS NETWORK

60 St Mary Road, Walthamstow, London E17 9RE; ☎020-8509 3440; fax 020-8509 3920.

London East Aids Network is an HIV/AIDS support agency providing home support and DIY/gardening, children and families support, complementary therapies, benefits, housing and money advice, and supportive groups to people directly affected by HIV/AIDS in East London. The Network also runs regular events and health promotion campaigns. About 35 volunteers annually are recruited to help in these areas. Minimum period of commitment is one year. Travel expenses are paid.

Applications at any time of year to the Volunteer Co-ordinator at the above address.

MARIE CURIE CANCER CARE

89 Albert Embankment, London SE1 7TP; ☎020-7599 7788; e-mail volunteering@mariecurie.org.uk; www.mariecurie.org.uk

Marie Curie Cancer Care is dedicated to the care of people affected by cancer and the enhancement of their quality of life through its caring services, research and education. The Charity provides care for today and hope for tomorrow.

As a hospice volunteer you can get involved with tasks ranging from ward assistance, helping in day care, working on reception, community and bereavement support, gardening, complementary therapies, admin support and much more. This role will help to enrich the experience of the patients who are with the organisation.

For a different perspective of the Charity, you can apply to be a volunteer fundraiser and play a vital role in the work of Marie Curie helping organise and run fundraising events. Alternatively, you can join the team of volunteers who work in the 170 Marie Curie shops.

Whatever your interests, skills and experience and however much time you can spare, volunteers are always made welome and given training and support.

Applications to your local fundraising office, hospice or shop.

MIND (NATIONAL ASSOCIATION FOR MENTAL HEALTH)

15-19 Broadway, London E15 4BQ; ☎020-8519 2122; fax 020-8522 1725; e-mail contact@mind.co.uk; www.mind.co.uk

Mind is the leading mental health charity in England and Wales. Working for a better life for everyone experiencing mental distress; Mind campaigns for their right to lead an active and valued life in the community and is an influential voice on mental health issues

*Local Associations.*Mind's network of 218 local associations throughout England and Wales offers a range of services including supported accommodation, drop-in and day centres, befriending, counselling, advocacy and employment schemes and cannot operate without substantial help from volunteers.

Minds Matter.Mind's trading arm runs a network of charity shops around the country, marketing selected Mind products, also available through mail order. Volunteers are vital to help run these shops.

MULTIPLE SCLEROSIS SOCIETY OF GREAT BRITAIN AND NORTHERN IRELAND

MS National Centre, 372 Edgware Road, London NW2 6ND; ☎020-8438 0700; helpline: 0808-800 8000; fax 020-8438 0701; e-mail info@mssociety,org.uk

The Society is the largest national organisation dedicated to supporting people living with MS. Its main roles include raising public awareness of MS and its consequences, campaigning to enable people with MS to participate fully in all areas of society, funding research into the causes of and treatments for MS and providing practical and financial support to people with MS and their families/carers.

It is a volunteer-based organisation, depending heavily on volunteers for the management of its national leadership structures. It also depends on volunteers to provide a range of local support services.

Enquiries should be sent to the Director of Development at the above address who will forward them to the appropriate Branch.

MUSCULAR DYSTROPHY CAMPAIGN
7-11 Prescott Place, London SW4 6BS; ☎020-7720 8055; fax 020-7498 0670; e-mail info@muscular-dystrophy.org; www.muscular-dystrophy.org
The Muscular Dystrophy Campaign is the only UK charity focusing on all muscular dystrophies and allied disorders. It has pioneered the search for treatments and cures for over 40 years and provides practical, medical and emotional support to people affected by the condition. There are over 400 branches and representatives throughout the UK and Northern Ireland, all of whom are anxious for local volunteers helpers to assist in their fundraising and other activities.

Write to the Branch Services Co-ordinator at the above address for the details of local branches.

NATIONAL ECZEMA SOCIETY
Hill House, Highgate Hill, London N19 5NA; ☎020-7281-3553; e-mail mcox@eczema.org; www.eczema.org
This Society aims to promote mutual support for individuals and families coping with eczema. Volunteers are required to assist with the day-to-day running of the National Office and they may find themselves working within any of the Society's departments. Help is required all the year round. Both travel and lunch expenses are paid.

Those interested should contact Simon Evans or Margaret Cox at the above address.

NATIONAL SOCIETY FOR EPILEPSY
Chalfont St Peter, Gerrards Cross, Buckinghamshire SL9 0RJ; ☎01494-601300; fax 01494-871927; e-mail jeanette.harley@epilepsy.org.uk
The NSE welcomes volunteers to assist their work caring for and rehabilitating people with epilepsy. Volunteers are needed to raise funds, provide caring assistance, provide transport and act as escorts for outings, help at social events and sporting activities.

Help is needed at any time, but especially during the holiday periods. No qualifications are necessary. Travelling expenses to and from the Society are not paid, but holidays and outings are paid for.

Applications to Jeanette Harley at the above address.

PHAB
Summit House, Wandle Road, Croydon CR0 1DF; ☎020-8667 9443; e-mail info@phabengland.org.uk; www.phabengland.org.uk
Phab works through its national network of clubs in which physically disabled and able bodied people work together on an equal basis. Phab also arranges holidays and courses in which physically disabled and able bodied people live, work and play together. Volunteers can help with all aspects of these programmes.

For further information and details of local clubs contact the Director of Operations at the above address.

PARKINSON'S DISEASE SOCIETY OF THE UNITED KINGDOM LTD
215 Vauxhill Bridge Road, London SW1V 1EJ; ☎020-7931 8080; fax 020-7233 9908; e-mail mailbox@pdsuk.demon.co.uk
The aims of the society are threefold: to help patients and their relatives with the problems arising from Parkinson's Disease; to collect and disseminate information on the disease; and to encourage and provide funds for research into it. Voluntary workers provide vital assistance in the achievement of these aims; they assist at the national headquarters and run about 230 local branches. Helpers are especially desirable if they can assist in the setting up of new branches, as at present many voluntary workers are relatives of sufferers from the disease, who already have many demands on their time. Drivers are always welcome at local branches, and fuel costs are reimbursed where appropriate.

Enquiries should either be directed to the Manager at the above address, or to the Honorary Secretary of the local branch of the applicant.

RICHARD CAVE MULTIPLE SCLEROSIS HOLIDAY HOME
Leuchie House, North Berwick, East Lothian EH39 5NT; ☎01620-892864; fax 01620-893761; e-mail leuchie@mssociety.scotland.org.uk
The Holiday Home is run by the Multiple Sclerosis Society in Scotland for sufferers of multiple sclerosis of all ages. Volunteers are taken on to assist with health care, taking patients for walks, writing postcards and to accompany them on special outings. Vacancies could be available from February to December. The duration of stay will depend on suitablity and other factors. Driving licences useful, nursing qualifications especially welcome but not essential, any other skills may also be useful.

Applicants should be aged 17+ up to any age as long as they are fit and healthy and English-speaking. No lodgings but pocket money will be provided. Applications to The Manager at the above address.

RIDING FOR THE DISABLED ASSOCIATION
Lavinia Norfolk House, Avenue 'R', Stoneleigh Park, Warwickshire CV8 2LY; ☎024-7669 6510; fax 024-7669 6532; admin@riding-for-disabled.org.uk; www.riding-for-disabled.org.uk.
The aim of the Association is to provide disabled people with the opportunity to ride and/or carriage drive to benefit their health and wellbeing. There are Member groups throughout the UK, whose voluntary helpers are drawn from many sources. Travel and accommodation expenses cannot be met by the Association.

For further details prospective overseas volunteers should contact the International Liaison Officer in writing at the above address.

RAD CENTRE FOR DEAF PEOPLE
Walsingham Road, Colchester, Essex CO2 7BP; ☎01206-509509; fax 01206-769755; minicom: 01206-577090; e-mail info@royaldeaf.org.uk; www.royaldeaf.org.uk
RAD promotes the social, spiritual, and general welfare of deaf people. It seeks to achieve this by providing deaf centres, specialist support services, sign language, interpreting and communication support, religious and cultural activities and training.

ROYAL NATIONAL INSTITUTE FOR THE BLIND (RNIB)
105 Judd Street, London WC1H 9NE; ☎020-391 2383; helpline: 0845-7669999; www.rnib.org.uk.
RNIB is Britain's largest organisation working with and for blind and partially sighted people. RNIB provides over sixty services, which rely on the commitment, skills and experience of its volunteers. Voluntary opportunities exist in the following areas: administration, research, management, events, fundraising, assisting with activities, providing transport, home visiting, and many more.

ROYAL NATIONAL INSTITUTE FOR DEAF PEOPLE
19-23 Featherstone Road, Street, London EC1Y 8SL; ☎020-7296 8000; fax 020-7296 8199; e-mail helpline@rnid.org.uk; www.rnid.org.uk
The RNID is the major service providing organisation for deaf people in the UK. Most of its work is highly specialised. However, approaches by volunteers with administrative or office skills are welcomed in national and local offices in London, Bath, Birmingham, Salford, Belfast and Glasgow. Offers of voluntary fundraising support are always appreciated. Volunteers hoping to work directly with deaf people should contact their local deaf club, details of which can be obtained from the RNID.

SIGN
13 Station Road, Beaconsfield, Bucks HP9 1YP; tel/minicom 01494-816777; fax 01494-812555; e-mail sign@charityheadoffice.freeserve.co.uk; www.signcharity.org.uk
Sign offers a range of support to deaf people with mental health problems, providing long-term supportive accommodation and care in the community. It runs a club house in South West London, and accommodation in London, Manchester, Leeds and Buckinghamshire. Sign is working towards further national provision.

About 6-24 volunteers are recruited annually to help with befriender schemes, assist at the Sign clubhouse in South West London, occasionally assist with other projects and at head office. For befriending and working at the clubhouse, a knowledge of British Sign language is useful but for clerical and administration duties it is not necessary. Applicants must be able to communicate clearly in English. Travel and lunch expenses will be covered by Sign. Applications all year round – positions will be arranged according to the volunteer's availability and Sign's requirements – to the Administrator at the above address.

Sign produce the following publications: *Mental Health Services for Deaf People: Are They Appropriate?* (£6.50 plus postage and packing); *Mental Health Services: Forging New Channels* (£12 plus postage and packing); available from Forest Bookshop, 8 St John's Street, Coleford, Gloucestershire GL16 8AR.

ST JOHN AMBULANCE
27 St. John's Lane, London EC1M 4BU; ☎020-7324 4000; www.sja.org.uk/ www.stjohnwales.co.uk
The St John Ambulance is a body of 300,000 volunteers worldwide who give millions of hours of unpaid service every year to their local communities, providing first aid cover at local and national events, welfare work in the local community and youth work opportunities. New recruits are always welcome, with a UK-wide membership now numbers of over 55,000

Young people aged 5 to 10 can join Badgers and 10 to 18-year-olds can join Cadets, with anyone over 18 joining as an adult member in a variety of roles from First Aider, Unit Leader or Youth Worker to Fundraiser, PR, Community First Responder, etc.

For further information either ring the number above or your local office on 08700 10 49 50. In Wales ring the Welsh National Headquarters on 029-2062 7627.

TERRENCE HIGGINS TRUST/LIGHTHOUSE
52-54 Gray's Inn Road, London WC12 8JU; ☎020-7831 0330; fax 020-7242 0121; e-mail londonvols@tht.org.uk; www.tht.org.uk

The Terrence Higgins Trust is the UK's largest AIDS charity and continues to expand to meet the many demands which AIDS and HIV infection present to all. There are currently over 1000 volunteers nationwide, who provide help, advice, information, support and training not only to people with HIV and AIDS, but also to anyone concerned about this health crisis. The Trust provides direct services in Sussex, the West Midlands, Yorkshire, Oxfordshire as well as sharing information and its expertise throughout the UK and Europe.

Volunteers work locally in the befriending scheme as a 'buddy',on the Helpline, in the advice centre, counselling and administration. Special skills may be needed, but training is provided. Volunteers must be over 18 years and either London-based or close to one of the THT regional centres. Minimum commitment after training is six months or a year depending on volunteer position. The Trust pays travel expenses and office-based volunteers will receive lunch costs.

Those interested should contact the Volunteer Coordinator at the above address.

United States of America

Children & Youth

CHILDREN'S HOSPICE INTERNATIONAL
2202 Mt. Vernon Avenue, Suite 3C, Alexandria, VA 22301, USA; ☎ +1 703 684-0330; fax +1 703 684-0226; e-mail chiorg@aol.com; www.chionline.org
Children's Hospice International (CHI) provides resources and referrals to children with life-threatening conditions and their families. Volunteers are required to operate the helpline, make referrals, send information on request and work on special events and programmes. About 10 volunteers a year work in the headquarters office and over 30 on special events and programmes. Help is needed all year round. Applicants must be English-speaking. Business-related expenses will be covered but not travel to and from work. A list of publications produced by CHI is available from the above address.
Applications to the Administrator at the above address.

YWCA OF THE CITY OF NEW YORK
610 Lexington Avenue at 53rd Street, New York, NY 10022, USA; ☎ +1 212 755 4500; fax +1 212 755 3362; e-mail info@ywcanyc.org; www.ywcanyc. org
The YWCA-NYC has been pioneering social change for young women since 1870. It runs innovative programmes that improve the lives of the women, girls and families of New York City. The YWCA serves New Yorkers with a range of programmes including employment training, leadership development, networking for youth with disabilities and fitness and cultural programmes. The YWCA-NYC is part of a worldwide organisation with 25 million members.
Volunteer opportunities include Sales and Membership Services (free fitness membership provided), Young Women's Leadership board members, mentors and internships. Internships include work on site to assist the Program Coordinator with planning and chaperoning field trips, developing and co-delivering workshops and developing and directing group activities including the project for community action. Volunteers and unpaid interns should be available for autumn and spring semesters. Minimum of one day a week and 12 months commitment preferred.
Applications to the above address.

TUCSON CHILDREN'S MUSEUM
200 South Sixth Avenue, PO Box 2609, Tucson, AZ 85702-2609, USA; ☎ +1 520 792-9985; fax +1 520 792-0639; e-mail tuchimu@azstarnet.com; www. azstarnet.com/tuchimu
Tucson Children's Museum is a non-profit organisation that aims to excite children about learning, inspire them to set goals important to their futures and challenge them to reach their full potential. It does this by using fun, interactive, educational exhibits and hands-on programmes.

The Museum is visited by over 40,000 children a year, and is run by a small staff of full-time employees who depend on the assistance of volunteers to aid both the daily operation of the Museum and special events. About 25-30 volunteers are recruited annually either as educators to lead school tours or as activity assistants to help develop and implement activities. Seasonal and year round voluntary opportunities are available. Internships are also offered to those interested in the fields of Graphic Design, Art, Public Relations and Education. Applicants must be able to speak and understand English and have a willingness to work with children. Volunteers must be entirely self-funding.

Applications to the Education Specialist at the above address.

Community, Social & Cultural Projects

BOND STREET THEATRE
2 Bond Street, New York, NY 10012, USA; tel/fax +1 212-254 4614; e-mail info@bondst.org; www.bondst.org
The Bond Street Theatre was founded in 1976 to create innovative theatre works that communicate across lingual and cultural borders and it takes these works to diverse audiences worldwide. It uses the performing arts to address social, political and environmental issues as well as to entertain. Its socially concerned actors have trained extensively in the physical and gestural arts to develop a theatrical language that includes mime, circus arts, mask, stilts etc. that is both captivating and communicates universally.

Volunteers and interns are regularly taken on. Some volunteer posts last just a few days or a couple of weeks mainly in the marketing and publicity departments. It also offers internships in arts administration that includes everything from answering the telephone to accompanying rehearsals during the creation of new works.

Prospective volunteers/interns should contact Joanna Sherman, Artistic Director at the above address/e-mail.

THE BOWERY MISSION
132 Madison Avenue D, New York, NY 10016, USA; ☎ +1 800-871-6347 (volunteer information) 212 684 2800 (admin); fax +1 212 684 3740; email info@chaonline.org; www.bowery.org
The Bowery Mission offers meals, shelter, showers and clothing to desperate people living on the street. Homeless men are then challenged to enter a six to nine-month residential programme to experience the beginning of a permanent change in their lives. Up to 62 men at a time are helped to break their destructive habits with a programme that includes seminars, computer classes, bible study and job training.

Volunteers who feel they can offer love and respect and directly minister to New York City's homeless, are needed to tutor, serve the homeless and work with children. To volunteer, you must call the volunteer hotline or e-mail volunteer@chaonline.org. You will be asked to complete some paperwork, usually booking one to two months ahead for weekday meal service or three to four months in advance for Saturday opportunities. Internships are also available.

THE 52ND STREET PROJECT
500 West 52nd Street, 2nd Floor, New York, NY 10019, USA; ☎ +1 212 333-5252; fax +1 212 333-5598.

The 52nd Street Project is an organisation that creates original theatre with children from the Hell's Kitchen neighbourhood of New York and professional volunteer theatre artists. They take two to three interns to assist in various aspects of production, classes and administration. Interns work closely with the staff of five, with children in classes and rehearsals as well as a large number of professional actors, directors, designers and writers from the New York theatre community.

Internships are unpaid and take at least 24 hours per week for three months. For complete details about intern positions, including information on how to apply, please visit our website and look under *library* and then intern positions. With any questions, please contact the Associate Artistic Director.

FOOLS COMPANY INC
423 W. 46th Street, New York, NY 10036-3510; ☎ +1 212-307-6000; fax +1 212 268 1289; e-mail foolsco@nyc.rr.com

Fools Company produces and presents experimental performances and creative-process workshops in the heart of midtown Manhattan's vibrant Times Square theatre district where it has been based since 1977. Its work has also been seen in London, Paris and Tokyo and has garnered commendations and support from public and private sources alike.

Five to ten volunteers are taken on annually. Jobs and activities that volunteers can be interns in include most aspects of production, administration and technical areas including fund raising, programme development, marketing, public relations and the artistic and the organisational aspects of the company.

Volunteers/interns can be any nationality, at least 18 years of age, with a good command of English and the ability to live independently in an urban setting. They should have the willingness to work hard under pressure, a strong desire to learn, a robust sense of humour, a mature and patient attitude towards work, and have an interest in the performing arts.

Applications direct to the above address.

JACKSON HOLE FILM FESTIVAL (JHFF)
50 West Broadway, Jackson, Wyoming 83002, USA; ☎ +1 307 733 8144; fax +1 307 733 8144; e-mail volunteer@jhff.org; www,jhff.org

The Jackson Hole Film Festival is a non-profit organisation dedicated to independent film-making. The Festival's diverse programming includes an international category and a global awareness category. The JHFF aims to provide an environment that promotes cultural diversity, education and encourages economic growth throughout the Jackson Hole community and provides an invaluable forum for independent film and film-makers from around the globe, while providing spectacular visions for audiences.

Volunteers are needed annually in September for the festival and also year round. In return for a commitment of a minimum 12 hours, you can experience the behind-the-scenes excitement of the independent film industry. There are also year round programmes and two festivals a year. Volunteering is a great way to get your face known and perhaps be considered for other opportunities. Volunteers can do a variety of tasks including ushering, working in the Festival office, driving, security, ticket and merchandise selling, press liaison, hospitality, film industry registration and marketing. More information on the website.

An application form can be completed online or mailed to Capital Campaign Coordinator, Jackson Hole Film Festival, P.O. Box 1601, Wilson, WY 83014, USA.

JUBILEE PARTNERS
P.O. Box 68, Comer, GA 30629, USA; ☎ +1 707-783 5131; fax +1 706-783 5134; www.jubilee.partners.org
Jubilee Partners is a Christian service community in Comer, Georgia, dedicated to serving the poor and oppressed. The primary ministry is resettling newly arrived refugees in the USA. JP also campaigns to abolish the death penalty and is involved in various peacemaking activities. Volunteers' jobs include teaching English as a second language to refugees, childcare, gardening, maintenance and grounds upkeep, cleaning and cooking, construction, auto repair. Most volunteers do a variety of tasks. Applicants should be over 19, in good health, able to speak good English and able to obtain an visitor's visa to the United States on their own behalf. Volunteers should also be able to come for a complete term of January through May, June through August or September through December. There are ten volunteers per term. Dormitory style housing, food and pocket money ($15 per week) provided. Volunteers must also be prepared to participate in the spiritual life of the community. Apply direct.

THE NEW CONSERVATORY THEATRE CENTER (NCTC)
25 Van Ness Avenue, San Francisco, CA 94102, USA; ☎ +1 415 861-4914; fax +1 415 861-6988; e-mail email@nctcsf.org; www.nctcsf.org
NCTC was established in 1981 as a non-profit theatre school and performing arts complex. Voluntary opportunities include administration, teaching assistance, technical and box office support. About 15 volunteers are required annually for periods of between 3 and 6 months all year round. Applicants must have previous experience and/or an interest in the performing arts. No help is given with expenses although qualified interns may receive a stipend or minimum wage.
Applications to the Conservatory Director at the above address.

NEW DRAMATISTS
424 W.44th Street, New York, NY 10036, USA; ☎ +1 212-757 6960; fax +1 212-265 4738; e-mail NewDramatists@NewDramatists.org; www.NewDramatists.org
New Dramatists is based in New York city. Volunteers are needed to work in person at their NY headquarters in Manhattan. ND is a non-profit, theatre-related organisation which needs about 30 volunteers throughout the year for a variety of activities from office management to special events and fundraising. Volunteers must be able to speak English, fund themselves and pay for their own accommodation.
Apply direct to the organisation above.

NEW YORK BOTANICAL GARDEN
200ᵗʰ Street and Kazimiroff Blvd, Bronx, New York 10458, USA ☎ +1 718 817 8614; fax +1 718-220- 6504; e-mail asnowden@nybg.org; www.nybg.org
The New York Botanical Garden comprises 250 acres of beautiful gardens and historic structures and is the largest and most significant horticultural attraction and authority combining recreation and education. Volunteers are much in evidence working as tour guides, retail assistants and children's and adults explainers. Explainers introduce families to gardening, plants, science and the natural world. Volunteers can also help with horticulture and propagation, special events and benefits.
Volunteers should contact Anthony Snowden, Associate Director of Volunteer Serv-

ices (718-817 8564) or the above e-mail.

THE POETRY PROJECT
St Mark's Church, 131 East 10th Street, New York, NY 10003, USA; ☎ +1 212 674-0910; fax +1 212 529-2318; e-mail info@poetryproject.com; www. poetryproject.com
The Poetry Project is a non-profit arts organisation devoted to contemporary poetry. The Project produces three reading series per week, a bimonthly newsletter, a literary magazine (*The World Literary Journal*), a website, writing workshops and special events. About 20 volunteers are recruited annually to assist preparing for readings, proofreading, mailings, publicity, data entry and copy-editing. Applicants must have a strong interest in contemporary poetry and be fluent in English. Help is needed from September to May. Volunteers must be entirely self-funding but workshop registration is free for volunteers.

Applications to the Programme Co-ordinator at the above address.

RAINBOW HOUSE
20 East Jackson Blvd., Suite 1550, Chicago, IL 60604, USA; ☎ +1 312-935-3430; fax +1 312-935-5071; www.solidprint.com/rainbow/
Rainbow House is a Chicago-based non-profit organisation, that works towards ending violence in the home. It provides a shelter for women and children who are the victims of domestic violence and offers counselling, outreach and programmes aimed at preventing violence. The shelter is also completely accessible to women and children with disabilities.

Volunteers are welcomed in several departments: you can give direct service as a children's activities assistant tutoring, playing games, doing arts and crafts, cooking and maintaining bedtime routines; also in providing childcare services at the centre, so that

women can attend the domestic violence support group. Volunteers are also needed in administration and building and house maintenance. Some positions ask for a regular weekly commitment of two to four hours. Regular volunteers must complete 40-Hour Domestic Violence Training, available through the Rainbow House organisation.

Anyone interested in volunteering should complete an online volunteer form or contact Dawn Dalton, Volunteer Coordinator at the above address.

TADA!
120 West 28th Street, New York, New York 10001, USA; ☎ +1 212 627-1732; fax +1 212 243-6736; e-mail tada@tadatheater.com; www.tadatheater.com
TADA! is a musical youth theatre company which requires about 100 volunteers annually to assist with administrative work in the office or help with ushering in the theatre. In return, volunteers receive essential theatre experience. Applicants must be entirely self-funding.

Applications accepted all year round to the Administrative Associate at the above address.

13TH STREET REPERTORY COMPANY
50 W 13th Street, New York, NY 10011, USA; ☎ +1 917 363 23 69 or +1 212 675-6677; e-mail SandraNord@aol.com; www.13thStreetRep.org
The 13th Street Repertory Company is an 80-member company which has been operating for 30 years, (including NYC's longest-running play, *Line* which was 28 years at this theatre) producing 5-8 different plays a week. About 20 volunteers are recruited annually to assist with stage managing, lighting, sound, literary management, and administration. Opportunities also exist for Directing internships. There is a weekly reading of new and published work. Help is required all year round for varying lengths of time. Applicants must be English-speaking and entirely self-funding.

Applications by e-mail to Sandra Nordgren, General Manager, at the above address.

THE VOLUNTEER CENTER OF SAN FRANCISCO
1675 California Street, San Francisco, CA 94109, USA; ☎ +1 415 982-8999; fax +1 415 982-0890
The Volunteer Center of San Francisco aims to improve the quality of life in the Bay area by supporting the efforts of non-profit organisations that seek to enlist volunteers to address community needs. Not only does the Center organise diverse voluntary placements for San Francisco residents, but it has begun a new programme, the Travellers' Volunteer Network (TVN), designed to outreach to visitors and travellers to San Francisco who have an interest in engaging in community involvement as a volunteer. All of the volunteer jobs selected to be a part of the TVN are special one-time events which require very little specialised skill or involvement on the part of the participants and still gives each person a chance to experience giving their time and energies to an agency's event. The jobs are usually large group type activities that can involve many at a time such as serving breakfast or lunch at a homeless shelter or planting trees at Golden Gate Park. Volunteers are required all year round for a variety of activities which can last from just a few hours a day to a more regular commitment.

Those interested in volunteering should contact the Community Service Co-ordinator of Volunteers at the above address.

THE WILMA THEATER
265 South Broad Street, Philadelphia, PA 19107, USA; ☎ +1 215-893-9456;

fax +1 215-893-0895; e-mailinfo@wilmatheater.org; www.wilmatheater.org
The Wilma Theater is a non-profit theatre based in Philadelphia which recruits about 25 volunteers/interns annually to work in the literary, development, marketing/publicity, and or Education departments and assist with all aspects of the departments' functions. Placements occur all year round and usually last from 3-5 months. Applicants must be fluent in English and entirely self-funding. Housing is not provided. Applications should be made to the Education Director at the above address.

WOMEN'S PROJECT AND PRODUCTIONS
55 West End Avenue, New York, New York 10023, USA; ☎ +1 212-765-1706; fax +1 212-765-2024; e-mail info@womensproject.org; www.womensproject. org
Women's Project and Productions is an off-Broadway theatre company dedicated to producing plays by women writers and directors. It also runs two developmental programmes for women artists: the Playwrights' Lab and Directors' Forum; and a weekly reading series. Opportunities exist for 30-35 volunteers annually in administration, marketing, development, literary management, education and production. Applicants should be fluent in English (written and spoken), and have a strong interest in New York City theatre; computer skills are a plus. Minimum age 17; high school students are only eligible for the administrative internship.

A minimum commitment of 10 weeks and 10 hours per week is required although most interns stay an entire semester, working at least 25-30 hours a week. Year-long interns are also accepted. Participants must be entirely self-funding.

Applications with resume and cover letter to the Intern Co-ordinator at the above address.

Conservation, the Environment and Heritage

THE ANIMAL RESCUE LEAGUE OF WESTERN PENNSYLVANIA WILDLIFE CENTER
6000 Verona Road, Verona, Pennsylbania 15147, USA; ☎ +1 412 793-6900; e-mail violeta0503@Comcast.net; www.pawildlifecenter.org
The Animal Rescue League of Western Pennsylvania is a clinic for the rehabilitation of injured and orphaned native wildlife. The centre also manages educational programmes provided to regional residents to foster an appreciation for conservation and ways to harmonise existence between humans and wildlife.

Volunteers are needed to help restore sick and injured animals and birds and care for orphaned wildlife. Volunteers help with a range of tasks from feeding patients and cleaning their cages, to helping stuff envelopes for a fund-raising mailshot. Besides learning about caring for wildlife, volunteers also learn about the behaviours and habitats of native wildlife, including birds, mammals, reptiles and amphibians. Volunteer applicants should be over 18.

Applications to Jamie Sehrer, Volunteer Coordinator at the above address or e-mail.

CAROLINA RAPTOR CENTER
PO Box 16443, Charlotte, NC 28027, USA; ☎ +1 704 875-6521 ext. 102; fax +1 704 875-8814; www.birdsofprey.org

Raptors are birds of prey such as eagles, owls, hawks, falcons, and vultures. They play a vital role in helping to maintain nature's balance. The Center is a non-profit organisation that exists to provide public education on environmental issues and about the importance of raptors to the environment, to care for the sick, injured and orphaned raptors, and to conduct and contribute research about birds of prey. As there are so few full-time staff and such extensive programmes, the majority of the work of the Center is carried out by volunteers from treatment of injured and orphaned raptors to fundraising, office work, volunteer co-ordinating and training, transport of injured birds, general or vehicle maintenance, cage building, assisting with special projects, working in the gift shop, landscaping, and trail-building. About 150 volunteers are taken on annually and more are always needed.

A commitment of 3 hours per week on a consistent basis or 6 hours every other week is required by volunteers for preferably a one year period although any time which can be spared is appreciated. Training is given and regular educational workshops are held. Applicants should be aged between 16 and 70.

Applications to the Director of Volunteer Programmes at the above address.

COOPER-HEWITT – NATIONAL DESIGN MUSEUM
Smithsonian Institution, 955 L'Enfant Plaza, Suite 7300, Washington, DC 20560, USA; ☎ +1 202 287-3271; www.si.edu/ndm/.
The Museum serves as a resource for architects, designers, studio artists, craftspeople and those interested in the decorative arts. Approximately ten internships (two with stipends) are available each summer at the National Design Museum. The ten-week programmes on offer to volunteers are designed to acquaint participants with the programmes, policies, procedures, and operations of the National Design Museum and of museums in general. Other paid internships are also available for those studying and considering careers in related areas such as art history, design, museum studies, etc.

Applications with résumés, college transcript, two letters of recommendation (with at least one of these to be from a recent or current tutor), and a 1-2 page essay describing career goals and specific areas of interest relating to the internship applied for, to the Intern Co-ordinator at the above address by the 31 March.

DOLPHIN RESEARCH CENTER
58901 Overseas Highway, Grassy Key, Florida 33050-6019, USA; ☎ +1 305 289-1121; fax +1 305 743-7627; e-mail drc-vr@dolphins.org; www.dolphins. org
The Dolphin Research Center recruits about 100 volunteers annually to assist with food preparation for the dolphins and sea lions, aviary care, Center's rubbish and recycling, monitoring of educational programmes, care of the Center's flora and any other support activity for the Center's departments. Any openings for staff are posted and volunteers are welcome to apply.

Applicants must be at least 18, speak English fluently, be in good health and able to lift heavy weights. Help is needed seasonally for periods of six weeks to three months. Volunteers must be entirely self-funding. The Center produces two publications, *Dolphin Society* ($40) and *Gray Cross* ($85) available at the above address.

Applications to Volunteer Resources at the above address.

THE FUND FOR ANIMALS
Campaign Office: 8121 Georgia Avenue, Suite 301, Silver Spring, MD 20910, USA; ☎ +1 301 585-2591; fax +1 301 585-2595; e-mail fundinfo@fund. org

Founded in 1967 by the author Cleveland Amory, the Fund for Animals works on a variety of issues but the primary focus is on the abolition of hunting and trapping. The Fund debunks the myth that these activities are a legitimate and necessary form of management, and educates the public about the true agenda of state wildlife agencies. The Washington DC-area office is also involved in various wildlife protection issues and ongoing anti-cruelty campaigns across the country. An intern at the Fund for Animals will benefit from an intensified experience of working close to the issues with a dedicated group of a activists, lobbyists and lawyers.

The Fund offers internships year-round. Interns may be required to do a variety of tasks depending on their skills including legal, legislative, outreach and administrative. Each internship is full-time and lasts three months. Work can be performed for a stipend or academic credit. Interns must be at least 18 years old.

uses education, litigation, legislation, direct action, and direct care to protect wildlife and domestic animals. Current campaigns include banning live pigeon shoots, halting the killing of bison outside Yellowstone Park, and promoting non-lethal solutions to human/wildlife conflicts.

If you would like to apply for an intern position, please send the following to Jennifer Allen at jallen@fund.org.

HAWK MOUNTAIN SANCTUARY ASSOCIATION
1700 Hawk Mountain Road, Kempton, Pennsylvania 19529, USA; ☎ +1 610 756 6961; fax +1 610-756 4468; e-mail info@hawkmountain.org; www.hawkmountain.org

Situated in south-eastern Pennsylvania, Hawk Mountain is a privately-run wildlife preserve covering 2,500 acres in the Appalachian mountains. It has 14 permanent employees and an army of volunteers who work in all departments from carrying out biological surveys to greeting visiting groups and from maintaining the archives and library to maintenance of the trails and gardening and keeping the grounds work. There is also the opportunity to take care of the non-releasable raptors, which are used for education programmes. Additionally, science students or those with a demonstrable personal interest in raptors, can apply for four month residential internships.

Contact the Volunteer Co-ordinator at the above address.

HEAL THE BAY
3220 Nebraska Avenue, Santa Monica, CA 90404 USA; ☎ +1 310-453-0395; fax +1 310-496-792701 585-2595; e-mail info@healthebay.org; www.healthebay.org

Heal the Bay is a non-profit environmental organisation dedicated to making the Santa Monica Bay and Southern Californian coastal waters safe and healthy for people and marine life.

About 250 volunteers are recruited annually to help in the office, carry out fieldwork such as chemical testing of water, carry out beach clean-ups and educating the public by giving talks to groups. Volunteers can work a few hours or a few days a week. Internships can be organised. No accommodation or expenses provided.

Contact the Volunteer Co-ordinator at the above address.

LAND TRUST ALLIANCE
1331 H Street NW, Suite 600, Washington, DC 20005-4711, USA; ☎ +1 202 638-4725; fax +1 202 638-4730; e-mail raldrich@lta.org; www.lta.org

The Alliance's mission is to strengthen the land trust movement by providing the information, skills, and resources land trusts need to protect land and to promote voluntary land conservation. About 3-4 volunteers are recruited annually to: update and produce factsheets, assist with various projects, do web research, stuff envelopes, help proofread journal articles and very occasionally help run programmes. Volunteers are placed on projects suited to their skills and interests. The Alliance also has a grassroots network for those interested in promoting public policies relating to land conservation.

Applicants should be English-speaking and able to commit themselves to a project for several weeks at any time of year although the Alliance is flexible. Only project expenses are paid. A list of publications produced by the Alliance is available from the above address.

Those interested should contact the Information Services Manager at the above address.

THE MARITIME AQUARIUM AT NORWALK
10 North Water Street, Norwalk, CT 06854, USA; ☎ +1 203 852-0700 ext. 225; fax +1 203 838-5416; e-mail slinskyl@aol.com; www.maritime-aquarium. org

The Aquarium provides volunteer programmes for a wide cross-section of the public: the young, the old, night people and day people. Activities are varied and range from administrative and other behind-the-scenes responsibilities to frontline jobs throughout the Aquarium and other areas where visitors are welcomed. Volunteers are relied upon to interpret and protect the Aquarium's marine and maritime collections while enhancing visitors' experiences about the maritime history of Long Island Sound and its marine life.

Applicants must be at least 15, English-speaking, and are expected to success-fully complete a Volunteer Training Programme of eight classes over a 4-week period followed by an 8-12 hour probationary period at work before starting their duties at the Aquarium. A $35 registration fee is required to cover the cost of this course. A minimum commitment of two 4-hour shifts per month is needed. Volunteers should be self-funding.

Applications all year round to the Assistant Director, Volunteer & Community Services, at the above address.

THE MUSEUM OF TELEVISION & RADIO
25 West 52nd Street, New York, NY 10019, USA; ☎ +1 212 621-6620; fax +1 212 621-6700; www.mtr.org

The Museum of Television & Radio is located both in New York City and Los Angeles, California. Its collections consist of television, radio and commercial programmes from around the world, but mainly from English-speaking countries. Volunteers assist museum staff members in nearly every phase of daily work. The departments which offer unpaid internship work are: curatorial, library research services and visitors services.

Applicants must be fluent in English (both written and spoken) and basic clerical and computer skills are usually required. The internship program is year round and starting and ending dates are flexible. No expenses are paid.

For an information pack and application form, please contact the internship coordinator at the above address.

NEW ENGLAND AQUARIUM
Central Wharf, Boston, MA 02110-3399, USA; ☎ +1 617 973-0222; fax +1 617 973-6552; e-mail vols@neaq.org; www.neaq.org

The New England Aquarium organises several volunteer programmes ranging from animal husbandry to aquarium administration, providing the necessary experience for those wishing to pursue a career in the relevant areas. The voluntary positions give participants the opportunity to become involved with behind and in front of the scenes operations of the Aquarium.

Over 900 volunteers are recruited annually all year round. The greatest need for help is during weekday business hours; some weekend positions are available on a limited basis. For most curatorial positions, especially those on weekends, there is a two-month waiting list. A six-month commitment is expected for all positions. Applicants for hands-on work with animals should be at least 18; those who are at least 16 can participate on the Aquarium Guide Training Programme. Qualifications required vary according to position applied for. No expenses are paid, volunteers must be self-funding and please note that the New England Aquarium cannot provide sponsorship for visas.

Applications to the Manager of Volunteer Programmes and Internships at the above address. An interview will follow application and successful candidates will receive training before beginning their duties.

PACIFIC ENVIRONMENT & RESOURCES CENTER (PERC)
1440 Broadway, Suite 306, Oakland, CA 94612, USA; ☎ +1 510 251-8800; fax +1 510 251-8838; e-mail info@pacificenvironment.org; www. pacificenvironment.org
Pacific Environment protects the living environment of the Pacific Rim by strengthening democracy, supporting grassroots activism, empowering communities, and redefining international policies. It supports over 100 small organisations in Russia, China and Japan with small grants and organisational capacity building. PERC are most interested in stopping or improving harmful resource extraction projects, especially in the forestry, oil and gas and fisheries sectors. They publish a free monthly newsletter, *Pacific Currents*, which you can subscribe to from their website homepage.

PERC has a few internships available for qualified, self-motivated people who can work with a minimal amount of supervision. Tasks include research and writing, administrative assistance, translating, and assistance with communications and outreach products. Internships are unpaid, though under some circumstances a travel stipend may be offered. No accommodation is provided. Knowledge of the following languages is advantageous but not essential: Russian, Cantonese, Mandarin and Japanese.

PEACE RIVER REFUGE & RANCH
PO Box 1127, 2545 Stoner Lane, Zolfo Springs, Florida 33890, USA; ☎ +1 863 735-0804; fax +1 863 735-0805; e-mail info@peaceriverrefuge.org; www.peaceriverrefuge.org
Peace River Refuge is a non-profit animal sanctuary and educational facility covering 70 acres and providing permanent care for unwanted, neglected or confiscated exotic animals. The sanctuary has a non-killing policy. Animals include cougars, tigers, leopards, bears, monkeys and any other captive wildlife in need. Many of the animals would have been destroyed by their original owners had they not been given sanctuary at Peace River Refuge.

Volunteer opportunities exist in the following departments: property maintenance (keeping the grounds attractive, land clearing, tree trimming etc); cage/fence construction (constructing new habitats to save more animals), veterinary care (licensed veterinarian or trained veterinary technician), animal care (volunteers needed every day to assist with basic animal care carried out under the guidance of experienced personnel until the volunteer is comfortable).

For further details contact Lisa Stoney at the above address.

SEATTLE AUDUBON SOCIETY
8050 35ᵗʰ Avenue, NE Seattle, Washington State 98115, USA ☎ +1 206-523-8243 ext. 12; fax +1 206-528-7779; www.seattleaudubon.org
The Audubon Society cultivates and leads a community that values and protects birds and the natural environment within the United States of America. About 650 active volunteers provide the organisation with their services. Volunteer opportunities can be found on the website and they include work in education, conservation, volunteer management, development, communications, land preservation, scientific research, merchandising for the Nature Shop, even management, bird censusing in Seattle parks, Christmas bird count, and many others.

Volunteers go through an application, screening and orienting process. The Society is flexible as regards the number of hours, but a regular commitment of time is requested. There is no pocket money or accommodation provided.

A newsletter *Earthcare Northwest* is published ten times a year and comes free with an annual subscription of $30 (50% reduction for full-time students and seniors)

Enquiries for volunteer work should be addressed to the Volunteer Program Manager at the above address.

SEATTLE AUDUBON SOCIETY
8050 35ᵗʰ Avenue, NE Seattle, Washington State 98115, USA ☎ +1 206-523-8243 ext. 12; fax +1 206-528-7779; www.seattleaudubon.org
The Audubon Society cultivates and leads a community that values and protects birds and the natural environment within the United States of America. About 650 active volunteers provide the organisation with their services. Volunteer opportunities can be found on the website and they include work in education, conservation, volunteer management, development, communications, land preservation, scientific research, merchandising for the Nature Shop, even management, bird censusing in Seattle parks, Christmas bird count, and many others.

Volunteers go through an application, screening and orienting process. The Society is flexible as regards the number of hours, but a regular commitment of time is requested. There is no pocket money or accommodation provided.

A newsletter *Earthcare Northwest* is published ten times a year and comes free with an annual subscription of $30 (50% reduction for full-time students and seniors)

Enquiries for volunteer work should be addressed to the Volunteer Program Manager at the above address.

UNITED STATES HOLOCAUST MEMORIAL MUSEUM
100 Raoul Wallenberg Place, S.W., Washington, D.C. 20024, USA; ☎ +1 202 479-9738; fax +1 202 488-6568; e-mail volunteer–services@ushmm.org; www.ushmm.org
The Memorial Museum recruits about 300-320 volunteers annually to assist with: public programmes, ushering and greeting visitors, collecting tickets; visitor services, giving information to visitors, enhancing visitors' experience in the Museum; behind-the-scenes, translating documents, fundraising, providing clerical support, updating the computer database, copy reading, editing, assisting with membership services. For those helping with visitor services a commitment of one year is required but for other positions this time is flexible.

Applicants should be English-speaking with a genial attitude, knowledge of other languages helpful. Volunteers must be entirely self-funding and over 16. An extensive list of publications produced by the Museum is available from the above address or on the website.

For an application form contact the Museum by post, telephone, or e-mail.

WARD-NASSE GALLERY
178 Prince Street, New York, NY 10012, USA; ☎ +1 212- 925-6951; fax +1 212 334-2095; e-mail wardnasse@hotmail.com; www.markherd@wardnasse. org
A respected gallery, exhibiting contemporary art, Ward-Nasse takes on about 10 volunteers annually to assist in all aspects of the gallery's work from greeting customers, making sales, preparing mailings, to hanging exhibitions and using various programmes on a computer. Help is required all year round for as much time as the volunteer can spare. Spanish and French are helpful as is a knowledge of Word or Quark computer programmes, but not essential. Computer skills are also desirable but not necessary. No expenses are paid so volunteers must be entirely self-funding.
Applications to the Gallery Assistant at the above address.

Fund Raising, Political Lobbying & Office Work

THE ASHBURN TRUST
P.O. Box 77164, Washington DC 20013-7164, USA; tel 202-220-1388; fax 202-220 1389; info@ashburninstitute.org; www.ashburninstitute.org
AI promotes Euro-Atlantic cooperation and the enlargement of the Euro-Atlantic community where newly democratic nations can find support in sustaining strong democracies. However, it has chosen a special path to achieve its goal: educational and cultural exchange among the representatives of the global community through academic conferences and student conferences, roundtable discussions, meetings, publications, distance learning programs, and scholarship grants. The programmes are conducted at the academic level and well as graduate, undergraduate and high school levels, utilising the latest state of the art technology to reach a large global audience.
Volunteers' activities involve clerical work, research, writing and event planning. Applicants must be in good health, speak English, be computer literate and have knowledge of political science and international relations. Volunteers are needed all year round from three to 18 months. Small stipend ($250 per month) is provided. AI produces a quarterly newsletter *Unite*.
For more information contact the above address or visit the website.

GLOBAL IMPACT
66 Canal Center Plaza, Suite 310, Alexandria, Virginia 22314, USA; tel ☎ +1 703-548 2200; fax 703 548 7684; mail@charity.org
Global Impact is a non-profit organisation dedicated to helping the poorest people on earth. It represents more than 50 of the most respected USA-based charities and organises workplace giving campaigns across the US. It provides a trustworthy, effective and efficient organisation through which Americans can direct their charitable contributions to where the need is greatest. It also manages the largest workplace giving campaigns in the world including the Federal Campaign of the National Capital Area (CFCNCA) in Washington.
Global Impact looks for volunteers to work in their Alexandria, Virginia office. Espe-

cially of interest are volunteers with skills in research, writing, editing web and information technology and/or administrative support and are willing to provide at least 20 hours a week for a minimum six-month commitment (one year is preferable). Applicants can be retired individuals and students, as well as anyone with availability between the hours of 8am and 5pm Monday to Friday. Volunteers will work with Global Impact staff on key projects. Although posts are unpaid, students doing internships get local travel expenses.

For further details contact the above address or e-mail. Applications to the above address.

GREEN PARTY OFFICE IN MANHATTAN
139 Fulton Street, Suite 215, New York, New York 10003, USA; tel ☎ +1 212-240-0501; fax 212-240 0503; e-mail info@greenpartyoffice.org; www. greenpartyoffice.org

The Green Party Office Committee is a group of Green Party members who have established a permanent office for the Green Party in Manhattan. The Committee is dedicated to facilitating Green organising of all kinds: activist, electoral and educational in New York City. The Office serves as a meeting place for Greens and supporters, a place to meet, discuss and plan Green activity. It also initiates contacts with other like-minded organisations, and provides information on the Green Party to interested individuals. The office space is open to all Greens, and the Committee is strictly non-partisan when it comes to differences that arise between various groups of Greens. The essential goal of the Committee is to help the Green Party grow and develop and become a major force for social and political change in New York City.

The office is staffed by volunteers and paid for by donations. There is always a need for volunteers to help with fundraising, party building, administration, volunteer coordination and outreach work such as registering voters in the disenfranchised communities in New York.

Anyone with an active interest in Green politics who is interested in becoming a volunteer should contact the above address. Undergraduate internships also offered.

HEARTS AND MINDS
3074 Broadway, New York, NY 10027, USA; ☎ +1-212 280 0333; fax +1 212 280 0336; help@change.net, www.change.net

Hearts and Minds is an all-volunteer, non-partisan, non-profit organisation working for meaningful change in issues including poverty, the environment, human rights, democracy and addiction recovery. Hearts and Minds websites and publicity campaigns serve as vital sources of information for people who want to get involved in socially beneficial activities such as volunteering, self-help and charitable giving. The aim of Hearts and Minds is to reach as many people as possible through mass communications locally, nationwide and worldwide. We direct people to effective resources that enable them to help themselves and others.

The website of Hearts and Minds, www.change.net provides motivation, resources and direction, moving individuals to make more effective contributions to society. The site has more than 500 web pages, has helped over 1,200,000 people and is being translated into ten other languages. The site is uniquely dedicated to countering apathy and fostering public involvement by inspiring and informing people to help solve persistent social problems. Furthermore, Hearts and Minds website is a clearinghouse of more than 750 other helpful organisations.

Hearts and Minds brings volunteers and experienced professionals of all ages together in a dynamic setting giving empowerment to the public and individuals. About

60 volunteers are taken on annually to work in a wide variety of areas from Journalism and fund-raising and from website designing to office work and maintenance. All ages from high school students to adults of all ages are welcome. Volunteers are welcome at any time. Pocket money and travel expenses provided but no accommodation.

Apply direct to the above address.

THE INSTITUTE FOR UNPOPULAR CULTURE

1592 Union Street, #226 San Francisco, CA 94123, USA; ☎ +1-415 986-4382; fax +1-415 986-4354; e-mail ifuc2003@yahoo.com; www.ifuc.org

About 30 volunteers a year are recruited to help the Institute in their work, assisting and sponsoring artists who attempt to challenge and destabilize the status quo. Duties include research, administration, and computer work. Applicants should have computer skills, knowledge of art history, and be able to speak English. Those who are multi-lingual are particularly desirable. Minimum age 18 and volunteers must be in good health. Help is needed all year round for periods of one month to a year. Volunteers must be entirely self-funding.

Applications to the above address.

INTERNATIONAL RESCUE COMMITTEE, DALLAS

Volunteer and Resource Development Department, 2515 Inwood Road, Suite 217 Dallas, Texas 75235, USA; ☎ +1-214 351 6864; fax 214 351 6876; Admin office: 7515 Greenville Ave, Suite 603, Dallas Texas 75231; ☎ +1-214-461-9781; fax +1-214-461 9782; www.the IRC.org/Dallas

The International Rescue Committee was founded in 1933 in the USA, and is the oldest and largest non-sectarian, independent agency dedicated to providing assistance to refugees and asylum seekers domestically and through its well-established global emergency relief operations. The Dallas office was opened in 1975 and it settles approximately 500 refugees and asylum seekers a year and seeks to integrate new arrivals into the Dallas area. Dallas office staff and volunteers have assisted refugees with obtaining housing, English language training, health care and finding employment.

Volunteers are needed in the Dallas offices to help with administration and fund raising. There are also openings for volunteers to help resettle refugees by working on programmes such as after-school tutoring of refugee children, helping refugees learn how to go about daily life in their new surroundings, using buses, grocery stores etc. and mentoring elderly refugees. The last one is very suitable for seniors and individuals.

For further details contact Kathy Mertens, the Resource Developer who is responsible for volunteer recruitment, at the Volunteer and Resource and Development Department at the above address.

MY SISTER'S PLACE

P O Box 29596, Washington, DC 20017; USA; ☎ +1 202-529 5261; fax +1 202-529 5991; www.mysistersplace.org

Temporary shelter for women who are victims of domestic violence and their children. Needs mainly office volunteers to help with the hotline, community education, plan children's outings and development and fundraising. May also occasionally need help with other areas including helping move families from the shelter to apartments and shelter maintenance.

Further details of how to help from the above address.

NATIONAL COUNCIL FOR INTERNATIONAL VISITORS
1420 K Street, NW, Suite 800, Washington, DC 20005-2401, USA; tel/fax + 1 202-289 4625; e-mail jlheureux@nciv.org; www.nciv.org
Volunteers are required to help all year round with specific programmes and projects and with general administrative tasks within the Washington office. Applicants must be fluent in English, both written and oral, have a good telephone manner and preferably knowledge of computers. About six volunteers are taken on annually to work for varying time periods. No expenses are paid so volunteers must be entirely self-funding.

The Council produces three publications at no cost: *The Art of Programming*, *Non-profit Management Resource Director*, and *Building Effective Boards of Directors*. For further information contact the Director of Communications at the above address.

PLANET DRUM
P.O. Box 31251, San Francisco, CA 94131, USA; ☎414-285 6556; fax 415-285 6563; e-mail planetdrum@igc.org; www.planetdrum.org
Planet Drum Foundation works to research, promote and disseminate information about bioregionalism, a grassroots approach to ecology that emphasises sustainability, community self-determination and regional self-reliance. 'We believe that people who know and care about the places where they live will work to maintain and restore them.'

It needs volunteers to work in office administration and public relations in its US office. These can be occasional volunteers and also those looking to make a more permanent commitment. Three to fifteen hours a week. Office hours 10am-4pm. No pay but occasionally a stipend for local travel. Three-month internships requiring 20 hours a week also offered.

Planet Drum also runs ecological projects in Ecuador and needs project workers to work on ecological projects in Ecuador. Knowledge of environmental issues and Spanish language is also considered prerequisite for Ecuador. Posts are unpaid and volunteers are responsible for all their own expenses.

Apply direct to the above address.

TRANSFAIR USA
1611 Telegraph Ave, Oakland, California 94612, USA; ☎ +1 510-663-5260; fax +1 510-663 5264; e-mail info@transfairusa.org; www.transfairusa.org
TransFair USA is the only non-profit organisation certifying Fair Trade products in the USA. It aims to increase the availability of Fair Trade certified goods throughout the US by forming partnerships with industry and also to increase consumer awareness and demand for fairly traded goods by penetration of mainstream markets and by educational outreach campaigns across the US.

Volunteer opportunities exist for working in the offices of Transfair USA and help with a very worthwhile campaign to make a real difference to disadvantaged farmers and growers of universal products such as cocoa, tea and coffee around the world. Firms and retailers that comply with the guidelines of Fair Trade earn the right to have their products endorsed with the Fair Trade logo showing that the farmer has received a fair price. Volunteers are needed to carry out general office duties for a few hours a week. Volunteers help send out educational and promotion materials.

A range of internships also exist lasting ten to twelve weeks each. Further details can be obtained from the above address and website.

Appendix 1

The Volunteer and the Job Seeker's Allowance

The definition of voluntary work is work for a non-profit organisation, or work for someone outside your family, where only out of pocket expenses are paid for.

Volunteers can claim Job Seeker's Allowance, provided they meet a few basic conditions. They must remain available either for a job interview or to begin work at a week's notice, and be actively seeking work. So this would mean for example that volunteers who gave a minimum commitment for say three months to their volunteer work might put their entitlement to the JSA at risk if it were at a time of day that would make them no longer available for work. Volunteers who work for organised emergency groups (e.g. staffing a lifeboat) would however be considered as available for work. It therefore makes sense to warn any organisation for which you are doing voluntary work that you may be required to attend a work interview at short notice.

Volunteers can also claim JSA and receive reasonable expenses, such as the payment of bus fares to wherever they will be helping, and the cost of meals.

People who are unemployed can also continue to receive JSA if they take part in a residential, voluntary workcamp lasting for up to fourteen days as long as they give their Benefit Office advance warning and the camp is run by either a charity or a local authority. The situation is less clear for those wanting to join a workcamp abroad, as it is at the discretion of their Benefit Officer whether or not they will be allowed to continue claiming. People claiming Incapacity Benefit can volunteer for any number of hours per week and this should not affect their benefit except in 'exceptional circumstances.'

Further information on volunteers and welfare benefits can be found in various booklets including: *JSAL7 – (Revised) Jobseeker's Allowance. voluntary work when you are unemployed and it needn't affect your benefits,* available free from your local Social Security office; also *WK-1- Financial help if you are working or doing voluntary work* which gives guidance on volunteering and benefits (www/jobcentreplus.gov.uk/pdfs/pflwk1v3.pdf.). Both the above are available from the Employment Service.

Volunteering and Welfare Benefits, and *Volunteers and Expenses,* both published by Volunteering England. You can order these free information sheets by telephone, post or online at www.volunteering.org.uk/work with/sheets.htm. Any further queries either contact your local Citizens' Advice Bureau, local Jobcentre Plus/Social Security office, or Volunteering England (Regent's Wharf, 8 All Saints Street, London N1 9RL; e-mail volunteering@volunteeringengland.org; www.volunteering.org.uk, or information line 0800 028 3304, Open Mon-Fri 10.30am-12.30pm and from 2pm-4pm..

Appendix Two
Further Reading

Please note that many of the organisations listed in this book produce their own literature and publications so do not hesitate to contact them if you would like further information about their particular activities. The organisations below produce some of the more extensive publications.

Many of these organisations also have useful websites which can provide useful data to the prospective volunteer.

American Hiking Society Volunteer Programmes: PO Box 20160, Washington, DC 20041-2160, USA; ☎+1 301 565-6704; fax +1 301 565-6714; e-mail info@americanhiking.org
Publishes *The AHS Hiker's Information Center* the online resource for volunteer opportunities. The *Hiker's Information Center* is an extensive database of volunteer opportunities, trail descriptions, local trail clubs, National Trails Day Events and House Trails Caucus members around the USA. Whether you are looking for a hike in your hometown or a volunteer opportunity across the country, you can find it in the *AHS Hiker's Information Center*. Visit the website www.americanhiking.org to access the *AHS Hiker's Information Center*.

Archaeological Institute of America: Boston University, 656 Beacon Street, Boston MA 02215; ☎+1 617-353 9364; fax +1 617 353 6550; e-mail afob@aia.bu.edu www. the yearly *Archaeological Fieldwork Opportunities Bulletin*.

Archaeology Abroad: 31-34 Gordon Square, London WC1H OPY; Tel/fax: 020-8537 0849; e-mail arch.abroad@ucl.ac.uk; www.britarch.ac.uk/archabroad. This organisation provides two information bulletins annually about forthcoming opportunities for archaeological fieldwork and excavations abroad. Publications are available by subscription. Enquiries should be sent to the Honorary Secretary at the above address enclosing a stamped and self-addressed envelope, or via e-mail to the address above, or pay subscription online at: www.britarch.ac.uk/shop.

Catholic Network of Volunteer Service (CNVS), 1410 Q Street, NW Washington DC 20009, USA; tel+1 301 270-0900; fax +1 301 270-0901; e-mail volunteer@cnvs.org; www.cnvs.org
Publishes *RESPONSE Volunteer Opportunities Directory*, which lists contact and other useful information about the member programmes and the full time volunteer opportunities CNVS offers throughout the world. Volunteer opportunities are from one week to two years or more in length. To receive a free copy of the *RESPONSE Volunteer Opportunities Directory* contact CNVS at the address above.

Christians Abroad: World Service Enquiry, 237 Bon Marché Centre, 241-251 Ferndale Road, London SW9 8BJ; tel 0870 700 3274; fax 0870 770 7991; e-mail wse@cabroad.

org.uk; www.wse.org.uk
Produces a free guide of over 200 voluntary work organisations and other information for those considering volunteering overseas. The guide is free on the website. If ordering by post a contribution of £3 is requested. See also *World Service Enquiry* below.

Christian Vocations: St.James House, Trinity Road, Dudley, West Midlands DV1 1JB; ☎01384-233011; fax 01384-233032; e-mail info@ChristianVocations.org; www. ChristianVocations.org
Publishes *Mission Matters* annually giving information about current long-term opportunities of interest to Christians, and the *Short-term Service Directory* which contains short term positions in the UK and abroad at a cost of £5 plus £12. Also a new publication *High Time* giving details of opportunities in the UK for the over 50s . Available free but there is a postage charge.

Co-ordinating Committee for International Voluntary Service (CCIVS): UNESCO, 1 rue Miollis, 75732 Paris Cedex 15, France; ☎+33-1 45 68 49 36; e-mail ccivs@unesco. org; www.unesco.org/ccivs
CCIVS is an international non-governmental organisation created in 1948 under the aegis of UNESCO to promote and co-ordinate voluntary work worldwide. CCIVS has 140 member organisations present in more than 90 countries.
Publications include *Volunteer's Handbook* a guide with useful addresses, and *African Directory* a detailed description of voluntary organisations in 28 sub-saharan African Countries. CCIVS is a structure of co-ordination, therefore it does not recruit volunteers directly. Volunteers have to contact a CCIVS organisation for the recruitment procedures. For a full list of publications, send your request to the above address with two International Reply Coupons.

Council for British Archaeology: Bowes Morrell House, 111 Walmgate, York Y01 9WA; ☎01904-671417; fax 01904-671384; e-mail info@britarch.ac.uk; www.britarch. ac.uk
Publishes *Briefing*, an information supplement to its magazine *British Archaeology*, which appears in the first week of February, April, June, August, October and December and carries announcements of forthcoming fieldwork opportunities on archaeological sites in Britain. An annual subscription for the magazine and *CBA Briefing* is £19 for the UK, £22 for Europe, and £28 for airmail outside Europe. US$ payments also accepted. Send an International Reply Coupon for details.

Directory of Social Change: 24 Stephenson Way, London NW1 2DP; ☎020-7391 4800; fax 020-7391 4804; e-mail info@dsc.org.uk; www.dsc.org.uk
Publishes *International Development Directory* (Sarah Harland and Dave Griffiths), £16.95 plus p&p. A comprehensive directory detailing 250 voluntary organisations involved in campaigning, development or emergency relief and funding for this type of work. Includes geographical and subject indexes.

International Health Exchange/RedR: 1 Great George Street, London SWIP 3AA; e-mail info@ihe.org.uk; ☎020-7233 1100; fax 020-7233 3590; e-mail info@ihe.org.uk
IHE is a clearing house for information on jobs and courses in health and developing countries. IHE maintains a register of health professionals, publishes *The Health Exchange* magazine (£3.50 per issue) and runs information workshops to prepare health professionals for work in developing countries.
For further information contact the Recruitment Department at the above address.

National Council for Voluntary Organisations: Regent's Wharf, 8 All Saints Street, London N1 9RL; ☎020-7713 6161; fax 020-7713 6300; e-mail ncvo@ncvo-vol.org.uk; www.ncvo-vol.org.uk
Established in 1919, NCVO is the umbrella body for the voluntary sector in England. Publishes *The Voluntary Agencies Directory* (£30) annually. Nearly 500 pages of voluntary organisations.

The National Youth Agency: 19-23 Humberstone Road, Leicester LE5 3GJ; tel 0116 2427350; e-mail nya@nya.org.uk
Visit www.youthinformation.com - The National Youth Agency's information toolkit for young people. The NYA also publishes a range of materials and lists important volunteer organisations' details on its website www.nya.org.uk.

OPTIONS: 3550 Afton Road, San Diego, CA 92123, USA; ☎+1 619 279-9690; fax +1 619 694-0294; e-mail patty@projcon.cts.com
Publishes a *Directory of Overseas Medical Facilities,* which includes complete information on approximately 150 current and past OPTIONS facilities. This comprehensive directory will include the addresses and contact numbers for all partner facilities. As a result, anyone interested in serving as an overseas medical volunteer will be able to utilise this information to directly inquire about hundreds of volunteer opportunities in a large number of countries around the world. For a copy of the directory, send a cheque for $15 made payable to OPTIONS at the above address.

Volunteering England: Regent's Wharf, 8 All Saints Street, London N1 9RL; ☎0845 305 6979; fax 020 7520 9810; information line 0800 028 3304 (open Mon-Fri 10.30am-12.30pm and 2pm-4pm; e-mail volunteering@volunteerengland.uk; www.volunteering. org.uk. Provides publications and services for anyone who works with volunteers. Does not provide volunteering opportunities or grants for individual volunteers. Of interest to volunteers is *Time Guide,* published in conjunction with TimeBank (see *Other useful Websites*). Can be ordered online from www.volunteering.org.uk VE also publishes free information sheets including *Finding Out About Volunteering in Your Area* and *Volunteering Overseas.* All the information sheets can be viewed on www.volunteering. org.uk/workwith/sheets.htm.

Returned Volunteer Action: 1 Amwell Street, London EC1R 1TH; 020-7278 0804. Publishes information pack *Thinking about Volunteering* and *Overseas Development: a Guide to Opportunities* which costs £3.50 plus a 44p stamped, self-addressed envelope and a monthly listing *Development Action* to which you can subscribe for £5 a year.

Vacation Work Publications: 9 Park End Street, Oxford OX1 1HJ; ☎01865-241978; www.vacationwork.co.uk. Publish a range of books covering both voluntary and paid work in Britain and around the world, including: *Work Your Way Around the World, Gap Years for Grown-ups, Taking a Gap Year* and also distributes *Green Volunteers, Archaeo-Volunteers* and *World Volunteers.* Send a stamped addressed envelope to the above address for a catalogue or visit www.vacationwork.co.uk.

Volunteer Vacations: Chicago Review Press/Independent Publishers Group, 814 N Franklin Street, Chicago, IL60610; ☎800-888-4741/www.ipgbook.com Publication updated every other year. Next due 2005.

Appendix Three
Other Useful Websites

Most of the organisations featured in this book are listed with their own websites which provide the latest details of the voluntary opportunities available and information on how to become a volunteer. Below are organisations which specifically use the internet to match volunteers up with voluntary positions which will most suit individual and organisation.

Association of Voluntary Services Organisations (AVSO)
174 rue Joseph II, 1000 Brussels, Belgium; ☎+32 (0)2 2306813; fax +32 (0)2 2311413; e-mail info@avso.org; www.avso.org.
AVSO is an NGO based in Belgium with details of hundreds of national and international non-profit organisations active in the field of voluntary service in their online *Directory of International Voluntary Service Resources* divided into four main sections: short-term, long-term, platforms & youth organisations and general info on voluntary service and non-profit resources.

Catholic Network of Volunteer Service (CNVS)
6930 Carroll Avenue, Suite 506, Takoma Park, MD 20912-4423 USA; ☎+1 301 270-0900; fax +1 301 270-0901; e-mail volunteer@cnvs.org; www.cnvs.org
People interested in volunteering can submit their profile (personal background information) online to CNVS and it is then passed on to volunteer programmes. In this way, if any programmes run by CNVS see a potential match between prospective volunteer and the needs of the programme, the programme(s) can contact the individual directly.

FullCircle: GoVolunteer:
Full Circle UK Office: (Norwood Park, Southwell, Notts. NG25 OPF; fax 01636-813117; Full Circle USA Office: 601 Crestmoore Place, Venice, Los Angeles, CA 90291. Lists various projects on its website: teaching English in Thailand, Creative Literacy and Medical Programmes in India and much more. If you can't find what you like on their website, you can e-mail them at info@fullcircle.org. uk and they will try to put you in touch with other volunteer placements. Fundraising required from volunteer to pay for trip and placements.

GoVolunteer:
GoVolunteer Office, Volunteering Australia, Level 3, Suite 2, 11 Queens Road, Melbourne, VIC 3004; ☎ 03 9820 4100; fax 03 9820 1206; e-mail govolunteer@govolunteer.com.au; www.GoVolunteer.com.au. GoVolunteer is Volunteering Australia's volunteering recruitment website. GoVolunteer provides volunteers with all the information they need to find out about volunteer opportunities in Australia, and helps them make the best match possible.

ImpactOnline:
325 B Forest Avenue, Palo Alto, CA94301, USA; ☎+1 650 327-1389; fax +1 650 327-1395; e-mail respond@impactonline.org; www.impactonline.org
The non-profit ImpactOnline uses the power of the internet to increase volunteerism and so build stronger, more involved, more connected communities. The aim is to use information technology to help people and organisations find each other online through

the www.volunteermatch.org website which makes direct linkages between people and organisations on behalf of specific local needs. Visitors to the website can input their details, their interests, and their time availability, and instantly retrieve a personalised list of local, up-to-date volunteer opportunities. The VolunteerMatch service saves money for non-profit organisations by reducing volunteer recruitment costs, while increasing volunteerism by making it easier to become involved. VolunteerMatch is an established service with thousands of opportunities available across the USA.

Areas of voluntary work include: animals, arts and culture, children and youth, human and civil rights, computer and technology, disabled, disaster relief, domestic violence, substance abuse, education and literacy, employment, environment, gay, lesbian, bi and trans, health and medicine, homeless and housing, international, legal aid, politics, race and ethnicity, religion, seniors, sports and recreation, volunteering and women.

For further information visit the ImpactOnline website at the above address.

NetAid: 267, Fifth Avenue, 11th Floor, New York, NY 10016 USA; ☎+1 212-537 0500; fax +1 212 537 0501; info@netaid.org; www.netaid.org. NetAid is the United Nations Online Volunteering arm. NetAid enables volunteers from all over the world to help organisations serving communities in developing countries without leaving their own communities. Online volunteers can help in any number of ways from translating documents, writing articles, data analysis, building websites, online mentoring, designing logos, programming and much more. Since starting in 2000, more than 12,000 individuals have volunteered online. There is a lot of guidance given on NetAid's website for prospective online volunteers.

Probono Australia Volunteer Match: PO Box 843, Hawthorn, Victoria 3122, Australia tel ☎ 03 9818 5533; e-mail probono@probonoaustralia.com.au; www.volunteermatch. com.au is a website offering a specialised service for matching skilled professional volunteers and non-profit organisations.

Quaker Information Center: 1501 Cherry Street, Philadelphia PA 19102; ☎+1 215 241 7024/ fax +1 215 567 2096/e-mail info@quakerinfo.org; wwwquakerinfo.org. Has a section on its website devoted to Volunteer and Service Opportunities which includes scores of volunteer opportunities from weekend workcamps to two-year internships. There are also some overseas assignments calling for specialised skills, experience and language abilities. These can be checked out at www.afsc.org/jobs/default.htm.

TakingITGlobal – Organisations: www.takingitglobal.org/opps/orgdir.html Directory giving details of 5544 organisations worldwide that take volunteers. Browse by type or region (e.g. Africa).

Worldwide Volunteering for Young People: www.worldwidevolunteering.org. uk/ Search and match database with nearly 1,000 organisations, 300,000 placements throughout the UK and in 214 countries worldwide. A comprehensive database of volunteer opportunities for 16-25 year olds. Projects last from a week to a year or more. Costs £10 for 3 separate sessions within a four-week period. Website also tells you where the database can be viewed for free.

ADDITIONAL WEBSITES

The following is simply a list of other websites which give details on particular voluntary opportunities available and information on volunteering.

www.idealist.org
The website of Action Without Borders. Includes huge worldwide charities such as The Peace Corps and local grassroots charities in 150 countries.

General Directories
www.afs.org
www.bolt.icestorm.com/lyric/volunteer.html (grassroots organisations)
www.do-it.org.uk (youth volunteering)
www.quakerinfo.org (religious organisations volunteering)
www.viaggiatori.net/public/odp/index.php?browse=/Recreation/Travel/Specialty_Travel/Volunteering/
www.volunteering.org.uk
www.volunteerinternational.org

Specific Fields of Interest

Archaeology:
www.britarch.ac.uk/archabroad
www.archaeological.org

Animal Rights:
www.arrs.envirolink.org

Financial Services Volunteer Corps:
www.fsvc.org/volunteer

Gap Year Opportunities:
www.gapyear.co.uk

Marine Biology:
www.coral.org

Online Volunteering:
www.onlinevolunteering.org
www.volunteermatch.org/virtual/

Index of Organisations

Vacation Work Publications

	UK Price	US price
Summer Jobs Abroad	£10.99	$18.95
Summer Jobs in Britain	£10.99	$18.95
Taking a Gap Year	£11.95	$19.95
Gap Years for Grown Ups	£11.95	$19.95
Teaching English Abroad	£12.95	$19.95
The Directory of Jobs & Careers Abroad	£12.95	$19.95
The International Directory of Voluntary Work	£11.95	$19.95
The Au Pair & Nanny's Guide to Working Abroad	£12.95	$17.95
The Good Cook's Guide to Working Worldwide	£11.95	-
Live & Work Abroad – A Guide for Modern Nomads	£11.95	-
Taking a Career Break	£11.95	-
Kibbutz Volunteer	£10.99	-
Work Your Way Around the World	£12.95	$21.95
Working in Tourism – The UK, Europe & Beyond	£11.95	$19.95
Working in Aviation	£10.99	$18.95
Working on Yachts and Superyachts	£10.99	$16.95
Working on Cruise Ships	£10.99	$18.95
Working in Ski Resorts – Europe & North America	£11.95	$19.95
Working with Animals – The UK, Europe & Worldwide	£11.95	$19.95
Working with the Environment	£11.95	$19.95
Workabout Australia	£10.99	$17.95
Live & Work in Australia & New Zealand	£10.99	$19.95
Live & Work in Belgium, The Netherlands & Luxembourg	£10.99	$19.95
Live & Work in China	£11.95	$19.95
Live & Work in France	£10.99	$19.95
Live & Work in Germany	£10.99	$19.95
Live & Work in Ireland	£10.99	$19.95
Live & Work in Italy	£10.99	$19.95
Live & Work in Japan	£10.99	$19.95
Live & Work in Portugal	£10.99	$19.95
Live & Work in Saudi & the Gulf	£10.99	$19.95
Live & Work in Scandinavia	£10.99	$19.95
Live & Work in Scotland	£10.99	$19.95
Live & Work in Spain	£10.99	$19.95
Live & Work in Spain & Portugal	£10.99	$19.95
Live & Work in the USA & Canada	£10.99	$19.95
Buying a House in France	£11.95	$19.95
Buying a House in Spain	£11.95	$19.95
Buying a House in Italy	£11.95	$19.95
Buying a House in Portugal	£11.95	$18.95
Buying a House on the Mediterranean	£13.95	$18.95
Starting a Business in France	£12.95	$18.95
Starting a Business in Spain	£12.95	$18.95
Starting a Business in Australia	£12.95	$19.95
Scottish Islands – Skye & The Western Isles	£12.95	$19.95
Scottish Islands – Orkney & Shetland	£11.95	$18.95
Drive USA	£10.99	$16.95

Vacation Work Publications, 9 Park End Street, Oxford OX1 1HJ
01865-241978   Fax 01865-790885

**Visit us online for more information on our unrivalled range of titles for work,
travel and gap years, readers' feedback and regular updates:**

www.vacationwork.co.uk

**Books marked with a dollar price are available in the USA from
The Globe Pequot Press, Guilford, Connecticut**

www.globepequot.com